A Special Issue of
Cognitive Neuropsychology

Words and Things:
Cognitive neuropsychological studies
in tribute to Eleanor M. Saffran

Edited by

Marlene Behrmann

Carnegie Mellon University, Pittsburgh, PA, USA

and

Karalyn Patterson

MRC Cognition and Brain Sciences Unit, Cambridge, UK

Routledge
Taylor & Francis Group
LONDON AND NEW YORK

First published 2004 by Psychology Press Ltd

Published 2018 by Routledge
2 Park Square, Milton Park, Abingdon, Oxon, OX14 4RN
52 Vanderbilt Avenue, New York, NY 10017

First issued in paperback 2018

Routledge is an imprint of the Taylor & Francis Group, an informa business

British Library Cataloguing in Publication Data
A catalogue record for this book is available from the British Library

This book is also a special issue of the journal *Cognitive Neuropsychology* and forms Issues 2, 3, and 4 of Volume 21 (2004).

Cover design by Joyce Chester
Typeset in the UK by Quorum Technical Services, Cheltenham, Glos

ISSN 0264-3294
ISBN 13: 978-1-138-87799-3 (pbk)
ISBN 13: 978-1-84169-964-6 (hbk)

COGNITIVE NEUROPSYCHOLOGY

Volume 21 Issue 2/3/4 March–June 2004

Contents

COGNITIVE NEUROPSYCHOLOGY, 2004, 21 (2/3/4), 99–100

PREFACE:
INTRODUCTION TO THIS SPECIAL ISSUE
OF *COGNITIVE NEUROPSYCHOLOGY*

Eleanor M. Saffran

A fitting tribute to Eleanor Saffran, and her exceptional contributions to our field, was published in *Cognitive Neuropsychology* in 2003 (Volume 20, p. 91). We recommend this "In Memoriam" piece to readers who have not already seen it: we did not write it but would have been pleased and proud to do so, and, accordingly, feel that we need not and should not offer another version of its contents here. This brief introduction will therefore merely explain why we wanted to prepare this special issue of the journal in Eleanor's honour.

Apart from all of her manifold accomplishments, Eleanor was a most extraordinary person to have as a colleague and friend. She exemplified the admirable goal of taking one's work, but not oneself, with great seriousness. We believe and indeed hope that Eleanor enjoyed her academic successes as much as any of us do; but she never seemed preoccupied with her own success or indeed with herself at all. The full force of her intellect was directed to advancing the 'career' of cognitive neuropsychology, not her own career—and, by the way, anyone who was lucky enough to work with her, or even to have a research-related discussion with her, will know how intense her intellectual force and focus could be.

99

DOI:10.1080/02643290342000636

Probably no human behaviour, and certainly not any behaviour as complex and long-lasting as a working life devoted to research, is singly or simply motivated. We nevertheless feel that, to the extent that it could be said of any researcher in our discipline, it would be appropriate to say of Eleanor Saffran that she was motivated almost purely by a drive to understand cognitive abilities and their neural implementation, and to help fellow researchers to do likewise. We were exceedingly lucky to have her in our field and in our lives.

Eleanor knew that we were preparing this special issue in her honour. Naturally we had hoped to complete it in time for her to see it, and were bitterly disappointed that the rapid progress of her illness thwarted this goal. We only hope that she would have been as pleased by the outcome and the honour as we were pleased to do it for her.

KARALYN PATTERSON AND MARLENE BEHRMANN

COGNITIVE NEUROPSYCHOLOGY, 2004, 21 (2/3/4) 101–102

SECTION I: SINGLE WORD PROCESSING

A note on Eleanor Saffran's contribution to this area

During her research career, Eleanor Saffran published nearly 100 papers and chapters on topics in human cognitive neurospychology (not to mention at least 1 paper on development of visual cortex in the rat!). As we will keep saying in our brief introductory notes to the four sections of this special issue in her honour, Eleanor's interests in, research on, and profound thoughtfulness about cognitive abilities and their disorders spanned many areas of cognition. She therefore defies pigeon-holing of the type that we are prone to in cognitive science ("he's a memory researcher; she studies visual attention; he's a psycholinguist" and so on); Eleanor contributed to all of these areas. If, however, one had to select one broad topic on which her research tended to focus, it would almost certainly be language. Because many of the papers in this special issue were written by researchers associated with her in one way or another, it is not surprising that many of the contributions here also concern language. We have chosen, a little arbitrarily, to divide these language-related contributions into two sections, the first concerning *Single Word Processing* and the second on *Language Beyond the Word Level*.

Eleanor's interests in lexical processing and their disorders took every imaginable shape with regard to tasks or modalities of input and output. Object naming, single-word reading, and single-word repetition all constituted an enduring focus. Consideration of each of these tasks on its own, and especially of the three together, offered Eleanor in her neurolinguistic "hat" a great richness of abnormal language behaviour to explore, which she did with the thoroughness and systematicity that pervaded her research. Her early work on deep dyslexia (e.g., Saffran, Bogyo, Schwartz, & Marin, 1980; Saffran & Marin, 1977) expanded into a set of important contributions on every major form of acquired dyslexia. Some of her most

elegant studies—first with Tim Shallice (Shallice & Saffran, 1986) and then in a number of papers with Branch Coslett (e.g., Coslett & Saffran, 1989, 1994; Coslett, Saffran, Greenbaum, & Schwartz, 1993; Saffran & Coslett, 1998)—were devoted to finding an account of pure alexia, also called alexia without agraphia because of its striking feature that the patients may fail to read even words that they themselves have written. Eleanor's work on alexia is described and praised further in the Introduction to Section 4, but it seemed appropriate to mention it here as part of her research on single word processing. Many of her papers on these topics are classics. For example, by demonstrating that reading in deep dyslexia is not disrupted by unusual word formats such as mixed case or vertical arrangement of the letters, Eleanor laid to rest the idea that these patients might be reading holistically, as if the words were pictures and the patients simply naming them. No one ever needed to ask this question again: Saffran (1980) had provided a succinct and definitive answer.

One of Eleanor's serious interests was always in speech production, at both single-word and sentence levels; and in the 1990s, with Gary Dell, Nadine Martin, and Myrna Schwartz, she embarked upon a challenging and highly productive enterprise: the application of computational models to the study of disordered lexical access and word production in tasks like naming and repetition (e.g., Dell, Schwartz, Martin, Saffran, & Gagnon, 1997; Martin, Dell, Saffran, & Schwartz, 1994; Martin & Saffran, 1992; Saffran, Dell, & Schwartz, 2000). This enterprise not only marked a significant change in Eleanor's approach but had a significant impact on other researchers' thinking. Although much of Eleanor's work consisted of careful single-case studies, she had always argued that it was important to think in terms of case series of patients if we were to make cumulative

DOI:10.1080/02643290342000474

progress in the field. With her turn to an interest in modelling of aphasic performance, this line of reasoning took another major step forward: instead of detailed accounts of individual cases, the goal was to explain sets of data from much larger groups of patients in terms of parameter changes in a network model of lexical processing. Always forward looking; never afraid of a new challenge: That was Eleanor Saffran.

REFERENCES

Coslett, H. B., & Saffran, E. M. (1989). Evidence for preserved reading in "pure alexia". *Brain, 112*, 327–359.

Coslett, H. B., & Saffran, E. M. (1994). Mechanisms of implicit reading in pure alexia. In M. J. Farah & G. Ratcliff (Eds.), *The neuropsychology of high level vision*. Hillsdale, NJ: Lawrence Erlbaum Associates Inc.

Coslett, H. B., Saffran, E. M., Greenbaum, S., & Schwartz, H. (1993). Reading in pure alexia: The effect of strategy. *Brain, 116*, 21–37.

Dell, G. S., Schwartz, M. F., Martin, N., Saffran, E. M., & Gagnon, D. A. (1997). Lexical access in aphasic and non-aphasic speakers. *Psychological Review, 104*, 811–838.

Martin, N., Dell, G. S., Saffran, E. M., & Schwartz, M. F. (1994). Origins of paraphasias in deep dysphasia: Testing the consequences of a decay impairment to an interactive spreading activation model of lexical retrieval. *Brain and Language, 47*, 609–660.

Martin, N., & Saffran, E. M. (1992). A computational account of deep dysphasia: Evidence from a single case study. *Brain and Language, 43*, 240–274.

Saffran, E. M. (1980). Reading in deep dyslexia is not ideographic. *Neuropsychologia, 18*, 219–223.

Saffran, E. M., Bogyo, L., Schwartz, M. F., & Marin, O. S. M. (1980). Does deep dyslexia reflect right hemisphere reading? In M. Coltheart, K. Patterson, & J. C. Marshall (Eds.), *Deep dyslexia* (pp. 381–406). London: Routledge & Kegan Paul.

Saffran, E. M., & Coslett, H. B. (1998). Implicit vs. letter-by-letter reading in pure alexia: A tale of two systems. *Cognitive Neuropsychology, 15*, 141–165.

Saffran, E. M., Dell, G. S., & Schwartz, M. F. (2000). Computational modelling of language disorders. In M. Gazzaniga (Ed.), *The new cognitive neurosciences* (pp. 933–948). Cambridge, MA: MIT Press.

Saffran, E. M., & Marin, O. S. M. (1977). Reading without phonology: Evidence from aphasia. *Quarterly Journal of Experimental Psychology, 29*, 515–525.

Shallice, T., & Saffran, E. M. (1986). Lexical processing in the absence of explicit word recognition: Evidence from a letter-by-letter reader. *Cognitive Neuropsychology, 3*, 429–458.

COGNITIVE NEUROPSYCHOLOGY, 2004, 21 (2/3/4) 103–123

THE NOUN/VERB DISSOCIATION IN LANGUAGE PRODUCTION: VARIETIES OF CAUSES

Marcella Laiacona
S. Maugeri Foundation, Veruno, Italy

Alfonso Caramazza
Harvard University, Cambridge, MA, USA

We report the performance of two patients who presented with complementary deficits in naming nouns relative to verbs: EA performed far worse with nouns than verbs, while MR performed worse with verbs than nouns. The two patients' grammatical category-specific deficits could not easily be explained in terms of damage to specific types of semantic knowledge prototypically associated with nouns (visual properties) and verbs (action features). One of the two patients, MR, also presented with a selective deficit in processing verbal as opposed to nominal morphology, in line with her impairment in naming verbs. The other patient, EA, showed no impairment in producing nominal and regular verbal morphology. The contrasting patterns of grammatical category-specific deficits in naming and morphological processing, along with other recently reported patterns, are interpreted as providing support for the claim that semantic and grammatical properties independently contribute to the organisation of lexical processes in the brain.

There are numerous reports documenting grammatical category-specific deficits—the disproportionate impairment in processing words of one grammatical category relative to other categories. In seminal reports, Goodglass, Klein, Carey, and Jones (1966) and Luria and Tsvetkova (1967) showed, respectively, that fluent (Wernicke's and anomic) aphasics have greater difficulty naming objects than actions and that patients with dynamic aphasia, involving damage to areas of the left frontal cortex, have greater difficulty producing names of actions than objects. Miceli, Silveri, Villa, and Caramazza (1984) confirmed this double dissociation: Anomic patients whose lesions tended to involve more posterior cortical areas were impaired at naming nouns relative to verbs while agrammatic aphasics whose lesions tended to involve more anterior areas were impaired with verbs relative to nouns. Many subsequent reports have replicated these findings (e.g., Berndt, Mitchum, Haendiges, & Sandson, 1997a, 1997b; Breedin, Saffran, & Schwartz, 1998; A. R. Damasio & Tranel, 1993; Daniele, Giustolisi, Silveri, Colosimo, & Gainotti, 1994; Miceli, Silveri, Nocentini, & Caramazza, 1988; Robinson, Rossor, & Cipolotti, 1999; for review, see Caramazza & Shapiro, in press; Druks, 2002; Silveri & Di Betta, 1997; Zingeser & Berndt,

Correspondence should be addressed to Alfonso Caramazza, Cognitive Neuropsychology Laboratory, Department of Psychology, Harvard University, 33 Kirkland St., Cambridge, MA 02446, USA (Email: caram@wjh.harvard.edu).

The work reported here was supported in part by NIG grant DC04542 and by a MIUR FIRST grant. We are grateful to EA and MR for their participation in this study. We also thank Erminio Capitani, Kathryn Link, Kevin Shapiro, and Brad Mahon for their helpful comments on this work and on an earlier version of the paper. Nadia Allamano and Lorena Lorenzi assisted with part of the patients' standard language examination.

1988, 1990), attesting to the robustness of the phenomenon. These results raise the possibility that noun retrieval is dependent on neural structures in the temporal lobe, while verb retrieval depends more on left prefrontal areas. Nonetheless, there are clear exceptions to this pattern. For example, there are patients with predominantly frontal-parietal damage who perform better at naming verbs than nouns (e.g., De Renzi & Di Pellegrino, 1995; Shapiro, Shelton, & Caramazza, 2000) and patients with spared left frontal cortex who are impaired in processing verbs (Silveri & Di Betta, 1997). Furthermore, there is disagreement about the causes of the observed deficits and their implications for the functional and neural organization of the lexicon. At issue is the cause of the seemingly grammatical class dissociations.

Following Bates, Chen, Tzeng, Li, and Opie (1991), we will distinguish three basic classes of explanations that have been offered for noun–verb dissociations in aphasia: "semantic-conceptual" explanations, which reduce differences between the two categories to effects of concreteness, imageability, or some other dimension related to lexical meaning; "lexical-grammatical" explanations, which trace dissociations between nouns and verbs to differences in form class; and "morphological" explanations, which are based on the different morphosyntactic roles nouns and verbs play in constructing sentences. We will refer to the latter two classes of theories generically as the "grammatical" accounts, since they both depend on morphosyntactic representations/processes.

Some researchers have interpreted the noun/verb dissociation to have a semantic basis. Two types of explanations have been proposed within this framework. One account is an extension of the sensory/functional theory of semantic category-specific deficits to the noun/verb dissociation (Bird, Howard, & Franklin, 2000, 2001; but see Shapiro & Caramazza, 2001a, 2001b). This account holds that semantic information is organised according to the modality of the represented attributes: for instance, properties referring to visual aspects of objects are stored in visual processing regions, while motor properties (associated with object use) are stored in movement perception and motor control areas. On this view, damage to a modality-specific semantic subsystem (e.g., visual semantic subsystem) will result in disproportionate impairment of those categories of concepts whose members differentially depend on that subsystem for identification. For example, it has been argued that members of the category "living things" are distinguished primarily on the basis of their visual attributes, and that therefore damage to the visual semantic subsystem will result in a category-specific deficit for living things (e.g., Humphreys & Forde, 2001; but see Capitani, Laiacona, Mahon, & Caramazza, 2003; Warrington & McCarthy, 1987). On the assumptions that nouns and verbs tend to correspond to objects and actions, respectively, and that objects are characterised primarily by their visual attributes while actions are characterised by their movement/motor attributes, damage to the visual semantic subsystem (temporal lobe) would be more likely to affect nouns while damage to motor and movement perception areas (frontal and posterior temporal) would be more likely to affect verbs.[1] In this way, seemingly grammatical category-specific deficits would actually have a semantic basis. However, it is unlikely that all cases of noun/verb dissociation can be explained in terms of the sensory/functional theory.

A central prediction made by the sensory/functional theory is that noun/verb grammatical category dissociations will vanish when the critical variable imageability (a sensory-based dimension of objects and events) is controlled. Results consistent with this prediction have been reported by Bird et al. (2000). However, not all grammatical

---

[1] Bird et al.'s (2000) proposal for the selective deficit of verbs is actually more complicated. They propose that difficulties in producing verbs result from deficits affecting low-imageability words. They propose that low imageability words have relatively sparse semantic representations and that widespread damage to the semantic system will disproportionately affect those words. Since verbs tend to be of low imageability, diffuse semantic damage will result in greater difficulty for words of this grammatical category.

category effects disappear when imageability is controlled. In a particularly well-designed study, Berndt, Haendiges, Burton, and Mitchum (2002) addressed the role of imageability on the production of nouns and verbs. They reported two crucial results. First, they documented cases in which a noun/verb dissociation remained even when imageability was tightly controlled. Second, they documented cases in which word retrieval was strongly affected by imageability but there was no corresponding grammatical class effect. Thus, while some reported noun/verb dissociations may arise due to semantic differences between nouns and verbs, it does not appear that all such dissociations can be explained by appeal to semantic factors.

The other semantic account of grammatical category-specific deficits does not make explicit claims about the representation of the semantic content of words but appeals to the fact that prototypical nouns and verbs tend to be objects and actions, respectively (A. R. Damasio & Tranel, 1993; McCarthy & Warrington, 1985). On this view, the apparent grammatical category-specific deficits are really deficits in processing object or action concepts. This account shares with the sensory/functional proposal the assumption that action concepts recruit primarily frontal lobe structures while object concepts are represented primarily in the temporal lobe. However, the object/action account is not committed to any particular claim about the organisation of the semantic content of nouns and verbs, and because of this it is not undermined by results demonstrating grammatical category-specific dissociations independently of imageability effects (e.g., Berndt et al., 2002). One major limitation of this proposal is that it is silent on how abstract nouns—such as "idea" and "intelligence"—and verbs—such as "inspire" and "think"—are represented. A further limitation of this account is that it leaves unspecified how and where, both functionally and neurally, grammatical class information is represented.

Other researchers have interpreted the noun/verb dissociation to have, in part, a grammatical basis (e.g., Caramazza & Hillis, 1991; Shapiro & Caramazza, 2003a; Tsapkini, Jarema, & Kehayia,

2002). The assumption here is that one dimension of the organisation of lexical knowledge in the brain is grammatical in origin. One source of evidence in favour of this hypothesis is the existence of modality-specific grammatical category deficits. These deficits are characterised by selective impairment/sparing of words of one grammatical class in only one modality of output (input)—either only speaking or only writing (Berndt & Haendiges, 2000; Caramazza & Hillis, 1991; Hillis & Caramazza, 1995; Hillis, Tuffiash, & Caramazza, 2002a; Hillis, Wityk, Barker, & Caramazza, 2002b; Rapp & Caramazza, 1998, 2002). For example in speaking, patient SJD (Caramazza & Hillis, 1991) flawlessly produced both the verb and noun forms of homonyms such as "to watch" and "the watch", but in writing she was severely impaired in producing the verb form (56% correct) while virtually unimpaired in producing the noun form (98% correct). The reverse pattern of modality-specific deficit for verbs was observed in patient MML (Hillis et al., 2002a), who presented with primary progressive aphasia. In the written modality, MML was able to consistently produce the verb and noun forms of homonyms with 90% accuracy, while in speaking she progressively and completely lost the ability to produce verbs (0% correct) while retaining the ability to produce nouns at the same level as in writing (90% correct). Finally, patient KSR (Rapp & Caramazza, 2002) made more errors with nouns than verbs in speaking but made fewer errors with nouns than verbs in writing.

These various patterns of modality-specific grammatical category deficits rule out a semantic *deficit* as the cause of the category-specific deficits. This conclusion follows from the fact that the semantic system in these patients had to be intact in order to support "normal" performance in the unimpaired modality of output. Furthermore, the observed differences in producing words of different grammatical classes could not be ascribed to a deficit at the phonological or orthographic levels since the words to be spoken or written had the same form for the two grammatical categories ("the watch" / "to watch"). Therefore, the most plausible locus of deficit in these patients is the level of lexical selection in the modality of output affected in each case, inviting the hypothesis that the phonological and orthographic lexicons are organised by grammatical category. If this hypothesis were correct, we would have the basis for truly *grammatical* category-specific deficits.

Although the existence of modality-specific grammatical category deficits suggests that the lexicon may be organised by grammatical category, it does not logically require such organisation. The fact that the deficits in these patients cannot be located at the semantic level does not exclude the possibility that their deficits have a semantic basis. If we were to assume that the semantic representations of nouns and verbs are (largely) segregated anatomically and that brain damage can functionally *disconnect* each of these semantic subsystems from modality-specific lexical components, we could have the basis for grammatical category effects restricted to only one modality (for discussion, see Rapp & Caramazza, 1998, 2002).

Stronger evidence for a grammatical cause of noun/verb dissociations is provided by recent studies that have explored morphological processing in patients with such dissociations. The crucial result is the reported association of difficulty in producing words of one grammatical category with difficulty in morphological production for that grammatical category (Shapiro et al., 2000; Shapiro & Caramazza, 2003a; Tsapkini et al., 2002). For example, patients were required to complete orally presented sentences with noun and verb homonyms that involved the addition/deletion of a nominal or verbal suffix (e.g., "This is a guide; these are ___"; "This person guides, these people ___"). Patient JR (Shapiro et al., 2000), who was impaired at naming nouns, was considerably worse at producing the plural/singular forms of nouns than he was at producing the phonologically identical third-person singular/plural forms of verbs; patient RC (Shapiro & Caramazza, 2003a), who was impaired at naming verbs, was considerably worse at producing the third-person plural/singular forms of verbs than he was at producing the phonologically identical singular/plural forms of nouns. Similar patterns of results were obtained in sentence completion tasks in which

these two patients were required to produce pseudowords in nominal or verbal contexts (e.g., "This is a wug; these are ___"; "This person wugs, these people ___") – JR performed worse when producing nominal morphology while RC performed worse when producing verbal morphology. The morphological processing results, and especially those with pseudowords, suggest that grammatical category-specific deficits can have a purely grammatical basis. This conclusion is based on the reasoning that since pseudowords do not have specific semantic content, their selective impairment when used in a particular grammatical context implies a difficulty in processing the contextually determined grammatical information.

One interpretation of the category-specific morphological processing dissociations in patients with grammatical category-specific naming deficits is that the phonological and orthographic lexicons are organised by grammatical category. Another possibility is that the lexicon is not organised by grammatical category but that the morphosyntactic processes for nouns and verbs are subserved by neuroanatomically dissociable mechanisms. On this view, it is not the lexicon itself that is organised by grammatical category but the processes that are applied to lexical representations in the course of sentence production. The latter possibility gains credence when we consider the fact that patients who present with verb naming difficulties are typically also more generally impaired in grammatical processing (e.g., Bastiaanse & Jonkers, 1998; Miceli et al., 1984; Myerson & Goodglass, 1972). Saffran (1982) noted the association between agrammatic production and difficulties in the use of verbs and argued that a deficit in retrieval of verbs plays a causal role in agrammatic production. Furthermore, she argued for a grammatical account of the verb retrieval deficit by further noting that agrammatic patients often produce the gerundive form of verbs (e.g., writing). This observation implies that the patients are nominalising the verbs they are unable to produce, suggesting that their deficit does not affect the conceptual content of verbs but their use as words of the grammatical category verb (see also Miceli et al., 1984).

From this brief review it is clear that we are still far from having a clear understanding of the causes of grammatical category-specific deficits. Although much of the discussion of these deficits has centred on whether the phenomenon of noun/verb dissociation has either only a semantic or only a grammatical basis, it is unlikely that the contrasting hypotheses are mutually exclusive. It is much more likely that both semantics and grammar play crucial roles in the organisation of lexical knowledge and processes in the brain. If such were the case we would expect to find patients with seemingly similar grammatical category-specific deficits but whose impairments ultimately have different causes. A case in point is the contrast between patients RC (Shapiro & Caramazza, 2003a) and HG (Shapiro & Caramazza, 2003b). Both patients presented with far greater difficulty at producing verbs than nouns. However, while RC was also severely impaired in sentence completion tasks requiring morphophonological processing of verbs (e.g., producing "jump" in response to: "He jumps; they ...."), patient HG performed the latter task flawlessly. The overall profile of performance observed for HG suggests that her seemingly grammatical category deficit in naming may actually have a semantic basis (although not necessarily due to a semantic deficit). The contrasting patterns of performance provided by RC and HG alert us to the need for further detailed investigations of the patterns of grammatical category effects in lexical access. Here we report the performance of two aphasic patients (EA and MR) whose grammatical category-specific impairments clearly have different causes, and at least one of them presents with a profile unlike other cases described thus far.

CASE HISTORIES

Patient EA

EA is a 54 year-old right-handed man, who suffered from herpes simplex encephalitis (HSE) in December 1990. CSF laboratory data showed HSV and HZV-specific IgG antibody. CT scans showed a severe left temporal lobe lesion, which MRI images (Figure 1) confirmed, involving the entire anterior half of the lobe and more posteriorly the middle and inferior temporal gyri, the medial and lateral occipito-temporal gyri and, less severely, the parahippocampal gyrus; abnormal intensity was also evident in the left hippocampus. In order to describe the damaged structures in a standard manner, MRI images were mapped onto the templates reported by H. Damasio and Damasio (1989); for the description of anatomical structures, reference was also made to Nieuwenhuys, Voogt, and Van Huijzen (1978).

In April 1991, the patient was referred to the Neuropsychology Unit of Veruno Hospital for evaluation. Neuropsychological assessment revealed a severe long-term verbal memory disorder, retrograde amnesia, and language impairment characterised by fluent production with lexical and semantic errors. EA also presented with a semantic category-specific deficit for biological kinds, which has been the subject of several reports (Barbarotto, Capitani, & Laiacona, 1996; Laiacona, Capitani, & Barbarotto, 1997; Laiacona, Capitani, & Caramazza, 2003b). The investigation reported here took place between November 2000 and August 2001. EA is currently well oriented in time and place and almost completely autonomous in everyday life. His principal complaint remains his word-finding difficulty.

On formal language examination (AAT test; Luzzatti, Willmes, & De Bleser, 1994b), EA showed significant improvement in naming (70/120 correct) over the previous assessment in 1992 (51/120 correct), but still presented with a mild amnestic aphasia. His spontaneous speech was fluent, well articulated, and grammatically correct, but with frequent and pervasive word-finding difficulties in speech and writing, which appeared to be more severe for nouns than verbs. He compensated for his word-finding difficulty by producing circumlocutions. An example of his speech is shown below—his attempt to describe what he remembers about the onset of his illness. Overall he produced more verbs than nouns (about one noun for every two verbs: nouns = 99, verbs = 183).

Quello che mi ricordo è che mi sono svegliato di giorno e ho visto dove ero, ma non riuscivo a capire cosa facevo in questo

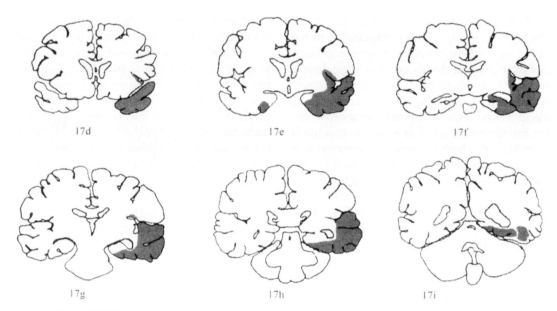

Figure 1. *Patient EA: MRI coronal sections showing the damaged structures. Right side of the diagram corresponds to the left side of the brain. On the left side, some temporal lesioned areas (shown in sections 17d, 17e) were almost destroyed and presented with wide cystic cavities. (Under each picture we indicate the template of reference in H. Damasio & Damasio, 1989; e.g., 17d means that we refer to the fourth template of the set A. 17.)*

posto, non sapevo neanche che era un Ospedale, ho sbagliato casa e stavo uscendo per andare a casa mia. ..E invece quando uscivo, mi han fermato, mi han bloccato, però io non conoscevo loro.

What I remember is that I awoke during the day and I saw where I was, but I couldn't understand what I was doing in that place, I didn't even know that it was a hospital ... I went to the wrong house, and I was about to leave to go home ... and instead when I was about to go out, they stopped me, they blocked me, but I didn't know who they were.

EA's reading and repetition performance was nearly flawless. He repeated without error 101 bi- or trisyllabic words and 30 nonwords, he read the nonwords perfectly, and he only made five errors in reading words, all involving the incorrect placement of stress (e.g., "fossile" [fossil] instead of "fòssile"). In writing to dictation, EA wrote all nonwords correctly ($N = 25$) but made "regularisation" errors (15/55) in writing words (e.g., "quota" [height] written as the nonword "cuota") (Luzzatti, Laiacona, Allamano, De Tanti, Inzaghi, & Lorenzi, 1994a). The stress errors in reading and the regularisation errors in writing indicate EA's overreliance on sublexical conversion procedures as a result of a deficit affecting lexical access.

Patient MR

MR is a 38-year-old right-handed woman who suffered a stroke in May 2001. CT scan showed a fronto-parietal lesion extending to the anterior part of the superior and middle temporal lobe. MRI images (Figure 2) confirmed the presence of a large area of abnormal intensity in the left hemisphere, mainly fronto-parietal, but encroaching upon the insula and the middle and posterior parts of superior and middle temporal gyri. The frontal lesion involved both cortical structures and subcortical white matter, whereas the temporal and parietal lesions were thin and affected only the cortex in a patchy pattern. MRI lesions were mapped in the same way as for EA.

Testing took place from August to October 2001 at the Neuropsychology Unit of Veruno Hospital. MR's language abilities were tested with

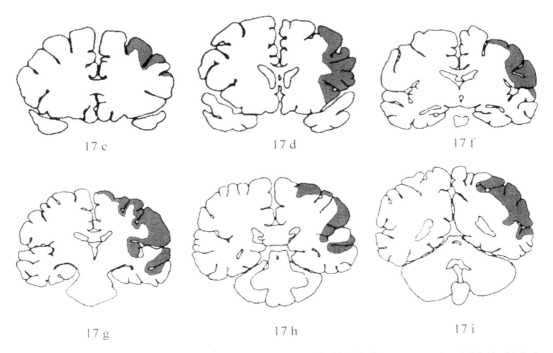

Figure 2. *Patient MR: MRI coronal sections showing the damaged structures. Right side of the diagram corresponds to the left side of the brain. (Under each picture we indicate the template of reference in H. Damasio & Damasio, 1989: e.g., 17c means that we refer to the third template of the set A.17.)*

the BADA (Miceli, Laudanna, Burani, & Capasso, 1994). MR performed well on phoneme discrimination and auditory-visual syllable matching tasks. She was impaired on all lexical processing tasks. She performed poorly in lexical decision (auditory and visual) and in reading and writing. Her reading errors included morphological substitutions or nominalisations (e.g., "regalo" [gift] instead of "regalato" [gave a gift]). Writing to dictation was severely affected: she could write only a few words, and many errors resulted in neologistic responses. She performed quite well on auditory and visual word–picture matching, but made a few errors with stimuli representing actions. In picture naming tasks, she performed better with nouns (80% correct) than verbs (39% correct); errors resulted from failures to respond, semantic substitutions, nominalisations of verb responses (e.g., "applauso" [applause] instead of "applaudire" [to applaud]) and substitutions of the object in an action instead of the action (e.g.,

"candela" [candle] instead of "accendere" [to light]). At the sentence level, she was severely impaired in all aspects examined (grammaticality judgements, sentence–picture matching). Spontaneous speech was agrammatic. An example of her speech is shown below.

un cacciatore … mentre dormiva … il lupo … la nonna e cappuccetto rosso andato fuori … e … uccide il … lupo e uccise … e poi la bambina … cappuccetto rosso e … la nonna … e il gendarme …

[a hunter … while he was sleeping … the wolf … the grandmother and little red riding hood went out … and … shoots the … wolf and shot … and then the girl … little red riding hood and … the grandmother … and the policeman …]

MR was tested with the transcoding tasks used with EA. She was too severely impaired to perform the writing tasks. She repeated correctly 100/101 (99%) words but only 20/30 (67%) nonwords. In reading aloud, she was 73% correct (74/101) with words, but could only read correctly 3% (1/30) of the nonwords. The majority of her reading errors were lexical substitutions. These findings suggest the presence of both lexical and sublexical processing deficits.

EXPERIMENTAL FINDINGS

This investigation focuses on EA's and MR's contrasting patterns of difficulty in producing nouns and verbs. In what follows, we first document the two patients' grammatical category naming deficits. We then describe various tasks designed to help determine the causes of the seemingly grammatical category-specific deficits.

Effects of grammatical category on lexical access

EA and MR were tested with the same set of words on the following tasks: picture naming, reading aloud, repetition, and picture–word matching (in which the target picture had to be distinguished from three other pictures randomly chosen from among those used for the picture naming task). The stimuli were 52 objects and 50 actions taken from the BADA test (Miceli et al., 1994). Objects and actions were presented blocked. Verbs are by inspection more frequent (41.32, SD = 42.17) than nouns (30.42, SD = 31.17) according to an Italian frequency lexicon (Bortolini, Tagliavini, & Zampolli, 1972). The tasks were presented in a fixed order, on separate days: first picture naming, then repetition, then reading, and finally the picture–word matching task.

Picturable objects and actions were not matched on imageability, a variable known to affect word production performance. To partially overcome this limitation, we tested the patients with a naming to definition task that included nouns and verbs. However, interpretation of performance on this task is necessarily limited by the fact that the patients differ in their ability to comprehend language. Thus, performance on this task will only indirectly reflect difficulties at the level of lexical access. Nonetheless, performance on this task can be used to complement the results of the single-word processing tasks. The patients were given definitions and they were required to produce the most appropriate name for the definition. EA was given the full set of 111 nouns and 88 verbs. The frequency of the target nouns was 53 (SD = 76.8) and that of target verbs was 71 (SD = 115.4). MR was unable to complete the full task because she found it too taxing: She refused to continue with the task after 82 stimuli (45 nouns and 37 verbs: mean frequency was 46, (SD = 76.5) for nouns and 88.9 (SD = 132.7 for verbs).

The patients were also given an instrument and action naming task. They were presented with 27 pictures showing an action being performed with an object (e.g., a woman sewing with a needle, a man reading a book, and so on). Patients were asked to respond to the question: What is he/she doing and what object is he/she using? This task allows us to assess action and object naming in response to the same picture stimuli.

Table 1 reports the patients' correct performance on these tasks: complementary dissociations for nouns and verbs are evident on the picture

Table 1. *EA and MR performances on screening tasks where a possible grammatical-specific deficit could be detected*

	EA		MR	
	Objects	*Actions*	*Objects*	*Actions*
Picture naming	42%	82%	90%	70%
Naming to definition	54%	66%	67%	46%
Reading aloud	100%	100%	98%	58%
Repetition	100%	100%	96%	96%
Picture–word matching task	98%	100%	100%	100%
Instrument and action naming task	22%	85%	93%	63%

naming, the naming to definition, the instrument and action naming, and the reading tasks. Figure 3 highlights the relevant contrasts. With the exception of the reading task, EA is worse in producing object names whereas MR is worse in producing action names. EA's flawless performance in reading reflects his ability to use sublexical conversion procedures in this task.

In order to assess the contribution of word frequency on the patients' performance, the responses of each patient on the picture naming and the naming to definition tasks were analysed with logistic regression, using the GLIM program (Aitkin, Anderson, Francis, & Hinde, 1989), which yields chi-square distributed values. The dependent variable was the response given by the patient, coded 1 (correct) or 0 (incorrect). The model considered both categorical (stimulus type, i.e., noun or verb) and continuous variables (log transformed word frequency). Table 2 shows the results of the analyses. A more detailed discussion of the patients' performance follows.

Case EA

In oral picture naming, EA was 42% (22/52) and 82% (41/50) correct with objects and actions, respectively. For objects, the majority of his errors were omissions or circumlocutions (23/30), followed by five semantic errors, one visual error, and one recognisable nonword. For actions, the majority of errors were semantic substitutions (7/9).

As shown in Table 2, the advantage of verbs over nouns was highly significant in a plain comparison as well as after covariance for word frequency. Ignoring grammatical category distinctions, the overall effect of frequency was significant. The interaction between grammatical class and frequency did not reach significance.[2]

In naming to definition, EA named correctly 54% (60/111) of nouns and 66% (58/88) of verbs. The majority of errors for nouns were omissions (24/51) and semantic substitutions (19/51); eight errors were semantically related responses belonging to another grammatical class (verb or adjective). For verbs, errors were semantic substitutions (19/30), followed by five adjectives semantically related to the target, five omissions, and one nominalisation. The dissociation between nouns and verbs was marginally significant in a plain comparison. Ignoring grammatical class, frequency was highly significant. There was no interaction between frequency and grammatical category ($\chi^2 <$ 1, n.s.). Because a significant advantage for verbs was obtained in the picture naming task, the hypothesis of a category effect is one-directional, and the significance level of about .09 suggests its presence also in this task.

Finally, in the instrument and action naming task, EA was 22% correct (6/27) in naming objects and 85% correct (23/27) in naming actions. This contrast is particularly interesting because it shows that EA's poor performance in naming objects is not due to an inability to recognise them, since recognition of the same objects was required in order to perform well in the action naming part of the test.

Case MR

In the oral Picture naming task, MR correctly produced 90% (47/52) of the object names and 70% (35/50) of the action names. For actions, errors were mostly omissions and circumlocutions (8/15), followed by semantic errors (4/15) and nominalisations (3/15). For objects, there were three semantic errors, an unrelated, word and a phonologically unrelated nonword. The dissociation between nouns and verbs was significant even

---

[2] On a separate occasion, EA was tested with *written* naming using the same pictures. His performance was similar to that observed in oral naming: He was 44% (23/52) and 86% (43/50) correct on written naming of objects and actions, respectively. The greater impairment for nouns than verbs was highly significant ($\chi^2 = 20.557$), even after covariance for word frequency ($\chi^2 = 20.035$). Also in this task, word frequency was significant by itself ($\chi^2 = 24.683$), but again there was no significant interaction between grammatical class and frequency. For objects, errors were mostly omissions and circumlocutions (22/29 errors), as well as a few semantic errors (7/29); for actions, the few errors were semantically related responses (5/7 errors).

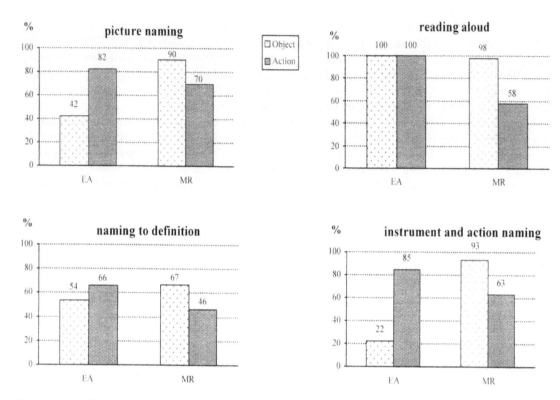

Figure 3. *EA and MR performances on tasks where complementary dissociations are evident.*

Table 2. *EA's and MR's performance on picture naming and on naming to definition tasks: Frequency effects and comparisons between nouns and verbs (in all cases the results derive from logistic regression analyses)*

	EA		MR	
	$\chi^2(1)$	p	$\chi^2(1)$	p
Picture naming (oral)				
Frequency effect (overall)	23.195	< .0001	2.743	.098
Frequency effect for nouns	21.840	< .0001	1.758	.185, n.s.
Frequency effect for verbs	4.408	.036	2.229	.135, n.s.
Noun/verb correct naming	42% / 82%		90% / 70%	
Noun/verb dissociation	17.711	< .0001	6.956	.008
Ruling out frequency effect	17.557	< .0001	7.953	.005
Naming to definition				
Frequency effect (overall)	26.774	< .0001	< 1	n.s.
Frequency effect for nouns	16.300	< .0001	< 1	n.s.
Frequency effect for verbs	10.646	.001	< 1	n.s.
Noun/verb correct naming	54% / 66%		67% / 46%	
Noun/verb dissociation	2.877	.09	4.366	.037
Ruling out frequency effect	2.814	.093	4.094	.043

after covariance for word frequency. The general role of word frequency, ignoring grammatical class distinctions, was not significant ($\chi^2 < 1$).

In naming to definition, MR was 67% correct (30/45) with nouns and 46% (17/37) with verbs. The majority of errors for verbs were omissions (16/20), followed by two nominalisations, one circumlocution, and one semantic substitution. For nouns, the most frequent error type was again omissions (10/15), followed by semantic substitutions (4/15) and one related verb response. The dissociation between nouns and verbs was present on a plain comparison and was also significant after covariance for word frequency. In this task, too, frequency did not significantly affect performance.

MR's performance in the instrument and action naming task is instructive. She named correctly 93% (25/27) of the objects but only 63% (17/27) of the actions. This contrast shows that MR's failure to name actions is unlikely to result from an inability to appreciate the relation among objects in a scene since she was able to use the picture context to interpret the nature of the instrument used in the action.

Comment

The results of the naming and reading tasks obtained with EA and MR indicate complementary dissociations in processing nouns and verbs: EA presented with greater difficulty in producing nouns than verbs in picture naming (both oral and written), whereas MR showed greater difficulty with verbs than nouns in naming and reading. EA did not show a grammatical class effect in reading but this may simply reflect the high transparency of Italian orthography and the fact that EA showed normal ability to convert orthography to phonology. MR's selective difficulty in reading verbs reflects her severe deficits in converting orthography to

phonology and in accessing the lexical representations of verbs. The two patients' seemingly normal performance in the picture–word matching task need not imply normal semantic processing since the task is rather simple and thus unable to reveal subtle semantic deficits.

In summary, then, the results confirm the clinical impression that the two patients presented with contrasting impairments in processing nouns and verbs, and we can proceed to identify the possible causes of the putative grammatical category effects.

Grammatical class distinctions or effects of concreteness/imageability?

Various authors (e.g., Bird et al., 2000, but see Shapiro & Caramazza, 2001a, 2001b; Marshall, Chiat, Robson, & Pring, 1996b; Marshall, Pring, Chiat, & Robson, 1996a) have argued that the putative effects of grammatical class in naming can be explained as resulting from the high correlation between grammatical categories and variables known to affect performance in word production tasks: concreteness and imageability. This correlation was also present in our picture naming stimuli: on a 5-point scale, a group of 40 normal controls judged the 52 nouns to be more concrete and imageable (4.58 and 4.44) than the 50 verbs (3.40 and 3.53). The strong correlation between imageability and grammatical category distinctions makes it extremely difficult to separate the contribution of these two factors by direct test of their effects on performance.[3] Consequently, we must turn to other evidence if we wish to argue that the putative grammatical category-specific effects are true grammatical effects. To this end, we will proceed in two directions. First, we will consider whether fine-grained consideration of the semantic hypothesis of putative grammatical class effects

---

[3] Nonetheless, for the sake of the completeness of the analyses we report the effects of imageability on naming performance. In picture naming, EA performed significantly better with verbs than with nouns even when imageability, concreteness, and word frequency were entered into the regression model ($\chi^2 = 6.816$, $p = .009$), whereas for MR the difference between nouns and verbs disappeared ($\chi^2 = 1.055$, $p = .304$, n.s.) In the naming to definition task the advantage of verbs for EA increased after covariance for concreteness and word frequency ($\chi^2 = 4.182$, $p = .041$), whereas for MR the advantage of nouns over verbs decreased ($\chi^2 = 2.760$, $p = .097$).

withstands scrutiny. Second, we will consider the relationship between grammatical class effects and morphological processing.

The semantic account of grammatical class effects

A sensory/functional account of EA's performance?

One hypothesis of the cause of selective difficulty in producing nouns is an extension of the sensory/functional theory of semantic category-specific deficits. On this view, the category-specific deficit for nouns is really a deficit in processing visual-semantic information. Since objects are, presumably, more dependent than verbs on such information, damage to the visual semantic subsystem will disproportionately affect nouns. Furthermore, the hypothesis predicts that within the category of nouns there should be greater impairment for living kind objects than for artifacts. These expectations are in line with EA's performance. Laiacona, Barbarotto, and Capitani (2003a) have shown that EA is much more impaired at naming biological kind objects than artifacts (13% vs. 50%). However, the underlying theory used to derive the prediction of an association between a deficit for biological kinds and sparing of action naming is not supported by EA's performance in the relevant tasks. Specifically, it is not the case that EA had greater difficulty in processing the visual as opposed to the functional attributes of objects generally and of biological kinds in particular. In an attribute judgment task, EA did not show greater difficulties for visuo-perceptual knowledge relative to functional knowledge for biological kind objects (58% vs. 50% correct, respectively). Thus, the theoretical motivation for the observed correlation between sparing of verb naming and greater impairment in naming biological kind objects than artifacts is undermined (see also Shapiro & Caramazza, 2001a, 2001b).

A further argument to consider is whether EA's poor performance for nouns merely reflects the inclusion of biological kind objects among the items to be named. As already noted, EA performed poorly in naming instruments in the instrument and action naming task. If we consider EA's performance in naming only artifacts in the picture naming task (N = 35), the dissociation between nouns and verbs remains strong: 46% correct with nouns and 82% correct with verbs (χ^2 = 12.337, p = .0004).

Finally, we note that in a picture naming task designed to investigate the possibility of a semantic category-specific deficit in patient MR (Laiacona, Barbarotto, Trivelli, & Capitani, 1993), this patient performed equally well with biological kind (83% correct) and artifact items (82% correct).

An action/object account of MR's performance?

In the introduction we noted that there are at least two hypotheses that could be entertained about the possible semantic causes of putative grammatical category-specific deficits. One of these is what we have labelled the *action/object account*. This hypothesis assumes that nouns and verbs are organised semantically according to whether they refer to objects or actions. To assess the viability of this hypothesis we investigated the two patients' ability to produce verbs that differ in "agentivity," that is, in the extent to which the meaning of a verb implicates an agent's action. Importantly, the "nonagentive" verbs did not involve specific (motor) actions. If the underlying cause of MR's verb production deficit were damage to the semantic representations of motor actions (as the prototypical action concepts) we would expect her to have particular difficulties with the clearly agentive verbs.

The patients were asked to name, in response to definitions, 35 verbs denoting a clear motor action (e.g., to draw), 26 verbs that do not have action features (e.g., to belong to), and 24 verbs of intermediate "agentivity" in the sense that the meaning can, but need not, imply an agent performing a specific motor action (e.g., to flood). The average frequencies of the three 3 verb groups were matched (Finocchiaro, 2002). Figure 4 displays the two patients' performance for the three groups of verbs. Both patients named verbs entailing a clear motor action *better* than intermediate ones, which in turn were named *better* than verbs without a motor action feature (EA: 97%, 79%, 73%, respectively; MR: 77%, 54%, 42%, respectively).

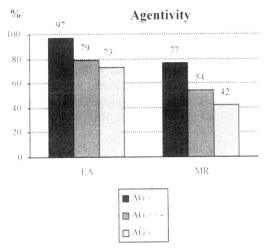

Figure 4. *EA and MR performances on naming to definition verbs differing in their agentivity meaning.*

These findings are at variance with the action/object account of MR's verb production deficit. To rule out the possibility that MR's performance with the three verb groups merely reflects intrinsic variation in difficulty for the three sets of verbs, we can express her performance as a function of EA's performance with the same stimuli. EA is, by hypothesis, supposed to have normal representation of action semantics. Therefore, his performance can serve as a nonceiling baseline for interpreting MR's performance. When we express MR's performance as a function of EA's performance we find that verbs entailing a clear motor action were still the best (27 correct for MR vs. 34 correct for EA = 79%), followed by the intermediate agentivity verbs (13 correct for MR vs. 19 correct for EA = 68%) and by verbs without any motor action feature (11 correct for MR vs. 19 correct EA = 58%). Thus we see that MR's performance is far better for clear action verbs (79%) than clear nonaction verbs (58%), and we can conclude that MR's verb production deficit is not the result of impairment in processing action semantics.

Comment
Consideration of specific aspects of the semantic accounts of grammatical category deficits shows little support for these accounts as explanations of the performance profiles observed in patients EA and MR. However, we recognise that the evaluation carried out here only addresses highly specific aspects of potentially much richer formulations of semantic accounts of grammatical class deficits. Therefore, our conclusion can only be tentative at this point. More powerful evidence against semantic accounts, at least for the deficits documented in our patients, would be provided by converging positive evidence in favour of grammatical accounts. We turn to such evidence next.

Evidence from morphosyntactic processing

In the introduction we noted that there are several results in the literature that support a grammatical basis for grammatical category-specific deficits in some patients (see Caramazza & Shapiro, in press). The evidence comes from evaluation of patients' ability to produce morphological variants of a target word. For example, patients could be asked to complete sentences in simple contexts such as "This is a guide; these are ___" and "This person guides, these people ___," where appropriate nominal and verbal morphology must be produced. Good performance on such tasks requires access to a word's grammatical class in order to apply the proper morphological transformation. Selective impairment for words of one grammatical class in this task would implicate specifically grammatical processes as the basis for the impairment. We carried out several morphological processing tasks with EA and MR.

Production of regular morphology
Patients were asked to complete sentence fragments of the form: "Oggi gioco, ieri _____" ("Today I play, yesterday I _____"), "Ieri ho giocato, oggi _____" ("Yesterday I played, today I _____"), and "Un vulcano, due ___" ("One volcano, two _____"). There were 204 verbal morphology trials; in 127 trials they had to produce the present tense and in 77 trials the present perfect). A smaller number of noun trials was used ($N = 74$) in which the patients had to produce the plural

form from the singular. For this latter task, we used the stimuli from Luzzatti and De Bleser (1996). The patients' performance is displayed in Figure 5.

EA did not show any impairment in the morphological processing task: he produced the correct morphological inflection for 71/74 nouns (96% correct) and for 202/204 verbs (99% correct).

A strikingly different pattern of performance was found for MR. She performed very poorly with verbs—137/204 (67%) correct—but performed nearly perfectly with nouns—72/74 (97%) correct. MR's errors in producing verbs were mostly failures to respond (59/67), followed by three perseverations of the input form, three infinitive forms, and two semantic substitutions ("semino" [I sow] instead of "mieto" [I reap] and "caduta" [fell] instead of "scivolata" [slipped]).

Although it would seem clear that MR has a severe deficit in processing verbal forms, even when the task merely requires producing a morphological variant of a cue word, this conclusion is undermined by the fact that the verb production task is more complex than the noun production task. The verbal morphology task requires producing phonological forms that are quite different from the cue word (e.g., "gioco" to "ho giocato")

whereas the noun production task involved minor phonological changes (e.g., "vulcano" to "vulcani" for masculine nouns, and "camera" to "camere" for feminine nouns). It is possible, therefore, that the dissociation observed for MR is not due to differences between grammatical classes but differences in the "complexity" of the phonological transformation to be produced for the two sets of words.

The most straightforward way to tackle the issue of phonological complexity is to use noun/verb homonyms in the morphological production task. In Italian, some nominal and verbal forms are homonyms: for example, "il suono" (the sound) versus "io suono" (I play [a musical instrument]) and "i suoni" (the sounds) versus "tu suoni" (you play). We constructed 56 pairs of nouns and verbs of this type and both patients were asked to complete sentence fragments involving the production of a morphological variant of a cue word (e.g., "io suono, tu _____" (I play, you _____). Figure 6 shows the results of this task.

EA was 100% correct on this task, both for nouns and verbs. By contrast, a clear dissociation is apparent in MR's performance: She was 100% correct with nouns, but only 52% correct with verbs. MR's errors (N = 27) were distributed as follows: 9 failures to respond, 2 infinitive forms (e.g. "suono" → "suonare"), one lexical substitution, and on 15 trials she produced the third-person singular

Inflectional morphology with regular nouns and verbs

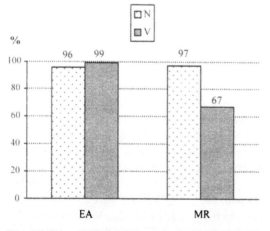

Figure 5. *EA and MR performances on tasks that require the use of morphological rules to correctly inflect regular nouns (N) and verbs (V).*

Homonyms-homophones

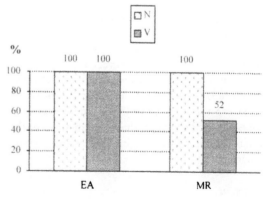

Figure 6. *EA and MR performances on homonyms/homophones nouns (N) and verbs (V) production.*

present form (e.g., "io suono" → "tu suona"), which is ungrammatical. Clearly, these errors cannot be ascribed to a deficit in processing the second-person singular present *form* (e.g., "suoni") because this form was produced flawlessly in the nominal morphology production task.

Production of irregular morphology
The regular morphology task could be solved, in principle, by analogy without necessarily involving an explicit morphological transformation. The patients could have treated the cue word as a string of sounds that had to be transformed into a related string of sounds. It is unlikely that this is the case since MR's performance clearly shows a selective deficit in applying the identical phonological transformation when functioning as a verb as opposed to a noun. Nonetheless, we can directly consider the two patients' ability to retrieve appropriate morphological forms by using a morphological transformation task with irregular verbs and nouns.

The two patients were tested with 156 irregular verb forms. Sixty verb forms were semiregular, in the sense that predictable inflections applied to an unpredictable stem for present perfect (e.g., "corro" [I run] → "ho corso" [I ran]), and 96 were irregular verb forms, such as "vado" (I go) → "sono andato" (I went). They were also tested with 37 irregular singular/plural nouns (e.g., "pirata" [pirate] → "pirati," "bue" [ox] → "buoi"). For the verb stimuli they were required to produce the present perfect in response to the present tense and vice versa and for the noun stimuli they were asked to produce the plural from the given singular noun. Figure 7 shows the two patients' performance for nouns and verbs.

EA was 96% correct with irregular verbs (150/156 correct productions), but he was only 76% (28/37) correct for irregular nouns. His errors with nouns were primarily over-regularisations (6/9;

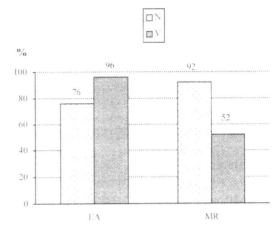

Inflectional morphology with nonregular nouns and verbs

Figure 7. *EA and MR performances on tasks requiring inflections of nonregular nouns (N) and verbs (V).*

e.g., "fantasma" [ghost] → "fantasme" [a neologism] instead of "fantasmi"). MR showed the reverse pattern of performance: She was impaired with irregular verbs, where she only produced 81/156 (52%) correct responses, but performed near-normally with irregular nouns, where she correctly produced 92% (34/37) of the morphological transformations. Her errors with verbs were distributed as follows: 46 no responses, 10 infinitive forms, 2 imperfect tense instead of the present perfect, 13 semantic substitutions, 1 regularisation, 2 perseverations of the input form, and 1 other incorrect inflection.[4]

The double dissociation obtained with EA and MR makes unlikely the interpretation that the patients' grammatical category-specific impairments are simply due to the greater difficulty of some inflections relative to others. Furthermore, logistic regression analyses that considered the contribution of word frequency on the two

---

[4] Note that MR's performance is the opposite from the pattern predicted by Ullman et al. (1997; see also Marslen-Wilson & Tyler, 1997), who claim that agrammatic patients should perform worse on regular than irregular morphological transformations, but is consistent with the performance of another agrammatic patient who also presented with greater difficulty producing irregular than regular past tense forms in English (Shapiro & Caramazza, 2003a).

patients' performance rules out an explanation of the observed effects in terms of frequency: In both cases $\chi^2 < 1$).

Comment

The results of the morphological production tasks are clear. Patient EA does not appear to have difficulties in morphological processing with either verbs or regular nouns. He does have difficulty producing the plural form of irregular nouns but this difficulty seems to be tied to a deficit in lexical access rather than in morphosyntactic processing, as he shows good performance with regular plurals. Patient MR presents a very different pattern. She is clearly impaired in processing verbal morphology, both regular and irregular. Her performance with nouns is near-normal. It is tempting to conclude from these data that the cause of EA's difficulty in noun production has a lexical-semantic basis while MR's difficulty in verb production has a true grammatical basis. However, as we will argue below, the picture may not be as straightforward as this.

DISCUSSION

We have reported the performance of two aphasic patients who present with complementary patterns of seemingly grammatical category-specific deficits: patient EA has considerably greater difficulty at naming nouns than verbs, while patient MR has greater difficulty at naming verbs than nouns. We have also reported various analyses of the two patients' naming performance as well as their performance on several tasks designed to help determine the cause of the naming deficit in each case. These analyses and results suggest that, whether or not the semantic properties of nouns and verbs contribute to the overall naming deficit in the two patients, there is a grammatical basis to MR's grammatical category-specific deficit and perhaps also to EA's deficit. Two arguments will be presented in support of this conclusion. First, consideration of the contribution of specific aspects of the semantic content of nouns and verbs, which have been hypothesised to be the basis for

the distinction between the two grammatical categories, fails to confirm the predicted role of these semantic properties on the two patients' performance. Second, consideration of the role of inflectional morphology on the patients' ability to produce words shows that MR is selectively impaired in the application of verbal but not nominal morphology, suggesting that her difficulty in processing verbs has a grammatical cause.

Semantic accounts of the noun/verb dissociation appeal to properties of the organisation of the semantic/conceptual system in order to explain the existence of putative grammatical category-specific deficits. One hypothesis of the cause of noun production deficits is based on the assumption that the semantic system is organised into modality-specific subsystems and that nouns, especially those referring to biological kind objects, depend more on the visual-semantic than other modality-specific subsystems (Bird et al., 2000). On this view, damage to the visual semantic subsystem should result both in disproportionate difficulty in naming biological kind objects and spared performance in naming actions. EA's performance profile in naming tasks is consistent with this expectation. However, detailed and systematic investigations of EA's ability to process visual as opposed to other semantic properties has consistently found that he is equally impaired for all semantic properties of biological kind objects (Laiacona et al., 1997). This result undermines the core assumption on which this particular semantic hypothesis of the noun/verb dissociation is based; namely, the assumption that EA has suffered damage to a visual semantic subsystem.

The major semantic hypothesis of the cause of selective deficit for verbs assumes that the underlying damage responsible for this putative grammatical category-specific deficit is to a semantic system that represents action concepts (A. R. Damasio & Tranel, 1993; McCarthy & Warrington, 1985; Tranel, Adolphs, Damasio, & Damasio, 2001). On this view, MR's impairment for verbs reflects the fact that words of this grammatical category tend to refer to action concepts, which can be selectively affected by lesions to the left frontal lobe. We have referred to this as the object/action hypothesis, which makes a straightforward prediction: Patients with selective deficits for verbs should be disproportionately impaired for verbs whose meanings implicate clear motor actions by comparison to verbs whose meanings do not implicate motor actions. MR's results are inconsistent with this prediction: She performed far better with verbs denoting clear actions (e.g., draw) than verbs that do not denote actions (e.g., belong to).

The results of the morphology processing tasks provide positive evidence in support of a grammatical basis for the noun/verb dissociation in MR. We found that MR performed near normal levels in producing nominal morphology but extremely poorly in producing verbal morphology, even when the words to be produced in the two cases were homonyms. That is, she had no difficulty producing "*suoni*" as a noun in the context "un suono, due _____" (one sound, two _____), but could not produce "*suoni*" as a verb in the context "io suono, tu _____" (I play, you _____). The selectivity of the morphological processing deficit—that is, the fact that it is restricted to words of the grammatical class she is unable to produce in naming tasks— invites the inference of a common cause responsible for both impairments: a deficit in processing the grammatical category "verb." If we were to accept this argument in support of a grammatical basis for MR's verb naming deficit, we would be required to conclude that EA's disproportionate difficulty in producing nouns does not have a grammatical basis. The latter conclusion would follow from the fact that he performed virtually flawlessly in the morphological processing tasks with both regular verbs and nouns, in contrast to his naming performance, where he was severely impaired in producing nouns but performed well with verbs.

Whatever the merits of this argument, the pattern of results obtained by EA is important for understanding MR's performance pattern. We have argued that the association of a selective naming deficit for verbs with a selective deficit in processing verbal morphology implies a deficit in processing words of a specific grammatical class. However, this inference does not have the force of

logic; it is purely pragmatically driven—it is the simplest hypothesis. Nothing in these results requires the conclusion we have drawn. Thus it could be argued that MR has a semantic deficit in processing verbs and that *as a consequence of this deficit* she is unable to process normally the lexical forms associated with the damaged meanings. That is, the claim could be made that the seemingly grammatical nature of the selective deficit for verbal morphology has a semantic basis, as argued previously for the simple naming task. The argument here is that a semantic deficit will necessarily affect lexical access, including morphological operations. However, this argument is undermined by EA's performance profile, which shows that a deficit in naming words of one grammatical class, presumably because of a semantic deficit, does not entail a morphological processing impairment for that class of words (see also Shapiro & Caramazza, 2003b). In other words, the existence of a dissociation between naming and morphological processing for words of a specific grammatical class increases our confidence that MR's morphological processing deficit does *not* have a semantic basis. The alternative we favour is that MR has a deficit in processing verbs by virtue of their grammatical category.

There are now a number of patients presenting with a noun/verb dissociation who have been studied for their ability to produce nominal and verbal morphology. Table 3 displays the relationship between naming and morphological

Table 3. *Observed patterns of association between deficits in single-word production and morphological processing tasks: Patients MR, RC, and HG are impaired in verb naming tasks; JR and EA are impaired in noun naming*

Patient	Grammatical category-specific morphological deficit?	
	Noun	Verb
MR	–	Yes
RC	–	Yes
HG	–	No
JR	Yes	–
EA	No	–

processing of nouns and verbs for the five patients studied in our laboratories.

As is apparent from the table, there are patients who show a grammatical category-specific deficit both in naming and in morphological processing tasks: MR, RC (Shapiro & Caramazza, 2003a), and JR (Shapiro et al., 2000). There are also patients who show a grammatical category-specific deficit in naming but *not* in morphological processing: EA and HG (Shapiro & Caramazza, 2003b). Furthermore, this contrast in performance patterns is not tied to a specific grammatical category. Thus, while patient EA has a grammatical category-specific deficit in naming nouns with normal morphological processing, patient HG shows the same relationship between naming and morphological processing but for the category "verb." As already noted, the existence of these patterns of performance is important because it shows that a putative semantic deficit for words of one grammatical class, either nouns (EA) or verbs (HG), does not imply a deficit in morphological processing for that category of words. As a consequence, the co-occurrence of grammatical category-specific deficits in naming and morphological processing for patients MR, RC, and JR can be more plausibly interpreted to have a grammatical as opposed to a semantic cause, both in the case of nouns and verbs. This last claim is based on the fact that, as shown in Table 3, the co-occurrence of grammatical category-specific naming and morphological processing deficits has been recorded both for verbs (MR and RC) and nouns (JR). In other words, the picture that is emerging is that even if some cases of putative grammatical category-specific deficit may actually have a semantic cause there are others for which a grammatical cause is the most plausible account.

Establishing the possible cause of a particular form of deficit does not completely determine the organization of the cognitive system involved in the behaviour of interest, but allows for various alternative organisations. Thus, for example, merely establishing that a particular case of grammatical category-specific deficit has a semantic cause or a grammatical cause is, in fact, consistent with several alternative theories of the organisation of the lexical system in the brain. Consider for illustrative purposes the case of EA. We have argued that his disproportionate difficulties in producing nouns may have a semantic cause. By this we mean that properties of the organisation of conceptual knowledge are *sufficient* to account for EA's noun/verb dissociation in naming. For example, it could be that the semantic representations of nouns (or a large part thereof) are "stored" in the temporal lobe(s), which, when damaged, make it difficult to access their corresponding lexical representations. Even if we were to grant this conclusion we would only have committed ourselves to a very narrow claim: The organisation of the semantic system is such that its organisation correlates very highly with grammatical category distinctions in the lexicon. We still have to answer the deeper questions: How and where are the grammatical features of a word represented? Does this information contribute to the organisation of the lexicon? The claim that semantic organisation correlates with grammatical category distinctions leaves these questions unanswered. And it is fully compatible with the possibility that grammatical category plays an independent role in the organisation of the lexicon.

Similar issues are raised by the conclusions we have reached from MR's performance. We have argued that MR's grammatical category-specific deficit has a grammatical cause. This position commits us only to the claim that some aspect of lexical access is structured in such a way that it distinguishes between nouns and verbs, strictly by virtue of their grammatical properties. This claim is not contrary to the proposal that the organisation of the semantic system may have a rough correspondence to grammatical category distinctions (e.g., see Tranel et al., 2001). In fact, it would be surprising if there were not a strong relationship between semantic structure and grammatical category. Furthermore, aside from the simple claim that grammatical category plays an independent role in the organisation of some aspect of the lexical system, it leaves open the issue of how and where a word's grammatical properties are represented. In the introduction we noted that there are at least two hypotheses that could be entertained in the latter regard. One possibility is that grammatical category determines how and where lexical representations are stored in the brain; that is, it could turn out that words of different grammatical categories are represented in distinct neural circuits, thereby allowing for the independent damage of words of one grammatical category. The other possibility is that grammatical category does not directly determine the organisation of lexical representations but that neural segregation by category emerges as a consequence of words undergoing neurally separable morphological processes in the course of language production. That is, if we were to assume that nominal and verbal morphological processes are carried out by distinct neural circuits that could be damaged independently of each other, we would have the basis for grammatical category-specific deficits (for further discussion of the two possibilities see Caramazza & Shapiro, in press; Shapiro & Caramazza, 2003c).

To conclude, we have reported the performance of two patients with grammatical category-specific deficits for nouns (EA) and verbs (MR). Consideration of their naming performance in relation to their morphophonological processing abilities suggests that only one of the two patients (MR) has a true grammatical category-specific deficit. The other patient (EA) did not show morphological processing difficulties of any sort and therefore we cannot exclude that his noun production deficit has a semantic basis. When we consider these cases in the light of other recently reported patients, who have been tested both with naming and morphological processing tasks, the picture that emerges is that grammatical category naming deficits can have different causes: In some cases a semantic basis is more plausible, whereas in others a grammatical account is preferred. One striking feature of the evidence that has accumulated over the years is that patients with verb naming deficits tend to have frontal lobe lesions and to be clinically classifiable as agrammatic aphasics (e.g., Miceli et al., 1984). This generalisation certainly applies to MR and it confirms a suggestion made some years ago by Saffran, Schwartz, and Marin (1980) that an *independent* difficulty in producing main verbs

plays an important part in determining the nature of the complex disorder of agrammatic production.

REFERENCES

Aitkin, M., Anderson, D., Francis, B., & Hinde, J. (1989). *Statistical modelling in GLIM*. Oxford: Oxford Science Publications.

Barbarotto, R., Capitani, E., & Laiacona, M. (1996). Naming deficit in herpes simplex encephalitis. *Acta Neurologica Scandinavica, 93*, 272–280.

Bastiaanse, R., & Jonkers, R. (1998). Verb retrieval in action naming and spontaneous speech in agrammatic and anomic aphasia. *Aphasiology, 12*, 951–969.

Bates E., Chen, S., Tzeng, O., Li, P., & Opie, M. (1991). The noun-verb problem in Chinese. *Brain and Language, 41*, 203–233.

Berndt, R., & Haendiges, A. (2000). Grammatical class in word and sentence production: Evidence from an aphasic patient. *Journal of Memory and Language, 43*, 249–273.

Berndt, R., Haendiges, A., Burton, M., & Mitchum, C. (2002). Grammatical class and imageability in aphasic word production: Their effects are independent. *Journal of Neurolinguistics, 15*, 353–371.

Berndt, R. S., Mitchum, C. C., Haendiges, A. N., & Sandson, J. (1997a). Verb retrieval in aphasia. 1. Characterizing single word impairment. *Brain and Language, 56*, 68–106.

Berndt, R. S., Mitchum, C. C., Haendiges, A. N., & Sandson, J. (1997b). Verb retrieval in aphasia. 2. Relationship to sentence processing. *Brain and Language, 56*, 107–137.

Bird, H., Howard, D., & Franklin, S. (2000). Why is a verb like an inanimate object? Grammatical category and semantic category deficits. *Brain and Language, 72*, 246–309.

Bird, H., Howard, D., & Franklin, S. (2001). Noun-verb differences? A question of semantics: A response to Shapiro & Caramazza. *Brain and Language, 76*, 213–222.

Bortolini, V., Tagliavini, C., & Zampolli, A. (1972). *Lessico di frequenza della lingua italiana contemporanea*. Milano: Garzanti.

Breedin, S., Saffran, E., & Schwartz, M. (1998). Semantic factors in verb retrieval: An effect of complexity. *Brain and Language, 64*, 1–31.

Capitani, E., Laiacona, M., Mahon, B., & Caramazza, A. (2003). What are the facts of semantic category-specific deficits? A critical review of the clinical evidence. *Cognitive Neuropsychology*, *20*, 213–261.

Caramazza, A., & Hillis, A.E. (1991). Lexical organisation of nouns and verbs in the brain. *Nature*, *349*, 788–790.

Caramazza, A., & Shapiro, K. (in press). The representation of grammatical knowledge in the brain. In L. Jenkins (Ed.), *Variation and universals in biolinguistics*. Amsterdam: Elsevier.

Damasio, A. R., & Tranel, D. (1993). Nouns and verbs are retrieved with differently distributed neural systems. *Proceedings of the National Academy of Sciences*, *90*, 4957–4960.

Damasio, H., & Damasio, A. R. (1989). *Lesion analysis in neuropsychology*. New York: Oxford University Press.

Daniele, A., Giustolisi, L., Silveri, M. C., Colosimo, C., & Gainotti, G. (1994). Evidence of a possible neuroanatomical basis for lexical processing of nouns and verbs. *Neuropsychologia*, *32*, 1325–1341.

De Renzi, E., & Di Pellegrino, G. (1995). Sparing of verbs and preserved, but ineffectual reading in a patient with impaired word production. *Cortex*, *31*, 619–636.

Druks, J. (2002). Verbs and nouns—a review of the literature. *Journal of Neurolinguistics*, *15*, 289–316.

Finocchiaro, C. (2002). Sensitivity to the verb [+−agentive] feature: The case of an aphasic subject. *Journal of Neurolinguistics*, *15*, 433–446.

Goodglass, H., Klein, B., Carey, P., & Jones, K. (1966). Specific semantic word categories in aphasia. *Cortex*, *2*, 74–89.

Hillis, A. E., & Caramazza, A. (1995). The representation of grammatical categories of words in the brain. *Journal of Cognitive Neuroscience*, *7*, 396–407.

Hillis, A. E., Tuffiash, E., & Caramazza, A. (2002a). Modality-specific deterioration in naming verbs in nonfluent, primary progressive aphasia. *Journal of Cognitive Neuroscience*, *14*, 1099–1108.

Hillis, A. E., Wityk, R. J., Barker, P. B., & Caramazza, A. (2002b). Neural regions essential for writing verbs. *Nature Neuroscience*, *6*, 19–20.

Humphreys, G. W., & Forde, E. M. E. (2001). Hierarchies, similarity, and interactivity in object recognition: "Category-specific" neuropsychological deficits. *Behavioural and Brain Sciences*, *24*, 453–509.

Laiacona, M., Barbarotto, R., & Capitani, E. (2003a). *Dissociation between the knowledge of animal and plant life stimuli during recovery from HSE. Case for an association between male gender and fruit–vegetables impairment?* Paper presented at the 21st European Workshop on Cognitive Neuropsychology, Bressanone, Italy.

Laiacona, M., Barbarotto, R., Trivelli, C., & Capitani, E. (1993). Dissociazioni semantiche intercategoriali: Descrizione di una batteria standardizzata e dati normativi. *Archivio di Neurologia, di Psicologia e di Psichiatria*, *59*, 209–248.

Laiacona, M., Capitani, E., & Barbarotto, R. (1997). Semantic category dissociations: A longitudinal study of two cases. *Cortex*, *33*, 441–461.

Laiacona, M., Capitani, E., & Caramazza, A. (2003b). Category-specific semantic deficits do not reflect the sensory/functional organization of the brain: A test of the "sensory quality" hypothesis. *Neurocase*, *9*, 221–231.

Luria, A. R., & Tsvetkova, L. S. (1967). Towards the mechanisms of "dynamic aphasia." *Acta Neurologica et Psichiatrica Belgica*, *67*, 1045–1057.

Luzzatti, C., & De Bleser, R. (1996). Morphological processing in Italian agrammatic speakers: Eight experiments in lexical morphology. *Brain and Language*, *54*, 26–74.

Luzzatti, C., Laiacona, M., Allamano, N., De Tanti, A., Inzaghi, M. G., & Lorenzi, L. (1994a). Un test per la diagnosi dei deficit di scrittura. *Ricerche di Psicologia*, *18*, 137–160.

Luzzatti, C., Willmes, K., & De Bleser, R. (1994b). *AAT, Aachener Aphasie Test: Manuale e dati normativi, seconda edizione.*S Firenze: Organizzazioni Speciali.

Marshall, J., Chiat, S., Robson, J., & Pring, T. (1996b) Calling a salad a federation: An investigation of semantic jargon. Part 2—verbs. *Journal of Neurolinguistics*, *9*, 251–260.

Marshall, J., Pring, T., Chiat, S., & Robson, J. (1996a) Calling a salad a federation: An investigation of semantic jargon. Part 1—nouns. *Journal of Neurolinguistics*, *9*, 237–250.

Marslen-Wilson W. D., & Tyler L. K. (1997). Dissociating types of mental computation. *Nature*, *387*, 592–594.

McCarthy, R. A., & Warrington, E. K. (1985). Category-specificity in an agrammatic patient: The relative impairment of verb retrieval and comprehension. *Neuropsychologia*, *23*, 709–723.

Miceli, G., Laudanna, A., Burani, C., & Capasso, R. (1994). *Batteria per l'analisi dei deficit afasici*. Roma: CEPSAG.

Miceli, G., Silveri, M. C., Nocentini, U., & Caramazza, A. (1988). Patterns of dissociation in comprehension and production of nouns and verbs. *Aphasiology*, *2*, 351–358.

Miceli, G., Silveri, M. C., Villa, G., & Caramazza, A. (1984). On the basis of agrammatics' difficulty in producing main verbs. *Cortex, 20,* 217–220.

Myerson, R., & Goodglass, H. (1972). Transformational grammars of three agrammatic patients. *Language and Speech, 15,* 40–50.

Nieuwenhuys, R., Voogt, J., & Van Huijzen, C. (1978). *The human central nervous system.* Berlin: Springer-Verlag.

Rapp, B., & Caramazza, A. (1998). A case of selective difficulty in writing verbs. *Neurocase, 4,* 127–140.

Rapp, B., & Caramazza, A. (2002). Selective difficulties with spoken nouns and written verbs: A single case study. *Journal of Neurolinguistics, 15,* 373–402.

Robinson, G., Rossor, M., & Cipolotti, L. (1999). Selective sparing of verb naming in a case of severe Alzheimer's disease. *Cortex, 35,* 443–450.

Saffran, E. S. (1982). Neuropsychological approaches to the study of language. *British Journal of Psychology, 73,* 317–337.

Saffran, E. M., Schwartz, M. F., & Marin, O. S. M. (1980). Evidence from aphasia: Isolating the components of a production model. In B. Butterworth (Ed.), *Language production, Vol. 1.* London: Academic Press.

Shapiro, K., & Caramazza, A. (2001a). Sometimes a noun is just a noun: Comments on Bird, Howard, & Franklin (2000). *Brain and Language, 76,* 202–212.

Shapiro, K., & Caramazza, A. (2001b) Language is more than the sum of its parts: A reply to Bird, Howard, & Franklin. *Brain and Language, 78,* 397–401.

Shapiro, K., & Caramazza, A. (2003a). Grammatical processing of nouns and verbs in left frontal cortex? *Neuropsychologia, 41,* 1189–1198.

Shapiro, K., & Caramazza, A. (2003b). Looming a loom: Evidence for independent access to grammatical and phonological properties in verb retrieval. *Journal of Neurolinguistics, 16,* 85–112.

Shapiro, K., & Caramazza, A. (2003c) The representation of grammatical categories in the brain. *Trends in Cognitive Sciences, 7,* 201–206.

Shapiro, K., Shelton, J., & Caramazza, A. (2000). Grammatical class in lexical production and morphological processing: Evidence from a case of fluent aphasia. *Cognitive Neuropsychology, 17,* 665–682.

Silveri, M. C., & Di Betta, A. (1997). Noun-verb dissociation in brain-damaged patients: Further evidence. *Neurocase, 3,* 477–488.

Tranel, D., Adolphs, R., Damasio, H., & Damasio, A. R., (2001). A neural basis for the retrieval of words for actions. *Cognitive Neuropsychology, 18,* 655–670.

Tsapkini, K., Jarema, G., & Kehayia, E. (2002). A morphological processing deficit in verbs but not in nouns: A case study in a highly inflected language. *Journal of Neurolinguistics, 15,* 265–288.

Ullman M. T., Corkin, S., Coppola, M., Hickok, G., Growdon, J., Koroshetz, W., et al. (1997). A neural dissociation within language: Evidence that the mental dictionary is part of declarative memory, and that grammatical rules are processed by the procedural system. *Journal of Cognitive Neuroscience, 9,* 266–276.

Warrington, E. K., & McCarthy, R. A. (1987). Categories of knowledge. Further fractionations and an attempted integration. *Brain, 110,* 1273–1296.

Zingeser, L. B., & Berndt, R. S. (1988). Grammatical class and context effects in a case of pure anomia: Implications for models of language production. *Cognitive Neuropsychology, 5,* 473–516.

Zingeser, L. B., & Berndt, R. S. (1990). Retrieval of nouns and verbs in agrammatism and anomia. *Brain and Language, 39,* 14–32.

COGNITIVE NEUROPSYCHOLOGY, 2004, 21 (2/3/4) 125–145

MODELS OF ERRORS OF OMISSION IN APHASIC NAMING

Gary S. Dell
University of Illinois at Urbana-Champaign, USA

Elisa N. Lawler
Georgia Institute of Technology, Atlanta, USA

Harlan D. Harris
University of Illinois at Urbana-Champaign, USA

Jean K. Gordon
University of Iowa, Iowa, USA

Five computational models of lexical access during production are tested for their ability to account for the distribution of aphasic picture-naming errors. The naming profiles ($N = 14$) were chosen from the literature to represent patients who make a relatively large number of omission errors. The most successful models combined the damage assumptions of the semantic-phonological model of lexical access (Foygel & Dell, 2000) with a treatment of omission errors as largely independent from overt errors (Ruml, Caramazza, Shelton, & Chialant, 2000). An explanation for the occurrence of omission errors was provided by the addition of a lexical-threshold parameter (Laine, Tikkala, & Juhola, 1998) to the model. Suggestions for further testing of these models are introduced, as is a new website that allows other researchers to make use of the models.

INTRODUCTION

Impaired word retrieval in aphasia leads to a variety of speech errors, all of which provide insight into the mechanisms of lexical access during speaking. Most research on aphasic errors focuses on *paraphasias*, errors of commission as opposed to errors of omission. Often, paraphasic utterances bear a semantic relation (e.g., "banana" instead of *strawberry*) or phonological relation (e.g., "treen" for *train*) to the intended word. These errors are studied, in part, because they provide specific information about hypothesised components of the lexical system (e.g., Buckingham, 1987; Caramazza & Hillis, 1990; Gagnon, Schwartz, Martin, Dell, & Saffran, 1997; Howard & Orchard-Lisle, 1984; Kay & Ellis, 1987; N. Martin & Saffran, 1997; Mitchum, Ritgert, Sandson, & Berndt, 1990; Nickels & Howard, 1995; Rapp & Goldrick, 2000).

In addition to overt errors, aphasic speakers also make errors of omission. These errors, commonly

---

Correspondence should be addressed to Gary S. Dell, Beckman Institute, University of Illinois, 405 N. Mathews Ave., Urbana IL 61801, USA (Email: gdell@s.psych.uiuc.edu).

This research was supported by DC-00191 (NIH), SBR 98-73450 (NSF), and a post-doctoral award from the National Sciences and Research Council of Canada to Jean Gordon. The authors wish to thank Myrna Schwartz and Adelyn Brecher for providing the breakdowns of the response categories for the profiles from Schwartz and Brecher (2000), and Eleanor Saffran, Nadine Martin, Zenzi Griffin, Prahlad Gupta, Karin Humphreys, Marlene Behrmann, Max Coltheart, and an anonymous reviewer for helpful comments on this work, and Judy Allen for work on the manuscript.

125

DOI:10.1080/02643290342000320

referred to as word-finding blocks, occur in all production tasks, and can be characterised by silence or by evidence of an unsuccessful word search, such as saying "I know what it is, but I can't say it," producing aborted attempts, or describing semantic features of the sought-after word, often called circumlocution (e.g., "It's some kind of animal"). These retrieval blocks have rarely been studied, and for good reason: Without an overt attempt to produce the target, it is difficult to come to any conclusions about the mental processes that are occurring. Nevertheless, clinical observations of word-searching behaviour have allowed some tentative hypotheses to be put forth. For example, comments such as "It's a, no, that's not it..." suggest that speakers sometimes inhibit incorrect responses that come to mind. Descriptions indicate that some of the target's semantic information is available, but not its phonological form. Unfortunately, word-finding difficulties frequently occur without such clues as to their origin.

In picture naming studies, trials on which subjects do not produce a naming attempt are typically excluded from analysis. Yet, such events are common. For example, in Mitchum et al.'s (1990) study of 28 unselected aphasic patients, no response occurred on 11% of naming trials, and for 7 of the patients, no response was the most common error. Mitchum et al.'s no-response category included silence, statements of no response (e.g., "I don't know"), and empty comments (e.g., "I have one of those"). In the studies providing the data for this article, the no-response category was expanded into a general *non-naming-response* category by including, in addition to silence, all responses in which the individual spoke but was not making an attempt to give the single-word name of the pictured object. For example, semantic descriptions were included.

This study seeks to understand errors of omission by developing computational models of naming and relating those models to aphasic data. Specifically, there are two goals. The first is to expand the data to which existing models can be applied. Current models make precise predictions only for errors of commission. By extending their application to non-naming responses, we can better discriminate among the models. The second goal is to begin to investigate the omission process itself, by formalising specific hypotheses. To realise these goals, we begin with two existing models that attribute errors of commission to pathological spreading activation within a lexical network: the *weight-decay* model of Dell, Schwartz, Martin, Saffran, and Gagnon (1997) and the *semantic-phonological* model of Foygel and Dell (2000). Both have been applied, with varying success, to aphasic naming and repetition errors (Caramazza, Papagno, & Ruml, 2000; Croot, Patterson, & Hodges, 1998; Cuetos, Aguado, & Caramazza, 2000; Dell, Schwartz, Martin, Saffran, & Gagnon, 2000; Gordon, 2002; Hanley, Kay, & Edwards, 2002; Hillis, Boatman, Hart, & Gordon, 1999; Ruml & Caramazza, 2000; Ruml, Caramazza, Shelton, & Chialant, 2000; Schwartz & Brecher, 2000; Schwartz & Hodgson, 2002). However, both models lack an account of non-naming responses, and have consequently only been tested using data sets in which such errors are uncommon.

To address this limitation, we consider three accounts of omission errors gleaned from the literature, the *independence model* (Ruml et al., 2000), the *lexical-editor model* (Baars, Motley, & MacKay, 1975), and the *lexical-threshold model* (Laine, Tikkala, & Juhola, 1998). Each of these is grafted onto the existing naming models to create compound models that can, in principle, explain both errors of commission and omission. The adequacy of these compound models is assessed by matching their performance to the naming profiles of aphasic individuals who make many non-naming responses.

The contrast between errors of commission and errors of omission applies to nonaphasic as well as aphasic speech. Overt speech errors in normal speakers are studied in analyses of natural error corpora (e.g., Garrett, 1975) and experimental tasks that create slips (e.g., Ferreira & Humphreys, 2001). Errors of omission in normal speakers are studied through "tip-of-the-tongue" states that often accompany such word-finding blocks (e.g., Burke, MacKay, Worthley, & Wade, 1991; Harley & Bown, 1998; Meyer & Bock, 1992; Miozzo &

Caramazza, 1997; Vigliocco, Antonini, & Garrett, 1997). Theories of normal production provide informal accounts of both omission and commission errors, but there has been no attempt to give a unified computational account of both (see, however, Levelt, Roelofs, & Meyer, 1999; MacKay, 1987, for work in this direction).

Models of non-naming responses

Independence model. The simplest treatment of errors of omission is to assume that they are independent of the processes that generate other responses (Ruml et al., 2000). The independence model is statistical rather than mechanistic; it specifies how errors distribute when non-naming responses occur, but does not attribute those responses to any particular processing system. To illustrate, consider a sample pattern without non-naming responses: 50% correct responses, 10% each of semantic, formally related, and unrelated word errors, and 20% nonword errors. Next, assume that an unspecified process converts a fraction of the overt responses to non-naming responses. If the independence model is correct, this conversion would leave the relative proportions of each of the overt response categories unchanged. For example, assuming 40% non-naming responses, the remaining categories would each be reduced by that percentage, to 30% correct, 6% semantic, 6% formal, 6% unrelated, and 12% nonwords. In essence, the independent non-naming process "steals" from the overt categories in proportion to their frequency.

Lexical-editor model. Speakers appear to monitor their planned output, suppressing it if it is linguistically deviant (Garnsey & Dell, 1984; Hartsuiker & Kolk, 2001; Levelt, 1983; Postma, 2000). The most commonly hypothesised process of this sort is the lexical editor. Baars et al. (1975) demonstrated that phonological exchange errors are less likely when they create nonwords, suggesting that potential nonword slips are caught and either suppressed or corrected before they are uttered (see also Dell, 1986; Dell & Reich, 1981; Humphreys & Swendson, 2002). This kind of editorial process may be responsible for many of the non-naming responses that aphasic patients produce (Mitchum et al., 1990). For example, in Schwartz and Brecher's (2000) study of recovery in naming, patient AK had a relatively low rate of nonword errors given the patient's low correctness, along with many no responses, suggesting that potential nonlexical output was converted to non-naming responses. Instead of converting responses from all overt categories like the independence model, the lexical-editor model converts only potential nonword responses.

Lexical-threshold model. The alternative to the claim that omission errors are caused by an editor suppressing deviant responses is that omissions are the consequence of a failure to retrieve any lexical item. This idea is implicit in accounts of the tip-of-the-tongue state (e.g., Burke et al., 1991) and was made concrete in a connectionist production model developed by Laine et al. (1998). The crucial component of this model for our purposes is the assumption that, to be spoken, words must exceed a minimum level of activation. Word units are retrieved by spreading activation, but if no unit's activation exceeds a specified threshold value, the model generates no response.

Interactive two-step models of lexical access in production

The weight-decay and semantic-phonological models of aphasic naming are derived from the interactive two-step model of lexical access (Dell & O'Seaghdha, 1991; N. Martin, Dell, Saffran, & Schwartz, 1994). Similar models in this domain include the restricted interaction model of Rapp and Goldrick (2000), the node-structure theory of MacKay (1987), and interactive activation models developed by Berg and Schade (1992; also Schade & Eikmeyer, 1998), Harley (1984, 1993), and Stemberger (1985). These are all associated with a bidirectional or interactive flow of activation, distinguishing them from discrete-stage (e.g., Levelt et al., 1999) and cascaded-stage theories (e.g., Caramazza, 1997; Cutting & Ferreira, 1999). First, we present the interactive two-step model's treatment of unimpaired processing, followed by the aphasia models derived from it.

Normal lexical access. Lexical access occurs through spreading activation in a network such as that shown in Figure 1. The network contains units for semantic features, words, and phonemes. Top-down excitatory connections link semantic features to words, and words to phonemes. Bottom-up excitatory connections do the reverse, thus providing interactive feedback from later to earlier levels. There are no inhibitory connections.

The "two-step" aspect of the model refers to distinct word-access and phonological access steps, a feature of many production models (e.g., Bock & Levelt, 1994; Griffin & Bock, 1998; Levelt et al., 1999; Rapp & Goldrick, 2000). Word access begins with a jolt of 10 units of activation to each of the target's semantic features. Activation then spreads through the network for eight time steps, according to a noisy linear activation rule:

$$A_{j,t} = A_{j,t-1} (1-decay) + \Sigma \, w_{ij} A_{i,t-1} + noise$$

where $A_{j,t}$ is the activation of unit j at time step t, *decay* is the decay rate, and w_{ij} is the connection weight from the source unit i to the receiving unit j. During each time step, each unit's activation level is perturbed by normally distributed noise, specifically the sum of two components, intrinsic noise (*SD* = .01) and activation noise (*SD* = .16$A_{j,t}$). After eight time steps, the most highly activated word unit of the appropriate syntactic category is selected, completing the word access stage.

During word access, the target (e.g., CAT) will normally obtain the most activation. However, a consequence of spreading activation is that other words, their phonemes, and their semantic features become active as well. Semantic neighbours (e.g., DOG) obtain activation from shared semantic features. Furthermore, because activation spreads from words to phonemes during word access, and feeds back from phonemes to words, phonologically related (or formal) neighbours such as MAT are also activated. Mixed semantic-phonological neighbours such as RAT are especially activated,

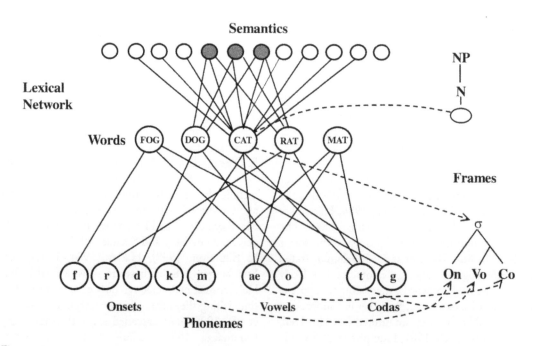

Figure 1. *The two-step interactive activation approach to lexical access in spoken word production, adapted from Dell et al. (1997).*

gaining activation from both top-down and bottom-up influences, leading to the "mixed-error effect," (e.g., N. Martin, Gagnon, Schwartz, Dell, & Saffran, 1996). Due to noise, any of these related words may be selected instead of the target. In extreme cases, an unrelated (LOG) word could also be incorrectly chosen.

Phonological access begins with a 100-unit jolt of activation to the selected word unit, and activation again spreads throughout the network, both in a top-down and bottom-up fashion, for eight more time steps. Finally, the most activated phonemes are selected and linked to slots in a phonological frame. The implemented model encodes only single-syllable CVC words. The possible phonemes are organised into sets of onsets, vowels, and codas, and the most active of each set is chosen and linked to the appropriate slot in a CVC frame. If one or more of these phonemes are not in the selected word, a phonological error—either real-word or nonword—occurs.

For the purposes of model evaluation, six categories were considered: *correct responses* (CAT); *semantic errors* (DOG); *formal errors* (MAT); *mixed errors* (RAT); *unrelated word errors* (LOG); and *nonword errors* (LAT). The model was initially set up to simulate the probability of these six categories in normal speakers' picture naming, based on the 175-item Philadelphia Naming Test (PNT; Roach, Schwartz, Martin, Grewal, & Brecher, 1996). This required specifying the model's lexical neighbourhoods and its connection weight and decay parameters (see Dell et al., 1997, for details).[1]

Aphasic lexical access. Dell et al. (1997) hypothesised that the error patterns produced by aphasic subjects fall on a continuum between the normal error pattern and a "random pattern." The random pattern is the proportion of each response category that would be observed if there were no lexical

influence on word-form retrieval, but the retrieved forms nonetheless respected the general phonological characteristics of (English) words. Dell et al. estimated the random pattern for English from a number of sources in order to reflect the opportunities afforded by the lexicon, such as the relative numbers of semantic and formal neighbours of words, and the proportion of phonologically legal strings that are words. The model's neighbourhoods were then constructed to simulate this estimate.

The continuum of possible response patterns from normal to random, referred to as *the continuity thesis*, constrains the error patterns that can occur in aphasia. With six response categories in the model, a particular pattern represents one point in a six-dimensional space, with the normal pattern at one end of the space and the random pattern at the other. For the continuity thesis to hold, the set of possible patterns should correspond to a simple continuous region connecting these two points. The weight-decay (Dell et al., 1997) and semantic-phonological (Foygel & Dell, 2000) models are methods of generating this region. Each model specifies how the normal model can be "lesioned," and this lesioning defines the region between the normal and random points. The semantic-phonological model is lesioned by reducing one or both of two parameters: s, the weight of the top-down and bottom-up connections between semantic features and words, and p, the weight of the corresponding connections between words and phonemes. The weight-decay model also has two lesionable parameters, a single weight parameter, w, which applies to both semantic and phonological connections, and *decay*.[2]

The two models were compared in a study of 21 patients (Dell et al., 1997; Foygel & Dell, 2000) and in another with 9 patients (Ruml et al., 2000). In these studies, both models performed fairly well in fitting the variety of patterns across the patients.

---

[1] Since the model's development, a small change has been made to the lexical neighbourhoods in response to observations that mixed errors were being under-predicted (Foygel & Dell, 2000; Rapp & Goldrick, 2000). In the current version, the chance opportunity for mixed errors has been increased from .004 to .008.

[2] Decay is set to a constant 0.6 for the semantic-phonological model.

The semantic-phonological model may be theoretically more valid, however, because the ability to create separate semantic and phonological lesions can better explain reported case studies of subjects demonstrating almost exclusively one or the other type of error (Rapp & Goldrick, 2000; Ruml et al., 2000). Moreover, this distinction allows the semantic-phonological model to make more accurate predictions about word repetition in aphasia. Repetition is assumed to depend more on lexical-phonological than lexical-semantic weights, since retrieval from semantics is not required (Foygel & Dell, 2000).

In the current study, we have an opportunity to test the effectiveness of the weight-decay and semantic-phonological models in explaining patterns of errors that previously could not be accounted for by either model; those of aphasic subjects who make many non-naming responses. In our study, we define naming models that account for non-naming responses in different ways, by combining the weight-decay and semantic-phonological models with the independence, lexical-editor, and threshold accounts, and assessing the fit of each to the error profiles of selected aphasic patients from the literature (Dell et al., 1997; Gordon, 2002; Ruml et al., 2000; Schwartz & Brecher, 2000).

MODEL COMPARISON STUDY

Methods

Data sets. Fourteen profiles were chosen from published studies of aphasic naming that used the PNT and its scoring standards. A profile consists of the proportions of correct, semantic, formal, mixed, unrelated, nonword, and non-naming responses to the 175 pictures of the PNT for a single patient. Included in the present study were all profiles from the four articles mentioned above that contained at least 18% non-naming responses,

or in which the non-naming responses comprised at least 80% of all erroneous responses.[3] The profiles were those of subjects GB and VP from Dell et al. (1997); IOC, JR1, EA, and JR2 from Ruml et al. (2000); S10, S16, S21, and S31 from Gordon (2002); and WR5, AS1, AK1, and AK2 from Schwartz and Brecher (2000). (Note that JR1 and JR2 are two different individuals, but AK1 and AK2 are profiles collected from the same person at two different times.) Information on these subjects is given in Table 1 and their naming profiles are presented in italic type in Table 2. Other background information can be obtained from the original publications.

The non-naming category comprises all responses in which the subject fails to provide a valid naming attempt. This includes null responses, in which the subject says nothing or otherwise indicates that he or she cannot name the picture, as well as overt responses that do not constitute a single-word attempt to name the target, such as

Table 1. *Characteristics of subjects contributing naming profiles*

Subject	Age (yrs)	Months post-onset	Education (yrs)
GB[a]	83	4.1	12
VP[a]	64	60.0	12+
IOC[b]	55	18.0	14
JR1[b]	50	36.0	12
EA[b]	65	216.0	15
JR2[b]	43	60.0	16
S10[c]	81	48.0	12
S16[c]	65	10.0	9
S21[c]	67	62.0	9
S31[c]	53	129.0	6
WR5[d]	62	14.5	12
AS1[d]	61	9.0	N/A
AK1[d]	77	14.0	N/A
AK2[d]	77	17.0	N/A

[a] From Dell et al. (1997).
[b] From Ruml et al. (2000).
[c] From Gordon (2002).
[d] From Schwartz and Brecher (2000).

---

[3] We originally required 20% non-naming responses, but then relaxed the criteria to include more subjects.

Table 2. Comparison of five models

Patient	Model	Correct	Semantic	Formal	Mixed	Unrelated	Nonword	Non-naming	Combined	RMSD[a]	χ^2	s / w	p / decay
GB	WD-ind	.39	.07	.09	.01	.03	.08	.32	.40	.011	2.31	.044	.695
	SP-ind	.39	.07	.07	.03	.03	.10	.32		.014	3.40	.017	.021
	WD-editor	.40	.07	.06	.02	.04	.10	.32	.35	.032	8.53	.004	.502
	SP-editor	.36	.08	.11	.02	.08			.39	.012	1.84	.021	.012
	SP-thresh (t = .019)	.41	.05	.09	.02	.03	.08	.31		.015	4.37	.013	.023
VP	WD-ind	.28	.07	.11	.05	.17	.04	.28	.32	.073	56.55	.085	.870
	SP-ind	.22	.08	.13	.04	.06	.19	.28		.024	10.71	.008	.028
	WD-editor	.28	.11	.14	.02	.14	.04	.28	.34	.039	13.93	.055	.764
	SP-editor	.26	.10	.16	.04	.10			.32	.026	9.61	.009	.015
	SP-thresh (t = .014)	.27	.10	.15	.02	.14	.04	.29		.022	9.25	.007	.029
IOC	WD-ind	.17	.03	.00	.01	.00	.00	.79	.79	.007	4.79	.096	.830
	SP-ind	.16	.02	.00	.01	.00	.01	.79		.008	6.36	.019	.035
	WD-editor	.16	.02	.01	.01	.01	.00	.79		.091	50.41	.002	.533
	SP-editor	.10	.06	.10	.01	.09			.63	.059	24.36	.091	.001
	SP-thresh (t = .030)	.18	.03	.08	.02	.03	.00	.78	.68	.012	7.23	.011	.041
JR1	WD-ind	.45	.03	.01	.01	.00	.00	.50	.50	.004	1.50	.056	.688
	SP-ind	.45	.03	.00	.01	.00	.01	.50		.005	1.93	.025	.044
	WD-editor	.46	.02	.01	.01	.00	.00	.50		.090	50.57	.004	.502
	SP-editor	.36	.08	.11	.02	.08			.35	.025	9.09	.099	.002
	SP-thresh (t = .032)	.45	.03	.04	.03	.01	.00	.49	.45	.007	3.78	.015	.055
EA	WD-ind	.34	.22	.03	.08	.11	.01	.21	.22	.078	74.23	.090	.871
	SP-ind	.34	.10	.12	.06	.05	.14	.21		.062	52.89	.009	.036
	WD-editor	.37	.12	.14	.03	.14	.01	.21		.073	38.54	.097	.904
	SP-editor	.35	.12	.18	.07	.07			.21	.075	53.43	.009	.021
	SP-thresh (t = .013)	.35	.12	.16	.03	.15	.01	.19	.17	.066	52.18	.008	.039

(continued overleaf)

Table 2. *Continued*

Patient	Model	Correct	Semantic	Formal	Mixed	Unrelated	Nonword	Non-naming	Combined	RMSD[a]	χ^2	s / w	p / decay
JR2		.67	.07	.01	.03	.00	.03	.19	.22				
	WD-ind	.67	.06	.01	.04	.00	.02	.19		.008	2.86	.075	.761
	SP-ind	.68	.05	.03	.01	.01	.02	.19		.014	8.86	.024	.029
	WD-editor	.63	.08	.07	.02	.04			.17	.040	21.69	.005	.504
	SP-editor	.74	.03	.01	.02	.00			.20	.034	10.05	.100	.004
	SP-thresh (t = .025)	.68	.05	.03	.02	.02	.03	.19		.014	9.07	.020	.030
S31		.04	.09	.05	.03	.07	.03	.68	.71				
	WD-ind	.08	.03	.06	.02	.03	.09	.68		.039	39.68	.095	.914
	SP-ind	.06	.05	.08	.01	.09	.03	.68		.023	16.13	.001	.025
	WD-editor	.06	.05	.10	.02	.09			.69	.030	14.22	.071	.890
	SP-editor	.06	.05	.09	.01	.10			.69	.029	15.89	.003	.005
	SP-thresh (t = .017)	.06	.06	.09	.01	.10	.04	.64		.028	15.72	.001	.025
S10		.55	.07	.02	.02	.02	.02	.30	.32				
	WD-ind	.54	.06	.03	.02	.01	.04	.30		.016	7.73	.040	.660
	SP-ind	.57	.06	.03	.02	.02	.01	.30		.010	2.68	.021	.032
	WD-editor	.51	.08	.09	.02	.06			.24	.048	18.75	.005	.506
	SP-editor	.55	.06	.07	.02	.03			.27	.030	9.80	.022	.015
	SP-thresh (t = .024)	.57	.06	.03	.02	.02	.02	.28		.014	2.89	.017	.032
S16		.66	.05	.02	.04	.02	.02	.19	.21				
	WD-ind	.63	.07	.03	.03	.01	.03	.19		.016	6.61	.056	.711
	SP-ind	.66	.06	.03	.02	.02	.01	.19		.012	8.66	.021	.032
	WD-editor	.64	.07	.07	.02	.04			.16	.033	17.38	.006	.508
	SP-editor	.66	.05	.06	.02	.01			.19	.020	10.69	.025	.017
	SP-thresh (t = .024)	.67	.06	.03	.02	.02	.02	.19		.011	7.23	.019	.033
S21		.61	.05	.06	.02	.00	.08	.18	.26				
	WD-ind	.60	.06	.04	.02	.02	.07	.18		.012	5.19	.028	.624
	SP-ind	.61	.05	.04	.01	.01	.09	.18		.013	6.00	.024	.021
	WD-editor	.59	.08	.08	.02	.05			.20	.035	13.76	.005	.500
	SP-editor	.60	.04	.06	.02	.01			.27	.007	2.29	.027	.014
	SP-thresh (t = .022)	.60	.06	.04	.02	.02	.08	.17		.013	6.10	.019	.024

Table 2. *Continued*

Patient	Model	Correct	Semantic	Formal	Mixed	Unrelated	Nonword	Non-naming	Combined	RMSD[a]	χ^2	s / w	p / decay
AK1		*.42*	*.05*	*.02*	*.01*	*.01*	*.01*	*.48*	*.49*				
	WD-ind	.41	.04	.02	.01	.01	.03	.48		.010	3.99	.041	.662
	SP-ind	.43	.04	.02	.01	.01	.00	.48		.003	0.30	.021	.035
	WD-editor	.35	.08	.11	.02	.08			.36	.076	36.02	.003	.501
	SP-editor	.43	.03	.04	.03	.01			.47	.015	6.66	.099	.002
	SP-thresh (t = .027)	.43	.04	.03	.01	.02	.01	.47		.006	0.79	.015	.037
AS1		*.15*	*.05*	*.11*	*.02*	*.21*	*.19*	*.27*	*.46*				
	WD-ind	.13	.06	.13	.03	.08	.29	.27		.064	44.94	.086	.895
	SP-ind	.15	.09	.14	.02	.15	.19	.27		.031	8.76	.005	.018
	WD-editor	.14	.07	.14	.03	.11			.50	.049	20.34	.051	.773
	SP-editor	.13	.10	.16	.02	.16			.44	.035	9.35	.003	.012
	SP-thresh (t = .011)	.13	.09	.15	.02	.16	.18	.27		.030	8.33	.003	.018
WR5		*.52*	*.07*	*.05*	*.03*	*.06*	*.05*	*.23*	*.28*				
	WD-ind	.49	.07	.06	.02	.03	.10	.23		.026	11.98	.035	.656
	SP-ind	.49	.08	.07	.02	.06	.05	.23		.017	3.64	.016	.027
	WD-editor	.50	.08	.09	.02	.06			.25	.024	5.78	.004	.503
	SP-editor	.52	.07	.08	.02	.04			.26	.018	5.41	.020	.016
	SP-thresh (t = .019)	.52	.08	.06	.02	.05	.05	.22		.010	2.22	.015	.027
AK2		*.85*	*.01*	*.00*	*.01*	*.00*	*.00*	*.13*	*.13*				
	WD-ind	.85	.01	.00	.01	.00	.00	.13		.001	0.05	.067	.583
	SP-ind	.84	.01	.00	.01	.00	.00	.13		.002	0.11	.064	.074
	WD-editor	.78	.06	.04	.01	.02			.09	.042	21.64	.007	.500
	SP-editor	.83	.02	.01	.01	.00			.12	.008	2.67	.069	.009
	SP-thresh (t = .207)	.87	.01	.00	.01	.00	.00	.12		.009	0.98	.059	.055

a These are raw *RMSD*s, with the averaging based on the number of proportions being fit: 6 for editor models and 7 for the others.

semantic descriptions and miscellaneous responses reflecting visual confusions or naming part of the picture.[4] Our rationale for lumping these together is both practical and principled. On the practical side, three of the experimental studies used an "other" category that closely corresponds to our definition (Dell et al., 1997, Ruml et al., 2000, and Gordon, 2002). Schwartz and Brecher (2000) had a non-naming category, defined as null responses and descriptions, and a miscellaneous category that, for consistency, were combined. The principled reason is that the non-naming responses are a natural class, insofar as the subject fails to provide a label, right or wrong, for the picture. Our treatment of this category is not without drawbacks, of course. There are important differences between silence and semantic description, notably with regard to the subjects' knowledge of the target, their awareness of their disability, and their strategies for adapting to it. However, these issues are beyond the scope of the current investigation.

Models. The weight-decay (WD) and semantic-phonological (SP) models were combined with the independence, lexical-editor, and threshold approaches to create the WD-independence, SP-independence, WD-editor, SP-editor, and SP-threshold models. (For reasons described later in footnote 5, we are not reporting a test of a WD-threshold model.) Each of the five models was fitted to the 14 profiles by finding parameter values that make the model's response proportions as similar as possible to the profiles, specifically by minimising the χ^2 goodness-of-fit value. Each model uses, for each profile, three free parameters to fit seven proportions constrained to add to 1.0. The weight-decay and semantic-phonological models each have two parameters, w and *decay*, and s and p, respectively. Dealing with the non-naming responses adds another free parameter. In the case of the independence models, the additional parameter is the proportion of non-naming responses.

For the lexical-editor models, it specifies the proportion of nonword responses that are converted to non-naming responses. For the SP-threshold model, the third parameter is the threshold, t, the minimum level of activation that the selected word unit must possess for the naming process to continue.

Non-naming response parameters were incorporated into the compound models in different ways depending on the approach taken to non-naming responses. For the independence and editor versions of the models, it was possible to reduce the number of explicitly fitted parameters from three to two, by adjusting the profiles. This adjustment was easy to make in the independence models. Because non-naming responses are assumed to be independent of the processes that generate overt responses, the non-naming proportion is simply removed from the profile, and the remaining proportions are normalised, that is, recalculated as a proportion of the modified total (Ruml et al., 2000). The normalised profile is fitted to determine the remaining two parameters as described below. The lexical-editor versions of the models were also fitted by making a simple adjustment. Because non-naming responses are assumed to correspond to suppressed nonwords, the proportion of non-naming responses is added to that for nonwords, and the adjusted profile is then fitted for the two remaining parameters. The SP-threshold model required an explicit search for all three parameters simultaneously.

Fitting routines for independence and editor models. The goal of the fitting procedure is to find the two parameters that generate the closest fits overall to the adjusted profiles. Because we required each model profile to be calculated over 10,000 runs, it is very time-consuming to search for the best fit. Consequently, we generated and stored model profiles in advance. In some areas of the space defined by the two parameters, small changes in

---

[4] The vast majority of non-naming responses consisted of null responses and semantic descriptions. To illustrate, the breakdown for the four profiles selected from Schwartz and Brecher (2000), the only study for which these numbers are available, is: 65% no responses, 29% semantic descriptions, 6% miscellaneous.

the parameters result in large changes in the model profiles; in other areas, small parameter changes result in insignificant profile changes. Rather than generate a uniformly dense array of model profiles to handle the areas in which small changes make a difference, a variable-resolution map was used, as in Foygel and Dell (2000).

We used a new method for determining which model profiles were stored—that is, which points on the variable-resolution map were occupied. Briefly, quasi-random points were generated iteratively, but the associated model profile was only generated and stored if the point's nearest neighbours (in parameter space) were sufficiently dissimilar (in model profile space). The result is a map consisting of model profiles that have very small differences from their neighbours, but that together define the space of possible error patterns as densely as necessary.

More specifically, points were generated using a Sobel' sequence, which is a way of subrandomly generating points that maximises coverage and minimises "lumpiness" (Press, Teukolsky, Vetterling, & Flannery, 1992). Five hundred initial points were generated, and the following procedure was then used to determine which subsequent points to keep. The average model profile of the eight nearest neighbours of a potential point was compared to each of those neighbours. If a χ^2 comparison between the average value and all eight of the neighbours was less than an arbitrary threshold (here, 8, using $N = 175$ for the PNT), then the point was determined to be superfluous and was skipped. Otherwise, the model profile for that point was generated and stored, and the process continued. The map was considered complete once 500 points in a row were skipped, giving 3782 stored model profiles for the semantic-phonological model, and 7481 stored model profiles for the weight-decay model. These fitting routines and the underlying model can be used at the following web address:
http://langprod.cogsci.uiuc.edu/cgi-bin/webfit.cgi

Fitting routine for SP-threshold model. A third free parameter, representing the lexical threshold t, was added to the lexical-semantic and lexical-phonological weight parameters, s and p, in the SP model. If the activation of no word unit is greater than t at the moment that the model chooses the most activated word unit, the trial is assigned to the non-naming-response category. Otherwise, the selected word undergoes phonological access and an overt response is generated.

Because three free parameters have to be specified in the SP-threshold model, it is not possible to use the variable-resolution two-dimensional map described above. Instead, we used a hill-climbing technique. First, we started with values of s and p generated from the SP-independence model, and made an educated guess about the best value of t, based on our experience from exploring the parameter space of the SP-threshold model. Then we evaluated the 26 locations adjacent to this starting location that are generated by increasing or decreasing at least one parameter by a step of .01. The location that led to the smallest value of χ^2 was then selected. The procedure was then repeated with the selected location replacing the starting location. This exploration continued until none of the adjacent locations led to a smaller χ^2 value than the current location. At this point, the step size was decreased to .001, and the process begun again. The final location was selected as the fitted parameter values. Note that this procedure does not guarantee finding the best fit for a profile, or even that the best fit is near the final location. We repeated the fitting process for each profile, starting from a randomly determined region of the parameter space (bounded by 0 and .1). In all cases, the fits starting from the initial locations described above were either better than or identical to those obtained from the random starting locations. Nonetheless, it must be recognised that the addition of a third parameter whose value must be discovered makes the fits of the SP-threshold model more likely to be suboptimal than the fits generated from the variable-resolution map.

Results and discussion

Table 2 presents the proportions of responses in each of the seven categories for each of the 14 profiles, along with the proportions and parameters generated from each of the five models. Two measures of goodness of fit are given for each profile: χ^2, the statistic used to discover the fit, and *root mean squared deviation* (*RMSD*). RMSD is the more intuitive measure of fit as it summarises the degree of deviation of the obtained proportions from the models' predictions. (An RMSD of .030 means that the model and patient proportions are on average .030 apart.) How close should these proportions be? It is hard to say, because there are no established benchmarks of quantitative modelling in this area. Until that is the case, measures of fit are best interpreted comparatively, rather than absolutely. Our discussion, therefore, focuses on which models provide the best fit.

There were clear differences among the models in overall quality of fit, with the most obvious being the superiority of the semantic-phonological models over the weight-decay models. The total χ^2 values for the SP-independence (130.4), SP-threshold (130.1), and SP-editor (171.1) models were much smaller than those for the WD-independence (262.4) and WD-editor (331.6) models.[5] The mean RMSD measures tell a similar story: SP-independence (.017), SP-threshold (.018), SP-editor (.028), WD-independence (.026), and WD-editor (.050). As Table 2 shows, there is no profile for which the two WD models fit better on average than the three SP models, and several where the SP models are much better (e.g., AS1, VP). In particular, the WD models have difficulty predicting the unrelated and nonword categories. The difficulty stems from the use of global parameters. Parameter settings that promote unrelated word errors necessarily also create many nonword errors. However, AS1's and VP's nonword errors are not particularly numerous relative to word errors. The ability of the SP models to separate influences on word errors (determined largely by the *s* parameter) from nonword errors (determined largely by *p*) gives them the edge in fitting these profiles.

A second result is that the independence and threshold models provide better fits than the lexical-editor models. Considering all five models, the SP-independence and SP-threshold models are the clear winners. The SP-independence model has significantly smaller RMSD's than both the SP-editor model, $t(13) = 2.52$,[6] and the WD-independence model, $t(13) = 2.20$. The SP-threshold model is also clearly superior to the SP-editor model, $t(13) = 2.73$, and (marginally) better than the WD-independence model $t(13) = 2.00$. The mean RMSD's for the SP-independence (.017) and SP-threshold (.018) models indicate a close agreement between model and profile proportions. Moreover, these two models account for 96.3% and 95.9% respectively of the variance in profile proportions.[7] The 96.3% value for the SP-independence model includes the variance within the non-naming category, which this model fits trivially by setting its third free parameter to the proportion of non-naming responses. Even if the non-naming category is left out, the model still accounts for 93.0% of the variance in the remaining categories.

Both the SP-independence and SP-threshold models fit the individual profiles fairly well, with one exception (EA, to be discussed later). There are no profiles for which the SP-editor model

---

[5] We explored the WD-threshold model as well, but were not able to find parameters that led to fits comparable to the WD-independence model. Given that the SP-threshold and SP-independence models had similar fits, more stringent parameter searches might lead to similar fits for the WD-threshold and WD-independence models. However, these would still be inferior to those for the SP-threshold and SP-independence models.

[6] The critical value for $t(13)$ is 2.16. The RMSDs for the two independence models used in these *t*-tests were adjusted upward so that these models were not credited for matching the non-naming response proportion (which they do perfectly because their third parameter is just this proportion). Specifically, the adjustment averages the total squared deviations over six rather than seven proportions for these models. The adjustment is conservative given our conclusion that the independence models are favoured over the editor models.

[7] This measure compares the squared deviations between the model and profile proportions to the squared deviations between each profile proportion and the mean proportion for that category across all profiles.

provides a close fit (say, RMSD < .020) and the SP-independence and SP-threshold models do not, while the reverse is clearly true. For example, the SP-independence and SP-threshold models are considerably better for IOC, JR1, JR2, S10, and S16. IOC's profile is a case in point. Under the SP-editor model, the many non-naming responses (.79) are assumed to be suppressed nonwords. To generate such a large proportion of nonwords, the model must set a very low value for p (.001). However, the processes that generate nonword errors create formal errors as well. With the parameters assigned to IOC by the SP-editor model, the

expected proportion of formals is .08, a significant contrast to the obtained proportion of zero.

This over-prediction of formal errors is a general problem with the SP-editor model when compared to the other SP models. Figure 2 illustrates how the predicted proportions for each model deviate from the obtained proportions in each response category, separately for each profile. (EA was left out because this profile was not fit well by any model; possible reasons for this will be discussed shortly.) A positive number indicates that the profile proportions exceed the model ones; a negative number means that the profile

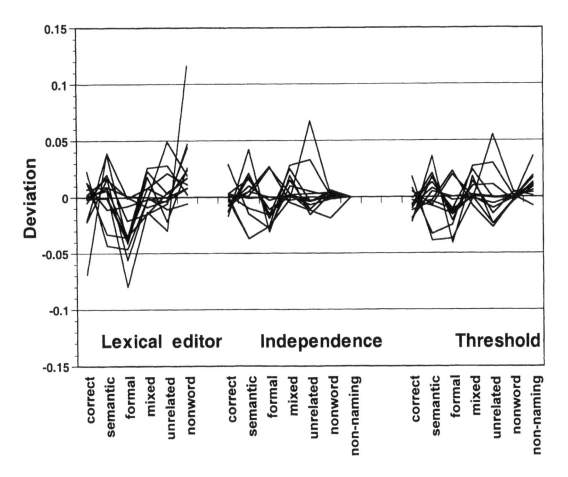

Figure 2. *Deviations between obtained response proportions and model response proportions, as a function of response category for the SP-editor model (left), the SP-independence model (middle), and the lexical threshold model (right). Each line represents a single profile (EA is not included).*

proportions are too small. The deviations for the SP-independence and SP-threshold models are small, and do not tend to one side or the other of zero. The SP-editor model not only has larger deviations, but they appear to be systematic. For example, the nonword category is almost always over-predicted, while the proportion of formals is underestimated. Although these deviations are largest for IOC (the most deviant line in the figure) they are present on most of the other profiles.

A third important finding is that none of the models fits EA's profile very well. The large number of semantic (.22), mixed (.08), and unrelated (.11) errors, along with a smaller proportion of formal errors (.03), challenges all of the models, even the SP models, which can assign lexical-semantic lesions without creating errors during phonological access. These models' neighbourhoods, however, do not support the generation of such high percentages of semantic and mixed errors. Moreover, when the SP models create many mixed and unrelated word errors, they must also generate a fair number of formal errors. Mixed errors suggest strong phonological feedback, which also activates formal neighbours of the target; unrelated errors signal that the target's activation is sufficiently degraded that these formal neighbours will often be selected instead of the target. Thus, EA's low proportion of formal errors presents a problem.

A clue to EA's naming pattern is the unusual finding that many of his semantic and mixed errors were verbs rather than nouns (Ruml et al., 2000). The naming models, however, assume that the processes ensuring selection of a noun operate without error, even for patients. Perhaps EA's profile reflects a failure of the syntactic system to constrain lexical access. Gordon and Dell (2003) implemented a model of such failure. Lesioning the weights from syntactic/sequential states to word units led to "agrammatic" production, and

specifically to naming deficits in which words were deleted or replaced by other words often not in the target syntactic category. We note that EA's sentence production was described as nonfluent, but lacking in articulatory problems (Ruml et al., 2000), and "agrammatic" (Berndt, Mitchum, Haendiges, & Sandson, 1997), which is consistent with the hypothesised lesion in syntactic/sequential states.[8]

The dominance of semantic and mixed errors along with the absence of phonological errors make EA's profile similar to three other cases in the literature that have challenged the semantic-phonological model: PW (Rapp & Caramazza, 1998; Rapp & Goldrick, 2000), JF (Foygel & Dell, 2000), and DP (Cuetos et al., 2000). Such cases might be consistent with the model if the naming difficulty occurs secondary to a problem with semantic representations. Recall that the models assume intact semantic input, and that semantic and other word errors occur in the process of mapping that input onto lexical units. The assumption of intact semantic input is probably false for EA, at least according to Shelton and Weinrich (1997), whose test of EA's single-word comprehension indicated that he had a "mild deficit to semantic knowledge" (p. 122). This explanation, however, does not hold for PW and DP, who are reported to have preserved semantic-level representations (Cuetos et al., 2000; Rapp & Goldrick, 2000). Instead, Rapp and Goldrick were able to account for PW's error pattern (which is similar to DP's) by positing that lexical-phonological feedback is restricted. That is, the bottom-up weights are weaker than the top-down ones. This restriction allowed Rapp and Goldrick's model to generate semantic errors without leading to formal errors at the word access stage, since the latter are promoted by strong feedback.

Restricted feedback, though, cannot by itself account for EA's profile. Ruml et al. (2000) explored restricted feedback versions of these

---

[8] Berndt et al. (1997) found that most examples of the uncommon verb-for-noun substitution were made by agrammatic aphasics. Those patients, however, were generally more impaired in accessing verbs, and more often replaced them with nouns than the other way around.

models and still were not able to generate high enough proportions of semantic, mixed, and unrelated errors. Consequently, we suggest that the failure to fit EA stems from the model's assumptions of intact semantic and syntactic inputs, either or both of which may have been violated in this case. In any event, this error pattern points to a clear limitation in the model as a general account of aphasic naming.

EA aside, the SP-independence and SP-threshold models provide a good account of the patient profiles in our sample, certainly better than the other three models examined. Consequently, the damage assumptions of the semantic-phonological model and the treatment of non-naming responses proposed in the independence and threshold models are supported over the weight-decay and lexical-editor models. This is not to say that the independence or threshold models apply universally or that the suppression of nonword responses—as assumed by the lexical-editor model—does not occur. Rather, the evidence from our sample is that the independence and threshold models are, on balance, more powerful in describing patient performance.

Moreover, they allow us to extend the observations that can be brought to bear on models of aphasic lexical access.

Thus far, we have treated the SP-independence and SP-threshold models together. On the basis of fit quality, they are indistinguishable, though clearly superior to the other models. This is true for the individual profiles as well as overall measures of fit. Only EA is poorly fit, both models having trouble matching the proportions in the formal, mixed, and semantic categories. For the remaining profiles, the two models fit reasonably well and offer similar characterisations. For example, for S10 the predicted profiles for SP-threshold and SP-independence differ only for the nonword (.02 and .01) and non-naming (.28 and .30) categories. The models assign similar values of s (.021 and .017) and p (.032 for both), characterising this patient as having more of a lexical-semantic than lexical-phonological deficit.

Clearly, the SP-threshold model behaves like the SP-independence model. Figure 3 shows why. The figure shows what types of responses a threshold tends to inhibit using a sample model with typical aphasic parameters. A model with $s = .02$

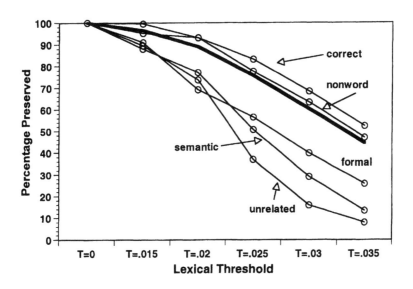

Figure 3. *The effect of threshold (T) on the proportions of each response category that are preserved. The bold line represents the average percentage of responses, across categories, preserved at each threshold value.*

and $p = .02$ and no threshold is compared to the same model with a variety of threshold values. The ordinate presents the percentage of responses exceeding the threshold. With t equal to zero (i.e., no threshold), all responses will emerge as overt responses. As the threshold increases, the proportions of supra-threshold responses are reduced. The narrow lines illustrate that the ability of the threshold to inhibit responses varies somewhat across response categories. Nevertheless, *all* of the categories decrease dramatically as t increases; the threshold robs from all response types and turns them into null responses. The single thick line indicates the mean percentage of responses preserved across all categories. In essence, this represents the independence model, in which non-naming responses are stolen from each category in proportion to its frequency of occurrence. The proximity of the narrow lines to the thick one thus demonstrates the degree of similarity between the SP-threshold and SP-independence models.

Despite their similarity, however, the two models are not identical. For example, the threshold is more likely to suppress a potential unrelated-word response than a correct response. A situation in which the most activated word unit corresponds to an unrelated word is most likely to be one in which all of the activations are very low, and hence subthreshold. Nevertheless, the differences between the two models are subtle with respect to their ability to account for the naming profiles. The overt response categories that are most common in the profiles are the correct and nonword categories. Figure 3 shows that the threshold takes away from these categories at about the same rate that it would take away if independence held. Consequently, the two models are difficult to distinguish.

Are there any reasons, then, to prefer either the SP-independence or the SP-threshold model? The SP-independence model has the advantage of being easy to use and can, therefore, be taken as the default assumption for treating non-naming responses when the focus of the analysis is on the overt error categories (e.g., Ruml et al., 2000). Its main drawback is that it does not specify a mechanism for non-naming responses. Although it succeeds in characterising error distributions

statistically, it does not explain them. The SP-threshold model may provide the missing explanation. Thresholds are common in biological systems, and particularly so in neural network models of such systems. Thus, an activation-level threshold governing whether or not a lexical unit proceeds to phonological access is a plausible mechanism. In the general discussion, we further consider the contrast between these models as well as other ramifications of our findings.

GENERAL DISCUSSION

The principal findings of the current model comparison were as follows:

1. The semantic-phonological model (Foygel & Dell, 2000) is better suited to matching naming profiles with a high percentage of non-naming responses than is the weight-decay model (Dell et al., 1997).

2. The distribution of non-naming responses is better accounted for by models incorporating an independence assumption (Ruml et al., 2000) or threshold mechanism (Laine et al., 1998) than a lexical-editor mechanism (Baars et al., 1975).

3. The SP-threshold model is largely indistinguishable from the SP-independence model in terms of its predictive power, but offers a more theoretically motivated mechanism for explaining the occurrence of non-naming responses.

4. The profile of EA, with its relatively high percentage of semantic and mixed errors, and low percentage of formal errors, is not fit well by any of the models, a finding that may call into question the models' assumptions of intact syntactic and semantic input.

It is important to put these conclusions in perspective. The superiority of the SP-independence and SP-threshold models does not mean that the suppression of deviant responses does not occur. On the contrary, one can construe a threshold as a strategically determined value that serves to prevent potentially erroneous responses. Moreover, the relatively poor performance of the lexical-editor models does not suggest that patients never preferentially suppress nonword errors. Rather, a pure lexical-editor account is less favoured by the current evidence. Given that any single account is unlikely to apply to all patients, it is worth noting that several of our profiles were well fit by the SP-editor model, for example, WR5, AK1, and AK2. Each of these profiles is associated with few nonword errors and a surfeit of non-naming responses. In one or more of these cases, the lexical-editor model might be the correct explanation. Nevertheless, we emphasise that the SP-independence and SP-threshold models also accounted for these profiles, as well as for other profiles that the SP-editor model was less successful in characterising.

Finally, we recognise that one can construct alternative editor models that may give more accurate results. For example, one can hypothesise that all semantically unrelated responses (non-words, formals, and unrelated errors) are subject to suppression. Models based on these broader editors, however, will be difficult to distinguish from the independence assumption because they, like the independence model, convert potential responses from multiple categories into non-naming responses. We have focused on a *lexical* editor because not only is it supported in the literature, but also it is maximally distinct from models that behave like the independence model. Model testing is best served by examining motivated models whose predictions stand in sharp contrast.

Ultimately, the decision about the best account of non-naming responses, both in general and for particular patients, cannot be made on the basis of naming profiles alone. In addition, the competing models should be used to generate and test predictions. Here we give two examples of this strategy: predicting word repetition performance from word naming performance, and predicting variations in naming profiles as a function of semantic neighbourhood.

Predicting repetition from naming

The semantic-phonological and weight-decay models assign parameters to profiles based on naming performance. Dell et al. (1997) and Foygel

and Dell (2000) used these parameters to predict auditory word repetition by identifying repetition performance with the phonological access stage of the naming process. This assumes that repetition entails access of the appropriate word unit through an intact perceptual system, followed by the mapping of that word unit onto its phonological representation (see R. C. Martin, Lesch, & Bartha, 1999, for evidence of separate input and output lexical-phonological mappings). Foygel and Dell found that naming parameters from the SP model predicted repetition performance better than did parameters from the WD model. This is because word repetition depends more on lexical-phonological mappings than on lexical-semantic mappings, and the SP model is able to characterise these differentially. The WD model's parameters do not isolate relatively impaired or preserved lexical-phonological abilities; hence, its repetition predictions are less accurate.

Predicting repetition can also discriminate between the independence/threshold and editor accounts of the non-naming responses. Note in Table 2 that the independence and threshold versions of the SP model assign higher values of p than s for 13 of 14 profiles, associating these patients with more severe lexical-semantic than lexical-phonological lesions. In contrast, the SP-editor model assigns a lower p than s in 10 of 14 cases, because treating non-naming responses as suppressed nonwords increases the evidence for a phonological deficit, by the model's logic. Because good repetition depends more on the lexical-phonological weight, the SP-independence and SP-threshold models predict that repetition should be relatively good for these patients in contrast to their naming, whereas the SP-editor model predicts poorer repetition.

Ruml et al. (2000) reported word repetition data for some of the subjects in their study, two of whom (EA and JR2) are represented in this study. Both EA and JR2 repeated the items of the PNT without error. Which of the models, if any, can account for this good performance? It turns out that that both the SP-independence and SP-threshold models can. Using the selected parameters for these two patients to carry out the repetition task, the two models perform at 97% and 98% correct respectively for EA, and 96% and 95% for JR2. The SP-editor model, on the other hand, predicts accuracy levels of only 76% for EA and 80% for JR2. The superiority of the SP-independence and SP-threshold models in predicting the repetition of EA and JR2 arises because they assigned larger values of p than did the SP-editor model, such that repetition was better preserved.

Semantic neighbourhood effects

In a study of naming errors by an aphasic individual (MW), Blanken, Dittmann, and Wallesch (2002) found that items differed in their propensity to create errors of either commission or omission. Target items that had close semantic competitors (as determined by independently gathered ratings) tended to create semantic errors, whereas those with few competitors often led, instead, to failures to respond. These two error types traded off such that the sum of the two categories differed very little as a function of the competitiveness of target's semantic neighbourhood. As semantic errors and no responses were the dominant error categories for MW, this trade-off implies that the proportion of correct responses was similar for competitive and less competitive neighbourhoods. Blanken et al.'s finding demonstrates, not surprisingly, that semantic-error probability increases with the opportunities for semantic errors. More importantly, though, it suggests that omissions are promoted more by the failure to strongly activate any lexical items, than by the activation of many competing items.

With respect to the current article, the trade-off between semantic errors and null responses is a clear prediction of the lexical-threshold model, provided that these are common error types for a particular patient. Consider an example using the SP-threshold model with $s = .02$, $p = .03$, and

$t = .03$. If the model neighbourhood with one semantic neighbour of the target (e.g., DOG for the target CAT) is tested, the model is correct 57% of the time, fails to respond 35% of time, and makes 3% semantic errors. If the neighbourhood is made more competitive by including DOG and RAT as semantic neighbours of CAT, these percentages become 60% correct, 28% no responses, and 9% semantic errors.[9] The increase in competition creates more semantic errors *at the expense of null responses*, just as was found by Blanken et al. (2002). The model behaves this way because competition increases the activation of both the target and its competitors. Activation reverberates between words and the shared properties of these words. The more competitors there are, and the more properties they share, the more reverberation occurs. The end result is that the most activated word unit, whether it is correct or not, has a greater chance of being above threshold. Hence, an overt response is more likely to occur. The presence of more competition, of course, leads to more semantic errors, but this is almost entirely compensated for by the decreased likelihood of an omission.

The lexical-editor approach does not make the same prediction. Consider a set of parameters (e.g., s and p both at .01) that creates a large number of nonwords, the responses that the editor can convert into omissions. Using the less competitive neighbourhood, the model generates 18% correct responses, 7% semantic errors, 52% nonwords, and 23% other errors (formals and unrelateds). When the more competitive neighbourhood is tested, the results are 18% correct, 15% semantic errors, 52% nonwords, and 15% other errors. Greater competition naturally leads to more semantic errors, but not at the expense of the nonword category, which remained at 52%. Rather it is at the expense of other errors. Consequently, the increase in semantic errors would not be associated with fewer omissions, on the assumption that these are suppressed nonwords.

---

[9] Note that RAT is also a phonological neighbour of CAT. This only tends to make it more of a competitor because of the model's interactive assumption, the point being to demonstrate that additional competition increases lexical substitution errors, while decreasing failures to respond.

It is difficult to say what the independence model would predict about Blanken et al.'s (2002) trade-off. Because that model lacks a true mechanism for generating no responses, it cannot create different proportions of omissions as a function of neighbourhood competitiveness without effectively adding parameters. So, unlike the lexical threshold model, which makes the correct prediction, and the lexical-editor model, which makes the wrong prediction, the independence model makes no prediction at all.

The repetition and semantic-neighbourhood predictions show how the models can be tested using data outside of the naming profiles. Predictions for repetition supported the SP-independence and SP-threshold models over the SP-editor model, and the semantic-neighbourhood prediction was consistent only with the SP-threshold model. These tests, though, are more illustrative than definitive, as they concerned only two cases for the repetition prediction, and only one for the semantic-neighbourhood prediction.

CONCLUSION

The current study demonstrates that it is possible to develop and test models of aphasic naming using errors of omission, as well as errors of commission. Our analysis favoured two models that were largely indistinguishable, the SP-independence model and the SP-threshold model. For the most part, these models provided close fits to the naming profiles of individuals who tend to make many non-naming responses. The analysis helps to constrain the interactive two-step theory of lexical access that is the basis of those models, and specifically supports the semantic-phonological approach to lesioning, as well as the independence and lexical-threshold accounts of non-naming responses. The weight-decay account of aphasic lesions suffered from its assumption that pathological parameter values are global, that is, they cannot differentially characterise lexical-semantic and lexical-phonological abilities (see Rapp & Goldrick, 2000; Ruml & Caramazza, 2000). The lexical-editor account of non-naming responses

forced the profiles to treat too many responses as nonwords. Although the lexical-editor account, in combination with the semantic-phonological model, fit several profiles quite well, the other approaches also worked well with these profiles.

By providing a method of analysing non-naming responses, we hope to expand the sources of evidence that can inform models of normal and aphasic speech production. Although the hypotheses presented here were able to explain a number of observations of aphasic behaviour in language production tasks, they must be considered preliminary. Further evidence from both normal and aphasic subjects, and from a variety of tasks, is needed to strengthen these findings and generate new predictions. We encourage other researchers interested in deficits in spoken word production to explore the models presented here using the website introduced in the Methods section of the study.

REFERENCES

Baars, B., Motley, M., & MacKay, D. (1975). Output editing for lexical status in artificially elicited slips of the tongue. *Journal of Verbal Learning and Verbal Behavior, 14,* 382–391.

Berg, T., & Schade, U. (1992). The role of inhibition in a spreading activation model of language production, Part 1: The psycholinguistic perspective. *Journal of Psycholinguistic Research, 22,* 405–434.

Berndt, R. S., Mitchum, C. C., Haendiges, A. H., & Sandson, J. (1997). Verb retrieval in aphasia. *Brain and Language, 56,* 68–106.

Blanken, G., Dittmann, J., & Wallesch, C.-W. (2002). Parallel or serial activation of word forms in speech production? Neurolinguistic evidence from an aphasic patient. *Neuroscience Letters, 325,* 72–74.

Bock, J. K., & Levelt, W. J. M. (1994). Language production: Grammatical encoding. In M. Gernsbacher (Ed.), *Handbook of psycholinguistics* (pp. 945–984). San Diego, CA: Academic Press.

Buckingham, H. W. (1987). Phonemic paraphasias and psycholinguistic production models for neologistic jargon. *Aphasiology, 1,* 381–400.

Burke, D. M., Mackay, D. G., Worthley, J. S., & Wade, E. (1991). On the tip of the tongue: What causes word finding failures in young and older adults? *Journal of Memory and Language, 30,* 542–579.

Caramazza, A. (1997). How many levels of processing are there in lexical access? *Cognitive Neuropsychology, 14*, 177–208.

Caramazza, A., & Hillis, A. (1990). Where do semantic errors come from? *Cortex, 26*, 95–122.

Caramazza, A., Papagno, C., & Ruml, W. (2000). The selective impairment of phonological processing in speech production. *Brain and Language, 75*, 428–450.

Croot, K., Patterson, K., & Hodges, J. R. (1998). Single word production in nonfluent progressive aphasia. *Brain and Language, 61*, 226–273.

Cuetos, F., Aguado, G., & Caramazza, A. (2000). Dissociation of semantic and phonological errors in naming. *Brain and Language, 75*, 451–460.

Cutting, J. C., & Ferreira, V. S. (1999). Semantic and phonological information flow in the production lexicon. *Journal of Experimental Psychology: Learning, Memory, and Cognition, 25*, 318–344.

Dell, G. S. (1986). A spreading activation theory of retrieval in language production. *Psychological Review, 93*, 283–321.

Dell, G. S., & O'Seaghdha, P. G. (1991). Mediated vs. convergent lexical priming in language production: Comment on Levelt et al. *Psychological Review, 98*, 604–614.

Dell, G. S., & Reich, P. A. (1981). Stages of sentence production: An analysis of speech error data. *Journal of Verbal Learning and Verbal Behavior, 20*, 611–629.

Dell, G. S., Schwartz, M. F., Martin, N., Saffran, E. M., & Gagnon, D. A. (1997). Lexical access in aphasic and nonaphasic speakers. *Psychological Review, 104*, 801–838.

Dell, G. S., Schwartz, M. F., Martin, N., Saffran, E. M., & Gagnon, D. A. (2000). The role of computational models in the cognitive neuropsychology of language: Reply to Ruml and Caramazza. *Psychological Review, 107*, 635–645.

Ferreira, V. S., & Humphreys, K. R. (2001). Syntactic influence on lexical and morphological processing in language production. *Journal of Memory and Language, 44*, 52–80.

Foygel, D., & Dell, G. S. (2000). Models of impaired lexical access in speech production. *Journal of Memory and Language, 43*, 182–216.

Gagnon, D. A., Schwartz, M. F., Martin, N., Dell, G. S., & Saffran, E. M. (1997). The origins of form-related paraphasias in aphasic naming. *Brain and Language, 59*, 450–472.

Garnsey, S. M., & Dell, G. S. (1984). Some neurolinguistic implications of prearticulatory editing in production. *Brain and Language, 23*, 64–73.

Garrett, M. F. (1975). The analysis of sentence production. In G. H. Bower (Ed.), *The psychology of learning and motivation* (pp. 133–175). San Diego, CA: Academic Press.

Gordon, J. K. (2002). Phonological neighborhood effects in aphasic speech errors: Spontaneous and structured contexts. *Brain and Language, 82*, 113–145.

Gordon, J. K., & Dell, G. S. (2003). Learning to divide the labor: An account of deficits in light and heavy verb production. *Cognitive Science, 27*, 1–40.

Griffin, Z. M., & Bock, J. K. (1998). Constraint, word frequency, and the relationship between lexical processing levels in spoken word production. *Journal of Memory and Language, 38*, 313–338.

Hanley, J. R., Kay, J., & Edwards, M. (2002). Imageability effects, phonological errors, and the relationship between auditory repetition and picture naming: Implications for models of auditory repetition. *Cognitive Neuropsychology, 19*, 193–206.

Harley, T. A. (1984). A critique of top-down independent levels models of speech production: Evidence from non-plan-internal speech errors. *Cognitive Science, 8*, 191–219.

Harley, T. A. (1993). Phonological activation of semantic competitors during lexical access in speech production. *Language and Cognitive Processes, 8*, 291–310.

Harley, T. A., & Bown, H. E. (1998). What causes a tip-of-the-tongue state? Evidence for lexical neighbourhood effects in speech production. *British Journal of Psychology, 89*, 151–174.

Hartsuiker, R. J., & Kolk, H. H. J. (2001). Error monitoring in speech production: A computational test of the perceptual loop theory. *Cognitive Psychology, 42*, 113–157.

Hillis, A. E., Boatman, D., Hart, J., & Gordon, B. (1999). Making sense out of jargon: A neurolinguistic and computational account of jargon aphasia. *Neurology, 53*, 1813–1824.

Howard, D., & Orchard-Lisle, V. (1984). On the origin of semantic errors in naming: Evidence from the case of a global aphasic. *Cognitive Neuropsychology, 1*, 163–190.

Humphreys, K. R., & Swendsen, A. (2002). *Asymmetric lexical bias in speech errors.* Presented at the 15th CUNY Conference in Human Sentence Processing, New York.

Kay, J., & Ellis, A. W. (1987). A cognitive neuropsychological case study of anomia: Implications for psychological models of word retrieval. *Brain, 110*, 613–629.

Laine, M., Tikkala, A., & Juhola, M. (1998). Modelling anomia by the discrete two-stage word production architecture. *Journal of Neurolinguistics, 11*, 275–294.

Levelt, W. (1983). Monitoring and self-repair in speech. *Cognition, 14*, 41–104.

Levelt, W., Roelofs, A., & Meyer, A. (1999). A theory of lexical access in speech production. *Behavioral and Brain Sciences, 22*, 1–75.

MacKay, D. G. (1987). *The organization of perception and action: A theory for language and other cognitive skills.* New York: Springer-Verlag.

Martin, N., & Saffran, E. M. (1997). Language and auditory-verbal short-term memory impairments: Evidence for common underlying processes. *Cognitive Neuropsychology, 14*, 641–682.

Martin, N., Dell, G. S., Saffran, E., & Schwartz, M. F. (1994). Origins of paraphasias in deep dysphasia: Testing the consequence of a decay impairment of an interactive spreading activation model of lexical retrieval. *Brain and Language, 47*, 609–660.

Martin, N., Gagnon, D. A., Schwartz, M. F., Dell, G. S., & Saffran, E. M. (1996). Phonological facilitation of semantic errors in normal and aphasic speakers. *Language and Cognitive Processes, 11*, 257–282.

Martin, R. C., Lesch, M. F., & Bartha, M. C. (1999). Independence of input and output phonology in word processing and short-term memory. *Journal of Memory and Language, 41*, 3–29.

Meyer, A. S., & Bock, K. (1992). The tip-of-the-tongue phenomenon: Blocking or partial activation? *Memory and Cognition, 20*, 715–726.

Miozzo, M., & Caramazza, A. (1997). The retrieval of lexical-syntactic features in tip-of-the-tongue states. *Journal of Experimental Psychology: Learning, Memory, and Cognition, 23*, 1410–1423.

Mitchum, C. C., Ritgert, B. A., Sandson, J., & Berndt, R. (1990). The use of response analysis in confrontation naming. *Aphasiology, 4*, 261–280.

Nickels, L., & Howard, D. (1995). Aphasic naming: What matters? *Neuropsychologia, 33*, 1281–1303.

Postma, A. (2000). Detection of errors during speech production: A review of speech monitoring models. *Cognition, 77*, 97–131.

Press, W. H., Teukolsky, S. A., Vetterling, W. T., & Flannery, B. P. (1992). *Numerical recipes in C: The art of scientific computing* (2nd ed.). Cambridge: Cambridge University Press.

Rapp, B., & Caramazza, A. (1998). A case of selective difficulty in writing verbs. *Neurocase: Case Studies in Neuropsychology, Neuropsychiatry, and Behavioural Neurology, 4*(2), 127–139.

Rapp, B., & Goldrick, M. (2000). Discreteness and interactivity in spoken word production. *Psychological Review, 107*, 460–499.

Roach, A., Schwartz, M. F., Martin, N., Grewal, R. A., & Brecher, A. (1996). The Philadelphia Naming Test: Scoring and rationale. *Clinical Aphasiology, 24*, 121–133.

Ruml, W., & Caramazza, A. (2000). An evaluation of a computational model of lexical access: Comments on Dell et al. (1997). *Psychological Review, 107*, 609–634.

Ruml, W., Caramazza, A., Shelton, J. R., & Chialant, D. (2000). Testing assumptions in computational theories of aphasia. *Journal of Memory and Language, 43*, 217–248.

Schade, U., & Eikmeyer, H.-J. (1998). Modeling the production of object specifications. In J. Grainger & A. Jacobs (Eds.), *Localist connectionist approaches to human cognition* (pp. 257–282). Mahwah, NJ: Lawrence Erlbaum Associates Inc.

Schwartz, M. F., & Brecher, A. (2000). A model-driven analysis of severity, response characteristics, and partial recovery in aphasics' picture naming. *Brain and Language, 73*, 62–91.

Schwartz, M. F., & Hodgson, C. (2002). A new multi-word naming deficit: Evidence and interpretation. *Cognitive Neuropsychology, 19*, 263–288.

Shelton, J. R., & Weinrich, M. (1997). Further evidence of a dissociation between output phonological and orthographic lexicons: A case study. *Cognitive Neuropsychology, 14*, 105–129.

Stemberger, J. P. (1985). *The lexicon in a model of language production.* New York: Garland.

Vigliocco, G., Antonini, T., & Garrett, M. F. (1997). Grammatical gender is on the tip of Italian tongues. *Psychological Science, 8*, 314–319.

COGNITIVE NEUROPSYCHOLOGY, 2004, 21 (2/3/4) 147–158

EVIDENCE FOR THE INVOLVEMENT OF A NONLEXICAL ROUTE IN THE REPETITION OF FAMILIAR WORDS: A COMPARISON OF SINGLE AND DUAL ROUTE MODELS OF AUDITORY REPETITION

J. Richard Hanley
University of Essex, Colchester, UK

Gary S. Dell
University of Illinois at Urbana-Champaign, USA

Janice Kay and Rachel Baron
University of Exeter, UK

In this paper, we attempt to simulate the picture naming and auditory repetition performance of two patients reported by Hanley, Kay, and Edwards (2002), who were matched for picture naming score but who differed significantly in their ability to repeat familiar words. In Experiment 1, we demonstrate that the model of naming and repetition put forward by Foygel and Dell (2000) is better able to accommodate this pattern of performance than the model put forward by Dell, Schwartz, Martin, Saffran, and Gagnon (1997). Nevertheless, Foygel and Dell's model underpredicted the repetition performance of both patients. In Experiment 2, we attempt to simulate their performance using a new dual route model of repetition in which Foygel and Dell's model is augmented by an additional nonlexical repetition pathway. The new model provided a more accurate fit to the real-word repetition performance of both patients. It is argued that the results provide support for dual route models of auditory repetition.

Two tasks that are commonly administered to aphasic patients in order to assess their ability to produce spoken words are auditory repetition (in which participants must repeat single words that they hear) and picture naming. The purpose of this paper is to evaluate two different theoretical accounts of the relationship between an individual's performance on these two tasks. Is it possible to predict accurately the number and nature of the

errors that a patient will make on a test of auditory repetition from their picture naming performance for the same set of items, as has been assumed by Dell, Schwartz, Martin, Saffran, and Gagnon (1997) and by Foygel and Dell (2000)? Alternatively, is it also necessary to take account of the individual's nonword repetition ability, as has been claimed by Hanley and Kay (1997) and Hanley, Kay, and Edwards (2002)? The answer to this

Correspondence should be addressed to Professor J. Richard Hanley, Department of Psychology, University of Essex, Wivenhoe Park, Colchester CO4 3SQ, UK (Email: rhanley@essex.ac.uk).

DOI:10.1080/02643290342000339

question should provide important evidence as to whether a nonlexical route is involved in the repetition of familiar words.

Hanley et al. (2002) argued that the relationship between picture naming and auditory repetition is best explained in terms of a dual route model of auditory repetition. They suggested that a lexical-semantic route and a separate nonlexical route both play an important role in the repetition of familiar words. According to this account, use of the nonlexical route involves the transfer of spoken items (regardless of their lexical status) from an auditory input layer/buffer to an output phoneme layer/buffer using auditory to phonological conversion. Use of the lexical-semantic route in repetition involves access of the meaning of a familiar spoken word in the conceptual system. The semantic representation is then used to generate an abstract output lexical representation of the word (its "lemma"). The phonological form of the word can then be generated in the output phoneme layer/buffer from its lemma. Consistent with Hillis and Caramazza's (1991) "summation" hypothesis, Hanley et al. suggested that the phonological representation of the word receives activation from both lexical and nonlexical routes when a familiar word is being repeated.[1] Picture naming, they argued, requires many of the same processes that are involved in repetition via the lexical-semantic route. Once the semantic representation of the pictured item has been accessed from its visual form, the lexical and phonological representations can be activated as in auditory repetition. But while auditory repetition can also benefit from the activity of the nonlexical route, picture naming relies entirely on the lexical-semantic route. As long as it is assumed that summation can occur even when both routes are partially impaired (Hillis & Caramazza, 1991), this model can explain why patients with impaired speech production typically perform better at repeating familiar words than at producing them in picture naming (e.g., Dell et al., 1997).

An alternative account of the relationship between auditory repetition and spoken picture naming was provided by Dell et al. (1997). It is becoming increasingly common to account for neuropsychological data using "lesioned" versions of connectionist models (e.g., Plaut & Shallice, 1993). Dell et al. used such a method to account for aphasic naming by lesioning a simple version of Dell's (1986) interactive activation model of speech production. The model states that picture naming involves accessing a word's lexical representation (lemma) by first activating its semantic features, and that the word's phonological representation in an output phoneme layer is then generated from its lemma. Dell et al.'s account of auditory repetition of familiar words, however, requires only a single route. They argued that repetition involves generation of a word's lexical representation directly from its representation in an input phoneme layer. The lexical representation then activates the word's phonological representation in the output phoneme layer, as in picture naming. A key difference between this account and the model put forward by Hanley et al. (2002) is the absence of any nonlexical route in familiar word repetition. Dell et al. did not rule out the existence of a separate nonlexical route; their claim was that it is not necessary to assume that such a route plays any role in the repetition of familiar words.

Dell et al. (1997) suggested that brain injury could produce two different types of impairment. It can reduce the strength of the associative connections between levels ("connection weight" lesions) and/or it can produce abnormally fast decay of nodes ("decay" lesions). The consequence of decay lesions is that information will be lost before it can be passed on to the next level (see Martin, Dell, Saffran, & Schwartz, 1994, for an application of decay lesions to repetition deficits in deep dysphasia). Dell et al. further claimed that when associative connections within the system are weakened, connection weights between *all* levels are reduced by the same extent. Similarly, they

---

[1] Summation means that activation from two sources converges. Interaction, by contrast, means two-way (top-down and bottom-up) flow of activation.

assumed that the decay rate of all nodes within the system is reduced equally by a decay lesion, regardless of level of processing. Dell et al. called these claims the "globality assumption."

On the basis of this account, Dell et al. (1997) predicted a close relationship between a patient's picture naming and auditory repetition performance as long as he/she could achieve "perfect recognition" of spoken words (i.e., intact auditory lexical decision). They assumed that patients with perfect recognition had an intact input phonological network (separate from the output phonological units) that produced normal levels of activation to the lexical units during auditory repetition. During picture naming, however, the lexical units will receive somewhat reduced levels of activation because of the weakened connections from the semantic units. Consequently, the model correctly predicts that repetition performance by aphasic patients with perfect recognition will generally be superior to their picture naming score. Furthermore, it follows from the globality assumption that the connection weight and decay lesions that reduce performance in picture naming should correspondingly impair performance in auditory repetition. As a consequence, the number of items that any patient with perfect recognition can repeat correctly from a particular set of words should be directly predictable from their picture naming performance for the same items.

In support of this claim, Dell et al. were able to predict the auditory repetition performance of 10/11 patients from their picture naming score with satisfactory levels of accuracy. Note that this should not be possible according to a dual route model of repetition because one should not be able to predict successfully a patient's auditory repetition performance from their picture naming score without also taking into account their ability to use the nonlexical route (i.e., their nonword repetition performance). However, Dell et al. did encounter problems in accounting for the repetition performance of the remaining patient (WR). WR's picture naming score was 8%, which produced a predicted auditory repetition score of 36%. In fact, WR scored 90% correct in a test of auditory repetition of the picture names. Dell et al. acknowledged that

their model of repetition could not explain such a large difference between picture naming and repetition scores in patients with perfect recognition as easily as models that incorporate a separate nonlexical pathway.

Hanley et al. (2002) provided a related empirical problem for Dell et al.'s account of auditory repetition. They reported two patients (MF and PS) whose picture naming scores were closely matched. It follows from the globality assumption that these two individuals should also be matched in terms of their ability to repeat words auditorily. However, MF was significantly better at auditory repetition than PS. Hanley et al. pointed out that this discrepancy could be explained in terms of a dual route model because MF was also much better than PS at auditory repetition of *nonwords*. They therefore suggested that MF was able to repeat familiar words more accurately than PS because his nonlexical route was better preserved.

Foygel and Dell (2000) produced an important reformulation of Dell et al.'s model. First, they abandoned the globality assumption. Second, they abandoned the claim that decay rate could be impaired by brain injury. They argued that picture naming impairments could be caused either by a reduction in the connection weights between the semantic layer and the lemma level (semantic impairment) or by a reduction in the connection weights between the lemmas and the output phoneme layer (phonological impairment). Following the abandonment of the globality assumption, it became possible for the connections between the lemmas and the output phoneme layer to be unimpaired despite picture naming problems caused by reduced connections between the semantic layer and the lemmas. Therefore, by assuming a relatively severe semantic lesion and a relatively mild phonological lesion for WR (Dell et al., 1997), the new model could in principle explain why auditory repetition was relatively good in spite of very poor picture naming.

Another advantage of Foygel and Dell's model compared with Dell et al. (1997) is that it can potentially explain why MF was so much better than PS at auditory repetition despite similar picture naming scores (Hanley et al., 2002).

Assume that MF has a more severe semantic impairment than PS,[2] whereas PS has a more severe phonological impairment than MF. MF might then perform much better at auditory repetition than PS because the semantic layer plays a smaller role in repetition than in naming. Hanley et al. argued that Foygel and Dell (2000) could not explain the performance of MF and PS because it was claimed that both patients had phonological lesions. Their rationale was that both patients made a preponderance of phonological rather than semantic errors in auditory repetition and therefore MF could not be suffering from a semantic lesion. However, Hanley et al. did not note the significance of the finding that MF made mainly formal (real word) errors whereas PS made mainly nonword errors. According to Foygel and Dell's model, real word errors (even when they are phonological) are characteristic of a semantic lesion whereas nonword errors are characteristic of a phonological lesion.

It is therefore possible that Foygel and Dell's model can explain the performance of these two patients by assuming that MF has a semantic lesion and that PS has a phonological lesion. The purpose of the present paper is to provide a detailed empirical investigation of this possibility. In Experiment 1, we examine whether the overall level of performance and the type of errors that these patients make in auditory repetition and picture naming can be simulated by Foygel and Dell's model. In Experiment 2, we examine whether the performance of these patients can be better accommodated by a new version of Foygel and Dell's model that incorporates a nonlexical repetition route.

CASE DETAILS

MF was aged 51 at the time that the tests reported below were carried out (for details, see Hanley et al., 2002). He had suffered a left-hemisphere CVA

a year earlier. A CT scan taken a day after his stroke revealed reduced attenuation in the left frontal and parietal lobes within the vascular territory of the left middle cerebral artery, consistent with a cerebral infarct. Up to that point, he had worked as a senior banker. PS was in his late forties when he suffered a left internal carotid artery dissection. A CT scan taken at the time showed evidence of an acute infarct in the left temporal region with a slight mass effect. PS worked as a bank manager at the time of his illness. The testing reported below took place 3 years later (for details, see Hanley & Kay, 1997).

Full details of the language processing problems suffered by PS (Hanley & Kay, 1997; Hanley & McDonnell, 1997) and MF (Hanley et al., 2002) have already been published. Their impairments were similar in a number of respects and can be summarised as follows. They both made phonological errors on a variety of tasks involving spoken production of familiar words and nonwords including auditory repetition, reading aloud, and picture naming. They both showed effects of imageability in auditory repetition, reading aloud, and writing. They both showed impaired ability to repeat nonwords. They both performed normally at auditory lexical decision and at comprehending the meanings of words (including words of low imageability). They were both significantly worse at oral than at written picture naming. More items were correct in auditory repetition than in oral picture naming when the same items were used in both tests.

Hanley et al. (2002) suggested that MF and PS were both suffering from three language production impairments. These three impairments are separate in the sense that the degree of impairment of each can vary from patient to patient. The first was a problem in activating lexical representations from an intact semantic system during word production (hence the imageability effect in reading aloud, repetition, and writing, but not comprehension). In terms of Foygel and Dell's (2000) model,

---

[2] A semantic lesion in this context refers to an impairment of the lexical retrieval process. It does not imply that MF has a central semantic/conceptual deficit.

this would be characterised as a semantic impairment to the process of lexical production. The second was a difficulty in accessing familiar phonological word forms from lexical representations during speech production (hence the greater number of errors in spoken than in written picture naming). This would be characterised as a phonological impairment in Foygel and Dell's model. The third deficit was an impairment to the auditory to phonological conversion component of the nonlexical repetition route (hence phonological errors in nonword repetition).

Experiment 1

Picture naming

The first step in attempting to discover whether Foygel and Dell's (2000) model can accommodate the results of MF and PS is to look at the patients' picture naming ability. We therefore examined their performance when naming 40 pictures from Test 53 of the PALPA Battery (Kay, Lesser, & Coltheart, 1992). Overall performance was very similar (see Hanley et al., 2002); MF named 22/40 of these pictures correctly whereas PS named 23/40 (control mean = 39.80, SD = 0.35).

Dell et al.'s (1997) and Foygel and Dell's (2000) models were designed to explain five basic types of error. These are semantic errors (semantically related real words), formal errors (phonologically related real words) mixed errors (semantically and phonologically related real words), unrelated errors (real word responses that met neither semantic nor formal criteria), and nonword errors (neologisms). Table 1 provides details of the performance of MF and PS using this terminology. Examples of the errors made by MF are: brush → "comb" (semantic), bread → "red" (formal), foot → "feet"

(mixed), monkey → "mudkey" (nonword). Examples of the errors made by PS are: yacht → "boat" (semantic), watch → "wash" (formal), glass → "tumble" (unrelated), arrow → "ayro" (nonword). It can be seen from Table 1 that PS makes more nonword errors than MF, whereas MF makes more real word errors than PS.

The next step is to attempt to simulate this pattern of impaired picture naming performance by altering the lesionable parameters of the Foygel and Dell (2000) model. These are the semantic parameter (s), the strength or weight of the bidirectional connections between semantic and lexical units, and the phonological parameter (f), the strength of the bidirectional connections between phonological and lemma units. Table 2 shows the best-fitting values of s and f for the picture naming proportions shown in Table 1, and the naming proportions predicted from the lesioned model. The search for best-fitting parameter values used a method similar to that of Foygel and Dell. It is described in Dell, Lawler, Harris, and Gordon (2004) (and can be accessed at http://langprod.cogsci.uiuc.edu/cgi-bin/webfit.cgi). The fitting minimised the deviations between predicted and obtained proportions as measured by chi-square, and made the same assumptions about the opportunities for mixed errors that Foygel and Dell did (10% sampling of the neighbourhood in which the target has a mixed semantic-formal neighbour). All other model characteristics and fixed parameters were as reported by Foygel and Dell, and are given as defaults at the URL above.

The model proportions in Table 2 show a good match to both PS, $\chi^2(3) = 4.09$, and MF, $\chi^2(3) = 6.86$. As anticipated, the match was achieved by a more severe semantic lesion for MF (s = .0146) than for PS (s = .0199), and a more severe

Table 1. *Observed performance by PS and MF on a test of picture naming (PALPA 53)*

		Error distribution				
	Correct	Semantic	Formal	Mixed	Unrelated	Nonword
PS	.58	.03	.15	0	.03	.23
MF	.55	.08	.20	.03	0	.15

Table 2. *Predicted performance for PS and MF on a test of picture naming by Foygel and Dell's (2002) model of naming*

	Error distribution							
	Correct	Semantic	Formal	Mixed	Unrelated	Nonword	s	f
PS	.52	.07	.09	.01	.04	.26	.0199	.0156
MF	.52	.11	.12	.01	.09	.14	.0146	.0211

phonological lesion for PS (f = .0156) than for MF (f = .0211). Crucially, Table 2 reveals equivalent levels of correct responses for the fits of both patients, with PS making more nonword errors, and MF making more real word errors.

Both MF and PS perform significantly better at written than at spoken picture naming; when asked to write the names of the pictures from PALPA 53, MF was .875 correct and PS was .90 correct. Although Foygel and Dell's model is not a model of written output, it seems likely that word nodes will be shared between the spoken and written systems. It would therefore be problematic if MF's relatively severe semantic lesion meant that predicted naming performance could never rise much higher than .52 even if the weakened lexical-phonological connections (f) were replaced by intact analogues for written naming. A simulation of written naming was therefore carried out in which lexical-orthographic connection strength (the written analogue to f) was set to its normal value of .1, and s was set to the lesioned values shown in Table 2. The outcome was a predicted naming score of .81 for MF and .89 for PS. It is therefore clear that significantly better written naming than spoken naming performance by these two individuals is consistent with the severity of the semantic lesions that we have used to predict their oral naming scores.

Auditory repetition

Table 3 provides details of the performance of MF and PS when they were given an auditory repetition test that used the picture names from PALPA 53 during different testing sessions. It can be seen that, as in picture naming, PS makes more phonological errors than real-word errors whereas MF makes more real-word errors than phonological errors. However, MF's overall performance level in auditory repetition is significantly higher than that of PS. The critical question is whether Foygel and Dell's model can simulate the auditory repetition performance of these patients using the same values for the parameters s and f that was used to simulate their picture naming performance.

Table 4 provides a summary of the results of this simulation. It can be seen that the model can successfully generate superior performance by MF over PS despite identical overall picture naming scores. Table 4 demonstrates that Hanley et al. (2002) were wrong to suggest that Foygel and Dell's model was inconsistent with such a pattern of performance.

It is also interesting to examine whether it is possible to simulate these findings in Dell et al.'s (1997) version of the model. The result of a simulation of the performance of MF and PS on the PALPA picture naming test using Dell et al.'s

Table 3. *Observed performance by PS and MF on a test of auditory repetition of real words (PALPA 53)*

	Error distribution					
	Correct	Semantic	Formal	Mixed	Unrelated	Nonword
PS	.83	0	.05	0	0	.13
MF	.95	0	.05	0	0	0

Table 4. *Predicted performance for PS and MF on a test of real word repetition by Foygel and Dell's (2002) model of repetition*

	Error distribution					
	Correct	Semantic	Formal	Mixed	Unrelated	Nonword
PS	.64	0	.08	0	0	.27
MF	.80	0	.05	0	0	.15

model was successful for both patients. PS had a "weight" lesion (weight = .0054, decay = .514), and MF had a "decay" lesion (weight = .0886, decay = .856) that produced equivalent overall levels of performance. However, the superiority of the Foygel and Dell model was apparent when repetition performance was predicted from these parameters. Predicted repetition was .70 for PS and .73 for MF (the real repetition scores were .83 for PS and .95 for MF). It is therefore clear that the global lesions cannot account for the large difference in repetition accuracy that was observed between these two patients.

Despite its success in predicting superior repetition by MF than PS, it is clear from Tables 3 and 4 that Foygel and Dell's model provides an underestimate of the repetition performance of both patients. MF's predicted repetition score is .80 whereas he actually achieved .95 correct. PS's predicted repetition score is .64 whereas he actually achieved .83 correct. The situation is reminiscent of what Foygel and Dell (2000) observed with patient WR. We pointed out earlier that Foygel and Dell's model did provide a much closer estimate of WR's auditory repetition performance than had been achieved by Dell et al.'s (1997) model. Nevertheless, the performance figure that Foygel and Dell's model produced (65%) still underestimated WR's total repetition performance (90%) by a wide margin.

In contrast, such an outcome might be consistent with a dual route model of auditory repetition in which there is an additional nonlexical repetition pathway. If WR, MF, and PS have access to two routes when repeating familiar words, then it would be expected that their repetition score should be higher than that predicted on the basis of a single lexical route. In Experiment 2, therefore, a

simulation of the repetition performance of MF and PS was carried out using a new version of Foygel and Dell's model that incorporated a nonlexical repetition pathway.

Experiment 2

A nonlexical route was added to Foygel and Dell's (2000) model in the following way. It was assumed that hearing a nonword sets up a temporary node for that event, a node whose activation is subject to decay and which has weights to (and from) the phoneme nodes for the nonword. This node can be considered a representation of the input phonology of the stimulus. The fact that it is a single node is not relevant here. The key is that it contributes directly to the activation of the output phonemes. The connections are two-way, in keeping with the general character of the model, the connections of which are all bidirectional. Making the nonlexical connections one-way, however, would not change the fundamental properties of the model, although one-way connections would need to have different weights from the two-way ones reported below to function in an equivalent manner. There are several other ways that a nonlexical route could be added. For example, one could assume that each output phoneme receives activation from its corresponding input phoneme, instead of from a single node representing the input as a whole. Although we did not explore this option, we suspect that would also suffice. The key is that the output phonemes of the string to be repeated must each receive activation regardless of the lexical status of the string. Without such a mechanism, the model cannot repeat nonwords accurately.

Fitting the model to the nonword repetition results of MF and PS again involved using the values of s and f derived from the simulation of their picture naming performance. The model was augmented with a single node for the nonword input stimulus. This node is given a jolt of 100 units of activation at the beginning of a repetition trial. As in Foygel and Dell's model, a repetition trial then involves the spread of activation for eight time steps and is concluded by the selection of the most activated phoneme units as the response. Because the implemented model had CVC words only, repetition of the CVC nonword "cog" was simulated. Any other CVC nonword would produce the same results. The input node was given two-way connections to its three phonemes, and a value for the weight of these connections (parameter nl) was determined that led the model to approximate each patients' nonword repetition accuracy.

Word repetition for MF and PS was then predicted (without any additional free parameters) simply by changing the nonlexical input node and its attendant connections to those of the word target (e.g., CAT) and running the model in repetition mode with both lexical and nonlexical routes active. This entails giving both the temporary phonological input node (e.g., "cat") and the lexical node for CAT a jolt of 100 activation units. The former represents the contribution of the word's input phonology translated directly to output phonology (which is assumed to be the same as for a nonword stimulus), and the latter represents the recognition of the target word through the comprehension system. In the single-route approach to word repetition taken by Foygel and Dell, only the jolt to the lexical node CAT would be applied. Figure 1 shows the complete dual route model assuming a repetition target of CAT.

Simulation of auditory repetition of nonwords

The results of the simulation of nonword repetition are shown in Table 5. The simulation provides a close match to the overall number of nonwords repeated correctly by both patients. In the simulation, as in real life, both patients make a preponderance of nonword errors rather than real-word errors, with the ratio of nonword errors to real-word errors being particularly high in the case of PS.

Simulation of auditory repetition of real words

Table 6 compares observed and simulated repetition performance for real words with both the lexical and nonlexical routes in operation. These values represent a good match to both MF, $\chi^2(3) = 7.22$, and PS, $\chi^2(3) = 1.56$. It can be seen that the relatively mild nl lesion that was used to simulate MF's nonword repetition has allowed his predicted real-word repetition performance (.97) to come very close to the observed performance level (.95). In the simulation, as in real life, the more severe nl lesion that was used to simulate nonword repetition by PS means that MF benefits more than PS from the addition of the nonlexical route. Nevertheless, estimated repetition performance by PS does derive some benefit from the nonlexical route (.76 correct in Table 6 compared to .64 correct in the Foygel and Dell simulation in Table 4), just as it does in the real data. It is therefore clear that the addition of a nonlexical route to Foygel and Dell's model has provided a much closer match to the real data than the simulation by the original version of the model, which does not incorporate a nonlexical route (see Table 4).

An important issue is whether the interaction of the two routes in this simulation produces higher scores than would be obtained when the two pathways operate independently. The simplest way to calculate the expected result from the independent operation of the routes is by using the equation P(lex) + P(nonlex) − [P(lex)*P(nonlex)]. For example, if one route produces the correct answer 50% of the time, and the other route produces the correct answer 40% of the time, then the correct answer will be produced by at least one of the routes 70% of the time.[3] For PS, the proportion correct from the pure nonlexical route was .10, and from the pure lexical route it was .64. The equation

---

[3] Even so, this is making the assumption that something "knows" which answer is the right one. Otherwise, "independent" performance would be lower still.

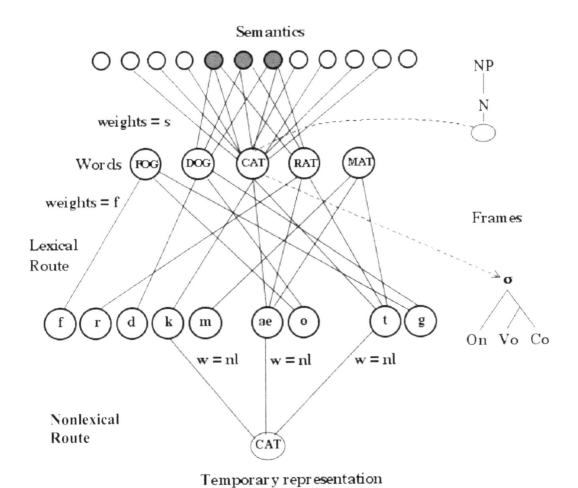

Figure 1. *A dual-route model of repetition based on Hanley et al. (2002) and Foygel and Dell (2000).*

Table 5. *A comparison of observed and predicted performance for PS and MF on a test of nonword repetition*

	Error distribution				
	Correct	*Nonword error*	*Real-word error*	*Other*	*nl*
PS					.009
Observed	.10	.73	.18	0	
Simulation	.10	.64	.17	.08	
MF					.033
Observed	.54	.30	.10	.06	
Simulation	.52	.30	.17	.01	

Table 6. *A comparison of observed and predicted performance for PS and MF on a test of real word repetition by a model that incorporates a nonlexical repetition route*

		Error distribution					
	Correct	Nonword error	Real-word error	Other	nl	s	f
PS					.009	.0199	.0156
Observed	.83	.13	.05	0			
Simulation	.76	.18	.06	0			
MF					.033	.0146	.0211
Observed	.95	0	.05	0			
Simulation	.97	.02	.01	0			

provides a predicted independent score of .68, which is lower than the combined model's score of .76. For MF, the proportion correct from the pure nonlexical route was .52, and from the pure lexical route was .80. The equation provides a predicted independent score of .90, which is lower than the combined model's score of .97. It is therefore clear that the two routes operating together do produce a higher overall level of performance than the independent operation of the same two routes. Such an outcome is consistent with Hillis and Caramazza's (1991) summation hypothesis, and indeed constitutes a computational demonstration of summation in action. It is also important to note that the interaction of the two routes provides a closer match to the observed real-word repetition performance of MF and PS than the independent performance of the two routes.

Imageability effects in repetition

When working on the simulations of performance by PS, it became clear that the model could also provide an account of the imageability effects that both PS and MF show in auditory repetition (Hanley et al., 2002). Following Newton and Barry (1997), Hanley et al. argued that imageability effects will occur when patients with impairments to the nonlexical repetition route also suffer impairments to the lexicalisation process. This is because the meanings of low-imageability words tend to be less specific than meanings of high-

imageability words (see Plaut & Shallice, 1993, for a similar proposal). If a patient has an impairment of the connections from the semantic system to the lemmas, then words of low imageability are likely to be particularly difficult to access. It therefore seems reasonable to simulate different levels of imageability in terms of different strengths of associative connections from the semantic to the lexical level in Foygel and Dell's model. In other words, the assumption is that the imageability effect involves a premorbid difference in semantic-lexical weights that favours concrete words. These differences become evident following brain injury that causes a general reduction in semantic-lexical weights.

In Foygel and Dell's model, one can think of the strength of the weight between the semantic and lexical levels for a particular word as reflecting two variables (the strength of the semantic lesion and imageability value of the word). For example, in the simulations described above, the strength of PS's semantic lesion was .0199. This can be construed as an average value for all the items in the set. To simulate performance on items of lower imageability, this value would be reduced. For example, when the setting of s was reduced to .01, then a simulation of PS's auditory repetition performance produced a drop from .76 to .71 correct. Increasing the value of s to .03 produced a simulated repetition score of .83 correct. Increasing the value of s to .06 produced a simulated repetition score of .97 correct.

Differences in the strength of the semantic lesion affect performance in auditory repetition because of the interactive properties of Foygel and Dell's model. During repetition, the lexical node resonates with its semantic representation, and consequently enhances its ability to activate its associated phonemes. The strength of the associative connections between the semantic and lexical levels will determine how much enhancement will occur. So, because of its interactive properties, the model predicts that repetition (a purely phonological task on the surface) is influenced by the semantic strength of items in repetition, as found in the effects of imageability in the observed repetition data (see also Martin, Saffran, & Dell, 1996).

DISCUSSION

The results of the simulations reported in this paper demonstrate that the model put forward by Dell et al. (1997) is unable to explain the performance of patients such as PS and MF (Hanley et al., 2002) who are matched for picture naming ability but differ significantly in terms of auditory repetition performance. The revised version of the model put forward by Foygel and Dell (2000) proved to be much more successful. By abandoning the globality assumption, Foygel and Dell allowed for the possibility that patients can suffer from phonological lesions that are of different severity from their semantic lesions. The simulation of their picture naming performance reported in Experiment 1 showed that PS could be seen as suffering from a more severe phonological impairment than MF, whereas MF could be seen as suffering from a more severe semantic impairment than PS. Because phonological lesions have a particularly marked effect on repetition performance, the next set of simulations clearly demonstrated that a patient with a mild phonological lesion (e.g., MF) could perform better at auditory repetition than a patient with a severe phonological impairment (e.g., PS), even though their picture naming scores were very similar.

Nevertheless, Foygel and Dell's model provided an underestimate of the auditory repetition scores obtained by both patients. Consequently, Experiment 2 investigated the effects of adding a nonlexical route to the model. The first set of simulations successfully simulated nonword repetition performance by both patients. The second set of simulations attempted to predict real-word repetition performance by MF and PS using appropriately lesioned lexical and nonlexical repetition routes. The most important finding was that the new version of the model provided a much closer match to the actual repetition scores that MF and PS achieved than that provided by Foygel and Dell's (2000) model. Taken together, the results of these two experiments provide strong support for the view that two routes (lexical and nonlexical) contribute to auditory repetition of familiar words (Hanley et al., 2002). The two routes converge at the output phonology, each contributing to the activation of the output units in a manner consistent with the summation hypothesis (Hillis & Caramazza, 1991).

If Foygel and Dell's model contains only one of the two repetition routes that are involved in auditory repetition of familiar words, it is somewhat surprising that they were able to successfully predict the repetition performance of many of the 11 patients that they discussed. Two important points must be borne in mind, however. First, the predictions of the two models will differ most markedly for patients whose picture naming scores are relatively low. When a picture naming score is high, both models predict that repetition performance will be close to the ceiling. It is therefore interesting to note that the predictions of Foygel and Dell's model were least accurate for patients with low naming scores (e.g., WR and JG). The repetition predictions made for WR and JG fell some way below the observed values (by .25 and .20, respectively). The second point to bear in mind is that some aphasic patients are totally unable to perform nonword repetition. This is the case for patients who are sometimes described as suffering from "deep dysphasia" (e.g., Franklin, Howard, & Patterson, 1994, 1995; Martin & Saffran, 1992). Because their nonlexical repetition route appears to be entirely abolished, the real-word repetition performance of these patients should be predicted equally well by models that do and do not incorporate a nonlexical repetition route. Indeed, Martin et al. (1994) were able to simulate successfully the repetition performance of a deep dysphasic patient with a model that that did not incorporate a nonlexical route. Nonword repetition scores were not available for the patients discussed by Foygel and Dell, so it is possible that some of them would have performed very badly at nonword repetition. A critical test of the two-route model will be to investigate whether it provides a more accurate prediction than Foygel and Dell (2000) of the picture naming and real-word repetition performance of new sets of patients for whom nonword repetition scores are also available.

In the meantime, it is encouraging that the dual route model can simultaneously account for the distribution of spoken naming responses (six proportions), the distribution of nonword repetition responses (four proportions), the distribution of word repetition responses (four proportions), and the accuracy of written naming (one proportion) using only three free parameters (s, f, and nl). It is also encouraging that it can do so for two patients who differ markedly in terms of the number and type of errors that they make in auditory repetition.

REFERENCES

Dell, G. S. (1986). A spreading activation theory of retrieval in sentence production. *Psychological Review, 93*, 283–321.

Dell, G. S., Lawler, E. N., Harris, H. D., & Gordon, J. K. (2004). Models of errors of omission in aphasic naming. *Cognitive Neuropsychology, 21*, 125–145.

Dell, G. S., Schwartz, M. F., Martin, N., Saffran, E. M., & Gagnon, D. A. (1997). Lexical access in aphasic and nonaphasic speakers. *Psychological Review, 104*, 801–838.

Foygel, D., & Dell, G. S. (2000). Models of impaired lexical access in speech production. *Journal of Memory and Language, 43*, 182–216.

Franklin, S., Howard, D., & Patterson, K. (1994). Abstract word meaning deafness. *Cognitive Neuropsychology, 11*, 1–34.

Franklin, S., Howard, D., & Patterson, K. (1995). Abstract word anomia. *Cognitive Neuropsychology, 12*, 549–566.

Hanley, J. R., & Kay, J. (1997). An effect of imageability on the production of phonological errors in auditory repetition. *Cognitive Neuropsychology, 14*, 1065–1084.

Hanley, J. R., Kay, J., & Edwards, M. (2002). Imageability effects and phonological errors: Implications for models of auditory repetition. *Cognitive Neuropsychology, 19*, 193–206.

Hanley, J. R., & McDonnell, V. (1997). Are reading and spelling phonologically mediated? Evidence from a patient with a speech production impairment. *Cognitive Neuropsychology, 14*, 3–33.

Hillis, A., & Caramazza, A. (1991). Mechanisms for accessing lexical representations for output: Evidence from a category specific semantic deficit. *Brain and Language, 40*, 106–144.

Kay, J., Lesser, R., & Coltheart, M. (1992). *Psycholinguistic Assessment of Language Processing in Aphasia*. Hove, UK: Lawrence Erlbaum Associates Ltd.

Martin, N., Dell, G. S., Saffran, E. M., & Schwartz, M. F. (1994). Origins of paraphasias in deep dysphasia: Testing the consequence of a decay impairment of an interactive spreading activation model of lexical retrieval. *Brain and Language, 47*, 609–660.

Martin, N., & Saffran, E. (1992). A computational account of deep dysphasia: Evidence from a single case study. *Brain and Language, 43*, 240–274.

Martin, N., Saffran, E. M., & Dell, G. S. (1996). Recovery in deep dysphasia: Evidence for a relation between auditory-verbal STM capacity and lexical errors in repetition. *Brain and Language, 52*, 83–113.

Newton, P. K., & Barry, C. (1997). Concreteness effects in word production but not word comprehension in deep dyslexia. *Cognitive Neuropsychology, 14*, 481–509.

Plaut, D. C., & Shallice, T. (1993). Deep dyslexia: A case study of connectionist neuropsychology. *Cognitive Neuropsychology, 5*, 377–500.

COGNITIVE NEUROPSYCHOLOGY, 2004, 21 (2/3/4) 159–186

ORIGINS OF NONWORD PHONOLOGICAL ERRORS IN APHASIC PICTURE NAMING

Myrna F. Schwartz
Moss Rehabilitation Research Institute, and Thomas Jefferson University, Philadelphia, PA, USA

Carolyn E. Wilshire
Victoria University of Wellington, New Zealand and Moss Rehabilitation Research Institute, Philadelphia, PA, USA

Deborah A. Gagnon
Cornell University, Ithaca, NY, USA

Marcia Polansky
Drexel University, and Moss Rehabilitation Research Institute, Philadelphia, PA, USA

A recent theory of lexical access in picture naming maintains that all nonword errors are generated during the retrieval of phonemic segments from the lexicon (Dell, Schwartz, Martin, Saffran, & Gagnon, 1997b). This theory is challenged by "dual origin" theories that postulate a second, post-lexical mechanism, whose disruption gives rise to "phonemic paraphasias" bearing close resemblance to the target. We tested the dual origin theory in a corpus of 457 nonword errors drawn from 18 subjects with fluent aphasia. The corpus was divided into two parts, based on degree of phonological overlap between error and target, and these parts were separately examined for proposed diagnostic characteristics of the postlexical error mechanism: serial order effects across the word, sensitivity to target length, and insensitivity to target frequency. Results did not support the dual origin theory but were consistent with a single, lexical origin account in which segment retrieval operates from left to right, rather than in parallel. Findings from this study also shed new light on how individual differences in the severity of the retrieval deficit modulate the expression of phonological errors in relation to target characteristics.

INTRODUCTION

Errors in which a phonologically related nonword is produced in place of the intended word (e.g., castle → /kæksəl/; chimney → /pɪnəli/) are a common feature of fluent aphasic speech. It is generally accepted that such errors result from a malfunction somewhere in the process of mapping from a lexical representation to a fully specified phonological representation. However, there are

Correspondence should be addressed to Myrna F. Schwartz, PhD, Associate Director, Moss Rehabilitation Research Institute, Philadelphia, PA 19106, USA (Email: mschwart@einstein.edu).

Eleanor Saffran, our friend and colleague, played a major role in this study. Her long-running NIH grant supported the data analysis and collection (#2 RO1 DC00191-21). Eleanor's scientific contribution to both the dual and single origin theories helped frame the questions we undertook to explore. Her enthusiasm and encouragement inspired us throughout. We miss her dearly.

Preliminary accounts of these findings were presented at annual meetings of the Psychonomic Society (1997), Academy of Aphasia (1997), and Theoretical and Experimental Neuropsychology (1996). We are grateful to Adelyn Brecher and Jason Smith for their invaluable help with the coding and analysis of errors, and to Gary Dell and Nina Silverberg for critical suggestions on earlier drafts of this manuscript.

competing accounts as to the precise stage at which these errors arise. In this paper, we assess the validity of some competing accounts by analysing a large corpus of nonword phonological errors gathered from a diverse group of fluent aphasic individuals.

The single-origin theory of aphasic phonological errors

A number of recent studies of naming impairment in aphasia centre on a naming model first described by Dell and O'Seaghdha (1991), which is one of a family of related models developed by Dell and his colleagues (Dell, 1986, 1988; Dell, Burger, & Svec, 1997a; Sevald & Dell, 1994; see also Harley, 1984; MacKay, 1987; Stemberger, 1985, 1990). Dell's naming model uses connectionist, interactive activation principles to explain how semantic representations are mapped onto the sequence of phonemes that express a target's pronunciation. In computer-implemented versions of the model, aphasic naming patterns (correct responses and various error types) have been simulated by altering ("lesioning") the spread of activation within the network. In one version, lesions were made by reducing connection weights and/or decay rates globally throughout the network (the weight-decay model: Dell, Schwartz, Martin, Saffran, & Gagnon, 1997b); in another version, lesions were made by reducing weights locally in semantic and/or phonological connections (the semantic-phonological model; Foygel & Dell, 2000). The implemented weight-decay and semantic-phonological models have been made available to other researchers[1] and this has encouraged a healthy debate on such topics as the use of computational models in aphasia research (Dell, Schwartz, Martin, Saffran, & Gagnon, 2000; Ruml & Caramazza, 2000), the validity of the models' processing assumptions (Rapp & Goldrick, 2000; Ruml & Caramazza, 2000), and whether there are naming patterns that cannot be

fit under these assumptions (Cuetos, Aguado, & Caramazza, 2000; Rapp & Goldrick, 2000; Ruml, Caramazza, Shelton, & Chialant, 2000).

A key assumption of the Dell family of naming models, and all models that share its properties, is that normal and aphasic naming errors arise from selection of incorrect units in the lexical network. In particular, the sole mechanism for aphasic phonological nonword errors is faulty selection at the phoneme level of the lexical network, as a result of lesion-induced changes in such factors as connection weights, decay rates, and/or noise levels. The misselection of phonemes can occur in conjunction with errors at the prior stage of lemma selection, but apart from these errors of compound origin, all nonword errors are assumed to arise from incorrect selection of the target's phonemes. Critically, the model does not recognise a *postlexical* origin for phonological errors. This aspect of the model has gone largely unchallenged in the debates surrounding the computational findings. However, it flies in the face of many previous accounts of normal and aphasic phonological errors.

The dual origin theory of aphasic phonological errors

During the 1970s and 1980s, research on phonological errors in aphasia was strongly influenced by a family of speech production theories developed by Fromkin (1971), Garrett (1975, 1982), and Shattuck-Hufnagel (1979, 1983, 1987, 1992). According to these theories, the recovery of phonological information from the lexicon is followed by a second, postlexical phonological processing stage, in which the retrieved phonological information is reorganised into the form it will ultimately take in the speech plan (see also Levelt, 1992; Levelt, Roelofs, & Meyer, 1999; Roelofs, 1997; Shattuck-Hufnagel, 1979, 1983; Wheeler & Touretzky, 1997). In these theories, a phonological nonword error can potentially arise not just at the lexical-phonological retrieval stage, but also

---

[1] A model-fitting process is available on the internet (http://langprod.cogsci.uiuc.edu/; follow links to "Projects" and then to "Aphasia Modeling Project (WebFit)."

during postlexical phonological processing. The spontaneous errors of normal speakers, which often involve movements of phonemes between words (e.g., "guinea *kig page*"; "the *pirst part*"), are generally attributed to a breakdown at the postlexical level. The idea is that the lexical-phonological information has been correctly retrieved for the target words, but the phonemes have become misordered during some later process that operates across the whole phrase.

The view that phonological errors can potentially arise not just during lexical-phonological recovery but also during postlexical phonological processing has been widely embraced in studies of aphasia, giving rise to what we will call the "dual origin" theory of aphasic phonological errors (e.g., Béland, Caplan, & Nespoulous, 1990; Bub, Black, Howell, & Kertesz, 1987; Buckingham, 1977, 1985, 1987; Caplan, Vanier, & Baker, 1986; Kohn, 1989; Kohn & Smith, 1990, 1994, 1995; Pate, Saffran, & Martin, 1987). The postlexical phonological stage is most strongly associated with the errors of conduction aphasic patients, which often involve relatively mild distortions of the target word and sometimes movement of phonemes within the word (e.g., apple → "papple"; see, e.g., Buckingham, 1987; Kohn, 1989; Kohn & Smith, 1990; Nespoulous, Joannette, Ska, Caplan, & Lecours, 1987; Pate et al., 1987). As in the case of nonaphasics' spontaneous slips, the failure in these instances is assigned to processes that act on the stored representation subsequent to its recovery from the lexicon.

If the dual origin theory is correct in ascribing a subset of aphasic phonological errors to a postlexical processing stage, a key assumption of Dell's and related naming models (the single origin assumption) is false, and the efforts to quantitatively model naming errors solely in terms of lexical retrieval failure must inevitably fall short. The question of a single versus dual origin therefore demands closer scrutiny.

Evaluating the dual origin theory

Despite the widespread influence of the dual origin theory in accounts of aphasic phonological errors, relatively few studies have tested it directly. One reason for this is that models which incorporate a postlexical phonological stage vary widely in the way they conceptualise this stage. The following paragraphs review a selection of the most influential studies, including the few that have generated and/or tested predictions directly associated with the dual origin theory.

Target-error overlap. Blumstein's (1973) seminal linguistic analysis of phonological errors in aphasic conversational speech established characteristics of these errors that resembled slips of the tongue. After this study, aphasic phonological errors would become assimilated into the theoretical paradigm of slips, and explained in terms of the same postlexical mechanisms that were used to explain slips at this time (e.g., Shattuck-Hufnagel, 1979). The error corpus analysed in Blumstein's study was unusually large—2800 phonological errors—and was drawn from the conversational speech of patients of the Broca, Wernicke, and conduction type. It was comprised of errors of a single consonant or syllable. Neologisms—nonwords bearing no phonemic similarity to any plausible target in that context—were deliberately excluded from the corpus. However, Blumstein's monograph makes no mention of errors of intermediate complexity, that is, errors that change multiple phonological units without rendering the target unrecognisable. This invites the inference that complex phonological errors of this kind were absent from the sample.

Buckingham and Kertesz (1976) addressed this issue directly in their systematic analyses of the phonological errors produced by a single jargon aphasic speaker, BF. Using material from conversational speech, they identified 258 nonword errors, 49 of which were phonologically related to a discernable target ("phonemic paraphasias" in their terminology). The vast majority of these differed by only one or two phonemes from the target. The rest of the errors in the corpus were neologisms, as defined above. The key finding was the rarity of errors of intermediate complexity. Buckingham and Kertesz (1976; also Buckingham, 1977, 1979) argued that if all phonological errors were the product of a single error-generating mechanism (phonemic substitution: Kertesz & Benson, 1970; transposition: Lecours & Lhermitte, 1969), then in a corpus that contains both simple and remote deviations from the target, there should also be deviations of intermediate complexity. The absence of intermediate errors suggests different mechanisms for the generation of phonemic paraphasias and neologisms.

In subsequent works, Buckingham (1985, 1987, 1992) argued that phonemic paraphasias bearing a close phonological relationship to the target are akin to normal speakers' slips of the tongue and, like them, originate from failure in postlexical phonological processing; the phonological form of a word has been correctly retrieved from the lexicon but distorted during subsequent processing. The more remote "neologisms", he argued, are like tip-of-the-tongue (TOT) states, wherein the patient experiences difficulty in retrieving the target item. However, instead of saying nothing, he or she fills in with phonemes selected at random or from a perseverated set (Butterworth, 1979).

Later evidence revealed that such lexical blocks are not necessarily complete. Like subjects in TOT states, aphasics may sometimes experience partial blocks, causing them to produce approximations that bear some similarity to the target (Ellis, 1985; Miller & Ellis, 1987). This observation extended the range of error phenomena that would be associated with lexical disturbances, which subsequently came to include so-called target-related neologisms.

The evidence just reviewed (along with the studies of Kohn and Smith, which will be described below) established error proximity (target-error overlap) as a property of phonological errors that potentially distinguishes lexical from postlexical errors. This accords with the fundamental premise of the dual origin theory, which is that the postlexical mechanism operates on a phonological representation that specifies the stored segmental information about the word. Disruptions of the

postlexical mechanism are unlikely to distort the word's segmental structure as seriously as failure to recover the correct segmental structure during lexical retrieval. Consequently, the average postlexical error is expected to contain more of the target's segments (i.e., have a higher overlap score) than the average lexical-phonological error.

Serial position effect. In a study directly addressing the dual origin theory, Kohn and Smith (1994) performed a detailed comparison of two phonologically impaired individuals (LW and CM) who were grossly matched in terms of overall naming accuracy but who differed in terms of specific language performance. For one thing, CM's errors tended to be more phonologically similar to their respective targets than those of LW. For another, there were differences in serial order effects: CM produced many "fragment" errors, which were cut short after just one or two initial phonemes (e.g., domino → /dom-/), and his accuracy decreased from the beginning to the end of the word. Neither effect was evident for LW. These serial position differences were further supported by a subsequent study (Kohn & Smith, 1995) in which the errors of four new patients (two of each hypothesised type) were added to the corpus. Adopting a model in which underspecified phonological representations were recovered (in parallel) from the lexicon and subsequently fleshed out via a sequential, postlexical process (see also Béland et al., 1990; Caplan et al., 1986), the authors argued that the pattern of phonologically close errors and strong serial position effects (as seen in CM) was symptomatic of a deficit in the sequential, postlexical process. In contrast, more remote errors and an absence of serial position effects (as seen in LW) were said to signal a problem with the (non-sequential) lexical-phonological recovery process. This study thus adds a second differentiating criterion—decline in segmental accuracy across the word—to the one previously mentioned (phonological proximity of error to target).[2] Other studies

---

[2] Kohn and Smith (1994) also noted a number of other differences between these two patients, particularly, with respect to the incidence of formal paraphasias and their sensitivity to lexical effects. The model they proposed also incorporated specific features designed to account for these differences. These aspects of the model are more speculative and will not be considered further here.

have also reported declining segmental accuracy across the word or syllable in phonological error corpora assumed to tap a postlexical mechanism (Goldrick, Rapp, & Smolensky, 1999; Romani & Calabrese, 1998; see also Wilshire & McCarthy, 1996).

Target lexical frequency. Another factor that might be expected to distinguish lexical and postlexical errors is sensitivity to the target's lexical frequency. A number of studies of normal word production indicate that a word's frequency of occurrence affects the strength of its lexical representation and hence the success of lexical-phonological retrieval (Brown & McNeill, 1966; Dell, 1990; Jescheniak & Levelt, 1994; Oldfield & Wingfield, 1965; for accounts within connectionist models, see Dell, 1988; Dell, Juliano, & Govindjee, 1993; Houghton, 1990; Stemberger, 1985). Lexical frequency is not, however, thought to influence the postlexical encoding mechanisms that operate on lexical-phonological representations (Goldrick et al., 1999; Jescheniak & Levelt, 1994; Nickels, 1995). There are reports that the incidence of phonological errors in aphasia is higher for low-frequency than for high-frequency targets (Ellis, Miller, & Sin, 1983; Gordon, 2002; Miller & Ellis, 1987; Nickels, 1995; Pate et al., 1987; Wilshire, 2002). The prediction from dual origin theory is that this negative relationship between phonological-error incidence and target frequency should hold more strongly for lexical than postlexical phonological errors.

Target length. One final variable that may be relevant to the dual origin debate is target length. The well-established length-sensitivity of phonological errors (more likely on longer words; see, e.g., Caplan et al., 1986; Nickels, 1995; Pate et al., 1987; Romani & Calabrese, 1998) is often cited as evidence for a postlexical site of origin: If, during phonological encoding, each segment or syllable has a certain probability of failing, or if the assembled segments are held in an output buffer with a pathologically fast decay rate, then the more segments or syllables in the target, the more probable

an error. Therefore, length effects might be expected to be stronger for postlexical errors than for lexical errors.

Overview of the present study

The present study examines a large corpus of phonological errors in search of the properties discussed above that have been hypothesised to signal disruption at either the lexical or postlexical stage. The task chosen to elicit errors was picture naming, which has the advantages that targets are known at the outset and the stimulus provides no clues to the target's phonology. The patients who contributed the errors were not selected to exemplify pure cases. However, Conduction aphasics—those individuals most often hypothesised to have postlexical deficits—were well represented in the participant group (9 of 18 participants). Thus, according to the dual origin theory, the corpus would be expected to contain a mixture of lexical and postlexical errors.

Part 1 investigates whether the corpus segregates naturally into high-overlap errors (i.e., those that are phonologically close to the target) and low-overlap errors (those that are phonologically remote from the target). Finding a natural split of this kind would provide support for dual mechanisms of phonological error creation, as maintained by the dual origin theory. It would also allow for tests of other predicted differences in the two subcorpora.

Looking ahead, we found that the corpus did not divide cleanly into high- and low-overlap errors. Thus, in subsequent sections, we adopted an arbitrary cut-off to form two subcorpora, one with relatively more target-error overlap, the other with relatively less. According to the hypothesis that postlexical errors tend to be phonologically closer to their targets than lexical errors, dividing the corpus in this way is expected to produce two groups of errors that differ in their relative proportions of lexical and postlexical errors. This should be true even though the exact cut-off values associated with the two types of errors are unknown, and even if there is some overlap in values. Adopting this strategy, we proceeded, in Parts 2 and 3, to test whether these subcorpora differ in the degree to which they instantiate serial order effects, sensitivity to target length, and sensitivity to target frequency, in accordance with predictions of the dual origin theory.

From the viewpoint of the single origin account, high- and low-overlap errors are different in degree, not kind. Taking this perspective, the final section investigates individual differences that influence the average overlap in phonological errors, in particular, differences that are associated with the severity of the naming deficit.

General methods

Materials

This study is based on archived records of the Philadelphia Naming Test (PNT), a test of confrontation naming consisting of 175 line drawings of objects (Roach, Schwartz, Martin, Grewal, & Brecher, 1996; see also Dell et al., 1997b). Target names in the PNT range from one to four syllables in length, one- and two-syllable targets being the most abundant (there are 101 monosyllabic, 52 bisyllabic, and 22 polysyllabic targets). Target frequencies range from 1 to 750 tokens per million (mean 30.5, range 0.47–45.6) based on the CELEX Cobuild lemmas corpus (Baayen, Piepenbrock, & Van Rijn, 1993).[3] Length and frequency are not balanced across the items: Monosyllabic targets tend to have the highest frequencies (mean 43.3, range: 0.7 to 745.6), followed by bisyllables (mean 16.9, range 0.7–117.8), with polysyllabic targets having the lowest frequencies (mean 3.8, range 0.4–16.6). The items of the PNT have been shown to have high name agreement: Healthy controls score just below ceiling (97%; Dell et al., 1997b).

Procedure

The PNT was administered and scored in the manner that is standard for this test (for details, see Roach et al., 1996). Subjects were shown the test items one at a time and instructed to name the pictured object using a single word response, as quickly as possible. After 30 seconds, or after the correct response was produced, the experimenter terminated the trial and provided the subject with the target name, regardless of whether the subject had produced it or not. The trial duration limit and feedback were imposed in an attempt to discourage aphasic subjects from perseverating on responses.

Administration of the PNT typically took place in a single 1-hour session, although a small number of subjects required two sessions to complete the items. Sessions began with a block of 10 practice items, none of which appeared as test items. Sessions were tape-recorded for later transcription.

Responses to each test item were transcribed by two trained, native speakers of English using a broad IPA phonemic transcription. In the phonological scheme used, syllabic consonants (e.g., butto*n*, cam*el*) and vowel + postvocalic r combinations (e.g., b*ir*d) were all coded as a vowel followed by a consonant (e.g., button = /bʌtən/, camel = /kæməl/, bird = /bʌrd/, hammer = /hæmər/). Transcribed responses were then coded as follows. For each trial, the first, complete (i.e., nonfragment) attempt at naming was assigned to one of six response categories: (1) correct; (2) semantic error; (3) phonological error; (4) formal error; (5) mixed error; and (6) other error. Descriptions of error categories are presented in Table 1. These categories are the same as those used in Dell et al. (1997b), with the exception that Dell et al.'s nonword category was subdivided into "phonological" errors (nonwords that bore a phonological relationship to the target, according to the definition shown in Table 1) and other nonword errors. This study concerns only the phonological errors. The exclusion of nonwords that failed the PNT's liberal target-relatedness criterion is appropriate, since the analyses to be presented involve comparisons between errors and designated PNT targets,

---

[3] In this study, all frequency measures were derived from the Celex corpus, rather than from Francis and Kucera (1982) as in previous studies using the PNT. This database was chosen because it is larger, and therefore provides better frequency discrimination at the lower end of the frequency range—a region where many of the test items fall.

Table 1. *Error taxonomy*

Error category	Description
Correct	Production of the target name.
Semanatic	A word response that bore a semantic relationship to the target. This included synonyms, category co-ordinates, superordinate/subordinate terms and associates (e.g., apple → "orange").
Phonological	A nonword response that was phonologically related to the target: target and response shared at least one phoneme in the same position or two phonemes in any position, excluding schwa (e.g., rake → /rɛsk/; pyramid → /mɪrəmɪd/).
Formal	A real-word response (as determined by its presence in an American English dictionary) that was phonologically related to the target according to the criterion stated above (e.g., camel → "candle").
Mixed	A real-word response that met the criteria for both semantic and formal errors (e.g., skunk → "squirrel").
Other	All other errors, including failures to respond, target descriptions, visual errors, blends, nonword responses that did not meet the phonological relatedness criterion, and unrelated real-word responses.

and the nonwords in question either have no discernable target or bear some resemblance to a semantic or other substitute. For the purposes of these analyses, we included these remaining nonwords into the category "other" (as in Schwartz & Brecher, 2000).

Subjects

Candidates for inclusion in this study were individuals who: (a) had suffered a cerebrovascular accident resulting in a fluent form of aphasia according to the Boston Diagnostic Aphasia Examination (BDAE) criteria (Goodglass & Kaplan, 1983), and (b) had produced at least 10 phonologically related nonword responses when tested on the PNT. We accepted only patients who were premorbidly right-handed, less than 80 years of age, and without significant visual or hearing impairment or articulatory disturbance (verbal apraxia; dysarthria). In total, 18 individuals were selected to participate. Based on the BDAE, 8 were classified as having Wernicke's aphasia, 9 conduction aphasia, and 1 anomic aphasia. Educational levels ranged from seventh grade to postgraduate studies. Additional demographic and language information is shown in Table 2.

Fourteen of 32 otherwise eligible candidates were rejected because they did not generate at least 10 phonologically related nonwords (9 anomic, 2 Wernicke's, 2 transcortical sensory, 1 conduction). Eleven of the 14 rejected candidates had mild naming impairments, by the criteria described below.

Data for this study were collected under a research protocol approved by the Institutional Review Board of Albert Einstein Healthcare Network (Philadelphia, PA). Each subject was reimbursed $15 per session (approximately 1 hour) for participating in the study.

Table 3 summarises each patient's performance on the PNT in terms of the percentage of targets correctly named, the rates of the major error types, and the number of phonological errors contributed to the study corpus. The table has subjects arranged from least to most correct on the PNT and grouped by naming severity, as in Schwartz and Brecher (2000). Patients who scored below 20% correct are called "severe," those who scored more than 20% but less than 70%, "moderate," and those who scored above 70%, "mild." This classification has been shown to correlate well with other, independent measures of aphasia severity, in particular, the BDAE severity rating (Schwartz & Brecher, 2000).

Table 2. Demographic and language profiles for the 18 participants

Patient	Age	Post CVA (mths)	Aetiology: lesion site	Boston Diagnostic Aphasia Exam (BDAE)[a]				Boston Naming Test[b] % corr	Philadelphia Repetition Test[c] % corr
				Classification	Severity level	Word rep[e]	Word[e] discrim		
EGa	60	8	CVA; left frontal; also bilateral lacunar infarction	Conduction	1	9	70.5	8	84
ET	78	9	CVA; left temporal, parietal	Wernicke's	1	2	34.5	0	18
WR	61	3	CVA; left frontal, parietal	Wernicke's	1	10	42.0	5	91
AH	64	7	CVA; left frontal, parietal	Wernicke's	1	5	18.0	10	50
ES	51	4	CVA; left frontal, parietal, occipital	Conduction	1	6	60.5	not tested	41
AS	61	9	CVA; territory of LMCA	Wernicke's	0	8	49.0	1	91
GL	45	9	Haemorrhagic CVA; left parietal, thalamus	Wernicke's	3	8	71.0	23	77
DS	38	3	CVA; left temporal, occipital	Wernicke's	1	5	42.5	43	29
JG	76	1	CVA; left basal ganglia, subinsular cortex	Conduction	2	9	70.0	35	90
CW	75	4	CVA; territory of LMCA	Conduction	2	7	71.0	50	69
HB	65		CVA; left parietal	Conduction	3	9	69.0	not tested	82
LH	47	2	CVA; left temporal, parietal	Conduction	5	9	71.0	55	not tested
GS	68	1	CVA; left temporal, parietal	Wernicke's	2	5	61.5	43	63
EF	68	8	CVA; left posterior parietal	Conduction	3	10	72.0	70	89
MA	28	23	Aneurysm; left temporal, parietal	Conduction	2	not tested[d]	58.5	43	not tested[d]
AF	77	2	Suspected embolic LMCA stroke (opercular branch); normal CT	Wernicke's	3	1	41.5	53	not tested
JL	36	2	Haemorrhagic CVA; left basal ganglia	Conduction	3	8	71.5	43	87
LB	77	10	Sudden onset loss of speech; 24-hr. CT shows lacunar infarcts	Anomic	4	9	69.0	78	90

[a] Goodglass and Kaplan (1983).

[b] Kaplan, Goodglass, and Weintraub (1983).

[c] Dell et al. (1997b).

[d] MA went by the initials NC in previous reports (Dell et al., 1997b; Foygel & Dell, 2000). At an earlier point in his clinical course, MA (NC) was diagnosed as a deep dysphasic because he produced semantic errors in repetition. Extensive analysis of this early pattern and its recovery over time is presented in Martin and Saffran (1992), Martin, Dell, Saffran, and Schwartz (1994) and Martin, Saffran, and Dell (1986).

[e] Raw score.

Table 3. *Patient performance on the Philadelphia Naming Test (PNT)*

Patient	BDAE diagnosis	PNT severity grouping	PNT (% responses)					Phonological corpus (no. err)		
			Correct	Phonological	Formal	Semantic	Mixed	All	Proximate	Remote
EGa[c]	Conduction	severe	3	12	27	4	2	20	7	13
ET[c]	Wernicke's	severe	3	20	8	1	0	35	14	21
WR[a,b,c]	Wernicke's	severe	8	13	15	6	5	23	6	17
AH[c]	Wernicke's	severe	11	15	13	5	3	26	4	22
ES[c]	Conduction	severe	13	43	14	2	3	75	28	47
AS[c]	Wernicke's	severe	15	8	11	5	2	13	5	8
GL[a,b,d]	Wernicke's	moderate	28	25	21	3	3	43	22	21
DS[c,d]	Wernicke's	moderate	51	11	13	7	4	20	12	8
JG[a,b]	Conduction	moderate	55	15	8	6	4	26	13	13
CW[c]	Conduction	moderate	59	19	13	5	1	34	18	16
HB[a,b]	Conduction	moderate	61	15	13	6	2	26	20	6
LH[a,b]	Conduction	moderate	69	13	7	3	1	23	17	6
GS[a,b,c]	Wernicke's	mild	70	13	6	2	1	23	16	7
EF[c,d]	Conduction	mild	74	13	2	3	3	22	17	5
MA[a,b,e]	Wernicke's	mild	75	7	7	3	1	10	8	2
AF[a,b,c]	Conduction	mild	75	6	3	2	6	13	9	4
JL[a,b,c]	Conduction	mild	76	6	1	3	3	10	7	3
LB[a,b]	Anomic	mild	82	9	2	4	1	15	10	5

The per cent response columns do not sum to 100 because the "Other" response category is not represented. Also, the percentages are not always based on 175 responses (the number of items in the PNT) due to occasional technical difficulties with stimulus presentation; actual totals range from 169–175. Patients ES, LH, and WR each made one phonological error that could conceivably be a dialectical variant of the target; while included in the error breakdown, these errors did not contribute to the phonological corpus. [a]PNT data previously reported in Dell et al. (1997a). [b]PNT data previously reported in Foygel and Dell (2000). [c]PNT data previously reported in Schwartz and Brecher (2000). [d]PNT and other relevant data reported in Wilshire (2002). [e]In previous reports, MA was identified as NC.

Not surprisingly, most of the study participants made more phonological than semantic errors (recall that the production of phonological errors was a criterion for inclusion). Formal errors were also common in this sample and were correlated with phonological errors (Spearman rho = .57; $p <$ .05). This may be because both were correlated with naming severity (rho = −.55 and −.77 for phonological and formal errors, respectively; $p <$ .05 for both) and/or because many formal errors are likely to be phonological errors that just happen to make words (Gagnon, Schwartz, Dell, Martin, & Saffran, 1997; Lecours, Deloche, & Lhermitte, 1973). The size of the phonological error corpus was 457, with individual patients contributing between 10 and 75 errors.

PART 1. DISTRIBUTION OF TARGET–ERROR OVERLAP

The absence of intermediate-overlap errors in the speech-error analyses of Blumstein (1973) and Buckingham and Kertesz (1976) might, on its own, constitute persuasive evidence against a single error-generation mechanism. However, this finding may be an artifact of the methods used for coding these spontaneously occurring errors. Because it is difficult to identify targets reliably in aphasics' spontaneous speech, a reasonable strategy is to code the most transparent errors as target-related and the remainder as abstruse neologisms. Such a strategy will yield a bimodal distribution consisting of very high overlap errors at one end and no-overlap errors (abstruse neologisms) at the other, as has been reported, but for reasons having nothing to do with the mechanism(s) generating the errors. On the other hand, if this finding were to replicate in a phonological error corpus that was derived from naming, using a liberal criterion for assigning target relatedness, it would indeed constitute strong evidence for dual mechanisms.

A potential criticism is that our chances of finding a peak in the very low overlap range is weakened by the necessity of excluding nonword errors that fail the PNT's target relatedness criterion (Table 1). Note, however, that while all errors were required to meet the PNT criterion for being phonologically related to the target, in some cases the relation was sufficiently weak that, had this been a spontaneous speech task (where the targets are unknown at the outset), they might have qualified as having no identifiable target, i.e., as abstruse neologisms. Thus, low-overlap errors were not excluded by our coding conventions. Moreover, it is important to note that the key piece of evidence from the spontaneous speech analyses was the absence of intermediate-overlap errors, not the prevalence of errors with low overlap. Thus, in seeking to replicate this finding with errors derived from naming, our primary interest lies in the relative frequency of errors in the intermediate-overlap range.

Methods

For each error–target pair in the corpus, we obtained a measure of error overlap, as follows: Two points were assigned for each phoneme that the target and response shared, and these points were summed and divided by the total number of target and error segments in the pair (Lecours et al., 1973). For instance, if the target was *frog* and the subject responded /flɛp/, two points would be assigned for the shared /f/, and this would be divided by the eight phonemes in the target and error combined (4 + 4), yielding a value of .25. This overlap proportion has the desirable feature of taking target and response length into account, allowing for direct comparisons across different target–response length combinations. On the

other hand, target length can still influence the data, since the outcomes for short words are highly restricted (ignoring additions, a three-phoneme word can yield only three values: 0, .33, and .67). With this in mind, we generated frequency histograms for the error corpus in its entirety, as well as broken down by target length (1, 2, and 3 or more syllables).

Results and commentary

Figure 1 shows the distribution of target–response overlap proportions for the entire corpus. The distribution is roughly bell-shaped, peaking at an overlap value of around .6. The graphs for targets of different lengths are shown in Figure 2. These frequency histograms are based on smaller numbers and are thus noisier than the summary graph, but they retain its basic shape. Critically, there is no indication of a dip in the middle range. On the contrary, errors with intermediate overlap are very common in this corpus.

As a follow-up, we examined overlap in a number of different ways, including proportion of

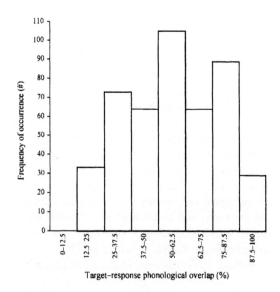

Figure 1. *Frequency histogram for errors at each level of target–error overlap.*

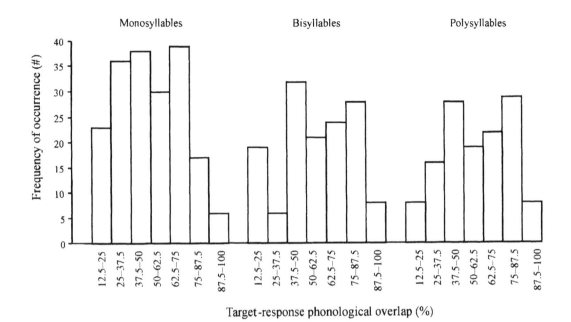

Figure 2. *Frequency histograms for errors at each level of target–error overlap, broken down for monosyllable, bisyllable, and polysyllable targets.*

target phonemes present in the error; the key feature criterion (Kohn & Smith, 1994); and a measure of target–response divergence that takes account of intrusion of foreign phonemes. In every case, the resulting frequency histograms were bell-shaped, without an intermediate-range dip.

Finally, we examined the frequency histograms for overlap proportions as generated by the 18 subjects individually. Only two provided a degree of support for the bimodality prediction: JL and AF, among the mildest patients in the sample, produced mostly high overlap errors (range .60 to .90) with occasional low values (range .20 to .40).

Contrary to the speech error analyses of Blumstein (1973) and Buckingham and Kertesz (1976), we did not find that the majority of phonological errors were limited to one or two segments, or that intermediate level errors were underrepresented. Most likely, this disagreement has to do with the different levels of confidence one has when associating phonological errors with

intended targets in connected speech versus naming. The low confidence afforded by conversational speech analyses creates a bias to identify as target-related only those errors that bear a transparent relation to the target. The higher confidence afforded by the naming task allows errors to be accepted where there is considerably less phonological overlap. When the more liberal criterion is applied, the appearance of bimodality in the overlap distribution disappears, and the prevalence of intermediate overlap errors becomes obvious. In previous work by our group, this has been shown even for connected speech samples (Goldmann, Schwartz, & Wilshire, 2001; Schwartz, Saffran, Bloch, & Dell, 1994).

Since the distribution of overlap scores in our corpus turned out to be roughly bell-shaped, it did not support a natural division of the corpus into likely lexical versus postlexical errors. We therefore proceeded to adopt an arbitrary separation point in order to test other predictions of the dual origin theory.

PART 2. SERIAL ORDER EFFECTS IN REMOTE AND PROXIMATE ERRORS

It has been noted that phonological errors in classic conduction aphasia tend to affect the ends of words more than the beginnings (Kohn, 1989; Wilshire & McCarthy, 1996). In their contrastive case studies of lexical and postlexical patients, Kohn and Smith (1994, 1995) identified increased vulnerability to phonological error production across the word (a type of serial position effect) as one of the consistent features of a postlexical disorder. A flat serial position function, on the other hand, was said to be indicative of a lexical retrieval disorder. In Part 2, we tested Kohn and Smith's differential serial order predictions by using another of their differentiating criteria—error proximity—to subdivide the corpus into two subsets: one that was more likely to contain postlexical errors (the proximate corpus) and another that was more likely to contain lexical errors (the remote corpus).

Methods

Each of the 457 errors in our corpus was classified as proximate or remote based on the percentage of the target's phonemes that was preserved in the error. Errors that preserved 50% or fewer of their target's segments were classified as "remote" and those that preserved more than 50% were classified as "proximate." The 50% criterion has been used before as a means of distinguishing closely related phonemic paraphasic errors from more distantly

Table 4. *Examples of assignment of target phonemes to the five normalised positions*

Target	IPA description	Normalised position				
		1	*2*	*3*	*4*	*5*
key	ki	k				i
map	mæp	m		æ		p
snake	snek	s	n		e	k
plant	plænt	p	l	æ	n	t
basket	bæskət	b	æ	s, k	ə	t
volcano	vɔlkeno	v, ɔ	l	k	e	n, o

related neologistic errors (e.g., Basso, Corno, & Marangolo, 1996).

Proximate and remote errors were separately analysed for serial order effects using the Wing and Baddeley method (1980; see also Miller & Ellis, 1987). This procedure assigns each phoneme of the target word to one of five normalised positions and calculates the proportion of phonemes correctly produced at each normalised position (see Table 4 for examples). This has the advantage of allowing for comparison across words of differing phonemic lengths. Preservation rates are obtained by summing the number of phonemes correctly produced in each position and expressing this as a proportion of the total target phonemes in that position.

In addition, in order to obtain a baseline measure of the chance rates of preservation at each of the five normalised word positions, a "pseudo-corpus" of errors was created by shuffling the entire error corpus and randomly re-pairing errors with targets. The serial position analysis was then repeated for this pseudocorpus. The figures obtained from this pseudocorpus provide some indication of the chance likelihood of correct phoneme reproduction at each of the five normalised positions.

Results and commentary

Overall, 51% of all errors in the corpus met the definition of proximate errors and the remaining 49% met the definition for remote errors. Every patient contributed at least some errors to each of the categories of proximate and remote errors (see Table 3).

Figure 3 shows the percentage of phonemes correctly reproduced in each of the five normalised positions, for proximate and remote errors respectively. For proximate errors, the distribution of preserved phonemes across positions did not differ significantly from a flat line, $\chi^2(4, N = 1277) = 4.2$, $p = .39$. Rates of phoneme preservation at all five positions were significantly higher than those obtained for the pseudocorpus, $\chi^2 = 306.7, 187.8, 213.9, 141.7,$ and 197.4 for positions one to five respectively, $p < .0001$ in all cases. For remote

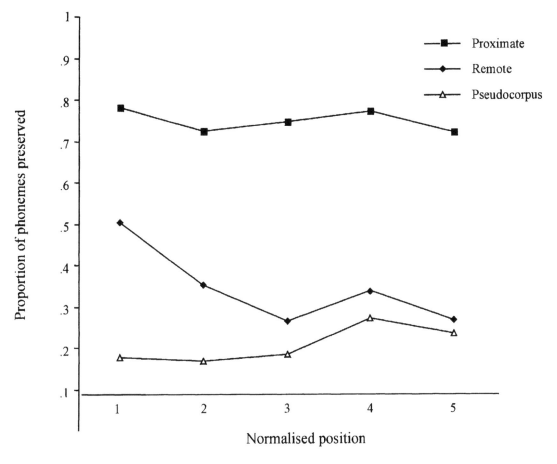

Figure 3. *Proportions of target phonemes correctly preserved in each of five normalised word positions for proximate, remote, and pseudocorpus errors.*

errors, however, the distribution of preserved phonemes *did* differ significantly from a flat line, $\chi^2(4, N = 1205) = 29.2, p < .0001$. Rates of phoneme preservation were significantly higher than those for the pseudocorpus for positions one to three, $\chi^2 = 99.9$ and 25.7 for positions one and two respectively, $p < .0001$ in both cases, and 5.19 for position three, $p < .05$. However, at positions four and five, preservation rates did not differ significantly from those of the pseudocorpus, $\chi^2 = 2.75, p = .10$, and 1.06, $p = .30$, for positions four and five respectively. Finally, a direct comparison between proximate and remote errors revealed that the differences in serial position effects between the two error types were statistically significant. If we compare error rates at the beginning and end positions—which, due to the symmetrical normal-ising procedure, contained equal numbers of targets and therefore equal opportunities for error—there was a significant interaction between position and error type, $\chi^2(1, N = 678) = 10.27, p < .01$.

It appears that proximate and remote errors do indeed exhibit differential serial order effects. However, the difference is the reverse of what was predicted based on Kohn and Smith (1994, 1995): Proximate errors—those most likely to have a postlexical origin—were found to exhibit a rela-tively flat distribution, with all word positions being equally susceptible to error. On the other hand, remote errors—those most likely to have a lexical origin—showed a strong primacy effect, with phonemes early in the word being the most likely to be correctly recalled.

Examination of the last two columns in Table 3 reveals that more of the remote errors were produced by the patients with severe naming deficits. This raises the possibility that the serial order effect in the remote errors reflects some particular characteristic of these severe patients. To check this, we examined the serial order data separately for mild, moderate, and severe subgroups. For the sake of simplicity, data are reported only for the first and last of the five normalised positions. For all three subgroups, remote errors showed a steeper decline from first to last positions than did proximate errors (see Figure 4). However, the trend reached significance only for the mild group: interactions between position and error type: mild: $\chi^2(1, N = 183) = 8.32, p < .01$; moderate: $\chi^2(1, N = 272) = 1.20, p = .27$; severe: $\chi^2(1, N = 223) = 2.33, p = .13$. Apparently, the serial position effect in remote errors is not restricted to the severe patients; on the contrary, the effect is most reliable in the mildest of the patients. We postpone further discussion of these findings until the General Discussion.

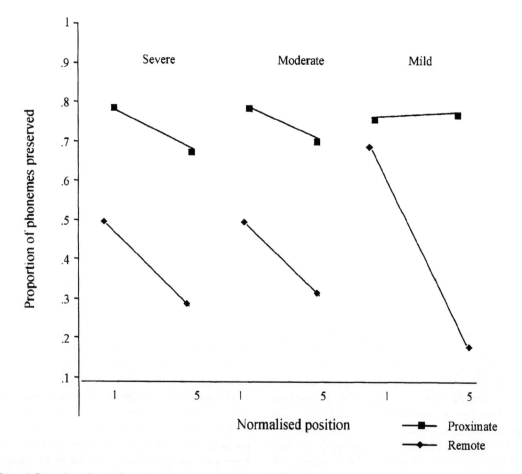

Figure 4. *Proportions of target phonemes correctly preserved in first and fifth normalised word positions in proximate and remote errors, for patients with severe, moderate, and mild deficits.*

PART 3. LENGTH AND FREQUENCY EFFECTS IN PROXIMATE AND REMOTE ERRORS

According to the dual origin theory, lexical and postlexical phonological errors should not only differ in their qualitative characteristics, but also in the way they are influenced by the properties of target words. Errors that arise during postlexical processing are expected to be strongly influenced by phonological characteristics of the target, including word length, and less influenced by lexical characteristics, whereas for lexical recovery errors the reverse is expected. The most extensively studied lexical characteristic is word frequency (e.g., Brown & McNeill, 1966; Dell, 1990; Jescheniak & Levelt, 1994; Oldfield & Wingfield, 1965), and this is the variable we focused on here. However, recent studies have also demonstrated the importance of another lexical characteristic, known as "neighbourhood density," which is defined as the number of words that are phonologically similar to a given target word. It appears that targets drawn from dense phonological neighborhoods are easier to produce than comparable words from sparse neighbourhoods, as indicated by their lower TOT and phonological-error rates (Gordon, 2002; Harley & Bown, 1998; Vitevitch, 2002; but see Goldrick & Rapp, 2001). The protective effect of neighbourhood density is thought to arise within the lexicon, as a result of activation feeding back from phoneme to lexical units (Gordon & Dell, 2003; Vitevitch, 2002).

Whatever the mechanism underlying this neighbourhood density effect, its existence has important methodological implications because density, frequency, and length are intercorrelated: short words are more frequent than long words (Zipf, 1965) and short, frequent words are more likely to have dense neighbourhoods (Landauer & Streeter, 1973).[4] Thus, density needs to be taken into consideration in any analysis of length and frequency effects.

Methods

Frequency analyses were based on frequency estimates obtained from the lemma corpus of the CELEX database and converted to log frequency values based on frequencies per million words. Density (phonological neighbourhood) values were obtained using a version of the Celex database that was modified to contain entries for American-English pronunciations. We identified all items in the Celex word forms corpus that differed from the target word by the substitution, addition, or omission of just one phoneme. The frequencies of these items were then summed to generate a single numerical measure of phonological neighbourhood density for each target word. Previous studies (e.g., Best, 1995; Gordon, 2002; Vitevitch, 2002) have used the same measure, albeit derived from different speech corpora. Target length was measured in number of syllables or number of phonemes, depending on the analysis.

Three separate analyses were performed. The first analysis examined the effect of target length on the incidence of proximate errors and remote errors. We fit simple least squares regression lines expressing the relation between number of errors per target and target length (in syllables) for proximate and remote errors separately and tested whether the slopes differed significantly from zero. The dual origin theory predicts a significant positive slope for proximate errors (more errors at longer lengths), but not necessarily for remote errors.

The second analysis examined the effect of target lexical frequency on proximate and remote error incidence and limited itself to monosyllabic targets (to avoid the confound with length). After subdividing the frequency range spanned by the monosyllabic targets into six equivalent ranges, we fit least squares regression lines and proceeded as described above. The dual origin theory predicts a significant negative slope (fewer errors to high-frequency targets) for remote errors, but not necessarily for proximate errors.

---

[4] A significant association among these variables also obtains for the targets of the PNT (syllabic length/log frequency: $r = -.44$; syllabic length/log density: $r = -.76$; log frequency/log density: $r = .51$; $p < .0001$ for all).

In the third analysis, the entire target set was examined using simultaneous multiple regression. We performed two separate analyses, in which the dependent variables were, respectively, number of proximate errors per target and number of remote errors per target. The independent variables in each analysis were log frequency, word length (number of phonemes), and log density. This enabled us to assess the independent contributions of target frequency (as well as length and density) using the full corpus, rather than just the errors involving monosyllabic targets.

Results and commentary

The linear relation between error incidence and target length was significant for both proximate and remote errors. For proximate errors, the slope of the least squares regression line was .92 ($N = $ 175; $t = 7.4$; $p < .0001$); for remote errors the slope was .59 ($N = 175$; $t = 4.9$; $p < .0001$). As expected, the slopes were positive, indicating that the error incidence was higher for longer words. For graphical representation of the length effects, the data were recalculated to express the probability of error at each word length, i.e., the sum total of errors at each length divided by the maximum number possible. The results are shown in Figure 5.

Turning to the target-frequency effect in monosyllabic targets, the slope of the of the least squares regression line was close to significant for the proximate errors (slope = −.18; $N = 100$; $t = $ −1.9; $p = .06$), with the negative sign indicating more errors to low-frequency targets. There was no effect for the remote errors (slope = −.05; $N = 100$; $t = 0.44$; $p > .50$). For graphical representation, the data were recalculated to express error probabilities in each frequency range, with results as shown in Figure 6.

In the multiple regression model for proximate errors, Adjusted $R^2(N = 174) = .28$. Parameter estimates are: for target length, .25 ($p < .01$); for log frequency, .46 ($p < .01$); and for log density, −.10 ($p > .20$). In the model for remote errors, Adjusted $R^2(N = 174) = .20$. Parameter estimates are: for target length, .35 ($p < .0001$), for log frequency, −.08 ($p > .50$); and for log density, .05 ($p > .50$).

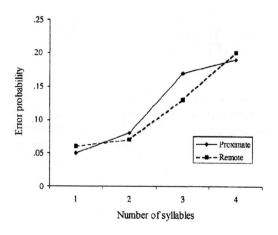

Figure 5. *Probability of proximate errors and remote errors as a function of target length in syllables. Probabilities were calculated by counting how many errors of each type (proximate, remote) were made for each of the word lengths and expressing the sum as a proportion of the maximum possible for that length (the number of targets multiplied by the number of subjects).*

Thus, for proximate errors, the significant predictors of error rate are length and frequency, whereas for remote errors the only significant predictor is length. The results comport with the length-effect analysis in showing that target length is a significant predictor of both proximate and remote errors. The results are also in basic agreement with the frequency analysis on monosyllabic targets, in that it shows that the effect is absent for remote errors but present for proximate errors. (That the frequency effect for proximates fell short of significance in the monosyllabic targets analysis was probably due to lower power.) The overall effects for target length and word frequency are quite different from what dual origin theory predicts.

Target density was not a significant predictor of either proximate or remote error rates. As a further check, we combined proximate and remote errors to create a new dependent variable—total number of errors per target—and we repeated the multiple regression analysis with this dependent variable. Results were as follows: Adjusted $R^2(N = 174) = .44$; parameter estimates for target length = .60 ($p < .0001$), for log frequency = −.53 ($p < .05$), and for log density = .05 ($p > .50$). Thus, in the corpus

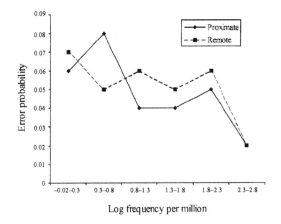

Figure 6. *Probability of proximate errors and remote errors as a function of target lexical frequency. Probabilities were calculated by counting how many errors of each type (proximate, remote) were made for each frequency level and expressing the sum as a proportion of the maximum possible for that level (the number of targets multiplied by the number of subjects).*

as a whole, target length and frequency each contributed to the prediction of error rate, whereas target density did not.

There is a potential confound in these analyses: Phonological errors on targets with many phonological neighbours are more likely to generate real words by chance than comparable errors on targets with few neighbors (cf. Gagnon et al., 1997; Nickels & Howard, 1995), but those real-word errors would be classified as formals in our taxonomy, not phonological errors. Since density, length, and frequency are correlated, excluding these "pseudoformals" from the analysis could have affected the results for any or all of the three variables. For example, by underestimating the true phonological error rate to short targets, it could have exaggerated the difference in error rate between short and long targets (yielding a spurious

length effect). Alternatively, by underestimating the phonological error rate to targets from dense neighbourhoods, it could have minimised the difference between dense- and sparse-neighbourhood targets (obscuring a true density effect).

With this in mind, we reanalysed the data, adding a correction for pseudoformals: For each target, we counted the number of formal errors that had been produced, took 40% of that number as our estimate of the number of misassigned phonological errors,[5] and added that to the "all errors" count for each target. Half that number was then added to the "proximate" count and half to the "remote" count, under the assumption that proximate and remote errors were equally likely to generate words by chance.

Adding the pseudoformals correction did not alter the conclusions. The effects depicted in Figures 4 and 5 were unchanged. The multiple regression analyses with the corrected data yielded slightly lower Adjusted R^2 values (.27, .17, and .42 for corrected proximate, remote, and all errors, respectively, compared with .28, .20, and .44 in the original model). There was no change in the significance of the factors for any of the three models. That is, just as in the uncorrected models, proximate errors and all errors were predicted by target length and word frequency, and remote errors by target length alone.

PART 4. FURTHER EXPLORATION OF THE FACTORS THAT INFLUENCE TARGET–ERROR OVERLAP

The foregoing analyses of proximate and remote phonological errors did not produce results in line with the dual origin theory. While the properties

---

[5] The 40% figure is based on an estimate of lexical density reported in Gagnon et al. (1997). When those authors generated all possible CVC (consonant-vowel-consonant) sequences from high-frequency English phonemes, they found that 40% of the sequences made real English words. This 40% lexical density estimate is based on a particularly dense space (CVC sequences comprised of high-frequency phonemes). It is therefore a high estimate, and especially so for longer words. Our pseudoformals correction is thus conservative, in that by exaggerating the phonological error counts for the longer (less dense, less frequent) words, it reduced the likelihood that we would see length (or density or frequency) effects in the reanalyses.

of the remote and proximate subcorpora did differ in several of the analyses, in most cases the observed properties ran counter to dual origin theory predictions. In this section, we explore characteristics of the full error corpus from the perspective of the single origin theory.

Severity, error incidence, and target–error overlap

Dell's naming theory explains all nonword phonological errors as arising from selection failure at the level of phoneme retrieval. The severity of the phoneme-retrieval deficit affects both the incidence of errors and the phonological proximity of errors to targets. Patients with a mild deficit are expected to make few phonological errors, with generally high target–error overlap; patients with a severe deficit are expected to make many phonological errors, with generally low target–error overlap (Schwartz & Brecher, 2000; see also Dell et al., 1997b). In Table 5, the data are displayed in a format that speaks to this prediction.

Results and commentary

It is apparent from the first four columns of Table 5 that naming accuracy and error-overlap scores are indeed related. The correlation between overall per cent correct and mean overlap score for phonological errors is .94 (Pearson r, $N = 18$, $p < .0001$), with poor namers having lower overlap scores. Thus, in this sample of fluent aphasics, 88% of the variance in overlap score is explained by overall naming severity. When we split the sample by aphasia classification, we find that the correlation between percent correct and mean overlap is .98 for Wernicke's aphasics ($N = 8$, $p < .0001$) and .89 for conduction aphasics ($N = 9$; $p = .0005$), indicating that the findings in the overall sample are representative of both fluent subtypes. (Recall that only one patient in the sample was classified as anomic.)

Severity and target length, frequency and density

Having determined that the overlap in phonological errors correlates strongly and positively with

Table 5. *Average error overlap and slopes of regression lines predicting error overlap from three target properties*

Patient	BDAE profile	PNT % correct	PNT severity grouping	Average error overlap	Slope of regresssion line		
					No. phonemes	Log frequency	Log density
EGa	Conduction	3	severe	.470	−.02	−.08	.01
ET	Wernicke's	3	severe	.423	.01	.08*	−.02
WR	Wernicke's	8	severe	.395	.03	−.06	−.03
AH	Wernicke's	11	severe	.391	−.03	.15**	.03
ES	Conduction	13	severe	.485	−.01	−.02	.01
AS	Wernicke's	15	severe	.467	−.01	.12	.00
GL	Wernicke's	28	moderate	.555	−.02	.04	.01
DS	Wernicke's	51	moderate	.595	−.02	.00	.02
JG	Conduction	55	moderate	.594	−.01	−.05	−.02
CW	Conduction	59	moderate	.601	.01	−.06	−.03
HB	Conduction	61	moderate	.680	−.02	.06	−.01
LH	Conduction	69	moderate	.670	.00	−.11	−.03
GS	Wernicke's	70	mild	.684	.00	.04	−.01
EF	Conduction	74	mild	.726	.02	−.11	−.05*
NC	Conduction	75	mild	.624	.01	.07	−.01
AF	Wernicke's	75	mild	.727	.04	−.28*	−.08*
JL	Conduction	76	mild	.620	.05*	−.20**	−.06*
LB	Anomic	82	mild	.693	.03*	−.22**	−.05*

*.05 < p ≤ .10; **p < .05.

naming correctness, we next investigated whether the properties of the words themselves also influence target–error overlap. Figure 7 depicts our intuitive prediction as to the direction of the effects for word length and frequency, as revealed by the slope of regression lines. The prediction is based on two assumptions: (1) that phonological retrieval is easier for targets that are shorter, and/or more frequent; and (2) that the easier the phonological retrieval, the greater the target-error overlap. The intuitive prediction is that the overlap/length function will have a negative slope and the overlap/frequency function a positive slope. We also predicted that these trends would be stronger in the relatively well-functioning systems of the milder patients, relative to the noise-dominated systems of those with more severe deficits.

Methods

For each of the subjects, we fit three simple least squares regression lines expressing the relation between the overlap in the patients' phonological errors and (1) the number of phonemes in the incorrectly named targets, (2) the targets' log frequency, and, for completeness, (3) the targets' log density. The slopes of these regression lines were examined for trends consistent with, or opposed to, the intuitive predictions.

Next, mixed-model multivariate analysis was performed on all the data from all patients. Three models were run, in which patient severity (mild, moderate, severe) and the three target properties (length, frequency, density) were entered as predictor variables, and interaction terms for the target properties and severity were included one at a time (i.e., one per model), because of the high

correlations among the target properties. The dependent variable was error-overlap score. The mixed model module of the SAS statistical package was used to perform the statistical analysis (Statistical Analysis Software, Release 8.1, N. Carolina: SAS Institute Inc.)

Results and commentary

The last three columns of Table 5 show the slopes of the individual regression lines. Overall, the slopes are small and not significantly different from zero. As expected, most of the significant or nearly significant slopes occur in the mild patients, but surprisingly, these go in the direction opposite to the intuitive prediction. That is, the mild patients tend to have positive slopes for length (less overlap in errors to short words) and negative slopes for frequency (less overlap in errors to high-frequency words). This counterintuitive finding could be artifactual. Since the possible values for very short words is restricted, a few errors on very short words could pull the slope in the negative direction for the mild patients, whose overlap scores are generally high. As a check on this possibility, we deleted errors to the shortest (two- and three-phoneme) targets from the corpus and recomputed the length/overlap functions for the mild patients. This produced very little change, other than to cause three of the slopes to become slightly *more* positive.

The slopes for log density, shown in the last column, are significant in the negative direction for four of the six mild patients, indicating that for these patients, targets from higher-density neighbourhoods tended to produce errors with *less* overlap than those from lower-density neighbourhoods. Given the intercorrelations among target density, length, and frequency, this was predictable from the length and frequency results reported in the preceding paragraph.

There was insufficient data in this individual subjects analysis to statistically control for the intercorrelation of target length, frequency, and density, but we did attempt to do this in the mixed model regression analyses. Recall that we ran three models, with the same four predictor variables but different interaction terms. All three models

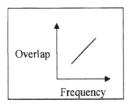
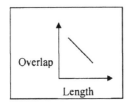

Figure 7. *Intuitive predictions regarding the direction of the slopes relating error overlap with target frequency and target length.*

showed significant main effects for patient severity ($p \leq .01$) and target log density ($p \leq .01$), whereas the main effects for target length reached only trend-level significance ($p = .06, .08, .12$); and the effect for log frequency was weaker still ($p = .13, .44, .45$). The interaction terms in all three models were significant, but slightly more so for log density × severity ($p = .02$) than for log frequency × severity ($p = .04$) or target length × severity ($p = .06$). The mixed model with the log density × severity interaction term is shown in Table 6. The main effect for density is negative, meaning that as log density increases, target–error overlap decreases; the interaction indicates that the decrease is greater for the mild group, just as we saw in the slopes from the individual subjects' data.

These results from the mixed model regressions suggest that neighbourhood density, possibly in combination with length, is the driving factor behind the significant slopes identified in Table 5. That is, what appeared to be significant effects for frequency were probably due to the correlation of frequency with density, which was not controlled in these individual analyses.

The emergence of density as an important factor suggests a possible explanation for why the intuitive predictions depicted in Figure 7 were not confirmed. Short, frequent words tend to have many phonologically related neighbours, and these neighbours are likely to become activated during the course of naming. So while short, frequent words may be less likely to elicit errors in the first place than longer, rarer ones, when they do, the errors produced may be more likely to contain phonemes belonging to these other, co-activated neighbours. This would result in errors that have low overlap because they contain phonemic material from more than one word. We could call this type of phonological error a "formal blend." The occurrence of even a few formal blends to these types of target could have affected overlap scores in the manner we observed, i.e., yielded slopes that were flatter than expected and, in some cases, reversed in sign.

Interestingly, Dell's interactive single origin model actually provides an explanation for why the reversed-sign slopes occurred only in the mild patients. The model predicts that mild patients are more likely to be influenced by phonological neighbourhood effects (in this case, the competition among phonological neighbours that sets the stage for formal blends) than will severe patients. This is because the activation of phonological neighbours results from the targets' phonemes feeding activation back up to the word level, and this feedback is most reliable in systems that are conducting activation efficiently. To support this reasoning, Table 7 shows what we found when we

Table 6. *Results from the mixed-model regression analysis with density in the interaction term*

Variable	Number	Denominator	f	p–value
Severity group[a]	2	15	28.33	.0001
Target log frequency[a]	1	434	0.56	.4545
Target length[b]	1	434	3.44	.0641
Target log density	1	434	9.39	.0023
Target log density × severity	2	434	3.89	.0212

[a]Mild, moderate, severe.
[b]In number of syllables.

Table 7. *Semantic (s) and phonological (f) connection weights in the best-fit semantic–phonological model*

Patient	PNT severity	s	f	RMSD	χ^2
EGa	severe	.001	.021	.084	41.2
ET	severe	.001	.007	.030	12.6
WR	severe	.001	.017	.065	27.1
AH	severe	.002	.016	.035	10.3
ES	severe	.015	.007	.026	10.0
AS	severe	.005	.018	.045	12.2
GL	moderate	.010	.016	.046	18.1
DS	moderate	.016	.019	.022	7.2
JG	moderate	.020	.018	.012	4.5
CW	moderate	.022	.017	.028	15.1
HB	moderate	.020	.018	.028	12.0
LH	moderate	.025	.018	.014	3.3
GS	mild	.025	.018	.019	4.6
EF	mild	.027	.020	.013	7.2
MA	mild	.026	.020	.027	10.6
AF	mild	.020	.025	.037	25.4
JL	mild	.027	.025	.013	6.3
LB	mild	.029	.022	.006	0.9

Optimal fits to control data are $s = .070, f = .100$ (Foygel & Dell, 2000).

ran the model-fitting routine for Foygel and Dell's (2000) semantic-phonological lesion model on each subject's PNT profiles. Note in particular the values for f—the phonological connection-weight parameter. These values are largest for the mild patients who exhibited significant or trend-level effects in direction opposite the intuitive predictions (EF, AF, JL, LB; see Table 5), thereby supporting the idea that their systems conducted activation between words and phonemes more efficiently than the more severe patients.[6]

GENERAL DISCUSSION

Failed tests of the dual origin theory

We sought to determine whether a theory of naming that explains all phonological errors as deriving from lexical-phonological retrieval (i.e., Dell's theory) has validity in the face of the dual origin theory, which claims a postlexical source for at least a subset of phonological errors. In a variation on the "corpus method" (cf. Nickels, 1995), we assembled phonological naming errors from a diverse group of fluent aphasic subjects and then subdivided the corpus into those that shared 50% or more of the targets phonemes (the proximate subcorpus) versus those in which the overlap was less than 50% (the remote corpus). The dual origin theory predicts that postlexical influences will be more apparent in the proximate corpus and lexical influences more apparent in the remote corpus. None of the three specific predictions we tested was supported.

1. Declining rates of segmental accuracy across the word—a type of serial position effect—are said to arise from the properties of the postlexical

mechanism. We found evidence for this effect in the Wing and Baddeley analysis, but it was the remote errors that showed the effect, not the proximate errors.

2. Target length is a phonological property that purportedly influences the accuracy of the post-lexical mechanism. We found in Part 3 that more phonological errors were made on long words than short words, even when frequency and density were statistically controlled. However, the length effect was strong and significant for both proximate and remote errors.

3. Lexical frequency is a variable thought to operate within the lexicon, and not at the post-lexical stage(s). Consequently, the effect of lexical frequency on phonological error rate is predicted to be stronger in the remote corpus than in the proximate corpus. We found the reverse; for example, in multiple regression analyses, target frequency was significant for proximate errors and for proximate and remote errors combined, but not for remote errors alone.

In summary, the four characteristics that the dual origin theory attributes to postlexical errors (high target–error overlap, declining segmental accuracy across the word, error rate sensitive to word length, error rate insensitive to word frequency) were not associated in the manner predicted by that theory.

Switching perspectives, Part 4 adopted the single-origin viewpoint on the matter of target–error overlap. We showed that subjects' average overlap score correlated strongly with the severity of their naming deficit ($r = .94$) (see also Schwartz & Brecher, 2000) and that for a subset of patients, namely those with relatively mild naming impairments, the overlap in "easy" words (i.e., shorter, higher-frequency, higher-density words) was *lower*

---

[6] Before running the model-fitting routine (see Footnote 1), we reassigned responses to the categories fit by the model, including dividing the category of "non-naming response" (null responses, descriptions and the small number of miscellaneous errors) among the remaining six categories: correct, nonword, formal, semantic, mixed, unrelated (Dell, Lawler, Harris, & Gordon, 2004; Ruml et al., 2000). The model-fitting routine outputs the model with the lowest value of chi-squared and reports as a goodness-of-fit measure the root mean square deviation (RMSD). Note that the only patients for whom $f \geq .02$ are the four mild patients mentioned in the text, plus patient EGa. EGa has the lowest correctness score of any patient, and the reliability of parameter fits in his case is rendered suspect by the relatively high RMSD, indicating a poor fit of model to data.

than for longer words. A mixed-model regression analysis indicated that this effect might be driven by neighbourhood density, leading us to suggest that dense neighbourhoods of short, frequent words might give rise to occasional "formal blends" (cf. Burns & Canter, 1977; Lecours, 1982), with lower than expected overlap. In mild patients, strong lexical-phonological connection weights, while generally keeping error rates low, would confer susceptibility to competition from phonological neighbours, and thereby to the occasional formal blend error. In fact, it may be that mild patients are unlikely to make errors to short, high-frequency words *except* in cases where the competitive pressure of a high-density neighbourhood predisposes them to formal blends. This would explain why mild patients make errors to easy targets in the first place, and why those errors are more remote than otherwise expected.

Though not initially predicted, the existence of formal blends, and the greater susceptibility of the milder patients, accords well with Dell's interactive, single origin model. Let us now consider how the model handles other key findings from this study.

The single origin account of key findings

The serial position effect

Part 2 revealed a strong serial position effect favouring early word positions. This is incompatible with single origin models that include parallel selection of target phonemes (e.g., Dell, 1988; Dell et al., 1997b), but it is consistent with models in which the segments are selected in sequence (e.g., Dell et al., 1993; Houghton, 1990; Sevald & Dell, 1994). For example, in the sequential model of Sevald and Dell, the phonemes at the beginning of a word become activated earlier than those towards the end, and thus have more opportunity to feed activation back to the lexical level. This means that neighbouring words with the same initial phoneme as the target receive more feedback than those sharing later phonemes. Consequently, onset-sharing neighbours compete more strongly with the target than do neighbours that share its end segments. Assuming that this competition also

affects the phonological level, the result is greater competition at later word positions than at earlier ones. Consider, for example, phonological retrieval as it operates for the word "cat." When the word node for "cat" is activated by semantics, its activation passes first to the initial sound /k/, which feeds activation back to all the words in the network that begin with /k/. Activation of the second phoneme strengthens feedback activation to cat and all other words beginning with /kae/. In this way, phonological neighbours like "cap" become strong competitors, passing activation down to their own constituent phonemes. As "cap" shares the targets first two phonemes, its co-activation with "cat" actually reinforces correct selection for these initial phonemes. However, when it comes to encoding of the final phoneme, there is divergence between the two candidates. If the "p" from "cap" is sufficiently strong, it could be selected in place of the target phoneme "t." In general, then, if there is interference between the two words at the phonological retrieval level, it will be likely to give rise to errors not at the beginning of the word but rather at the end.

This account of the serial position effect rests on two assumptions: the sequential activation of phonemes, and the interactive feedback between words and phonemes. Without strong interactive feedback, there is no competition among lexical neighbours and hence no mechanism for phoneme competition at the later word positions. This explains why the serial position effect proved to be particularly robust in the mild patients (Figure 4): As noted above, the mild patients have less disrupted connection weights and, consequently, are better able to form and sustain strong word-to-phoneme feedback loops.

As noted in connection with formal blends, lexical competition creates competitive forces that drive phonological errors to become more remote, since the activated phonemes of multiple lexical neighbours compete for selection with the target phonemes. Here we have a possible explanation for why the serial position (primacy) effect showed up only in remote errors: Both effects—primacy and remoteness—may be manifestations of the same phenomenon, lexical competition.

Length and frequency effects on target error rate

In the full error corpus (proximate and remote combined), error probability was significantly influenced by both target frequency and target length (Part 3). This is entirely consistent with the single origin account. Within a spreading activation framework, both length and frequency will influence the likelihood of successfully activating the target's phonemes from its corresponding lexical representation. In such models, frequency is often represented in terms of the lexical nodes' resting levels of activation (e.g., Dell, 1988; Stemberger, 1985) or the strength of the connections that relate a word to its phonological constituents (e.g., Houghton, 1990; Vousden, Brown, & Harley, 2000). Both accounts predict that lower-frequency words will be less likely to successfully activate their phonemes than higher-frequency ones, leading to an increased incidence of phonological errors. In these types of model, word length also influences this process because lexical-phonological retrieval is not a single-step process: The probability of failing to successfully select at least one phoneme increases as the length of the target word increases.

Caveats and conclusions

The characteristics of postlexical errors examined in this study by no means exhaust those that have been proposed in association with a presumed postlexical origin. In particular, we did not look for differences between proximate and remote errors with respect to effects of the target's phonological structure (e.g., syllable sonority, frequency, or markedness; phoneme frequency or position within the syllable; cf. Béland et al., 1990; Christman, 1994; Goldrick et al., 1999; Romani & Calabrese, 1998). We elected to examine characteristics that are least dependent on the specific model adopted, hence less controversial.

We did not find, as others have, that dense neighbourhoods *facilitate* phonological retrieval. In nonaphasic speakers, dense neighbourhoods have been associated with reduced incidence of TOTs (Harley & Bown, 1998; Vitevitch & Sommers,

1999); reduced vulnerability to errors (Vitevitch, 1997, 2002); and shorter latencies to name pictures (Vitevitch, 2002). The few studies that have examined neighbourhood density effects in connection with aphasic production have produced conflicting findings (Best, 1995; Goldrick & Rapp, 2001; Gordon, 2002). The most extensive analysis was performed by Gordon, who found that neighbourhood density influenced, among other things, aphasics' accuracy scores on the PNT. In a multiple regression analysis predicting error rates to PNT targets, log density and log frequency made significant contributions to the models (denser and more frequent targets yielded lower error rates), whereas target length in syllables did not enter the model. In contrast, we found significant effects for target frequency and target length, but not density (i.e., in the analysis of total errors).

Neither Gordon's study nor our own were specifically designed to tease apart density effects from the many other influences with which it correlates, among which are lexical frequency, length, and phonotactic markedness. Pending future experiments with better controlled materials (e.g., Vitevitch, 2002) and more thorough consideration of the methods used to define neighbourhoods (Goldrick & Rapp, 2001), conclusions regarding the influence of target neighbourhood density on aphasic phonological error production must be considered tentative. From a broader perspective, however, Gordon's findings and ours are consistent in showing that across a large sample of aphasic patients, targets that are longer and lower in frequency are more likely to give rise to phonological errors.

The corpus analysis is unorthodox, and we need to consider the ways in which the method elucidated some phenomena and possibly obscured others. One obvious advantage is that the large number of errors that enter into the various analyses affords greater power to detect effects than the typical single case or small group study. For example, single case studies have sometimes denied the presence of lexical frequency effects on errors assumed to arise post-lexically when there was arguably insufficient power to reject the null hypothesis (e.g., Cohen, Verstichel, & Dehaene,

1997; Goldrick et al., 1999; Kohn, 1989; Newsome & Martin, 2000).

Another advantage is that the patients who contributed to our error corpus were a relatively unselected group, the sole requirements being that they carried one of the fluent aphasia diagnoses (to avoid contamination with apraxia and other articulatory disturbance) and that they produced at least 10 phonological errors on the PNT. This minimises one danger associated with single case designs: that the methods used to select cases of sufficient "purity" might be contaminated by the theoretical orientation of the researcher.

One final benefit was that the corpus method enabled us to examine the modulating effect of individual patient characteristics. It was clearly of great benefit that the subjects represented a wide range of severity, as severity was found to exert an important influence on the characteristics of errors (and see Dell et al., 1997b). It was also important that the subjects were not restricted to any one subtype; since conduction aphasics generally have milder deficits than Wernicke's aphasics, restricting participation to only one group would have risked confounding subtype with severity.

On the other hand, one could object that since claims for a postlexical locus for errors have been based primarily on data from Conduction aphasics, those are the patients in whom the dual origin theory should be tested. Note, however, that Conduction aphasics were well represented in our patient sample: 9 of the 18 patients who contributed errors to our corpus had a diagnosis of Conduction aphasia, and more than 50% of the phonological errors themselves were produced by these individuals. Therefore, any properties of phonological errors that are unique to Conduction aphasics would be expected to be clearly evident in our corpus. Furthermore, our findings are consistent with those of a companion study based on a more conventional case-study design, which featured a large number of Conduction aphasics. Wilshire (2002) examined a group of seven individuals, highly susceptible to phonological errors— five of whom had a diagnosis of Conduction aphasia—and found no evidence for a relationship between the patients' average error proximity, their relative sensitivity to word length and frequency, and/or the extent to which they showed serial order effects across the word. Thus, even when individuals with the most favourable profile are singled out and examined on their own, the associations predicted by the dual origin theory are not always obtained.

It may be significant that the poor support for the dual origin theory obtained in this study and in Wilshire (2002) came from errors that were generated in a picture naming task. Arguably, picture naming places particularly strong demands on lexical-phonological retrieval, compared to other commonly used tasks such as word reading and repetition, and may obscure phenomena associated with postlexical phonological impairment. Error features commonly associated with postlexical deficits, such as phoneme movement, do appear to be less common in naming than in other word production tasks (Wilshire, 2002). On the other hand, many studies of phonological error production in Conduction aphasia have found that the rate and characteristics of these errors remain constant across tasks and materials that vary in their lexical demands. Indeed, this finding is frequently cited in support of the idea that these errors originate subsequent to lexical-phonological retrieval (Caplan et al., 1986; Pate et al., 1987). Given the questions that surround the task-specificity issue, it is probably prudent to limit the present conclusions to phonological errors in picture naming and the models aimed at explaining them. This caveat applies also to healthy speakers' errors. The present data lend support to the single origin account of naming errors, both normal and pathological, but they do not rule out the possibility that postlexical mechanisms are implicated in the phonological speech errors that healthy speakers generate during conversational or narrative speech.

We argued that most of the findings in this study are consistent with Dell's interactive-activation naming model (Dell & O'Seaghdha, 1991; Dell et al., 1997b; Foygel & Dell, 2000), and some findings provide new support for the model (e.g., the effects that emerged selectively or more strongly in the mild patients). However, the serial order effect we found in Part 2 contradicts that model's assumption of parallel retrieval of target segments and calls instead for a sequential account of segmental retrieval (e.g., Dell et al., 1993; MacKay, 1987; Meyer & Schriefers, 1991; Roelofs, 1997; Sevald & Dell, 1994).

Finally, we note that the model's explanation for the findings in Parts 2 and 4 highlighted a set of properties that have hitherto received little attention, namely: (1) how competition at the word level encourages phoneme selection to go awry; (2) how properties of the target can promote or minimise such interference (e.g., density of its phonological neighbourhood; see Gordon, 2002; Vitevitch, 2002); and (3) how individual differences can modulate these effects. This study highlighted one key difference among the patients—severity. However, it is possible that patients at the same severity level might differ in their response to lexical neighbourhood effects, such that some experience more of the facilitation effects of density (e.g., Gordon, 2002) while others experience interference. Subjecting this to empirical test will be difficult, as it will require large collections of errors from individual subjects at the same severity level.

In conclusion, it would appear that computational models that account for phonological errors in naming solely in terms of lexical-phonological retrieval failure are not seriously threatened by the possibility of a second, postlexical error source. We did not find any association among the characteristics that the dual origin theory assigns to postlexical errors, which would have supported the existence of such errors. We maintain that the totality of findings are best explained within a single origin, interactive activation framework that views all phonological naming errors as failures of lexical-phonological retrieval.

REFERENCES

Baayen, R. H., Piepenbrock, R., & van Rijn, H. (1993). *The CELEX lexical database (CD-ROM)*. Pennsylvania: Linguistic Data Consortium, University of Pennsylvania, PA.

Basso, A., Corno, M., & Marangolo, P. (1996). Evolution of oral and written confrontation naming errors in aphasia. A retrospective study on vascular patients. *Journal of Clinical and Experimental Neuropsychology, 18*, 77–87.

Béland, R., Caplan, D., & Nespoulous, J.-L. (1990). The role of abstract phonological representations in word production: Evidence from phonemic paraphasias. *Journal of Neurolinguistics, 5*, 125–164.

Best, W. (1995). A reverse length effect in dysphasic naming: When elephant is easier than ant. *Cortex, 31*, 637–652.

Blumstein, S. E. (1973). *A phonological investigation of aphasic speech*. The Hague: Mouton.

Brown, R., & McNeill, D. (1966). The "tip of the tongue" phenomenon. *Journal of Verbal Learning and Verbal Behaviour, 5*, 325–337.

Bub, D., Black, S., Howell, J., & Kertesz, A. (1987). Damage to input and output buffers: What's a lexicality effect doing in a place like that? In E. Keller & M. Gopnik (Eds.), *Motor and sensory processes of language*. Hillsdale, NJ: Lawrence Erlbaum Associates Inc.

Buckingham, H. W. (1977). The conduction theory and neologistic jargon. *Language and Speech, 20*, 174–184.

Buckingham, H. W. (1979). Linguistic aspects of lexical retrieval disturbances in the posterior fluent aphasia. In H. Whitaker & H. A. Whitaker (Eds.), *Studies in neurolinguistics* (Vol. 4). New York: Academic Press.

Buckingham, H. W. (1985). Perseveration in aphasia. In S. Newman & R. Epstein (Eds.), *Current perspectives in dysphasia* (pp. 113–154). Edinburgh: Churchill Livingstone.

Buckingham, H. W. (1987). Phonemic paraphasias and psycholinguistic production models for neologistic jargon. *Aphasiology, 1*, 381–400.

Buckingham, H. W. (1992). Phonological production deficits in conduction aphasia. In S. E. Kohn (Ed.), *Conduction aphasia*. Hillsdale, NJ: Lawrence Erlbaum Associates Inc.

Buckingham, H.W., & Kertesz, A. (1976). Neologistic jargon aphasia. In R. Hoops & Y. Lebrun (Eds.), *Neurolinguistics*. Amsterdam: Swets & Zeitlinger.

Burns, M. S., & Canter, G. J. (1977). Phonemic behavior of aphasic patients with posterior cerebral lesions. *Brain and Language, 4*, 492–507.

Butterworth, B. (1979). Hesitation and the production of verbal paraphasias and neologisms in jargon aphasia. *Brain and Language, 8*, 133–161.

Caplan, D., Vanier, M., & Baker, C. (1986). A case study of reproduction conduction aphasia. I: Word production. *Cognitive Neuropsychology, 3,* 99–128.

Christman, S. H. (1994). Target-related neologism formation in jargonaphasia. *Brain and Language, 46,* 109–128.

Cohen, L., Verstichel, P., & Dehaene, S. (1997). Neologistic jargon sparing numbers: A category-specific phonological impairment. *Cognitive Neuropsychology, 14,* 1029–1061.

Cuetos, F., Aguado, G., & Caramazza, A. (2000). Dissociation of semantic and phonological errors in naming. *Brain and Language, 75,* 451–460

Dell, G. S. (1986). A spreading-activation theory of retrieval in sentence production. *Psychological Review, 93,* 283–321.

Dell, G. S. (1988). The retrieval of phonological forms in production: Test of predictions from a connectionist model. *Journal of Memory and Language, 27,* 124–142.

Dell, G. S. (1990). Effects of frequency and vocabulary type on phonological speech errors. *Language and Cognitive Processes, 5,* 313–349.

Dell, G. S., Burger, L. K., & Svec, W. R. (1997). Language production and serial order: A functional analysis and a model. *Psychological Review, 104,* 123–144.

Dell, G. S., Juliano, C., & Govindjee, A. (1993). Structure and content in language production: A theory of frame constraints in phonological speech errors. *Cognitive Neuroscience, 17,* 149–195.

Dell, G. S., Lawler, E. N., Harris, H. D., & Gordon, J. K. (2004). Models of errors of omission in aphasic naming. *Cognitive Neuropsychology, 21,* 125–145.

Dell, G. S., & O'Seaghda, P. G. (1991). Mediated and convergent lexical priming in language production: A comment on Levelt et al. *Psychological Review, 98,* 604–614.

Dell, G. S., Schwartz, M. F., Martin, N., Saffran, E. M., & Gagnon, D. A. (1997b). Lexical access in aphasic and nonaphasic speakers. *Psychological Review, 104,* 801–838.

Dell, G. S., Schwartz, M. F., Martin, N., Saffran, E. M., & Gagnon, D. A. (2000). The role of computational models in neuropsychological investigations of language: Reply to Ruml and Caramazza (2000). *Psychological Review, 107,* 635–645.

Ellis, A. W. (1985). The production of spoken words: A cognitive neuropsychological perspective. In A. W. Ellis (Ed.), *Progress in the psychology of language* (Vol. 2). Hove, UK: Lawarence Erlbaum Associates Ltd.

Ellis, A. W., Miller, D., & Sin, G. (1983). Wernicke's aphasia and normal language processing: A case study in cognitive neuropsychology. *Cognition, 15,* 111–144.

Foygel, D., & Dell, G. S. (2000). Models of impaired lexical access in speech production. *Journal of Memory and Language, 43,* 182–216.

Francis, W., & Kucera, H. (1982). *Frequency analysis of English usage.* New York: Houghton Mifflin.

Fromkin, V. A. (1971). The non-anomalous nature of anomalous utterances. *Language, 47,* 27–52.

Gagnon, D. A., Schwartz, M. F., Martin, N., Dell, G. S., & Saffran, E. M. (1997). The origins of formal paraphasias in aphasics picture naming. *Brain and Language, 59,* 450–472.

Garrett, M. F. (1975). The analysis of sentence production. In G. Bower (Ed.), *Psychology of learning and motivation* (Vol. 9). New York: Academic Press.

Garrett, M. F. (1982). Production of speech: Observations from normal and pathological language use. In A. W. Ellis (Ed.), *Normality and pathology in cognitive functions.* London: Academic Press.

Goldmann, R. E., Schwartz, M. F., & Wilshire, C. E. (2001). The influence of phonological context on the sound errors of a speaker with Wernicke's aphasia. *Brain and Language, 78,* 279–307.

Goldrick, M., & Rapp, B. (2001). What makes a good neighbor? Evidence from malapropisms. *Brain and Language, 79,* 141–143.

Goldrick, M., Rapp, B., & Smolensky, P. (1999). Lexical and postlexical processes in spoken word production. *Brain and Language, 69,* 367–370.

Goodglass, H., & Kaplan, E. (1983). *The assessment of aphasia and related disorders* (2nd ed.). Philadelphia: Lea & Feibiger.

Gordon, J. K. (2002). Phonological neighborhood effects in aphasic speech errors: Spontaneous and structured contexts. *Brain and Language, 82,* 113–145.

Gordon, J. K., & Dell, G. S. (2003). Learning to divide the labor: An account of deficits in light and heavy verb production. *Cognitive Science, 27,* 140.

Harley, T. A. (1984). A critique of top-down independent levels models of speech production: Evidence from non-phrase-internal errors. *Cognitive Science, 8,* 191–219.

Harley, T. A. (1984). A critique of top-down independent levels models of speech production: Evidence from non-phrase-internal errors. *Cognitive Science, 8,* 191–219.

Harley, T. A., & Bown, H. E. (1998). What causes a tip-of-the-tongue state? Evidence for lexical neighbourhood effects in speech production. *British Journal of Psychology, 89*, 151–174.

Houghton, G. (1990). The problem of serial order: A neural network model of sequence learning and recall. In R. Dale, C. Mellish, & M. Zock (Eds.), *Current research in natural language generation.* London: Academic Press.

Jescheniak, J.D., & Levelt, W. J. M. (1994). Word frequency effects in speech production: Retrieval of syntactic information and of phonological form. *Journal of Experimental Psychology: Learning, Memory, and Cognition, 20*, 824–843.

Kaplan, E., Goodglass, H., & Weintraub, S. (1983). *The Boston Naming Test.* Philadelphia: Lea & Febiger.

Kertesz, A., & Benson, D. F. (1970). Neologistic jargon: A clinicopathological study. *Cortex, 6*, 362–386.

Kohn, S. E. (1989). The nature of the phonemic string deficit in conduction aphasia. *Aphasiology, 3*, 209–239.

Kohn, S. E., & Smith, K. L. (1990). Between-word speech errors in conduction aphasia. *Cognitive Neuropsychology, 7*, 133–156.

Kohn, S. E., & Smith, K. L. (1994). Distinctions between two phonological output deficits. *Applied Psycholinguistics, 15*, 75–95.

Kohn, S. E., & Smith, K. L. (1995). Serial effects in phonemic planning during word production. *Aphasiology, 9*, 209–222.

Landauer, T. K., & Streeter, L. A. (1973). Structural differences between common and rare words: Failure of equivalence assumptions for theories of word recognition. *Journal of Verbal Learning and Verbal Behavior, 12*, 119–131.

Lecours, A. R. (1982). On neologisms. In J. Mehler, E. C. T. Walker, & M. F. Garrett (Eds.), *Perspectives on mental representation.* Hillsdale, NJ: Lawrence Erlbaum Associates Inc.

Lecours, A. R., Deloche, G., & Lhermitte, F. (1973). Paraphasies phonémiques: Description et simulation sur ordinateur. In *Colloquies-IRIA—Informatique Medical.* Rocquencourt, France: Institut de Recherche d'Informatique et d'Automatique.

Lecours, A. R., & Lhermitte, F. (1969). Phonemic paraphasias: Linguistic structures and tentative hypotheses. *Cortex, 5*, 193–228.

Levelt, W. J. M. (1992). Accessing words in speech production: Stages, processes and representations. *Cognition, 42*, 122.

Levelt, W. J. M., Roelofs, A., & Meyer, A. S. (1999). A theory of lexical access in speech production. *Behavioral and Brain Sciences, 22*, 175.

MacKay, D. G. (1987). *The organization of perception and action.* New York: Springer Verlag.

Martin, N., Dell, G. S., Saffran, E. M., & Schwartz, M. F. (1994). Origins of paraphasias in deep dysphasia: Testing the consequences of a decay impairment to an interactive spreading activation model of lexical retrieval. *Brain and Language, 47*, 609–660.

Martin, N., & Saffran, E. (1992). A computational account of deep dysphasia: Evidence from a single case study. *Brain and Language, 43*, 240–274.

Martin, N., Saffran, E. M., & Dell, G. S. (1996). Recovery in deep dysphasia: Evidence for a relationship between auditory-verbal STM capacity and lexical errors in repetition. *Brain and Language, 52*, 83–113.

Meyer, A. S., & Schriefers, H. (1991). Phonological facilitation in picture-word interference experiments: Effects of stimulus onset asynchrony and types of interfering stimuli. *Journal of Experimental Psychology: Learning, Memory, and Cognition, 17*, 1146–1160.

Miller, D., & Ellis, A. (1987). Speech and writing errors in "neologistic jargonaphasia": A lexical activation hypothesis. In M. Coltheart, G. Sartori, & K. Job (Eds.), *The cognitive neuropsychology of language.* Hove, UK: Lawrence Erlbaum Associates Ltd.

Nespoulous, J. L., Joanette, Y., Ska, B., Caplan, J. D., & Lecours, A. R. (1987). Production deficits in Brocas and conduction aphasia: Repetition versus reading. In E. Keller & M. Gopnik (Eds.), *Motor and sensory processes of language. Neuropsychology and neurolinguistics* (pp. 5381). Hillsdale, NJ: Lawrence Erlbaum Associates Inc.

Newsome, M. R., & Martin, R. C. (2000). *Lexical versus segmental deficits in phonological retrieval: Implications for models of naming.* Poster presented at the 41st Annual Meeting of the Psychonomic Society, November, 2000, New Orleans, LA, USA.

Nickels, L. (1995). Getting it right? Using aphasic naming errors to evaluate theoretical models of spoken word production. *Language and Cognitive Processes, 10*, 13–45.

Nickels, L., & Howard, D. (1995). Phonological errors in aphasic naming: Comprehension, monitoring and lexicality. *Cortex, 31*, 209–237.

Oldfield, R. C., & Wingfield, A. (1965). Response latencies in naming objects. *Quarterly Journal of Experimental Psychology, 17*, 273–281.

Pate, D. S., Saffran, E. M., & Martin, N. (1987). Specifying the nature of the production impairment in a conduction aphasic: A case study. *Language and Cognitive Processes, 2*, 43–84.

Rapp, B., & Goldrick, M. (2000). Discreteness and interactivity in spoken word production. *Psychological Review, 107*, 460–503.

Roach, A., Schwartz, M. F., Martin, N., Grewal, R. S., & Brecher, A. (1996). The Philadelphia Naming Test: Scoring and rationale. *Clinical Aphasiology, 24*, 121–133.

Roelofs, A. (1997). The WEAVER model of word-form encoding in speech production. *Cognition, 64*, 249–284.

Romani, C., & Calabrese, A. (1998). Syllabic constraints in the phonological errors of an aphasic patient. *Brain and Language, 64*, 83–121.

Ruml, W., & Caramazza, A. (2000). An evaluation of a computational model of lexical access: Comment on Dell et al. (1997). *Psychological Review, 107*, 609–634.

Ruml, W., Caramazza, A., Shelton, J. R., & Chialant, D. (2000). Testing assumptions in computational theories of aphasia. *Journal of Memory and Language, 43*, 217–248.

Schwartz, M. F., & Brecher, A. (2000). A model-driven analysis of severity, response characteristics, and partial recovery in aphasics' picture naming. *Brain and Language, 73*, 6291.

Schwartz, M. F., Saffran, E. M., Bloch, D. E., & Dell, G. S. (1994). Disordered speech production in aphasic and normal speakers. *Brain and Language, 47*, 5288.

Sevald, C. A., & Dell, G. S. (1994). The sequential cueing effect in speech production. *Cognition, 53*, 91–127.

Shattuck-Hufnagel, S. (1979). Speech errors as evidence for a serial ordering mechanism in sentence production. In W. E. Cooper & E. C. T. Walker (Eds.), *Sentence processing: Psycholinguistic studies presented to Merrill Garrett.* Hillsdale, NJ: Lawrence Erlbaum Associates Inc.

Shattuck-Hufnagel, S. (1983). Sublexical units and suprasegmental structure in speech production planning. In P. F. MacNeilage (Ed.), *The production of speech.* New York: Springer-Verlag.

Shattuck-Hufnagel, S. (1987). The role of word onset consonants in speech production planning: New evidence from speech error patterns. In E. Keller & M. Gopnik (Eds.), *Motor and sensory processes of language.* Hillsdale, NJ: Lawrence Erlbaum Associates Inc.

Shattuck-Hufnagel, S. (1992). The role of word structure in segmental serial ordering. *Cognition, 42*, 213–259.

Stemberger, J. P. (1985). An interactive activation model of language production. In A. Ellis (Ed.), *Progress in the psychology of language.* Hove, UK: Lawrence Erlbaum Associates Ltd.

Stemberger, J. P. (1990). Wordshape errors in language production. *Cognition, 35*, 123–157

Vitevitch, M. S. (1997). The neighborhood characteristics of malapropisms. *Language and Speech, 40*, 211–228.

Vitevitch, M. S. (2002). The influence of phonological similarity neighborhoods on speech production. *Journal of Experimental Psychology: Learning, Memory, and Cognition, 28*, 735–747.

Vitevitch, M. S., & Sommers, M. (1999). Neighborhood density, the tip-of-the-tongue phenomenon and aging. *Research on Spoken Language Processing: Progress Report No. 23.* Bloomington, IN: Speech Research Laboratory, Indiana University.

Vousden, J. I., Brown, G. D. A., & Harley, T. A. (2000). Serial control of phonology in speech production: A hierarchical model. *Cognitive Psychology, 41*, 101–175.

Wheeler, D. W., & Touretzky, D. S. (1997). A parallel licensing model of normal slips and phonemic paraphasias. *Brain and Language, 59*, 147–201.

Wilshire, C. E. (2002). Where do aphasic phonological errors come from? Evidence from phoneme movement errors in picture naming. *Aphasiology, 16*, 169–197.

Wilshire, C. E., & McCarthy, R. A. (1996). Experimental investigations of an impairment in phonological encoding. *Cognitive Neuropsychology, 13*, 1059–1098.

Wing, A. M., & Baddeley, A. (1980). Spelling errors in handwriting: A corpus and a distributional analysis. In U. Frith (Ed.), *Cognitive processes in spelling.* New York: Academic Press.

Zipf, G. K. (1965). *The psycho-biology of language: An introduction to dynamic philology.* Cambridge, MA: MIT Press.

COGNITIVE NEUROPSYCHOLOGY, 2004, 21 (2/3/4) 187–210

"PHONOLOGICAL" DYSPHASIA: A CROSS-MODAL PHONOLOGICAL IMPAIRMENT AFFECTING REPETITION, PRODUCTION, AND COMPREHENSION

Carolyn E. Wilshire and Caroline A. Fisher

Victoria University of Wellington, New Zealand

In this paper we describe an aphasic patient, MS, who is impaired across a wide range of auditory input processing and spoken word production tasks. MS's performance on all these tasks shows phonological features: (1) his performance is poorest on auditory tasks with a strong phonological component, such as phoneme discrimination, auditory lexical decision, and word–picture matching featuring phonologically related distractors; and (2) in spoken word production tasks, his errors are mainly phonemic and formal paraphasias. MS's single word repetition is particularly poor and exhibits some of the features of deep dysphasia, including lexicality effects (MS is unable to repeat nonwords) and imageability effects. However, unlike in deep dysphasia, there are no semantic errors. We show that MS's condition, although apparently heterogeneous when viewed from a functional architecture perspective, can be described quite elegantly within an interactive-activation framework by proposing a single abnormality—a pathologically fast rate of decay within phonological representations.

The cognitive neuropsychological approach to aphasia is founded on the premise that we can decompose language processing into smaller components, each of which may become independently impaired after brain damage. Over the past three decades, much of the theoretical work in this tradition has focused on identifying and mapping these various language components in a way that is neutral as to the precise processing mechanisms involved. This is often called the "functional architecture" approach (see, e.g., Coltheart, 1987, 2002; Howard & Franklin, 1988; Marshall & Newcombe, 1973; Patterson & Shewell, 1987; Shallice & Warrington, 1980). Patterson and Shewell's (1987) diagrammatic account of single word processing, shown in Figure 1, is a classic example of this approach. It specifies the components involved in a range of single word tasks, including auditory comprehension, spoken production, reading, and writing. Accounts like these

Correspondence should be addressed to Carolyn Wilshire, School of Psychology, Victoria University of Wellington, PO Box 600, Wellington, New Zealand (Email: Carolyn.Wilshire@vuw.ac.nz).

Caroline A. Fisher is now at Department of Psychology, Monash University, Australia.

A portion of this research was conducted as part of a fourth-year undergraduate project by the second author and was presented at the Australian Conference for Cognitive Neuropsychology and Neuropsychiatry, Deakin University, Australia, July 2001. The research was supported in part by a grant from the Marsden Fund of the Royal Society of New Zealand (to C. Wilshire PI). We would like to thank MS for his enthusiasm, generosity, and good humour throughout this study. We are also grateful to Leonie Keall for her valuable contributions to the design, running, and analysis of these experiments and to Liz Stuart for assistance with testing, transcription, and statistical analysis. Thanks also to Maryanne Garry and the Applied Memory Research Group at Victoria University for their many helpful suggestions on an earlier draft. Finally, we thank David Howard for suggesting the name "phonological dysphasia."

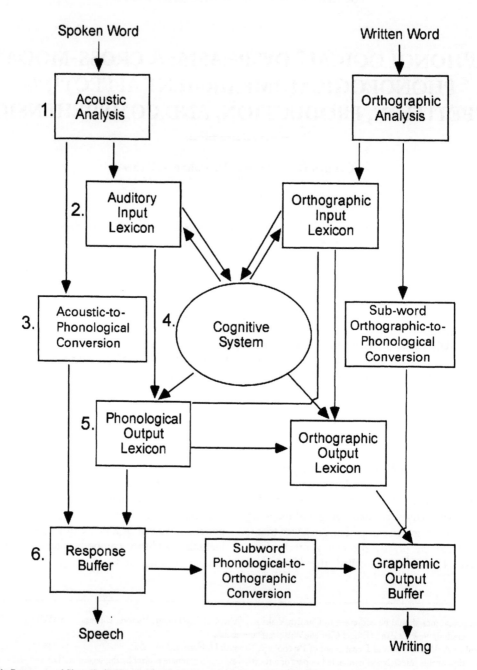

Figure 1. *Patterson and Shewell's (1987) model of language processing (adapted from Patterson & Shewell, 1987).*

are extremely useful, because they enable us to capture many sources of variation amongst aphasic patients: The degree of involvement of each component varies from task to task, so we can compare a patient's performance across tasks to determine which component(s) are damaged. This assessment can then be used to make predictions about other aspects of performance.

Nevertheless, some aphasic conditions are difficult to capture within this kind of simple schematic framework. Instead, they seem to require an explanation at a finer-grained level of description. The most striking example is the syndrome of deep dysphasia (see, e.g., Coslett, 1991; Howard & Franklin, 1988; Katz & Goodglass, 1990; Majerus, Lekeu, Van der Linden, & Salmon, 2001, and references therein; N. Martin, Dell, Saffran, & Schwartz, 1994; N. Martin & Saffran, 1992; Michel & Andreewsky, 1983; Valdois, Carbonnel, David, Rousset, & Pellat, 1995, and references therein). Deep dysphasia is, by definition, a repetition disorder: In repetition, patients produce semantic paraphasias (camel → "horse"), show concreteness/imageability effects, and are completely unable to repeat nonwords. However, typical cases also produce other types of repetition errors, including phonemic paraphasias (camel → "copple") and formal paraphasias (form-related real-word substitutions, e.g., camel → "candle"). Patients are also impaired on a range of other auditory processing and spoken production tasks. For example, they typically perform poorly on word–picture matching tasks and, in picture naming, produce a range of error types including phonemic paraphasias, and to varying degrees, formal and semantic paraphasias (see cases reported by Duhamel & Poncet, 1986; Howard & Franklin, 1988; Katz & Goodglass, 1990; Majerus et al., 2001; N. Martin & Saffran, 1992; Michel & Andreewsky, 1983; Trojano, Stanzione, & Grossi, 1992; Valdois et al., 1995; but see also Metz-Lutz & Dahl, 1984, for an exception).

Within functional architecture accounts, the pattern of deficits seen in deep dysphasia can only be captured by proposing a number of separate and independent impairments. For example, in terms of Patterson and Shewell (1987)'s account (Figure 1),

the disproportionate difficulty with nonword repetition suggests damage to the acoustic-to-phonological conversion route, the pathway that accomplishes nonlexical repetition (no. 3 in Figure 1). In addition, the poor real-word repetition—with its characteristic semantic features—suggests that there is damage to some part of the direct lexical pathway that maps between the auditory input lexicon and the phonological output lexicon (no. 4), and that repetition must be mediated by the cognitive/semantic system (no. 5). Other features of this disorder are likely to involve further impairments. For example, the phonological errors produced in both naming and repetition suggest impairment to the phonological output lexicon (no. 6) and/or the response buffer (no. 7); the difficulties in auditory input processing suggest impairment to the auditory input lexicon (no. 2), the acoustic analysis system (no. 1), and/or their associated pathways (for detailed examples, see Howard & Franklin, 1988; Katz & Goodglass, 1990).

However, within a model based at a finer-grained level of description, an alternative, more economical account of deep dysphasia is available. In a series of influential papers, N. Martin, Saffran, and colleagues proposed an account of deep dysphasia within an interactive activation model (N. Martin & Saffran, 1992; N. Martin et al., 1994; N. Martin, Saffran, & Dell, 1996). Their account was based on Dell and O'Seaghdha's (1991, 1992) model of word production (see also Dell, 1986; Dell, Schwartz, Martin, Saffran, & Gagnon, 1997; Foygel & Dell, 2000). The model they used, illustrated in Figure 2, comprises a network of localist nodes representing units at three levels of description—phonological, lexical, and semantic. Nodes at each level are connected to related nodes at the next level (for example, in Figure 2, the lexical node for "cat" is connected to semantic nodes representing its meaning and to phonological nodes representing its phonemes). During production, activation spreads down the network from semantic to lexical nodes, then to phonological nodes. At each level, the most highly activated node is selected and then receives an additional activation boost. Activation can also partially feed back up

Semantic nodes

Lexical nodes

Phonological nodes

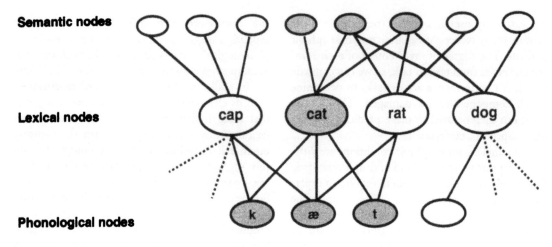

Figure 2. *An example lexical network based on the word production model of Dell and O'Seaghda (1991, 1992). The figure shows that part of the lexical network associated with the presentation of the word "cat."*

the system: For example, activated phonological nodes (/k/, /æ/ and /t/ in Figure 2) feed some portion of their activation back to all lexical nodes containing those phonemes, thereby activating words that are phonologically related to the target (e.g., *cap* and *rat* in Figure 2).

N. Martin, Saffran, and colleagues accounted for the key symptoms of their deep dysphasic patient, NC, by postulating just one impairment to this model: an abnormally rapid rate of activation decay throughout all nodes in the network. NC's pattern of errors in naming—which were primarily formal and phonemic paraphasias—was quite well predicted by this "lesioned" version of the model. This model predicts a high rate of formal paraphasias because activation spreads to form-related lexical items relatively late in the planning process, as a result of feedback from phonological to lexical nodes. Therefore, at the time of lexical selection, the nodes of form-related words will have experienced less activation decay than those activated earlier in the production process and, as a result, they will compete strongly with the target. Phonemic paraphasias also occur, because a rapidly decaying lexical node may be unable to fully activate its phonemes; also, those phonemes that are activated may themselves decay too fast to be selected. Consequently, some or all may be

replaced by more strongly activated, nontarget phonemes.

N. Martin, Saffran, and colleagues accounted for a number of other, non-naming features of NC's performance by extending their basic model to encompass other tasks. Their extended model included an auditory input system with direct connections to phonological nodes. During auditory input tasks, this system activates the relevant phonological nodes, and this activation then spreads up the network to lexical and then to semantic nodes. In addition to this upward activation spread, there is also feedback: Activated nodes at each level transmit a portion of their activation back to the preceding level. This simple extended model could account for the three key "deep dysphasic" features of NC's repetition: (1) a pattern of errors that includes semantic paraphasias, as well as phonemic and formal paraphasias; (2) fewer errors on imageable than on nonimageable words; and (3) an inability to repeat nonwords. Phonemic and formal paraphasias arise as a result of similar mechanisms to the ones outlined for naming. Semantic errors occur because in repetition, semantic nodes are the last to become activated, and so are the least subject to the effects of decay. These nodes therefore have ample opportunity to activate the lexical nodes of semantically related words, which may then compete with the target. Imageability effects can be accounted for by making the additional assumption that high-imageable words receive more activation support from semantic nodes than low-imageable words. Finally, extremely poor nonword repetition is also consistent with this model, because unlike real words, the phonological activation pattern associated with a nonword would receive little or no stabilisation from the lexical level, and thus would be particularly vulnerable to the effects of fast decay.

N. Martin, Saffran, and colleagues' decay model constituted one of the first attempts to interpret aphasic data within an interactive-activation framework. Although the fits between their model and the data were not perfect (a point we return to later), its ability to predict a diverse range of phenomena with just a small number of assumptions set it apart from other contemporary accounts. Two features of the theoretical framework made this possible. First, it was based at a finer-grained level of description than purely architectural schemes. The model went beyond mere labelling of the relevant language components, and addressed what actually took place *within* those components. In particular, the principles of activation summation and interaction provided a mechanism for explaining how a single event could affect multiple levels of processing simultaneously, and conversely, how multiple influences could converge to affect a single level of processing. Second, and perhaps most importantly, the model incorporated time-course properties. This enabled it to offer an account of aphasia that was centred on the notion of impaired *temporal dynamics*—or more specifically, temporal instability of linguistic representations, modelled in terms of abnormally fast activation decay. The idea that deep dysphasia might involve temporal instability had been put forward by earlier authors (see, e.g., Michel & Andreewsky, 1983), but N. Martin, Saffran and colleagues' decay model offered a more formal framework for describing this notion. Since then, the decay model has been applied to a number of more recent cases of deep dysphasia (e.g., Croot, Patterson, & Hodges, 1998; Majerus et al., 2001;

Tree, Perfect, Hirsh, & Copstick, 2001). In addition, the concept of fast decay has formed the basis of a recent account of an aphasic impairment in phonological input processing (R. C. Martin, Breedin, & Damian, 1999) and the notion has also been incorporated into a more comprehensive model of aphasic inter-patient variability (see Dell et al., 1997).

In this paper, we describe an aphasic condition that has a great deal in common with deep dysphasia. Like deep dysphasia, it appears complex and heterogeneous when viewed from a functional architecture perspective, but it can be described quite elegantly within an interactive-activation framework via the concept of fast decay. We report data from a single case. Patient MS exhibits many of the classic features of deep dysphasia: He is unable to repeat nonwords, and in repetition tasks he is sensitive to imageability. Also, like other deep dysphasics, he produces phonemic paraphasias and formal paraphasias in repetition as well as picture naming. Finally, he shows significant impairment on a number of auditory input-processing tasks. However, MS differs from deep dysphasics in that he does not produce semantic errors in repetition. Indeed, his profile is rather more "phonological" overall: Performance across all modalities exhibits strong phonological characteristics. We account for MS's pattern of performance within a simple interactive-activation model in which a decay impairment is restricted to phonological representations.

CASE DESCRIPTION

MS is an 83-year-old retired real estate agent and a native speaker of New Zealand English. On February 28, 2000, he suffered a sudden onset CVA. On admission to hospital, he presented with slurred speech, was unable to name objects, and had difficulty following verbal instructions. A CT scan performed on March 1, 2000 revealed a small region of hypodensity in the posterior parietal area of the left cerebral hemisphere. On initial speech-language assessment, MS exhibited a fluent aphasia with both receptive and expressive features. He had severely reduced auditory comprehension and his speech was characterised by paraphasias and word-finding difficulties. By July 2000, following 4 months of speech-language therapy, he was described as being "generally able to express himself, although paraphasias and word finding difficulties still occur."

MS was first tested by us in January 2001, 11 months after his stroke. At this time, his speech was fluent and grammatically well formed, but was often interrupted by pauses and paraphasic errors (see Table 1 for example). Error types included: phonemic paraphasias (e.g., losing → /ludɪŋ/; walkway → /tɔkswe/), formal paraphasias (e.g., articles → "artists"; nest → "node"), semantic paraphasias (e.g., hear → "sound"; dark → "black") and neologisms (e.g., petrol → /fʌtɪn/). MS also appeared to have some difficulty following conversations: from time to time, he asked for a word or sentence to be repeated. On the Boston Diagnostic Aphasic Examination (BDAE; Goodglass & Kaplan, 1983), MS's diagnosis was borderline Wernicke's/conduction aphasia: His overall auditory comprehension score, which was moderately low, fell directly in between the critical range for both subtypes. MS's other notable area of weakness on the BDAE was repetition: On the sentence repetition subtest, his score was zero. Below we report MS's performance on specific language tests; all were administered between January and July 2001 (that is, 11 to 17 months post-stroke).

Phoneme discrimination

MS was impaired on tests of phoneme discrimination. On the PALPA Word Minimal Pair Discrimination test (PALPA; Kay, Lesser, & Coltheart, 1996), which involves identifying whether two successive words are the same (e.g., *cub–cub*) or different (e.g., *cup–cut*), MS scored 54/72 ("same" pairs 24/36; "different" pairs 30/36). There was a trend towards a frequency effect ("same" pairs: high frequency 14/18 vs. low frequency 10/18). On "different" pairs, the majority of MS's misses involved place of articulation distinctions (5 out of 6 errors). There were no effects of phoneme position. On the nonword version of this test, MS scored a poorer 41/72 ("same" pairs 20/36; "different" pairs 21/36). Again, there were more errors involving place of articulation (9 errors) than voicing or manner (2 and 5 errors respectively) but, again, there was no position effect.

Auditory lexical decision

MS was impaired on tasks of auditory lexical decision. On the PALPA test of imageability and frequency in lexical decision, he scored 127/160. He correctly rejected 73 of 80 nonwords, but correctly identified only 54 of the 80 real words. This poor performance again indicates a marked impairment in the ability to access lexical representations from phonology. There was no significant

Table 1. *Excerpts from MS's description of the Cookie Theft Picture from the Boston Diagnostic Aphasic Examination (Clear examples of errors are underlined)*

What I see on (tgt: in) this picture is a man (tgt: woman) at the (tgt: in the?), a young lady at the kitchen, she's doing the… /krʊkəri/, crockery, supposed to be doing those, but the… she's been /l/ /lʌst/ (tgt: lost) of (tgt: or?) something or other, because all the water from the tank (tgt: sink) is overflowing, is running over out into (tgt: onto) the skin (tgt: floor) into the…floor, the /tɪŋk/… the sink is full of water, she could be looking out of the… window… with (tgt: at?) the kitchen garden and a-nother /wɪlbo/ (tgt: window)… 'nother window, window… [*MS then describes several features of the kitchen benches and the and items on them*] Her son, presumably a boy, is /tɪtɪŋ/, /stɪtɪŋ/ /ov-/, on the stool and was taking the cookie jar out of the jar upstairs (tgt: on the top shelf?) and he's (tgt: his) s-sister was got her left /hɛ-/ (tgt: hand) out for a cookie, handing (tgt: taking it?) from the right hand from (tgt: of?) her… brother, and she's having some afternoon /fʌm/ (tgt: fun) out helping herself from the cookie jars (tgt: jar?) while her mother is not taking the slightest notice of the boys (tgt: children) and she's doesn't seem to be, seems to be lot what she is doing because she's not doing anything in particular.

effect of frequency (MS's scores were identical for high- and low-frequency words) or of imageability (scores were 28/40 and 26/40 for high- and low-imageability words respectively).

Auditory word–picture matching

On word-picture matching tasks from the Philadelphia Comprehension Battery (PCB; Saffran, Schwartz, Linebarger, Martin, & Bochetto, 1989), MS's performance was influenced by the nature of the distractor pictures. He performed at ceiling on items with semantically related distractors (16/16) and perceptually related distractors (12/12). However, on those featuring phonologically-related distractors, he scored a lower 7/12. On an unpublished word–picture matching test featuring phonologically-related word triplets (e.g., target: *comb*; distractors: *cone, coat*), MS scored a poor 14/24. Most errors involved the distractor that was featurally closest to the target (e.g., comb → cone). There were no notable trends with respect to phoneme position or type of feature distinction (voice, manner, or place). These findings further suggest that MS's auditory comprehension deficit involves an early level of processing at which phonological information is critical.

Digit span

MS's digit span was moderately impaired: On the PALPA auditory digit repetition span test, he scored 8/10 each for two-digit and three digits strings, and 4/10 for four-digit strings, giving him an estimated digit span of three. The number of digits correctly recalled at each sequential position was as follows: two-digit strings 10-8; three-digit strings 10-9-8; four-digit strings 10-10-8-4.

Spoken naming

MS's picture naming performance was severely impaired. On the Graded Naming Test (McKenna & Warrington, 1983) he scored only 5/30 correct, which placed him below the 4th percentile for older New Zealanders (Harvey & Siegert, 1999).

Errors on this difficult test were primarily phonemic paraphasias (e.g., turtle → /tɛpəl/; thimble → /θʌmsɪk/) and neologisms (e.g., periscope → /kæmərɪn/). There were three unrelated word substitutions (e.g., chopsticks → "thistle"), but no semantic paraphasias. A more detailed analysis of errors in naming appears below. Verb naming appeared to be at least as impaired as noun naming: On the Zingeser and Berndt (1988) Noun-Verb Naming test, MS scored 20/30 correct for verbs, 26/30 for nouns that were matched on the basis of verb cumulative frequency, and 24/30 for nouns matched on verb base frequency.

Single word repetition

Single word repetition was severely impaired. On the PALPA word repetition test featuring items varying in frequency and imageability, MS scored a low 36/80. Phonemic paraphasias were the most common error type (e.g., funnel → /fɛnərəl/; length → /lɪŋktjuə/), followed by formal paraphasias (e.g., folly → "colic"; character → "cataract"), and no responses. There was one unrelated word substitution (pig → "table"), but no semantic paraphasias. There was a significant imageability effect: MS correctly repeated 12/40 low-imageable words and 24/40 high-imageable words, $\chi^2(1, N = 80) = 6.11, p < .05$. There was no effect of frequency. MS was completely unable to repeat nonwords. On the PALPA nonword repetition test, he scored 0/30. His errors were mainly phonologically related nonwords (e.g., ality → /ælifod/; lerman → /lʌrnɪm/). Even when asked to repeat the simpler, monosyllabic words from the PALPA nonword reading task, MS still scored zero. His errors were again mainly phonologically related nonwords.

Reading

In comparison to spoken word tasks, MS's reading was remarkably well preserved. On the difficult Schonell Graded Word Reading Test (Nelson & McKenna, 1975) his score (68/80) was within 1 *SD* of the mean for adult controls. Most of his errors were phonological, and a number were regularisations (e.g., postage → /postɪg/; imagine →

/ɪməgin/). On the PALPA regularity reading test, MS scored 30/30 on the regular words, but made 4 errors on the exception words (e.g., mortgage → /mɔːtɪdʒ/; pint → /pɪnt/). On the PALPA non-word reading test, he scored a surprising 22/24. Reading comprehension was also well preserved: On a written form of the PCB Lexical Comprehension test, MS performed at ceiling.

Summary

MS is impaired across a range of auditory/spoken language tasks, including production, auditory comprehension, and repetition. Many features of his performance are similar to those observed in deep dysphasia. First, repetition is markedly impaired, and shows strong lexicality effects and imageability effects. Second, phonemic and formal paraphasias occur in significant numbers in repetition as well as in picture naming. Third, visual input processing is vastly superior to auditory processing. Nevertheless, MS rarely, if ever, produces semantic paraphasias in repetition, a feature that is diagnostic of the deep dysphasic profile. Rather, his performance across all spoken language tasks suggests an impairment involving phonological representations. In tasks requiring spoken output, the vast majority of errors are phonologically related to their targets. In tasks requiring auditory input-processing, performance is poorest on tasks that emphasise early, sound-based processing, such as phoneme discrimination, auditory lexical decision, and word–picture matching involving phonologically related distractors. On the other hand, tasks of a more semantic nature, such as word–picture matching with semantically related distractors, are performed relatively well.

Experiments 1–3 further examine the nature of MS's impairment in both input and output processing by comparing his performance across tasks, and investigating the influence of variables such as word length, frequency, and imageability.

Experiment 1 compares picture naming and word repetition and examines the types of errors produced as well as the influence of word length and frequency. Experiment 2 examines the role of word length and imageability on three tasks with an auditory input component—word repetition, auditory lexical decision, and semantic similarity judgment. Experiment 3 compares performance on four tasks, all of which require word production, but which vary as to the modality of presentation of the stimulus (auditory vs. picture stimulus) and the modality of output (spoken vs. written).

EXPERIMENT 1: DETAILED COMPARISON OF NAMING AND REPETITION

Experiment 1 directly compares MS's naming and repetition using a large target word set. The set is orthogonally controlled for length and frequency, thereby enabling us to examine both these variables. The experiment was run in late January 2001 (that is, 11 months post-stroke).

Method

The set of target words was taken from the Length and Frequency Naming Test, an unpublished, 180-item test that contains equal numbers of monosyllabic, bisyllabic, and polysyllabic items in each of three frequency groups—low (0.1 to 1.8 occurrences per million), medium (above 1.8 and up to 5 per million) and high (above 5 per million: see Wilshire, 2002, for further information). The pictures in the test each yielded at least 80% name agreement when presented to a group of 10 normal subjects.[1] In the naming task, MS was presented with each picture and asked to provide its name. There was no time limit. In the repetition task, MS was presented auditorily with each picture's name, and was asked to repeat it out loud. Items were presented in a new, randomised order. The naming

---

[1] Eleven pictures had target names that were appropriate for US English only. These items were excluded from the total naming scores in all relevant conditions.

task was given first, followed by the repetition task 1 week later.

Data was analysed using logistic regression: For each task, effects of word length and frequency on accuracy were analysed using simple simultaneous logistic regression; z-scores for the Wald statistic are reported. For cross-task analyses, which incorporate task as a repeated measure, the model was fitted using Generalised Estimating Equations, and run on SAS (GENMOD procedure). The z-scores reported in the text are based on empirical standard error estimates.

Results

Naming. MS correctly named 47% of the stimulus items on the first attempt. Table 2 gives a breakdown of the errors he produced based on the first complete attempt at each picture (that is, excluding attempts that were interrupted or consisted only of fragments). It can be seen that phonemic paraphasias were the most common error type (e.g., peacock → /pikrо/; tambourine → /tʌmpinə/), followed by formal paraphasias (e.g., saddle → "sandal"; mushroom → "marshmallow"). Formal paraphasias were also common, and accounted for a substantial 41% of all phonological errors. This exceeds the percentage that would be expected by chance, which, according to Best's (1996) estimates, would be likely to be somewhere between 19% and 31%, depending upon the corpus—and for this corpus of mainly bi- and polysyllabic words, would probably lie towards the lower end of the range.[2] In contrast, semantic paraphasias and mixed errors were rare. Finally, MS also produced a number of unrelated real-word substitutions (e.g., cigarette → "elephant") and neologisms (a nonword with no phonological relation to the target, e.g., calculator → /grændspɪə/). Table 3 shows MS's overall performance as a function of

Table 2. *Experiment 1: Breakdown of responses on naming and repetition tasks (classifications based on first complete attempt)*

Response type[a]	% of responses	
	Naming	Repetition
Correct	47.3	30.1
Phonemic paraphasia	19.5	34.7
Formal paraphasia	13.6	14.5
Semantic paraphasia	4.7	0.6
Unrelated word	6.5	3.5
Neologism	4.1	7.5
Mixed[b]	0.6	0
Morphological error	0	2.3
No response	1.2	4.6
Other	2.4	2.3

[a] To qualify as phonologically-related (for phonemic paraphasias and formal paraphasias), a response had to contain the correct first or last phoneme *or* at least two other phonemes in their correct position, *or* at least 30% correct phonemes in any position.
[b] Semantic + formal error.

Table 3. *Experiment 1: Percentage correct on naming and repetition as a function of length and frequency group (based on first complete attempt)*

	% targets correct	
	Naming	Repetition
Frequency group		
Low	25.0	27.3
Medium	51.7	25.9
High	62.7	36.7
Length group		
Monosyllabic	50.0	29.3
Bisyllabic	52.7	25.5
Polysyllabic	39.7	35.0

[2] Best (1996) calculated these estimates using the phonological errors of a single patient, MF. From these errors, she created a "pseudocorpus" by substituting a phoneme at random in each position where the error diverged from the target. She then calculated the proportion of "pseudoerrors" that formed real words. Estimates based on this method would be expected to vary depending upon the length of the target words that were failed: An error corpus with a high proportion of short words will generate a higher estimate of chance than one with many long words. Given that our word set included a large proportion of polysyllabic words, and that MS made slightly more errors on the longer words, the chance rate for our corpus is likely to be at the lower end of Best's range.

target length and frequency There was a significant effect of word frequency, $z = 14.49$, $p < .001$, but not of length, $z = 0.97$, $p = .32$, n.s.

Repetition. MS correctly repeated only 30% of the stimulus items on the first attempt, a score that was significantly below that on the naming task, $z = 3.26$, $p < .01$. As can be seen in Table 2, phonemic paraphasias were again the most common error type (e.g., camel → /krʌntəl/; octopus → /ɒmtəməs/) followed by formal paraphasias (e.g., comb → "council"; penguin → "pyramid"), and there was also a small number of neologisms (e.g., parachute → /baɪsɛlf/) and unrelated word substitutions (e.g., canoe → "umbrella"). Formal paraphasias accounted for 29% of all phonological errors. Semantic paraphasias and mixed errors were rare. The main difference between repetition and naming appeared to be in the higher incidence of phonemic paraphasias. Turning now to the effect of length and frequency (Table 3), the effect of frequency failed to reach significance on this task, $z = 1.41$, $p = .23$. The effect of length was again non-significant, $z = 0.59$, $p = .44$.

Summary and comment

In picture naming, a task that requires spoken production but not auditory input processing, the vast majority of MS's errors were phonological. Performance was influenced by lexical frequency and the errors themselves showed sensitivity to lexical status (formal paraphasias were common). In repetition, MS's overall error profile was very similar to that in naming: Again, the vast majority of errors were phonological, and again, a substantial proportion of these were real words. Nevertheless, MS's performance was substantially poorer overall, and in particular, there were considerably more phonemic paraphasias. However, unlike naming, there was no significant frequency effect. In neither task was there a significant length effect.

MS's high rate of phonological errors in naming and repetition indicates a primary impairment in phonological encoding. In the aphasia literature, there are now many documented cases of patients who exhibit a selective impairment in phonological

encoding (see, e.g., Caplan, Vanier, & Baker, 1986; Caramazza, Papagno, & Ruml, 2000; Kohn, 1989; Kohn & Smith, 1990; Pate, Saffran, & Martin, 1987; Shallice, Rumiati, & Zadini, 2000; Wilshire, 2002; Wilshire & McCarthy, 1996). Nevertheless, MS's performance differed in a number of important respects from these classic phonological encoding cases. First, in both naming and repetition, formal paraphasias occurred at a rate that well exceeded chance. These errors are relatively rare in "classic" phonological encoding cases (for other cases that produce large numbers and formal paraphasias, see Best, 1996; Blanken, 1990; N. Martin & Saffran, 1992). Second, unlike most of these classic cases, MS did not exhibit word length effects. Finally, and perhaps most importantly, MS's performance was markedly poorer in word repetition than in naming. It appears that for MS, initiating word production from an auditory representation increases the incidence of phonological errors in particular. This contrasts with typical phonological encoding cases, for whom repetition is generally at least as good as, if not better than, naming.

EXPERIMENT 2: EFFECTS OF WORD LENGTH AND IMAGEABILITY IN THREE AUDITORY INPUT PROCESSING TASKS

The data so far suggest that MS's difficulties in auditory input processing involve phonological processing, rather than semantic processing. Nevertheless, some aspects of MS's repetition appear to be at odds with this account. One is the absence of an effect of word length, a variable that would be expected to influence phonological processing. The other is the presence of an imageability effect, a variable generally associated with semantic processing (see discussions in Franklin, Howard, & Patterson, 1994, 1995; Hanley & Kay, 1997; Hanley, Kay, & Edwards, 2002; Nickels, 1995). Experiment 2 gathers more information about the role of these two variables across three different auditory input-processing tasks—repetition, auditory lexical decision, and semantic similarity judgment. The experiment was performed 1 year after our initial examination of MS, between January and March 2002 (23 to 25 months post-stroke).

Method

Materials. The stimuli were 120 words with familiarity ratings ranging from 4.00 to 5.15 according to the MRC Psycholinguistic database (Coltheart, 1981). The set comprised 60 words of low imageability (ratings between 2.50 and 4.00), and 60 of high imageability (ratings between 5.50 and 6.50). Word familiarity was matched across the subsets. Within each imageability subset, there were 20 monosyllabic, 20 bisyllabic, and 20 polysyllabic words, and familiarity was also matched across these groups. For the auditory lexical decision task, there was an additional set of 120 pronounceable nonwords (40 monosyllables, 40 bisyllables, and 40 polysyllables). Finally, for the semantic similarity judgement task, each stimulus word was also paired with: (1) a related word; and (2) a distractor word. The discrimination between these two words required access to fine-grained semantic information about the stimulus word: The related word was either a synonym or near-synonym (e.g., *income* for *revenue*), or a member of the same narrow semantic category (e.g., *giraffe* for *camel*). The distractor word was a member of a broader superordinate category (e.g., *rat* for *camel*, instead of *giraffe*), or was indirectly related to the target (e.g., *work* for *revenue*).

Procedure. In the repetition task, each stimulus word was presented auditorily in random order, and MS was asked to repeat it. In the auditory lexical decision task, the stimulus word set and the set of nonwords were combined and randomised. MS was then presented with each item auditorily and asked to respond "yes" if it was a real word and "no" if it was a nonword. In the semantic similarity judgment task (henceforth, the *semantic similarity* task), each stimulus was presented auditorily, and at the same time MS was shown a card with the corresponding related and distractor words written side by side. He was asked to choose the word that

was closest in meaning to the one he had just heard. Items were presented in random order. Data was analysed using logistic regression: For each of the three tasks, effects of imageability and length on accuracy were analysed using simple simultaneous logistic regression; z-scores for the Wald statistic are reported. For cross-task analyses, which incorporate task as a repeated measure, the model was fitted using Generalised Estimating Equations, and run on SAS (GENMOD procedure). The z-scores reported are based on empirical standard error estimates.

Results

Table 4 shows MS's performance on each of the three tasks. It is not possible to directly compare performance across tasks, because they are associated with different chance baselines. Nevertheless, MS does appear to be substantially impaired on all three. Across all tasks considered together, there was a significant effect of imageability, $z = 2.21$, $p < .05$. However, on individual tasks, the imageability effect was generally small: For the auditory lexical decision task, it was not significant, and for the semantic similarity and repetition tasks it fell just short of significance under a conservative, two-tailed test, $z = 3.27$, $p = .07$, and $z = 2.95$, $p = .09$, respectively.

The effect of length, on the other hand, varied dramatically across tasks. In the semantic similarity task, performance was weakest on monosyllabic words and strongest on polysyllabic words. This effect fell just short of significance, $z = 3.39$, $p = .07$. In contrast, for repetition, performance was weakest on *polysyllabic* words and strongest on *monosyllabic* words. Again, this effect fell just short of significance, $z = 2.98$, $p = .09$. On auditory lexical decision, there was no significant effect of word length. Nevertheless, the data appear to pattern more closely with those from the semantic similarity task than those from the repetition task. When all tasks were considered together, a repeated measures logistic regression analysis for task, word length, and including a Task × Word Length interaction term yielded a significant interaction, Chi square value (type 3 analysis): $\chi^2 = 6.29$, $p < .05$.

Table 4. *Experiment 2: Percentage of items correct on each of the three tasks*

| | % correct | | | |
	Monosyllables	Bisyllables	Polysyllables	Total
Semantic similarity				
High imageability	70.0	90.0	85.0	81.7
Low imageability	60.0	65.0	80.0	68.3
Total	65.0	77.5	82.5	75.0
Auditory lexical decision[a]				
High imageability	65.0	55.0	75.0	65.0
Low imageability	60.0	55.0	60.0	58.3
Total	62.5	55.0	67.5	61.6
Repetition				
High imageability	45.0	40.0	30.0	38.3
Low imageability	35.0	20.0	15.0	23.3
Total	40.0	30.0	22.5	30.8

[a] Figures reported are for correct identification of real words. The overall score for nonwords (percentage of correct rejections) was 71.7%.

Summary and comment

In this experiment, MS was found to be impaired on a range of auditory input tasks, including repetition, semantic similarity judgment, and auditory lexical decision. On all tasks, he tended to perform better on highly imageable words. For the experiment as a whole, this effect was significant and for the repetition and semantic similarity judgment tasks, considered separately, it fell just short of significance under a two-tailed hypothesis (a criterion that may be unnecessarily conservative given the strong a priori prediction concerning the direction of the effect).

The effect of word length varied dramatically across tasks. This can be seen most clearly by comparing repetition and semantic similarity judgment: In repetition, a task that involves both input and output processing, there was a trend towards a "forward" length effect—that is, better performance on shorter words. However, in semantic similarity judgment, a task that does not require spoken output, this trend shifted towards a "reverse" length effect, with better performance on *longer* words. These findings suggest that for MS,

word length has opposite effects in input and output processing: Output phonological encoding is associated with weak forward length effects, most probably due to the fact that longer words contain more phonemes, and therefore more opportunities for a phonological error. On the other hand, auditory input processing is associated with reverse length effects. Longer words are likely to have fewer phonological neighbours, so this may protect them from being confused with other words even when the input phonological representation is incomplete or degraded. By this account, the overall effect of length in any one task will depend upon the load it places on input and output processing respectively. Length effects may be weak in repetition because this task has both input and output processing requirements, which may partially cancel each other out. MS is not the first aphasic patient who has been reported to show a shift in the direction of length effects across tasks: Franklin, Turner, Lambon Ralph, Morris, and Bailey (1996) report another case for whom "forward" length effects in output tasks give way to "reverse" effects on input tasks. We return to this issue in the General Discussion.

EXPERIMENT 3: DIRECT COMPARISON OF FOUR WORD PRODUCTION TASKS

Our data so far indicate that MS has difficulty at "both ends" of the phonological processing system—both input and output processing are impaired. Experiment 3 gathers more data on this issue by comparing four production tasks that vary as to stimulus modality (a picture or an auditory word) as well as output modality (a spoken or a written response). If phonological input processing is impaired, then tasks that use auditory word stimuli—such as repetition and writing to dictation—should be more difficult than those using picture stimuli—such as written or spoken naming. Similarly, if phonological output processing is impaired, then tasks that require full phonological encoding—spoken naming and repetition—should be more difficult than written naming or writing to dictation where this process may be bypassed (see Hanley & McDonnell, 1997, and references therein, for evidence). The experiment was run between February and April 2002 (that is, 24 to 26 months post-stroke).

Method

Materials. Stimuli comprised 150 pictures, the majority of which were black-and-white line drawings (a small number were coloured to enhance recognisability). The pictures had names of one to four syllables (there were 69 monosyllables, 51 bisyllables, and 30 polysyllables), with Celex lemma frequencies ranging from 0 to 331.16 occurrences per million (mean = 17.64).

Procedure. MS performed four tasks: spoken naming, written naming, repetition, and dictation. In the spoken and written naming tasks, he was presented with each picture and asked to name it orally or write its name, depending upon the task. In the repetition task, the experimenter spoke the name of each picture, and MS had to repeat it. In the dictation task, the procedure was the same, except that MS had to write the word. The experiment was run across four sessions, as follows:

Session 1—repetition; Session 2—spoken naming (first half of pictures), then written naming (second half of pictures); Session 3—written naming (first half of pictures) then spoken naming (second half of pictures); Session 4—dictation. The effect of stimulus modality and output modality on response accuracy was analysed using logistic regression: The repeated measures model was fit using generalised estimating equations and run on SAS (GENMOD procedure). The z-scores reported in the text are based on empirical standard error estimates.

Results

Table 5 summarises MS's performance on the four tasks. As predicted, tasks involving auditory stimuli (repetition and dictation) elicited more errors overall than those involving pictorial stimuli (spoken and written naming). In addition, those involving spoken responses (naming and repetition) elicited more errors than their written counterparts. The effect of both stimulus modality and output modality was significant, $z = 5.96, p < .0001$ and $z = 3.28, p < .01$, respectively. There was no significant interaction between these two variables.

Turning now to the errors themselves, the spoken naming and repetition tasks elicited fewer errors overall than in Experiment 1—perhaps due to the higher average frequency of the targets used here. However, error patterns were similar. As previously, form-related nonword errors (that is, phonemic paraphasias) were the most common error type, followed by form-related word substitutions (formal paraphasias). On the dictation task, the error pattern was similar: Form-related nonword errors were most common (e.g., broom → *broon*; scale → *scound*; halo → *hellode*), followed by form-related word substitutions (e.g., slide → *slave*; cross → *croft*; olive → *orange*), and there were also several unrelated word substitutions (e.g., arm → *owed*; island → *window*) and unrelated nonword errors (cactus → *outry*; dragon → *keldbug*). In contrast, on the written naming task, form-related errors were rare; there were only four instances in total, all of which were nonwords (e.g., broccoli → *brocillo*; avocado → *ovado*). Indeed, on

Table 5. *Experiment 3: Breakdown of responses (first complete attempt) on each of the four tasks*

Response type[a]	% of total responses			
	Spoken naming	Written naming	Repetition	Dictation
Correct	72.0	84.0	50.0	56.7
Form-related nonword error	10.7	2.7	28.0	17.3
Form-related word substitution	5.3	0	12.7	8.0
Semantic substitution	1.3	4.7	1.3	0.7
Unrelated word	3.3	0	0	5.3
Unrelated nonword error	2.0	0	1.3	5.3
Mixed (semantic + formal) substitution	0.7	0.7	0	0
Morphological error	0	0	0.7	0.7
No response	3.3	4.0	5.3	5.3
Other	1.3	4.0	0.7	0.7

[a] The standard terms used in spoken error classifications have been replaced with modality-neutral terms. For spoken tasks, "form-related" was defined in the same way as "phonologically related" in Experiment 1. For written tasks, a response was considered form-related if it contained the correct first or last letter of the word or at least two other letters in their correct position, or at least 30% correct letters in any position.

this task, semantic errors were in fact more common (e.g., compass → *barometer*).

Summary and comment

In this word production experiment, the tasks were varied with respect to both the modality of the stimulus (whether a picture or spoken word) and the modality of output (whether spoken or written). We argued that, if both input and output phonological processing are impaired in MS, then there should be significant effects of both these manipulations. This prediction was confirmed. Tasks using auditory stimuli were performed more poorly than those using picture stimuli, and tasks requiring a spoken response were performed more poorly than those requiring a written response. The effects of these two variables were independent and noninteractive.

An analysis of error types supported the hypothesis that both input and output impairments involve the phonological level of representation: On spoken naming, repetition, and writing to dictation, the three tasks that require a significant degree of phonological processing (either input phonological processing, output phonological encoding, or both), the vast majority of errors were form related. Also, the relative incidence of form-related errors across tasks was consistent with each task's phonological processing requirements: Repetition, a task that requires both input *and* output phonological processing, elicited roughly the same number of form-related errors as the spoken naming and dictation tasks combined. In contrast with spoken naming, repetition, and dictation, the written naming task, which has no input phonological processing requirements and probably little or no phonological encoding requirement, elicited very few form-related errors.

GENERAL DISCUSSION

In this paper, we have described an aphasic patient (MS) who suffers from a phonological impairment that affects both auditory comprehension and spoken language production. The key features of MS's performance are as follows.

1. *Picture naming.* In naming tasks, MS's errors were mostly phonemic and formal paraphasias. Semantic paraphasias were rare. There were effects of word frequency but not of length.

2. *Repetition.* Repetition was poorer than picture naming. Errors were again mainly phonemic and formal paraphasias. Semantic

paraphasias were extremely rare. Performance was strongly affected by target lexicality, word imageability, and possibly also word length (there was a significant forward effect in some tasks). It was not affected by word frequency.

3. *Auditory comprehension.* MS performed poorly on tasks of phoneme discrimination and auditory lexical decision. On word–picture matching tasks, performance was considerably poorer with phonological distractors than with semantic distractors. Most auditory input tasks showed weak imageability effects, and some showed reverse length effects.

4. *Written tasks.* Comprehension of written stimuli was much better than that of auditory stimuli. Oral reading was also superior to naming or repetition, although irregular words elicited some errors. Nonword reading was preserved. Written tasks were performed better than their spoken counterparts, and in particular elicited fewer form-related errors.

MS's condition shares a number of similarities with deep dysphasia. Like deep dysphasia, it selectively affects auditory/spoken language (rather than written) and encompasses impairment on both input and output processing tasks. Also, like deep dysphasia, one of its most notable features is markedly impaired single word repetition, which shows imageability effects and strong lexicality effects (nonword repetition is extremely impaired). And finally, like deep dysphasia, phonemic and formal paraphasias are produced in both repetition and naming. However, MS's performance differs from that of deep dysphasics in one critical manner: Semantic paraphasias are not produced in repetition. Indeed, in all his tasks, MS's performance is more "phonological" in quality—hence our choice of the name "phonological dysphasia" for his condition. MS's pattern of performance can also be contrasted with that of patients with a selective impairment in phonological encoding. Like these individuals, MS produces phonemic paraphasias as his primary error type in production tasks. However, he differs in that he is also impaired on auditory input processing tasks, particularly those with a strong phonological

component. He also performs much more poorly on word repetition than on more pure tasks of production such as picture naming. MS's picture naming also exhibits some features not often seen in classic phonological encoding cases, most notably a high rate of formal paraphasias and an absence of strong word length effects.

MS's pattern of errors in repetition is quite similar to that of N. Martin, Saffran, and colleagues' patient NC in later testing phases (around 1 year to 18 months post-onset: see N. Martin et al., 1994, 1996). At this time, NC continued to produce phonemic and formal paraphasias in repetition, but made almost no semantic paraphasias—just as was the case for MS. This raises the question as to whether the difference between MS and classic deep dysphasics might be one of degree only: Severe cases may generate semantic errors in repetition, but milder cases might produce only phonological errors. However, two observations argue against this. First, even during initial testing, MS was not uniformly better than NC; he actually performed considerably *more poorly* on some input tasks such as minimal pair discrimination. Second, although the partially recovered NC produced similar error patterns to MS in repetition, other error patterns were quite different: In picture naming, he produced a large number of semantic paraphasias, whereas MS produced few such errors. These differences suggest that MS's condition is not simply a milder version of NC's, but rather differs in quality—most notably, it appears to be more "phonological" in nature.

Theoretical interpretation

To explain MS's pattern of performance within a functional architecture framework, we would need to propose multiple independent impairments. For example, within Patterson and Shewell's (1987) scheme (see Figure 1): (1) the extremely poor nonword repetition would indicate an impairment to the acoustic-to-phonological conversion route); (2) the phonological errors in naming, and evidence of sensitivity to lexical factors in naming, would indicate an impairment to phonological output lexicon itself; and (3) the impairment in auditory input tasks would indicate impairment to at least one of the components involved in auditory word processing (the acoustic analysis system and/or the auditory input lexicon). In addition, the imageability effects seen in repetition (and possibly some other tasks) indicate that MS is sensitive to semantic variables, which, in terms of Patterson and Shewell's model, would implicate the cognitive system itself.[3]

In an interactive-activation framework, however, a simpler account is available. Within this framework, we can capture the major features of MS's condition by proposing that phonological representations decay at an abnormally fast rate. We will describe how such an account would deal with our key findings using a very simple, hypothetical interactive-activation model (we return to the issue of model choice later). Our hypothetical model, like that of N. Martin, Saffran, and colleagues, incorporates three interconnected layers of localist nodes—phonological, lexical, and semantic—and permits two-way flow of activation between successive layers. Nodes, once activated, decay at a predetermined rate. In this mini-model, there is only one layer of phonological representations that subserves both input and output processing (we return to this issue later). We'll imagine that individual connection strengths are a function of the model's previous experience with a particular association (a Hebbian learning algorithm could achieve this: see examples in Farrar & Van Orden, 2001; Hartley & Houghton, 1996; Houghton, 1990; Vousden, Brown, & Harley, 2000). This provides a simple mechanism for modelling frequency effects. And finally, since imageability effects need to be within the explanatory domain of the model, we will make the further assumption that highly imageable words are represented in

the semantic layer by a greater number of nodes than nonimageable words. This is consistent with previous suggestions that highly imageable words may have richer or more easily accessible semantic representations (see, e.g., Jones, 1985; N. Martin & Saffran, 1992; N. Martin et al., 1994; Plaut & Shallice, 1993).[4,5]

This simple model can be used to describe performance on a range of single word tasks, including production tasks like picture naming; auditory tasks like word–picture matching; and "mixed" tasks like word repetition. Consider first the task of picture naming. This involves translating a pattern of activation in the semantic layer into a pattern in the phonological layer. Activation is transmitted from the semantic to the lexical layer in the first instance, and then later spreads to the phonological layer. Activation continues to flow back and forth between adjacent layers until the process is deemed complete (either a particular end-state is reached in the phonological nodes, or a certain period of time elapses). On the other hand, a word–picture matching task would involve almost the reverse sequence of events. Here, the input representation involves the phonological layer, and the output involves the semantic layer. In this task, there is also another source of input: Semantic nodes corresponding to the target and distractor words will become activated as a result of exposure to the pictures. This "top-down" activation will spread to the corresponding lexical and phonological nodes. Finally, in word repetition, the input and output states involve the same level of representation—that is, both involve a pattern of activation across phonological nodes. There is no need to translate the input into another type of representation. Nevertheless, the correct pattern of phonological activation must be *maintained* by the network long enough for an articulatory-motor

---

[3] Other possibilities are available within other functional architecture accounts: see for example, Hanley and Kay (1997) and Hanley, Kay, and Edwards (2002).

[4] This is very much a shorthand approximation. We are in fact sympathetic to the idea that imageability effects may actually reflect the *uniqueness* of the semantic-lexical mappings, rather than their richness per se (see also Newton & Barry, 1997).

[5] A complete version of this model would need to include some further features. There would need to be separate nodes for phonemes at each word position. Also, there would need to be a mechanism for keeping the spread of activation in check, for example, inhibitory connections between nodes within a layer. However, these issues are beyond the scope of the current discussion.

plan to be constructed, and this process is likely to involve some considerable delay.[6] The backward and forward activation flow that occurs between the phonological, lexical, and semantic layers is beneficial because it helps to maintain phonological activation, even after the (normal) effects of decay have begun to exert themselves.

Now, imagine what would happen if this model were "lesioned" so that activation within the phonological nodes decayed at an abnormally fast rate. Consider first the task of picture naming. In this task, activation spreads from the semantic layer to the lexical layer and then subsequently to the phonological layer. Activation will also feed back in the reverse direction. However, unlike in the normal system, activation within the phonological nodes will decay rapidly. By the time articulation is initiated, some phonological nodes may no longer be active enough to win the competition for selection, so phonological errors will be common. In addition, there will be a bias towards phonological errors with real-word outcomes, because the (late-acting) effects of feedback between the phonological and lexical layers will reinforce any pattern of phonological activation that corresponds to a real word. Semantic paraphasias will be rare because activation spreads normally between the semantic and lexical layers, and both layers can sustain activation for a normal period of time. Consequently, the lexical representations of semantically related words will have little opportunity to become activated above the level of the target. Performance will be influenced by word frequency and length. Frequent words are associated with stronger lexical–phonological connections, so their phonological nodes are likely to receive strong activation. This may help to partially offset the effects of decay. In addition, the stronger lexical–phonological activation may mean that the network reaches its end-state sooner, so decay may have less time to operate before a response is made. The effect of word length will be complex. In general, the transmission of activation from the

lexical to the phonological layer will be more accurate for shorter words. This is because they contain fewer phonemes, and therefore fewer opportunities for a phonological error to occur. However, this effect might be partially offset by feedback activation, which will have a greater reinforcing effect for long than for short words. This is because longer words tend to have fewer phonological neighbours with which to "share" feedback activation.

In an auditory comprehension task, the initial input will be to the phonological nodes, which are inherently unstable. By the time activation is transmitted to the lexical layer, the pattern of activation across phonological nodes is likely to be partially (or even completely) degraded. The input to the lexical layer may therefore be insufficient to activate the target lexical representation above that of other words that are also consistent with the degraded phonological activation pattern—that is, other phonologically related words. Short words, which tend to have more phonologically related neighbours, will be particularly prone to error. Performance will also depend upon task requirements. In word–picture matching, the top-down activation from the target and distractor pictures will generally enhance the activation of the target relative to its (phonologically related) competitors—so long as the distractor(s) aren't also phonologically related to the target. Hence, performance would be expected to be better on tasks involving semantic distractors than on those involving phonological distactors. In tasks such as auditory lexical decision, where there are no top-down influences, performance will be entirely dependent upon the integrity of the activation reaching the lexical layer. If this is at all degraded, there may not be enough information to establish whether the stimulus was in fact a real word or a highly word-like nonword.

Auditory repetition will be severely compromised by this rapid phonological decay for two reasons. First, successful repetition depends

---

[6] Even in university undergraduates, there can be a delay of more than 1 second between the onset of the auditory stimulus and the onset of a repetition response (Vitevitch, 2002).

heavily upon the model's ability to sustain the correct pattern of activation at the phonological level. Second, in repetition, both input and output representations involve phonological descriptions, so errors can occur at both "ends" of the process: The input pattern of phonological activation may become degraded before it is even transmitted to the lexical layer, and it can also become degraded later in the process, as activation begins to spread from the lexical back down to the phonological layer. Performance will be influenced by lexical and semantic variables. This is because repetition will depend entirely on the extent to which the (rapidly decaying) phonological representation can be maintained by backward and forward activation involving the lexical and semantic layers. Therefore, nonword repetition would be expected to be particularly difficult, because these items can presumably benefit little from such lexical-semantic support. For real words, highly imageable words may also be at a slight advantage, because activation at the lexical level can be sustained longer for these words by virtue of the greater number of lexical-semantic connections. Again, the role of word length will be complex. As noted above, while the spread of activation from the phonological to lexical layer favours longer words, that from the lexical to the phonological layer favours shorter words. Since both these opposing processes are critical for the maintenance of phonological-level activation, they may partially cancel each other out.

So far, our model's predictions appear to be consistent with the key features of MS's performance. Of course, these predictions were generated informally, and would need to be confirmed through computational simulation. Nevertheless, the account does seem promising. Other findings not yet considered—such as MS's well-preserved reading and writing, and his reduced digit span—also seem to be compatible in principle with our model. The preserved writing skills would not be unexpected, because written production does not rely solely on the generation of a correct pattern of activation in the phonological nodes (see Hanley & McDonnell, 1997, and references therein). Better performance in oral reading than in other word production tasks would also not be unexpected:

Several recent models of oral reading suggest that output phonological representations receive direct activation not just from their dominant lexical representations, but also from their corresponding graphemic representations (see, e.g., Coltheart, Rastle, Perry, Langdon, & Ziegler, 2001). This additional source of activation support may partially offset the effects of phonological-level decay. MS's occasional errors on irregularly spelled words would certainly be consistent with this account, because for these words, the normal grapheme-to-phoneme correspondence rules do not apply, so input from graphemic representations does not provide consistent, accurate support to phonological representations. Finally, MS's reduced digit span, although well beyond the scope of our model, is nevertheless not incompatible with it. A number of recent authors have suggested that performance on span tasks relies heavily on the ability to sustain activation within phonological representations (see, e.g., N. Martin & Saffran, 1997; R. C. Martin, Shelton, & Yaffee, 1994; Saffran & Martin, 1990).

The concept of a phonological decay impairment is not entirely new to the literature. R. C. Martin et al. (1999) recently offered a similar account for an aphasic individual with impaired auditory input processing. Patient AP exhibited a number of abnormalities, including (1) moderately impaired auditory lexical decision, most notably an inability to reject nonwords, particularly those with very close real-word neighbours; (2) occasional errors in real-word repetition, most of which were formal paraphasias; and (3) preserved minimal pair discrimination at short ISIs (500 msec), but some difficulty at longer ISIs. Using an auditory-phonological adaptation of McClelland and Rumelhart's (1981) interactive-activation model of visual word recognition, the authors modelled AP's behaviour by increasing the decay rate in the phonological nodes. They showed that this lesion results in the misrecognition of nonwords as real words, and to a lesser extent, gives rise to confusions amongst similar-sounding real words. It would also have a detrimental effect on any task with a high phonological retention load, such as minimal pair discrimination at long ISIs. AP differs in several respects from MS, at least on auditory tasks (there is no data on AP's production). Some of these differences are ones of degree: AP performs well on standard minimal pair discrimination tasks, and scores higher than MS on both auditory lexical decision and word repetition. However, some differences are qualitative—for example, unlike MS, AP has greater difficulty with nonwords than with words in lexical decision, and he produces mainly formal paraphasias in repetition. It is unclear whether a single model could account for the features of both individuals. Nevertheless, it is still possible that both suffer from the same *type* of impairment (that is, phonological decay), but vary in terms of the *extent* of that impairment (that is, the rate of that decay). Such variation would be likely to have qualitative as well as quantitative effects on performance. Further cross-patient comparisons and more formal model simulations would be required to explore these issues.

Finally, let us consider briefly how our hypothetical model compares with the model of Dell and O'Seaghdha (1991) used in the deep dysphasia studies of Martin, Saffran, and colleagues. We chose not to base our description of MS on this type of model because it has several problematic features for describing data from aphasic phonological errors. Specifically, it incorporates a property known as "signalling activation," which effectively limits the extent of cascading activation between levels of representation. One consequence of this is that large numbers of formal paraphasias are produced only if there is a lesion that affects lexical selection.[7] This aspect of the model sits uncomfortably with recent data from aphasic errors, which shows that substantial rates of formal paraphasias are more likely to co-occur with other types of phonological errors (that is, phonemic paraphasias) than with other types of lexical errors such as semantic paraphasias (see Foygel & Dell,

2000, Table 4, for supporting evidence; and Wilshire & Saffran, 2002, for further discussion). This property of the Dell models was also problematic in Martin, Saffran, and colleagues' own simulations of deep dysphasia: For example, in picture naming, phonemic paraphasias were underpredicted while semantic paraphasias were overpredicted. Since our present aim was to demonstrate the advantages of the interactive-activation approach *in general*, we instead opted for a formulation that would provide an optimum framework for illustrating this approach.

Evaluation

Our interactive-activation account of MS's condition has a number of parallels with functional architecture accounts. Many of the operations performed by our model have direct counterparts within a functional architecture framework. For example, the process of transmitting activation from the lexical to the phonological layer corresponds roughly to accessing the phonological output lexicon. Similarly, activation transmission from the phonological to the lexical layer corresponds roughly to accessing the auditory input lexicon. However, despite these similarities, there is one fundamental difference between the two frameworks when applied to MS's condition: Within a functional architecture framework, the condition is seen as arising from a constellation of functionally unrelated deficits, whereas within an interactive-activation framework, it is underpinned by a single abnormality. Of course, the suggestion that MS's condition reflects a single unitary functional impairment is no more than an assumption. It is entirely possible that MS indeed suffers from a number of separate and independent impairments, and it would be difficult to imagine a test that could potentially falsify such an account. Nevertheless, the interactive-activation model

---

[7] In this model, formal paraphasias can arise as a result of two different mechanisms: (1) a phoneme selection error; and (2) a lexical selection error. The first mechanism—when operating alone—generates formal paraphasias at a rate close to (or perhaps just slightly above) chance. The second mechanism, however, can generate high rates of formal paraphasias. For MS, the incidence of formal paraphasias is too high to be attributable to the first mechanism alone.

offers a novel perspective by showing that the various features of MS's condition *need not necessarily* arise from separate and independent functional impairments.

The interactive-activation framework has two additional advantages. The first is that it can generate interesting predictions for future research. One example concerns the effect of word position on phonological errors. In our hypothetical mini-model above, we have not considered the issue of phoneme serial order. However, it has recently been suggested that phonological encoding is sequential, and that word-final phonemes may be more sensitive to a phonological level impairment than word-initial phonemes, because they do not receive as much direct activation support from lexical and higher levels (N. Martin & Saffran, 1997; Wilshire & Saffran, 2002). Such an effect might be likely to be particularly pronounced in the case of a phonological decay impairment, in which successful production (particularly in repetition) is strongly dependent upon feedback and feedforward between the phonological and lexical/semantic levels. These kinds of predictions could be addressed in various ways, for example by looking at serial position effects across phonological errors, and perhaps even manipulating the extent of activation of early and late phonemes through priming (see also Wilshire & Saffran, 2002). There are also predictions regarding word and digit span. According to recent proposals, a phonological decay impairment would have specific consequences for performance on span tasks—specifically, performance should be more strongly influenced by modality of presentation than that of normal subjects, and may show stronger effects of semantic variables such as imageability (see N. Martin & Saffran, 1997; R. Martin et al., 1994; Saffran & Martin, 1990). Some studies investigating a number of these predictions are currently underway in our laboratory.

A second advantage of the interactive-activation framework is that it may be useful for cross-patient comparison. In interactive-activation models, differences amongst patients are accounted for by varying a small number of parameters. They can therefore be used as the basis for creating multidimensional models of inter-patient variability. Dell and colleagues have suggested two primary parameters along which fluent aphasic patients may vary: (1) the *quality* of the processing impairment—whether it involves pathologically fast decay, or weakened transmission of activation between levels (Dell et al., 1997); and (2) the *locus* of the impairment—whether it involves lexical–phonological connections and/or lexical–semantic connections (e.g., Foygel & Dell, 2000). Both these parameters may be useful in capturing the similarities and differences between MS and other patients. For example, it could be proposed that MS's condition is similar to deep dysphasia in that both involve pathologically fast decay, but differ in terms of the *locus* of that decay impairment. While MS's condition would be attributed to phonological-level decay, the mixed pattern of performance seen in deep dysphasia would be attributed to a more global impairment affecting all levels of representation. In the same vein, the differences between MS and patients with classic output phonological encoding impairments could be captured by varying the "quality" parameter. While both impairments would involve phonological representations, the deficit in classic "output" cases would be attributed not to pathologically fast decay, but rather to weakened connections between lexical and phonological nodes. Such an impairment would be consistent with the input–output asymmetries seen in these patients, because production tasks—which involve a one-to-many mapping between lexical and phonological representations—would be more severely affected than input tasks, where there is a convergent, many-to-one mapping.

This brings us to one important issue raised by our account—that concerning the relationship between phonological input and output processing. Our model contained only a single layer of phonological nodes that subserved both input and output processing. It was not necessary to propose separate sets of input and output phonological representations in order to account for MS's performance. However, the question arises as to whether this type of architecture may suffice as a more general model of phonological processing.

On the one hand, several studies have reported dissociations between input and output phonological processing impairments in aphasic patients (see, for example, Nickels & Howard, 1995; Romani, 1992; Shallice et al., 2000.). However, N. Martin and Saffran (2002) have recently argued that many of these apparent dissociations may be accommodated within a model with a single level of phonological representation, if we take into account the difference in the direction of information flow in input and output processing tasks, and the way in which this influences overall task difficulty and the strategies available to the individual. Indeed, a recent correlational study by these authors provides some direct evidence in support for a functional relationship between input and output phonological processing (N. Martin & Saffran, 2002). Our present study offers a further argument in support of the common input-output hypothesis, because it documents a condition that is awkward to accommodate within a model with separate input and output phonological representations, but is quite elegantly captured within a common input-output model. Only the latter type of model enables us to account for MS's impairment in terms of a single abnormality—any other conceptualisation would involve the postulation of multiple independent impairments.

CONCLUSION

The fundamental difference between functional architecture models of aphasia and those based on interactive-activation frameworks is one of grain size. Indeed, many of the components and pathways proposed in functional architecture accounts translate directly into levels of representation and/or specific processes in interactive-activation models. However, some differences between the two frameworks have direct consequences for accounts of aphasia. Specifically, the finer grain size of interactive-activation models allows them to capture similarities in the nature of the impairment across different language components. Certain types of conditions, which appear complex and heterogeneous when viewed in functional

architecture terms, can therefore be seen as the result of a single unitary impairment. This is most clearly evident in conditions with strong dynamic qualities, such as deep dysphasia.

The present study contributes another example of a condition with distinct temporal qualities that lends itself particularly well to an interactive-activation account. The cross-modal nature of the condition and the high prevalence of feedback-related errors, such as formal paraphasias, both suggest that it may best be captured in terms of fast decay. Further, the phonological quality of the patient's impairment across all tasks argues for an impairment restricted to a (non-modality-specific) phonological level of representation. This single impairment account can accommodate a wide range of the features of MS's performance that would otherwise require the postulation of multiple independent impairments. The model proposed here is tentative and informal, but it nonetheless offers a number of interesting possibilities for future investigation.

REFERENCES

Best, W. (1996). When racquets are baskets but baskets are biscuits, where do the words come from? A single case study of formal paraphasic errors in aphasia. *Cognitive Neuropsychology, 13*, 443–480.

Blanken, G. (1990). Formal paraphasias: A single case study. *Brain and Language, 38*, 534–554.

Caplan, D., Vanier, M., & Baker, C. (1986). A case study of reproduction conduction aphasia. I: Word production. *Cognitive Neuropsychology, 3*, 99–128.

Caramazza, A., Papagno, C., & Ruml, W. (2000). The selective impairment of phonological processing in speech production. *Brain and Language, 75*, 428–450.

Coltheart, M. (1981). The MRC Psycholinguistic Database. *Quarterly Journal of Experimental Psychology, 33A*, 497–505.

Coltheart, M. (1987). Functional architecture of the language-processing system. In M. Coltheart, G. Sartori, & R. Job (Eds.), *The cognitive neuropsychology of language.* (pp. 1–25). Hove, UK: Lawrence Erlbaum Associates Ltd.

Coltheart, M. (2002). Cognitive neuropsychology. In H. Pashler & J. Wixted (Eds.), *Stevens' handbook of* experimental psychology. Vol. 4: Methodology in experimental psychology (3rd ed., pp. 139–174). New York: Wiley.

Coltheart, M., Rastle, K., Perry, C., Langdon, R., & Ziegler, J. (2001). DRC: A dual route cascaded model of visual word recognition and reading aloud. Psychological Review, 108, 204–256.

Coslett, H. B. (1991). Read but not write "idea." Evidence for a third reading mechanism. Brain and Language, 40, 425–443.

Croot, K., Patterson, K., & Hodges, J. R. (1998). Single word production in nonfluent progressive aphasia. Brain and Language, 61, 226–273.

Dell, G. S. (1986). A spreading activation theory of retrieval in sentence production. Psychological Review, 93, 283–321.

Dell, G. S., & O'Seaghda, P. G. (1991). Mediated and convergent lexical priming in language production: A comment on Levelt et al. (1991). Psychological Review, 98, 604–614.

Dell, G. S., & O'Seaghda, P. G. (1992). Stages of lexical access in language production. Cognition, 42, 287–314.

Dell, G. S., Schwartz, M. F., Martin, N, Saffran, E. M., & Gagnon, D. A. (1997). Lexical access in aphasic and nonaphasic speakers. Psychological Review, 104, 801–838.

Duhamel, J.-R., & Poncet, M. (1986). Deep dysphasia in a case of phonemic deafness: Role of the right hemisphere in auditory language comprehension. Neuropsychologia, 24, 769–779.

Farrar, W. T., & Van Orden, G. C. (2001). Errors as multistable response options. Nonlinear Dynamics, Psychology and Life Sciences, 5, 223–264.

Foygel, D., & Dell, G. S. (2000). Models of impaired lexical access in speech production. Journal of Memory and Language, 43, 182–216.

Franklin, S., Howard, D., & Patterson, K. (1994). Abstract word meaning deafness. Cognitive Neuropsychology, 11, 1–34.

Franklin, S., Howard, D., & Patterson, K. (1995). Abstract word anomia. Cognitive Neuropsychology, 12, 549–566.

Franklin, S., Turner, J., Lambon Ralph, M. A., Morris, J., & Bailey, P. J. (1996). A distinctive case of word meaning deafness? Cognitive Neuropsychology, 13, 1139–1162.

Goodglass, H., & Kaplan, E. (1983). The assessment of aphasia and related disorders (2nd ed.). Philadelphia: Lea & Feibiger.

Hanley, J. R., & Kay, J. (1997). An effect of imageability on the production of phonological errors in auditory repetition. Cognitive Neuropsychology, 14, 1065–1084.

Hanley, J. R., Kay, J., & Edwards, M. (2002). Imageability effects, phonological errors, and the relationship between auditory repetition and picture naming: Implications for models of auditory repetition. Cognitive Neuropsychology, 19, 193–206.

Hanley, J. R., & McDonnell, V. (1997). Are reading and spelling phonologically mediated? Evidence from a patient with a speech production impairment. Cognitive Neuropsychology, 14, 3–33.

Hartley, T., & Houghton, G. (1996). A linguistically constrained model of short-term memory for nonwords. Journal of Memory and Language, 53, 1–31.

Harvey, J. A., & Siegert, R. J. (1999). Normative data for New Zealand elders on the Controlled Oral Word Association Test, Graded Naming Test and Recognition Memory Test. New Zealand Journal of Psychology, 28, 124–132.

Houghton, G. (1990). The problem of serial order: A neural network model of sequence learning and recall. In R. Dale, C. Mellish, & M. Zock (Eds.), Current research in natural language generation. London: Academic Press.

Howard, D., & Franklin, S. (1988). Missing the meaning?: A cognitive neuropsychological study of the processing of words by an aphasic patient. Cambridge, MA: MIT Press.

Jones, G. V. (1985). Deep dyslexia, imageability and ease of predication. Brain and Language, 24, 1–19.

Katz, R. B., & Goodglass, H. (1990). Deep dysphasia: Analysis of a rare form of repetition disorder. Brain and Language, 39, 153–185.

Kay, J., Lesser, R., & Coltheart, M. (1992). Psycholinguistic Assessments of Language Processing in Aphasia. Hove, UK: Lawrence Erlbaum Associates Ltd.

Kohn, S. E. (1989). The nature of the phonemic string deficit in conduction aphasia. Aphasiology, 3, 209–239.

Kohn, S. E., & Smith, K. L. (1990). Between-word speech errors in conduction aphasia. Cognitive Neuropsychology, 7, 133–156.

Majerus, S. Lekeu, F., Van der Linden, M., & Salmon, E. (2001). Deep dysphasia: Further evidence on the relationship between phonological short-term memory and language processing impairments. Cognitive Neuropsychology, 18, 385–410.

Marshall, J. C., & Newcombe, F. (1973). Patterns of paralexia: A psycholinguistic approach. Journal of Psycholinguistic Research, 2, 175–199.

Martin, N., Dell, G. S., Saffran, E. M., & Schwartz, M. F. (1994). Origins of paraphasias in deep dysphasia: Testing the consequences of a decay impairment to an interactive spreading activation model of lexical retrieval. *Brain and Language, 47,* 609–660.

Martin, N., & Saffran, E. M. (1992). A computational account of deep dysphasia: Evidence from a single case study. *Brain and Language, 43,* 240–274.

Martin, N., & Saffran, E. M. (1997). Language and auditory-verbal short-term memory impairments: Evidence for common underlying processes. *Cognitive Neuropsychology, 14,* 641–682.

Martin, N., & Saffran, E. M. (2002). The relationship of input and output phonological processing: An evaluation of models and evidence to support them. *Aphasiology, 16,* 107–150.

Martin, N., Saffran, E. M., & Dell, G. S. (1996). Recovery in deep dysphasia: Evidence for a relation between auditory-verbal STM capacity and lexical errors in repetition. *Brain and Language, 52,* 83–113.

Martin, R. C., Breedin, S. D., & Damian, M. F. (1999). The relation of phoneme discrimination, lexical access, and short-term memory: A case study and interactive activation account. *Brain and Language, 70,* 437–482.

Martin, R. C., Shelton, J. R., & Yaffee, L. S. (1994). Language processing and working memory: Neuropsychological evidence for separate phonological and semantic capacities. *Journal of Memory and Language, 33,* 83–111.

McClelland, J. L., & Rumelhart, D. E. (1981). An interactive activation model of context effects in letter perception: I. An account of basic findings. *Psychological Review, 88,* 375–407

McKenna, P., & Warrington, E. K. (1983). *Graded Naming Test.* Windsor, UK: NFER-Nelson.

Metz-Lutz, M., & Dahl, E. (1984). Analysis of word comprehension in a case of pure word deafness. *Brain and Language, 23,* 13–25.

Michel, F., & Andreewsky, E. (1983). Deep dysphasia: An analog of deep dyslexia in the auditory modality. *Brain and Language, 18,* 212–223.

Nelson, H. E., & McKenna, P. (1975) The use of current reading ability in the assessment of dementia. *British Journal of Clinical Psychology, 14,* 259–267.

Newton, P. K., & Barry, C. (1997). Concreteness effects in word production but not word comprehension in deep dyslexia. *Cognitive Neuropsychology, 14,* 481–509.

Nickels, L. (1995). Getting it right? Using aphasic naming errors to evaluate theoretical models of spoken word production. *Language and Cognitive Processes, 10,* 13–45.

Nickels, L. A., & Howard, D. (1995). Phonological errors in aphasic naming: Comprehension, monitoring and lexicality. *Cortex, 31,* 209–237

Pate, D. S., Saffran, E. M., & Martin, N. (1987). Specifying the nature of the production impairment in a conduction aphasic: A case study. *Language and Cognitive Processes, 2,* 43–84.

Patterson, K., & Shewell, C. (1987). Speak and spell: Dissociations and word class effects. In M. Coltheart, G. Sartori, & R. Job (Eds.), *The cognitive neuropsychology of language* (pp. 273–294). Hove, UK: Lawrence Erlbaum Associates Ltd.

Plaut, D. C., & Shallice, T. (1993). Deep dyslexia: A case study of connectionist neuropsychology. *Cognitive Neuropsychology, 10,* 377–500.

Romani, C. (1992). Are there distinct input and output buffers? Evidence from an aphasic patient with an impaired output buffer. *Language and Cognitive Processes, 7,* 131–162.

Saffran, E. M., & Martin, N. (1990). Neuropsychological evidence for lexical involvement in short-term memory. In G. Vallar & T. Shallice (Eds.), *Neuropsychological impairments of short-term memory* (pp. 145–166). Cambridge: Cambridge University Press.

Saffran, E. M., Schwartz, M. F., Linebarger, M., Martin, N., & Bochetto, P. (1989). *The Philadelphia Comprehension Battery.* Unpublished.

Shallice, T., Rumiati, R. I., & Zadini, A. (2000). The selective impairment of the phonological output buffer. *Cognitive Neuropsychology, 17,* 517–546.

Shallice, T., & Warrington, E. (1980). Single and multiple component central dyslexic syndromes. In M. Coltheart, K. E. Patterson, & J. C. Marshall (Eds.), *Deep dyslexia.* London: Routledge.

Tree, J. J., Perfect, T. J., Hirsh, K. W., & Copstick, S. (2001). Deep dysphasic performance in non-fluent progressive aphasia: A case study. *Neurocase, 7,* 473–488.

Trojano, L., Stanzione, M., & Grossi, D. (1992). Short-term memory and verbal learning with auditory phonological coding defect: A neuropsychological case study. *Brain and Cognition, 18,* 12–33.

Valdois, S., Carbonnel, S., David, D., Rousset, S., & Pellat, J. (1995). Confrontation of PDP models and dual route models through the analysis of a case of deep dysphasia. *Cognitive Neuropsychology, 12,* 681–724.

Vitevitch, M. S. (2002). Influence of onset density on spoken-word recognition. *Journal of Experimental Psychology: Human Perception and Performance, 28,* 270–278.

Vousden, J. I., Brown, G. D. A., & Harley, T. A. (2000). Serial control of phonology in speech production: A hierarchical model. *Cognitive Psychology*, *41*, 101–175.

Wilshire, C. E. (2002). Where do aphasic phonological errors come from? Evidence from phoneme movement errors in picture naming. *Aphasiology*, *16*, 169–197.

Wilshire, C. E., & McCarthy, R. A. (1996). Experimental investigations of an impairment in phono-logical encoding. *Cognitive Neuropsychology*, *13*, 1059–1098.

Wilshire, C. E., & Saffran, E. M. (2002) Contrasting effects of phonological priming in aphasic word production. *Manuscript under review*.

Zingeser, L. B., & Berndt, R. S. (1988). Grammatical class and context effects in a case of pure anomia: Implications for models of language production. *Cognitive Neuropsychology*, *5*, 474–513.

COGNITIVE NEUROPSYCHOLOGY, 2004, 21 (2/3/4) 211–212

SECTION II: BEYOND SINGLE WORD PROCESSING

A note on Eleanor Saffran's contribution to this area

Unlike many language researchers, Eleanor Saffran did not restrict herself to the relatively "safe" world of single words; she also tackled a more challenging set of issues concerning the comprehension and production of connected speech. This dimension of her research revealed itself in a number of separate, though related, topics.

One of the most important of these was the development of a quantitative analysis technique for assessing speech production, particularly its grammatical structure. Quantitative Production Analysis (or QPA, as it is fondly known) was applied in the original article (Saffran, Berndt, & Schwartz, 1989) to aphasic patients' narrative samples from telling the story of "Cinderella"; but the procedure can be applied to any narrative for which the context is well-enough known to assist the researcher's interpretation of (sometimes severely aphasic) patients' speech. The development of QPA was a massive and scholarly undertaking; the fact that it is alive and well 14 years after its publication confirms its status as one of Eleanor's many outstanding contributions to the world of aphasia research.

Needless to say, Eleanor's work on agrammatism went well beyond the quantification of agrammatic speech production. With her colleagues Myrna Schwartz, Oscar Marin, and Marcia Linebarger, she did a substantial amount of basic research on both receptive and expressive aspects of agrammatism (e.g., Linebarger, Schwartz, & Saffran, 1983; Saffran, Schwartz, & Linebarger, 1998; Saffran, Schwartz, & Marin, 1980; Schwartz, Saffran, & Marin, 1980); and she also investigated treatments for agrammatic comprehension and production (e.g., Saffran, Schwartz, Fink, Myers, & Martin, 1992; Schwartz, Fink, & Saffran, 1995; Schwartz, Saffran, Fink, Myers, & Martin, 1994).

Another arena in which Eleanor moved beyond traditional single-word language tasks was in her research on the relationship between language and verbal short-term memory. At a time in the field when these were typically treated as unrelated cognitive skills, Eleanor and Nadine Martin were struck by how un-separate they were, and set about investigations of aphasic patients that firmly linked disorders in the two domains (e.g., Martin & Saffran, 1990, 1997; Saffran & Martin, 1990a, 1990b).

It is not possible to describe all of Eleanor's contributions to language beyond words in this short tribute; but one more topic demands mention, as it relates to Eleanor's deep interest in semantics (covered in Section III). These two aspects merged in her work on the degree of independence of semantic and syntactic components of sentence processing. Although Eleanor's general views on cognition tended to emphasise graded effects and interaction rather than modularity and dissociation, her studies of patients with semantic impairments persuaded her that syntactic processing was surprisingly immune to semantic disruption (e.g., Breedin & Saffran, 1999). Many other researchers studying semantic dementia have also found this a dramatic and challenging dissociation; but, as so often, Eleanor and her colleagues (e.g., Schwartz, Marin, & Saffran, 1979) were there way ahead of the "pack".

REFERENCES

Breedin, S. D., & Saffran, E. M. (1999). Sentence processing in the face of semantic loss: A case study. *Journal of Experimental Psychology: General, 128,* 547–562.

Linebarger, M., Schwartz, M. F., & Saffran, E. M. (1983). Sensitivity to grammatical structure in so-called agrammatic aphasics. *Cognition, 13,* 361–392.

http://www.tandf.co.uk/journals/pp02643294.html

DOI:10.1080/02643290342000483

Martin, N., & Saffran, E. M. (1990). Repetition and verbal STM in transcortical sensory aphasia: A case study. *Brain and Language, 39,* 254–288.

Martin, N., & Saffran, E. M. (1997). Language and auditory verbal short-term memory impairments: Evidence for common underlying processes. *Cognitive Neuropsychology, 14,* 641–682.

Saffran, E. M., Berndt, R. S., & Schwartz, M. F. (1989). The quantitative analysis of agrammatic production: Procedure and data. *Brain and Language, 37,* 440–479.

Saffran, E. M., & Martin, N. (1990a). Neuropsychological evidence for lexical involvement in STM. In G. Vallar & T. Shallice (Eds.), *Neuropsychological impairments of short-term memory* (pp.145–166). Cambridge: Cambridge University Press.

Saffran, E. M., & Martin, N. (1990b). Short-term memory impairment and sentence processing: A case study. In G. Vallar & T. Shallice (Eds.), *Neuropsychological impairments of short-term memory* (pp. 428–447). Cambridge: Cambridge University Press.

Saffran, E. M., Schwartz, M. F., Fink, R. B., Myers, J. L., & Martin, N. (1992). Mapping therapy: An approach to remediating agrammatic sentence comprehension and production. *Aphasia Treatment: Current Approaches and Research Opportunities.* NIDCD Monograph (Vol. 2).

Saffran, E. M., Schwartz, M. F., & Linebarger, M. C. (1998). Semantic influences on thematic role assignment: Evidence from normals and aphasics. *Brain and Language, 62,* 255–297.

Saffran, E. M., Schwartz, M. F., & Marin, O. S. M. (1980). The word order problem in agrammatism: II. Production. *Brain and Language, 10,* 263–280.

Schwartz, M. F., Fink, R. B., & Saffran, E. M. (1995). The modular treatment of agrammatism. *Neuropsychological Rehabilitation, 5,* 93–127.

Schwartz, M. F., Marin, O. S. M., & Saffran, E. M. (1979). Dissociations of language function in dementia: A case study. *Brain and Language, 7,* 277–306.

Schwartz, M. F., Saffran, E. M., Fink, R. B., Myers, J. L., & Martin, N. (1994). Mapping therapy: A treatment program for agrammatism. *Aphasiology, 8,* 19–54.

Schwartz, M. F., Saffran, E. M., & Marin, O. S. M. (1980). The word order problem in agrammatism: I. Comprehension. *Brain and Language, 10,* 249–262.

COGNITIVE NEUROPSYCHOLOGY, 2004, 21 (2/3/4) 213–228

EXPLORING THE RELATIONSHIP BETWEEN WORD PROCESSING AND VERBAL SHORT-TERM MEMORY: EVIDENCE FROM ASSOCIATIONS AND DISSOCIATIONS

Nadine Martin

Temple University and Moss Rehabilitation Research Institute,
Philadelphia, PA, USA

Prahlad Gupta

University of Iowa, Iowa City, USA

A theory of the cognitive organisation of lexical processing, verbal short-term memory, and verbal learning is presented along with a summary of data that bear on this issue. We conceive of verbal STM as the outcome of processing that invokes both a specialised short-term memory and the lexical system. On this model, performance of verbal STM tasks depends on the integrity of lexical knowledge, access to that knowledge, and processes that encode serial order information.

INTRODUCTION

The goal of this article is to present a theoretical view of the relationship among three cognitive capacities: Lexical processing, verbal short-term memory (STM), and the ability to learn new verbal material. We operationalise "lexical processing" to mean the processes that, during comprehension, map the phonological representation of a word onto its meaning, and that, during production, map a meaning onto a phonological representation to be produced in spoken form. We operationalise "verbal short-term memory" to mean the set of processing mechanisms that are invoked in performance of an immediate serial recall task. By "learning new verbal material," we mean the learning of either a single new word, or a list (set) of new words.

Two considerations have motivated our examination of relationships between these abilities.

First, although there is now a wealth of evidence from studies of STM performance from normal and impaired populations that indicates relationships among these abilities (e.g., Baddeley, Gathercole, & Papagno, 1998; Craik & Lockhart, 1972; Freedman & Martin, 2001; Gathercole & Baddeley, 1993; Hulme, Maughan, & Brown, 1991; N. Martin & Saffran, 1997, 1999; Saffran, 1990), the nature of these relationships is not well understood. Second, individuals with neurologically based language deficits frequently demonstrate deficits of verbal STM and verbal learning. The development of more effective interventions for individuals with these deficits will be enhanced considerably with increased understanding of the integrated roles of word processing and verbal STM in learning.

Our theoretical orientation is one that views performance of verbal STM tasks as being

---

Correspondence should be addressed to Nadine Martin, PhD, Dept of Communication Sciences, Temple University, Weiss Hall, 1701 N 13th Street, Philadelphia, PA 19122, USA (Email: nmartin@temple.edu).

http://www.tandf.co.uk/journals/pp02643294.html

DOI:10.1080/02643290342000447

inextricably linked with the lexical processing system (rather than as drawing only on an independent short-term memory system). This theoretical view has evolved from four lines of work.

First, in several studies investigating the relationship between verbal STM and lexical processing in normal subjects, we have found evidence of very robust relationships between these abilities (Gupta, 2003; Gupta, MacWhinney, Feldman, & Sacco, in press). We have also provided evidence of serial position effects in repetition of individual polysyllabic nonwords similar to those in immediate serial recall of lists (Gupta, in press). These results have led us to a view of the relationship between verbal short-term memory and lexical processing that extends previous formulations, suggesting that the sequencing mechanisms underlying immediate serial recall of lists are also engaged in nonword repetition and in word learning.

Second, we have found that language impaired individuals (with aphasia) demonstrate differential influences of semantic and phonological abilities on primacy and recency effects in repetition span tasks (N. Martin & Saffran, 1997; N. Martin, Ayala, & Saffran, 2002). That is, the semantic and phonological processing abilities of aphasic patients impact their serial recall performance in systematic ways. We also have identified more specific correlations between span measures and semantic or phonological processing that reflect an interaction of the task demands and the nature of the lexical processing impairment (whether it is semantic or phonologically based). These results complement a large body of evidence indicating that properties of the language system impact performance in verbal short-term memory tasks, suggesting that the relationship between lexical processing and verbal short-term memory is bidirectional.

Third, we have been influenced by our study of the recovery patterns of an aphasic patient NC, who demonstrated severe STM and repetition impairment at acute stages of his illness. As NC recovered from his aphasia, his profile of "deep dysphasia" (semantic errors in single word repetition) gave way to a pattern more like that of a short-term memory deficit (semantic errors in multiple word repetition), suggesting continuity in the mechanisms underlying verbal STM and lexical processing (N. Martin, Dell, Saffran, & Schwartz, 1994; N. Martin, Saffran, & Dell, 1996). This, together with other results, has led us to the hypothesis of a continuum in the relationship between severity of lexical processing impairment in aphasia and verbal span, once again suggesting that impairments of lexical processing and verbal STM share a common underlying deficit.

In a fourth line of work, we have attempted to integrate evidence from the three domains, word processing, verbal STM, and word learning, through development of a computational model of various aspects of these relationships (Gupta, 1995, 1996a; Gupta & MacWhinney, 1997; N. Martin et al., 1996) that explicitly characterises the performance of verbal STM tasks as involving lexical processing mechanisms and the performance of lexical processing tasks as involving verbal short-term memory mechanisms. This effort is in keeping with other current models that aim to describe the ways in which the linguistic and non-linguistic aspects of word processing and STM are functionally integrated as a system that supports the development, use, and temporary and long-term storage of language (e.g., Cowan, 1995; Crosson, 1992; R. C. Martin, & Freedman, 2003; Ruchkin, Corcoran, Grafman, & Berndt, in press).

Below, we discuss each of these lines of work, and how they together lead to the theoretical framework outlined above. The discussion of computational models will be interleaved with discussion of experiments, reflecting the co-evolution of our theoretical ideas and empirical investigations.

IMMEDIATE SERIAL RECALL, NONWORD REPETITION, AND WORD LEARNING

Recent thinking has emphasised the importance of verbal short-term memory (as measured by immediate serial recall) in the study of word learning and in the processing of nonwords. In children, reliable correlations have been obtained between digit span, nonword repetition ability, and vocabulary achievement, even when other possible factors such as age and nonverbal intelligence have been factored out (e.g., Gathercole & Baddeley, 1989; Gathercole, Service, Hitch, Adams, & Martin, 1999; Gathercole, Willis, Emslie, & Baddeley, 1992). Nonword repetition ability has been shown to be an excellent predictor of language learning ability in children learning English as a second language (Service, 1992; Service & Kohonen, 1995), and is also associated with more rapid learning of the phonology of new words by children in experimental tasks (Gathercole & Baddeley, 1990b; Gathercole, Hitch, Service, & Martin, 1997; Michas & Henry, 1994). It also appears that there is a population of neuropsychologically impaired patients in whom language function is largely preserved, but who exhibit relative difficulty in immediate serial recall, nonword repetition, and word learning ability (Baddeley, 1993; Baddeley, Papagno, & Vallar, 1988). Overall, there is now a considerable body of evidence to suggest that word learning, immediate serial recall, and nonword repetition are a related triad of abilities, at least in children and in neuropsychologically impaired populations (Baddeley et al., 1998; Gathercole & Baddeley, 1993). An emerging view of this relationship is that immediate serial recall and nonword repetition are both tasks that draw on the mechanisms of verbal short-term memory fairly directly, and that the learning of new words is also in some way supported by verbal short-term memory (e.g., Baddeley et al., 1998; Brown & Hulme, 1996; Gathercole et al., 1999).

There are, of course, many questions that remain unanswered by this very general formulation. In particular: What are the mechanisms underlying these abilities? How do they work? Why are performances on these tasks related? Attempting to answer these questions, Gupta (1995, 1996b; Gupta & MacWhinney, 1997) proposed a computational model that provided a mechanistically specified account of relationships between immediate serial recall, nonword repetition, and word learning. The essence of this model is depicted in Figure 1. This work incorporates a

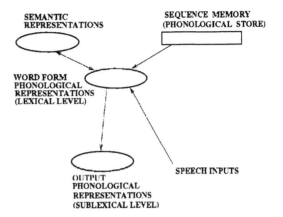

Figure 1. *A model of immediate serial recall, nonword repetition, and word learning (Gupta & MacWhinney, 1997).*

simple model of lexical and sublexical processing, and a sequence memory. For present purposes, the relevant aspects of the lexical model are that when a sequence of sounds constituting a word form (either known or unknown) is input to the system (as a sequence of phonemic representations), this leads to the activation of an internal phonological representation of the word form (again, known or unknown). The output (sublexical) level consists of representations of phonological constituents. The connection weights from the lexical to the sublexical level constitute an encoding of what the sublexical constituents of a word form are, and what their serial order is; these connection weights thus represent long-term phonological knowledge. Immediate repetition of a nonword requires the rapid creation of connection weights from the lexical to the sublexical level. Learning a new word requires that these weights be encoded sufficiently strongly to resist decay over time, and additionally that long-term connection weights be created between the lexical and semantic levels.

The sequence memory has short-term connection weights to the word form (lexical) level of representation. When a list of words is presented to the system, as in immediate serial recall, this leads to a sequence of activations at the lexical level. The sequence memory encodes the serial order of this sequence of activations at the lexical level via temporary learning in its short-term connection weights to the lexical level. That is, the sequence memory takes "snapshots" of the activations of linguistic representations as they occur in sequence at the lexical level of representation as a result of presentation of a list of word forms. As long as its short-term connection weights have not decayed too much, the sequence memory can cause that sequence of activations to be replayed and thus recalled; in the model, such recall exhibits typical serial position effects. The sequence memory is thus a specialised short-term sequencing mechanism; it corresponds roughly to the working memory model's phonological store, but with the important difference that it is not really a store into which items are entered (which appears to be the view outlined in Baddeley et al., 1998), but rather a serial ordering device that sets up associations to a sequence of activations in the lexical system. In this respect, the sequence memory's function is akin to one function of Cowan's (1988) central executive that regulates voluntary attention and selective recall of temporarily activated representations in STM. Moreover, it is also consistent with serial order devices in several other recent models of immediate serial recall (e.g., Brown, Preece, & Hulme, 2000; Burgess & Hitch, 1992, 1999; Hartley & Houghton, 1996; Page & Norris, 1998; Vousden, Brown, & Harley, 2000), and indeed incorporates mechanisms from some of the earlier models (in particular, Burgess & Hitch, 1992; Hartley & Houghton, 1996). However, the aims of the Gupta model were largely complementary to the aims of these other models, being concerned more with explaining relationships between immediate serial memory and aspects of linguistic processing and less with accounting for the many phenomena of immediate serial recall per se. It offered an account of word learning, nonword repetition, and immediate serial recall, incorporating the notion that verbal short-term memory mechanisms work closely with linguistic representations at the lexical level. It suggested that the relationship between these abilities arises because performance in all three tasks is dependent on the integrity of linguistic knowledge, especially the long-term phonological knowledge embodied in the connection weights from the lexical to the

sublexical levels of representation. It has remained the only implemented computational model that directly addresses the relationships between verbal short-term memory and lexical processing and learning, and the only implemented model to address issues of serial ordering at both the lexical and sublexical levels.

It seems intuitively obvious why there might be a relationship between nonword repetition and word learning; after all, every known word was once a nonword to the learner, so we might expect greater facility in processing nonwords to lead to greater facility in eventually learning them. But what is the relationship between nonwords and immediate serial memory? Why are these abilities correlated? Our computational model offered one account: Nonword repetition and verbal short-term memory both rely on the integrity of phonological knowledge (Gupta, 1996b) and so these abilities are correlated during development, as phonological knowledge is developing.

However, another possibility is that a nonword is literally processed like a list when it is first encountered; this notion is implicit in some accounts of the phonological loop (e.g., Baddeley et al., 1998), although it has not previously been made explicit. If this were the case, it would make sense that sequencing mechanisms similar to those underlying recall of a list of verbal stimuli in a typical immediate serial recall task might also be engaged in recall of the sequence of sounds comprising a nonword; this would provide a simple explanation of the relationships observed between immediate serial recall and nonword repetition.

How might we examine such a hypothesis? One of the hallmark characteristics of performance in immediate serial recall tasks is the presence of primacy and recency effects that result in a bowed serial position curve. If mechanisms similar to those underlying immediate serial recall are operative in the repetition of nonwords, we would expect to observe serial position effects in repetition of the sequence of sounds comprising nonwords. This raises the question of what might constitute the "list items" in a nonword. There is considerable evidence to suggest that the syllable, rather than the phoneme, is a natural unit of

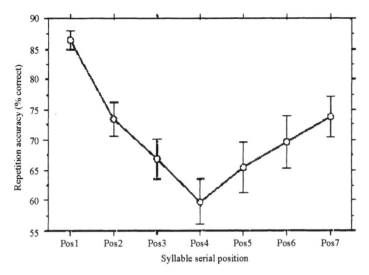

Figure 2. *Primacy and recency effects in repetition of four-syllable nonwords (results of Experiment 3, Gupta, in press).*

phonological analysis (e.g., Jusczyk, 1986, 1997; Massaro, 1989). It therefore seems plausible that, if nonwords are in some sense lists, the list items are syllables. Therefore, it should be possible to detect effects of syllable serial position on repetition of polysyllabic nonwords.

We conducted three experiments to test this prediction (Gupta, in press). Experiment 1 demonstrated significant primacy and recency effects in repetition of four-syllable nonwords. Experiments 2 and 3 showed that these effects were not due to the controlled duration of the nonwords, nor to the requirements of concurrent articulation, nor to the procedure by which nonwords were created. Figure 2 shows the results of Experiment 3, which used seven-syllable nonwords. Both primacy and recency effects were statistically significant (Gupta, in press).

These results suggest a possible revision of the computational model described earlier (Gupta, 1995, 1996b; Gupta & MacWhinney, 1997), to have the conceptual structure shown in Figure 3. For our present purposes, the key aspect of the reformulation is the addition of direct short-term connections from the sequence memory to the sublexical level of representation, which introduces a direct role for the sequence memory in temporarily

maintaining and repeating the sequence of sublexical constituents (i.e., syllables) that comprise an individual nonword. This would offer a simple account of the finding of primacy and recency effects in repetition of individual polysyllabic nonwords: They arise for the same reason as in serial recall of lists of lexical items, because of the involvement of the sequence memory at both levels.

The original model also allowed for serial position effects in repetition of individual nonwords,

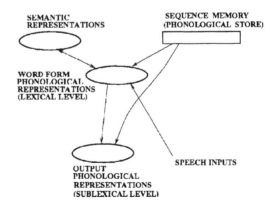

Figure 3. *Revised model of immediate serial recall, nonword repetition, and word learning (Gupta, in press).*

but attributed them to independent serial order encoding mechanisms contained within each word form level representation, rather than to the sequence memory. Which of the two accounts is to be preferred? The two formulations of the model can be distinguished by differing predictions with regard to correlations between immediate serial recall, nonword repetition, and word learning. The earlier formulation offered an account of the developmentally observed correlations between these measures, but predicted that these correlations would not persist in adulthood. In that model, as noted briefly above, the correlations between these abilities arose from the development of the linguistic system; as this system is no longer developing in adulthood, there is a predicted loss of correlations. The revised formulation predicts that such correlations will obtain not only developmentally, but also in adulthood because of the direct involvement of the sequence memory in sequencing at both the lexical and sublexical levels. Correlations between immediate serial recall, nonword repetition, and word learning in adults would thus serve to discriminate between the two models.

Two experiments designed to investigate this issue (Gupta, 2003). established that the developmental association between word learning, nonword repetition, and immediate serial recall extends into adulthood. The results are shown in Table 1, which compares the two experiments in Gupta with the developmental correlations (e.g., Gathercole, Willis, Baddeley, & Emslie, 1994). These experiments thus supported the revised model over the original model.

The correlations between nonword repetition, immediate serial recall, and word learning suggest that the relationships between these abilities may be a fundamental aspect of the human cognitive architecture, holding up as they do in normal children (e.g., Gathercole et al., 1994) and normal adults (Gupta, 2003), and under conditions of delayed linguistic development in children (e.g., Gathercole & Baddeley, 1990a) and under neurological insult in adults (e.g., Baddeley, 1993; Baddeley et al., 1988). The revised version of our model in effect incorporates such a view, in that there is a functional relationship between the abilities, all of which invoke the same sequencing mechanisms. But how robust are these correlations?

Little is known about the impact of early neurological injury on the development of these abilities. In the case of early lesions, there is a real possibility for remission of deficits as a result of developmental neural plasticity. Previous studies of the development of language in children with early focal lesions suggest that there is a generally favourable prognosis for language acquisition, although this is accompanied by selective deficits

Table 1. *Correlations between nonword repetition, immediate serial recall, and word learning in children and adults*

Correlation between	Gathercole et al. (1994)				Correlation between	Gupta (2003) (Adults)		Gupta et al. (in press) (5–10 years)	
	4 yrs	5 yrs	8 yrs	13 yrs		Expt 1	Expt 2	Exptl	Control
Span & CN rep					Span & NWR				
Simple	.520‡	.667‡	.445†	.320‡	Simple	.409‡	.363†	.891**	.522**
Partial					Partial	.314†	.267†	.658†	
Span & vocab					Span & WL				
Simple	.284†	.376‡	.355‡	.450‡	Simple	.388†	.373†	.898**	.447**
Partial	.107	.122	.266†	.390‡	Partial	.284†	.281†	.804*	
Vocab & CN rep					WL & NWR				
Simple	.413‡	.419‡	.284†	.390‡	Simple	.357†	.353†	.798‡	.657**
Partial	.397‡	.387‡	.151	.370‡	Partial	.236	.252	.600	

† $p < .05$; ‡ $p < .01$; * $p < .005$; ** $p < .001$.

or delays, especially in the more complex aspects of language processing (e.g., Aram, Ekelman, Rose, & Whitaker, 1985; Aram, Ekelman, & Whitaker, 1986; Lenneberg, 1967; MacWhinney, Feldman, Sacco, & Valdès-Pérez, 2000; Marchman, Miller, & Bates, 1991; Thal, Marchman, Stiles, Trauner, Nass, & Bates, 1991). If the relationship between nonword repetition, immediate serial recall, and word learning is indeed a fundamental functional aspect of cognition, we would expect relationships between them to obtain even following early injury across a variety of lesion sites.

Gupta et al. (in press) examined this question by administering tests of vocabulary learning, nonword repetition, and immediate serial recall to two groups of children aged 5 through 10 years. One group of 11 children had suffered perinatal brain injury that resulted in focal lesions; all but two of the lesions were to the left hemisphere, but across a variety of sites. The second group consisted of age-matched controls. The experimental group of children was part of a large-scale investigation, other aspects of which were reported in MacWhinney et al. (2000). It was therefore possible to compare results from the present investigations with a broader profile of results that has been established for the same children. Table 1 shows the patterns of correlation, both simple and partial, between these abilities in the experimental and control groups in the Gupta et al. study and also summarises developmental results for normally developing children (e.g., Gathercole et al., 1994). The results suggest that the relationships between digit span, nonword repetition, and word learning are similar to those observed in the other populations, even under conditions of early brain injury. Given that the lesions in the experimental group were quite widely varied (as detailed in Gupta et al., in press), it seems very unlikely that the brain areas subserving immediate serial recall, nonword repetition, and word learning were uniformly impaired across the experimental group. Gupta et al. therefore suggested that the results were best interpreted as indicating that this triad of abilities is functionally related. These findings thus provide further support for the functional architecture of our revised model.

EFFECTS OF LINGUISTIC VARIABLES ON VERBAL STM

So far, we have emphasised the role of verbal short-term memory mechanisms in lexical processing and learning. However, it is also important to keep in mind that the mechanisms of verbal short-term memory do not operate independently of linguistic representations or the lexical system. Evidence from normal (Hulme et al., 1991) and brain-damaged adults (e.g., R. C. Martin, Shelton, & Yaffee, 1994; Patterson, Graham, & Hodges, 1994) as well as developmental populations (e.g., Gathercole & Martin, 1996) indicates the impact of long-term linguistic knowledge on immediate serial recall and also on nonword repetition (e.g., Gathercole, 1995). These influences include phonological (e.g., Brooks & Watkins, 1990), lexical (Gathercole & Martin, 1996), semantic (Saffran & Marin, 1975; R. C. Martin et al., 1994), and conceptual (Potter, 1993; Saffran & Martin, 1999) aspects of language.

An important aspect of the computational model of Gupta (1995; Gupta & MacWhinney, 1997) was its suggestion that nonword repetition, immediate serial recall, and word learning each depend crucially on the strength of long-term phonological knowledge in the lexical system. Additionally, through interactive connections between phonological and semantic representations, this model allows for the influence of semantic factors on word repetition (e.g., imageability effects). Thus, it is quite conceivable that the mechanisms of verbal short-term memory may themselves draw on aspects of the linguistic system, rather than consisting of an isolated verbal short-term memory buffer that stores or temporarily maintains traces derived from a completely separate lexical system. That is, although one aspect of the functional relationship between these abilities is that they share a dependence on the serial ordering mechanisms of the sequence memory or phonological store, they are also related in that they depend on the fundamentals of lexical processing. A similar point has been made by Gathercole et al. (1997), who noted that the "phonological store" on which immediate serial recall, nonword repetition, and word learning rely is perhaps better conceived of as a system whose performance depends on both a specialised short-term sequence memory and the activation of representations in the lexical system. This notion is akin to formulations of the relation between linguistic processing and storage advanced by Cowan (1988), Crosson (1992), Ruchkin et al. (in press), and others.

Focusing on the linguistic contribution to verbal STM and serial order, N. Martin and Saffran found that performance on tests of lexical-semantic processing is strongly associated with primacy in immediate recall, while performance on tests of phonological processing ability is associated with recency. In that study, Martin and Saffran tested 15 aphasic subjects on one- and two-word strings varied for frequency and imageability. The word pairs were sufficiently taxing to these subjects' spans to reveal primacy and recency effects and their associations with semantic and phonological processing ability. We recently replicated this finding with a larger group of aphasic subjects with a wider range of span capacity (1–4 items) and aphasia severity (N. Martin & Ayala, 2003; N. Martin et al., 2002), which enabled us to observe associations between lexical processing and serial position effects at longer string lengths. As N. Martin and Saffran (1997) observed, performance on lexical semantic tests correlated with primacy in retrieval of phonemes within a single word and words within a two-word string.

N. Martin and et al. (2002) offered an account of the influences of linguistic processing on serial position effects within an interactive activation model of word processing that illustrates how the temporal course in which phonological and semantic representations are activated in a repetition span task affects the probabilities that words from different serial positions will be recalled. Their account assumes an interactive activation model based on Dell and O'Seaghdha, (1992) but with modifications introduced by Foygel and Dell (2000) that allowed for lesions of semantic-lexical and lexical phonological mappings instead of global lesions. For the present account, we will make the further assumption that deficits in

mapping involve decay rate rather than reduced connection weight. Also, this account of linguistic influences on serial position is an elaboration of the contribution of the word processing components of Gupta's model above. It does not address the sequence memory's involvement in maintaining serial order, but assumes that linguistic processes work in conjunction with the action of a sequence memory to encode serial order.

When activation spreads between levels of representations within an interactive activation model of word processing, a series of feedforward-feedback cycles of activation are set into motion. These cycles of spreading activation serve to maintain the activation of a word's lexical representation over the course of speech comprehension or production. In the repetition task, lexical and semantic representations of words are activated after phonological representations. The cumulative effect of many interactive spreading activation cycles is that words in a sequence will have different proportions of semantic and phonological support. All things being otherwise equal, the first word in a sequence will have the greatest amount of semantic activation accumulated over the course of the span task, increasing its relative probability of being recalled (see Figure 4).

If activation of semantic representations decays too quickly, the lexical representations of initial words in an input string will not benefit from accumulating semantic support of these words and will be less active at recall (Figure 5). If activation of phonological representations decays too quickly, feedback from activated semantic representations will keep initial words active. This support from semantic feedback is *weakest at the end of the list*. Under conditions of rapid phonological decay, then, final words in a sequence would be supported by weak semantic support and recently activated but rapidly decaying phonological activation (Figure 6). Compared to earlier activated items with accumulated semantic support (from feedforward-feedback cycles) the probability of retrieving these final items would be lowered. These same principles would apply in repetition of nonwords or nonword sequences, but in that case, initial segments of a nonword or initial nonwords

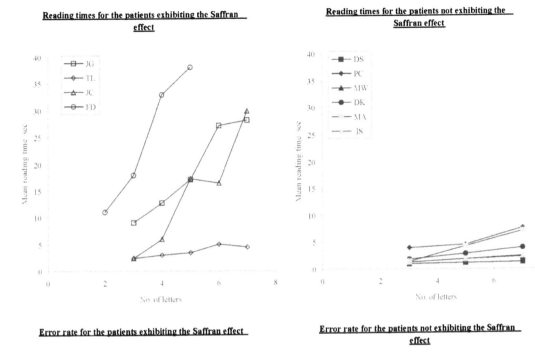

Reading times for the patients exhibiting the Saffran effect

Reading times for the patients not exhibiting the Saffran effect

Error rate for the patients exhibiting the Saffran effect

Error rate for the patients not exhibiting the Saffran effect

Figure 4. *Hypothesised activation of phonological* ←→ *lexical and lexical* ←→ *semantic mappings of word representations at time of recall in a three-word repetition span task.*

in a sequence would normally receive extra support from spreading of activation between phonological and lexical levels.

An important implication of these data and the model is that the linguistic contribution to serial order is not linguistic per se, but is more related to processes that enable access to linguistic knowledge. This point is further supported by several findings and observations. First, we would expect primacy in nonword span to be less robust than in word span overall, because there is altogether less support from linguistic processes, but it should not be reduced in relation to recency. This was confirmed in one of our recent studies (N. Martin, 2003) examining recall of words and nonwords by normal adult subjects (aged 20–70 years). We found that overall, more items were recalled in word span than in nonword span, but primacy (as measured by % correct in position 1 / % correct in all positions) was no greater for words than nonwords. A similar finding was obtained when the

same word and nonword span task was administered to 13 adult aphasic speakers. We found no difference in this group between word and nonword span tasks in either primacy: two words, $t(12) = -0.58$. $p = .47$; three words, $t(12) = -1.67$, $p = .12$: or recency effects: two words, $t(12) = -0.65$, $p = .52$; three words, $t(12) = 0.52$, $p = .62$.

We have shown that in aphasia, poor performance on tasks measuring lexical-semantic ability is associated with loss of primacy in serial recall tasks (N. Martin & Saffran, 1997). In semantic dementia, a disorder leading to degradation of representations, this same selective depression of recall at primacy positions is not observed (Knott, Patterson, & Hodges, 1997). This population performs similarly to aphasic patients with lexical-semantic impairment in that they both fail tests that require processing semantic information about words. However, the origins of their failures on these measures are very different. In cognitive terms, this difference is typically characterised in

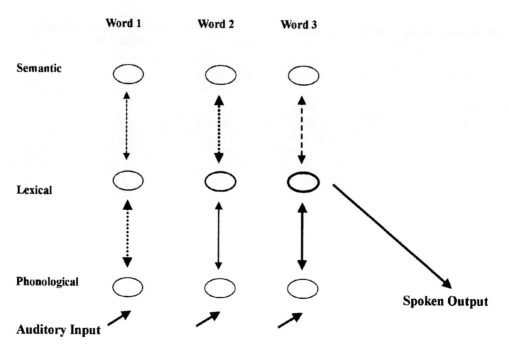

Figure 5. *Hypothesised activation of phonological ←→ lexical and lexical ← → semantic mappings of word representations at time of recall in a three-word repetition span task under conditions of impaired lexical ←→ semantic connections.*

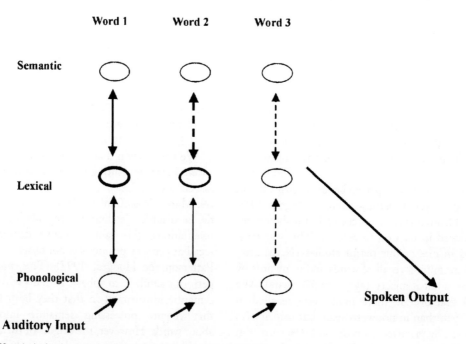

Figure 6. *Hypothesised activation of phonological ←→ lexical and lexical ← → semantic mappings of word representations at time of recall in a three-word repetition span task under conditions of impaired phonological ←→ lexical connections.*

terms of access vs. knowledge deficits; aphasics have difficulty accessing semantics and individuals with semantic dementia experience a degradation of the semantic representations themselves (see discussion below). If the association between primacy and performance on lexical-semantic tasks were related to the integrity of semantic knowledge per se, we would expect a loss of primacy in the verbal span performance of these individuals. This is not observed, providing further evidence that primacy is supported by the integrity of processes that access and maintain representations of words rather than the long-term semantic knowledge of words.

Our account of the lexical-semantic deficit in aphasia is one of access caused by premature decay of activation spreading to lexical-semantic representations. This account predicts that imageability and frequency variables associated with lexical and semantic representations should *not* lead to selective increases or reductions in recall of items from primacy portions of the input string in a span task. Rather, their effects should be constant across the word string with no *additional* advantage in recalling primacy portions of the word string. We investigated this hypothesis in a repetition span task that varied imageability and frequency effects on serial position in an immediate serial recall task (19 aphasic participants) and found that both variables affected overall accuracy of recall. Span was greater on average for high- than low-imageability words (2.62 vs. 2.21, $p < .0045$) and greater for high- than low-frequency words (2.53 vs. 2.25, $p < .0002$). Importantly, the difference between accuracy on high- and low-imageability words and high- and low-frequency words was significant for *all positions* of the input string. There was no additional advantage related to imageability or frequency at initial positions. Thus, recall of initial items in a list does not seem to benefit because of lexical or semantic status per se, but rather because of the temporal course over which these representations are activated and its effect on the cumulative activation support to the maintenance of these words during an immediate recall task.

How does the interactive activation model account for the observation that repetition span in semantic dementia does not suffer from loss of primacy in the way that semantic access aphasia does, but in both disorders, word retrieval is impaired? In a repetition task, phonological activation spreads upward to lexical and then semantic representations and then feeds back down to lexical and phonological representations again. In naming, conceptual semantic representations send activation to corresponding and related lexical nodes and then to phonological representations. When impairment affects the mapping between lexical and semantic representations (as in aphasia), this should disrupt semantic encoding and its support to short-term maintenance of words and subsequent learning of new verbal information. This should result in a reduction of imageability effects and tendency to show reduced primacy. It should also affect the output mapping between semantic and lexical representations and disrupt naming. When the conceptual representations that constitute semantic representations are degrading, as presumed in the case of semantic dementia, spreading activation from phonological input should access lexical and semantic representations of words with varying stability. Those semantic representations that are only partially degraded should provide support to primacy that would not be evident in an access impairment. This support, however, would be dependent on the severity of degradation; if substantial (i.e., if the meaning of these words is no longer "known" to the individual), there would be little support to primacy because there would be no representations for intact access processes to retrieve. Thus, as semantic memory becomes increasingly degraded, we might expect to observe a reduction in primacy in verbal span tasks. In contrast, naming would be disrupted by semantic feature degradation even in milder cases because it is this very stage of processing where naming begins.

In a further set of investigations of how the properties of the lexical processing system impact performance in verbal short-term memory tasks, we have identified a number of associations between word processing measures and immediate verbal span. We began with two word processing measures that engage both semantic and phonological processing, picture naming and auditory lexical decision. We obtained data from 50 subjects on these two tasks as well as on four measures of verbal span: pointing and repetition span for digits and for words. Both the pointing and repetition span tasks involve auditory input of the stimuli to be recalled but differ with respect to the response mode. In the pointing task, the subject hears the sequence of words or digits and points to this same sequence from an array of nine items or nine pictures depicting the objects denoted by the words. The array is rearranged on each trial. In the repetition span task, the heard sequence is repeated immediately by the subject. First, we examined the relationship of two abilities that engage both semantic and phonological processing, word recognition, (auditory lexical decision) and word production (picture naming) with four span measures (pointing and repetition span for digits and for words). Span size was positively correlated with performance on each of these measures (Tables 2 and 3 below). The association of word recognition with span was robust and significant for concrete words and less so for abstract words. It is reasonable to suppose that this difference is most likely to be due to the fact that our span measures used concrete words, although the assumption needs to be investigated.

We used two measures of overall naming ability, percentage correct and percentage of "no response" errors. As the table indicates, all four span measures correlated with our two measures of naming. This finding is not altogether unexpected, although models with separate input and output buffers (e.g., Romani, 1992) might not predict an association between pointing span tasks that require no verbal output and a production task such as naming.

DEFICITS AND RECOVERY IN DEEP DYSPHASIA: A CONTINUUM BETWEEN LEXICAL PROCESSING AND STM

Additional support for a model of qualitative links between word processing and verbal span comes from studies of recovery from acquired language and verbal STM impairments. N. Martin and colleagues (1994, 1996) studied a deep dysphasic subject, NC, whose error pattern in the early stages of his recovery from a stroke included semantic errors in single word repetition. At that time, his repetition and pointing spans for digits or words were limited to a single item. With recovery, NC's span increased to two–three items and, although

Table 2. *Correlations between verbal span measures and measures of auditory word recognition (D-prime scores, n = 50, df = 48)*

Auditory lexical decision measure	Digit point	Word point	Digit repetition	Word repetition
Concrete	.24*	.44**	.32**	.43**
Abstract	.13	.24*	.19	.21
Total	.20	.39**	.27*	.39**

* $p < .05$, one-tailed test; ** $p < .01$, two-tailed test.

Table 3. *Correlations between performance on the Philadelphia Naming Test (percent correct and percent of 'No response' errors) and four measures of verbal span performance (n = 50, df = 48)*

Response type	Digit point	Word point	Digit repetition	Word repetition
Correct	.39**	.52**	.43**	.50**
No response	−.35**	−.37**	−.30**	−.35**

** $p < .01$, two-tailed test.

semantic errors were no longer present in single word repetition, they re-emerged in repetition of two words, particularly in recall of the second word. The Dell model assumes that activation processes that mediate lexical retrieval are regulated by two parameters, connection strength (the rate of activation spread) and decay rate (the rate of activation decline toward resting level). We hypothesised that NC's error pattern resulted from a pathologically rapid decay of primed nodes in the semantic-lexical phonological network. This hypothesis was tested and supported in a series of simulations that successfully reproduced NC's error pattern in *both* naming and repetition, with the same lesion to the model (N. Martin et al., 1994, 1996). The key notion that we have derived from this computational work is that interactive activation in the lexical system constitutes a means of maintaining information over time in the lexical system (via persistence of the activation of representations). That is, it is a form of short-term memory.

Models of this general type have been successfully applied not just to a single case like NC but characterising the deficits of a case series of 21 aphasic subjects (Dell, Schwartz, Martin, Saffran, & Gagnon, 1997). We were able to fit the model to patients' errors in picture naming quite accurately. Analysis of how the model fitted each patient led to a classification scheme in which each patient's deficits could be characterised in terms of two key parameters: connection strength and decay rate. This model consolidated our ideas about the importance of interactive activation in the lexical system as a form of memory, and demonstrated the value of fitting computational models to data from individual aphasic subjects.

Thus in our view, the ability to comprehend or produce single or multiple words is impacted by the severity of the impairment to those spreading activation processes responsible for maintaining activation of the representations of a word. If the impairment is severe enough, activation of representations of even a single word is affected, and disrupts performance on both single and multiple word language tasks (e.g., verbal span). In milder forms of this deficit, activation processes may be adequate to support processing of a single word but not multiple words, giving the appearance of an independent disruption of verbal short-term memory. On this proposed severity continuum, it is the case that all individuals with aphasia should also present with verbal STM deficits, but not all individuals with verbal STM deficits should present with obvious aphasia. In addition to the severity of impairment to activation maintenance, word processing and span impairments vary according to the level(s) of word representation that is affected (e.g., semantic or phonological; R. C. Martin et al., 1994) and the task used to measure span (affecting the linguistic processes deployed, N. Martin, 1999; N. Martin & Ayala, 2003). These variables together determine the activation available to support maintenance of linguistic information in STM.

REFERENCES

Aram, D., Ekelman, B., Rose, D., & Whitaker, H. (1985). Verbal and cognitive sequelae following unilateral lesions acquired in early childhood. *Journal of Clinical and Experimental Neuropsychology, 7*, 55–78.

Aram, D., Ekelman, B., & Whitaker, H. (1986). Spoken syntax in children with acquired unilateral hemisphere lesions. *Brain and Language, 27*, 75–100.

Baddeley, A. D. (1993). Short-term phonological memory and long-term learning: A single case study. *European Journal of Cognitive Psychology, 5*, 129–148.

Baddeley, A. D., Gathercole, S. E., & Papagno, C. (1998). The phonological loop as a language learning device. *Psychological Review, 105*, 158–173.

Baddeley, A. D., Papagno, C., & Vallar, G. (1988). When long-term learning depends on short-term storage. *Journal of Memory and Language, 27*, 586–595.

Brooks J. O., III, & Watkins, M. J. (1990). Further evidence of the intricacy of memory span. *Journal of Experimental Psychology: Learning, Memory, and Cognition, 6*, 1134–1141.

Brown, G. D. A., & Hulme, C. (1996). Nonword repetition, STM, and word age-of-acquisition. In S. E. Gathercole (Ed.), *Models of short-term memory* (pp. 129–148). Hove, UK: Psychology Press.

Brown, G. D. A., Preece, T., & Hulme, C. (2000). Oscillator-based memory for serial order. *Psychological Review, 107*, 127–181.

Burgess, N., & Hitch, G. J. (1992). Toward a network model of the articulatory loop. *Journal of Memory and Language, 31*, 429–460.

Burgess, N., & Hitch, G. J. (1999). Memory for serial order: A network model of the phonological loop and its timing. *Psychological Review, 106*, 551–581.

Cowan, N. (1988). Evolving conceptions of memory storage, selective attention, and their mutual constraints within the human information processing system. *Psychological Bulletin, 104*, 163–191.

Cowan, N. (1995). *Attention and memory: An integrated framework* [Oxford Psychology Series, No. 26]. New York: Oxford University Press.

Craik, F. I. M., & Lockhart, R. S. (1972). Levels of processing: A framework for memory research. *Journal of Verbal Learning and Verbal Behavior, 11*, 671–684.

Crosson, B. (1992). *Subcortical functions in language and memory*. New York: Guilford Press.

Dell, G. S. (1986). A spreading activation theory of retrieval in sentence producion. *Psychological Review, 93*, 283–321.

Dell, G. S., Schwartz, M. F., Martin, N., Saffran, E. M., & Gagnon, D. A. (1997). Lexical access in normal and aphasic speakers. *Psychological Review, 104*, 801–838.

Dell, G. S., & O'Seaghdha, P. G. (1992). Stages in lexical access in language production. *Cognition, 42*, 287–314.

Dunn, L., & Dunn, L. (1981). *Peabody Picture Vocabulary Test—Revised*. Circle Pines, MN: American Guidance Service.

Foygel, D., & Dell, G. S. (2000). Models of impaired lexical access in speech production. *Journal of Memory and Language, 43*, 182–216.

Freedman, M. L., & Martin, R. C. (2001). Dissociable components of short-term memory and their relation to long-term learning. *Cognitive Neuropsychology, 18*, 193–226.

Gathercole, S. E., & Baddeley, A. D. (1989). Evaluation of the role of phonological STM in the development of vocabulary in children: A longitudinal study. *Journal of Memory and Language, 28*, 200–213.

Gathercole, S. E., & Baddeley, A. D. (1990a). Phonological memory deficits in language-disordered children: Is there a causal connection? *Journal of Memory and Language, 29*, 336–360.

Gathercole, S. E., & Baddeley, A. D. (1990b). The role of phonological memory in vocabulary acquisition: A study of young children learning arbitrary names of toys. *British Journal of Psychology, 81*, 439–454.

Gathercole, S. E., & Baddeley, A. D. (1993). *Working memory and language*. Hove, UK: Lawrence Erlbaum Associates Ltd.

Gathercole, S. E., Hitch, G. J., Service, E., & Martin, A. J. (1997). Short-term memory and new word learning in children. *Developmental Psychology, 33*, 966–979.

Gathercole, S., & Martin, A. (1996). Interactive processes in phonological memory. In S. E. Gathercole (Ed.), *Models of working memory* (pp. 149–178) Hove, UK: Psychology Press.

Gathercole, S. E., Service, E., Hitch, G. J., Adams, A.-M., & Martin, A. J. (1999). Phonological short-term memory and vocabulary development: Further evidence on the nature of the relationship. *Applied Cognitive Psychology, 13*, 65–77.

Gathercole, S. E., Willis, C., Emslie, H., & Baddeley, A. D. (1992). Phonological memory and vocabulary development during the early school years: A longitudinal study. *Developmental Psychology, 28*, 887–898.

Gathercole, S. E., Willis, C. S., Baddeley, A. D., & Emslie, H. (1994). The children's test of nonword repetition: A test of phonological working memory. *Memory, 2*, 103–127.

Gupta, P. (1995). *Word learning and immediate serial recall: Toward an integrated account*. PhD thesis, Department of Psychology, Carnegie Mellon University, Pittsburgh, PA.

Gupta, P. (1996a). Verbal short-term memory and language processing: A computational model. *Brain and Language, 55*, 194–197.

Gupta, P. (1996b). Word learning and verbal short-term memory: A computational account. In G. W. Cottrell (Ed.), *Proceedings of the Eighteenth Annual Meeting of the Cognitive Science Society* (pp. 189–194). Mahwah, NJ: Lawrence Erlbaum Associates Inc.

Gupta, P. (2003). Examining the relationship between word learning, nonword repetition, and immediate serial recall in adults. *Quarterly Journal of Experimental Psychology, 56A*, 1213–1236.

Gupta, P. (in press). Primacy and recency in nonword repetition. *Memory*.

Gupta, P., & MacWhinney, B. (1997). Vocabulary acquisition and verbal short-term memory: Computational and neural bases. *Brain and Language, 59*, 267–333.

Gupta, P., MacWhinney, B., Feldman, H., & Sacco, K. (in press). Phonological memory and vocabulary learning in children with focal lesions. *Brain and Language.*

Hartley, T., & Houghton, G. (1996). A linguistically constrained model of short-term memory for non-words. *Journal of Memory and Language, 35*, 1–31.

Hulme, C., Maughan, S., & Brown, G. D. A. (1991). Memory for familiar and unfamiliar words: Evidence for a long-term memory contribution to short-term memory span. *Journal of Memory and Language, 30*, 685–701.

Jusczyk, P. W. (1986). Toward a model of the development of speech perception. In J. S. Perkell & D. H. Klatt (Eds.), *Invariance and variability in speech processes.* Mahwah, NJ: Lawrence Erlbaum Associates Inc.

Jusczyk, P. W. (1997). *The discovery of spoken language.* Cambridge, MA: MIT Press.

Knott, R., Patterson, K., & Hodges, J. R. (1997). Lexical and semantic binding effects in short-term memory: Evidence from semantic dementia. *Cognitive Neuropsychology, 14*, 1165–1218.

Lenneberg, E. H. (1967). *Biological foundations of language.* New York: Wiley.

MacWhinney, B., Feldman, H., Sacco, K., & Valdès-Pèrez, R. (2000). Online measures of basic language skills in children with early focal brain lesions. *Brain and Language, 71*, 400–431.

Marchman, V., Miller, R., & Bates, E. (1991). Babble and first words in children with focal brain injury. *Applied Psycholinguistics, 12*, 1–22.

Martin, N. (1999). Measurements of auditory-verbal STM abilities in aphasic subjects with word retrieval deficits. *Brain and Language, 69*, 358–361.

Martin, N. (2003). *Word and nonword span in normal and language impaired adults.* Manuscript in preparation.

Martin, N., & Ayala, J. (2003). *Measurements of auditory-verbal STM in aphasia: Effects of task, item and word processing impairment.* Manuscript submitted for publication.

Martin, N., Ayala, J., & Saffran, E. M. (2002). Lexical influences on serial position effects in verbal STM span in aphasia. *Brain and Langauge, 83*, 92–95.

Martin, N., Dell, G. S., Saffran, E. M., & Schwartz, M. F. (1994). Origins of paraphasias in deep dysphasia: Testing the consequences of a decay impairment to an interactive spreading activation model of language. *Brain and Language, 47*, 609–660.

Martin, R. C., Freedman, M. L. (2001). Neuropsychology of verbal working memory: Ins and outs of phonological and lexical-semantic retention. In H. L. Roediger, J. S. Nairne, I. Neath, & A. M.

Surprenant (Eds.), *The nature of remembering: Essays in honor of Robert G. Crowder.* Washington, DC: American Psychological Association.

Martin, N., & Saffran, E. M. (1997). Language and auditory-verbal short-term memory impairments: Evidence for common underlying processes. *Cognitive Neuropsychology, 14*, 641–682.

Martin, N., & Saffran, E. M. (1999). Effects of word processing and short-term memory deficits on verbal learning: Evidence from aphasia. *International Journal of Psychology, 34*, 330–346.

Martin, N., Saffran, E. M., & Dell, G. S. (1996). Recovery in deep dysphasia: Evidence for a relation between auditory-verbal STM capacity and lexical errors in repetition. *Brain and Language, 52*, 83–113.

Martin, R. C., Shelton, J., & Yaffee, L. (1994). Language processing and working memory: Neuropsychological evidence for separate phonological and semantic capacities, *Journal of Memory and Language, 33*, 83–111.

Massaro, D. W. (1989). *Experimental psychology.* Orlando, FL: Harcourt Brace Jovanovich.

Michas, I. C., & Henry, L. A. (1994). The link between phonological memory and vocabulary acquisition. *British Journal of Developmental Psychology, 12*, 147–164.

Page, M. P. A., & Norris, D. (1998). The primacy model: A new model of immediate serial recall. *Psychological Review, 105*, 761–781.

Patterson, K. E., Graham, N., & Hodges, J. R. (1994). The impact of semantic memory loss on phonological representations. *Journal of Cognitive Neuroscience, 6*, 57–69.

Potter, M. C. (1993). Very short-term conceptual memory. *Memory & Cognition, 21*, 156–161.

Romani, C. (1992). Are there distinct input and output buffers? Evidence from an aphasic patient with an impaired output buffer. *Language and Cognitive Processes, 7*, 131–162.

Ruchkin, D. S., Grafman, J., Cameron, K., & Berndt, R. S. (in press). Working memory retention systems: A state of activated long-term memory. *Brain and Behavioral Sciences.*

Saffran, E. M. (1990). Short-term memory impairment and language processing. In A. Caramazza (Ed.), *Cognitive neuropsychology and neurolinguistics: Advances in models of cognitive function and impairment.* Mahwah, NJ: Lawrence Erlbaum Associates Inc.

Saffran, E. M., & Martin, N. (1999). Meaning but not words: Neuropsychological evidence for very short-term conceptual memory. In V. Coltheart (Ed.),

Fleeting memories: Cognition of brief visual stimuli. Cambridge, MA: MIT Press.

Service, E. (1992). Phonology, working memory, and foreign-language learning. *Quarterly Journal of Experimental Psychology, 45A*, 21–50.

Service, E., & Kohonen, V. (1995). Is the relation between phonological memory and foreign language learning accounted for by vocabulary acquisition? *Applied Psycholinguistics, 16*, 155–172.

Thal, D., Marchman, V., Stiles, J., Trauner, D., Nass, R., & Bates, E. (1991). Early lexical development in children with focal brain injury. *Brain and Language, 40*, 491–527.

Vousden, J. I., Brown, G. D. A., & Harley, T. A. (2000). Serial control of phonology in speech production: A hierarchical model. *Cognitive Psychology, 41*, 101–175.

Warrington, E. K., Logue, V., & Pratt, R. T. C. (1971). The anatomical localisation of selective impairment of short-term memory. *Neuropsychologia, 9*, 377–387.

Warrington, E. K., & Shallice, T. (1969). The selective impairment of auditory verbal short-term memory. *Brain, 92*, 885–896.

COGNITIVE NEUROPSYCHOLOGY, 2004, 21 (2/3/4) 229–244

COMPREHENSION OF REVERSIBLE SENTENCES IN APHASIA: THE EFFECTS OF VERB MEANING

Rita Sloan Berndt, Charlotte C. Mitchum, Martha W. Burton,
and Anne N. Haendiges

University of Maryland School of Medicine, Baltimore, USA

Comprehension of semantically reversible active and passive voice sentences was tested in a timed sentence/picture verification task. Three sets of six verbs were identified that incorporated different features of meaning relevant to the assignment of nouns to the thematic role of agent. Normal control subjects showed an effect of verb set on their response times, with significant effects between sets in the predicted direction. A group of aphasic patients without sentence comprehension disorder also showed a significant effect of verb set despite long and variable response times. A group of patients with reversible comprehension disorder in screening tasks showed weaker effects, primarily because of the use of consistent response biases that ignored the sentence verb. An experimental treatment of active/passive comprehension was conducted with two of these latter patients; one patient reached ceiling in post-testing, and the other showed significant improvement but demonstrated residual comprehension problems that indicated differences across verb sets. Results support the critical importance of verb meaning to normal and aphasic sentence comprehension.

The study of sentence comprehension in aphasia has focused on the ability of patients with intact comprehension of single words to understand sentences that are "semantically reversible." Such sentences, which can take a variety of structural forms, typically employ agentive verbs and contain more than one noun that could plausibly fill the thematic role of agent. A determination of sentence meaning—understanding who is doing what to whom—requires interpretation of sentence structure as well as of word meaning. Many studies of reversible comprehension impairments have concentrated on aphasic patients with the "agrammatic" pattern of sentence production,

although other types of aphasic speakers can demonstrate this comprehension pattern (e.g., Berndt, Mitchum, & Wayland, 1997; Caramazza & Zurif, 1976).

In work spanning almost 25 years, Saffran and colleagues have conducted numerous studies of sentence comprehension in aphasia that have contributed to our understanding of the disorder (Saffran, 2001). Many studies of this issue have focused on complex sentences, such as those with relative clauses ("the monkey that the elephant hit is brown," e.g., Caramazza & Zurif, 1976) and clefted elements. Relative complexity has even been argued to be a major determinant of aphasic

---

Correspondence should be addressed to Rita Sloan Berndt, Department of Neurology, University of Maryland School of Medicine, 22 South Greene Street, Baltimore, Maryland 21201, USA (Email: rberndt@umaryland.edu).

This research was supported by grant number R01-DC00262 from the National Institute on Deafness and Other Communication Disorders to the University of Maryland School of Medicine. A portion of this report was presented at the Academy of Aphasia (2000) in Montreal, Canada. The authors are grateful to Sarah Wayland, PhD, for assistance in the development of the stimulus materials. We are most grateful to the subjects who participated in the study.

DOI:10.1080/02643290342000456

performance (Miyake, Carpenter, & Just, 1994). However, in a seminal study with agrammatic patients, Schwartz, Saffran, and Marin (1980) demonstrated that such patients often failed to interpret even simple active and locative sentences correctly. This paper provided the basis for many follow-up studies of these issues using one-clause sentences tested with a sentence/picture matching task, and it also suggested that the comprehension impairment did not emanate from failure to interpret grammatical morphemes (such as "that") in complex sentences (see Saffran, 1982). However, comprehension was shown in a post hoc analysis to be affected by the meaning of the verbs used in the test materials, with purely relational verbs (such as "follow") giving rise to twice the error rate of verbs that were "inherent" in the agent (such as "applaud," Saffran, Schwartz, & Marin, 1980).

The earliest interpretation of reversible comprehension impairment in agrammatic patients was that such patients have difficulty computing a syntactic structure, either because of problems processing grammatical markers (Bradley, Garrett, & Zurif, 1980), or because of a more generalised syntactic impairment implicating word order (Berndt & Caramazza, 1980). Saffran and colleagues presented a major challenge to such interpretations, however, by demonstrating that patients with poor understanding of reversible sentences performed well on tasks requiring judgment of sentence grammaticality (Linebarger, Schwartz, & Saffran, 1983). These findings, which have been widely replicated, indicate that many patients can generate a correct syntactic analysis of a sentence type while failing to interpret its meaning correctly. Saffran and colleagues have argued that, rather than reflecting a syntactic deficit, comprehension breakdown arises in some aspect of the process of "mapping" from syntactic structure to thematic roles such as agent of the action (Linebarger et al., 1983; Schwartz, Linebarger, & Saffran, 1985). Such difficulties might implicate whatever procedures are involved in aligning syntactic constituents and thematic roles, or they may reflect impairment of verb-specific information about how a verb's arguments are associated with its thematic roles. In either case, the problem appears to emanate from failure to integrate aspects of (at least grossly intact) syntactic structure with semantic information.

In an elegant demonstration of such failure of integration, Saffran and colleagues used a sentence plausibility task employing distinct types of violations of relations between verbs' thematic roles and nouns that could potentially fill those roles (Saffran, Schwartz, & Linebarger, 1998). Surprisingly, patients had much difficulty rejecting sentences in which only one of the sentence nouns could plausibly fill the thematic role of agent of the action (e.g., "the cheese ate the mouse"), while they were much better able to reject as implausible sentences in which either noun could fill the verb's thematic roles, but which were nonetheless implausible because of the meaning of the proposition as a whole (e.g., "the puppy is carrying the child"). The strong semantic constraints operating in the first type of sentence (i.e., mice can eat, but cheese cannot) apparently outweighed conflicting syntactic cues about which sentence noun was the agent of the action. The second type of sentence, without such strong semantic constraints to agency (i.e., both puppies and children can carry), were interpreted in accordance with their syntactic structure.

Saffran and colleagues interpreted this finding to be a reflection of patients' tendency to rely on semantic information when syntax and semantics are in conflict (see also Saffran & Schwartz, 1994). Such a tendency may reflect an exacerbation of normal speakers' use of semantic information in the earliest stages of thematic role assignment during comprehension (e.g., MacDonald, Pearlmutter, & Seidenberg, 1994; Tabossi, Spivey-Knowlton, McRae, & Tanenhaus, 1994). For example, there is evidence that the thematic roles associated with specific verbs may carry with them semantic features that are likely to characterise the nouns that fill those roles (McRae, Ferretti, & Amyote, 1997). That is, a verb such as "frighten" fills the thematic role of agent with nouns that are likely to be viewed as mean, scary, ugly, big, etc. (see Table 1 in McRae et al., 1997). Aphasic speakers, whose syntactic processing of sentences may be somewhat weakened (although not abolished), may be more sensitive than normal to the semantic features linking verbs and their thematic roles.

The relevance of these considerations for aphasic performance in the sentence/picture matching task may not be readily apparent, since many studies have taken some pains to assure that the reversible sentences tested contained nouns that could equally plausibly fill the thematic role of agent (Schwartz et al., 1980). Thus, the predictability with which each of two nouns might fill the sentence's thematic roles should be equivalent; in such cases, semantic influences (in the form of role/filler typicality) should not influence comprehension. However, other semantic factors might still influence comprehension of reversible sentences—even those with equi-probable "agent" nouns—when tested in sentence/picture matching.

The idea that there are verb-specific conceptual representations associated with thematic roles, described above, reflects to some extent a linguistic reconsideration of the entire concept of thematic roles, in which the typical thematic role hierarchy (e.g., Jackendoff, 1987) is replaced by prototypical thematic roles. Within this framework, the arguments of a verb may bear either of two "proto-roles" (proto-agent or proto-patient) to different degrees, depending on the distribution of proto-role features entailed by the verb's meaning (Dowty, 1991). For example, the cluster concept "proto-agent" is associated with features such as "volitional involvement in the event or state … sentience … causing an event or change of state in another participant … movement (relative to the position of another participant) … exists independently (of the event named by the verb)" (Dowty, 1991, p. 572). The cluster concept "proto-patient" involves complementary features, such as undergoing a change of state, being stationary relative to the movement of another participant, etc. Verbs may differ in the number of features falling into each of these concept clusters, resulting in more or less clear assignment of arguments to (deep) subject and object.

This view of the relationship between thematic roles and verbs' arguments suggests that the semantics of some verbs will compellingly assign the agent role to the (deep) subject argument, while for other verbs this assignment may be semantically less clear, thereby shifting more of the interpretive burden to syntactic analysis. If so, the specific verbs used in tests of sentence comprehension could affect how easy or difficult it may be to identify the agent in reversible sentences, as suggested by Saffran et al. (1980). It is also possible that the manner in which actions are depicted in tests of sentence/picture matching could enhance, or mitigate, these verb-specific tendencies toward assignment of roles.

Tests of sentence comprehension in aphasia have not controlled for such factors, and many have not even identified the verbs used in comprehension tests (but see Jones, 1984, for a notable exception). We have previously used the features described by Dowty as being associated with the proto-agent role in a post-hoc analysis of the sentence comprehension performance of a patient who, following an experimental treatment that resulted in significant improvement in comprehension to levels approaching normal, still failed to understand sentences containing certain verbs (Berndt & Mitchum, 1998). The sentences that this patient failed after treatment contained verbs whose meanings entailed few proto-agent features. These observations motivated the present study, in which we set out to determine whether a verb hierarchy based on differences in proto-agent/proto-patient features would affect comprehension performance for semantically reversible active and passive voice sentences. Since these features might produce detectable effects on even normal listeners' comprehension of reversible sentences, we designed the experiment so that reaction time data could be collected.

In addition to a group of normal control subjects, we tested two groups of aphasic patients. One aphasic group showed no selective difficulty understanding semantically reversible sentences, and they demonstrated good comprehension in clinical testing. These patients were included to explore the possible effects of general processing limitations, including increased response times, on the factors of interest. The second patient group showed relatively intact comprehension of sentences tested with lexical distractors, and they could judge sentence grammaticality, but they performed at chance levels with semantically reversible materials.

TIMED SENTENCE/PICTURE VERIFICATION

Methods

Subjects

Control subjects. Nine neurologically intact adults (three male and six female) were paid to participate in this and a number of other language experiments conducted over a period of several weeks. Mean age of the group was 50 years (range = 36–73); mean education was 14.6 years (range = 9–18).

Aphasic patients. Eleven chronic aphasic patients were tested. Descriptive information is provided in Table 1. These patients demonstrated a variety of aphasic symptoms and a range of clinical types of aphasia. However, all patients were free from uncompensated neglect or other impairments that

might interfere with picture analysis, and all showed good auditory comprehension (> .87) of picturable single words on the PALPA high imageability synonyms subtest (Kay, Lesser, & Coltheart, 1992). These patients were divided into two subgroups based on their sentence comprehension on the Philadelphia Comprehension Battery (Saffran, Schwartz, Linebarger, Martin, & Bochetto, 1988). This unpublished test includes two sentence/picture matching subtests in which patients must select one of two pictures that corresponds to a spoken sentence. Ten tokens of six sentence types (including active and passive voice and more complex sentences) are tested against lexical distractors in one subtest (lexical), and against distractor pictures that represent a reversal of thematic roles in another (reversible) subtest. This test battery also includes two sets of grammaticality judgments. The more difficult set, reported here, includes 60 items probing detection of six different structural violations (e.g., "the boy was carried the man").

One group of five patients, labelled the "good comprehenders," scored well above chance on sentences with both reversible and with lexical

Table 1. *Description of patients tested, grouped by comprehension of semantically reversible sentences*

Patient	Age at onset	Yrs post onset	Education (yrs)	Occupation	Philadelphia sentence comprehension[a]	
					Lexical	Reversible
Good comprehenders						
JH	53	5	16	Engineer	1.00	1.00
BN	55	3	12	Executive	1.00	.90
RS	53	2	20	Toxicologist	1.00	.85
DS	46	5	10	Machine operator	.98	.88
CF	59	2	18	Engineer	1.00	.92
Poor comprehenders						
ML	46	15	18	Judge/attorney	.97	.67
JQ	59	1	16	Executive	.93	.67
TP	38	2	12	Machine operator	.98	.70
RE	34	4	12	Librarian	.87	.50
AM	67	1	9	Machine operator	.87	.61
ST	63	1	18	Teacher	.85	.55

[a] Proportion correct on Philadelphia Comprehension Battery, N = 60 per condition.

distractors (.85 correct or greater). The other six patients also performed well with the lexical contrasts (.85 correct or greater), but performed much more poorly with the reversible items. Chi-square analyses conducted on the number correct in the two conditions showed highly significant differences between reversible and lexical subtests for all patients in the "poor comprehenders" group (all two-tailed p-values < .003). In contrast, performance on grammaticality judgments ($N = 60$) was good for all patients who were tested (A-primes ranged from .88–.99; ML and RS were not tested).

Materials

Selection of verbs. An initial set of 58 agentive, transitive verbs was selected from WordNet (Fellbaum, 1998) on the basis that they could plausibly enter into a picturable reversible sentence with two animate nouns, without the necessity of a prepositional phrase. Because of the requirement that verbs be capable of taking animate nouns as agents, all verbs selected entailed three of the properties for proto-agent—sentience, volitional involvement, and existence independent of the event. The important discriminating properties on which verbs were grouped thus involved the extent of relative motion of the participants, and the extent to which the verb's meaning requires a change of state in the undergoer participant. Three sets of six verbs were identified as exhibiting these properties to different extents.

1. Set 1 (bury, wash, kick, shoot, slap and spray): For these verbs, the thematic agent is actively moving, while thematic patient is almost completely stationary; agent causes a clear change of state in patient.

2. Set 2 (drop, lift, shove, trip, shake, drag)[1]: These verbs require relatively little movement by agent, and more movement by patient; agent is still causal and patient affected.

3. Set 3 (pull, push, chase, follow, guide, lead): Both agent and patient are moving for these verbs; both actors participate. The agent is less clearly causal of the event, with minimal change of state in the patient.

Frequency of usage and imageability were not parameters considered in grouping the verbs. Mean cumulative frequencies calculated from the MRC database (Coltheart, 1981) showed that Set 1 verbs were lower in frequency ($M = 20$, $SD = 13$) than Set 2 ($M = 33$, $SD = 30$) or Set 3 ($M = 61$, $SD = 43$). Mean imageability from the same database showed the opposite trend. Set 1 verbs were higher in imagability ($M = 533$, $SD = 26$) than Set 2 ($M = 473$, $SD = 52$) or Set 3 ($M = 452$, $SD = 42$).

Construction of sentences and pictures. Each of the 18 verbs was combined with a pair of nouns (man and woman, or boy and girl) to create two reversible active and two passive sentences (one with the male and one with the female as agent). For example, sentences tested for the verb "bury" were: "the boy is burying the girl"; "the girl is burying the boy"; "the girl is buried by the boy"; and "the boy is buried by the girl." Black-and-white line drawings were prepared by a graphic artist to depict the meaning of each sentence in a context chosen to highlight the characteristics of the verb sets. For example, the Set 1 verb "bury" was tested in the context of a beach scene in which one child "buries" another with sand; the agent is thus shown moving sand onto a completely stationary patient, who is caused to be covered with sand. Particular care was taken to distinguish clearly the gender of the actors in the picture. Examples of the sentence stimuli and pictures are given in Figure 1.

Sentences were recorded by a male speaker and digitised on a Power Macintosh computer at 22 kHz using SoundEdit. Sound files were edited so that the end of the file corresponded as closely

---

[1] This set includes three verbs (drop, trip, shake) that allow an intransitive (unaccusative) interpretation in which the subject fills the thematic role of theme, e.g., "the boy is shaking." The testing context in which all sentences are pictured as transitive is likely to suppress this possible interpretation, but these verbs will be analysed separately in cases where Set two verbs demonstrate any unpredicted effects.

Verbs: Type 1 (bury, wash, kick, shoot, slap, spray)

Change of state in patient caused by agent
Agent movement > Patient movement

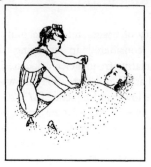

Verbs: Type 2 (drop, lift, shove, trip, shake, drag)

Change of state in patient caused by agent
Patient movement > Agent movement

Verbs: Type 3 (pull, push, chase, follow, guide, lead)

Change of state in patient: minimal
Agent movement = Patient movement

Figure 1. *Example of sentence and picture stimuli.*

as possible to the termination of the sentence. Pictures were scanned using Apple Scan, and were sized uniformly.

Filler sentences. Each of the 18 verbs was also used in an active and passive nonreversible sentence with a larger set of agent nouns and an inanimate object (e.g., "the dog is burying the bone"). Distractor pictures for the filler sentences showed the referents of the named nouns engaged in some other action relationship (e.g., a dog *eating* a bone).

Experimental design. Reversible sentences employed 18 verbs, with two agents, each in both active and passive voice, for a total of 72 distinct sentences tested. In order to prevent the use of spatial strategies affecting the outcome of the testing (Chatterjee, Maher, Gonzalez-Rothi, & Heilman, 1995), each sentence was tested once with the agent shown on the right of the picture, and once with the agent on the left. This was accomplished by using mirror reversals of each picture. These 144 sentence/picture combinations were tested once with a correct pairing of sentence and picture ("yes" trials), and once with a picture showing a reversal of thematic roles ("no" trials), for a total of 288 reversible trials.

The filler sentences employed the same 18 verbs in active and passive voice, each of which was tested once with the agent shown on the right and once with agent on the left, for a total of 72 trials. Each of these was paired once with the correct depiction, and once with a distractor picture showing the same two nouns with a different verb. Thus, there were a total of 144 filler trials.

The 432 trials were divided into four blocks such that each verb appeared six times per block, twice in filler sentences and four times in the semantically reversible sentences. Sentence type (reversible/filler), target response (yes/no), sentence voice (active/passive), and agent position (left/right) were balanced within each block and across blocks for all conditions. Trials within each block were pseudorandomised such that the same verb did not appear in consecutive trials; order of administration of blocks was counterbalanced across subjects.

Verb meaning control. Each of the 18 verbs was also tested in an experiment probing verb comprehension outside the context of a sentence. This condition was included to assure that patients understood the meaning of the verbs, and to evaluate the time taken by normal subjects to process the pictures and decide that the picture portrayed the spoken verb. Thus, it served as a means of evaluating differences among the three verb sets that might be attributable to differences in picture complexity, or to the ease of imageability of the individual verbs.

Each of the 18 verbs was tested in two "yes" and two "no" trials using the pictures from the reversible sentence trials, and one "yes" and one "no" from the nonreversible fillers. The "yes" trials paired the spoken verb with two depictions from the reversible trials (one with each of the two agents) and the "yes" pictures from the filler sentences. The "no" trials substituted depictions of one of the other verbs from the same set for reversible trials, and used the distractor picture from the nonreversible sentences for the filler trial. Thus, each verb was tested in three "yes" and three "no" trials, one of each using the filler materials. The spoken stimuli for these 108 trials, using the "-ing" form of the individual verbs, were recorded and digitised as described above. Sentences were divided into two blocks with equal representation of verbs and of target (yes/no) responses, pseudorandomised to avoid consecutive use of any verb. The order of administration of the blocks was counterbalanced across subjects. The verb meaning control test was completed prior to administration of the sentence verification test.

Procedures

Each subject was seated comfortably before a Macintosh Apple Vision 17-inch monitor, approximately 20 inches from the screen. Auditory stimuli were presented via the computer's internal speaker and enhanced by dual monitor speakers. A standard button box was placed on the table between the monitor and the subject, and was connected to the computer to record responses. The left (yellow) button was marked "NO", and the right (green) button was marked "YES" for response. A marker placed between the two buttons on the button box indicated where the subject should place his/her index finger between trials. Each trial began with an audible beep simultaneously with the appearance of a fixation cross (+) that remained at the centre of the monitor screen for 2 s. With fixation offset, the screen became blank as the spoken sentence was played. A picture appeared on the screen upon termination of the spoken sentence. The picture remained visible until the subject responded by depressing one of the two response keys. Reaction time (RT) data were collected from the initiation of the picture to the button box key press. The inter-trial interval was 2000 ms. Trials advanced automatically, with examiner-controlled "rest" points following every nine trials. No repetitions were given. Each subject was familiarised with the task during 33 practice trials using nontest stimuli.

RESULTS

Control subjects

Accuracy

The mean proportion correct for reversible sentences in each condition is shown in the top half of Table 2. The proportion correct included only those responses that occurred within 2 SDs of the mean RT of correct reversible sentences for an individual subject. The 2 SD threshold was used to eliminate outlier responses from the reaction time analysis (see below). Overall, the control group performed well on the semantically reversible sentences (mean accuracy across subjects = .94, range .92 to .96). Accuracy was statistically analysed using repeated measures analysis of variance (ANOVA) with three factors, Response ("yes" vs. "no"), Voice (active vs. passive), and Verb Set (Set 1 vs. Set 2 vs. Set 3). The ANOVA on accuracy revealed significant main effects of Response, $F(1, 8) = 10.888$, $p = .011$, $MSe = 0.003$, Voice, $F(1, 8) = 9.903$, $p = .014$, $MSe = 0.04$, and Set, $F(2, 16) = 6.782$, $p = .007$, $MSe = 0.05$. "Yes" responses were significantly more accurate than "no" responses (mean proportion correct for " yes"

Table 2. *Mean proportion correct and response time for control subjects in each of the reversible conditions (SDs are in parentheses)*

| | Accuracy (proportion correct) | | | | | | Response time (ms) | | | | | |
| | Active | | | Passive | | | Active | | | Passive | | |
	Set 1	Set 2	Set 3	Set 1	Set 2	Set 3	Set 1	Set 2	Set 3	Set 1	Set 2	Set 3
Yes	.97	.99	.97	.98	.94	.91	1212	1263	1220	1286	1320	1414
	(.04)	(.02)	(.05)	(.02)	(.04)	(.09)	(270)	(293)	(261)	(293)	(327)	(366)
No	.94	.97	.94	.94	.93	.84	1328	1392	1412	1490	1488	1587
	(.05)	(.04)	(.07)	(.05)	(.06)	(.08)	(335)	(363)	(348)	(416)	(390)	(439)

= .96, for "no" = .93). In addition, active sentences were more accurate than passive (mean active = .96, mean passive = .93). Newman-Keuls post hoc tests showed that Set 3 verbs were significantly less accurate than either Set 2 or Set 1 (*p* < .05). However, the lower accuracy for Set 3 was mainly in the passive condition, as reflected by a significant Voice × Verb Set interaction, *F*(2, 16) = 6.391, *p* = .009, *MSe* = 0.003. Newman-Keuls post hoc tests revealed that passive Set 3 sentences were significantly less accurate than any other condition. No other comparisons were significantly different.

Response times

For each control subject, the mean response time and standard deviation of all correct reversible sentences were calculated. Any trials with response times greater than 2*SD*s above the mean for an individual subject were eliminated from further analysis for that subject. An analysis of variance on the trimmed response times (RT) was performed using the same factors as in the accuracy analysis. The bottom half of Table 2 shows the mean response times for each condition. As in the accuracy analysis, there were significant main effects of Response, *F*(1, 8) = 13.519, *p* = .006, *MSe* = 53388, Voice, *F*(1, 8) = 22.240, *p* = .002, *MSe* = 19427, and Set, *F*(2, 16) = 14.247, *p* < .0001, *MSe* = 7965. "Yes" response times (mean = 1286 ms) were significantly faster than "no" responses (mean = 1450 ms); active responses (mean = 1304 ms) were significantly faster than passives (mean = 1431 ms). Figure 2 shows that the response times to the verb sets varied parametrically with the proto-agent features of the verb. Newman-Keuls post hoc tests comparing the verb sets showed that sentences containing Set 1 verbs (mean = 1329 ms) were significantly faster than either those contained in Set 2 (mean = 1366 ms; *p* < .05) or in Set 3 (mean = 1408; *p* < .01). Furthermore, Set 2 was significantly faster than Set 3 (*p* < .05). The response time analysis also indicated that there was a significant Voice × Set interaction, *F*(2, 16) = 4.924, *p* = .022, *MSe* = 85634. Post-hoc analyses revealed that the passive conditions were all significantly slower than the active conditions for each of the sets. In addition, Passive Set 3 sentences were significantly slower than either those in passive Set 1 (*p* < .01) or in passive Set 2 (*p* < .01).

To ensure that the verb set effects were not due to systematic differences in the portrayal of the verbs in the pictures, or to imageability differences across the verb sets, accuracy and response time to

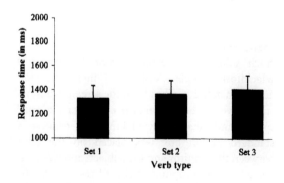

Figure 2. *Mean response times for verb set conditions for control subjects. Error bars show standard error.*

the verb meaning control task were analysed. Overall, the control subjects were highly accurate in verifying that the verbs matched the pictures (mean proportion correct = .93). Separate one-way analyses of variance with one factor (verb set) were performed on the "yes" trials using accuracy and response time as dependent measures. There was no main effect of verb set for the accuracy analysis, $F < 1$, or the response time analysis, $F(2, 16) = 1.243$, $p = .315$, $MSe = 13814$. Thus, the verb set effects seen in the sentence verification task cannot be attributed to differences in picture complexity or to systematic differences in ease of imageability across the three sets.

Good comprehenders

Accuracy

The data from the five patients without reversible sentence comprehension impairment were analysed using the same 2 SD cutoff for outliers and the same factors as in the analyses of variance for the control subjects. Overall accuracy in sentence/picture verification was slightly depressed relative to controls (mean accuracy = .91, range .88 to .93). Table 3 shows the mean accuracy and response times in each condition for the good comprehenders. The three-way analysis of variance for proportion correct (Response × Voice × Set) showed a main effect of Voice, $F(1, 4) = 9.718$, $p = .036$, $MSe = 0.053$, with actives (mean = .96) more accurate than passives (mean = .87). No other main effects were significant. The three-way interaction Response × Voice × Set was significant, $F(2, 8) =$

4.291, $p = .054$, $MSe = 0.004$. Newman-Keuls post-hoc tests indicated that for the "no" responses, passive sentences in Sets 2 and 3 were significantly different from most other conditions, including each of the "no" active conditions, "yes" actives in Sets 1 and 3 and "yes" passives in Set 2. Thus, similar to the control subjects, accuracy for the good comprehenders on passive Set 3 sentences was lower than on other sentences. In addition, the passives in Set 2 were also more difficult than sentences in other conditions. However, these effects appeared more consistently for the "no" responses in the good comprehension group of patients, in contrast to results for the control subjects where the Set 3 verbs were significantly less accurate for both "yes" and "no" responses.

Response times

The analysis of variance on response time using the same factors as the accuracy analysis showed a similar pattern of results to the control subjects with significant main effects of Response, $F(1, 4) = 15.788$, $p = .016$, $MSe = 138806$; Voice, $F(1, 4) = 10.540$, $p = .031$, $MSe = 157650$; and Set, $F(2, 8) = 5.266$, $p = .035$, $MSe = 969918$. None of the interactions was significant. "Yes" responses (mean RT = 2312 ms) were significantly faster than "no" responses (mean RT = 2694 ms). In addition, active sentences were responded to significantly faster than passive sentences (difference = 333 ms).

Figure 3 shows the significant verb set effect, in which the pattern of response times mirrored that of the controls, even though the patients' response times were much longer and more variable than

Table 3. *Mean proportion correct and response times for good comprehenders in each of the reversible conditions (SDs are in parentheses)*

| | Accuracy (proportion correct) | | | | | | Response time (ms) | | | | | |
| | Active | | | Passive | | | Active | | | Passive | | |
	Set 1	Set 2	Set 3	Set 1	Set 2	Set 3	Set 1	Set 2	Set 3	Set 1	Set 2	Set 3
Yes	.99	.91	.97	.91	.94	.85	2275	2633	2537	2638	3053	2915
	(.02)	(.04)	(.05)	(.09)	(.02)	(.02)	(849)	(1332)	(971)	(856)	(1527)	(1003)
No	.95	.98	.98	.89	.83	.81	2781	2869	3079	3106	3236	3579
	(.06)	(.02)	(.03)	(.10)	(.13)	(.11)	(961)	(1091)	(1344)	(1353)	(1359)	(1408)

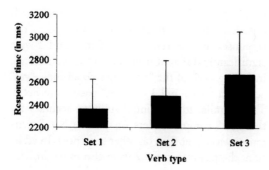

Figure 3. *Mean response times for verb set conditions for good comprehenders. Error bars show standard error.*

those of control subjects. Newman-Keuls post-hoc tests indicated that there was a significant difference between Set 1 and Set 3. However, this group differed from controls in that their verb set effect did not show a reliable difference between Set 2 and Set 3. Since Set 2 contained three verbs (trip, shake, drop) that could yield an unaccusative interpretation if used intransitively (see footnote 1), it was possible that an attenuated difference between Set 2 and Set 3 resulted from some confusion about the thematic role that should be associated with the subject nouns in Set 2 sentences. That is, the unaccusative interpretation of those verbs would assign the subject noun to the thematic role of theme (as in "the girl is tripping"), which would be associated with the incorrect picture choice. To assess the possibility that poor performance for Set 2 reflected confusion about these three verbs, we compared the response times for this group for these three verbs to their response times for the other three verbs in Set 2. There was no difference between the two subsets of Set 2, $t(4) = 1.13$, $p = .32$, indicating that this particular difference between verbs in Set 2 was not responsible for their slower responses to Set 2 verbs (compared to controls' relative performance across sets). Rather, the lack of a significant difference between Set 2 and Set 3 is likely attributable to the large variability in the patients' RTs.

Unlike the controls, the good comprehenders showed some difficulty with the verb meaning control condition. Although the overall mean

proportion correct across the good comprehension patients on the verb meaning control tasks was high (mean = .91, $SD = .05$), an analysis of variance on the accuracy data for "yes" responses showed a significant effect of Verb Set, $F(2, 8) = 24.667$, $p < .0001$, $MSe = 0.004$. Newman-Keuls tests showed that Set 2 (.81) differed both from Set 1 (1.00) and from Set 3 (.97) ($p < .01$). Differences in RTs on the "yes" responses based on verb set did not reach significance, $F(2, 8) = 3.676$, $p = .074$, $MSe = 35900$.

Poor comprehenders

Accuracy

Overall accuracy for the six patients with reversible sentence comprehension impairment was quite poor (.55 correct overall, see Table 4). However, these difficulties could not be attributed to problems in comprehension of the pictures. Accuracy in the verb meaning control task was high across all of these patients (mean = .95, $SD = .05$). Furthermore, there was no significant verb set effect in the verb meaning control task ($F < 1$).

Despite large individual differences in response biases in the sentence comprehension task (discussed below), the group showed some effects of response similar to the normal controls and the good comprehenders. A three-way analysis of variance (Response × Voice × Set) revealed a significant main effect of Response, $F(1, 5) = 12.123$, $p = .018$, $MSe = 0.277$, where the mean proportion of correct "yes" responses (mean = .77) was greater than those in the "no" conditions (mean = .37). Although there was no main effect of Voice, $F(1, 5) = 3.035$, $p = .142$, $MSe = 0.297$, or Verb Set, $F(2, 10) = 1.620$, $p = .246$, $MSe = 0.024$, there was a significant interaction of Voice × Verb Set, $F(2, 10) = 5.749$, $p = .022$, $MSe = 0.015$. This interaction reflected the fact that, although performance on passive voice sentences was much poorer than on active sentences for all verb sets, active sentences in Set 3 were also poorer than the active sentences for the other verb sets. Figure 4 depicts the response accuracy for each verb set for the active and passive sentences. RTs were not analysed for this group because of the high error rate.

Table 4. *Mean proportion correct for poor comprehenders in each of the conditions (SDs are in parentheses)*

| | Accuracy (proportion correct) | | | | | |
| | Active | | | Passive | | |
	Set 1	Set 2	Set 3	Set 1	Set 2	Set 3
Yes	.89	.91	.83	.64	.65	.68
	(.08)	(.09)	(.10)	.39	(.34)	(.37)
No	.48	.53	.34	.20	.22	.24
	(.26)	(.25)	(.32)	(.13)	(.19)	(.11)

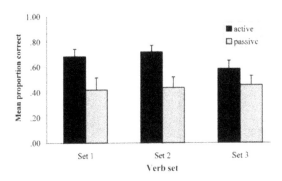

Figure 4. *Mean accuracy for poor comprehenders for active versus passive sentence for each verb set.*

These results in patients' accuracy emerged despite substantial heterogeneity. As shown in Figure 5, two clear response patterns emerged in their data. Four of the six patients had a strong bias to respond "yes" (patients to the left of the solid line in Figure 5), and two patients seemed to interpret the first noun of the sentence as the agent of the action in most trials, resulting in many correct responses for active sentences and incorrect responses for passives (patients to the right of the solid line in Figure 5).

MANIPULATING APHASIC RESPONSE STRATEGIES

The patients with poor understanding of reversible sentences tested here did not demonstrate an obvious sensitivity to verb type. However, each of

them relied on an apparent response strategy in which their judgment reflected information other than the full meaning of the sentence. In fact, the contrasting response strategies shown in Figure 5 seem to indicate different sources of difficulty and different levels of attention to the experimental stimuli. A bias to respond "yes" in a sentence/picture verification paradigm, especially when (as here) filler sentences contained catch trials with lexical distractors, may represent a reliance on lexical semantic content and inattention both to structure and to the relationship between the actors shown in the picture. That is, a "yes" response to virtually all semantically reversible sentences, regardless of voice, may reflect a patient's judgment that the picture accurately depicts the lexical content of the sentence, i.e., the two nouns and a verb. If so, such a strategy may represent an extreme example of reliance on semantic information (in this case, lexical semantics) at the expense of structure (Saffran et al., 1998).

In an attempt to test this possibility, we selected one patient with strong "yes" bias (TP, Figure 5) and presented him with a forced-choice version of the test sentences in which he was asked to choose between a correct depiction of the sentence and one showing its thematic reversal. TP's overall proportion correct was significantly better (.80) in the forced-choice format than in yes/no verification (.64), $\chi^2 = 11.44$, $p < .001$. Moreover, his performance on the forced-choice task improved to ceiling levels (.98 correct) following an experimental treatment in which he was simply given feedback as to the correctness of his response in exercises using a single picture and sentence

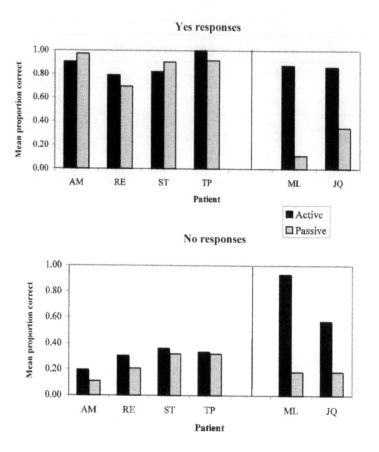

Figure 5. *Mean proportion correct for "yes" and "no" responses in the active and passive sentences for each patient in the poor comprehension group. The four patients to the left of the solid line demonstrate a strong "yes" bias in their responses, whereas the two patients to the right of the solid line have adopted a first-noun-as-agent strategy.*

(pre- vs. post-treatment), McNemar χ^2 = 9.29, p < .0001. Although we have no evidence regarding the other patients with strong "yes" bias, for TP the syntactic processing skills needed to assign agent in active and passive sentences were presumably available but not employed until the task (forced choice) and the feedback procedure made clear that more than a lexical/semantic judgment was required. His performance then was at ceiling, so no verb effects emerged.

The second response pattern shown in the right section of Figure 5 appears to reflect a strategy of interpreting the first noun heard to be the agent of the action. This pattern has been argued to reflect a basic perceptual strategy (Bever, 1970) in which

the order of nouns around the verb is interpreted in line with its most frequent mapping to thematic roles in English. Note that this "first noun = agent" strategy, which has been hypothesised previously to underlie aphasic comprehension performance (e.g., Caplan & Futter, 1996), requires attention to the order of nouns in the spoken sentence and interpretation of the thematic relations displayed in the picture—with an inappropriate mapping rule linking the two. Because this heuristic involves the systematic application of an incorrect rule, we expected it to be more difficult to attenuate than the simple "yes" bias.

We investigated this issue with JQ (see Figure 5), who performed significantly better with active

(.72) than passive (.26) sentences in the sentence/picture verification task, $\chi^2 = 60.53$, $p < .0001$. Re-testing using the two-picture forced-choice procedure produced similar results (active = .76; passive = .26), $\chi^2 = 32$, $p < .0001$. Because JQ's consistent response strategy appeared to treat active and passive voice sentences as equivalent, experimental treatment began with passive listening exercises in which each picture was presented along with pairs of spoken active and passive voice sentences. JQ was told that despite the fact that the sentences were different, both described the picture correctly. Following two sessions of passive listening, a more formal treatment using response feedback in single sentence/picture verification was undertaken (see Mitchum, Haendiges, & Berndt, 2000). Briefly, the treatment sentences and pictures (64 different combinations of nouns and pictures for four verbs) were presented in a verification format with an equal number of "yes" and "no" trials. Each response was followed by immediate feedback that either verified a correct response (and repeated the sentence) or corrected an erroneous response.

JQ required eight runs through the materials before reaching a performance criterion of .95 correct, and an additional five runs to achieve that criterion with no repetitions of the spoken sentence. Thereafter, he showed significant improvement in the forced-choice sentence/picture matching task employing all untreated sentences (pre/post = .51/.82), McNemar $\chi^2 = 5.96$, $p < .0001$. Despite these significant gains, JQ failed to show the near-perfect performance in the post-test noted for TP. Accuracy for both active (.85), $z = 5.94$, $p < .0001$, and passive (.74), $z = 4.00$, $p = .0001$, was significantly better than chance, with only a marginally significant advantage for active voice, $\chi^2 = 2.20$, $p = .08$. Further analysis of JQ's post-treatment forced-choice performance (untreated stimuli only) revealed differences in performance across verb sets, which had not been present before the treatment. As shown in Figure 6, *untreated* sentences with Set 1 verbs (.96, active/passive combined, $n = 24$) were correct more often than either sentences with Set 2 verbs (.77, $n = 56$), Fisher's Exact Test = 4.28, $p = .05$, or Set 3 verbs (.75, $n = 56$); Fisher's Exact Test = 4.95, $p = .03$.

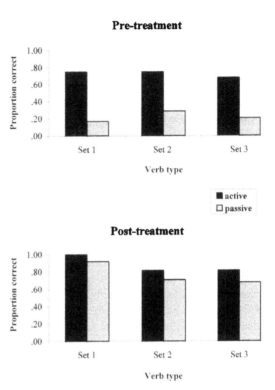

Figure 6. Mean proportion correct performance for patient JQ on untreated active and passive sentences with verbs from the three sets. The top panel shows results prior to the feedback treatment, and the bottom panel shows post-treatment. $N = 12$ trials with untreated verbs of Set 1; $N = 28$ trials each for Sets 2 and 3.

These data indicate that it is possible to convince patients to give up a consistent response strategy and attend to structural differences between sentences that had previously been ignored. Both patients presumably learned that the differences between active and passive voice sentences have implications for meaning, although we did not explicitly teach them the details of structure/meaning mappings. For present purposes, the important point is that, for JQ, improved appreciation of the two sentence types could not be applied equally easily to all sentences. Rather, sentences with verbs from Sets 2 and 3 continued to be more difficult than untrained verbs from Set 1. Importantly, these verb effects were not detectable in his pre-treatment performance because of his consistent use of a response strategy that essentially ignored the verb.

SUMMARY OF RESULTS

All groups tested showed some effects of the verb set manipulation in the direction predicted, although some differences emerged across the groups. The response times of the normal controls showed the precise hierarchy predicted, with Set 1 verb sentences faster than Set 2, which in turn were faster than Set 3. The control subjects also showed an interaction of verb set with voice in both accuracy and response times, with Set 3 passives being the slowest and most error prone. These verb set differences did not apparently reflect differential difficulty in interpreting the actions shown in the pictures, or systematic differences "picturing" the actions described, as no differences emerged across sets in a separate test of verb meaning/ picture verification. That is, verb set effects were evident only when the task required a judgment on whether the picture showed the *thematic relations stated in the sentence*.

The response times of the aphasic participants with good comprehension also showed a main effect of verb set in the predicted direction. However, the post hoc analysis showed a reliable difference only for Set 3 vs. each of the other two sets, probably because response times were highly variable. However, these findings for the two groups of subjects who performed relatively accurately on the task suggest that the factors of verb meaning identified by Dowty (1991) may have a measurable effect on performance, at least in the sentence/ picture matching task. The difficulty of assigning noun arguments to the thematic roles of agent and patient in reversible sentences, when either noun is equally likely to play either role, appears to reflect aspects of verb meaning and/or of its depiction.

It is not as clear that these semantic factors had any effect on the performance of the patients who had difficulty understanding even the sentences employing the easiest verb set. As a group, they responded incorrectly to passive voice sentences more often than active, especially for the Set 3 verbs. Otherwise, they relied on a consistent response strategy—either favouring the "yes" response or assigning thematic agent to the first noun heard. Our attempts to obviate these strate-

gies and induce attention to sentence structure suggested that the "chance" performance associated with such strategies reflected different underlying impairments. One patient who demonstrated a "yes" response bias in sentence/picture verification performed much better in a forced-choice task with two pictures, and ultimately reached ceiling performance. This rapid improvement in performance supports the hypothesis that his initial strategy reflected his judgment that the meaning of the content words in the sentences was reflected in the picture. A second patient who showed a "first noun = agent" strategy did not improve in the forced-choice procedure, and never approached ceiling performance. Moreover, although accuracy improved significantly overall, with above-chance performance on both active and passive sentences, this patient now demonstrated a significant effect of verb set: Sentences with Set 1 verbs were understood significantly better than were sentences with either of the other two verb sets.

DISCUSSION

Interpretation of sentence comprehension impairments in aphasia has tended to adopt a "modular" view of sentence processing in which syntactic parsing and semantic interpretation are discrete steps in the creation of meaning. Within that framework, attention has focused on the integrity of syntactic processing in patients with comprehension disorder, with differences of opinion about whether syntactic processes are largely intact (Linebarger et al., 1983) or are impaired in specific ways (Grodzinsky, 1984). The recent research of Saffran and colleagues (Saffran et al., 1998) has adopted a more interactive approach, emphasising recent psycholinguistic studies of sentence comprehension in which information from a wide range of sources plays a role from the earliest points (e.g., Tabossi et al., 1994).

Much of this recent work has focused on assignment of thematic roles, and evidence has accumulated that semantic factors influence normal subjects' willingness to fill a specific verb's thematic roles with specific nouns (McRae et al., 1997). Our study tested a more general hypothesis that did not consider the role/filler typicality of noun/verb pairs, but looked at verb role features in isolation from "typical" filler nouns. That is, we showed that, *even when the nouns were deliberately kept neutral with respect to the meaning of the verb* (such that either of two nouns could fill either role in transitive sentences), features of verb meaning still exerted a measurable effect on thematic role assignments for normal subjects and aphasic patients. Across all the data collected, there was a tendency for verb meaning to interact with sentence syntax, such that passive voice sentences were more difficult with the more difficult verb sets.

Our division of verbs into sets was motivated by a linguistic theory that has not been subjected to empirical test; thus, there was no operational definition of the role features at issue. Our division of verbs into sets may not have captured the target distinctions optimally, and this may have led to our findings of an imperfect hierarchy in some of the data. Set 2 did not appear to fall out as intermediate to the other sets in all cases, but frequently clustered with Set 3. This suggests that a different division of verbs might present a better match to the data.

Earlier considerations of the effects of the verb on aphasic sentence comprehension have identified verbs such as those in our Set 3 as particularly difficult. Saffran and colleagues (Saffran, 1982; Saffran et al., 1980) were the first to point out that purely relational verbs ("chase") are more difficult than verbs that "inhere" in the agent, such as "smile at." This distinction seems to involve a difference between verbs that can be pictured as an action carried out by a single agent (even though another participant in the action is named in the sentence), and one that can be pictured only as a relation between two actors. This dichotomy might serve to distinguish our Set 1 from Set 3, although imperfectly, but it is less clear how to fit the Set 2 verbs into this scheme.

Another view of the effects of specific verbs on aphasic patients' comprehension was contributed by Jones, who also identified the relative difficulty of the "relational" verbs discussed by Saffran and colleagues. According to Jones (1984), these verbs

constitute a class of "directional motion verbs" that dictates the direction in which the actors are moving. For example, understanding the thematic mappings for a verb such as "follow" requires knowledge of the spatial relationships between the actors, i.e., which participant is in front given the direction in which they are travelling. Although this type of spatial/directional analysis may contribute to the difficulty of the Set 3 verbs, it does not allow straightforward application to the Set 2 verbs, which were as difficult as Set 3 in several of the analyses.

Our division of verbs into sets was based in part on how clearly the proto-role features could be pictured in the testing materials. Thus, the pictures employed here explicitly emphasised the relative motion and change of state of the sentences' participants. It is, of course, not clear to what extent these depiction manipulations contributed to the verb set effects reported here. This is an important question that must be addressed before our results can be attributed unequivocally to elements of verb meaning in isolation from the testing context.

Even though our findings of verb set effects may be open to other interpretations, they suggest that the ease with which thematic roles can be interpreted may differ across sentence/picture combinations in this task. Some verbs' agents are more easily identified than others'. Further, noun arguments do not appear to be assigned to thematic roles strictly on the basis of the sentence's syntactic structure, but through a dynamic process in which verb meaning and sentence structure interact as they are compared to the sentence's depiction. All of these factors must be considered when attempting to determine the source of aphasic comprehension impairments.

REFERENCES

Berndt, R. S., & Caramazza, A. (1980). A redefinition of the syndrome of Broca's aphasia: Implications for a neuropsychological model of language. *Journal of Applied Neurolinguistics, 1,* 225–278.

Berndt, R. S., & Mitchum, C. C. (1998). An experimental treatment of sentence comprehension. In N. Helm-Estabrooks & A. L. Holland (Eds.), *Approaches to the treatment of aphasia*. Boston: Singular Publishing.

Berndt, R. S., Mitchum, C. C., & Wayland, S. C. (1997). Patterns of sentence comprehension in aphasia: A consideration of three hypotheses. *Brain and Language, 60*, 197–221.

Bever, T. G. (1970). The cognitive basis for linguistic structures. In J. R. Hayes (Ed.), *Cognition and the development of language*. New York: John Wiley.

Bradley, D., Garrett, M. L., & Zurif, E. (1980). Syntactic deficits in Broca's aphasia. In D. Caplan (Ed.), *Biological studies of mental processes*. Cambridge, MA: MIT Press.

Caplan, D., & Futter, C. (1996). Assignment of thematic roles to nouns in sentence comprehension by an agrammatic patient. *Brain and Language, 27*, 117–134.

Caramazza, A., & Zurif, E. B. (1976). Dissociation of algorithmic and heuristic processes in language comprehension: Evidence from aphasia. *Brain and Language, 3*, 572–582.

Chatterjee, A., Maher, L. M., Gonzalez-Rothi, L. J., & Heilman, K. M. (1995). Asyntactic thematic role assignment: The use of a temporal-spatial strategy. *Brain and Language, 49*, 125–139.

Coltheart, M. (1981). The MRC psycholinguistic database. *Quarterly Journal of Experimental Psychology, 33A*, 497–505.

Dowty, D. (1991). Thematic proto-roles and argument selection. *Language, 67*, 547–619.

Fellbaum, C. (1998). *WordNet: An electronic lexical database*. Cambridge, MA: MIT Press.

Grodzinsky, Y. (1984). The syntactic characterization of agrammatism. *Cognition, 16*, 99–120.

Jackendoff, R. (1987). The semantic organization of some simple nouns and verbs. *Journal of Verbal Learning and Verbal Behavior, 18*, 141–162.

Jones, E. V. (1984). Word order processing in aphasia: Effect of verb semantics. In F. C. Rose (Ed.), *Progress in neurology* (pp. 159–181). New York: Raven Press.

Kay, J., Lesser, R., & Coltheart, M. (1992). *The Psycholinguistic Assessment of Language Processing in Aphasia (PALPA)*. Hove, UK: Lawrence Erlbaum Associates Ltd.

Linebarger, M. C., Schwartz, M. F., & Saffran, E. M. (1983). Sensitivity to grammatical structure in so-called agrammatic aphasics. *Cognition, 13*, 361–392.

MacDonald, M. C., Pearlmutter, N. J., & Seidenberg, M. S. (1994). Lexical nature of syntactic ambiguity resolution. *Psychological Review, 101*, 676–703.

McRae, K., Ferretti, T. R., & Amyote, L. (1997). Thematic roles as verb-specific concepts. *Language and Cognitive Processes, 12*, 137–176.

Mitchum, C. C., Haendiges, A. N., & Berndt, R. S. (2000). Using treatment to unmask verb complexities in sentence comprehension. *Brain and Language, 74*, 463–466.

Miyake, A., Carpenter, P. A., & Just, M. A. (1994). A capacity approach to syntactic comprehension disorders: Making normal adults perform like aphasic patients. *Cognitive Neuropsychology, 11*(6), 671–717.

Saffran, E. M. (1982). Neuropsychological approaches to the study of language. *British Journal of Psychology, 73*, 317–337.

Saffran, E. M. (2001). Effects of language impairment on sentence comprehension. In R. S. Berndt (Ed.), *Handbook of neuropsychology* (Vol. 3, pp. 157–171). Amsterdam: Elsevier Science Publishers.

Saffran, E. M., & Schwartz, M. F. (1994). Impairments of sentence comprehension. *Philosophical Transactions of the Royal Society of London, 346*, 47–53.

Saffran, E. M., Schwartz, M. F., & Linebarger, M. C. (1998). Semantic influences on thematic role assignment: Evidence from normals and aphasics. *Brain and Language, 62*, 255–297.

Saffran, E. M., Schwartz, M. F., Linebarger, M. C., Martin, N., & Bochetto, P. (1988). *The Philadelphia Comprehension Battery*. Unpublished battery.

Saffran, E. M., Schwartz, M. F., & Marin, O. S. M. (1980). Evidence from aphasia: Isolating the components of a production model. In B. Butterworth (Ed.), *Language production* (Vol. 1). London: Academic Press.

Schwartz, M. F., Linebarger, M. C., & Saffran, E. M. (1985). The status of the syntactic deficit theory of agrammatism. In M.-L. Kean (Ed.), *Agrammatism*. Orlando, FL: Academic Press.

Schwartz, M. F., Saffran, E. M., & Marin, O. S. M. (1980). The word order problem in agrammatism: Comprehension. *Brain and Language, 10*, 249–262.

Tabossi, P., Spivey-Knowlton, M. J., McRae, K., & Tanenhaus, M. K. (1994). Semantic effects on syntactic ambiguity resolution: Evidence for a constraint-based resolution process. In C. Umiltà & M. Moscovitch (Eds.), *Attention and performance XV. Conscious and nonconscious information processing*. Cambridge, MA: MIT Press.

COGNITIVE NEUROPSYCHOLOGY, 2004, 21 (2/3/4), 245–265

SEMANTIC RELATEDNESS EFFECTS IN CONJOINED NOUN PHRASE PRODUCTION: IMPLICATIONS FOR THE ROLE OF SHORT-TERM MEMORY

Monica L. Freedman, Randi C. Martin, and Kelly Biegler

Rice University, Houston, TX, USA

Speech error data and empirical studies suggest that the scope of planning is larger for semantic than for phonological form representations in speech production. Previous results have demonstrated that some patients show dissociable impairments in the retention of semantic and phonological codes. The effect of these STM deficits on speech production was investigated using a phrase production paradigm that manipulated the semantic relatedness of the words in the phrase. Subjects produced a conjoined noun phrase to describe two pictures (e.g., "ball and hat") or produced the same phrases in response to pairs of written words. For the picture naming condition, control subjects showed an interference effect for semantically related pictures relative to unrelated pictures. This interference effect was greatly exaggerated for two patients with semantic short-term memory deficits but not for a patient with a phonological STM deficit. For the written words, control subjects showed a small facilitatory effect for the onset of phrases containing semantically related words. One of the patients with a semantic STM deficit who was tested on picture naming was also tested on these materials and showed a small facilitatory effect within the range of controls. The findings support the contention that speech planning is carried out at a phrasal level at the lexical-semantic level and that the capacities that support semantic retention in list recall support speech production planning.

INTRODUCTION

In a series of papers beginning in 1990, Eleanor Saffran and Nadine Martin and colleagues explored the relation between lexical processing and short-term memory (N. Martin, Dell, Saffran, & Schwartz, 1996; N. Martin & Saffran, 1990, 1992, 1997; N. Martin, Saffran, & Dell, 1996; Saffran & Martin, 1990). Their approach has been a major influence on the approach taken in our lab. In fact, in the model of short-term memory presented by R. C. Martin, Lesch, and Bartha (1999) (depicted in Figure 1), the lexical processing network shown on the left-hand side is equivalent to that used by N. Martin and Saffran in providing an account of the effects of lexical factors such as word frequency and concreteness on short-term memory performance. Their model is closely related to the interactive activation model of word production initially presented by Dell and O'Seaghdha (1992) and used by Dell, Schwartz, Martin, Saffran, and Gagnon (1997) to account for accuracy and error patterns in normal and aphasic patients' picture naming. The model includes phonological, lexical, and semantic nodes and bidirectional connections between them; however, unlike the lexical network on the

---

Correspondence should be addressed to Randi C. Martin, Department of Psychology, MS-25, Rice University, PO Box 1892, Houston, TX 77251, USA (Email: rmartin@rice.edu).

This research was supported NIH grant DC-00218 to Rice University. These studies were carried out as part of Monica Freedman's dissertation research (Freedman, 2001).

http://www.tandf.co.uk/journals/pp/02643294.html

DOI:10.1080/02643290342000528

left-hand side of Figure 1, there is no distinction between input and output phonology. The model has global activation and decay parameters and variations in these parameters (i.e., decreases in activation and increases in decay) have been used to simulate both naming disorders (Dell et al., 1997) and short-term memory deficits (N. Martin et al., 1996).

The major difference between our approach and theirs is that we have emphasised the role of buffers on the right-hand side of the model, which are used to maintain several representations simultaneously (R. C. Martin et al., 1999). We have claimed that there are separate buffers for maintaining input phonological representations, output phonological representations, and lexical-semantic representations, and that brain damage can selectively affect these buffers, leaving lexical processing intact. Our

work has been concerned with the effects of restricted buffer capacity on language processing and the current study investigates the role of the lexical-semantic buffer in language production. In earlier instantiations of the model, we assumed that representations were copied from the long-term knowledge structures into the buffers; however, in more recent formulations we have argued that the buffers have nodes that serve as placeholders and these nodes are linked to the appropriate representations in the knowledge structure (R. C. Martin et al., 1999; Romani, McAlpine, Olson, & Martin, 2003). Bidirectional activation between the knowledge structure and the buffers is assumed such that the attachment of a representation to a placeholder node results in activation of the node, and activation of the placeholder node feeds back activation to the representations in the knowledge structure.

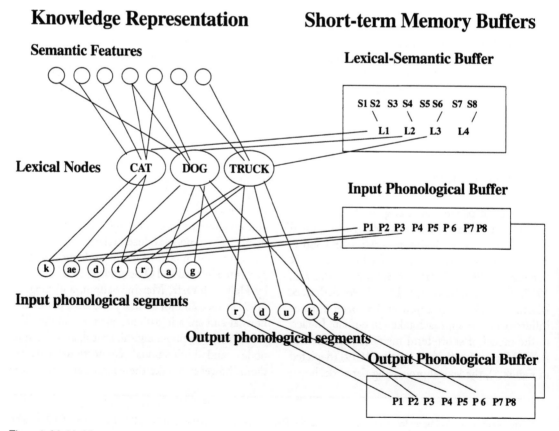

Figure 1. *Model of short-term memory proposed by R. C. Martin et al. (1999).*

The separation between knowledge structure and buffers is motivated by dissociations between single word processing and short-term memory that have been reported in our lab (R. C. Martin & Lesch, 1996) and others (e.g., Vallar & Baddeley, 1984) and by other theoretical considerations. Various researchers have claimed that short-term memory consists of currently activated representation in long-term memory (Crowder, 1993; Ruchkin, Grafman, Cameron, & Berndt, in press). Although the principle may sound reasonable at a general level, applying this principle to the knowledge structure in Figure 1 raises problematic issues such as how the activation of several different words would be maintained simultaneously such that different words could be distinguished at recall. The problem would be particularly severe in the case in which a word is repeated in a list (e.g., "chair grass chair book"). Subjects would presumably have little difficulty repeating such a list, but it is unclear how the two presentations of chair would be represented in the lexical network. Also, if one assumes that the parameters of activation and decay that are used in single word processing in such a network also apply to short-term memory, then the differences in the timescales over which the activation would need to be maintained also raise questions. That is, in modelling picture naming (as in Dell et al., 1997), many cycles through the lexical network are assumed to occur during the 600–900 ms that normal subjects require to name a picture. It is unclear what would be left of the activation in the lexical network after the much longer time periods that might be involved in list recall (e.g., five or more seconds from presentation to recall when a five-item list is presented at one word per second). To avoid this difficulty in our model, we assume that the rate of decay of the connections between the buffer and the lexical representations is much slower than the decay within the lexical network.

In previous discussions of the model in Figure 1, we have hypothesised that the capacity of the buffer may be reduced due to brain damage, but have not been specific about the nature of this capacity restriction. Given the variation in memory span for a given individual related to different features of the words to be recalled (e.g., better recall for concrete

than abstract words, Walker & Hulme, 1999), it seems unworkable to assume a fixed number of nodes for controls and a smaller number for patients with STM deficits. Instead, one might assume that there is a fixed amount of capacity for each buffer that can be allocated to form the connections between the lexical network and the buffer, and that this capacity is smaller for the patients. Alternatively, one might assume that initial connections of equal strength are formed for normal subjects and patients, but that decay of these connections is overly rapid for the patients. Without computational modelling of these assumptions, it is unclear whether they would lead to different predictions. In the present investigation, we assume overly rapid decay is the underlying cause of STM deficits, though we have no strong commitment to this option.

Speech production models and relation to short-term memory

Predictions regarding the consequences of a short-term memory deficit on production depend on the stages in the production process, the representations involved in these stages, and the scope of planning at each stage. There is general agreement on the stages of planning and the levels of representations involved in each stage (Bock & Levelt, 1994; Dell, 1986). At the highest level, the message to be expressed is represented in a nonverbal format. The message is used to select the lexical representations and syntactic structures used to convey the message. The lexical representations at this level are assumed to be nonphonological representations, often termed "lemmas," containing semantic and syntactic specifications of words, but not phonological information (Kempen & Huijbers, 1983; Levelt, 1989). In some models lemmas are sometimes claimed to contain only syntactic information (Bock & Levelt, 1994; Levelt, Roelofs, & Meyer, 1999), but graphical depictions of these models indicate that the lemmas are essentially empty nodes that link semantic and syntactic representations for words. We will use the term lemma to refer to this type of representation that provides a means of linking semantic and syntactic representations. Further downstream in the production process, phonological representations for words are retrieved.

Despite the general agreement on the stages of planning, there is a great deal of debate on the scope of planning at each stage and whether the scope differs for different levels of representation. Some speech error and experimental data have been interpreted as indicating that the scope is larger at the lemma level than at the phonological level. Some researchers have hypothesised that, at the lemma level, the scope of planning might be as large as a clause, whereas at the phonological level the scope might span only a few adjacent words (Garrett, 1975, 1982). This view is supported by speech error data showing that word exchanges frequently occur between words in different phrases but within the same clause (e.g., "My chair seems empty without my room") whereas sound exchanges tend to occur between adjacent words (e.g., "Children interfere with your nife lite..."). Some experimental data have also been taken to support a clausal scope of planning at the lemma level (e.g., Bock & Cutting, 1992; Meyer, 1996) and the planning of only one or two phonological words (that is, content words with associated function words) at the phonological level (e.g., Costa & Caramazza, 2002; Jescheniak, Schriefers, & Hantsch, 2003).

Other researchers have argued that planning at the lemma level occurs at the phrasal level (e.g., Smith & Wheeldon, 1999) or at the single word level (Griffin & Bock, 2000; Meyer, Sleiderink, & Levelt, 1998). Smith and Wheeldon (1999) showed that onset latencies for describing moving pictured objects were about 70 ms longer when the initial noun phrase contained two nouns (e.g., "The ball and the faucet move above the wall") than when the initial noun phrase contained a single noun (e.g., "The ball moves above the faucet and the wall"). They interpreted these results as indicating that subjects planned the entire initial noun phrase prior to the beginning of articulation. The onset latency difference between the two sentence types would not have been expected if subjects were planning at the clausal level or at the single word level. Evidence supporting the claim that planning is only at the single word level comes from studies in which eye movements have been recorded while participants describe pictures. Studies using this methodology have shown a tight linkage between the timing of participants' fixation of an object in the scene and the onset of the word corresponding to the name of the fixated object (Griffin, 2001; Griffin & Bock, 2000; Meyer et al., 1998). For example, Griffin (2001) showed that, in producing a sentence beginning with a conjoined noun phrase, gaze durations and onset latencies for the first noun were related to the encodability of the picture and frequency of the name for the first noun, but unaffected by these variables for the second noun. In order to account for word exchanges across a long distance, those taking a single word or phrasal planning approach argue that these errors arise from errors or interference at the message level (Griffin & Bock, 2000; see also Smith & Wheeldon, 1999, for discussion). Phonological errors spanning several words have been attributed to malfunctioning of the system that is designed to plan only a single phonological word at a time (e.g., a failure to inhibit one phonological representation before proceeding to the planning of the next).

Previous results from our lab support a phrasal scope of planning. Studies of sentence comprehension (R. C. Martin & He, in press; R. C. Martin & Romani, 1994) showed that patients with semantic STM deficits, but not a patient with a phonological STM deficit, had difficulty comprehending sentences for which semantic representations for several individual words had to be maintained in STM before they could be integrated into higher-order propositions (e.g., for sentences with several adjectives preceding a noun). Because these patients performed much better when individual words could be immediately integrated into propositions (e.g., when the adjectives followed the noun), the results indicated that their deficit was specifically at a lexical-semantic level rather than at a more general conceptual level. R. C. Martin and Freedman (2001a, 2001b) showed that the same patients also had difficulty producing adjective-noun phrases and adjective-adjective noun phrases, although they were able to produce the adjectives and nouns in isolation. (A patient with a phonological retention deficit performed at a normal level.)

Thus, they argued that the same lexical-semantic retention capacity is involved in comprehension and production.

In terms of the production model described previously, these lexical-semantic representations might be equated with lemma representations and the buffer holding these representations might be equated with the capacity involved in planning at the level (or levels) intervening between the message level and the phonological level. This level has been assumed to be a level of grammatical encoding (Bock & Levelt, 1994; Fromkin, 1973) and consequently the buffer might be assumed to hold the lexical-semantic representations that are associated with positions in a syntactic frame, or alternatively, the buffer might itself be assumed to be a syntactic frame. As discussed at greater length in Martin, Miller, and Vu (in press), it is unclear that these patients' deficit is a deficit in maintaining lemmas, primarily because there is currently no evidence that these patients have difficulty maintaining syntactic information about several individual words simultaneously, and the term "lemma" necessarily implies that syntactic information is involved. In fact, these patients have been found to perform well on grammaticality judgments even when several words intervene between the words signaling the grammatical errors (R. C. Martin & He, in press; R. C. Martin & Romani, 1994). Consequently, these patients do not seem to have difficulty in holding onto syntactic structure per se, but rather in holding onto the semantic representations that might be linked to slots in such a structure. Thus, we will continue to use lexical-semantic rather than "lemma" in describing the representation involved in these patients' STM deficit.

SEMANTIC RETENTION AND PRODUCING SEMANTICALLY RELATED WORDS

The current experiments follow up on the R. C. Martin and Freedman (2001a, 2001b) findings by examining the effects of semantic relatedness on the production of conjoined noun phrases for patients with different types of short-term memory deficits. If speakers are planning both nouns in a conjoined noun phrase simultaneously, then one might expect an effect of the semantic relatedness of the two words on onset latencies for the phrase. Results from a variety of paradigms involving picture naming suggest that the concurrent activation of two related semantic representations causes an interference effect. For example, in the picture–word interference paradigm described earlier, semantically related distractor words produce greater interference than unrelated words in naming pictures (e.g., Damian & Martin, 1999; Glaser & Dungelhoff, 1984). Other studies have found interference effects that persist across trials. Wheeldon and Monsell (1994) showed that priming a likely competitor for an object's name on one trial had a significant inhibitory effect on naming latency and error rate for those objects, even with several intervening trials between prime and probe. Kroll and Curley (1988) found that when subjects named pictures presented in lists of items from the same category, their reaction time was significantly slower than when they named the pictures presented in an unrelated condition. Kroll and Stewart (1994) replicated this finding with picture naming but showed that word naming was unaffected by this manipulation.

The interference effects in picture naming are thought to arise because the process of word selection is fundamentally competitive (Wheeldon & Monsell, 1994). Models of word production typically assume that speakers access a semantic representation of the picture to be named, which is then used to select an appropriate lexical representation. This lexical representation then provides access to a phonological representation of the word. In going from the semantic representation to the lexical representation, most models assume that several lexical representations are activated in proportion to the degree of semantic overlap between the target and related words. (For example, a picture of a lion will activate the lexical representation for "lion" and, to a lesser degree, "tiger," "leopard," etc.) A lexical representation is chosen when its activation exceeds some absolute or relative threshold. Wheeldon and Monsell put forward two possible causes of interference in picture naming. One possibility is lateral inhibition, in which activation of the target causes related items to be inhibited so that the target can be selected rather than other related competitors. In a semantically related naming task, when one category member is activated, other category members may be inhibited, making it a slower process to activate these related items in ensuing trials. However, one would not expect that such items would be inhibited below baseline, so it is unclear why these items would be at a disadvantage relative to items on unrelated lists. Thus, lateral inhibition does not seem to provide a very satisfying explanation of categorical interference. A second possibility is that, in order for a given lexical representation to be selected, its activation must be a certain proportion above the highest competitor. When competitors are activated from previous trials, the target for any given trial will take longer to move above the critical difference threshold for selection.

These findings on interference and their interpretation have been concerned with interference from a distractor during single picture naming or with the lingering effects of producing a word for one trial on producing a related word later. For the present study, the task is to produce a phrase to describe two objects using a conjoined noun phrase. If speakers carried out the naming process through to phonological access sequentially for each pictured object in turn, then there would be no load on STM and one might expect similar findings for controls and for patients with short-term memory deficits, as these patients do not have difficulty producing single words. However, if speakers attempt to plan both words simultaneously, then they are trying to maintain two different semantic representations simultaneously and a short-term memory deficit could potentially cause difficulties in production. R. C. Martin, Miller, and Vu (in press) recently reported findings supporting the contention that both words in a conjoined noun phrase are planned at a lexical-semantic level prior to speech onset and that a semantic STM deficit impairs production of such phrases. They replicated Smith and Wheeldon's (1999) study showing that onset latencies for describing moving pictured objects were longer when the initial noun phrase

contained two nouns compared to when it contained a single noun. Control subjects showed an effect of about 60 ms whereas a patient with a semantic STM deficit showed an effect of 1027 ms. A patient with a phonological STM deficit showed an effect within normal range.

In terms of the model in Figure 1, the assumption is that speakers who are producing a conjoined noun phrase will first link semantic representations for both nouns in the knowledge structure to nodes in the lexical-semantic buffer and to a syntactic frame for the conjoined noun phrase. (As discussed earlier, it is possible that the buffer and the syntactic frame are one and the same.) Then, attention will be directed towards the noun to be produced first (i.e., the leftmost object in our task) so that phonological retrieval can take place. In order for this to occur, we assume that activation of the lexical node in the knowledge representation for the first object will have to exceed that for the other object by some proportion. We will assume that direction of attention to the first object to be named will serve to increase the activation of its node in the buffer, and consequently, in the knowledge structure. Once this node has reached the activation criterion, its phonology will be retrieved and then attention can be directed to the second object. For semantically related objects, activation of the knowledge representation for one object will serve to activate the knowledge representation for the other (as discussed previously) and thus boost the activation of the associated node. Hence, the time for the node for the first object to reach the critical proportion above that for the other will be longer than when the words are unrelated. Thus, we would expect that even for normal subjects, onset latencies for production of phrases with related nouns should be longer than latencies for phrases with unrelated nouns.

For patients with a semantic short-term memory deficit, planning both items could lead to a strain on their limited capacity. As discussed earlier, the patients' short-term memory deficit is assumed to result from overly rapid decay in the links between the nodes and the knowledge structure. That is, activation in the knowledge structure deriving from the pictured object is assumed to accrue in a normal fashion, and the linkage to a node in the buffer also proceeds normally. However, once these linkages are made, they decay rapidly. When attempting to produce the first item, increases in activation due to attention being directed toward this object would be counteracted by rapid decay. Consequently, activation for the two items ends up being more similar than it would if decay were less rapid. Thus, it might take a very long time for the first item to reach the necessary proportion of activation above that of the other item in order to reach the criterion for the selection of phonology. This difficulty would be particularly severe when the two items are related and each is activating the other. Thus, a patient with a semantic STM deficit may demonstrate increased interference effects from naming pairs of semantically related pictures.

Patients with a phonological STM deficit would not be expected to show this exaggerated interference effect, since their difficulty is not at the level of maintaining lexical-semantic representations. If the patient's deficit is on the input side, that is, in terms of retaining input phonological representations, then no deficit in speech production would be expected (Shallice & Butterworth, 1977). If the patient's deficit is on the output side, then speech production would be expected to show some phonological disorder (Romani, 1992; Shallice, Rumiati, & Zadini, 2000); however, the patient would not be expected to show greater than normal susceptibility to semantic relations between items in the target phrase.

This study tested the hypothesis that semantic relatedness of two nouns in a conjoined noun phrase would produce interference in onset latencies for the phrase and that this effect would be exaggerated for patients with a semantic STM deficit. Patients and controls were presented with one or two pictures to name. In the paired picture conditions, the pairs were either unrelated or semantically related. For the semantically related pairs, both pictured objects were drawn from the same semantic category. Performance on the picture pairs was compared to onset latencies for the same words and word pairs but with written words rather than pictures as input. Reading does not put the same demands on selecting a lexical

representation from semantic input that is involved in picture naming (Kroll & Stewart, 1994). Consequently, one would not expect the same interference effect for semantically related word pairs in oral reading for normal subjects. Moreover, patients with a semantic STM deficit would be predicted to perform in a normal fashion.

PATIENT DESCRIPTIONS

Patient ML

ML was 60 years old at the time of testing. He suffered a left-hemisphere CVA in 1990. CT scan indicated an infarction involving the left frontal and parietal operculum, with atrophy in the left temporal operculum and mild diffuse atrophy. He had completed 2 years of college and had been employed as a draftsman. ML demonstrates good comprehension on single word tasks. For example, he obtained a standardised score of 117 on the Peabody Picture Vocabulary Test (PPVT; Dunn & Dunn, 1981). (See Freedman & Martin, 2001; R. C. Martin & Lesch, 1996, for further information.) His speech is halting and characterised by reduced phrase length. In continuous speech, he sounds anomic. However, he is not classically anomic in that he performs at a high level on tests of single picture naming. On the Philadelphia Naming Task (PNT), he scored 98% correct, which is above the control mean of 96% correct (Saffran, Schwartz, Linebarger, & Bochetto, 1989).

Patient GR

GR was 57 years old at the time of testing. He had received his bachelor's degree in English and History and was working at the Texas Employment Commission before suffering a stroke in 1989. CT scan revealed a large left fronto-parietal-temporal infarction following a middle cerebral artery stroke. GR exhibits good comprehension but reduced output. His speech is characterised by short utterances, which are grammatically correct, and by word-finding difficulty. Similar to ML, he performs within normal range on accuracy in single word comprehension tasks (see Freedman & Martin, 2001). For example, he scored 117 on the PPVT. He scores at the low end of the normal range on picture naming tasks (e.g., 84% correct PNT, where control mean = 96% and SD = 7%).

Patient EA

EA was 73 years at the time of testing. She is a college-educated woman who is a homemaker and participates in a competitive synchronised swimming team. She suffered a left-hemisphere stroke in 1975, involving the left temporal and parietal lobes, including the primary auditory cortex, Wernicke's area, and the superior and inferior parietal lobules. She demonstrates good comprehension and fluent speech, with very occasional phonological paraphasias in multisyllable words. Her performance on single word processing tasks has been reported in several previous publications (Freedman & Martin, 2001; R. C. Martin & Lesch, 1996; R. C. Martin, Shelton, & Yaffee, 1994). She obtained a score of 117 on the PPVT and 93% correct on the PNT.

All three of the patients have reduced memory span. For example, in spoken recall of three-word lists, EA recalled 33% of items in the correct serial position, ML recalled 76%, and GR recalled 79%. In terms of lists recalled in the correct order, EA's word span is 1.5 items with auditory presentation and 2.5 items with visual presentation. ML's word span is 2.5 items with auditory presentation and 1.5 with visual. GR's word span is 3.3 items with auditory presentation and 2.2 items with visual. Patients ML and GR have been identified as having semantic STM deficits (Freedman & Martin, 2001; R. C. Martin & Lesch, 1996), whereas patient EA has been identified as having an input phonological STM deficit (R. C. Martin et al., 1994). Freedman and Martin (2001) tested ML, GR, and EA (plus two other patients) on a variety of tasks that required the retention of semantic or phonological information. Their scores on each of the tasks were converted to z-scores and added together to yield a composite semantic STM score and a composite phonological STM score.

The semantic STM score included performance on four tasks: a category probe task, the difference between a three-choice and a two-choice relatedness judgment task, an attribute judgment task, and the difference between word vs. nonword span, where better performance with words was assumed to reflect a benefit from retention of the words' semantic representations. The phonological STM score included performance on three tasks: a rhyme probe task, the difference between repetition of long (three- and four-syllable) and short (one- and two-syllable) nonwords, and the difference between phoneme discrimination between items presented one after the other and those having a 5-second filled delay between them. Of the five patients in the study, EA had the lowest composite phonological STM score (−4.14) and the highest composite semantic STM score (3.86). Both ML and GR showed the opposite pattern of higher phonological STM scores than semantic STM scores. ML scored −0.23 on the phonological STM score vs. −2.59 on the semantic STM score. While ML may show some impairment of phonological retention, it is much better preserved than his semantic retention ability. GR scored 0.98 on the phonological STM score compared to 0.53 on the semantic retention score. Thus GR was not as impaired as ML on these retention tasks, but he showed the same pattern of better preserved phonological than semantic retention. While the difference was slight, he was clearly more impaired than EA on semantic retention, and thus, differences in the pattern of performance for EA and GR could plausibly be attributed to GR's worse semantic retention ability.

Evidence that EA's phonological retention deficit is on the input side comes from findings indicating that she performs poorly on tests that tap phonological retention even when no output is required (such as on rhyme probe tasks and matching span tasks) (R. C. Martin et al., 1994). Her narrative production is normal in terms of speech rate, sentence length, and grammatical complexity. Assuming that a phonological output buffer is used in spontaneous production, then the normal quality of her speech would suggest that this output buffer is preserved.

METHOD

Participants

Twelve control subjects (aged 55 to 75) and patients ML, GR, and EA were tested in the picture naming condition. Six control subjects (aged 60 to 75) and patients ML and EA completed the word naming task. Patient GR withdrew from the study after completing the picture naming task.

Materials

In the picture naming condition, 10 line-drawing pictures (Snodgrass & Vanderwart, 1980) from each of eight different semantic categories (see Appendix A) were presented on a Macintosh computer using the PsyScope experiment-construction software (Cohen, MacWhinney, Flatt, & Provost, 1993). In the word naming condition, the written names corresponding to these pictures were presented.

Design and procedure

Stimulus pre-testing. A group of 13–15 pictures from each of the eight different categories were presented to six control subjects. They were asked to name each picture as quickly and accurately as possible, in order to determine consistency of the names used across subjects. Naming reaction time was measured using a voice key, which was triggered at the onset of the subject's utterance. Next, the subjects were shown each of the pictures and asked to determine how good an exemplar each picture was of the given category. The purpose of these ratings was to obtain a set of pictures for which there was high agreement that the item belonged to a particular category. For each category, subjects were given a preview of all the pictures. Then, they were shown each picture again and rated the goodness of the exemplar on a scale of 1 (very poor exemplar) to 5 (very good exemplar). From these pictures, the best 10 pictures from each category were chosen, based on naming reaction time, naming consistency, and goodness of category membership. First, the means of the naming

reaction times for each category were calculated and all pictures were discarded with means falling 2 SDs above or below the categorical mean. Of the remaining pictures, those with the highest naming consistency and category exemplar rating scores (M = 4.6, SD = 0.6) were selected. Of the 80 pictures that were selected, 69 had perfect agreement among all subjects tested, 9 had agreement from all but one subject (e.g., violin named as fiddle), and 2 were named incorrectly by two of the subjects tested (boat named as sailboat, and car named as automobile). These pictures were used despite imperfect agreement because agreement was fairly high and, in the actual experiment, subjects were shown the labelled pictures before completing the naming task, so they would know the expected name.

Picture naming task. Subjects were first shown a preview of all the pictures that would be seen during the experiment with the intended name of the picture presented below. Then they completed a practice block in which they named each picture and received feedback from the experimenter if they produced an incorrect name. Next, subjects completed three test blocks of pictures. On the first block, they named the pictures one at a time, with the stipulation that no two pictures from the same category be shown within three trials of each other. In the second and third blocks, pictures were shown in pairs, side by side on the computer screen, and the subjects were asked to produce descriptions such as "nose and hat." They were asked to name the picture on the left first. The second block presented unrelated pairs of pictures from two different categories with the stipulation that no two pictures from the same category be viewed within two trials of each other. In the third block, semantically related pairs were presented, with both pictures from the same category. No two consecutive pairs could come from the same category. The blocks were presented in the same order for each subject as we wanted to examine individual patient data and compare data across patients. Subjects were instructed to name the picture or pair of pictures as quickly and as accurately as possible. The picture(s) disappeared from the screen as soon as the subject began the utterance. The pictures were removed in order to force subjects to attend to both objects before speech onset. The time to onset of the response was measured using a voice-activated relay that was monitored by the computer, and the session was recorded on cassette tape. After each trial, the examiner pressed a key to indicate whether their response was correct, an error, or a voice key error.

In an earlier version of this task, all of the semantically related pairs were presented in a blocked design (all animal pairs, then all vehicle pairs, etc.). Both patients ML and GR showed a large, significant interference effect (474 ms and 244 ms, respectively), while patient EA showed a 68 ms facilitation effect. In the present paradigm, results for ML and GR were similar to those of the early version, but EA showed a marginally significant result in the other direction. Thus, she was tested again several weeks later using the same materials in order to determine the reliability of this finding. Both testing sessions for EA are reported.

Word naming task. The words corresponding to the picture names were presented in 36-point Geneva font in the centre of the screen. The conditions were the same as in the picture naming task and were presented in the same order (single word reading, unrelated word pairs, semantically related word pairs). Each trial began with a fixation "****" for 500 ms followed by the presentation of the word or pair of words presented side by side. There were five practice trials before each block. Subjects were instructed to read each word or pair of words (going from left to right) as quickly and accurately as possible, inserting "and" between the two when producing a pair of words (e.g., "nose and hat"). Words remained on the screen until the onset of the subject's response. The experimenter pressed a key to indicate whether the response was correct, incorrect, or a voice key error.

The picture naming and word naming conditions were presented in different sessions separated by at least 2 weeks. The patients completed the picture naming condition before the word naming condition. Different control subjects completed picture naming and word naming tasks.

RESULTS

Picture naming

Controls

Reaction times. Results for controls and the patients are presented in Table 1. All trials containing response errors or voice key errors were removed from the reaction time data. For the control subjects, 2.0% of the data were removed for voice key errors, and 3.7% for response errors. Next all reaction times that fell more than 2SDs above or below that subject's conditional mean were discarded, which amounted to 4.3% of the data. Control subjects showed an overall effect of picture naming condition, $F(2, 22) = 31.05$, $p < .0005$. They were significantly faster to name single ($M = 758$, $SD = 83$) than unrelated paired ($M = 868$, $SD = 89$), $t(11) = 6.6$, $p = .0001$, or semantically related paired pictures ($M = 909$, $SD = 106$), $t(11) = 5.7$, $p < .0001$. Importantly, they were significantly slower (41 ms; range of effect −20 to 142 ms) to name the semantically related than unrelated pairs, $t(11) = 2.84$, $p = .02$.

Errors. The mean number of trials with an error in each condition for controls and patients is shown in Table 2. Controls also showed an effect of naming condition in the number of errors, $F(2, 22) = 8.34$, $p = .002$. They made fewer errors in the single picture condition ($M = 1.8$, $SD = 1.3$) than the paired unrelated ($M = 3.6$, $SD = 1.9$), $t(11) = 2.9$, $p = .01$, or the paired semantically related ($M = 3.8$, $SD = 1.7$) conditions, $t(11) = 5.0$, $p = .0004$. There was no difference in error rates between the unrelated and semantically related paired conditions, $p > .05$. Most of the control subjects' errors involved the substitution of a semantically related word, usually one of the words in the response set.

Patients

Reaction times. Collapsed across all conditions, the percentage of data removed due to voice key errors was 0% for ML, 11.3% for GR, and 4.0% for EA. There was no difference in the number of voice key errors between the semantically related and unrelated pairs. The percentage of data removed due to response error was 15.8% for ML, 22.5% for

Table 1. *Utterance initiation times for single and paired pictures and words*

	Pilot picture naming	Picture naming	Word naming
Controls[a]			
Single		758 (835)	625
Paired unrelated		868 (901)	658
Paired related		909 (984)	641
Relatedness effect	N/A	41* (83***)	−17**
(range)		(−20 to 142)	(−4 to −26)
ML[a]			
Single		1370 (1169)	732
Paired unrelated		1788 (1562)	1027
Paired related		2371 (2291)	1019
Relatedness effect	474	583** (728***)	−8
GR			
Single		1073	
Paired unrelated		1363	
Paired related		1670	
Relatedness effect	244	307**	
EA[b]			
Single		1347	872
Paired unrelated		1588	895
Paired related		1595	913
Relatedness effect	−68	13	18

* $p < .05$; ** $p < .01$; *** $p < .001$.
[a] Values in parentheses are from retest with related condition preceding unrelated.
[b] The results for EA are averaged cross two sessions.

GR, and 17.7% for EA. When all data that fell more than 2 *SD*s above or below each subject's conditional mean were removed, this amounted to an additional 5% for ML, 3.3% for GR, and 4.0% for EA.

The two patients with semantic short-term memory deficits, ML and GR, showed significant effects of single vs. paired picture naming, and they showed a category interference effect in paired picture naming that was well outside the range of controls (see Table 1). ML showed a significant overall effect of picture naming condition, $F(2, 188) = 13.6$, $p < .0005$. He was significantly faster to name single ($M = 1370$, $SD = 871$) compared to unrelated ($M = 1788$, $SD = 1148$), $t(188) = 2.2$, $p = .03$, or semantically related paired pictures ($M = 2371$ ms, $SD = 1319$), $t(188) = 5.2$, $p < .0005$. He was also faster (583 ms) to name the unrelated pairs than the semantically related pairs, $t(112) = 2.8$, $p = .005$. Though controls also showed

a significant effect of semantic relatedness, ML's effect was more than 14 times larger than the mean effect for controls and 4 times larger than the largest effect for any of the controls.

GR also showed a significant overall effect of picture naming condition, $F(2, 147) = 33.5$, $p < .0005$. He was faster to name the single pictures ($M = 1073$ ms, $SD = 187$) compared to the unrelated pairs ($M = 1363$ ms, $SD = 380$), $t(147) = 3.8$, $p < .0005$, or the semantically related pairs ($M = 1670$ ms, $SD = 533$), $t(147) = 8.2$, $p < .0005$. He was also significantly faster (307 ms) to name the unrelated pairs than the semantically related pairs, $t(147) = 3.8$, $p < .0005$. Though this relatedness effect was not quite as large as ML's, it was 7.5 times larger than the mean effect for controls and more than twice as large as the largest effect for controls. The somewhat smaller effect for GR corresponds to his less severe impairment in semantic retention.

Table 2. *Percentage of errors for single and paired pictures and words*

	Picture naming	Word naming
Control mean[a]		
Single	1.8　(2.5)	0.3
(range)	(0–4)	(0–1)
Paired unrelated	3.6　(2.5)	1.0
(range)	(1–7)	(0–3)
Paired related	3.5　(5.0)	0.5
(range)	(1–6)	(0–2)
ML[a]		
Single	2　(3)	0
Paired unrelated	19　(4)	5
Paired related	17　(5)	11
GR		
Single	6	–
Paired unrelated	27	–
Paired related	22	–
EA[b]		
Single	6	2
Paired unrelated	21	15
Paired related	16	13

[a] Values in parentheses are from re-test with related condition preceding unrelated.

[b] The results for EA are averaged across two sessions.

In EA's first session, she showed a significant effect overall of naming condition, $F(2, 170) = 7.56$, $p = .001$. She was faster in the single picture condition ($M = 1350$, $SD = 482$) compared to the unrelated condition ($M = 1575$, $SD = 638$), $t(170) = 2.03$, $p = .04$, or the semantically related condition ($M = 1773$, $SD = 680$), $t(170) = 3.9$, $p < .0005$. The 198 ms interference for semantically related picture pairs was marginally significant, $t(170) = 1.7$, $p = .09$. As the effect was only slightly outside the range of controls, of marginal significance, and going in the opposite direction to that observed for her in the pilot testing, EA was re-tested on this task several months after completing the first version. In the second session, she also showed a significant effect of naming condition, $F(2, 181) = 4.15$, $p = .02$. She was significantly faster to name single pictures ($M = 1343$, $SD = 554$) than unrelated pictures ($M = 1599$, $SD = 563$), $t(181) = 2.85$, $p = .005$, but not paired semantically related pictures ($M = 1426$, $SD = 349$), $t(181) = 0.93$, $p = .36$. However, she showed

marginally significant facilitation (173 ms) with the semantically related compared to unrelated picture pairs, $t(181) = 1.85$, $p = .07$. Collapsing across the two sessions, she was significantly faster to name single pictures ($M = 1347$, $SD = 518$) than paired unrelated pictures ($M = 1588$, $SD = 597$), $t(354) = 3.36$, $p = .001$, or paired semantically related pictures ($M = 1595$, $SD = 561$), $t(354) = 3.5$, $p = .001$. However, the 13 ms difference between unrelated and semantically related picture pairs failed to reach significance, $t(354) = 0.10$, $p = .92$. As mentioned earlier, both ML and GR were tested previously on another very similar version of this task, in which they showed a qualitatively similar pattern of results to those reported here. Both showed significant interference in the semantically related vs. unrelated picture pairs, well outside the range of controls (474 ms interference for ML and 244 ms for GR).

Errors. In the single picture naming condition, the patients' number of errors was either within or slightly outside the range of controls. In the paired conditions, the number of errors for all patients was far outside the range of controls. Using a Chi-Square test, ML, GR, and EA showed significantly more errors in the unrelated or semantically related paired condition than in the single picture naming condition, all ps < .05. None of the patients showed a significant difference between the number of errors for the unrelated vs. semantically related pairs, $p > .05$.

For all of the patients (as for controls) the largest percentage of errors in the paired conditions consisted of the substitution of a semantically related word. The pattern of errors for the two patients with a semantic STM deficit differed somewhat in that 44% of ML's errors were long hesitations between the production of the first and second picture name whereas GR had only a few such hesitations. A fairly large proportion of GR's errors (19%) involved the omission of one (or both) words whereas ML never made an omission error. Patient EA made a large proportion of word omission errors (36% of her errors on the paired conditions). In these cases, EA consistently produced the name of the first object in the pair but failed to produce the name of the second. Also, EA made 10% phonological errors (e.g., "aliprocter" for helicopter) in each of the two testing sessions in contrast to ML and GR, who made no such errors. These phonological approximations only occurred for three words, all having multiple syllables.

Word naming

Controls

Reaction times to initiate responses are shown in Table 1 and error rates in Table 2. All trials containing subject or voice key errors were removed from the reaction time data. This amounted to 1.6% of the controls' data removed for voice key errors, and 0.7% for subject errors. Next all reaction times that fell more than 2 SDs above or below that subject's conditional mean were discarded, which amounted to 3.3% of the data.

Controls showed a marginally significant overall effect of word naming condition, $F(2,10) = 3.77, p = .06$. In planned comparisons, controls were faster in the single word ($M = 625$ ms, $SD = 145$) than in the paired unrelated word condition ($M = 658$ ms, $SD = 127$), though this difference was only marginally significant, $t(5) = 2.3, p = .07$. The difference between single word naming and semantically related word pair naming ($M = 641$ ms, $SD = 134$) was not significant, $p = .31$. However, controls showed a 17 ms facilitation effect (range = 4 to 26) for the semantically related compared to the unrelated word pair naming, which was significant, $t(5) = 4.5, p = .006$. Error rates for controls were very low for all conditions (see Table 2).

Patients

Collapsed across all conditions, the percentage of data removed due to voice key errors was 3.8% for ML, and 3.8% for EA. There was no difference in the number of voice key errors between the semantically related and semantically unrelated pairs. Data removed due to response error was 6.7% for ML and 12.3% for EA. When all data that fell more than two standard deviations above or below each subject's conditional mean were removed, this amounted to 6.7% for ML, and 3.5% for EA.

Patient ML's utterance initiation times were almost 300 ms longer for the paired than the single conditions, compared to a 20–30 ms effect for controls. The difference between the single ($M = 732$ ms, $SD = 107$) and paired unrelated conditions was significant ($M = 1027$ ms, $SD = 395$), $t(194) = 5.5, p < .0005$, as was the difference between the single and the paired semantically related condition ($M = 1019$ ms, $SD = 374$), $t(194) = 5.1, p < .0005$. In striking contrast to the large category interference effect he showed in the picture naming task, ML showed no interference effect between the unrelated and semantically related word pairs, $p = .9$. The 8 ms facilitation effect was well within the range of effects shown by controls. While he showed no interference effect with respect to onset times, ML did produce a somewhat larger number of errors in the semantically related compared to paired unrelated word naming; however, this difference was not significant, $\chi^2 = 2.5, p = .11$.

As patient EA was tested twice on the picture naming task, she was also tested twice on the word naming task and the results are combined across two testings. She showed no overall effect of word naming condition, $F(2, 390) = 1.9, p = .15$. There was no significant difference between single word naming ($M = 872$, $SD = 147$) and paired unrelated word naming ($M = 895$, $SD = 162$), $t(390) = 1.0, p = .3$, but single word naming was faster than paired related word naming ($M = 913$, $SD = 210$), $t(390) = 2.0, p = .05$. Importantly, she showed no significant difference between naming unrelated and semantically related word pairs, $t(390) = 0.84, p = .4$, though her 18 ms interference effect for semantically related pairs was outside the range of effects for controls. EA showed no significant difference in error rates between the two paired conditions.

DISCUSSION

Picture naming

Previous studies have reported a category interference effect in single picture naming (e.g., Kroll & Curley, 1988; Kroll & Stewart, 1994). In this experiment, control subjects demonstrated a significant interference effect in reaction times for paired picture naming for pairs drawn from the same category vs. pairs drawn from different categories. The interference in onset latency due to the semantic relationship between the first and second noun indicates that subjects were planning both items at the lexical-semantic level. Thus, the results support the contention that both lexical representations in a single phrase are planned before articulation is initiated.

The primary question of interest was whether the nature of the patients' short-term memory deficit would relate to the presence or size of this interference effect. Both patients with a semantic STM deficit, ML and GR, demonstrated a significant semantic interference effect in onset latencies that was well outside the range of controls. In contrast to the exaggerated semantic interference effect demonstrated by the semantic STM deficit patients, patient EA showed a small interference effect when averaged across the two sessions. There was considerable variability in the size of the effect shown by individual control subjects, and the effect for EA fell within their range (see Table 1).

A reviewer questioned whether the picture naming results for the semantic STM patients might be attributed to fatigue, as the paired related condition was always the last condition. ML was re-tested with the single picture condition first, the paired related condition second, and the paired unrelated condition third. Six new control subjects were also tested with this order. The results from the re-test are shown in parentheses in Tables 1 and 2. The results were quite similar to those obtained previously. ML's latencies were overall somewhat faster and his errors were substantially fewer, but he showed an even larger semantic interference effect (728 ms) that was highly significant ($p < .001$). Control subjects also showed a highly significant semantic interference effect with this order of conditions: 83 ms, $p < .001$.

All of the patients produced substantially more errors in the paired than the single picture conditions, with no difference between the two paired conditions. Thus, the exaggerated interference effect for the semantic STM deficit patients was

evident only in their onset latencies. (It should be noted that the interference effect for controls was also evident only in onset latencies.) The errors of the patient with a phonological STM deficit differed from those of the patients with a semantic STM deficit in that EA made substitutions of phonologically related words or nonwords on some trials. A large number of EA's errors in paired picture naming seemed to reflect a forgetting of the second item of the pair, which is similar to her performance on memory span tasks. For example, on two-item list recall, she often reports the first item and fails to recall the second item (R. C. Martin & Lesch, 1996). (This pattern coincides with what N. Martin & Saffran, 1997, reported for patients with a phonological deficit.) It is possible that EA tried to encode both items phonologically before beginning the utterance. That is, because the pictures disappeared with voice onset, she may have been worried that she would forget the second item by the time she was able to utter its name, and thus wished to fully encode both items before beginning articulation. Such a strategy was not very effective for EA, however, as she has difficulty retaining more than one item in a phonological form.

If EA had adopted such a strategy, then one might hypothesise that the other patients had as well. If so, then the evidence for simultaneous planning and the very large interference effect for the patients with a semantic STM deficit may have derived from this strategy of trying to plan both items at a lexical-semantic and phonological level prior to voice onset because of the disappearance of the pictures. Without the constraint of the pictures disappearing, there may be no need to encode both items at a lexical-semantic level. To address this concern, patient ML was asked to name the pictures in Experiment 1 again while they were left in view until the end of his response. (GR was no longer available for testing.) He still showed a large and significant interference (270 ms) effect, $t(131) = 1.98$, $p = .05$ (unrelated picture pairs: $M = 1272$ ms, $SD = 688$; semantically related paired pictures: $M = 1542$, $SD = 875$). Consequently, the findings suggest that simultaneous planning of both nouns occurs even under conditions in which there is no artificial constraint that might force such a strategy.

Word naming

The word naming results for controls were interesting in that they showed facilitation due to semantic relatedness, which contrasted with the interference demonstrated for picture naming. Most models of reading assume that one route for accessing a phonological representation from print is a semantic route—that is, a route in which the orthographic representation activates a semantic representation and the semantic representation then activates a phonological representation (e.g., Hillis & Caramazza, 1995; Plaut, McClelland, Seidenberg, & Patterson, 1996). The semantic to phonological links are assumed to be the same links involved in picture naming. Consequently, one might have expected some degree of interference from semantic relatedness due to the operation of this route, though the effect should have been smaller than in picture naming because of the direct orthographic to phonological connections that are available in word reading.[1] One might hypothesise that the route involving orthographic to phonological representations operates more quickly for most words and thus a contribution of the semantic route is hard to detect. However, if written word naming is not influenced by semantics, then why should there have been any effect at all with respect to the semantic relationship between the words? Damian, Vigliocco, and Levelt (2001) suggested that the semantic facilitation they observed in naming words in categorised lists may have resulted from some interaction between semantic and orthographic activation of target phonological representations. However, they did not spell out how the addition of activation due to input from orthography to phonology could turn a semantic

interference effect into a facilitatory effect. Another possibility involves the assumption that there are separate lexical-semantic and lexical-phonological representations (Levelt, 1989) and that the facilitation is due to associative connections between words at a lexical-phonological level. That is, words that co-occur may be linked such that activation spreads from one to the other (Lupker, 1984; Shelton & Martin, 1992; but see McRae & Boisvert, 1998). At least some of the semantically related words in the present experiment would be expected to have such associative links (e.g., lion and tiger). This hypothesis could be tested by comparing latencies for related pairs that are or are not associatively related—only those with an associative relation would be expected to give rise to facilitation. In order for such spreading activation to explain the different results from picture naming and reading, however, one would have to hypothesise different selection processes at the lexical-semantic and lexical-phonological levels such that coactivation at one level leads to interference but coactivation at the other level leads to facilitation. In addition, since picture naming should involve activation of both lexical-semantic and lexical-phonological representations, one would have to hypothesise that competition at the lexical-semantic level outweighs the facilitation at the lexical-phonological level.

The results from patients on the word naming task provide evidence that the large interference effect for ML in picture naming was not due to some difficulty in articulating semantically related words that was independent of the semantic selection process involved in picture naming. The word naming results for ML are also interesting with regard to their implications for models of reading. Lesch and Martin (1998) showed that ML is a phonological dyslexic patient in that he was able to read all kinds of real words normally, including

---

[1] Traditional dual route models assume that this orthographic to phonological route encodes grapheme–phoneme correspondences, and thus subserves the reading of regularly spelled words and nonwords (Hillis & Caramazza, 1995). Some connectionist models assume that this route encodes orthographic to phonological correspondences for both regular and irregular words and for nonwords (Plaut, McClelland, Seidenberg, & Patterson, 1996). However, both types of models also assume a semantic route that might be expected to produce some interference in naming related words.

irregular words, but was impaired in his ability to read nonwords (38% correct). His impaired nonword reading ability indicates that a route converting orthography to phonology was operating sub-optimally.[2] Consequently, one might have expected a greater contribution of a semantic route to his reading compared to that for controls for whom the orthographic to phonological route operates quickly and accurately. The fact that he showed a small facilitatory effect within the range of controls goes against this prediction. One means of accounting for the results for ML is to hypothesise a third route—that is, a direct route from lexical orthography to lexical phonology (Coltheart, Rastle, Perry, Langdon, & Ziegler, 2001; Coslett, 1991; Schwartz, Saffran, & Marin, 1980), that is preserved for ML. In a recent study, Wu, Martin, and Damian (2002) provided further evidence that ML reads via this third route, as a dual route model could not adequately account for his data. Wu et al. argued that according to a dual route model (with a sublexical orthography to phonology route and a semantic route), a patient with damage to the sublexical route should show longer latencies for reading words for which there is some damage to the semantic route. Although the combined operation of the two routes could lead to the correct response (as argued by Hillis & Caramazza, 1995, in their summation hypothesis), reaction times should be longer. They provided an interactive activation dual route model that substantiated this prediction. Thus, as ML has difficulty in naming body parts (from pictures and from definitions), one would have expected his reading times for body part names to be longer than those for control words. However, this was not found to be the case—reading times for body part names were equivalent to those for control words. The present results provide further evidence consistent with the hypothesis that ML is reading by this third route.

Relation between short-term memory and language processing

The results from the patients provided evidence that the lexical-semantic capacity that is tapped in speech planning is that which is also tapped in word list recall and sentence comprehension. Two patients with lexical-semantic STM deficits showed greatly exaggerated semantic interference effects in conjoined noun phrase production. Thus, the results from ML add to those from R. C. Martin and Freedman (2001) and R. C. Martin et al. (in press) in showing that patients with a lexical-semantic STM deficit have great difficulty in producing phrases containing two or more content words. It should be noted that ML's spontaneous speech has a hesitant, stop-and-start quality, and measures of spontaneous speech show very reduced speech rate and reduced noun phrase and verb phrase complexity. It seems likely that the same capacity restriction that underlies his difficulties in performing the tasks reported here also gives rise to these features of his spontaneous speech.

Patient EA, with a phonological STM deficit, showed considerable variability in results across different testing sessions. However, she never showed the large and highly significant interference effects that were demonstrated by ML in conjoined noun phrase production. When averaging across different administrations of the same task, her interference effects were more similar to controls. EA's more normal pattern of performance may have arisen either because her phonological STM deficit is on the input side and the tasks were tapping output, or because phonological planning proceeds over a more narrow scope than planning at a lexical-semantic level. In order to address the scope of phonological planning in the present paradigm, it would be necessary to manipulate factors related to phonological retrieval and examine whether such factors for the second noun

---

[2] Phonological dyslexics' difficulties in reading nonwords have sometimes been attributed to general difficulty with phonological processing that affects their ability to produce unfamiliar phonological sequences (i.e., nonwords) more than familiar sequences (i.e., words). As a test of phonological processing, R. C. Martin and Lesch (1996) had ML repeat nonwords. They showed that his ability to repeat different types of nonwords was unrelated to his ability to read these nonwords.

in the phrase or sentence influence onset latencies for the first noun. Freedman (2001) made two attempts along these lines. She manipulated number of syllables and word frequency for the two nouns in a conjoined noun phrase. However, for control subjects, an effect of number of syllables was elusive even for the first noun. Word frequency of the first noun had an effect, but frequency of the second noun had no effect on onset latency for the first. These results may indicate that subjects only plan one word at a time at a phonological level.[3] If so, then a phonological STM deficit may have no impact on production even for patients with an output phonological buffer deficit as one word may be within the capacity of such patients.

Relation to other patients with deficits in naming in context

Recently, other patients have been reported who, like the semantic STM deficit patients reported here, have demonstrated much better single picture naming than naming in the context of other pictures to be named. McCarthy and Kartsounis (2000) and Wilshire and McCarthy (2002) each reported a case that showed a significant decrement in accuracy in naming pictures when the pictures were blocked by semantic category compared to unblocked presentation, particularly when the pictures were presented at a fast rate. They hypothesised that this decrement was due to a difficulty in selecting among competing lemma representations. These patients appear similar to the semantic STM deficit patients reported here in that their spontaneous speech was halting and seemingly anomic, yet their single picture naming (and single word comprehension) was well preserved. Short-term memory performance was not reported for these patients and thus it is unclear whether they would show a similar pattern to ML and GR. One difference between these patients' performance and that of ML and GR is that semantic relatedness had

an effect on accuracy. The effects of semantic relatedness for ML and GR appeared in their onset latencies and not in accuracy. However, it is possible that ML's and GR's deficits are simply less severe, and thus a more subtle reaction time effect of semantic relatedness is all that can be observed. Of course, there are substantial differences in the naming tasks presented here and those used by McCarthy and Kartsounis and Wilshire and McCarthy, making direct comparison difficult.

Schwartz and Hodgson (2002) also reported a patient (MP) who demonstrated a contextual effect on naming. This patient performed much better in naming single pictures at a self-paced rate than in naming the same items in a scene containing several of the pictures. A similar contextual decrement was seen even when the multi-picture condition consisted of two or more pictures in a row that were to be named from left to right. Unlike the cases reported by McCarthy and Kartsounis (2000) and Wilshire and McCarthy (2002), MP was unaffected by semantic relatedness in speeded picture naming. However, Schwartz and Hodgson did not report naming latencies. They did report short-term memory performance, and concluded that MP showed a deficit in both phonological and semantic retention. MP, unlike ML and GR, produced a considerable proportion of phonological errors in naming pairs of pictures. Schwartz and Hodgson concluded that access to multiple lemmas occurred normally for MP, but serial selection of an appropriate lexical-phonological representation (i.e., lexeme) was impaired because of a failure of syntactic control processes that boost the activation of the appropriate lemma when it is to be selected for production.

For all of these cases, we and the other authors are proposing that these patients have preserved lexical-semantic representations but deficient processes that act upon these representations— retention processes in our view, selection processes in the view of McCarthy and Kartsounis (2000) and

---

[3] As discussed earlier, phonologically based speech errors that span more than a single phonological word have been attributed to the malfunctioning of a system designed to produce a single word.

Wilshire and McCarthy (2002), and a syntactic process in the view of Schwartz and Hodgson (2002). All of these patients have lesions that are limited to or include frontal regions, consistent with the notion of a disruption of control processes. Because of differences in tasks administered and in dependent measures (i.e., reaction time vs. accuracy) it is difficult to determine at this point the extent of similarity or dissimilarity amongst the symptoms and underlying deficits in all of these cases. Further research will be needed to determine whether several independent control mechanisms need to be postulated to account for the seeming differences in the cases. In any event, all of these suggest that there are frontal mechanisms involved in lexical selection for language production that are important when producing words in the context of other words—which, of course, is critical for ordinary communication.

REFERENCES

Bock, K., & Cutting, J. C. (1992). Regulating mental energy: Performance units in language production. *Journal of Memory and Language, 31*, 99–127.

Bock, K., & Levelt, W. (1994). Language production: Grammatical encoding. In M. A. Gernsbacher (Ed.), *Handbook of psycholinguistics* (pp. 945–984). San Diego, CA: Academic Press.

Cohen, J. D., MacWhinney, B., Flatt, M., & Provost, J. (1993). PsyScope: A new graphic interactive environment for designing psychology experiments. *Behavioral Research Methods, Instruments, and Computers, 25*, 257–271.

Coltheart, M., Rastle, K., Perry, C., Langdon, R., & Ziegler, J. (2001). DRC: A dual route cascaded model of visual word recognition and reading aloud. *Psychological Review, 108*, 204–256.

Coslett, H. B. (1991). Read but not write "idea": Evidence for a third reading mechanism. *Brain and Language, 40*, 425–433.

Costa, A., & Caramazza, A. (2002). The production of noun phrases in English and Spanish: Implications for the scope of phonological encoding in speech production *Journal of Memory and Language, 46*, 178–198.

Crowder, R. (1993). Short-term memory: Where do we stand? *Memory and Cognition, 12*, 142–145.

Damian, M. F., & Martin, R. C. (1999). Semantic and phonological codes interact in single word production. *Journal of Experimental Psychology: Learning, Memory, and Cognition, 25*, 345–361.

Damian, M. F., Vigliocco, G., & Levelt, W. J. M. (2001). Effects of semantic context in the naming of pictures and words. *Cognition, 81*, B77–B86.

Dell, G. S. (1986). A spreading-activation theory of retrieval in sentence production. *Psychological Review, 93*, 283–321.

Dell, G. S., & O'Seaghdha, P. G. (1992). Stages of lexical access in language production. *Cognition, 42*, 287–314.

Dell, G. S., Schwartz, M. F., Martin, N., Saffran, E. M., & Gagnon, D. A. (1997). Lexical access in aphasic and nonaphasic speakers. *Psychological Review, 104*(4), 801–838.

Dunn, L., & Dunn, L. (1981). *Peabody Picture Vocabulary Test-Revised*. Circle Pines, MN: Guidance Service.

Freedman, M. L. (2001). *Effects of short-term memory deficits on speech planning and production*. Unpublished doctoral dissertation, Rice University.

Freedman, M. L., & Martin, R. C. (2001). Dissociable components of short-term memory and their relation to long-term learning. *Cognitive Neuropsychology, 18*, 193–226.

Fromkin, V. (1973). *Speech errors as linguistic evidence*. The Hague: Mouton.

Garrett, M. F. (1975). The analysis of sentence production. In G. H. Bower (Ed.), *The psychology of learning and motivation* (pp. 133–177). New York: Academic Press.

Garrett, M. F. (1982). Production of speech: Observations from normal and pathological language use. In A. W. Ellis (Ed.), *Normality and pathology in cognitive functions* (pp. 19–76). London: Academic Press.

Glaser, W. R., & Dungelhoff, F.-J. (1984). The time course of picture-word interference. *Journal of Experimental Psychology: Human Perception and Performance, 10*, 640–654.

Griffin, Z. M. (2001). Gaze durations during speech reflect word selection and phonological encoding. *Cognition, 82*, B1–B14.

Griffin, Z. M., & Bock, K. (2000). What the eyes say about speaking. *Psychological Science, 11*, 274–279.

Hillis, A. E., & Caramazza, A. (1995). Converging evidence for the interaction of semantic and sublexical phonological information in accessing lexical representations for spoken output. *Cognitive Neuropsychology, 12*, 187–227.

Jescheniak, J. D., Schriefers, H., & Hantsch, A. (2003). Utterance format affects phonological priming in the picture-word task: Implications for models of phonological encoding in speech production. *Journal of Experimental Psychology: Human Perception and Performance, 29,* 441–454.

Kempen, G., & Huijbers, P. (1983). The lexicalization process in sentence production and naming: Indirect election of words. *Cognition, 14,* 185–209.

Kroll, J. F., & Curley, J. (1988). Lexical memory in novice bilinguals: The role of concepts in retrieving second language words. In M. Gruneberg, P. Morris, & R. Sykes (Eds.), *Practical aspects of memory* (Vol. 2, pp. 389—395). London: John Wiley.

Kroll, J. F., & Stewart, E. (1994). Category interference in translation and picture naming: Evidence for asymmetric connections between bilingual memory representations. *Journal of Memory and Language, 33,* 149–174.

Lesch, M. F., & Martin, R. C. (1998). The representation of sublexical orthographic-phonologic correspondences: Evidence from phonological dyslexia. *Quarterly Journal of Experimental Psychology, 51A,* 905–938.

Levelt, W. J. M. (1989). *Speaking: From intention to articulation.* Cambridge, MA: MIT Press.

Levelt, W. J. M., Roelofs, A., & Meyer, A. S. (1999). A theory of lexical access in speech production. *Behavioral and Brain Sciences, 22,* 1–75.

Lupker, S. J. (1984). Semantic priming without association: A second look. *Journal of Verbal Learning and Verbal Behavior, 23,* 709–733.

Martin, N., Dell, G. S., Saffran, E. M., & Schwartz, M. F. (1996). Origins of paraphasias in deep dysphasia: Testing the consequences of a decay impairment to an interactive spreading activation model of lexical retrieval. *Brain and Language, 47,* 609–660.

Martin, N., & Saffran, E. (1990). Repetition and verbal STM in transcortical sensory aphasia: A case study. *Brain and Language, 39,* 254–288.

Martin, N., & Saffran, E. (1992). A computational account of deep dysphasia. Evidence from a single case study. *Brain and Language, 43,* 240—274.

Martin, N., & Saffran, E. (1997). Language and auditory-verbal short-term memory impairments: Evidence for common underlying processes. *Cognitive Neuropsychology, 14,* 641–682.

Martin, N., Saffran, E., & Dell, G. S. (1996). Recovery in deep dysphasia: Evidence for a relation between auditory-verbal short-term memory and lexical errors in repetition. *Brain and Language, 52,* 83–113.

Martin, R. C. (1990). Neuropsychological evidence on the role of short-term memory in sentence processing. In G. Vallar & T. Shallice (Eds.), *Neuropsychological impairments of short-term memory* (pp. 390–427). Cambridge: Cambridge University Press.

Martin, R. C. (1993). Short-term memory and sentence processing: Evidence from neuropsychology. *Memory and Cognition, 21,* 176–183.

Martin, R. C., & Freedman, M. L. (2001a). The neuropsychology of verbal working memory: The ins and outs of phonological and lexical-semantic retention. In H. L. Roediger, J. S. Nairne, I. Neath, & A. M. Surprenant (Eds.), *The nature of remembering: Essays in honor of Robert G. Crowder.* Washington, DC: American Psychological Association Press.

Martin, R. C., & Freedman, M. L. (2001b). Short-term retention of lexical-semantic representations: Implications for speech production. *Memory, 9,* 261–280.

Martin, R. C., & He., T. (in press). Semantic short-term memory deficit and language processing: A replication. *Brain and Language.*

Martin, R. C., & Lesch, M. (1996). Associations and dissociations between language processing and list recall: Implications for models of short-term memory. In S. Gathercole (Ed.), *Models of short-term memory* (pp. 149–178). Hove, UK: Lawrence Erlbaum Associates Ltd.

Martin, R. C., Lesch, M. F., & Bartha, M. C. (1999). Independence of input and output phonology in word processing and short-term memory. *Journal of Memory and Language, 40,* 1–27.

Martin, R. C., Miller, M., & Vu, H. (in press). Lexical-semantic retention and speech production: Further evidence from normal and brain-damaged participants for a phrasal scope of planning. *Cognitive Neuropsychology.*

Martin, R. C., & Romani, C. (1994). Verbal working memory and sentence comprehension: A multiple-components view. *Neuropsychology, 8,* 506–523.

Martin, R. C., Shelton, J., & Yaffee, L. S. (1994). Language processing and working memory: Neuropsychological evidence for separate phonological and semantic capacities. *Journal of Memory and Language, 33,* 83–111.

McCarthy, R. A., & Kartsounis, L. D. (2000). Wobbly words: Refractory anomia with preserved semantics. *Neurocase, 6,* 487–497.

McRae, K., & Boisvert, S. (1998). Automatic semantic similarity priming. *Journal of Experimental Psychology: Learning, Memory and Cognition, 24,* 558–572.

Meyer, A. S. (1996). Lexical access in phrase and sentence production: Results from picture-word interference experiments. *Journal of Memory and Language, 35,* 477–496.

Meyer, A., Sleiderink, A., & Levelt, W. (1998). Viewing and naming objects: Eye movements during noun phrase production. *Cognition, 66,* B25–B33.

Plaut, D. C., McClelland, J. L., Seidenberg, M. S., & Patterson, K. (1996). Understanding normal and impaired word reading: Computational principles in quasi-regular domains. *Psychological Review, 103,* 56–115.

Roelofs, A. (1992). A spreading-activation theory of lexical representation retrieval in speaking. *Cognition, 42,* 107–142.

Romani, C. (1992). Are there distinct input and output buffers? Evidence from an aphasic patient with an impaired output buffer. *Language and Cognitive Processes, 7,* 131–162.

Romani, C., & Martin, R. (1999). A deficit in the short-term retention of lexical-semantic information: Forgetting words but remembering a story. *Journal of Experimental Psychology: General, 128,* 56–77.

Romani, C., McAlpine, S., Olson, A., & Martin, R. C. (2003). *Concreteness effects in serial recall: Evidence for semantic STM.* Manuscript submitted for publication.

Ruchkin, D., Grafman, J., Cameron, K., & Berndt, R. (in press). Working memory retention systems: A state of activated long-term memory. *Behavioral and Brain Sciences.*

Saffran, E. M., & Martin, N. (1990). Neuropsychological evidence for lexical involvement in short-term memory. In G. Vallar & T. Shallice (Eds.), *Neuropsychological impairments of short-term memory* (pp. 145–166). London: Cambridge University Press.

Saffran, E., Schwartz, M., Linebarger, M., & Bochetto, P. (1989). *The Philadelphia Comprehension Battery.* Unpublished.

Schwartz, M. F., & Hodgson, C. (2002). A new multiword naming deficit: Evidence and interpretation. *Cognitive Neuropsychology, 19,* 263–288.

Schwartz, M. F., Saffran, E. M., & Marin, O. S., (1980). Fractionating the reading process in dementia:

Evidence for word-specific print-to-sound associations. In M. Coltheart, K. E. Patterson, & J. C. Marshall (Eds.), *Deep dyslexia.* London: Routledge & Kegan Paul.

Shallice, T., & Butterworth, B. (1977). Short-term memory impairment and spontaneous speech. *Neuropsychologia, 15,* 729–735.

Shallice, T., Rumiati, R. I., & Zadini, A. (2000). The selective impairment of the phonological output buffer. *Cognitive Neuropsychology, 17,* 517–546.

Shelton, J. R., & Martin, R. C. (1992). How semantic is automatic semantic priming? *Journal of Experimental Psychology: Learning, Memory, and Cognition, 18,* 1191–1210.

Smith, M., & Wheeldon, L. R. (1999). High level processing scope in spoken sentence production. *Cognition, 73,* 205–246.

Snodgrass, J. G., & Vanderwart, M. (1980). A standardized set of 260 pictures: Norms for name agreement, image agreement, familiarity, and visual complexity. *Journal of Experimental Psychology: Human Learning and Memory, 6,* 174–215.

Vallar, G., & Baddeley, A. D. (1984). Fractionation of working memory: Neuropsychological evidence for a phonological short-term store. *Journal of Verbal Learning and Verbal Behavior, 23,* 151–161,

Walker, I., & Hulme, C. (1999). Concrete words are easier to recall than abstract words: Evidence for a semantic contribution to short-term serial recall. *Journal of Experimental Psychology: Learning, Memory, and Cognition, 25,* 1256–1271.

Wheeldon, L. R., & Monsell, S. (1994). Inhibition of spoken word production by priming a semantic competitor. *Journal of Memory and Language, 33,* 332–356.

Wilshire, C. F., & McCarthy, R. A. (2002). Evidence for a context-sensitive word retrieval disorder in a case of nonfluent aphasia. *Cognitive Neuropsychology, 19,* 165–186.

Wu, D. H., Martin, R. C., & Damian, M. F. (2002). A third route for reading? Implications from a case of phonological dyslexia. *Neurocase, 8,* 274–293.

APPENDIX A

Stimuli used in picture naming and word naming

Kitchen things	Animals	Fruits/ vegetables	Clothing	Body parts	Musical instruments	Vehicles	Tools
cup	cat	banana	belt	eye	bell	car	hoe
glass	elephant	corn	shoe	ear	harmonica	bicycle	hammer
pitcher	horse	pineapple	dress	hand	violin	helicopter	rake
knife	camel	carrot	mitten	finger	xylophone	wagon	wrench
ladle	giraffe	onion	pants	foot	piano	airplane	scissors
toaster	bear	strawberry	skirt	shoulder	guitar	train	saw
spoon	dog	grapes	sock	arm	saxophone	bus	pliers
refrigerator	owl	pear	glove	nose	harp	sled	shovel
bowl	cow	apple	shirt	thumb	drum	truck	screw
fork	zebra	pumpkin	coat				

COGNITIVE NEUROPSYCHOLOGY, 2004, 21 (2/3/4), 267–282

THE ROLE OF PROCESSING SUPPORT IN THE REMEDIATION OF APHASIC LANGUAGE PRODUCTION DISORDERS

Marcia C. Linebarger[1]

Psycholinguistic Technologies, Inc and Moss Rehabilitation Research Institute, Philadelphia, PA, USA

Denise McCall and Rita S. Berndt

University of Maryland School of Medicine, Baltimore, MD, USA

Performance factors such as resource or memory limitations, as opposed to loss of linguistic knowledge per se, are increasingly implicated in aphasic language impairments. Here we investigate the consequences of this hypothesis for the remediation of aphasic language production. Two nonfluent aphasic subjects used a computerised communication system (CS) to practice narrative production. The CS serves primarily as a "processing prosthesis," allowing the user to record spoken sentence elements, replay these elements, and build them up into larger structures by manipulating icons on the screen. Use of the CS in conjunction with explicit training of syntactic structure has been reported to bring about gains in unaided language production. Here we examine the treatment impact of CS-based processing support alone. Eleven weeks of independent home use of the CS resulted in some marked changes in one subject's production of unaided spoken narratives. The most striking and consistent changes involved more structured and informative speech. The second subject, who presented with far more severe lexical impairments, did not show comparable gains in the structural properties of his unaided speech, but was able to produce markedly more structured narratives when aided by the CS. These results support the performance hypothesis because the CS provided no structure-modelling or feedback. In addition, the first subject's treatment gains indicate that practising narrative production with processing support may be effective in bringing about increased structural complexity and informativeness in aphasic speech. This is congruent with other claims in the literature that increasing the complexity or difficulty of the training material may in some cases increase the efficacy of the treatment.

---

[1] ML owns shares in Psycholinguistic Technologies, Inc., which will release commercially the software described in this paper. In order to guard against any conflict of interest, therefore, ML did not participate in subject testing or in the scoring of raw data.

Correspondence should be addressed to Marcia Linebarger, Psycholinguistic Technologies, Inc, 1520 Spruce Street, Suite 406, Philadelphia, PA 19102, USA (Email: linebarger@alum.mit.edu).

This research was supported by NIH grants R01DC00856 and R01DC00262 to the University of Maryland School of Medicine. We are grateful to Michael Weinrich, Myrna Schwartz, Karalyn Patterson, and an anonymous reviewer for helpful comments. Above all, we gratefully acknowledge the influence of our friend and colleague Eleanor M. Saffran, whose ideas and findings directly underpin the current study through her seminal work on the preservation of linguistic knowledge in agrammatism, the role of memory in language processing, and the development of quantitative methods and psycholinguistic models for the analysis of aphasic language disorders.

DOI:10.1080/02643290342000537

INTRODUCTION

The performance hypothesis

A major focus of research into aphasic language disorders over the past quarter century has been to exploit our increasingly rich understanding of the structure and complexity of linguistic information to construct models of normal and aphasic language processing. Deviant utterances or interpretations are central to this enterprise, but cannot necessarily be taken as the transparent reflections of underlying ability. Rather, such errors may arise through the interplay between linguistic knowledge and performance factors such as memory or resource limitations. Interpretations of aphasic error patterns differ in the extent to which these patterns are attributed to loss of knowledge or ability (the "competence hypothesis") or to the disruptions caused by limitations of memory or resources (the "performance hypothesis"). This latter view has been articulated in considerable detail by Kolk and colleagues (Haarmann & Kolk, 1991; Hartsuiker & Kolk, 1998; Kolk, 1995), who have argued that delayed activation or rapid decay of lexical, syntactic, or semantic information may trigger structural degradation through a reduced temporal window available for linguistic computations, even if parsing or grammatical encoding mechanisms are themselves intact.

The challenge undertaken by researchers in recent years has been to discover the sources of this disruption, to spell out the memory or access impairments underlying aphasic language deficits. The range of possibilities is vast. As regards memory, investigators have linked aphasic impairments to a global resource deficit (Blackwell & Bates, 1995) but also to more specific disruptions, e.g., working memory for comprehension (Miyake, Carpenter, & Just, 1994), working memory for receptive syntax (Caplan & Waters, 1995), or impaired retention of lexico-semantic information (Martin & Freedman, 2000). Studies of lexical processing also reveal a range of possibilities for performance-based (rather than knowledge-based) word-finding disorders in aphasia. The finding that some aphasic patients experience more difficulty with naming in connected speech (Williams & Canter, 1982) or in multiword nonsentential utterances (Schwartz & Hodgson, 2002) than with confrontation naming lends support to the performance account. Whether this effect arises from semantic refractoriness (Forde & Humphreys, 1995; Warrington & Cipolotti, 1996) or from item selection deficits (Thompson-Schill, D'Esposito, Aguirre, & Farah, 1997; Wilshire & McCarthy, 2002), it underscores the complex relationship between linguistic knowledge and real-time exploitation of that knowledge.

This interplay between competence and performance has been most prominently discussed in the context of the aphasic category of "agrammatism." The ill-formed, structurally and/or morphologically impoverished output of agrammatic aphasics is often seen in conjunction with a pattern of comprehension errors turning on the same grammatical devices that are implicated in production (Caramazza & Zurif, 1976; Heilman & Scholes, 1976; Saffran, Schwartz, & Marin, 1980; Salomon, 1914; Schwartz, Saffran, & Marin, 1980). The most transparent interpretation would be that these patterns directly reflect the agrammatic subjects' grammatical knowledge or ability to perform grammatical operations.

There are several pieces of evidence weighing against this competence-based account of the symptoms included in agrammatism. First, the comprehension impairment that is often found in such patients does not apparently reflect a loss of syntactic competence. Evidence on this point includes the near-normal sensitivity of these patients to grammatical structure on grammaticality/acceptability judgment tasks (Friederici, 1982; Linebarger, Schwartz, & Saffran, 1983; Shankweiler, Crain, Gorrell, & Tuller, 1988; Wulfeck, Bates, & Capasso, 1991) and the induction of agrammatic comprehension patterns in normal subjects in dual task paradigms (Blackwell & Bates, 1995; Miyake et al., 1994).

The complex relationship between aphasic error patterns and underlying competence is exemplified in the results of a study by Saffran and co-workers (Saffran, 2001; Saffran & Schwartz, 1994; Saffran, Schwartz, & Linebarger, 1998) using a plausibility judgment task. Aphasic subjects performed well above chance in detecting the implausibility of sentences like "The squirrel dropped the puppy," in which neither subject nor object noun violates semantic constraints associated with the verb (since both squirrels and dogs can be agents or themes of "drop"), but the proposition taken as a whole is implausible. The same subjects showed a marked decline in performance when the lexical content was manipulated so that the syntactically correct interpretation was the *opposite* of the interpretation supported by lexico-semantic heuristics based upon these constraints, as in "The cheese ate the mouse," in which the subject noun violates semantic constraints of the verb (cheese cannot be the agent of "eat"). The insensitivity to these latter anomalies cannot be attributed to an inability to use word order cues to meaning, given the same subjects' ability to detect the proposition-based anomalies, but must rather reflect the influence of extra-grammatical heuristics operating in parallel with grammar-based interpretive processes. When syntactic control is diminished as a result of decreased automaticity or limitations of resource or memory, the influence of the lexico-semantic heuristics is increased. Such reduction of grammatical influences has been invoked to explain reaction time effects in normal sentence processing (Bever, 1970; Slobin, 1966; Trueswell, Tanenhaus, & Garnsey, 1994), but in aphasic language processing it is also associated with error effects.

Other evidence against a global competence account of agrammatism is the apparent heterogeneity of that descriptive category. Not all patients exhibiting the agrammatic speech pattern demonstrate problems with sentence comprehension (Berndt, Mitchum, & Haendiges, 1996), and elements of the production pattern considered emblematic of "agrammatism" have been shown to dissociate. Saffran and colleagues, using a reliable quantitative system for analysing aphasic speech samples, showed that the structural symptoms of agrammatism (fragmentary speech and simplified structures) can occur in the context of relatively normal use of grammatical morphemes (Saffran, Berndt, & Schwartz, 1989). More fine-grained analyses (e.g., Rochon, Saffran, Berndt, &

Schwartz, 2000) have established the dissociability of freestanding versus bound grammatical morphemes, with impaired use of bound grammatical morphemes linked to "structural" agrammatism. These dissociations suggest that different functional disorders may underlie the distinct symptoms that have been described as "agrammatism."

Studies of sentence production have also provided support for the performance hypothesis. The variability of agrammatic production is the most compelling datum. Individual speakers show sometimes marked variation in the syntactic structure of their utterances across different modalities (writing versus speech), task demands, or other contextual factors (Bastiaanse, 1994; Isserlin, 1922; Micelli, Mazzucchi, Menn, & Goodglass, 1983; Kolk & Heeschen, 1992). Furthermore, the ability to induce otherwise unavailable syntactic structures by syntactic priming techniques in agrammatic speakers (Hartsuiker & Kolk, 1998; Saffran & Martin, 1990) suggests that these structures are at least weakly present.

Very strong experimental support for the performance-based account of agrammatic production comes from a study (Linebarger, Schwartz, Romania, Kohn, & Stephens, 2000) in which agrammatic aphasics produced spoken video narratives using a communication system (CS) designed for aphasic speakers. The purpose of the CS is to alleviate some of the specific performance factors underlying aphasic production (e.g., the impact of slowed retrieval and/or rapid decay of linguistic information), thereby serving as a "processing prosthesis." The CS allows aphasic subjects to record words or phrases on the computer. These elements are then associated with icons that can be replayed or moved to different areas of the screen to build up larger units such as sentences and narratives. Five of the six agrammatic subjects in this study produced significantly more structured utterances on the CS than they were able to produce unaided. Since the CS provided no linguistic information (a limited word-finding tool having been disabled for testing), the more structured utterances produced on the CS (henceforth termed the *aided/unaided effect*) provide evidence in support of the performance hypothesis.

It is worth noting that improved structure in the CS-aided condition in this study was demonstrated using the quantitative analysis system devised by Saffran et al. (1989), which has been shown to be reliable across subjects over multiple samples, and across scorers on the same samples (Rochon et al., 2000). This system makes it possible to investigate improvements in specific aspects of aphasic production resulting from the use of assistive technology (e.g., the aided/unaided effect noted above) or from treatment interventions.

Implications for language therapy

To the extent that aphasic language disorders reflect processing limitations rather than loss of linguistic knowledge, the focus of language therapy shifts away from language instruction and toward the goal of remediating or compensating for these processing limitations. Increasing the automaticity of linguistic operations (e.g., lexical access or grammatical encoding) may compensate for diminished resources. Alternatively, it is possible that certain kinds of training may be able to ameliorate the underlying processing limitations themselves, e.g., by increasing the subject's ability to retain certain kinds of linguistic material in working memory. Finally, a treatment protocol which brings about functional reorganisation of the language production system may compensate for processing deficits (Springer, Huber, Schlenck, & Schlenck, 2000). In all cases, however, the focus is upon restoring access to linguistic knowledge rather than upon re-inculcating that knowledge.

Approaches to treatment may be classified along the dimension of task difficulty. At one end of the continuum lies an approach which may be termed "bottom up." The focus here is on isolating the component parts of a cognitive process in the hope that increased automaticity in these processes will scale up to more demanding and naturalistic contexts. On this approach, one might train subjects on syntactically unelaborated structures and simplify message level processing by the use of single pictures designed to elicit the target structure. At the other end of the continuum, a "top-down" approach would be to practise language production under more challenging circumstances, either in syntactically complex sentences or in message-level contexts approaching normal complexity; for example, eliciting descriptions of a videotaped series of interconnected events. The latter task increases the demands of message level processing (e.g., Marshall, Pring, & Chiat, 1993), thereby increasing the drain on resources and also complicating lexical access and grammatical encoding through the potential of more complex material to activate competing lexical and syntactic choices. That is, since a complex event can typically be parsed into subevents in many more ways than can a single picture designed to elicit a specific sentence, competing event parses may have the effect of activating competing linguistic material even if the event itself has been processed accurately. In addition, if the message incorporates a series of actions, this may result in the simultaneous activation of words and structures that are not relevant to a particular sentence under construction.

The impact of increased narrative-level complexity on aphasic speech is demonstrated dramatically in Weinrich, Shelton, McCall, and Cox (1997). Following intensive training of a small set of vocabulary items and syntactic structures, aphasic subjects showed improved production of single sentences in response to single pictures depicting isolated propositions, but this improvement did not generalise to even a minimally more difficult task, the elicitation of two-sentence narratives (retelling short videotaped vignettes, each depicting two distinct actions). Most evident was the degradation of syntactic structure in this latter task, which employed exactly the same trained vocabulary and sentence structures as the single-sentence task. Because the subjects in this study were severely aphasic and may not have had many syntactic structures even weakly available, their poor performance on the narrative task is not surprising. Nonetheless, the contrast between their performance on single vs. multi-sentence production tasks illustrates the impact of message-level complexity.

More generally, the limitations of "bottom-up" training are suggested by the typical (although not universal) failure of sentence level treatment interventions to generalise to narrative production (e.g., Berndt & Mitchum, 1995; although see, e.g., Jacobs & Thompson, 2000). There is considerable evidence that the degradation of performance in such multisentence tasks is not due to impaired message-level processing (Ulatowska, Weiss-Doyell, Friedman-Stern, & Macaluso-Haynes, 1983; Weinrich et al., 1997). The most plausible hypothesis is that the increased processing load imposed by narrative production tasks disrupts language production in aphasic patients, and that treatment interventions that do not increase the automaticity of language processing or ameliorate the underlying processing limitations will not lead to gains in narrative production.

Thompson, Shapiro, and Ballard (1998) propose a top-down approach, training aphasic subjects on complex structures incorporating wh-movement. Their interestingly counterintuitive finding is that training on linguistically complex syntactic structures is more effective than working up to such structures through training in their simpler subcomponents. Thompson et al. frame their Complexity Account of Treatment Efficacy (CATE) in terms of syntactic complexity, although the account remains to be more fully specified, especially as regards the reasons for this effect and whether it derives from grammatical properties of the more complex structures or from the more intense processing demands they presumably impose. Nonetheless, the CATE paradigm has been associated with treatment effects that do generalise to narrative production.

Narrative production itself is a highly demanding task. Thus a testable prediction of the top-down approach is that practising narrative production may bring about more automaticity in the production of a given syntactic structure—assuming that this structure is at least weakly available—than will practising this same syntactic structure under less demanding circumstances (e.g., eliciting descriptions of single pictures designed to elicit the target structure). There is, however, an important "catch-22": The task of producing a complex narrative is so resource-demanding that syntactic structure typically degrades markedly in such

contexts, and hence a target structure that can be elicited in a single picture description task may never be produced in a multisentence narrative production task. (Note, however, that an approach such as the Reduced Syntax Therapy—REST—of Springer et al., 2000, may allow the user to practise assembling more complex syntactic structures, because it limits processing demands by explicitly discouraging morphological encoding.) This raises the possibility that the CS might be used to test the above prediction, since it allows patients to practise spoken language under the demanding conditions of multisentence production. Linebarger, Schwartz, and Kohn (2001) explored this possibility, reporting that two subjects who used the CS to produce narratives in a language therapy programme made impressive treatment gains, showing increases of length and structural complexity in *unaided* multisentence productions, as demonstrated by the quantitative analysis system of Saffran et al. (1989). However, the two subjects in this study used the CS in conjunction with a second computer program that employed speech recognition and natural language understanding to facilitate "bottom-up" practice of specific structures, using single pictures designed to elicit the target structure. The impact of CS-supported narrative production was not assessed in isolation. Here we report the results of a study in which two chronically aphasic subjects used the CS alone to practice narrative production.

SUBJECTS

Two subjects (S1, S2) with severe chronic non-fluent aphasia are reported in this study. Both subjects were right-handed, had suffered single left-hemisphere strokes, and had been aphasic for at least 4 years. Residual effects of their strokes included mild right hemiparesis, mild dysarthria, and aphasia. Demographic information and pre-training narrative production samples for the two subjects are presented in Table 1. Prior to this study, both subjects had undergone individual outpatient speech treatment in a number of settings. S1 had undergone intensive speech

Table 1. *Subject information*

	S1	*S2*
Age	70	54
Date of onset	11/83	7/97
Education	PhD	High school
Occupation	CEO/engineer	Bricklayer
Lesion	Large infact, L posterior frontal lobe extending to L anterior temporal, L parietal lobes and ventral basal ganglion	Large infarct, L-MCA extending into L posterior frontal, temporal and parietal lobes
Narrative sample[a]	the /ma/ the boy go out and drink ... snowman ... snowman and pretty good ... and then uh ... it's uh drink champagne or something like that and then ... go out ... and then big ball ... and then drink ... and then and then ok finished ... eyes nose mouth and {unintelligible} ... and neck and two buttons ... and then finished ... and then uh man and woman ... uh uh come back big complex ... and then and then a man 9 o'clock upstairs ... and then go out ... and then sleeping upstairs /upsru/ ... it's pretty good ... a coat ... and slowly down and uh it's here ... and man the snowman is ah ha ha...and then sit down and uh go out and uh uh	ok kid's ... walking the /sn/snow ... he's look there and kids kids kid /prob/ kid let's see ... big ok the kid is making a ... /no/snowman ... ok and the kid get cold stuff for him and his mom open the door ... come here the house ... it cold and time food ... he did ... and the kid again kid like ... kid again get up get up ... and the and the and the snowman again ... and up ... o.k. the time time it's it's time to sleep ... the kid's open the door ... his his pop there ... his mom there and it's something {unintelligible} something there and the kid going to the bedroom asleep he sleeps /slink/ sleep and then get up

[a] First 100 words of pre-training narrative.

therapy in a residential programme and several psycholinguistic treatments (Haendiges, Berndt, & Mitchum, 1996; Mitchum, Haendiges, & Berndt, 1993). S2 had participated in individual outpatient speech treatment for approximately 1 year. Additionally, both subjects had completed an intensive sentence production treatment programme using a computerised visual communication system, C-VIC (Weinrich, McCall, Weber, Thomas, & Thornburg, 1995). Briefly, C-VIC training involved intensive practice constructing a limited number of simple syntactic structures using iconic symbols, and verbally producing the English sentences corresponding to these iconic sequences. Despite making positive changes specific to the various treatment contexts, the subjects remained severely aphasic with markedly impaired spoken production (Weinrich, McCall, Boser, & Virata, 2002).

Detailed assessment of the subjects' comprehension and production abilities was completed at the outset of this study. Both subjects were nonfluent speakers compared to the normal fluency range

(107–232 words/minute), with S1's rate (61 words/ minute) reflecting a more severe nonfluency than S2's (91 words/minute). Qualitative observation of their connected speech (exemplified in Table 1) indicated that S1 produced fragmentary speech with infrequent production of both bound and free grammatical morphemes (i.e., classic "agrammatism"), while S2 produced many free-standing grammatical morphemes in his structurally impoverished speech (i.e., the "nonfluent, nonagrammatic" pattern described by Saffran et al., 1989).

Preliminary testing revealed that the subjects performed comparably on comprehension measures. Both subjects showed relatively intact auditory comprehension (S1 .93; S2 .83) at the single word level on the word–picture matching subtest of the Psycholinguistic Assessments of Language Processing in Aphasia (PALPA; Kay, Coltheart, & Lesser, 1992). On the Philadelphia Sentence Comprehension Battery (Saffran, Schwartz, Linebarger, Martin, & Bochetto, 1988), both subjects demonstrated relatively intact lexical comprehension (.97) with difficulty comprehending semantically reversible sentences in forced-choice sentence–picture matching (S1 .57; S2 .70). Although performing above chance, both subjects also had difficulty detecting grammatical violations in complex sentences (S1 .70; S2 .77).

The subjects' language profiles differed significantly in terms of their performance on lexical retrieval tasks. On the PALPA, both subjects were able to repeat single words flawlessly but had some difficulty orally naming pictures (S1 .65; S2 .88). However, when production of frequency-matched nouns and verbs was assessed using a shortened version ($N = 40$) of the Noun/Verb Naming Test (Zingeser & Berndt, 1990), the difference between the two subjects was striking for both nouns (S1 .30; S2 .80, Fisher's Exact = 10, $p = .004$, two-tailed) and verbs (S1 .15; S2 .50; Fisher's Exact = 5.5, $p = .04$, two-tailed).

METHODS

The communication system (CS)

As indicated above, the CS is a computerised program designed to provide processing support to aphasic speakers by allowing the user to replay and order words and phrases already created. In addition, the system can store and replay multisentence productions. Although previous studies using the CS have employed a touch screen for operating the program, the subjects of this study used a computer mouse to complete operations. Figure 1 displays the computer screen during a typical session. The user records utterances by touching (or clicking) the "On" button (bottom centre left), which controls a sound recorder. After speaking, the user selects a second button (bottom centre right) that turns off the sound recorder and causes the utterance to be saved as a sound file. This sound file is associated with an arbitrary coloured shape (e.g., an orange circle) that immediately appears in a large area in the centre of the screen termed the work area; in Figure 1 there are four such shapes in the work area. Touching or clicking

a shape causes the system to replay the recorded utterance associated with that shape. Shapes can be dragged to the top of the screen into an ordered series of slots (the sentence assembly area, containing five shapes in Figure 1) or discarded in the trashcan in the upper right-hand corner of the screen. The user attempts to order the shapes in the available slots to create a well-formed sentence or, more rarely, a phrase or multisentence sequence. The order in which shapes are placed in the slots determines the order in which they are replayed by the system when the user selects a "play sentence" icon (represented by musical notes in the upper left-hand corner of the screen). Shapes can be replayed, reordered, or dragged into the trash or back into the work area. These "sentences" can then be assembled, using a similar incremental procedure, to form multisentence productions in the narrative assembly area (right side of the screen in Figure 1: In this example, the narrative assembly area contains three green rectangles, each playing the concatenation of a sequence of chunks from the sentence assembly area).

Lexical support is provided by 20 labelled side buttons and by a noniconic word-finding tool (the word finder or WF). The side buttons (see Figure 1) display the printed text of key elements such as verbs and prepositions; touching or clicking a side button causes the system to play a pre-recorded sound file pronouncing the word displayed on the button. The WF contains printed words displayed in a semantic hierarchy; touching or clicking a printed word in this hierarchy causes the system to play its pre-recorded pronunciation. Since the on/off buttons are visible from within the WF, subjects record the target word (playing the WF item repeatedly as a model when needed) from within the WF, and then return to the main CS screen where the recorded item is found associated with a new shape in the work area.

For this study, the vocabulary required to describe the training materials was determined from normal control samples and was added to the WF. In addition, the side buttons were programmed to play 13 verbs and 7 prepositions that were frequently used by the control subjects to describe the training materials.

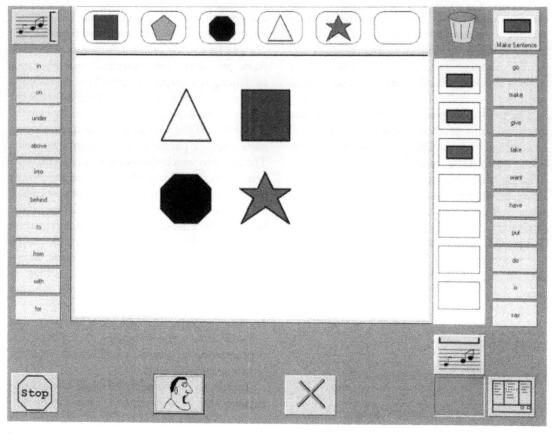

Figure 1. *The communication system (CS). Sentence assembly area containing five recorded segments is at top of screen; narrative assembly area with three multisegment utterances is on the right; workspace with four as yet unintegrated segments is in the middle.*

Training

Subjects completed five 1-hour sessions of training in the lab on the mechanics of using the CS. Specifically, subjects were instructed on how to record, manipulate, and replay productions on the CS using the mouse. They learned to store multi-sentence productions and to revise productions when necessary. Additionally, the prerecorded vocabulary available on the side buttons and in the WF was reviewed. Finally, subjects were required to watch a videotaped episode of a television programme (*Gomer Pyle, USMC*) and to use the CS to recount the story. Subjects were provided with assistance locating vocabulary in the WF when requested. Feedback regarding the accuracy of their productions and cues to correct errors were provided during this brief training session.

The subjects were then provided with a computer to use at home and were required to use the CS to describe a different videotaped episode of this television programme each week. Each episode was approximately 20 minutes in length and involved the same main characters. Both subjects reportedly practised using the CS for about 1 hour per day. Subjects were permitted to watch the episodes repeatedly; however, they both reportedly watched the videotaped episode once and then created their narratives across several days. Subjects did not receive assistance creating these narratives or feedback regarding the accuracy of their productions. CS narratives were collected weekly, using a handheld tape recorder (S2) or zip disk (S1), when they were seen for observation at the lab. During these visits, subjects were asked to demonstrate use of the CS. No explicit linguistic instruction or detailed feedback regarding their narrative productions was provided. However, suggestions and feedback designed to refine their use of the system were provided as needed. Suggestions consisted largely of reminding subjects to record material in small chunks (for easier revision), to use the word-finding support, and to monitor their productions regularly, both for accuracy and to facilitate lexical retrieval. Each subject described the same nine episodes in the same order across 11 weeks using the CS.

Pre/Post test

A story retelling task was administered to establish a profile of subjects' narrative abilities before and after CS training. The subjects viewed a silent video adaptation of a children's book, *The Snowman* (Briggs, 1989), edited to approximately 5 minutes in length, and were then asked to verbally describe the story. The subjects' spoken responses were recorded on tape. Note that the semantic content of the test video was considerably different from the content of the programme episodes used in training.

Measures

Structural analyses. These pre/post-narrative samples were transcribed and analyzed using a modification of the Quantitative Production Analysis (QPA; Rochon et al., 2000; Saffran et al., 1989). Analyses were based on the first 150 "narrative" words uttered (i.e., excluding neologisms, habitual starters, repairs, and direct responses to questions). Intonational, pausal and syntactic information was used to segment narrative words into "utterances." The segmented utterances were then scored independently by two raters, using the detailed scoring criteria available for the QPA.

Semantic analyses. To evaluate the communicative informativeness and efficiency of the subjects'

narratives, a standard rule-based scoring system for content, the Correct Information Unit (CIU) analysis (Nicholas & Brookshire, 1993), was applied to the subjects' full narrative samples (not just to elements counted as "narrative words" under the QPA analysis). A CIU is a single word that is "accurate, relevant, and informative relative to the eliciting stimulus" (Nicholas & Brookshire, 1993, p. 36). Time, word, and CIU counts were used to calculate the percentage of words that were correct information units (proportion of CIUs), and correct information units per minute. Two raters scored the transcripts independently.

RESULTS

Use of CS

From the outset of the study, both subjects demonstrated the ability to independently create multi-sentence productions to describe the training materials. Because the study employed a version of the CS incorporating lexical support (side buttons, word finder), no attempt was made to replicate the aided/unaided effect reported in Linebarger et al. (2000), which was argued to index the impact of "pure" processing support. However, S1's aided and unaided narratives of comparable stimuli are discussed below.

Impact on unaided narrative production

Transcriptions of subjects' pre/post narratives were analysed in accordance with the structure- and content-based methodologies outlined above.

Structural analyses

Inter-judge reliability on the application of the QPA procedures to the pre- and post-CS narrative samples for the two subjects ranged from 92% to 100% across the individual structural indices.

Table 2 presents the subjects' performance on selected measures of the QPA, which are roughly divided into those that index structural improvement and those that focus on morphological factors, i.e., use of closed class words and

Table 2. *Structural, morphological, and content measures for narrative samples elicited from S1 and S2 before and after a period of CS use (control data for Quantitative Production Analysis from Rochon et al., 2000, N=12; for Correct Information Unit Analysis system, estimated from Nicholas & Brookshire, 1993, N=20)*

	Control mean (range)	S1 Pre	S1 Post	p	S2 Pre	S2 Post	p
Quantitative Production Analysis (QPA)							
Structural							
Median length of utterance	8.17 (6.5–10.5)	2	4		4	6	
Mean sentence length	10.95 (7.6–11.3)	5.4	4.76	>.20	4.78	6.35	.004
Prop. of utterances that are sentences	.94 (.76–1.0)	.29	.41	>.20	.62	.80	.07
Prop. of words in sentences	.98 (.84–1.0)	.50	.54	>.20	.73	.81	.04
Morphological							
Prop. of narrative words that are closed class	.54 (.47–61)	.39	.36	>.20	.50	.47	>.20
Prop. of sentences that are well-formed	.95 (.75–1.0)	.36	.47	>.20	.39	.30	>.20
Prop. of verbs that are inflected	.92 (.53–1.0)	.32	.35	>.20	.41	.52	>.20
Correct Information Unit (CIU) analysis							
Prop. of words that are CIUs	.86 (.71–.93)	.32	.35	>.20	.46	.71	.0001
CIUs/minute	145 (92–178)	19.0	25.0		41.0	51.0	

inflections. The sentence well-formedness measure is included in the latter group because most violations of well-formedness involved agreement errors and other morphological problems. The pre-CS analyses for both subjects indicate structural abnormalities (both subjects are well outside the normal range on all structural measures), although S2 demonstrates better use of closed class vocabulary than does S1, scoring within the normal range on closed class usage.

S2. Samples of S2's test narratives are presented in Table 3. Note that underlined portions include the core narrative content defined by the QPA methodology, i.e., false starts, repairs, and repetitions are deleted from the transcript before application of QPA methods. The QPA analysis of S2's unaided narratives before and after training showed marked improvement in several structural aspects

of narrative discourse. For measures that can be expressed as counts of items in specific categories (e.g., closed class vs. open class words, yielding a proportion of total words that were closed class), analyses were performed using 2×2 chi-square tests. A significant improvement was observed in the proportion of words that occurred in sentences, $\chi^2 = 3.20$, $p = .04$, one-tailed, as was a marginally significant improvement in the proportion of utterances produced that were sentences, $\chi^2 = 2.23$, $p = .07$, one-tailed. It is noteworthy that S2's performance on this measure moved into the normal range on post-testing. Mean sentence length, evaluated with an unpaired t-test across items produced before and after treatment, improved significantly, $t(41) = 3.03$, $p = .004$, two-tailed. Median length of all utterances also increased and approached the normal range after CS use.

Table 3. *S2's pre- and post-training unaided narrative production samples: Transcripts up to first 150 narrative words (underlining identifies items counted as narrative words in QPA analysis)*

Pre-training	Post-training
ok. kid's … walking the /sn/snow … he's look there and kids kids kid /prob/ kid let's see … big ok the kid is making a … / no/snowman … ok and the kid get cold stuff for him and his mom open the door…come here the house… it cold and time food … he did … and the kid again kid like … kid again get up get up … and the and the and the snowman again … and up … o.k. the time time it's it's time to sleep… the kid's open the door…his his pop there…his mom there and it's something {unintelligible} something there and the kid going to the bedroom asleep he sleeps /slink/ sleep and then get up open the window and the noseman it's what's it called now … he's uh it's a something what's it called yeah yeah and o.k … and the kid getting uh it's a it's a not a scap not a scope not a sledder or something there he going to … he going to the … going he gone to open door gone to look no nowman there and then … snowman's get up now he's like now he a kid he's a boy now … and o.k. and uh the boy … come here my house come let's go nowman come here and maybe in a little bit something looks up there and snowman sit the /st/ chair and / la/ try the t.v. /bel/ the house the house hot though	kid is making a /nom/ snowman then kid's shovel more snow then the kid's then the kid's take a ball snowman's head the kid's yeah I try that take on kid's put put snowman's head on her shoulders o.k.and the kid's thinking he o.k. going to the house a hat and scarf and the kid's walk to the snowman the kid's take this … kid's put the head the … I got it … wait a minute hat hat kid's put hat on his head and the kid's rolling no tie a scarf snowman's arms no neck o.k. the kid's looking the kid's looking thinking more o.k. walking to the kid's walking to the house he get buttons and an orange kid's walking to the snowman again … get buttons on the head of the eyes and your buttons on your … belly no not neither … kid's putting buttons on the kid the snowman his chest and the kid's put on the orange on the snowman head and the kid's draw his snowman's mouth o.k. getting getting night so the kid go no his mom open the door call kid come here come to your house o.k. o.k. o.k. the kid's walk walk running to the house and the kid's his pop there too

S1. Analysis of S1's pre- and post-unaided narratives revealed no differences in the structural properties of his productions, with the exception of median length of utterance, which increased from 2 to 4.

No significant changes were observed for either subject in morphological measures of production (verb inflection index, proportion of closed class words, proportion of well-formed sentences). However, S2's preposition use increased markedly following training. In the transcript of the first 150 narrative words used for the QPA analysis, the number of prepositions rose from 3 to 13.

Content analyses

The CIU analysis was carried out on the full narrative samples, following published procedures, to assess changes in the semantic content of the subjects' narratives. Interjudge agreement for number of words and number of CIUs, calculated using the procedures described by Nicholas and Brookshire (1993), exceeded 94% for words and CIUs for both subjects' transcripts.

S2. S2 demonstrated significant improvements in the proportion of CIUs produced, $\chi^2 = 83$, $p < .001$, as well as a modest increase in CIUs per minute. These data reflect a marked decline of partial words, unintelligible utterances, and filler words ("let's see"; "I mean") following exposure to the CS, as well as a decline in nonspecific (low content) vocabulary (e.g., "gets cold *stuff*"; "*something there*").

S1. CIU analysis of S1's narratives revealed far more limited treatment gains. The minimal increase in proportion of CIUs produced (pre-CS .32; post-CS .35) was not significant, and CIUs per minute increased only slightly (pre-CS 19; post-CS 25).

S1's failure to show robust treatment gains from CS training cannot be attributed to his failure to master use of the system. In fact, his mastery of the CS was quite impressive, given the severity of his aphasia. Although, as noted above, the study was not designed to assess the aided/unaided effect, it is nevertheless possible to establish his competence in use of the CS by comparing aided and unaided descriptions of two highly comparable training videos recounting *Gomer Pyle, USMC* episodes. The lexical support provided by the WF no doubt facilitated his language production in the aided condition, although this support was present in a more limited form in the unaided condition through the considerable practice he had received in producing the vocabulary appropriate to this television series. We do not claim that S1's aided/unaided disparity reflects the "pure" processing support reported in Linebarger et al. (2000), since the CS provided linguistic information in the form of word-finding assistance. In fact, we assume that the CS exercised its effects for S1 largely through support of word retrieval, given the severity of his word-finding impairments in natural speech. If so, the availability of appropriate vocabulary support appears to have contributed substantially to his structural success.

Table 4 presents the first 10 utterances that were classified as English sentences (under the QPA methodology) produced by S1 in the *unaided* condition contrasted with the first ten "narrative chunks" that he produced in the corresponding *aided* narrative. The term "narrative chunk" is used here to refer to the material occupying a single slot in the narrative assembly area of the CS. As is evident from Table 4, these narrative chunks produced by S1 tended to correspond to English sentences, although it must be emphasised that this outcome is not in any way dictated by the system (i.e., feedback is not provided).

Note that the narrative chunks produced on the CS are far more elaborated than even the *sentences* in the corresponding unaided condition, and arguably contain embedded clauses. A limited QPA analysis was performed on the entire transcripts of the aided and unaided narrative samples (including both sentential and nonsentential utterances). Both proportion of utterances that were sentences: unaided .38; aided .89, $\chi^2 = 14$, $p = .0003$, two-tailed; and mean sentence length: unaided 4.5; aided 6.3; $t(34) = 3.13$, $p = .003$, two-tailed; were significantly higher in the aided narrative.

DISCUSSION

As noted above, sentence-level treatment interventions rarely lead to gains in multisentence production. This failure to "scale up" is particularly unfortunate because improved performance on such more complex laboratory tasks may index functionally important language gains (Ross & Wertz, 1999). From a clinical standpoint, then, S2's improved narrative production following CS use is highly encouraging, especially since this result was achieved following a largely independent home-based protocol.

The specificity of the treatment effects is of some interest. S2's unaided narratives following CS use showed greater structural elaboration, but morphological measures remained stable. This is

Table 4. *CS-"aided" vs. unaided narratives produced by S1: First 10 sentences (nonsentential utterances excluded) of unaided transcript contrasted with first 10 "narrative chunks" (elements in narrative assembly area) of aided transcript*

Unaided (sentences only)	Aided (narrative chunks)
It's a big one, two, three, four.	Sergeant Carter scold at Gomer Pyle for break the law.
It's good.	Gomer Pyle feel sorry Goober without work.
It's a man.	Gomer Pyle feel sad Goober can't work.
It's a Private Riley.	Gomer Pyle tells Goober in hotel.
It's pretty good.	Lieutenant takes Goober hike takes shoes.
Let me see.	Gomer Pyle finds Goober in Marines.
This Private Riley shake hands.	Lieutenant may Goober at jeep.
It's a Private Riley.	Goober don't know for psychiatrist.
It's here.	Gomer Pyle tells Lieutenant feel sorry Goober.
Give me money.	Psychiatrist take Sergeant Carter.

consistent with the finding that the *aided/unaided* effect of Linebarger et al. (2000) was also largely confined to structural as opposed to morphological measures (although a trend toward improvement in the aided condition was observed for bound but not freestanding grammatical morphemes). The specificity of the system's effects tends to support the dissociability of structural and morphological production impairments, although the current data are not conclusive; it is possible that morphological encoding requires more processing support than the CS provides.

The limited treatment gains achieved by S1 are also of interest because he differed from S2 primarily in the severity of his lexical impairment. Furthermore, S1's impressive use of the CS, enhanced to provide word-finding support, underscores the difficulty of teasing apart lexical and syntactic aspects of impaired production. As noted above, aphasic error patterns are rarely interpretable as transparent reflections of underlying knowledge or ability. With regards to S1, what looks like structural failure may well be lexical in origin.

The current data do not provide a definitive answer to the question of how, exactly, the CS brought about these changes in S2's speech. As noted in Linebarger et al. (2001), there are many different ways in which CS use might lead to improved unaided production.

One possibility is that the impact of the CS is largely *strategic*, in the sense that it may teach the user more effective "habits" for language production. For example, CS use may train the user to devote more effort to creating full sentences rather than isolated phrases, by virtue of the architecture of the CS with its three distinct "levels." The emphasis on sentence construction may also lead users to narrow the lexical search space to conform to the requirements of the sentence currently under construction. Because the CS allows users to record whatever comes to mind, and to build on it, CS use may foster a certain flexibility, an appreciation that there is more than one way to express a particular idea. (Similarly, use of the verbs and prepositions on the CS side buttons may train subjects to circumlocute more effectively.) Avoiding "lexical perfectionism" and exploiting imperfect but available words or phrases may free up resources for structure-building. Finally, the CS may train the user to actively maintain elements already retrieved, because the CS itself models such maintenance by allowing the user to replay elements previously produced.

A second possibility is that the CS helps the user to develop *automaticity* in one or another aspect of grammatical encoding. Because the CS makes it possible for aphasic speakers to assemble sentences, this structure may facilitate practice in sentence construction. Furthermore, this practice may tap into deeper processes than practice to single pictures designed to elicit a particular structure; specifically, it may exercise the construction of the underlying predicate-argument structures. A single picture designed to elicit a particular structure will normally depict an unambiguous, isolated event, and one which maps onto a single sentence in the target language. In contrast, retelling a video narrative normally requires the speaker to identify "language-ready" propositions in the flow of events. The mapping from complex nonlinguistic conceptual representations to sentences requires that each sentence be cut, so to speak, from the whole cloth of the message. Training on isolated pictures may not exercise this "chunking" of the message into linguistically expressible propositions, and narrative production without CS support may lead to such syntactic degradation that even if a "language-ready" proposition is identified, it cannot be encoded in a sentence.

A third possible explanation for the observed treatment effects is that the CS *ameliorates the processing limitations* implicated in aphasic language production deficits. It may be that practice in the resource-demanding task of narrative production, which the CS makes possible, allows aphasic users to increase their ability to retain linguistic information. Further research is required to tease apart these and other possibilities.

The results reported here add further support to the performance hypothesis. As noted above, the aided/unaided effect reported in Linebarger et al. (2000) supports this account, since the CS used in that study provided no lexical support or other linguistic cueing. S1's aided/unaided effect was accomplished with the addition of lexical support, but nonetheless his CS-aided productions demonstrate considerable preserved structural ability, in support of the performance hypothesis. S2's treatment gains add to this evidence that impaired activation and retention of linguistic information are at the core of aphasic language production deficits, since the CS-based protocol brought about structural changes but provided no explicit training in linguistic structure, and no feedback regarding the correctness of his productions; its primary function was to provide processing support.

Finally, S2's treatment gains may be seen as providing support for a "top-down" approach to the remediation of language production. The CS made it possible for S2 to practise sentence construction in the context of a resource-demanding task. Although further research is required to understand more precisely the reasons for his treatment gains, and the role played by the CS in these gains, we conclude that supported narrative production represents a potentially effective approach to retraining language production in more demanding and, ultimately, more naturalistic contexts.

REFERENCES

Bastiaanse, R. (1994). Broca's aphasia: A syntactic and/ or a morphological disorder? A case study. *Brain and Language, 48*, 1–32.

Berndt, R. S., & Mitchum, C. C. (1995). Cognitive neuropsychological approaches to the treatment of language disorders. *Neuropsychological Rehabilitation, 5*, 1–6.

Berndt, R. S., Mitchum, C. C., & Haendiges, A. N. (1996). Comprehension of reversible sentences in "agrammatism": A meta-analysis. *Cognition, 58*, 289–308.

Bever, T. G. (1970). The cognitive basis for linguistic structures. In R. Hayes (Ed.), *Cognition and language development*. New York: Wiley.

Blackwell, A., & Bates, E. (1995). Inducing agrammatic profiles in normals: Evidence for the selective vulnerability of morphology under cognitive resource limitation. *Journal of Cognitive Neuroscience, 7*, 228–257.

Briggs, R. (1989). *The Snowman*. New York: Random House.

Caplan, D., & Waters, G. S. (1995). Aphasic disorders of syntactic comprehension and working memory capacity. *Cognitive Neuropsychology, 12*, 637–649.

Caramazza, A., & Zurif, E. B. (1976). Dissociation of algorithmic and heuristic processes in language comprehension: Evidence from aphasia. *Brain and Language, 3*, 572–582.

Forde, E. M. E., & Humphreys, G. W. (1995). Refractory semantics in global aphasia: On semantic organisation and the access-storage distinction in neuropsychology. *Memory, 3*, 265–307.

Friederici, A. (1982). Syntactic and semantic processes in aphasic deficits: The availability of prepositions. *Brain and Language, 15*, 249–258.

Haarmann, H., & Kolk, H. H. J. (1991). A computer model of the temporal course of agrammatic sentence understanding: The effects of variation in severity and sentence complexity. *Cognitive Science, 15*, 49–87.

Haendiges, A. N., Berndt, R. S., & Mitchum, C. C. (1996). Assessing the elements contributing to a "mapping" deficit: A targeted treatment study. *Brain and Language, 532*, 276–302.

Hartsuiker, R. J., & Kolk, H. H. J. (1998). Syntactic facilitation in agrammatic sentence production. *Brain and Language, 62*, 221–254.

Heilman, K. M., & Scholes, R. J. (1976). The nature of comprehension errors in Broca's, conduction, and Wernicke's aphasics. *Cortex, 12*, 258–265.

Isserlin, M. (1922). Uber agrammatismus. *Zeitschrift fur die gesamte Neurologie und Psychiatrie, 75*, 322–416.

Jacobs, B. J., & Thompson, C. K. (2000). Cross-modal generalization effects of training noncanonical sentence comprehension and production in agrammatic aphasia. *Journal of Speech, Language, and Hearing Research, 43*, 5–20.

Kay, J., Coltheart, M., & Lesser, R. (1992). *PALPA— Psycholinguistic Assessment of Language Processing in Aphasia*. Hove, UK: Psychology Press.

Kolk, H. H. J. (1995). A time-based approach to agrammatic production. *Brain and Language, 50*, 282–303.

Kolk, H. H. J., & Heeschen, C. (1992). Agrammatism, paragrammatism, and the management of language. *Language and Cognitive Processes, 7*, 82–129.

Linebarger, M. C., Schwartz, M. F., & Kohn, S. E. (2001). Computer-based training of language production: An exploratory study. *Neuropsychological Rehabilitation, 11*, 57–96.

Linebarger, M. C., Schwartz, M. F., Romania, J. F., Kohn, S. E., & Stephens, D. L. (2000). Grammatical encoding in aphasia: Evidence from a "processing prosthesis." *Brain and Language, 75*, 416–427.

Linebarger, M. C., Schwartz, M. F., & Saffran, E. M. (1983). Sensitivity to grammatical structure in so-called agrammatic aphasics. *Cognition, 13*, 361–392.

Marshall, J., Pring, T., & Chiat, S. (1993). Sentence processing therapy: working at the level of the event. *Aphasiology, 7*, 177–199.

Martin, R. C., & Freedman, M. (2000). Language and memory impairments. In R. S. Berndt (Ed.), *Handbook of neuropsychology* (Vol. 2, 2nd ed.). Amsterdam: Elsevier.

Micelli, G., Mazzucchi, A., Menn, L., & Goodglass, H. (1983). Contrasting cases of Italian agrammatic aphasia without comprehension disorder. *Brain and Language, 19*, 65–97.

Mitchum, C. C., Haendiges, A. N., & Berndt, R. S. (1993). Model-guided treatment to improve written sentence production: A case study. *Aphasiology, 7*, 71–109.

Miyake, A., Carpenter, P., & Just, M. A. (1994). A capacity approach to asyntactic comprehension: Making normal adults perform like aphasic patients. *Cognitive Neuropsychology, 11*, 671–717.

Nicholas, L. E., & Brookshire, R. H. (1993). A system for quantifying the informativeness and efficiency of the connected speech of adults with aphasia. *Journal of Speech and Hearing Research, 36*, 338–350.

Rochon, E., Saffran, E. M., Berndt, R. S., & Schwartz, M. F. (2000). Quantitative analysis of aphasic sentence production: Further development and new data. *Brain and Language, 72*, 193–218.

Ross, K. B., & Wertz, R. T. R. (1999). Comparison of impairment and disability measures for assessing severity of, and improvement in, aphasia. *Aphasiology, 13*, 113–124.

Saffran, E. M. (2001). Effects of language impairment on sentence comprehension. In R. S. Berndt (Ed.), *Handbook of neuropsychology. Vol. 3: Language and aphasia* (2nd ed.). Amsterdam, Elsevier.

Saffran, E. M., Berndt, R. S., & Schwartz, M. F. (1989). The quantitative analysis of agrammatic production: Procedure and data. *Brain and Language, 37*, 440–479.

Saffran, E. M., & Martin, N. (1990). Effects of syntactic priming on sentence production in an agrammatic aphasic. Paper presented at the 28th Annual Meeting of the Academy of Aphasia, Baltimore, MD.

Saffran, E. M., & Schwartz, M. F. (1994). Impairments of sentence comprehension. *Philosophical Transactions of the Royal Society of London, Series B, 346*, 47–53.

Saffran, E. M., Schwartz, M., & Linebarger, M. C. (1998). Semantic influences on thematic role assignment: Evidence from normals and aphasics. *Brain and Language, 62*, 255–297.

Saffran, E. M., Schwartz, M. F., Linebarger, M. C., Martin, N., & Bochetto, P. (1988). *The Philadelphia Comprehension Battery.* Unpublished battery.

Saffran, E. M., Schwartz, M. F., & Marin, O. S. M. (1980). The word order problem in agrammatism: II. Production. *Brain and Language, 10*, 263–280.

Salomon, E. (1914). Motorische aphasia mit agrammatismus und sensorisch agrammatischen storungen. *Monatsschrift fur Psychiatrie und Neurologie, 35*, 181–208.

Schwartz, M., & Hodgson, C. (2002). A new multiword naming deficit: Evidence and interpretation. *Cognitive Neuropsychology, 19*, 263–287.

Schwartz, M. F., Saffran, E. M., & Marin, O. S. M. (1980). The word order problem in agrammatism. I: Comprehension. *Brain and Language, 10*, 249–262.

Shankweiler, D., Crain, S., Gorrell, P., & Tuller, B. (1988). Reception of language in Broca's aphasia. *Language and Cognitive Processes, 4*, 1–33.

Slobin, D. I. (1966). Grammatical transformations and sentence comprehension in childhood and adulthood. *Journal of Verbal Learning and Verbal Behavior, 2*, 219–227.

Springer, L., Huber, W., Schlenck, K.-J., & Schlenck, C. (2000). Agrammatism: Deficit or compensation? Consequences for aphasia therapy. *Neuropsychological Rehabilitation, 10*, 279–309.

Thompson, C. K., Shapiro, L. P., & Ballard, K. J. (1998). Role of syntactic complexity in training *wh*-movements structures in agrammatic aphasia: Order for promoting generalization. *Journal of International Neuropsychological Society, 4*, 661–674.

Thompson-Schill, S. L., D'Esposito, M., Aguirre, G. K., & Farah, M. J. (1997). Role of left prefrontal cortex in retrieval of semantic knowledge: A re-evaluation. *Proceedings of the National Academy of Science, 94*, 14792–14797.

Trueswell, J. C., Tanenhaus, M., & Garnsey, S. M. (1994). Semantic influences on parsing: Use of thematic role information in syntactic disambiguation. *Journal of Memory and Language, 33*, 285–318.

Ulatowska, H. K., Weiss-Doyell, A., Friedman-Stern, R., & Macaluso-Haynes, S. (1983). Production of narrative discourse in aphasia. *Brain and Language, 19*, 317–334.

Warrington, E. K., & Cipolotti, L. (1996). Word comprehension: The distinction between refractory and storage impairments. *Brain, 119*, 611–625.

Weinrich, M., McCall, D., Boser, K. I., & Virata, T. (2002). Narrative and procedural discourse production by severely aphasic patients. *Neurorehabilitation and Neural Repair, 16*, 249–274.

Weinrich, M., McCall, D., Weber, C., Thomas, K., & Thornburg, L. (1995). Training on an iconic communication system for severe aphasia can improve natural language production. *Aphasiology, 9*, 343–364.

Weinrich, M., Shelton, J. R., McCall, D., & Cox, D. M. (1997). Generalization from single sentence to multisentence production in severely aphasic patients. *Brain and Language, 58*, 327–352.

Williams, S. E., & Canter, G. J. (1982). The influence of situational context on naming performance in aphasic syndromes. *Brain and Language, 17*, 92–106.

Wilshire, C. E., & McCarthy, R. A. (2002). Evidence for a context-sensitive word retrieval disorder in a case of nonfluent aphasia. *Cognitive Neuropsychology, 19*, 165–186.

Wulfeck, B. B., Bates, E., & Capasso, R. (1991). A cross-linguistic study of grammaticality judgments in aphasia. *Brain and Language, 41*, 311–336.

Zingeser, L., & Berndt, R. S. (1990). Retrieval of nouns and verbs in agrammatism. *Brain and Language, 39*, 13–32.

SECTION III: CONCEPTUAL AND SEMANTIC REPRESENTATIONS

A note on Eleanor Saffran's contribution to this area

Although so much of Eleanor Saffran's research was in the arena of language, in one sense it seems that language was just the context or framework for an exploration of her most central research passion: semantic memory or conceptual knowledge. The earliest manifestations of this quest for knowledge about knowledge came in two main forms. The first was her pioneering study, with Myrna Schwartz and Oscar Marin (Schwartz, Marin, & Saffran, 1979), of patient WLP, who had a neuro-degenerative condition that we would now call semantic dementia. Eleanor, Myrna, and Oscar mainly studied WLP's performance on language tasks (and some picture-processing tasks as well); but what they were actually documenting and dissecting was the patient's progressive deterioration of conceptual knowledge. This paper should be considered a case study in two senses: not only of WLP but also, as a lesson to cognitive neuropsychologists, of the most elegant, logical and subtle ways in which to conduct such research. The second early manifestation of this interest was Eleanor's work on deep dyslexia (e.g., Saffran, Bogyo, Schwartz, & Marin, 1980; Saffran & Marin, 1977), in which she explored the fascinating and curious phenomena of a reading system that "knows" what a written word means but not how it sounds.

Many other aspects of semantic knowledge came to the forefront of Eleanor's intellectual curiosity over the years of her research career. From the days of her research on deep dyslexia, and picked up again later in her 1990s studies of semantic dementia, she was intrigued by the nature of semantic representations for concrete vs. abstract concepts (e.g., Breedin, Saffran, & Coslett, 1994) and how this might relate to left-vs. right-hemisphere contributions to semantics and language (Coslett & Saffran, 1998). In some of her most recent work, she explored (with Laurel Buxbaum: Buxbaum & Saffran, 2002) the distinction between our knowledge of what objects are used for and of how we manipulate or use them, and with Branch Coslett (Coslett, Saffran, & Schwoebel, 2002) the semantic domain of body knowledge.

In a provocative and forward-looking paper (Saffran & Schwartz, 1994, with a cleverly punned/rhyme title: see references below), she and Myrna championed a model of semantic memory that is now, a decade later, becoming widely favoured (see also Saffran, 2000, and Saffran & Sholl, 1999). They argued that different kinds of conceptual knowledge (such as visual vs. action-related attributes of objects), and different modalities of access to semantic memory (such as words vs. pictures or real objects) are represented neither in one undifferentiated system nor in a collection of completely separate modules, but rather in an interconnected network of auto-associated activity patterns, where parts of the pattern are closely linked to the appropriate modality or attribute type. Thus, knowledge about the visual features of an object might reflect activation of part of the visual stream of processing; but the distributed nature of the full concept's representation means that there is no separate visual-semantic system.

REFERENCES

Breedin, S. D., Saffran, E. M., & Coslett, H. B. (1994). Reversal of the concreteness effect in a patient with semantic dementia. *Cognitive Neuropsychology, 11,* 617–660.

http://www.tandf.co.uk/journals/pp02643294.html
DOI:10.1080/02643290342000492

Buxbaum, L. J., & Saffran, E. M. (2002). Knowledge of object manipulation and object function: Dissociations in apraxic and nonapraxic subjects. *Brain and Language, 82,* 179–199.

Coslett, H. B., & Saffran, E. M . (1998). Reading and the right hemisphere: Evidence from acquired dyslexia. In M. Beeman & C. Chiarello (Eds.), *Right hemisphere language comprehension: Perspectives from cognitive neuroscience.* Mahwah, NJ: Lawrence Erlbaum Associates Inc.

Coslett, H. B., Saffran, E. M., & Schwoebel, J. (2002). Knowledge of the human body: A distinct semantic domain. *Neurology, 59,* 357–363.

Saffran, E. M. (2000). The organization of semantic memory: In support of a distributed model. *Brain and Language, 71,* 204–212.

Saffran, E. M., Bogyo, L., Schwartz, M. F., & Marin, O. S. M. (1980). Does deep dyslexia reflect right hemisphere reading? In M. Coltheart, K. Patterson, & J. C. Marshall (Eds.), *Deep dyslexia* (pp. 381–406). London: Routledge & Kegan Paul.

Saffran, E. M., & Marin, O. S. M. (1977). Reading without phonology: Evidence from aphasia. *Quarterly Journal of Experimental Psychology, 29,* 515–525.

Saffran, E. M., & Schwartz, M. F. (1994). Of cabbages and things: Semantic memory from neuropsychological perspective—a tutorial review. In C. Umiltà & M. Moscovitch (Eds.), *Attention and performance XV: Conscious and nonconscious information processing* (pp. 507–536). Cambridge, MA: MIT Press.

Saffran, E. M., & Sholl, A. (1999). Clues to the functional and neural architecture of word meaning. In C. M. Brown & P. Hagoort (Eds.), *The neurocognition of language* (pp. 241–272). Oxford: Oxford University Press.

Schwartz, M. F., Marin, O. S. M., & Saffran, E. M. (1979). Dissociations of language function in dementia: A case study. *Brain and Language, 7,* 277–306.

COGNITIVE NEUROPSYCHOLOGY, 2004, 21 (2/3/4) 285–298

REPRESENTATIONS OF THE HUMAN BODY IN THE PRODUCTION AND IMITATION OF COMPLEX MOVEMENTS

John Schwoebel
Department of Psychology, Cabrini College, Radnor, PA, USA

Laurel J. Buxbaum
Moss Rehabilitation Research Institute and Thomas Jefferson University, Philadelphia, PA, USA

H. Branch Coslett
University of Pennsylvania, Philadelphia, PA, USA

Previous investigations suggest that there are at least three distinct types of representation of the human body. One representation codes structural information about body part location (body structural description), the second codes knowledge about body parts (body semantics or body image), and the third provides a dynamic mapping of the current positions of body parts relative to one another (body schema) (Buxbaum & Coslett, 2001; Schwoebel, Coslett, & Buxbaum, 2001; Sirigu, Grafman, Bressler, & Sunderland, 1991). In this study we used an influential "two route" model of gesture performance (Gonzalez Rothi, Ochipa, & Heilman, 1991) to derive predictions about the body representations expected to underlie the production and imitation of meaningful and meaningless movements. The relationships between these measures were examined in 55 patients with unilateral left-hemisphere lesions. Multiple regression analyses demonstrated that performance on body semantics and body schema tasks were significant and unique predictors of meaningful gesture performance, whereas the body schema measure alone predicted imitation of meaningless movements. Body structural descriptions did not enter into any of the models. These findings are consistent with performance of meaningful actions via a semantic route that accesses body semantics and other action knowledge, and performance of meaningless movements via a "direct" route that bypasses this information.

INTRODUCTION

Recent studies of body representation are consistent with classic accounts (Head & Holmes, 1911–12; Pick, 1922) in suggesting that there are at least three distinct types of representation of the human body. The first, termed the "body schema," has been characterised as an on-line representation of the current configuration of the body, derived from numerous motor and sensory inputs (e.g., proprioceptive, vestibular, tactile, visual, efference copy), that is involved in the production of action (e.g., Schwoebel, Boronat, & Coslett, 2002a). The second, which has been called the "body image" or

Correspondence should be addressed to Laurel J. Buxbaum at Moss Rehabilitation Research Institute, Korman Bldg., Suite 213, 1200 West Tabor Rd., Philadelphia, PA, 19141, USA (Email: LBuxbaum@einstein.edu).

In fond memory of Eleanor Saffran, whose insights, guidance, and friendship are sadly missed. We are grateful to Rukmini Menon, who assisted with subject testing and data analysis. This research was supported by NIH Grant R01 NS36387 awarded to Dr Buxbaum and R01 NS37920 awarded to Dr Coslett.

© 2004 Psychology Press Ltd

http://www.tandf.co.uk/journals/pp02643294.html

DOI:10.1080/02643290342000348

"body semantics," represents semantic and lexical information about the body, such as functions of body parts, associations between body parts and objects, and body part names (Coslett, Saffran, & Schwoebel, 2002). The third type of representation, termed the "body structural description," is a topological map of locations derived from visual input that defines body part boundaries and proximity relationships (Buxbaum & Coslett, 2001; Sirigu, Grafman, Bressler, & Sunderland, 1991). A number of lines of evidence support the validity and distinctiveness of these three types of representation (see Schwoebel, Coslett, & Buxbaum, 2001, for detailed review).

The body schema or on-line representation of the body in space is central to an understanding of action. Recent models of motor control suggest that sensory and efference copy information may be integrated in order to allow for the on-line correction of motor errors as well as to generate a more accurate estimate of current body posture (e.g., Desmurget, Epstein, Turner, Prablanc, Alexander, & Grafton, 1999; Desmurget & Grafton, 2000; Wolpert & Ghahramani, 2000; Wolpert, Ghahramani, & Jordan 1995). Furthermore, neurophysiological studies support the possibility that the brain computes a dynamic body representation derived from multiple sensory inputs. For example, the firing rate of individual neurons in parietal area 5 of the monkey is influenced by proprioceptive information coding the position of the monkey's own unseen arm as well as visual input concerning the position of a "dummy" arm. These neurons were suggested to "form the basis of the complex body schema that we constantly use to adjust posture and guide movement" (Graziano, Cooke, & Taylor, 2000, p. 1782).

In addition to guiding action, the body schema may also contribute to the perception of the postures and actions of others. For example, Parsons (1987, 1994) and others have demonstrated that response times to judge the laterality of a depicted hand are highly correlated with actual movement time, depend on the current position of the subjects' own hands, and respect the biomechanical constraints of the human body. This suggests that participants judge the laterality of pictured hands

by imagining their own hand moving from its current position into the orientation of the stimulus hand (Coslett, 1998; Parsons, 1987, 1994; Schwoebel et al., 2002a; Schwoebel, Coslett, Bradt, Friedman, & Dileo, 2002b; Schwoebel, Friedman, Duda, & Coslett, 2001). Functional neuroimaging findings suggest that hand laterality tasks as well as explicit motor imagery tasks are associated with activation in inferior and superior parietal areas and motor and premotor areas that substantially overlap with areas activated during actual movements (e.g., Gerardin et al., 2000; Grezes & Decety, 2001; Jeannerod, 2001; Parsons & Fox, 1998). In addition, Decety et al. (1997) found that when subjects viewed the actions of others with instructions to imitate them at a later time, increased activity was observed in parietal and premotor areas typically involved in the planning of actions.

There is also growing evidence that the body schema may dissociate from other body representations. Sirigu et al. (1991) and Buxbaum and Coslett (2001) reported patients who were unable to point to named body parts on themselves or others (i.e., "autotopagnosia"). Both patients were able, in contrast, to point to objects taped to the body surface. This is consistent with an adequate map of the dynamic position of the body in space (body schema), but poor knowledge of the structural boundaries between body parts (body structural descriptions) without the extra cue afforded by the extraneous objects. Body semantics may also dissociate from other body representations. The autotopagnosic patient reported by Sirigu et al. performed normally on a task assessing body part function (e.g., "what is the mouth for?"), and the autotopagnosic patient we reported (Buxbaum & Coslett, 2001) performed perfectly when asked to point to body parts associated with items of clothing or grooming tools (see also Coslett et al., 2002; Suzuki et al., 1997 for evidence of selective preservation and impairment of body semantics).

An important question that has rarely been empirically investigated is the status of these body representations in patients with deficits in complex gesture and movement production and imitation, i.e., ideomotor apraxia (IM). IM is a disorder common in left-hemisphere stroke and degenerative dementia that is characterised by spatiotemporal errors in pantomime and/or imitation of complex movements and postures (Heilman & Gonzalez Rothi, 1993). For example, a patient with IM might imitate a hammering gesture with an increased frequency, low-amplitude movement in the horizontal plane, with the hand open rather than clenched. Recent evidence has focused attention on the fact, first noted by De Renzi and colleagues (De Renzi, 1985; De Renzi, Faglioni, Lodesani, & Vecchi, 1983; De Renzi & Luchelli, 1988), that in addition to their deficits in production and imitation of meaningful gestures, many such patients may be deficient in the imitation of meaningless movements and postures (Goldenberg, 1995). Given that the disorder may affect both meaningful and meaningless movements, and both production and imitation, it provides a rich opportunity to explore the role of body representations in complex motor tasks.

Among the few previous investigations that have addressed the relationship of body representations and praxis is a study by Heilman, Gonzalez Rothi, Mack, Feinberg, and Watson (1986) reporting a patient with damage to the right superior parietal lobe, who was profoundly impaired in pantomiming gestures when deprived of vision of the hand, but who improved with visual input. The authors attributed her impairment to deficits in a proprioceptive "comparator" system that compares efference copy from motor and premotor areas with proprioceptive feedback, and corrects mismatches. A related study by Buxbaum, Giovannetti, and Libon (2000) reported a degenerative dementia patient with primary progressive apraxia whose imitation of meaningless movements was significantly more impaired than her imitation of meaningful gestures matched for complexity. We attributed this pattern of performance to deficits in dynamic procedures coding the locations and movements of the body parts of self and others—that is, the body schema. Goldenberg and colleagues (Goldenberg, 1995; Goldenberg & Hagmann, 1997) demonstrated that left-hemisphere stroke patients who were impaired in imitating meaningless hand postures were also

impaired when required to manipulate a mannequin to copy the same meaningless poses. This pattern of performance was interpreted as a deficit in structural knowledge of the human body. However, the status of body structural representations or of other body representations was not tested directly.

One factor complicating the interpretation of the studies reviewed above is that different types of praxis tasks (e.g., imitation of meaningful and meaningless gestures, production of gesture to verbal command) may bear different relationships to the three putative types of body representations. Fortunately, an influential model of ideomotor apraxia (Gonzalez Rothi et al., 1991) can be used to generate specific predictions about these relationships. The model posits that complex movement production and imitation may be performed via two routes. Production of gestures to command is thought to be performed via the semantic route. On this account, auditory-lexical input contacts semantic information, including information about gesture meaning, which then activates a "visuo-kinesthetic motor engram" or "praxicon" providing information about the body shapes and movements entailed in the particular gesture. Imitation of meaningful gestures can be performed via this route as well. In this case, visual information about the spatial configuration and movements of the body parts of another person are proposed to contact the action praxicon and semantic systems.

Imitation of meaningful gestures may also be performed via an alternative, nonsemantic route to action. The nonsemantic route bypasses the information stored in the praxicon and action semantic systems, and thus provides a more "direct" translation between visual input and motor output. While the model was not developed to account for meaningless movement and posture imitation, it would appear that such movements, lacking semantic content, must be performed via the second, so-called direct route. To summarise, then, on the two route model, gesture to command is performed via the semantic route, meaningful gesture imitation by either the semantic or the direct route, and meaningless movement imitation via the direct route.

If we assume that body semantics are aligned most closely with the semantic route, and the body schema with the direct route, we can generate relatively straightforward predictions about the types of body representations expected to be involved in gesture to command and in meaningful and meaningless movement imitation tasks. Because all have movement production as a final output, all three tasks might be predicted to require access to the body schema. Gesture to command might be predicted to depend additionally upon body semantics. If performed via the semantic route, meaningful gesture imitation would similarly be expected to access both the body schema and body semantics; on the other hand, if performed via the direct route, only the body schema should be required. Meaningless movement imitation, if indeed performed via a direct route as conceptualized by Gonzalez Rothi et al. (1991), would not be expected to activate semantic information informing gesture or body part meaning, and so should rely solely upon the body schema. The two route model does not lend itself to strong predictions about the relationship of body structural descriptions to praxis tasks, but this relationship remains of interest, particularly as this representation has been postulated to be relevant to the imitation of meaningless gestures (e.g., Goldenberg & Hagmann, 1997).

In this study we assessed a group of left-hemisphere stroke patients with a battery of tests of praxis and body representation. Our aim was to determine whether the body representation tasks contributing to praxis performance were consistent with the predictions of the two route model as outlined above.

STUDY 1: PREDICTING MEANINGFUL GESTURE IMITATION

Methods

Participants

We examined a group of 55 patients (mean age 58 years, SD 12; mean education 14 years, SD 3)

with left-hemisphere stroke as diagnosed by clinical information (i.e., right hemiparesis, aphasia) and, in the vast majority of cases (46 patients), documented by CT or MRI scans (see Table 1). In addition, 18 normal controls (mean age 47 years, SD 11; mean education 15 years, SD 2) were tested on the body representation tasks and 10 normal controls (mean age 65 years, SD 11; mean education 14 years, SD 3) were tested on the praxis and comprehension tasks. The Institutional Review Boards of the University of Pennsylvania and Albert Einstein Healthcare Network approved the research, and all subjects gave informed consent. Subjects were paid for the approximately 1 hour testing session.

Procedure

Participants completed three tasks designed to assess the integrity of the body schema, body structural description, and body semantics representations described above, as well as gesture imitation and language comprehension tasks. All of these tasks, which are described below, involved nonverbal responses.

Body representation tasks. The hand laterality task developed by Parsons (1987) was used to investigate the body schema. On each of 64 trials, subjects were shown a digitised colour picture of a hand and asked if it was a left or a right hand. The stimuli were presented in the subjects' midline in palm up or palm down views and in one of four orientations: fingers pointing away, fingers pointing toward the subject, fingers pointing to the left, and fingers pointing to the right. Subjects responded by moving their left or right hands. Hemiplegic subjects pointed with the ipsilesional hand to the contralesional hand, when appropriate. Accuracy for each hand was calculated.

A body part localisation task was used to investigate the body structural description. On each of 20 trials, subjects were seated with their eyes closed, facing the investigator, and the investigator touched one part of their bodies with a brush (left: foot, shin, thigh, index finger, wrist, elbow, upper arm, shoulder, ear; right: ankle, knee, thigh, hip, thumb, hand, forearm, upper arm, eyelid; centre:

Table 1. *Summary of patient demographic and lesion data*

Patient	Education	Age	Handedness	Months post-lesion	Locus of lesion
Study 2					
S1	16	49	R	24	subcortical
S2	16	80	R	53	NA
S3	12	49	R	22	fronto-parietal, occipital
S4	18	53	L	41	NA
S5	12	49	R	8	temporal, subcortical
S6	16	43	R	9	frontal
S7	12	68	R	61	temporo-parietal
S8	11	78	R	12	temporo-parietal
S9	13	48	R	43	occipital, subcortical
S10	18	56	R	93	fronto-parietal, subcortical
S11	14	49	R	124	parietal
S12	16	71	R	8	NA
S13	14	63	R	9	subcortical
S14	13	49	R	11	temporal
S15	12	41	R	24	temporo-parietal
S16	16	61	R	35	subcortical
S17	23	73	R	86	NA
S18	14	53	R	14	frontal
S19	12	58	R	24	subcortical
S20	12	68	R	34	temporal
S21	13	68	Ambi	33	occipital
S22	15	55	R	54	subcortical
S23	20	70	R	70	subcortical
S24	13	75	Ambi	16	NA
S25	14	48	Ambi	16	temporal
S26	12	63	R	14	frontal
S27	12	38	R	8	fronto-parietal
S28	13	57	R	54	temporo-parietal
S29	12	52	R	23	NA
S30	13	40	R	9	frontal, subcortical
Study 3					
S31	12	50	R	29	temporal
S32	12	79	R	9	temporal
S33	12	63	R	132	temporo-parietal, DLF
S34	12	67	R	9	subcortical
S35	16	79	R	25	NA
S36	14	56	R	9	temporo-parietal
S37	10	50	R	27	temporo-parietal
S38	16	42	R	11	temporo-parietal
S39	16	42	R	14	temporo-parietal, DLF
S40	10	58	R	6	temporo-parietal
S41	14	67	R	62	temporo-parietal, DLF
S42	10	39	R	78	temporo-parietal, DLF
S43	12	77	R	9	NA
S44	14	51	R	9	temporal, DLF
S45	12	58	R	87	temporal, DLF
S46	12	51	R	16	temporo-parietal
S47	3	58	R	50	subcortical
S48	16	71	R	10	NA
S49	18	50	R	11	DLF
S50	8	51	R	26	temporal, DLF
S51	12	80	R	39	subcortical
S52	18	55	R	77	subcortical
S53	12	56	R	8	subcortical
S54	16	74	R	52	subcortical
S55	18	54	L	73	temporo-parietal

All 55 patients participated in Study 1. DLF = (dorsolateral frontal), NA = patients without scans or with normal scans.

lips, nose). Touch intensity was determined in preliminary testing to provide a suprathreshold stimulus at all sites; i.e., tactile stimuli were suprathreshold for both ipsilesional and contralesional body parts. After each tactile stimulus was delivered, subjects opened their eyes and pointed to the same body part on the investigator. Responses were coded as correct if the subject identified the correct body part, regardless of laterality.

A task requiring the matching of body parts by function was used to investigate body semantics. On each of 24 trials, four pictures of isolated body parts were presented in the subjects' midline. Subjects were instructed to point to one of three body parts that was most closely related to a target body part in terms of its function—"the thing that it does, or is used for." Foils included body parts contiguous with the target body part and unrelated body parts. For example, on one trial, the target was an elbow and response options included a knee (the correct choice), a forearm, and a nose.

Meaningful gesture imitation task. Subjects were asked to imitate 10 different meaningful gestures (i.e., 6 transitive: comb hair, brush teeth, cut with scissors, hammer a nail, flip a coin, pour water from a pitcher into a glass; four intransitive: wave goodbye, beckon to come here, salute, hitch-hike). Subjects were asked to execute each gesture as precisely as possible immediately after viewing the experimenter demonstrate the gesture. Gestures were coded based on the guidelines of the Test of Oral and Limb Apraxia (TOLA; Helm-Estabrooks, 1992). Thus, they were scored as correct if perfectly performed, or if performed with subtle spatial or temporal errors, and incorrect if they had moderate or severe spatial or temporal errors. For transitive gestures, subjects were instructed to perform the gesture as if they were holding the object and not to use a body part as an object (e.g., using a finger as a toothbrush). If

subjects did use a body part as an object, they were reminded of the instructions and asked to perform the gesture again. If they made this type of error a second time, the gesture was coded as incorrect.

Language comprehension task. Thirty of the subjects were asked to complete six comprehension tasks that involved following instructions of increasing difficulty. Responses were coded as errors if they included omissions, additions, or were performed in the wrong order. The remaining 25 subjects were given the comprehension subtests of the Western Aphasia Battery (Kertesz, 1982), which included requirements to answer 20 yes/no questions (e.g., Do you cut grass with an axe?), point to 60 named objects, and follow 11 instructions of increasing difficulty.[1]

Results

Table 2 provides a summary of subjects' performance on the tasks of Study 1, as well as on the additional praxis tasks reported in Studies 2 and 3.

Before examining the relations between the body representation tasks and meaningful gesture imitation performance, we first explored the relations between the body representation and comprehension measures. Factor analysis with principle component extraction and varimax rotation was used to examine the relations between proportion correct measures for the following tasks: (1) body schema (ipsilesional hand), (2) body schema (contralesional hand), (3) body structural description, (4) body semantics, and (5) language comprehension. The appropriateness of factor analysis for the observed correlations was suggested by a value of .65 resulting from the Kaiser-Meyer-Olkin (KMO) measure of sampling adequacy (Tabachnick & Fidell, 1989). Examination of an initial scree plot suggested two factors. These two factors accounted for a substantial

---

[1] It is possible that the failure of language comprehension to enter the regression model of Study 1 may be due to the internal inconsistency caused by the use of these different measures in subsets of the patients. However, we note that language comprehension also failed to enter the regression models in Studies 2 and 3 despite the fact that only one measure was used in each of these studies.

Table 2. *Means (proportions correct) and standard deviations (SD) for patients and normal controls on the body representation, comprehension, and apraxia tasks*

Tasks	Patients			Controls		
	Mean	SD	N	Mean	SD	N
BSi	.86	.15	55	.86	.11	18
BSc	.86	.15	55	.88	.09	18
BSD	.95	.09	55	1.00	.00	18
BSe	.80	.16	55	.88	.11	18
Mf-im	.85	.20	55	.97	.05	10
Mf-co	.79	.20	30	.94	.07	10
Ml-im	.78	.24	25	.99	.03	10
WAB	.89	.11	25	.99	.02	59[a]
Comp	.76	.21	30	1.00	.00	10

BSi = body schema (ipsilesional for patients; left for controls); BSc = body schema (contralesional for patients; right for controls); BSD = body structural description; BSe = body semantics; Mf-im = meaningful gesture imitation; Mf-co = meaningful gestures to command; Ml-im = meaningless gesture imitation; WAB = comprehension subtests of Western Aphasia Battery; Comp = comprehension task.

[a] = Control data reported by Kertesz (1982).

amount of variance in each of the variables, as indicated by the communalities in Table 3, suggesting that the variables are well defined by the two-factor solution.

The first factor (sum of squared loadings, or SSL = 2.39) was defined by the body schema (ipsilateral and contralateral) and body structural description tasks. The second factor (SSL = 1.49) was defined by the body semantics and language comprehension measures.

Next, standard multiple regression was performed to examine the degree to which the different body representation and language comprehension measures predicted performance in the meaningful gesture imitation task. The predictor variables entered simultaneously into the analysis were the same variables used in the factor analysis above.

Table 4 displays the correlations between each of the variables and the results of the regression analysis. The regression model accounted for a significant amount of variability in gesture imitation performance, $F(5, 49) = 9.32$, $p < .001$. Further, only body semantics and body schema (contralesional) measures contributed significantly to the prediction of gesture imitation performance. More specifically, only body semantics and body schema

(contralesional) accounted for significant and unique (i.e., variance in gesture imitation performance not accounted for by any of the other predictors) variability in gesture imitation performance, as indicated by the semipartial correlations (i.e., sr) in Table 4.

We note that while both the body schema (ipsilateral) and body structural description measures were moderately correlated with meaningful gesture imitation performance, neither of these measures contributed significantly to the regression. This suggests that body schema (ipsilateral) and body structural description measures may be

Table 3. *Factor loadings (F1 and F2), communalities (Com), and percent of variance accounted for, for principle component extraction with varimax rotation*

Task	F1	F2	Com
BSi	.89	.13	.80
BSc	.92	.07	.85
BSD	.81	.05	.65
BSe	.31	.81	.75
WAB/Comp	−.09	.90	.82
% variance	48%	30%	

For abbreviations see Table 2. Italicised numbers indicate factors with the highest loadings.

Table 4. *Standard multiple regression: Predictors of meaningful gesture imitation performance*

Variables	Correlations					Regression			
	Mf–im	BSi	BSc	BSD	BSe	B	β	t	sr
BSi	.46					−.04	−.03	−0.19	
BSc	.55	.81				.55	.41	2.23*	.23
BSD	.45	.49	.56			.28	.12	0.97	
BSe	.54	.27	.25	.31		.45	.37	2.91**	.30
WAB/Comp	.24	.03	−.02	−.02	.47	.08	.08	0.67	
R = .70**; R² = .48									

For abbreviations, see Table 2. B = unstandardised coefficient; β = standardised coefficient; sr = semipartial correlation.
* p < .05; ** p < .01.

indirectly related to gesture imitation performance as a result of their correlations with the body schema (contralesional) and body semantics measures.

Discussion

The factor analysis suggests that the body representation tasks load on two factors. This is in partial agreement with previous findings suggesting distinctions between body representations; we will consider this in the General Discussion. There are several ways in which the two factors might be characterised. They may be broadly characterised in terms of their relationship to language processes, i.e., as "lexical-semantic" (language comprehension and body semantics) and "nonsemantic" (body structural descriptions and body schema) forms of information. Alternatively, they may be labelled in accordance with the two route model of action; thus, the body semantics and language comprehension tasks may to be related to the "semantic" route to action, whereas the body schema and body structural description tasks might be characterised as related to "direct" or "nonsemantic" forms of information.

In agreement with the predictions derived from the two route model of IM outlined above, regression analyses suggest that both the on-line coding of postural information (i.e., body schema) as well as semantic knowledge of the body (i.e., body semantics) predict imitation of meaningful gestures. Further, we note that the relatively low correlation between language comprehension and gesture imitation and the failure of language comprehension to contribute to the regression suggest that the observed relations between imitation performance and the body schema and body semantics measures may not be accounted for in terms of a general comprehension deficit.

Although subjects could have arguably performed the meaningful gesture imitation task via either the direct or semantic routes, the regression analysis is consistent with the possibility that many subjects did so via the semantic route. On the two route model of action, performance of meaningful gestures to command should result in a similar pattern of performance, i.e., reliance upon both body semantics and dynamic body posture information. We examined this possibility in Study 2.

STUDY 2: PREDICTING MEANINGFUL GESTURES TO COMMAND

Methods

Participants

A subset of 30 patients from Study 1 (see Table 1) participated in additional praxis testing. Due to scheduling constraints, all Study 1 participants were randomly assigned to undergo additional testing for either Study 2 or for Study 3 during the same session as the Study 1 testing.

Procedure

The body representation and language comprehension tasks were the same as described above. In addition, patients were asked to pantomime meaningful gestures to command. The gestures were the same as those imitated in Study 1. For each gesture, patients were given the verbal label of the gesture (e.g., brush teeth) and asked to pantomime the gesture as precisely as possible. Gestures were coded as described in Study 1.

Results

Standard multiple regression analysis was performed to examine the degree to which the different body representation and language comprehension measures predicted performance in the meaningful gesture to command task. The predictor variables simultaneously entered into the analysis consisted of the proportion correct measures for the following tasks: (1) body schema (contralesional),[2] (2) body semantics, and (3) language comprehension. Unfortunately, due to ceiling effects for the body structural description task in this subset of patients (100% correct performance by > 75% of patients), we were unable to include it as a predictor in the regression analysis.

Table 5 displays the correlations between each of the variables and the results of the regression analysis. The regression model accounted for a significant amount of variability in the gesture to command task, $F(3, 26) = 8.38$, $p < .001$. As in Study 1, only body semantics and body schema (contralesional) measures contributed significant and unique predictions of performance on the meaningful gesture to command task.

Discussion

As we have previously argued (e.g., Buxbaum et al., 2000), the results of Study 2 suggest that both semantic information about the body and on-line postural information about the body may be involved in producing meaningful gestures to command. Although we were unable to assess the contribution of structural descriptions in this study, it should be noted that the results of the regression models in Studies 1 and 2 were highly similar, and that structural descriptions did not contribute to the regression model in Study 1. However, it remains possible that we would have observed their contribution to the model of Study 2 had subjects not performed at ceiling on this measure.

Table 5. *Standard multiple regression: Predictors of meaningful gesture to command performance*

Variables	Correlations			Regression			
	Mf-co	BSc	BSe	B	β	t	sr
BSc	.55			.79	.37	2.37*	.33
BSe	.60	.44		.59	.55	3.04*	.43
Comp	.20	.27	.56	−.20	−.21	−1.22	
R = .70**; R² = .49							

For abbreviations, see Table 2 and Table 4.
* $p < .05$; ** $p < .01$.

[2] Based on the results of the regression analysis in Study 1 and in order to reduce the number of predictor variables to reflect the reduced number of patients (i.e., Tabachnick & Fidell, 1989, recommend having at least five times more subjects than predictor variables) in this study, we included only the contralesional portion of the body schema task. When the regression was run with the ipsilesional portion included, it did not contribute significantly to the regression and it did not alter the reported findings.

The two route model of praxis suggests that meaningless movement imitation must be performed via the "direct" route and thus should not require access to body semantics. We assessed this prediction in Study 3.

STUDY 3: PREDICTING MEANINGLESS GESTURE IMITATION

Methods

Participants

A different subset of 25 patients tested in Study 1 (see Table 1) participated in additional praxis testing.

Procedure

The body representation and language comprehension tasks were the same as described above. In addition, patients were asked to imitate meaningless movements. These movements were created in accordance with the methods reported by Buxbaum et al. (2000) so that they were spatially and temporally analogous to meaningful gestures in terms of the plane of gesture (e.g., horizontal or vertical) and the joints around which the movement occurred. The hand posture was also modified so as to be unlike the meaningful gestures. For example, the movement analogous to hammering was a vertical movement performed by the side of the body, with movements of the elbow and shoulder joints, and the hand in a claw shape.

Each patient imitated 10 meaningless movements derived from transitive gestures and 5 meaningless movements derived from intransitive gestures (see Buxbaum et al., 2000, for detailed descriptions). Patients performed each movement immediately after viewing a videotape of a model performing the movement. Movements were scored by a trained coder according to the same guidelines as in Studies 1 and 2.

Results and discussion

The predictor variables simultaneously entered into the multiple regression consisted of the proportion correct measures for the following tasks: (1) body schema (contralesional), (2) body structural description, (3) body semantics, and (4) language comprehension.

Table 6 displays the correlations between each of the variables and the results of the regression analysis. The regression model accounted for a significant amount of variability in the meaningless gesture imitation task, $F(4, 20) = 11.31$, $p < .001$. In contrast to the findings of Studies 1 and 2, only the body schema (contralesional) measure contributed significantly to the prediction of performance on the meaningless gesture imitation task.

As in Study 1, other measures were correlated with performance on the meaningless imitation task, but failed to contribute to the regression. This suggests that these measures may be indirectly related to imitation performance through their relations with the body schema (contralesional) task.

Variables	Correlations				Regression			
	Ml-im	BSc	BSD	BSe	B	β	t	sr
BSc	.57				.52	.38	2.31*	.29
BSD	.78	.51			.81	.35	1.59	
BSe	.53	.03	.58		.41	.20	1.19	
WAB	.55	.05	.64	.61	.37	.18	0.96	
R = .83**; R² = .69								

For abbreviations, see Table 2 and Table 4.
* $p < .05$; ** $p < .01$.

GENERAL DISCUSSION

Data from 55 patients with left-hemisphere stroke support previous evidence for distinctions between three types of body representation, and extend previous knowledge of the relationships between these representations and performance of meaningful gestures and complex meaningless movements. The results demonstrate that body semantics and the body schema both play a role in the production of spatially and temporally accurate movements when the task is to imitate meaningful gestures or produce meaningful gestures to command (Studies 1 and 2). In contrast, only the body schema appears to be directly involved in the ability to imitate meaningless movements (Study 3). There are three main implications of these findings that will be discussed in turn.

First, the present results are consistent with previous findings derived primarily from single case studies suggesting that there are dissociable representations of the human body (e.g., Buxbaum & Coslett, 2001; Coslett et al., 2002; Ogden, 1985; Sirigu et al., 1991). In the factor analysis performed in Study 1, the body semantics task did not load on the same factor as the body schema and body structural description tasks, supporting previous evidence for a distinction between semantic knowledge of the body and structural and on-line postural representations of the body. The body semantics measure did load on the same factor as the language comprehension measure, suggesting a relation between semantic knowledge of the body and other lexical-semantic information. However, only the body semantics task contributed significantly to the prediction of meaningful gesture imitation, suggesting that body semantics plays a role in gesture production beyond that predicted by its relationship with other semantic information.

Previous single case reports of patients with autotopagnosia (a deficit in body part identification) have demonstrated dissociations between the body schema and body structural description (Buxbaum & Coslett, 2001; Sirigu et al., 1991). In the present study, tasks designed to assess these representations loaded on the same factor. However, only the body schema measure contributed

significantly to the prediction of complex movement production and imitation, suggesting a distinction between body schema and body structural description representations in terms of their relations to complex movements.

The second contribution of the present findings is a clarification of the body representations involved in meaningful and meaningless movement performance. In the domain of meaningless movements, Goldenberg and colleagues (Goldenberg, 1995; Goldenberg & Hagmann, 1997) demonstrated that IM patients have difficulty imitating meaningless hand and arm postures as well as positioning a mannequin in such imitative postures. Goldenberg and Hagmann (1997) suggested that "... the transposition of the demonstrated gesture to the patient's own body could be achieved by coding of the meaningless gestures with reference to knowledge about the human body. A generally valid structural description of the human body provides a classification of significant body parts and specifies the boundaries that define them" (p. 339). Further, Goldenberg (1995) argued that "defective imitation of gestures on oneself and on a manikin cannot be ascribed to the disturbance of a personal 'body schema' which integrates information about the extension and position of one's own body" (p. 70). The present data conversely suggest that the body schema is important in complex movement imitation and production, but that body structural descriptions are unlikely to play a direct role. There were, however, significant correlations between measures of the body structural description and praxis and between body structural description and body schema measures. Thus, it appears likely that body structural descriptions may contribute indirectly to praxis performance, perhaps through an influence on body schema representations. Given that body structural descriptions correlate more strongly with meaningless than meaningful movements (see Tables 4 and 6), this relationship may be particularly strong when other potential sources of information (e.g., body semantics information, the presence of tools/objects) contributing to the body schema are absent.

One additional finding of interest is that although subjects performed equivalently on the hand laterality task with pictures of the contra-lesional and ipsilesional hands (86% on both), only performance with stimuli depicting the contra-lesional hand predicted ability to gesture to imitation or command. This pattern of performance is not predicted by accounts that posit that the left hemisphere is "dominant" for motor planning (e.g., Sirigu, Duhamel, Cohen, Pillon, Dubois, & Agid, 1996). Additional investigations will be required to determine the relative contributions of the right and left hemispheres to motor imagery and action.

Finally, the present findings are consistent with the predictions derived from the two-route model of praxis described in the Introduction (Gonzalez Rothi et al., 1991). Imitation and production of meaningful gestures appeared to depend both on body semantics (aligned with the semantic route) as well as the body schema (aligned with the direct route). Imitation of meaningless gestures, on the other hand, appeared to rely only on the body schema. We suggest that body semantics and the body schema may both contribute to the production of meaningful gestures to command in that body semantics may permit the linking of lexical-semantic information about action (called "action semantics" in the model of Gonzalez Rothi et al., 1991) to body schema representations involved in the on-line guidance of the gesture.

Both body semantics and body schema representations also appeared to play a role in imitating meaningful gestures. Thus, while it is theoretically possible for this task to be performed solely via the body schema (direct route), the body semantics measure made an independent contribution to the prediction of meaningful gesture imitation performance beyond that predicted by the body schema measure. We suggest that body semantics information may serve to augment body schema representations through top-down information concerning the goal of the observed movements. This type of understanding of the purpose of the movements may help to simplify the task by distinguishing between the important aspects of the observed behaviour and incidental movements; it may allow for "replicating a person's *intent* rather than going through the motions" (Pinker, 2002,

p. 62). On this account, it may be expected that patients with selective impairment on body semantics tasks will be able to imitate meaningful gestures via the body schema (direct route), but the imitation may be impaired or slowed relative to normal controls. More interestingly, such patients may also be expected to be more likely than controls to imitate incidental or "mistaken" aspects of an observed gesture.

REFERENCES

Buxbaum, L. J., & Coslett, H. B. (2001). Specialised structural descriptions for human body parts: Evidence from autotopagnosia. *Cognitive Neuropsychology, 18,* 289–306.

Buxbaum, L. J., Giovannetti, T., & Libon, D. (2000). The role of the dynamic body schema in praxis: Evidence from primary progressive apraxia. *Brain and Cognition, 44,* 166–191.

Coslett, H. B. (1998). Evidence for a disturbance of the body schema in neglect. *Brain and Cognition, 37,* 527–544.

Coslett, H. B., Saffran, E. M., & Schwoebel, J. (2002). Knowledge of the human body: A distinct semantic domain. *Neurology, 59,* 357–363.

Decety, J., Grezes, J., Costes, N., Perani, D., Jeannerod, M., Procyk, E., Grassi, F., & Fazio, F. (1997). Brain activity during observation of action: Influence of action content and subject's strategy. *Brain, 120,* 1763–1777.

De Renzi, E. (1985). Methods of limb apraxia examination and their bearing on the interpretation of the disorder. In E. A. Roy (Ed), *Neuropsychological studies of apraxia and related disorders* (pp. 45–64). Amsterdam: Elsevier, North Holland.

De Renzi, E., Faglioni, P., Lodesani, M., & Vecchi, A. (1983). Performance of left brain-damaged patients on imitation of single movements and motor sequences: Frontal and parietal-injured patients compared. *Cortex, 19,* 333–343.

De Renzi, E., & Lucchelli, F. (1988). Ideational apraxia. *Brain, 111,* 1173–1185.

De Renzi, E., Motti, F., & Nichelli, P. (1980). Imitating gestures: A quantitative approach to ideomotor apraxia. *Archives of Neurology, 37,* 6–10.

Desmurget, M., Epstein, C. M., Turner, R. S., Prablanc, C., Alexander, G. E., & Grafton, S. T.

(1999). Role of the posterior parietal cortex in updating reaching movements to a visual target. *Nature Neuroscience, 2,* 563–567.

Desmurget, M., & Grafton, S. T. (2000). Forward modeling allows feedback control for fast reaching movements. *Trends in Cognitive Sciences, 4,* 423–431.

Di Pellegrino, G., Fadiga, L., Fogassi, L., Gallese, V., & Rizzolatti, G. (1992). Understanding motor events: A neurophysiological study. *Experimental Brain Research, 91,* 176–180.

Fadiga, L., Fogassi, L., Gallese, V., & Rizzolatti, G. (2000). Visuomotor neurons: Ambiguity of the discharge or "motor" perception? *International Journal of Psychophysiology, 35,* 165–177.

Gallese, V., Fadiga, L., Fogassi, L., & Rizzolatti, G. (1996). Action recognition in the premotor cortex. *Brain, 119,* 593–609.

Gerardin, E., Sirigu, A., Lehericy, S., Poline, J.-B., Gaymard, B., Marsalt, C., Agid, Y., & Bihan, D. L. (2000). Partially overlapping neural networks for real and imagined hand movements. *Cerebral Cortex, 10,* 1093–1104.

Goldenberg, G. (1995). Imitating gestures and manipulating a manikin—The representation of the human body in ideomotor apraxia. *Neuropsychologia, 33,* 63–72.

Goldenberg, G. (2000). Disorders of body perception. In M. J. Farah & T. E. Feinberg (Eds.), *Patient based approaches to cognitive neuroscience.* Boston: MIT Press.

Goldenberg, G., & Hagmann, S. (1997). The meaning of meaningless gestures: A study of visuo-imitative apraxia. *Neuropsychologia, 35,* 333–341.

Gonzalez Rothi, L. J., Ochipa, C., & Heilman, K. M. (1991). A cognitive neuropsychological model of limb apraxia. *Cognitive Neuropsychology, 8,* 443–458.

Goodale, M. A., Milner, A. D., Jakobson, L. S., & Carey, D. P. (1991). A neurological dissociation between perceiving objects and grasping them. *Nature, 349,* 154–156.

Graziano, M. S. A., Cooke, D. F., & Taylor, C. S. R. (2000). Coding the location of the arm by sight. *Science, 290,* 1782–1786.

Grezes, J., & Decety, J. (2001). Functional anatomy of execution, mental simulation, observation, and verb generation of actions: A meta-analysis. *Human Brain Mapping, 12,* 1–19.

Head, H., & Holmes, G. (1911–1912). Sensory disturbances from cerebral lesions. *Brain, 34,* 102–254.

Heilman, K. M., & Gonzalez Rothi, L. J. (1993). Apraxia. In K. M. Heilman & E. Valenstein (Eds.), *Clinical neuropsychology* (3rd ed., pp. 141–150). New York: Oxford University Press.

Heilman, K. M., Gonzalez Rothi, L. J., Mack, L., Feinberg, T., & Watson, R. T. (1986). Apraxia after a superior parietal lesion. *Cortex, 22,* 141–150.

Helm-Estabrooks, N. (1992). *Test of Oral and Limb Apraxia.* Itasca, IL: Riverside Publishing Company.

Iacoboni, M., Woods, R. P., Brass, M., Bekkering, H., Mazziotta, J. C., & Rizzolatti, G. (1999). Cortical mechanisms of human imitation. *Science, 286,* 2526–2528.

Jeannerod, M. (2001). Neural simulation of action: A unifying mechanism for motor cognition. *NeuroImage, 14,* S103–S109.

Kertesz, A. (1982). *Western Aphasia Battery.* New York: Grune & Stratton.

Lackner, J. R. (1988). Some proprioceptive influences on the perceptual representation of body shape and orientation. *Brain, 111,* 281–297.

Lacquaniti, F., Guigon, E., Bianchi, L., Ferraina, S., & Caminiti, R. (1995). Representing spatial information for limb movement: Role of area 5 in the monkey. *Cerebral Cortex, 5,* 391–409.

Mishkin, M., Ungerleider, L. G., & Macko, K. A. (1983). Object vision and spatial vision: Two cortical pathways. *Trends in Neuroscience, 6,* 414–417.

Ogden, J. A. (1985). Autotopagnosia: Occurrence in a patient without nominal aphasia and with an intact ability to point to parts of animals and objects. *Brain, 108,* 1009–1022.

Parsons, L. M. (1987). Imagined spatial transformations of one's body. *Journal of Experimental Psychology: General, 116,* 172–191.

Parsons, L. M. (1994). Temporal and kinematic properties of motor behavior reflected in mentally simulated action. *Journal of Experimental Psychology: Human Perception and Performance, 20,* 709–730.

Parsons, L. M., & Fox, P. T. (1998). The neural basis of implicit movements used in recognising hand shape. *Cognitive Neuropsychology, 15,* 583–615.

Pick, A. (1922). Storrung der orientierung am eigenen korper. *Psychologische Forschung, 2,* 303–318.

Pinker, S. (2002). *The blank slate: The modern denial of human nature.* New York: Viking.

Rizzolatti, G., Camarda, R., Fogassi, L., Gentilucci, M., Luppino, G., & Matelli, M. (1988). Functional organization of area 6 in the macaque monkey. II. Area F5 and the control of distal movements. *Experimental Brain Research, 71,* 491–507.

Rizzolatti, G., Fadiga, L., Gallese, V., & Fogassi, L. (1996). Premotor cortex and the recognition of motor actions. *Cognitive Brain Research, 3,* 131–141.

Schwoebel, J., Boronat, C. B., & Coslett, H. B. (2002a). The man who executed "imagined" movements: Evidence for dissociable components of the body schema. *Brain and Cognition, 50*, 1–16.

Schwoebel, J., Coslett, H. B., Bradt, J., Friedman, R., & Dileo, C. (2002b). Pain and the body schema: Effects of pain severity on mental representations of movement. *Neurology, 59*, 775–777.

Schwoebel, J., Coslett, H. B., & Buxbaum, L. J. (2001). Compensatory coding of body-part location in autotopagnosia: Evidence for extrinsic egocentric coding. *Cognitive Neuropsychology, 18*, 363–381.

Schwoebel, J., Friedman, R., Duda, N., & Coslett, H. B. (2001a). Pain and the body schema: Evidence for peripheral effects on mental representations of movement. *Brain, 124*, 2098–2104.

Sirigu, A., Duhamel, J. R., Cohen, L., Pillon, B., Dubois, B., & Agid, Y. (1996). The mental represen-tation of hand movements after parietal cortex damage. *Science, 273*, 1564–1568.

Sirigu, A., Grafman, J., Bressler, K., & Sunderland, T. (1991). Multiple representations contribute to body knowledge processing. *Brain, 114*, 629–642.

Suzuki, K., Yamadori, A., & Fujii, T. (1997). Category-specific comprehension deficit restricted to body parts. *Neurocase, 3*, 193–200.

Tabachnick, B. G., & Fidell, L. G. (1989). *Using multi-variate statistics* (2nd ed.). New York: Harper Collins.

Wolpert, D. M., & Ghahramani, Z. (2000). Computa-tional principles of movement neuroscience. *Nature Neuroscience, 3*, 1212–1217.

Wolpert, D. M., Ghahramani, Z., & Jordan, M. I. (1995). An internal model for sensorimotor integra-tion. *Science, 269*, 1880–1882.

COGNITIVE NEUROPSYCHOLOGY, 2004, 21 (2/3/4) 299–315

A CIRCUMSCRIBED REFRACTORY ACCESS DISORDER: A VERBAL SEMANTIC IMPAIRMENT SPARING VISUAL SEMANTICS

Elizabeth K. Warrington
University College, London, UK

Sebastian J. Crutch
University College and Imperial College, London, UK

We report the case of a patient (AZ) with a semantic refractory access dysphasia. On matching-to-sample tests assessing comprehension of the spoken word, AZ shows all the hallmarks of a refractory access disorder, namely inconsistent performance on repeated testing and sensitivity to both presentation rate and the semantic similarity between competing responses. However, on tasks examining her visual knowledge, such as matching two structurally different exemplars of the same item, AZ's performance is quantitatively and qualitatively different. In a series of experiments testing her knowledge of animate and inanimate items, AZ demonstrated significantly worse performance with verbal–visual matching than with visual–visual matching. Furthermore, response accuracy was observed to decrease with successive probing of an item in the verbal conditions but not the visual conditions. We also demonstrate that this discrepancy cannot be explained on the basis of either task difficulty or presentation rate. We attribute our results to a build-up of refractoriness in the systems mediating verbal comprehension whilst those underlying visual comprehension remain unaffected. We argue that our data speak against a unitary amodal semantic system and in favour of at least partially separate verbal and visual semantic processing.

INTRODUCTION

Semantic memory is a mental thesaurus of organised knowledge about the meanings of words, objects, symbols, and all manner of factual information. An individual's verbal vocabulary is one major component of this storehouse. However objects, quite apart from having verbal labels, have clearly defined attributes, functions, and associations. The question of whether this level of representation is stored in a unitary all-purpose amodal system or whether there are multiple semantic systems is more controversial (for a review, see Saffran & Schwartz, 1994). Investigations that address this issue stress either the concordance or rather the lack of concordance between knowledge experienced in the verbal and the visual domains. Is information from the verbal and visual

Correspondence should be addressed to Professor Elizabeth Warrington, Dementia Research Group, The National Hospital for Neurology and Neurosurgery, 8–11 Queen Square, London WC1N 3BG, UK (Email: e.warrington@dementia.ion.ucl.ac.uk).

We are most grateful to Dr D. Cohen for allowing us to study a patient under his care. We are also indebted to Katie Cohen for her assistance and provision of language assessment information.

We were very pleased to welcome Eleanor Saffran to the Department of Neuropsychology as a visiting scientist for the 1981–1982 academic year. We still have a video recording she made of the first semantic access dysphasic (VER). Indeed it was a remark of hers which led to our documentation of VER's refractory behaviour.

DOI:10.1080/02643290342000546

domains integrated within a unified semantic representation (e.g., Caramazza, Hillis, Rapp, & Romani, 1990; Lambon Ralph, Graham, Patterson, & Hodges, 1999; Riddoch, Humphreys, Coltheart, & Funnell, 1988)? Alternatively, do verbal and visual semantic processes operate in parallel or have a degree of autonomy (e.g., McCarthy & Warrington, 1988; Shallice, 1988, 1993)?

There are three sources of neuropsychological data that point to a dissociable neural substrate for visual and verbal knowledge. First, there is the evidence of two classical neurological syndromes, *transcortical sensory aphasia* (Lichtheim, 1885) and *visual associative agnosia* (Lissauer, 1890), each with distinct anatomical correlates. The former is characterised by fluent dysphasia with loss of comprehension in the context of intact repetition. The visual associative agnosic is unable to recognise common objects by sight despite normal vision and perception. The orthodox, classical interpretation of these syndromes was in terms of a *disconnection* between sensory processing and more central meaning centres (for a review, see Geschwind, 1965). However, an alternative view equates transcortical sensory aphasia with an impaired verbal knowledge base and visual associative agnosia with an impaired visual knowledge base (Warrington, 1975).

These syndromes, in which the semantic impairment is confined (or nearly so) to either the verbal or the visual domain, are recognised to pose difficulties for the adherents of the unimodal semantics hypothesis. The evidence of transcortical sensory aphasia has been rejected on the grounds that a visual representation supplies superordinate knowledge of "affordances" (i.e., access to information in the structural description) that support identification in the visual domain but not in the verbal, where the linkage between phonology and the concept is arbitrary (e.g., Rapp, Hillis, & Caramazza, 1993). Lauro-Grotto, Piccini, and Shallice (1997), however, have described a semantic dementia patient with a profound verbal comprehension deficit in whom, they argue, the preservation or use of affordances could not possibly account for her sophisticated knowledge of foodstuffs and kitchen utensils.

An alternative escape clause that has been proposed is the notion of visual primacy. This claim relates to the relationship between words/objects and their meaning; words are held to have an arbitrary relationship to their meaning, whereas the meaning of an object is dependent upon its properties (e.g., Caramazza et al., 1990). To sustain this position it is necessary to reject the evidence of visual associative agnosia. Indeed, proponents of a unitary semantics model directly acknowledge the significance of this phenomenon: "These cases supposedly represent instances in which a deficit can be unequivocally localised within the semantic system and yet the impairment is apparent for one input modality but not for others. If this indeed were an accurate characterisation of the performance patterns exhibited by certain neurologically impaired patients it might constitute a serious problem for OUCH [the Organised Unitary Content Hypothesis]" (Rapp et al., 1993). The suggestion that subtle visual or perceptual impairments undermine their visual recognitions skills is hardly compelling in face of well-documented cases (e.g., FRA: McCarthy & Warrington, 1986; CAV: Warrington, 1981; DRS: Warrington & McCarthy, 1994). Clear evidence of well-preserved perceptual and spatial skills were demonstrated in these patients.

The second source of data supporting the multiple semantics position comes from impairments of conceptual knowledge in patients with cortical degenerative conditions. In the original study that described the selective impairment of semantic knowledge there were unequal verbal and visual impairments. One patient had particular difficulty in defining the names of objects, which nonetheless could be identified. More critical was the evidence of the second patient, who was unable to identify the object though still able to define its name (Warrington, 1975). In subsequent cases the emphasis has been placed on the concordance between items lost in the verbal or visual domain (Lambon Ralph et al., 1999). This argument has particular force in those cases of congruent category-specific impairments in the two modalities. For example, in some patients an animate/inanimate dissociation has been observed for both verbal and visual stimuli (Caramazza & Shelton, 1998; Farah, Hammond, Mehta, & Ratcliff, 1989; Sartori & Job, 1988; Warrington & Shallice, 1984). However, Warrington and Shallice (1984) demonstrated that this congruence broke down with a more detailed item analysis. Such reports of associated deficits are entirely compatible with, though alone perhaps do not compel, the multiple semantics model.

Third, and more compelling still, are those patients in whom the modality-specific deficit is selective to one category of knowledge. The first clear-cut example of such a pattern of deficit was observed in a patient whose visual knowledge appeared to be intact for all objects, animate and inanimate. However, within the verbal domain his knowledge of names of animate objects was much degraded as compared with inanimate. For example, presented with the word *swan* he responded, "can't tell you any functions" but to a picture of a swan "large bird, seen on canals and rivers, nesting at this time of year" (TOB: McCarthy & Warrington, 1988). The evidence of category specificity indicated that the locus of the deficit was at the level of semantic processing. That it was also modality specific is difficult to accommodate within a unitary system. There are now a number of other instances of a modality by category interaction in the literature. For example, a category-specific visual agnosia for inanimate stimuli was demonstrated in a patient whose verbal knowledge base was entirely intact (DRS: Warrington & McCarthy, 1994). Incisa della Rocchetta, Cipolotti, and Warrington (1998) described a patient (DK) who had a selective deficit for countries restricted to the visual domain. Kartsounis and Shallice (1996) reported a patient whose only deficit was an inability to recognise visual representations of famous historical figures or famous buildings. Counter-arguments involving task difficulty and resource capacity have difficulty withstanding the evidence of these "quadruple" dissociations. Once again, the significance of such behavioural patterns has been acknowledged: "Category by modality interactions such as these would appear to be difficult to accommodate within a unitary semantics framework" (Rapp et al., 1993).

In addition to highlighting unexpected category and modality dissociations, some investigations have focused on the dynamics of the impairment. A major distinction is drawn between patients in whom there is a degradation of the semantic knowledge base and those in whom there is a temporary unavailability of stored information, termed storage cases and access cases respectively. Specifically, the temporary unavailability can be decreased by the introduction of a delay between a response and the following stimulus. In some patients, temporal factors appear to be crucial in that the system appears to become "refractory" for a variable period of time after activation (Cipolotti & Warrington, 1995; Warrington & McCarthy, 1983). Typically using matching-to-sample techniques to assess verbal comprehension, items in an array are probed several times. Strong serial position effects are observed in the refractory cases, with overall decrement in performance across trials (Forde & Humphreys, 1995). In a direct comparison of the two types of syndrome, the response accuracy of the access cases could be modulated by temporal factors whereas the storage cases were unaffected (Warrington & Cipolotti, 1996). Refractoriness may nevertheless be restricted to a semantic category and, within a category, to near semantic neighbours. The pattern of this spread of refractoriness has been interpreted to reflect the organization of our semantic knowledge base (Crutch & Warrington, 2003; Warrington & McCarthy, 1987). In this context, it has been argued that the semantic distance effects observed in patients with degenerative conditions have a different basis (Warrington & Cipolotti, 1996).

Patients with a static degradation of their semantic knowledge base have provided most of the evidence adduced for and against the unitary amodal theory of semantic representations. The one notable exception is the detailed experiments of Forde and Humphreys (1997). They reported a patient with a semantic refractory access deficit that was harnessed to address the issue of multiple semantics. In two experiments, they compared verbal–visual matching with visual–visual matching (based on similarity of function or association). A comparable deficit was observed on the visual within-modality task as on the cross-modality task. In a further experiment, they examined the effect upon the patient's strong serial position effects of switching the response modality. Specifically, after repeated testing of items with spoken word–written word matching, there was a fourth trial involving a switch to matching the same spoken words to pictures. They reported a spread of refractoriness across modalities. Both these results were interpreted as favouring the amodal model of semantic knowledge. It is, however, worth noting that the latter effect was somewhat weak and not obtained in all conditions, added to which the modality switch was not complete as the stimulus item was a spoken word in all conditions. If the refractory state derives at least as much from processing the stimulus input as from rejecting distracter items in an array, then this is not a critical test of the multiple semantics hypothesis.

Qualitative differences between storage deficits and refractory deficits may be observed not only within a cognitive system but also between systems. A refractoriness that affects the performance of a particular cognitive task sparing a related task has been interpreted to indicate a degree of independence of the neural substrates mediating the two tasks. In the case of language processing, word retrieval skills were shown to become refractory whilst word comprehension was spared (McCarthy & Kartsounis, 2000), and in object recognition, semantic processing was impaired, sparing perceptual processing (Forde & Humphreys, 1997). In the case of a dyslexic patient (VYG: Crutch & Warrington, 2001) it was observed that his reading accuracy could be modulated by temporal factors, whereas neither his naming nor repetition were susceptible. Indeed, his naming and propositional speech was quite free from the phonological errors that so characterised his reading. It was on the basis of these qualitative differences that a model proposing multiple phonological output systems was preferred to the more orthodox unitary output model. An analogous argument applies to the present case.

Our aim in this paper is to describe our further observations of a refractory dysphasic patient. In this series of experiments we focus on the qualitative, dynamic differences between her performance on tasks with a verbal component and those that can be performed entirely within the visual domain. We shall claim that our findings provide further evidence in support of the multiple semantics system hypothesis.

CASE REPORT

AZ, a 72-year-old right-handed housewife was admitted to Northwick Park Hospital under the care of Dr Cohen following the acute onset of right-sided weakness and a severe language comprehension impairment. A CT scan demonstrated a large cerebral infarction in the territory of the left middle cerebral artery involving the parietal, temporal, and posterior frontal regions but sparing the basal ganglia (see Figure 1). On examination she was globally and severely dysphasic, dysgraphic, and dyslexic. Her expressive speech was a mixed phonemic and semantic jargon. Her language

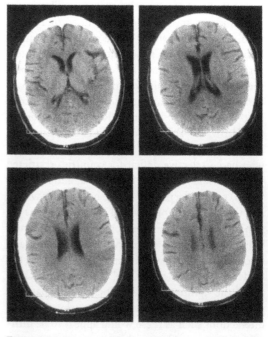

Figure 1. *A CT scan of AZ showing damage to the left middle cerebral territory.*

comprehension was also compromised. There was a mild right-sided hemiparesis. There were no other neurological signs of note and, in particular, she had full visual fields.

NEUROPSYCHOLOGICAL ASSESSMENT

AZ was gravely dysphasic, such that any task requiring a verbal output, with the exception of verbal repetition, could not be administered. Her propositonal speech was reduced to a few stereo-typed phrases. Her attempts to express more complex messages were characterised by florid fluent jargon in which both semantic and phonemic errors were observed. She was unable to name even very high-frequency objects; her attempts were effortful and bore little resemblance to the target. She was unable to read aloud high-frequency monosyllabic words. Again her attempts to read were effortful, succeeding only in producing perseverative phonemic jargon responses. She was totally unable to spell aloud or to write words to dictation. Her ability to repeat was poor but much superior to her word retrieval and word production skills (39/99 correct; subset of the Patterson & Hodges, 1992, corpus).

AZ's comprehension was relatively preserved and it was possible to obtain quantitative measurements using matching-to-sample and recognition techniques. On a lexical decision task (PALPA) she obtained the creditable score of 71/80. On the short form of the BPVT she obtained the weak score of 22/32 with oral presentation and a similarly weak score of 23/32 with written stimuli. She attempted the Peabody Picture Vocabulary Test (Version A, first 100 items) with both written and orally presented target items, producing comparable scores with each presentation modality (Spoken = 75/100, Written = 77/100). Although well below average, her performance demonstrated relative preservation of her comprehension as compared with expressive speech functions. She attempted two versions of the Pyramids and Palm Trees Test (written word–written word and picture–picture matching), completing the task

slowly at her own pace. She scored 38/52 on both versions. While acknowledging that neither her verbal nor visual comprehension is intact, it is AZ's susceptibility to refractoriness that we are concerned with in the following experiments.

EXPERIMENTAL PROCEDURES

Experiment 1

Our overall aim in these experiments was to compare AZ's performance on tasks within the visual domain with her performance on tasks with a verbal component. AZ was gravely globally aphasic and even her ability to repeat monosyllabic words was impaired. It was therefore important to establish that any observed visual superiority could not be attributed to an auditory acoustic impairment. This experiment was devised to establish that her verbal comprehension deficit resulted from damage at the level of semantic processing. We compared her ability to match a spoken word to a target in an array of pictures that were either phonologically (rhyming names) or semantically related.

Procedure

This verbal–visual matching test consisted of 23 sets of rhyming triplets of picturable stimuli (e.g., *plate, grate, gate*). The morphology of the English language is such that these arrays are at the same time semantically distant. These same 69 stimuli were rearranged to make 23 sets of semantically related triplets (e.g., *plate, mug, spoon*; see Appendix A). Each item was probed four times and the stimuli were presented at a natural pace with approximately 1s between AZ's response and the presentation of the next stimulus. The two types of array were tested in blocks of 12 and 11 using an ABBA design.

Results

Her percentage correct score for the semantically related triplets was significantly worse than for the phonological triplets (74% and 88% respectively); $\chi^2(1) = 18.7$, $p < .001$. We would interpret AZ's superior performance on the phonologically similar triplets as compared with the semantically related triplets as an indication that a significant component of her verbal comprehension deficit was at the level of semantic processing. Indeed, considering the extreme phonemic similarity of the rhyming stimuli, we would suggest her acoustic word perception was very satisfactory.

Experiment 2

In Experiment 1 we established that AZ's comprehension deficit encompassed semantic processing, her performance being affected more by semantic similarity than by phonological similarity. Our aim in this experiment was to assess whether temporal factors also contributed to her deficit. This was achieved by comparing her performance on a verbal–visual matching test using two presentation rates.

Procedure

The test stimuli consisted of 36 line drawings of common inanimate objects (taken from Warrington & McCarthy, 1987, Experiment 6). These were grouped into six arrays of six semanti-

cally similar items (furniture, crockery, vehicles, clothes, personal items, office items; see Figure 2). AZ was presented with an array of six pictures. The name of each picture was presented three times in total (i.e., 18 probes altogether) in a pseudorandom order (e.g., stool, table, television, chair, desk, sofa, desk, television, stool, table, desk, etc.…). Using a similar procedure for all six arrays, each array was tested at two presentation rates: at a natural pace with a 1 s response–stimulus interval (RSI; the "fast" condition) and at a slower pace with a 10 s RSI (the "slow" condition). The slow and fast conditions were administered using an ABBA design. Each stimulus in each array was probed three times in a pseudorandom order such that successive stimuli were not the same.

Results

The percentage correct score for the fast presentation condition was significantly worse than for the slow presentation condition (80% and 92% respectively); $\chi^2(1) = 6.4$, $p < .02$. The number of errors on the first, second, and third probe of each item, summing across each array and each presentation rate, is given in Figure 3. There was a significant increase in the number of errors as a function of probe number, $\chi^2(2) = 9.2$, $p = .01$.

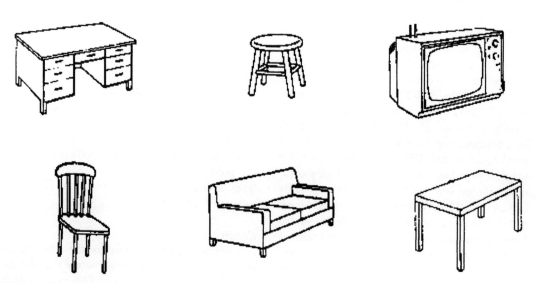

Figure 2. *An example of the arrays of semantically similar items used in Experiment 2.*

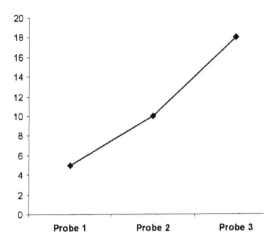

Figure 3. *The serial position curve showing the increasing number of errors observed with successive probes of the test items in Experiment 2.*

In this experiment we have shown that her response accuracy was affected by presentation rate. The facilatatory effect of a short delay after each response indicates that the system supporting this verbal–visual matching task became refractory with use. The results of this experiment, together with the semantic relatedness effect observed in Experiment 1, establish that AZ had all the core hallmarks of a semantic refractory access dysphasia.

Experiment 3

In Experiments 1 and 2 we have demonstrated facilitatory effects of semantic distance and slow presentation rates on verbal–visual matching tests. AZ's performance on comprehension tasks is indicative of evidence of a semantic refractory access syndrome. Her naming and reading aloud skills were so impaired that it was not possible to investigate whether these too would be influenced by temporal factors. However, her ability to repeat, though impaired, was sufficiently viable to assess whether a degree of refractoriness in the phonological transcoding system was limiting her performance. Our aim in this experiment was to document whether temporal factors affected her performance on a repetition task. This experiment was conducted in two sections to assess (1) the

effect of a slow presentation rate, and (2) the effect of repeated probes of the same item.

Procedure

1. The test stimuli consisted of 80 three-letter words (CVCs), 40 of which were high frequency (Thorndike Lorge, A and AA) and 40 lower frequency (1–50 per million). The words were presented singly and AZ attempted to repeat them at two presentation rates: Fast (1 s RSI) and slow (5 s RSI). She was tested in blocks of 10 words alternating the fast and the slow conditions.

2. The test stimuli consisted of 24 monosyllabic and 24 bisyllabic words, of which half were high frequency and half low frequency (selected from the McCarthy & Warrington, 1984, corpus). The words were arranged in 12 sets of four words and each set was repeated four times in pseudorandom order.

Results

1. The percentage correct scores for each presentation rate condition are shown in Table 1. Overall her performance with the fast rate is almost the same as with the slow rate for both the high- and the low-frequency words. Her correct responses were clearly and promptly produced. She made a small number of perseverative responses after a lag of up to six intervening responses.

2. The percentage correct repetitions for the monosyllabic and bisyllabic words for each level of frequency are given in Table 2. There were no significant differences between one- and two-syllable words or between low- and high-frequency words. Many of her errors were jargon utterances and difficult to transcribe accurately. There was not a significant trend for her errors to increase with successive attempts at the same target

Table 1. *The percentage correct scores for repeating high-frequency (HF) and low-frequency (LF) single words at each of two different presentation rates (Experiment 3a)*

RSI condition	HF	LF	Total
1 second	50%	58%	54%
5 seconds	58%	48%	53%

Table 2. *The percentage correct scores for repeating high-frequency (HF) and low-frequency (LF) monosyllabic and bisyllabic words (Experiment 3b)*

Words	HF	LF	Total
Monosyllabic	54%	40%	47%
Bisyllabic	44%	54%	49%

stimulus with one- or two-syllable words (see Figure 4); $\chi^2(3) = 2.5, p > .4$ and $\chi^2(3) = 1.5, p > .6$, respectively. Nevertheless response inconsistency was demonstrated. The distribution of her errors conformed to the pattern expected by chance for both monosyllabic and bisyllabic words, $\chi^2(2) = 4.9, p > .05$ and $\chi^2(2) = 4.5, p > .05$, respectively.

In these experiments, which document AZ's single word repetition skills there was no evidence of a contribution of temporal factors. Her performance was not influenced by presentation rate, nor was there any deterioration in her performance with successive attempts to repeat the target. Thus the refractoriness that characterised her performance on verbal-visual matching tasks was not observed in repetition tasks. These observations provide further evidence of the functional specificity of access disorders.

Experiment 4

In the previous experiments we have established that AZ's performance was affected both by semantic relatedness (Experiment 1) and by rate of presentation (Experiment 2). These were both cross-modality experiments. A verbal–visual matching task demands not only the comprehension of the spoken word but also the identification of the visual representation. Our aim in this and the following three experiments was to compare her visual recognition skills with her verbal comprehension. The integrity of visual semantics can be probed independently of verbal semantics by devising visual–visual matching tests. Such tests, which require matching by semantic similarity (i.e., two types of kettle) rather than by physical similarity (i.e., two views of a kettle) are held to access a level of visual object identification beyond that of a mere structural description. For example, to match a wristwatch to a wall clock demands processing to a semantic level and cannot be solved by the detection of common features. Our aim was to replicate the experiment contrasting a visual–visual matching task with a verbal–visual matching task reported previously by McCarthy and Warrington (1986).

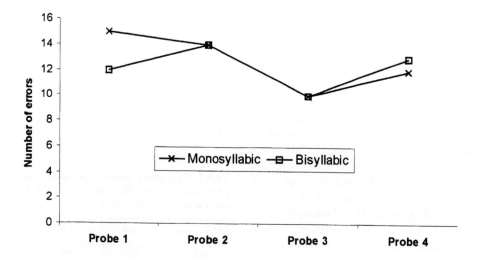

Figure 4. *The serial position curves for successive repetition of monosyllabic and bisyllabic words (Experiment 3b).*

Procedure

The stimuli consisted of line drawings of 30 objects. These were grouped into six sets of five semantically similar items. Five-item arrays were constructed by selecting one picture of each object. There were two conditions. In the visual–visual matching task, AZ was required to match an alternate, visually dissimilar example of the same kind of object to the picture in the array. In the verbal–visual matching task, AZ was required to match the spoken word to an array of the same pictures. Each item in the array in each condition was probed four times at a natural pace of a 1 s RSI.

Results

AZ scored 112/120 correct on the visual–visual condition. On three of the arrays her performance was flawless. On one array she made the consistent error or confusing a vase for a jug and on another array she consistently confused a door with a window frame (in both instances there was perceptual ambiguity). Her score on the verbal–visual condition was significantly worse than on the visual-visual condition (89/120 correct); $\chi^2(1) = 16.2, p < .001$. Moreover, there was no suggestion of a serial position effect in the visual–visual condition but such an effect was present in the verbal–visual condition (see Figure 5); $\chi^2(3) = 1.1, p > .7$ and $\chi^2(3) = 8.1, p < .05$, respectively.

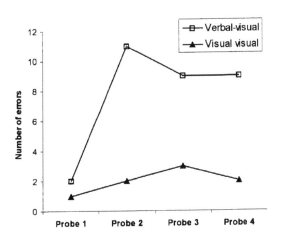

Figure 5. *The serial position curve for the verbal–visual and visual–visual conditions in Experiment 4.*

We have demonstrated a clear-cut dissociation between the two conditions. There was only a significant deficit on the task with a verbal component, sparing the within-modality matching task. Furthermore, AZ's performance was relatively intact as compared with three earlier patients tested on the visual–visual task. One earlier patient with a classical highly selective visual associative agnosia was tested on this task and was significantly more impaired on the visual–visual than the verbal–visual version: FRA, 86/120 and 101/120 respectively, $\chi^2(1) = 5.45, p < .05$; (McCarthy & Warrington, 1986). Three of the same arrays were also attempted twice by a further patient with a visual associative agnosia who was reported to have a more significant impairment in the visual–visual than verbal–visual condition: DRS, 66/120 and 92/120 respectively, $\chi^2(1) = 12.52, p < .001$; (Warrington & McCarthy, 1994). We would argue therefore that this visual–visual matching task was sufficiently demanding to require access to a semantic knowledge base.

Experiment 5

In Experiment 4 we demonstrated AZ's relatively intact performance on a visual–visual matching task that had previously been used to demonstrate deficits of visual knowledge. Our aim in this experiment and in Experiment 6 was to compare AZ's performance on such visual–visual matching tasks with that on verbal–visual matching tasks. This was attempted using arrays of greater semantic similarity than those in Experiment 4.

Procedure

The stimuli consisted of 16 inanimate objects. These were grouped into four sets of four semantically similar items. As in Experiment 4, for each object name two dissimilar photographs were selected such that there were obvious structural differences (see Figure 6). One picture of each object was selected and arranged in an array. There were two testing conditions: Verbal–visual matching and visual–visual matching. In the visual–visual matching task AZ was required to match the alternate example of the object picture

Figure 6. *An example of the inanimate visual–visual matching task conducted in Experiment 5.*

to the one in the array. Each item in the array was probed four times with a 1 s RSI. The two conditions were tested in an ABBA design and the same stimuli represented using a BAAB order. The time taken to present and elicit a response to each array was recorded.

Results

AZ's performance on the visual–visual matching test was virtually at ceiling (93% correct). Her performance on the verbal–visual matching test (summing across both presentations of the experiment) was significantly worse (76% correct);

$\chi^2(1) = 14.3$, $p < .001$. The total time to administer each array was only recorded on the first presentation of the test. However, the mean time to complete the visual–visual and verbal–visual matching test was not significantly different (54.3 s and 48.0 s respectively; Mann-Whitney U test: $Z = 1.3$, $p > .1$). The number of errors on all four probes of each item in each condition are shown in Figure 7. Only the verbal–visual matching showed a significant change in response accuracy across probes, $\chi^2(3) = 11.7$, $p < .01$.

In this experiment we have observed both a quantitative and a qualitative difference in AZ's

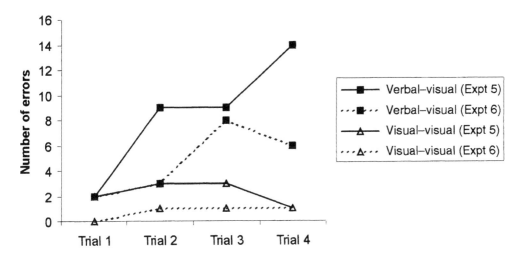

Figure 7. *The serial position curve for both verbal–visual and visual–visual matching conditions in Experiments 5 and 6 combined, showing the number of errors observed on successive probes of individual inanimate test items.*

performance on the cross-modal task as compared with the task completed within the visual modality. Her performance on the verbal task was inconsistent, deteriorating with successive probes. With the visual task not only was her performance superior but also there was no hint of a serial position effect. This difference could not be attributed to an overall slower presentation rate. Furthermore, her few errors on this task appeared to be a consistent misrecognition of two items (lamp and drawers). It was clear that the refractoriness that characterises her verbal comprehension was absent in the visual domain, which was in fact relatively intact.

Experiment 6

Our aim in this experiment was to replicate our findings of Experiment 5 and to obtain further evidence for dissociation between verbal and visual processing. This was again attempted using a task involving arrays of semantically similar items, the probing of which would be expected to induce a refractory state.

Procedure

The test stimuli consisted of 24 inanimate object names, 4 from each of six semantically close categories. As in Experiment 5, two dissimilar, structurally different pictorial representations were selected for each object. One picture of each object was selected and arranged in an array of 4 items. There were again two presentation conditions: verbal–visual matching and visual–visual matching. In the visual–visual matching task the alternate object picture was required to be matched to the picture in the array. Each item in the array was probed four times at a natural pace using a 1 s RSI. Each stimulus item was tested in both presentation conditions using an ABBA design such that half the arrays were tested first in the verbal–visual matching condition and half in the visual–visual matching condition. The time taken to present and elicit a response to each array was recorded.

Results

AZ's performance on the visual–visual matching condition was close to ceiling, scoring 97% correct; her score of 83% correct on the verbal–visual matching test was significantly lower, $\chi^2(1) = 9.87$, $p < .001$. In the verbal–visual matching condition there was a mild serial position effect but this did not reach significance (see Figure 7), $\chi^2(3) = 5.6$, $p > .1$. As before, the total time to present and elicit responses for each array was recorded; there was no difference between the verbal–visual and visual–visual conditions (mean = 44.5 s and 42.3 s respectively; Mann-Whitney U test: $Z = 1$, $p > .2$). It was also of note that the only three errors on the visual–visual matching test were a consistent misrecognition of *shorts* for *trousers*.

Experiment 7

Our aim in this experiment was to compare AZ's visual and verbal knowledge within a different broad semantic category. In all the previous experiments the stimuli have been inanimate objects. In this experiment we wished to establish whether our observations would generalise to animate stimuli.

Procedure

The test stimuli consisted of 16 animals, 4 selected from each of four semantically similar groups (zoo animals, farm animals, birds, domestic animals). For each animal two alternative structurally different pictures were selected, one of which was arranged in an array of four semantically similar items (see Figure 8). As in the previous two experiments there were two conditions: Verbal–visual matching and visual–visual matching, in which each picture stimulus had to be matched to its alternate in the array. Each item in each array was probed four times at a natural pace using a 1 s RSI. Each stimulus item was tested in both conditions using an ABBA design. The time taken to present and elicit a response to each array was recorded.

Results

AZ's performance on the verbal condition (66% correct) was significantly worse than her performance on the visual condition. (89% correct); $\chi^2(1) = 10.0$, $p < .01$. There was also a qualitative difference in her performance on the two conditions. On the visual condition four of the seven errors were a consistent mismatching of a lion to the picture of the tiger in the array. Moreover, there was a serial position effect on the verbal–visual task but not the visual–visual task (see Figure 9); $\chi^2(3) = 9.7$, $p < .05$ and $\chi^2(3) = 0.5$, $p > .9$, respectively. Once again, these differences could not be attributed to an

imbalance in the mean time to complete each array in the verbal–visual and visual–visual conditions (mean = 47.3 and 46.3 respectively; Mann-Whitney U test: $Z = 0.29$, $p > .5$).

Comment

The design of Experiments 4–7 all incorporate a visual–visual matching task, which was compared with a verbal–visual matching test. The rationale of this procedure is that it provides a direct measure of visual semantic processing on a task that does not have a verbal component. This measure can then be compared with the same stimuli in a cross-modal format. AZ's performance was close to ceiling on the visual tasks, and her few errors tended to be consistent misrecognitions. Typical serial position effects were observed with the verbal–visual matching tasks such that on the first probe her performance was virtually error-free and on subsequent probes she made an increasing number of errors. Thus in the tasks with a verbal component we have obtained evidence of refractoriness that is not present in the visual tasks. We shall interpret these results as providing evidence of a degree of independence between the representations underpinning verbal and visual semantics.

DISCUSSION

In this series of experiments we have documented a semantic refractory access deficit in a globally dysphasic patient. The main aim was to establish the modality specificity of this syndrome and in particular to compare her performance on tasks with a verbal component with those conducted entirely within the visual domain.

AZ was globally dysphasic; her language functions were impaired to the extent that propositional speech, naming, and reading aloud were profoundly impaired. Using matching-to-sample techniques to assess her comprehension, it was possible to demonstrate that semantic and temporal factors strongly influenced her performance. In particular, in Experiment 1 we established that her performance on a verbal–visual matching test was

Figure 8. *An example of the animate visual–visual matching task conducted in Experiment 7.*

superior with phonologically related than with semantically related arrays. In Experiment 2, again using a verbal–visual matching task, we showed a significant presentation rate effect by introducing a delay between each response and the subsequent target item. In addition there were strong serial position effects such that with successive probes of a target her performance deteriorated. These facilatatory effects of semantic distance and delay between successive probes typify a semantic refractory access dysphasia. AZ thus presented with a very similar syndrome to other earlier cases in the literature.

Experiments 4, 5, 6, and 7 were devised to assess the same contrast: Performance on a verbal–visual matching task as compared with visual–visual matching. Typically her performance on the verbal–visual matching and visual–visual matching conditions was equivalent and also at ceiling on the first probe. This equivalence mirrors the equivalence of her performance on the two versions of the Pyramids and Palm Trees test. However, AZ's performance on the verbal–visual matching task then deteriorated with each successive probe. This build-up of refractoriness did not occur on the visual–visual matching condition, where a ceiling

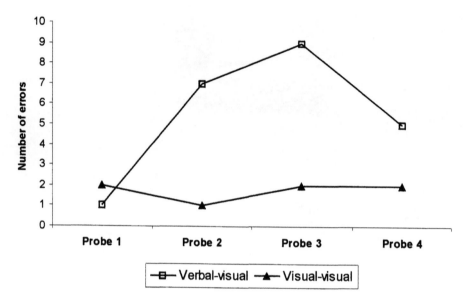

Figure 9. *The serial position curve for both verbal–visual and visual–visual matching conditions in Experiment 7, showing the number of errors observed on successive probes of individual animate test items.*

level of performance was maintained. Significant serial position functions were obtained on the verbal–visual matching condition of three of the four experiments and there was a trend in the fourth. By contrast, no significant serial position functions were found with the visual–visual conditions. Thus there was a clear-cut qualitative as well as quantitative difference in her performance on the verbal-visual as compared with the visual-visual conditions. We interpret these findings as evidence for a refractory deficit that is only present in the task with a verbal component; visual processing appears to be spared. Moreover, with repetition tasks on which AZ was significantly impaired, her performance showed no evidence of refractoriness (see Experiment 3). Thus AZ provides a further example of a dissociation based on the presence or absence of refractory phenomena (Forde & Humphreys, 1997; McCarthy & Kartsounis, 2000). It is AZ's circumscribed refractory deficit that we argue provides evidence of modality specificity of the semantic systems. The force of this argument rests on the assumption that visual–visual matching of structurally dissimilar objects is mediated by semantic processing.

Tasks that require object matching by name or function rather than by physical identity were introduced by De Renzi and Spinnler (1966) to obtain evidence for a two-stage process in object recognition: a perceptual processing stage and a semantic processing stage. This discontinuity has proved to be robust. Impairments at a semantic stage of processing in patients with intact perceptual processing have been demonstrated both in group studies (De Renzi, Scotti, & Spinnler, 1969; Warrington & Taylor, 1978) and more importantly in single case studies (Albert, Reches, & Silverberg, 1975; Hécaen, Goldblum, Masure, & Ramier, 1974). Furthermore, Forde and Humphreys reported a discontinuity between a task that required matching by physical identity, which was error-free, and matching by name, which was impaired in a patient (MJ). This they interpreted as a deficit at the semantic level of processing.

It is necessary also to be satisfied that the visual–visual matching tests are sufficiently demanding to permit a valid comparison with the comparable verbal–visual matching tasks. We would claim that the visual–visual matching test used in Experiment

4 was sufficiently sensitive to detect a visual semantic processing deficit, because two previously reported visual agnosic patients in whom verbal skills were intact were more impaired than on the visual–visual matching task than the verbal–visual matching task (FRA: McCarthy & Warrington, 1986; DRS: Warrington & McCarthy, 1994). AZ thus provides a double dissociation, which effectively counters a task difficulty explanation of her good performance. Although we do not have comparable evidence of a double dissociation, for Experiments 5, 6, and 7, we would nevertheless argue that these tasks are of comparable difficulty.

Our interpretation of the dissociation demonstrated in AZ between her performance on verbal–visual and visual–visual matching tasks in favour of the multiple semantics hypothesis is predicated by the assumption that visual–visual matching of structurally dissimilar objects having the same name or function access a semantic representation. Accepting Forde and Humphreys' position that the parallel deficit observed on verbal–visual and visual–visual matching tests provided evidence in favour of the unitary semantics hypothesis, it then follows that a dissociation between the ability to perform these tasks provides support for the multiple semantics position. In the case of AZ, it would appear that access to verbal semantics becomes refractory whereas access to visual semantics does not. It is this qualitative difference that provides converging evidence in the unitary/multiple semantics debate and adds weight to those studies that report quantitative differences in verbal and visual processing.

In general the unitary hypothesis relies heavily on the association of deficits. The most quoted evidence is the correspondence between animate and inanimate categories in the visual and verbal domains. These category correspondences, it is argued, would be most improbable in a multiple semantics organisation. Although to date asymmetries of knowledge in the two domains are on record, there is as yet no case in which there is a crossover, that is, an animate deficit in the verbal domain and an inanimate deficit in the visual domain. However, if an association breaks down, then the onus will be on the proponents of the unitary semantics position to offer an alternative account.

REFERENCES

Albert, M. L., Reches, A., & Silverberg, R. (1975). Associative visual agnosia without alexia. *Neurology, 25,* 322–326.

Caramazza, A., Hillis, A. E., Rapp, B. C., & Romani, C. (1990). Multiple semantics or multiple confusions? *Cognitive Neuropsychology, 7,* 161–168.

Caramazza, A., & Shelton, J. R. (1998). Domain-specific knowledge systems in the brain: The animate-inanimate distinction. *Journal of Cognitive Neuroscience, 10,* 1–34.

Cipolotti, L., & Warrington, E. K. (1995). Towards a unitary account of access dysphasia: A single case study. *Memory, 3,* 309–332.

Crutch, S. J., & Warrington, E. K. (2001). Refractory dyslexia: Evidence of multiple task-specific phonological output stores. *Brain, 124,* 1533–1543.

Crutch, S. J., & Warrington, E. K. (2003). Spatial coding of semantic information: Knowledge of country and city names depends upon their geographical proximity. *Brain, 126,* 1821–1829

De Renzi, E., Scotti, G., & Spinnler, H. (1969). Perceptual and associative disorders of visual recognition. Relationship to the side of the cerebral lesion. *Neurology, 19,* 634–642.

De Renzi, E., & Spinnler, H. (1966). Visual recognition in patients with unilateral cerebral disease. *Journal of Nervous Mental Disorders, 142,* 515–525.

Farah, M. J., Hammond, K. M., Mehta, Z., & Ratcliff, G. (1989). Category-specificity and modality-specificity in semantic memory. *Neuropsychologia, 27,* 193–200.

Forde, E. M. E., & Humphreys, G. W. (1995). Refractory semantics in global aphasia: On semantic organisation and the access-storage distinction in neuropsychology. *Memory, 3,* 265–307.

Forde, E. M. E., & Humphreys, G. W. (1997). A semantic locus for refractory behaviour: Implications for access-storage distinctions and the nature of semantic memory. *Cognitive Neuropsychology, 14,* 367–402.

Geschwind, N. (1965). Disconnexion syndromes in animals and man. I. *Brain, 88,* 237–294.

Hecaen, H., Goldblum, M. C., Masure, M. C., & Ramier, A. M. (1974). Une nouvelle observation d'agonsie d'objet. Deficit de l'association ou de la categorisation, specifique de la modalite visuelle? [A new case of object agnosia. A deficit in association or categorization specific for the visual modality?] *Neuropsychologia, 12*, 447–464.

Incisa della Rocchetta, A., Cipolotti, L., & Warrington, E. K. (1998). Countries: Their selective impairment and selective preservation. *Neurocase, 4*, 99–109.

Kartsounis, L. D., & Shallice, T. (1996). Modality specific semantic knowledge loss for unique items. *Cortex, 32*, 109–119.

Lambon-Ralph, M. A., Graham, K. S., Patterson, K., & Hodges, J. R. (1999). Is a picture worth a thousand words? Evidence from concept definitions by patients with semantic dementia. *Brain and Language, 70*, 309–335.

Lauro-Grotto, R., Piccini, C., & Shallice, T. (1997). Modality-specific operations in semantic dementia. *Cortex, 33*, 593–622.

Lichtheim, L. (1885). On aphasia. *Brain, 7*, 433–484.

Lissauer, H. (1890). Ein Fall von Seelenblindheit nebst einem Beitrag zur Theorie derselben. *Archiv für Psychiatrie, 21*, 222–270.

McCarthy, R. A., & Kartsounis, L. D. (2000). Wobbly words: Refractory anomia with preserved semantics. *Neurocase, 6*, 487–497.

McCarthy, R. A., & Warrington, E. K. (1986). Visual associative agnosia: A clinico-anatomical study of a single case. *Journal of Neurology, Neurosurgery and Psychiatry, 49*, 1233–1240.

McCarthy, R. A., & Warrington, E. K. (1988). Evidence for modality-specific meaning systems in the brain. *Nature, 334*, 428–430.

Patterson, K., & Hodges, J. R. (1992). Deterioration of word meaning: Implications for reading. *Neuropsychologia, 30*, 1025–1040.

Rapp, B. C., Hillis, A. E., & Caramazza, A. (1993). The role of representations in cognitive theory: More on multiple semantics and the agnosias. *Cognitive Neuropsychology, 10*, 235–249.

Riddoch, M. J., Humphreys, G. W., Coltheart, M., & Funnell, E. (1988). Semantic systems or system? Neuropsychological evidence re-examined. *Cognitive Neuropsychology, 5*, 3–25.

Saffran, E. M., & Schwartz, M. F. (1994). Of cabbages and things: Semantic memory from a neuropsychological perspective—a tutorial review. *Attention and Performance, 25*, 507–536.

Sartori, G., & Job, R. (1988). The oyster with four legs: a neuropsychological study on the interaction of visual and semantic information. *Cognitive Neuropsychology, 5*, 105–132.

Shallice, T. (1988). *From neuropsychology to mental structure.* Cambridge, UK: Cambridge University Press.

Shallice, T. (1993). Multiple semantics: Whose confusions? *Cognitive Neuropsychology, 10*, 251–261.

Warrington, E. K. (1975). The selective impairment of semantic memory. *Quarterly Journal of Experimental Psychology, 27*, 635–657.

Warrington, E. K., & Cipolotti, L. (1996). Word comprehension. The distinction between refractory and storage impairments. *Brain, 119*, 611–625.

Warrington, E. K., & McCarthy, R. (1983). Category specific access dysphasia. *Brain, 106*, 859–878.

Warrington, E. K., & McCarthy, R. A. (1987). Categories of knowledge. Further fractionations and an attempted integration. *Brain, 110*, 1273–1296.

Warrington, E. K., & McCarthy, R. A. (1994). Multiple meaning systems in the brain: A case for visual semantics. *Neuropsychologia, 32*, 1465–1473.

Warrington, E. K., & Shallice, T. (1984). Category specific semantic impairments. *Brain, 107*, 829–854.

Warrington, E. K., & Taylor, A. M. (1978). Two categorical stages of object recognition. *Perception, 7*, 695–705.

Warrington, E. K. (1981). Concrete word dyslexia. *British Journal of Psychology, 72*, 175–196.

APPENDIX A

Experiment 1: Stimuli

Semantic triplets

mug	paw	louse	red	fan	bread	tart	moon
plate	tail	frog	blue	plug	rice	cake	star
spoon	fin	snake	brown	hook	pear	bun	sun
ice	clown	plane	clog	ear	mouse	boat	lake
rain	cook	saw	coat	heart	crow	train	shore
snow	nun	vice	shoe	toe	slug	car	pier
can	screw	deer	plan	hair	house	log	
pail	nail	goat	book	crown	gate	bin	
jar	pin	bear	chart	head	room	grate	

Phonological triplets

bin	coat	hook	saw	snow	pail	plan	plate
fin	boat	cook	shore	crow	nail	can	gate
pin	goat	book	paw	toe	tail	fan	grate
tart	rice	louse	bread	frog	screw	pier	bear
chart	ice	house	red	clog	blue	ear	hair
heart	vice	mouse	head	log	shoe	deer	pear
crown	rain	lake	nun	star	room	plug	
brown	train	snake	sun	jar	moon	mug	
clown	plane	cake	bun	car	spoon	slug	

COGNITIVE NEUROPSYCHOLOGY, 2004, 21 (2/3/4) 317–330

SENTENCE COMPREHENSION IN SEMANTIC DEMENTIA: A LONGITUDINAL CASE STUDY

Elizabeth Rochon
University of Toronto, Canada

Gitit Kavé
Hebrew University, Jerusalem, Israel and Baycrest Centre for Geriatric Care, Toronto, Canada

Jennifer Cupit
University of Toronto, Canada

Regina Jokel
University of Toronto and Baycrest Centre for Geriatric Care, Toronto, Canada

Gordon Winocur
Baycrest Centre for Geriatric Care, Toronto, Canada

Sentence comprehension abilities were investigated in a patient with semantic dementia who was administered tests of semantic knowledge and sentence comprehension over a 5-year period. Results showed that despite a severe and continual degradation in semantic knowledge, syntactic comprehension abilities remained largely intact. Evidence was also found for a codependency between semantics and syntax in a task in which knowledge about conceptual number influenced subject–verb agreement in the patient and in control participants. Results are discussed in relation to the nature of the sentence comprehension impairment in semantic dementia and with reference to the modularity of the components of the language processing system.

Semantic dementia (SD) is a neurodegenerative disorder characterised by a breakdown of word meaning. Its features include impaired word comprehension and severe anomia in the presence of effortless, fluent speech (see Hodges, 2001). It has been established that while naming is impaired in SD, word repetition and phonology are remarkably spared (e.g., Hodges, Patterson, & Tyler, 1994; Hodges, Patterson, Oxbury, & Funnell, 1992; Patterson, Graham, & Hodges, 1994; Patterson & Hodges, 1992). In contrast to impaired single

word comprehension, understanding of even complex sentences appears to be intact (Breedin & Saffran, 1999; Hodges et al., 1994). Despite the loss of semantic knowledge (e.g., Bozeat, Lambon-Ralph, Patterson, Garrard, & Hodges, 2000; Graham, Patterson, & Hodges, 2000), individuals with SD are capable of carrying out most activities of daily living (Hodges, 2001).

Although it appears to be accepted that syntactic comprehension abilities are intact in patients with SD (e.g., Hodges et al., 1992, 1994), as

Correspondence should be addressed to Elizabeth Rochon, Graduate Department of Speech-Language Pathology, University of Toronto, Rehabilitation Sciences Building, 500 University Ave., Toronto, Canada M5G 1V7 (Email: elizabeth.rochon@utoronto.ca).

We thank AK for her continued willingness to participate in our research and Dr Morris Freedman, Baycrest Centre for Geriatric Care, for referring her to us. We also thank Dr Karalyn Patterson and an anonymous reviewer for helpful comments. This research was supported in part by a University of Toronto Connaught grant to Elizabeth Rochon.

http://www.tandf.co.uk/journals/pp02643294.html   DOI:10.1080/02643290342000357

Breedin and Saffran (1999) noted in their study, there exist very little data to support this claim. To date, sentence processing has been studied most extensively in Breedin and Saffran's SD patient, DM, who was followed for 2 years. His lexical semantic knowledge declined over time, yet many aspects of his sentence-processing abilities remained intact. For instance, he performed remarkably well when making grammaticality judgements, indicating that he was sensitive to a variety of syntactic constraints. He also demonstrated intact thematic role assignment in two sentence comprehension tasks, showing understanding of *who does what to whom* in the sentence. Assigning correct thematic roles (e.g., agent, theme, etc.) to sentence constituents is a necessary step in deriving a syntactic interpretation and arriving at the correct underlying meaning of a sentence (see Breedin & Saffran, 1999, for discussion). Breedin and Saffran demonstrated that DM could assign thematic roles reliably, even in syntactically complex sentences, and regardless of whether he had conceptual knowledge of the lexical items in the sentences. In a word monitoring task, DM also demonstrated syntactic facilitation but, unlike controls, benefited less from a semantic coherence condition on the same task. Last, DM's sentence production in a narrative retelling task was found to be within the normal range on a number of structural measures.

Hodges et al. (1994) tested their patient, PP, on two sentence comprehension tasks; a simplified version of the Token Test (De Renzi & Faglioni, 1978) and the Test for the Reception of Grammar (TROG; Bishop, 1983). PP responded correctly to 10/12 complex commands on the Token Test and achieved 68% correct on the TROG, in which her errors were largely lexical rather than grammatical. In addition, PP benefited from syntactic facilitation in a word monitoring task. The conclusion from the findings with both these patients was that syntactic processing abilities can remain almost unaffected, even in the presence of severely impaired semantic abilities. DM's performance led Breedin and Saffran (1999) to argue against a fully integrated model of sentence processing, in which structural and semantic information is interwoven,

with little representational difference between the operations (e.g., Bates & MacWhinney, 1989; McClelland, St John, & Taraban, 1989). Instead, they argued that DM's performance supported a more modular interpretation of the syntactic and semantic operations carried out during sentence processing and that models such as the one put forth by Frazier (1990) best accounted for their data. Based upon the findings of both their sentence processing study (Breedin & Saffran, 1999) and another study they carried out with DM (Breedin, Saffran, & Coslett, 1994) they also raised another possibility, namely, that there may exist a codependency between syntactic operations and related semantic abilities, in line with a view of sentence processing in which there may be some interaction between largely independent modules (MacDonald, Pearlmutter, & Seidenberg, 1994; Trueswell, Tanenhaus, & Garnsey, 1994).

We present the case of a patient whom we have followed longitudinally for 5 years. In light of the paucity of evidence regarding sentence processing in semantic dementia, we undertook a study focused in particular on sentence comprehension, sentence production, and narrative production. In this paper we present our investigations related to sentence comprehension. Inspired by Breedin and Saffran's (1999) study, we attempted to investigate the question of whether certain syntactic operations might be influenced by semantic factors.

CASE DESCRIPTION

AK was a 61-year-old right-handed woman when she first presented with difficulty retrieving names and understanding words in 1998. With follow-up testing she received a diagnosis of SD approximately 1 year later. AK is a native English speaker, has a university education, and worked in a professional capacity.

Magnetic resonance imaging (MRI) revealed left anterior temporal atrophy in 1998. AK also participated in a research project in which high-resolution structural MRI data were acquired (Kovacevic, Lobaugh, Bronskill, Levine, Feinstein,

& Black, 2002).[1] AK's regional atrophy was compared to the same brain regions derived from a set of eight age-matched healthy controls (Dade et al., 2003). In April 2001, quantitative analysis of regional atrophy of AK's MRI indicated the greatest atrophy over bitemporal regions, with greater atrophy in the left than in the right hemisphere; the greatest atrophy was over the left anterior temporal lobe. Atrophy was also noted in left ventral frontal regions, though to a lesser degree than in temporal regions. Dorsolateral frontal and posterior volumes were within the normal range, relative to the age-matched control subjects. A second high-resolution structural MRI was acquired in August 2002. Temporal lobe atrophy remained the most prominent feature; further bilateral atrophic changes were noted, with left greater than right, and anterior greater than posterior. Bilateral frontal atrophy was now evident, with left greater than right, and ventral greater than lateral. The

parietal and occipital lobes remained less affected, though no longer within the normal range.

We have followed AK annually since 1998, though she was not tested in our research in 1999. After that, AK was usually seen every 12 to 15 months. Due to a lengthy trip undertaken by AK and her husband, the time between the fourth and fifth years of testing was 19 months.

Semantic knowledge

Table 1 shows AK's performance on a number of tests over a 5-year time period. As can be seen in the table, her score on the Mini-Mental State Exam (MMSE; Folstein, Folstein, & McHugh, 1975) remained within normal limits until 2002, when there was a precipitous drop. Her anomia, as measured by the Boston Naming Test (BNT; Kaplan, Goodglass, & Weintraub, 1983), was severe in 1998 and continued to deteriorate, until

Table 1. *AK's performance on repeated administrations of several cognitive and language tests*

Test	1998	2000	2001	2002
MMSE[a] (n = 30)	29	28	28	10
BNT[b] (n = 60)	16	5	4	1
PPVT[c] (n = 175)	163	135	22	19[d]
PPT[e] 3 pictures (n = 52)	–	37	39	29
PALPA[f] Visual lexical Decision (n = 60)	59	55	51	49
Oral reading Regular words (n = 36)	36	36	36	32
Irregular words (n = 36)	35	30	28	8

Dash indicates that the test was not administered in that year.

[a] MMSE = Mini-Mental State Examination (Folstein, Folstein, & McHugh, 1975).

[b] BNT = Boston Naming Test (Kaplan, Goodglass, & Weintraub, 1983).

[c] PPVT = Peabody Picture Vocabulary Test (Dunn & Dunn, 1981).

[d] PPVT-III (Dunn & Dunn, 1997) was used in this year, (n = 204).

[e] PPTT = Pyramids and Palm Trees Test—3 pictures (Howard & Patterson, 1992).

[f] PALPA = Psycholinguistic Assessments of Language Processing in Aphasia (Kay, Lesser, & Coltheart, 1992).

[1] We thank Dr Brian Levine, Rotman Research Institute, Baycrest Centre for Geriatric Care, for providing us with these data.

she could name only one item ("house") in 2002. AK's word comprehension declined considerably over time, with performance ranging from the 66th percentile in 1998, to less than the first percentile in the last 2 years of testing (Peabody Picture Vocabulary Test; Dunn & Dunn, 1981). Her loss of nonverbal semantic knowledge is also seen on the Pyramids and Palm Trees test (PPT; Howard & Patterson, 1992). Visual lexical decisions and oral reading of regular words show that despite gradual deterioration, access to and decoding of orthographic information remained relatively intact. Over time, the difference between reading of regular and irregular words showed the pattern of surface dyslexia expected in patients with SD (Graham et al., 2000; Noble, Glosser, & Grossman, 2000; Patterson & Hodges, 1992). In light of a clear pattern of severe and progressive deterioration in semantic knowledge, we undertook an investigation of AK's sentence processing abilities.

Sentence processing

PCB grammaticality judgements (Saffran, Schwartz, Linebarger, Martin, & Bochetto, 1988). AK was administered the grammaticality judgements subtest from the Philadelphia Comprehension Battery (PCB; Saffran et al., 1988). The test includes 60 sentences: Half are grammatically well formed and half contain grammatical violations. The test includes several classes of rule violation such as subject–auxiliary inversion (e.g., *Are the*

boys fix the radio?) and empty elements (e.g., *That's who thought could win*). Sentences are presented auditorily and the participant must indicate with a "yes" or a "no" whether the sentence is "good" or "bad" English. A practice set precedes the test stimuli. Results are shown in Table 2. AK's performance was 97% when she was first tested in 1998, and remained stable for the next 2 years at 92%. Her performance remained close to that of normal controls over the 3 years in which she was tested. In the last year of testing, 2002, AK was unable to understand the instructions for the test despite a number of attempts at explanation by the examiner. For example, when asked to indicate whether a sentence was "good English" or "bad English," she asked: "English is where? London?"

Test for the Reception of Grammar (TROG; Bishop, 1983). AK was also administered the TROG, a sentence–picture matching task that contains 20 blocks of four items each, testing lexical knowledge as well as a variety of morphosyntactic and syntactic constructions. As can be seen in Table 2, until 2002, AK's performance was well within the range reported by Croot, Hodges, and Patterson (1999) for normal controls.

Despite strong evidence that AK was very impaired on tasks requiring semantic knowledge, it appeared that she retained the ability to comprehend sentences, at least as measured by the PCB grammaticality judgement task and the TROG. However, although AK performed very well on the grammaticality judgements test, indicating that

Table 2. *Performance of AK and control participants on administrations of sentence processing tests*

Test	AK				Control participants
	1998	2000	2001	2002	
PCB[a] grammaticality judgements (n = 60)	58	55	55	–	58.2[b]
TROG[c] (n = 20)	20	18	19	2	17–20[d]

Dash indicates that the test was not administered in that year.

[a] PCB = Philadelphia Comprehension Battery (Saffran, Schwartz, Linebarger, Martin, & Bochetto, 1988).

[b] Data from Breedin and Saffran (1999).

[c] TROG = Test for the Reception of Grammar (Bishop, 1983).

[d] Range of scores for controls, reported in Croot, Hodges, and Patterson (1999).

she was sensitive to the syntactic constraints of sentences, this did not necessarily guarantee that she would perform within the normal range on other syntactic measures. For instance, many aphasic patients retain the ability to perform grammaticality judgements accurately while demonstrating an impairment in thematic role assignment in sentence interpretation (e.g., Schwartz, Linebarger, Saffran, & Pate, 1987). While AK demonstrated sentence comprehension abilities that were comparable to normals on the TROG, this test was not designed to test thematic role assignment per se. In addition, it was difficult to determine whether the errors she did make on this test were syntactic or lexical-semantic in nature. As with Breedin and Saffran's (1999) DM, we were interested in determining whether AK had access to syntactic knowledge that would allow her to assign thematic roles to sentences. We were also interested in whether her sensitivity to syntactic constraints was affected by her semantic impairment. We therefore undertook a more extensive examination of AK's sentence processing abilities.

THEMATIC ROLE ASSIGNMENT

To examine AK's sentence comprehension abilities in more detail, we administered a sentence picture matching test taken from Rochon, Waters, and Caplan (1994), which was designed to test participants' abilities to (a) assign thematic roles to the constituents of sentences, and (b) understand sentences with differing numbers of propositions. In this test, syntactic processing is examined by manipulating whether thematic role order in the stimulus sentences is canonical or noncanonical. For instance, an active sentence like *The pig chases the lion* has canonical thematic role assignment because the first noun, which is the subject of the sentence, is also the agent of the action in the sentence. However, a passive sentence, such as *The lion was chased by the pig*, has noncanonical thematic role assignment because the first noun is the theme or the recipient of the action and the last noun is the agent. This test also includes sentences that differ in number of propositions. In previous

work with patients with Alzheimer's disease (e.g., Rochon et al., 1994; Waters, Caplan, & Rochon, 1995; Waters, Rochon, & Caplan, 1998), we examined syntactic processing by comparing participants' performance on five pairs of sentences that differ in terms of whether thematic roles are assigned canonically but are matched as closely as possible for number of words, propositions, verbs, and thematic roles (i.e., active vs. truncated passive; active conjoined theme vs. passive; active conjoined theme vs. cleft object; object subject vs. subject object; conjoined vs. subject object sentences). We also examined the number of proposition effect in sentence comprehension by looking at performance on three sentence pairs that differ in terms of number of propositions but are matched for length and canonicity of thematic roles (i.e., active conjoined theme vs. object subject; active conjoined theme vs. conjoined; cleft object vs. subject object sentences).

Method

Participants
AK was 61 years old when first tested on this task. Eleven control subjects were also tested. The mean age of control subjects was 70.7 years ($SD = 6.1$), and their mean number of years of education was 13.8 years ($SD = 2.9$). All controls spoke English as their primary language.

Stimuli and procedure
Comprehension was tested on nine sentence types, chosen to represent different levels of syntactic complexity. A limited set of lexical items (six animals and seven verbs) was used in creating the stimuli. The stimulus sentences were all semantically reversible (i.e., either actor could accomplish or be affected by the action of the verb). Pictures of the target sentences were each matched with a picture depicting a syntactic foil sentence (i.e., the sentence *The cow kicked the horse* was depicted with a correct picture and a picture depicting a horse kicking a cow). Testing on the sentence–picture matching test began with a brief pretest to establish that participants could identify the animals and actions used

in the test. Following the pretest, the sentence–picture matching test was administered. On each trial, the examiner read the target sentence with the two drawings in full view, and the participant was required to choose the drawing that matched the sentence. In 2001 and 2002, cues for AK were incorporated into the procedure, as will be explained in the results, below. Performance was tested on 20 sentences of each of nine types, administered in two equivalent versions of 90 sentences each. Responses were scored for accuracy.

Results

As can be seen in Table 3, on this task AK scored well within the 95% confidence interval for control subjects in the first 2 years of testing. In 2001, her performance dropped to 83%. Several features of her performance were notable and led us to allow her to use a set of cues that she spontaneously developed for the second version of the test. First, inspection of her errors on the test indicated that they were evenly spread across all sentence types. No effects of syntactic complexity emerged such as have been found with aphasic patients (e.g., Caplan & Waters, 1996), and no effects of number of propositions emerged such as have been found with patients with Alzheimer's disease (Rochon et al., 1994; Waters et al., 1995, 1998). Second, AK was exceedingly slow to complete the test. It took her 51 minutes to respond to 90 sentences. In our experience, it usually takes participants approxi-

mately half that time. Her slowness appeared to be due to her uncertainty regarding the meaning of the actors in the sentences (despite having passed the pretest, in which she accurately identified all the animals and actions). For instance, she often asked the examiner to tell her which animal was which, and she began to write herself notes to help herself identify the animals. The examiner did not identify the animals for her, and she was asked to complete the task without referring to her notes. At the end of the task she said: "If you knew the words you could do it so fast."

In light of her difficulties on the first version of the sentence–picture matching task, we asked AK to complete the cue sheet she had begun for herself, and she used this sheet in the administration of the second set of 90 sentences. Six other experimental tasks were administered between the administration of the two versions of the sentence–picture matching task. Figure 1 shows AK's cue sheet. As can be seen, she used differences in colour and size, as well as some physical features (e.g., udder for cow and hooves—misspelled as hoowes—for pig), to help her disambiguate the animals. "Chased" is written at the bottom because she said she was sometimes unsure about its meaning. As shown in Table 3, using this method she achieved 98% correct (neither of her two errors contained the verb chased). In addition, despite having to check her cue sheet for virtually every sentence, she completed the task in 26 minutes; half the time it had taken her originally.

Table 3. *Percentage correct sentence–picture matching scores for AK and control participants*

Test	AK				Control participants
	1998	*2000*	*2001*	*2002*	
Sentence–picture matching[a]					
Without cues	97	95	83	–	95
CI lower limit					92.2
CI upper limit					98.5
With cues	–	–	98	63[b]	–

Dash indicates that the test was not administered in that manner.

CI = 95% confidence interval.

[a] Sentence-picture matching (Rochon, Waters, & Caplan, 1994).

[b] Based on four sentence types only; see text.

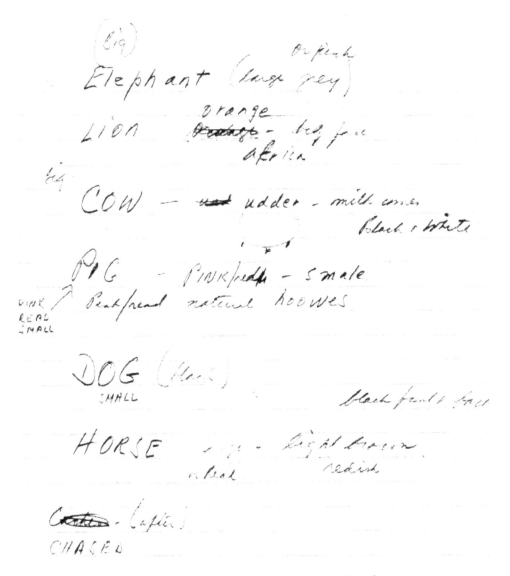

Figure 1. *AK's cue sheet for disambiguating the nouns used in the sentence–picture matching task.*

At the last testing session, AK was unable to complete the sentence–picture matching task on her own. Although the cues she had previously used were offered to her, these did not help, as she did not appear to know colours or other lexical items such as "udder." Given how overwhelming the task appeared to be for AK, the examiner wrote the names of the six animals on small cards, and it was decided to present only the sentences that had

two actors: these were active, passive, truncated passive, and cleft object sentences. For each sentence, the examiner placed labels above the animals and AK read the labels while pointing to the animals, then the examiner provided the sentence in the usual way. As seen in Table 3, when carried out in this way, AK scored 63% correct. This result is above chance (Binomial test, $p < .04$), though it does not fall within the 95% confidence interval for control participants on the full version of this test (see Table 3). It should also be noted that AK did appear to have more difficulty with some verbs than others (e.g., chasing and pushing vs. kicking and following) at this time. While we cannot make any strong conclusions, based on the small number of data points and because verb comprehension problems may have contributed to AK's performance, it is interesting to note that the two sentence types on which she made the most errors were both passive. Of her 15 errors only 1 was on an active sentence and 2 were on cleft object sentences (nouns and verbs are evenly distributed across sentence types in this task). AK retained the ability to assign thematic roles on both a simple sentence type (actives) and a complex sentence type (cleft objects), though she had difficulty doing so in two other complex constructions (passives and truncated passives).

In summary, like Breedin and Saffran (1999), we have presented evidence that a person with SD can retain the ability to correctly assign thematic roles for syntactic interpretation, even in the face of a devastating loss of semantic knowledge. In our next experiment, we wished to investigate the extent to which semantic knowledge might influence some aspects of grammatical encoding.

EFFECTS OF CONCEPTUAL NUMBER IN GRAMMATICALITY JUDGEMENTS

Another way to look at the relationship between semantics and syntax is by examining whether subject–verb agreement processing is purely syntactic or whether it is affected by conceptual knowledge. Several studies have focused on errors in agreement of number between the sentential subject and the verb (e.g., Bock & Miller, 1991; Eberhard, 1997, 1999; Vigliocco, Butterworth, & Garrett, 1996, among others). In these studies, participants were presented with a sentential subject and were asked to complete the sentence. The subject noun (i.e., the "head" noun) was always separated from the verb by another noun (i.e., the "local" noun) that was either matched or

mismatched in number with the first noun (i.e., given a singular head noun, the local noun was either singular or plural). The mismatch led to errors in subject–verb number agreement, which were found to be more common when the subject head noun was grammatically singular but conceptually plural (GS/CP: "the label on the bottles") than when the subject head noun was both grammatically and conceptually singular (GCS: "the blanket on the babies"). Notice that the head noun in a phrase such as "the label on the bottles" necessarily refers to more than one label, whereas this is not the case in a phrase such as "the blanket on the babies" that may refer to one blanket over several babies.

According to Vigliocco and Franck (1999), such findings indicate that conceptual features, such as number, influence grammatical subject–verb agreement processes. Moreover, Bock, Nicol, and Cutting (1999) found that collective nouns, such as "the jury for the trials," led to more agreement errors than noncollective nouns, such as "the judge for the trials," even though these errors are found more commonly with pronoun agreement than with verb agreement. The conceptual plurality inherent in collective nouns appears to be similar in its influence on agreement processes to the plurality inferred from distributive nouns such as "the label on the bottles." However, it must be noted that the effects of conceptual number on processing of subject–verb agreement have not been universally obtained, especially in comprehension tasks (e.g., Nicol, Forster, & Veres, 1997; Pearlmutter, Garnsey, & Bock, 1999).

In light of these mixed results, and the relative scarcity of research on the interface between conceptual and grammatical knowledge affecting comprehension processes, we chose to develop a grammaticality judgement paradigm to investigate this question further in AK and in normal control participants.

Method

Participants

AK was 63 years old when first tested on this task. In addition to AK, a different group of 10 control participants was also administered the test described below. The mean age of the control group was 70.4 (*SD* = 6.5) years, and the mean number of years of education was 16.5 (*SD* = 3.8).

Stimuli and procedure

The experiment included two conditions. In the first condition sentences were grammatically singular but conceptually plural (i.e., GS/CP sentences). These sentences had either collective or distributive head nouns. In the second condition sentences were grammatically and conceptually singular (i.e., GCS sentences). These sentences had either noncollective or nondistributive head nouns. All head nouns were singular and all local nouns were plural, as this combination has the largest effect on the production of subject–verb agreement errors (Eberhard, 1997). In both conditions, sentences included a verb in either a singular form (and therefore grammatical and congruent with the head noun) or a plural form (and therefore ungrammatical and incongruent with the head noun).

All nouns were easy to picture in order to facilitate their distributive reading (following Eberhard, 1999). Noun phrases used by investigators in other studies (Bock et al., 1999; Eberhard, 1999; Pearlmutter et al., 1999) were incorporated into our stimuli where possible. Table 4 shows examples of the stimuli. Each collective and distributive noun was matched to a noncollective and nondistributive noun respectively, such that they appeared with the same verb and thus the argument structure of the verb was held constant.

The verb was selected so that the resulting sentence would be plausible whether the head noun or the local noun was taken to be the sentence subject. Thus, errors could not be attributable to a mere lack of plausibility. All verbs appeared in the present tense.

Four experimental lists of stimuli were compiled and every verb appeared once in a list. Each list included 48 target sentences; 6 of each of the 8 possible combinations of congruity and type of noun. Each list also included 24 filler sentences whose head nouns were plural. Presentation of lists was counterbalanced across control participants, such that each participant saw one list that included all types of stimuli. AK was administered one list in 2000 and two lists in 2001. Participants were instructed to read the sentence out loud and say whether the sentence was "good" or "bad" English, without describing the reason for their judgement. Responses were scored for accuracy.

Results

The data from one of the control participants were removed from the analysis, as her scores were more than 2 *SD*s below the mean for the group. The average scores on each sentence type for the remaining nine participants are shown in Table 5. As expected, controls' performance was significantly better for sentences that were not influenced by conceptual number (i.e., GCS sentences) in each of the two comparisons that tested this hypothesis. Participants performed better on noncollective than collective sentences, $t(8) = 3.77$,

Table 4. *Examples of the stimuli in the conceptual number grammaticality judgement task*

	Grammatical	Ungrammatical
Grammatically singular/Conceptually plural sentences (GS/CP)		
Collective	The gang of boys fights.	*The gang of boys fight.
Distributive	The wheel on the toys squeaks.	*The wheel on the toys squeak.
Grammatically and conceptually singular sentences (GCS)		
Noncollective	The hunter of the rabbits hides.	*The hunter of the rabbits hide.
Nondistributive	The hat by the dresses shocks.	*The hat by the dresses shock.
Filler sentences	The lamps on the tables shatter.	*The racks for the ties crumples.

Table 5. *Proportion correct performance (SD in parentheses) in the conceptual number grammaticality judgement task for control participants*

Sentence type	Mean (SD)	CI Lower	CI Upper
Noncollective	.93 (.11)	.84	1.00
Collective	.72 (.21)	.56	.89
t_{diff}	3.77**		
Nondistributive	.94 (.08)	.88	1.00
Distributive	.84 (.18)	.70	.98
t_{diff}	2.23[a]		
Fillers	.99 (.02)	.97	1.00

CI = 95% confidence interval.
[a] This value is significant at $p < .056$.
** $p < .01$.

$p < .01$, and better on nondistributive than distributive sentences, though the latter difference was only marginally significant, $t(8) = 2.23$, $p < .056$. An additional analysis showed that the difference between the collective and distributive sentences was also significant, $t(8) = 2.31$, $p < .05$, with better performance seen on the distributive than on the collective sentences.

AK's scores on this task are shown in Table 6. AK's pattern of performance was similar to controls' in both years in which she was tested, although her accuracy was reduced compared to control participants. In fact, her ability to carry out this task might be questioned, given her poor performance on most of the experimental sentences. However, it is important to note that AK performed significantly above chance on the filler

sentences in both years of testing (Binomial test, $p < .001$, for both years), though outside the range of the 95% confidence interval for control participants (see Table 5).

As can be seen in Table 6, AK's overall performance on GS/CP sentences was poorer than her performance on GCS sentences. In 2000, this is seen in performance that is below chance on collective sentences ($p < .02$, Binomial test) compared to non-collective sentences, which were at chance, and performance that is marginally above chance on nondistributive ($p < .07$, Binomial test) compared to distributive sentences, which were at chance. The same pattern is seen in 2001 for the collective versus noncollective comparison, but not in the distributive versus nondistributive comparison.

AK's scores indicate that, like controls, she responded differently to the two types of sentences in the GS/CP condition (i.e., collective and distributive sentences). Her below-chance performance on the collective sentences in both years suggests that she was using a consistent yet incorrect strategy to arrive at her responses. Her above-chance performance on nondistributive sentences in 2000, albeit marginal, suggests that AK may have been processing these sentences, in contrast to all other experimental sentences, in a manner similar to controls. By 2001, AK was performing at chance when attempting to determine the grammaticality of all sentences (except fillers), adopting a strategy only when faced with collective nouns, which she detected as being different from the rest.

A similar differentiation between the sentence types was observed in an analysis of AK's errors, which indicated that she was more likely to make

Table 6. *Proportion correct performance for AK on the conceptual grammaticality judgement task*

	Sentence type				
	Noncollective	Collective	Nondistributive	Distributive	Fillers
2000	.58	.24*	.75[a]	.50	.96*
2001	.46	.29*	.54	.38	.90*

[a] This value is significantly above chance by the Binomial test, $p < .073$.
* Significantly below chance, Binomial test, $p < .05$.

false positive errors, accepting ungrammatical sentences as correct. Interestingly, in 2000, this tendency was seen neither for the filler sentences nor for either of the GCS sentences, where the number of false positive and false negative errors was equivalent, even though they contained more errors than the filler sentences. However, false positive errors were three times more prevalent in the GS/CP than in the GCS condition, compared to false negative errors, which remained the same. These differences may in part reflect the mismatch between nouns in sentences (as seen in the difference between AK's scores in filler sentences, in which the two nouns have the same number, and GCS sentences in which the two nouns have different number). That it is not due solely to this mismatch is seen by the fact that when conceptual number is added to the manipulation, as in collective sentences, AK's performance fell well below chance. This provides further support that conceptual number (in the GS/CP collective and distributive sentences) led AK to make the most errors. In 2001, her tendency to provide false positive errors increased across the board. Unfortunately, as for most of our tests, she was unable to complete this test in the last testing session in 2002.

DISCUSSION

We have presented data from a patient with SD whose syntactic abilities appeared to be remarkably preserved despite a significant loss of semantic knowledge. AK's severe impairment in conceptual knowledge was demonstrated on a number of tasks, over a period of 5 years. Despite this loss of word meaning and conceptual knowledge, and until the final year of testing, she performed almost flawlessly on a grammaticality judgement task (i.e., PCB), and on a sentence comprehension task designed to examine her ability to assign thematic roles. In the last years of testing, she would have appeared much more impaired in her syntactic processing abilities than she actually was, had she not used cues to disambiguate the lexical items in the sentences. Our findings replicate those

reported by Breedin and Saffran (1999) and add to the understanding of the sentence processing abilities of persons with SD. Like DM's performance (Breedin & Saffran, 1999), AK's performance also supports the view that components of the language processing module are functionally distinct, at least to a certain degree. Our results add to a body of literature in which other patients with semantic deficits but intact syntactic abilities have provided evidence for arguments in favour of the modularity of language (e.g., Hodges et al., 1994; Schwartz, Marin, & Saffran, 1979; Whitaker, 1976).

Although we have argued that AK presented with intact syntactic processing in the face of impaired semantic abilities, our evidence also suggests that a codependency between syntax and semantics may exist, at least for some operations (Breedin & Saffran, 1999). For instance, although AK's ability to derive correct thematic roles from sentence constituents implies preserved syntactic processing, the operations that result in correct syntactic interpretations of these sentences also require a certain amount of semantic knowledge, such as information about verb arguments. Until the last testing session, AK appeared to have retained this knowledge, in the absence of core semantic knowledge about words.

More to the point, our grammaticality judgement task, in which participants' performance was influenced by conceptual number, constitutes evidence for a co-dependency between syntax and semantics. While these effects have been found previously in sentence production in normal subjects (e.g., Bock et al., 1999; Eberhard, 1997, 1999), we have demonstrated them here in a comprehension task. First, sensitivity to conceptual number was significant in the control participants. Second, AK performed poorly in the conceptual number condition, relative both to controls and to her own performance on sentences in which conceptual number had no effect. This suggests that, like controls, AK was sensitive to incongruity between semantic and syntactic information as found in the GS/CP sentences. That AK's performance was below chance on the collective sentences suggests that she was making her grammaticality judgements in a different way from controls. AK could have computed agreement on the basis of the local noun but such a strategy would have affected her performance on the other sentence types as well. Alternatively, her knowledge of the plurality inherent in the collective nouns could have overridden her syntactic computation. Such an interpretation may seem unlikely in light of her severe semantic deficit, yet it is possible that the knowledge of plurality remains preserved despite a loss of other conceptual aspects of word meaning. Thus, she could be unable to tell the difference between "group" and "crowd," while knowing that both words refer to "many."

While we have emphasised the difference in performance between GS/CP and GCS sentences, it is also important to highlight the differences that emerged between collective and distributive sentences within the GS/CP condition. Control participants' performance was poorer on collective than on distributive sentences, and AK's performance mirrored controls'. This may reflect an inherent difference underlying the conceptual plurality in each sentence type. In collective sentences plurality is implied in the meaning of the collective noun (e.g., "the jury"); in distributive sentences plurality relies on the syntactic relationship between the two nouns (e.g., "the label on the bottles"). It is particularly interesting that AK appeared to have greatest difficulty with the sentence type that may have been most reliant on her knowledge about the underlying meaning of words; this is consistent with her pervasive semantic impairment.

It must be noted that overall, AK performed more poorly on the GCS sentences on this task than she did on the PCB grammaticality judgement task. AK was highly accurate in the filler sentences on the conceptual number grammaticality judgement task, suggesting that she was able to perform the task. Nor do we think that syntactic complexity might have been exerting an effect, as the PCB grammaticality judgement task contains more complex sentences such as passives. However, we cannot rule out the possibility that there may have been factors related to aspects of the stimuli, such as verb comprehension difficulties, or the particular sentence types used in the conceptual

number task, that were especially difficult for AK. The fact that she performed at chance on both types of GCS sentences in 2001, as well as the fact that she needed cues to complete the sentence picture matching task in that testing session, are compatible with the likelihood that increasing cerebral atrophy may have been affecting her cognitive abilities more and more. Indeed, by the last testing session in 2002, not only could she not perform any of the grammaticality judgement tasks, but her performance on the sentence–picture matching task suggested that she may have developed difficulties with thematic role assignment, at least in complex sentence structures. Since AK's atrophy extended into inferior frontal areas (among others) by this time, our findings are consistent with imaging studies that have localised syntactic processing to the left inferior frontal cortex (e.g., Caplan, Alpert, & Waters, 1998; Friederici, Opitz, & von Cramon, 2000).

Another question raised by our findings relates to the nature and extent of verb comprehension problems in SD, which have been previously documented by other investigators (e.g., Rhee, Antiquena, & Grossman, 2001). Although there were indications that AK had difficulty understanding some verbs, her verb deficit did not appear to be as marked as her difficulty with nouns, and it appeared relatively late in the progression of her disease. It is quite possible that, similar to the pattern found in production in SD patients, this apparent discrepancy between noun and verb comprehension may be explained by the fact that verbs tend to be of a higher frequency than nouns (Bird, Lambon-Ralph, Patterson, & Hodges, 2000). It is also possible that verb comprehension, including the processes involved in thematic role assignment or in agreement, may rely more heavily on syntactic parsing.

We have presented evidence for the preservation of syntactic abilities concomitant with impaired semantic abilities on the one hand, together with evidence for the codependency of syntax and semantics for some operations. While these findings await corroboration with other sentence comprehension measures, and while our evidence in this study comes solely from offline measures, our results are in keeping with Breedin and Saffran's (1999) suggestion that a codependency between syntax and semantics may exist for certain operations, as well as with theoretical models of sentence processing that predict such a relationship (e.g., MacDonald, 1997; MacDonald et al., 1994). For instance, it may be that the effect of brain damage in AK resulted in the equivalent of reduced experience in MacDonald and Christiansen's (2002) terms, leading in turn to greater difficulty in sentential contexts that might be construed as being less regular (i.e., our GS/CP sentences). These possibilities, while intriguing, remain highly speculative and await further investigation. We are currently examining the degree to which AK's sentence production abilities are affected by similar processes.

REFERENCES

Bates, E., & MacWhinney, B. (1989). Functionalism and the competition model. In B. MacWhinney & E. Bates (Eds.), *The crosslinguistic study of sentence processing* (pp. 3–73). Cambridge: Cambridge University Press.

Bird, H., Lambon-Ralph, M. A., Patterson, K., & Hodges, J. R. (2000). The rise and fall of frequency and imageability: Noun and verb production in semantic dementia. *Brain and Language, 73*, 17–49.

Bishop, D. V. M. (1983). *Test for the Reception of Grammar*. Abingdon, UK: Thomas Leach Ltd.

Bock, K., & Miller, C. A. (1991). Broken agreement. *Cognitive Psychology, 23*, 45–93.

Bock, K., Nicol, J. L., & Cutting, J. C. (1999). The ties that bind: Creating number agreement in speech. *Journal of Memory and Language, 40*, 330–346.

Bozeat, S., Lambon-Ralph, M. A., Patterson, K., Garrard, P., & Hodges, J. R. (2000). Non-verbal semantic impairments in semantic dementia. *Neuropsychologia, 38*, 1207–1215.

Breedin, S. D., & Saffran, E. M. (1999). Sentence processing in the face of semantic loss: A case study. *Journal of Experimental Psychology: General, 128*, 547–562.

Breedin, S. D., Saffran, E. M., & Coslett, H. B. (1994). Reversal of the concreteness effect in a patient with

semantic dementia. *Cognitive Neuropsychology, 11*, 617–660.

Caplan, D., Alpert, N., & Waters, G. (1998). Effects of syntactic structure and propositional number on patterns of regional cerebral bloodflow. *Journal of Cognitive Neuroscience, 10*, 541–552.

Caplan, D., & Waters, G. S. (1996). Syntactic processing in sentence comprehension under dual task conditions in aphasic patients. *Language and Cognitive Processes, 11*, 525–551.

Croot, K., Hodges, J. R., & Patterson, K. (1999). Evidence for impaired sentence comprehension in early Alzheimer's disease. *Journal of the International Neuropsychological Society, 5*, 393–404.

Dade, L., Kovacevic, N., Gao, F., Roy, P., Rockel, C., O'Toole, C. M., et al. (2003). *Semi-automatic brain region extraction (SABRE): A method of parcellating brain regions from structural magnetic resonance images*. Manuscript submitted for publication.

De Renzi, E., & Faglioni, P. (1978). Normative data and screening power of a shortened version of the Token Test. *Cortex, 14*, 41–49.

Dunn, L. M., & Dunn, L. M. (1981). *Peabody Picture Vocabulary Test–Revised*. Circle Pines, MN: American Guidance Service.

Dunn, L. M., & Dunn, L. M. (1997). *Peabody Picture Vocabulary Test–Third Edition*. Circle Pines, MN: American Guidance Service.

Eberhard, K. M. (1997). The marked effect of number on subject–verb agreement. *Journal of Memory and Language, 36*, 147–164.

Eberhard, K. M. (1999). The accessibility of conceptual number to the processes of subject-verb agreement in English. *Journal of Memory and Language, 41*, 560–578.

Folstein, M. F., Folstein, S. E., & McHugh, P. R. (1975). Mini-Mental State: A practical method for grading the state of patients for the clinician. *Journal of Psychiatric Research, 12*, 189–198.

Frazier, L. (1990). Exploring the architecture of the language-processing system. In G. T. M. Altmann (Ed.), *Cognitive models of speech processing: Psycholinguistic and computational perspectives* (pp. 407–433). Cambridge, MA: MIT Press.

Friederici, A. D., Opitz, B., & von Cramon, D. Y. (2000). Segregating semantic and syntactic aspects of processing in the human brain: An fMRI investigation of different word types. *Cerebral Cortex, 10*, 698–705.

Graham, N. L., Patterson, K., & Hodges, J. R. (2000). The impact of semantic memory impairment on spelling: Evidence from semantic dementia. *Neuropsychologia, 38*, 143–163.

Hodges, J. R. (2001). Fronto-temporal dementia (Pick's disease): Clinical features and assessment. *Neurology, 56*, S6–10.

Hodges, J. R., Patterson, K., Oxbury, S., & Funnell, E. (1992). Semantic dementia: Progressive fluent aphasia with temporal lobe atrophy. *Brain, 115*, 1783–1806.

Hodges, J. R., Patterson, K., & Tyler, L. K. (1994). Loss of semantic memory: Implications for the modularity of mind. *Cognitive Neuropsychology, 11*, 505–542.

Howard, D., & Patterson, K. (1992). *The Pyramids and Palm Trees Test.* Bury St Edmunds, UK: Thames Valley Test Company.

Kaplan, E., Goodglass, H., & Weintraub, S. (1983). *Boston Naming Test.* Philadelphia, PA: Lea & Febiger.

Kay, J., Lesser, R., & Coltheart, M. (1992). *Psycholinguistic Assessments of Language Processing in Aphasia.* Hove, UK: Lawrence Erlbaum Associates Ltd.

Kovacevic, N., Lobaugh, N. J., Bronskill, M. J., Levine, B., Feinstein, A., & Black, S. E., (2002). A robust method for extraction and automatic segmentation of brain images. *Neuroimage, 17*, 1087–1100.

MacDonald, M.C. (1997). Lexical representations and sentence processing: An introduction. *Language and Cognitive Processes, 12*, 121–136.

MacDonald, M. C., & Christiansen, M. H. (2002). Reassessing working memory: Comment on Just and Carpenter (1992) and Waters and Caplan (1996). *Psychological Review, 109*, 35–54.

MacDonald, M. C., Pearlmutter, N. J., & Seidenberg, M. S. (1994). The lexical nature of syntactic ambiguity resolution. *Psychological Review, 101*, 676–703.

McClelland, J. L., St John, M., & Taraban, R. (1989). Sentence comprehension: A parallel distributed processing approach. *Language and Cognitive Processes, 4*, SI287–SI335.

Nicol, J. L., Forster, K. I., & Veres, C. (1997). Subject–verb agreement processes in comprehension. *Journal of Memory and Language, 36*, 569–587.

Noble, K., Glosser, G., & Grossman, M. (2000). Oral reading in dementia. *Brain and Language, 74*, 48–69.

Patterson, K., Graham, K. S., & Hodges, J. R. (1994). The impact of semantic memory loss on phonological representations. *Journal of Cognitive Neuroscience, 6*, 57–69.

Patterson, K., & Hodges, J. R. (1992). Deterioration of word meaning: Implications for reading. *Neuropsychologia, 30*, 1025–1040.

Pearlmutter, N. J., Garnsey, S. M., & Bock, K. (1999). Agreement processes in sentence comprehension. *Journal of Memory and Language, 41*, 427–456.

Rhee, J., Antiquena, P., & Grossman, M. (2001). Verb comprehension in frontotemporal degeneration: The role of grammatical, semantic and executive components. *Neurocase. Special Issue: Frontotemporal dementia: Part II, 7*, 173–184.

Rochon, E., Waters, G. S., & Caplan, D. (1994). Sentence comprehension in patients with Alzheimer's disease. *Brain and Language, 46*, 329–349.

Saffran, E. M., Schwartz, M. F., Linebarger, M., Martin, N., & Bochetto, P. (1988). *Philadelphia Comprehension Battery.* Unpublished test.

Schwartz, M. F., Linebarger, M. C., Saffran, E. M., & Pate, D. S. (1987). Syntactic transparency and sentence interpretation in aphasia. *Language and Cognitive Processes, 2*, 85–113.

Schwartz, M. F., Marin, O. S. M., & Saffran, E. M. (1979). Dissociations of language function in dementia: A case study. *Brain and Language, 7*, 277–306.

Trueswell, J. C., Tanenhaus, M. K., & Garnsey, S. M. (1994). Semantic influences on parsing: Use of thematic role information in syntactic ambiguity resolution. *Journal of Memory and Language, 33*, 285–318.

Vigliocco, G., Butterworth, B., & Garrett, M. F. (1996). Subject–verb agreement in Spanish and English: Differences in the role of conceptual constraints. *Cognition, 61*, 261–298.

Vigliocco, G., & Franck, J. (1999). When sex and syntax go hand in hand: Gender agreement in language production. *Journal of Memory and Language, 40*, 455–478.

Waters, G. S., Caplan, D., & Rochon, E. (1995). Processing capacity and sentence comprehension in patients with Alzheimer's disease. *Cognitive Neuropsychology, 12*, 1–30.

Waters, G. S., Rochon, E., & Caplan, D. (1998). Task demands and sentence comprehension in patients with dementia of the Alzheimer's type. *Brain and Language, 62*, 361–397.

Whitaker, H. (1976). A case of the isolation of the language function. In H. Whitaker & H. A. Whitaker (Eds.), *Studies in neurolinguistics* (Vol. 2, pp. 1–58). New York: Academic Press.

COGNITIVE NEUROPSYCHOLOGY, 2004, 21 (2/3/4) 331–352

NATURAL SELECTION: THE IMPACT OF SEMANTIC IMPAIRMENT ON LEXICAL AND OBJECT DECISION

Timothy T. Rogers
MRC Cognition & Brain Sciences Unit, Cambridge, UK

Matthew A. Lambon Ralph
University of Manchester, UK

John R. Hodges
MRC Cognition & Brain Sciences Unit and Addenbrooke's Hospital, Cambridge, UK

Karalyn Patterson
MRC Cognition & Brain Sciences Unit, Cambridge, UK

This study was designed to investigate the impact of semantic deficits on the recognition of words and objects as real/familiar. Two-alternative forced-choice tasks of lexical decision and object decision were each administered to a case series of patients with semantic dementia. In both tasks, the critical manipulation was whether the real word or object was more or less "natural" (i.e., typical of its domain) than the nonword or nonobject with which it was paired. For lexical decision, typicality of the words and nonwords was manipulated in terms of bigram and trigram frequencies of the letter strings. For object decision, high typicality in real and chimeric objects consisted in having only or mainly visual features that are standard for objects in that category. This manipulation of relative typicality of real and made-up stimuli exerted a dramatic influence on the patients' success in both lexical and object decision. The patients' strong tendency towards "natural selection" was further modulated by both the frequency/familiarity of the real words/objects and the degree of semantic degradation of the individual patients. This outcome is in line with the authors' model of semantic knowledge and the impact of its degradation on a wide range of cognitive behaviour.

INTRODUCTION

When normal adult humans encounter a familiar object or word, they can easily judge that it is known to them; we characterise this phenomenon by saying that they have recognised the stimulus. The mechanisms for such recognition are not, however, especially well understood, and one unresolved question is this: Can recognition be achieved on the basis of the familiarity of structural features alone, or does semantic information about the concept contribute crucially to normal, efficient recognition of it? Phrasing the question in this manner makes it immediately apparent why neuropsychological evidence is pertinent to this issue. If there are patients who have normal ability

Correspondence should be addressed to Dr T. T. Rogers or Dr K. Patterson, MRC Cognition & Brain Sciences Unit, 15 Chaucer Road, Cambridge CB2 2EF, UK (Email: tim.rogers@mrc-cbu.cam.ac.uk or karalyn.patterson@mrc-cbu.cam.ac.uk).

This article is lovingly and grievingly dedicated to the memory of our colleague Eleanor M. Saffran. KP had several discussions with Eleanor about the expected impact of semantic impairment on lexical decision, and had hoped to benefit from her theoretical insights and experimental wisdom in investigating this issue. This paper therefore seems a particularly apt contribution to the issue of CN in honour of Eleanor and her outstanding contributions to the field of cognitive neuropsychology.

to process the structural features of objects or words but lack a normal complement of knowledge about the concepts represented by such stimuli, their degree of success on tests of object or word recognition might provide telling evidence on the question.

Note that when we speak of recognition in this article, we shall always mean the term in the sense just conveyed—i.e., "it is an object or a word that I know"—rather than in the episodic, recognition-memory sense of "I recognise this word or object as one that I encountered in an earlier phase of this experiment, or on some other specific occasion in place and time." The kind of recognition in focus here is typically measured by tests of lexical decision (LD) for words and of object decision (OD) for concrete objects, and those are the tests employed in this study.

Prevailing opinion, if there is such a thing, on the question of whether recognition depends on knowledge beyond structure seems to be that it does not. That is, most language researchers would probably say that positive lexical decisions are the result of a match between the stimulus and a stored representation corresponding to a word node or lemma that, in the processing sequence, precedes access to any semantic information about the word. For example, "...when we know what the word is, we then have access to all the information about it, such as what it means" (Harley, 1995, pp. 31–32). Likewise, most researchers concerned with object recognition have argued that positive object decisions occur when the stimulus activates a stored structural description for the known object where, once again, the structural description necessarily precedes—and indeed is a gateway to—conceptual knowledge about the object (e.g., Riddoch & Humphreys, 1987). Some models of word and object processing, however, incorporate the assumption of automatic and functionally significant interaction between perceptual processing and conceptual knowledge, and predict that significant semantic impairment will necessarily disrupt recognition (see, for example, Plaut, 1997, and Seidenberg & McClelland, 1989, with respect to lexical decision). The proposal of the current paper is in line with this latter position. Our hypothesis

is that recognising an object or word is not the result of matching it to a structural description or a lemma, but is the result of the interactive perceptual and semantic processing of the stimulus item itself, when that item consists of properties that have been encountered together in past experience. A likely corollary of this position is that there is no need to assume the existence of item-specific representations like structural descriptions or lemmas that intervene between perceptual and semantic aspects of processing, and furthermore that there is no sharp demarcation between these aspects (Barsalou, 2003; Dixon, Bub, & Arguin, 1997; Gloor, 1997; Smith, 2000); but the experiments presented below are addressed to the more modest question of the role of semantic knowledge in object and word recognition, and the interpretation of the results will be largely confined to this question.

The full account of our thoughts on this issue will be developed after the results have been presented, but the basis for our predictions should be presaged at least briefly here. In our view (see, for example, McClelland & Rogers, 2003; Plaut, 1997; Plaut, McClelland, Seidenberg, & Patterson, 1996; Rogers, Lambon Ralph, Garrard, Bozeat, McClelland, Hodges, & Patterson, in press; Rogers & Plaut, 2002), knowledge about orthographic word form, the visual structure of objects, and the meanings of words and objects is encoded in the brain in a network of interacting distributed representations. The interactions among different kinds of representations are governed by weighted connections, whose strengths in turn are shaped by experience, so that each processing episode influences to some degree the complete system of knowledge encoded in the network. As a consequence, the connection weights that emerge after extensive experience are jointly determined by information specific to particular items and by information general to the domain. An important general property of such networks is that they are sensitive both to the frequency with which individual stimulus items are encountered in the learning environment, and to the regularities that occur across items. Information about frequently encountered items will be more robustly ingrained in the weights than information about less common items; but even for infrequent exemplars, the characteristics that they share with their neighbours will be more robustly represented than will their unique or individuating features.

For example, in the orthographic domain, typical or consistent spelling patterns will tend to be robust whilst atypical ones (letter combinations that occur in few words, like the *acht* in *yacht*) will be more fragile. Apart from typicality of spelling pattern, word frequency is the most important determinant of strength. As explained in detail in Plaut et al. (1996), frequency and consistency to some extent offset one another: A word can be strongly represented and efficiently processed even if it has atypical characteristics, so long as it is frequently encountered and thus overlearned. Likewise a word can be robust even if it is rarely encountered so long as it is consistent with most of its neighbours.

Because recognition in our account arises from an interaction of perceptual and conceptual processing, these two components also offset one another to some extent. Thus recognition of written words that are either orthographically unusual or of lower frequency, and especially of words that are both inconsistent and infrequent, will rely more on a semantic contribution (Plaut, 1997). We therefore predict that a deficit of conceptual knowledge will necessarily disrupt written-word lexical decision, but only for words with atypical orthographic structure, particularly when these are infrequent words, and increasingly so with greater semantic deterioration.

Similarly, in the visual domain, attributes that are shared across many instances of a conceptual category should be more robust to impairment than the idiosyncratic visual attributes that differentiate related items (Bozeat et al., 2003; Rogers et al., in press), as should the visual properties of very frequently encountered, familiar items. Our theoretical stance thus offers the same predictions about object decision, i.e., that it should be impaired in patients with SD but only for objects with atypical visual-object structure, particularly when these are less familiar objects, and increasingly so with greater semantic deterioration.

How does our proposal accommodate the published neuropsychological evidence that has been claimed to support the alternative position? This evidence consists of demonstrations that some patients with impaired semantic memory (or impaired access to semantic memory) can achieve scores within or at least close to the normal control range on tests of LD (e.g., Breedin, Saffran, & Coslett, 1994; Ward, Stott, & Parkin, 2000) or OD (e.g., Humphreys, Riddoch, & Quinlan, 1988; Lambon Ralph & Howard, 2000). Our account of these results in the domain of OD can be found in Rogers, Hodges, Lambon Ralph, and Patterson (2003); the line of argument in the domain of LD is precisely parallel but has not yet been published, and that is what we shall emphasise in the Introduction.

The first clue to our account derives from the fact that semantically impaired patients—more specifically, patients with semantic dementia (Hodges, Patterson, Oxbury, & Funnell, 1992; Snowden, Goulding, & Neary, 1989)—can apparently have almost any degree of success or failure in lexical decision. Published reports of accuracy in LD to written or spoken words range from essentially normal (Ward et al., 2000), to mildly impaired (Breedin et al., 1994; Lambon Ralph & Howard, 2000), to mildly but increasingly impaired with semantic deterioration (Tyler & Moss, 1998), to performance no better than chance (Moss, Tyler, Hodges, & Patterson, 1995). As usual, these various investigations have used a substantial variety of different stimulus materials and procedures and, moreover, are all single-case studies, making it difficult to draw any general conclusions.

The second and more important clue comes from the fact that two researchers studying LD in semantically impaired patients have been clever enough to manipulate the LD experimental conditions, and have also documented performance ranging from good to poor—within a single patient. Diesfeldt (1992), in studies of case BHJ with semantic dementia (SD), varied the characteristics of the nonword stimuli in a yes/no written-word LD task. When the nonwords were orthographically illegal, BHJ's success at discriminating between words and nonwords was essentially perfect (97% correct); when the non-words were orthographically legal, he was significantly less accurate (79% correct); and when the nonwords were carefully matched to the words on orthographic characteristics, his discrimination was only just above chance (64% correct). Bub, Cancelliere, and Kertesz (1985) studied case MP, in whom a severe and unusually focal head injury had damaged the left inferior temporal lobe, yielding a profound semantic impairment that resembled a nonprogressive version of SD (see also Behrmann & Bub, 1992; Bub, Black, Hampson, & Kertesz, 1988; and Patterson & Behrmann, 1997, for other studies of MP). Bub et al. (1985) varied the characteristics of both the word and nonword stimuli in a two-alternative, forced-choice, written-word LD task, and again documented a wide range of success in this single case, ranging from good (though not perfect: 85% correct) when orthographically regular words were paired with orthographically irregular nonwords (e.g., *block* vs. *macht*), to chance (41% correct) when regularity characterised the nonwords but not the words (e.g., *yacht* paired with *plock*).

The outcome of these two studies is exactly in line with our predictions, but an attempt at replication seemed valuable for a number of reasons. First, this phenomenon has only been demonstrated for two individual cases and with different materials/procedures; we had access to a larger group of semantically impaired patients (SD) in whom the prediction could be tested with the same set of stimulus materials and the same paradigm. Second, at least one of the two patients in whom the phenomenon has been established (MP; Bub et al., 1985) had severe semantic impairment. Her reasonable success in LD for pairs like *block* vs. *macht* obviates to some extent the concern that her poor scores in other conditions might simply reflect the fact that profound brain damage disrupts all cognitive performance; nevertheless, it

would be valuable to assess the impact on lexical decision of semantic deficits over a range of severities. Third, neither Bub et al. (1985) nor Diesfeldt (1992) included word frequency as a factor to be manipulated in their selection of stimulus materials, whereas our account treats frequency as a crucial component of the story. Fourth, and perhaps most important: Assuming that we would replicate the findings of Bub et al. and Diesfeldt, we wanted to set this phenomenon into a theoretical context that would emphasise its significance and its generality.

Lexical decision data for a cohort of SD patients constitute Experiment 1, and object decision data constitute Experiment 2. In both cases—as the title of this article suggests—our hypothesis is that a degraded semantic system pushes word and object recognition towards the "natural" selection of forms that are typical of their domains, whether these correspond to real or unreal stimuli.

EXPERIMENT 1: LEXICAL DECISION: THE OVER-REGULAR WORD TEST (OWT)

Methods

Participants

Twenty-two patients with a clinical diagnosis of semantic dementia (SD)—based on both cognitive and neuroradiological criteria as outlined by Hodges et al. (1992)—participated in Experiment 1. Sixteen of these cases were identified through the Memory and Cognitive Disorders Clinic at Addenbrooke's Hospital, Cambridge, UK (under the direction of consultant neurologist, and author, JRH); the remaining six cases were recruited via clinics at either St Martin's Hospital or Royal United Hospital in Bath, UK.[1] Four of the 22 patients were tested at two different time points roughly a year apart, yielding a total of 26 scores for

[1] We are extremely grateful to Dr R. W. Jones, St Martin's Hospital, Bath and Dr David Bateman, Royal United Hospital, Bath, for their permission to publish results from some of the patients under their care, and to Elizabeth Jefferies, Department of Experimental Psychology, University of Bristol, for collecting some of the data from the patients in Bath.

the 22 patients on this test.[2] Table 1 gives some basic background data on the patients. Sex, age, and scores on the Mini-Mental State Examination as a general measure of cognitive status are self-explanatory. The next two entries in the table correspond to two tests from the semantic battery used in our research programme in Cambridge (Bozeat, Lambon Ralph, Patterson, Garrard, & Hodges, 2000; Hodges, Graham, & Patterson, 1995): (a) Word–Picture Matching as a test of comprehension in which, for each of the 64 concrete concepts in the battery, the patient hears the spoken name of the object and is asked to point to the corresponding picture in an array of 10 line drawings (the target plus 9 distractors), all from the same category; (b) Object Naming as a combined test of semantic knowledge and word-production ability, in which each of the 64 items is presented as a single line drawing and the patient is asked to name it. The patients in the table are ordered in terms of their Word–Picture Matching scores, from highest to lowest; these scores demonstrate a substantial range of semantic impairment, from essentially normal (control participants perform perfectly on this test) to near chance. The Object Naming scores indicate that all patients, even the least impaired (AN), had some degree of anomia, as control participants also score at ceiling on this naming task. Note that AN was something of an outlier in the range of naming ability, with all other cases more notably anomic, and many of them strikingly so.

The final entry in Table 1 gives the patients' proportions correct in reading aloud a list of 42 high-frequency words with regular spelling–sound patterns from Patterson and Hodges (1992). This reading measure is included here to establish that none of these patients had any major impairment in the basic early visual processes required for the main experimental task of interest here, written-word lexical decision. In oral reading, all 22

Table 1. *Background data for the OWT participants with semantic dementia, including each patient's sex, age, Mini-Mental State Exam score at (or very close to) the time of experimental testing, Word–Picture Matching as an assessment of comprehension, Object Naming as an assessment of semantic knowledge and word production, and proportion correct in reading words with regular spelling–sound correspondences as a measure of accuracy of letter/word perception*

Patient	Sex	Age	MMSE[a]	Word-Pic Match[b]	Object Naming[b]	Read reg words[c]
AN	M	64	29	.98	.91	1.00
JP-2	M	65	26	.98	.77	1.00
LS	M	60	26	.98	.56	1.00
JP-1	M	64	27	.92	.80	1.00
ATe-1	M	65	25	.91	.16	.93
MG	F	77	20	.91	.13	1.00
NS-1	F	68	24	.89	.20	.90
MA	M	63	29	.89	.20	1.00
JTh	F	55	25	.86	.67	1.00
WM	F	55	24	.81	.22	1.00
SJ	F	60	23	.80	.17	.88
DV	M	64	21	.77	.27	.98
JC	M	58	15	.72	.52	.93
AT	M	62	22	.70	.20	NT
NS-2	F	69	25	.66	.13	.86
KH	M	61	10	.64	.34	1.00
BS	M	68	25	.63	.45	.95
EK	F	60	26	.61	.27	.95
KI	M	65	23	.56	.23	.98
JTw	M	66	25	.53	.08	.98
ATe-2	M	67	24	.45	.08	NT 2nd
GT	M	71	22	.42	.17	1.00
PS	F	75	23	.39	.13	1.00
JG-1	F	68	19	.38	.18	1.00
DC	F	78	15	.30	.05	NT
JG-2	F	70	19	.17	.03	NT 2nd

No reading scores (NT = not tested) were available for two patients (AT and DC); and for two of the four patients given the OWT lexical decision test twice (ATe-2 and JG-2), reading was tested only in conjunction with the first administration of the OWT and was not repeated the second time (NT 2nd).

[a]Score /30. [b]Proportion correct /64. [c]Proportion correct /42.

---

[2] Four patients were tested twice, simply because their yearly testing rounds came about twice within the 13 or so months during which these data were collected. We include both measurements here to present a complete portrait of the data. Observations were treated as independent in statistical analyses, as the patients have progressive neurological disorders and thus can show very different patterns of performance on testing rounds separated by a long period of time (see Lambon Ralph & Howard, 2000, for discussion).

patients were surface dyslexic, and thus made regularisation errors in reading aloud words with an atypical relationship between spelling pattern and pronunciation (e.g., reading *pint* to rhyme with "mint"). Furthermore, as Table 1 indicates, a few of the patients were less-than-perfect at reading even regular words, making mainly two types of error: (a) so-called LARC errors (legitimate alternative reading of components: Patterson, Suzuki, Wydell, & Sasanuma, 1995), in which a regular word like *hoot* is pronounced like its irregular neighbours "foot" and "soot"; and (b) word substitutions (e.g., *trial* → "trail") of the kind made by any and every reading-impaired individual. Such word substitutions were, however, rare; and both the generally high scores for reading regular words—even in some of the most semantically impaired patients—and the other error types (regularisations of irregular words and LARC errors to regular words) are all indicative of correct letter perception/identification. It therefore seems reasonable to conclude that, if the patients reveal the predicted deficits in lexical decision, this will not be attributable to problems in correctly perceiving the target words.

With the goal of demonstrating that our prediction of "natural selection" in word recognition applies specifically to the impact of semantic impairment, we also administered the OWT not only to a group of normal control subjects (*N* = 11, from the MRC-CBU subject panel) who were age- and education-matched to the SD patients, but also to a small set of neurological patients with Broca's aphasia consequent on left perisylvian lesions from cerebrovascular accidents (*N* = 5).

Stimulus materials

We constructed a two-alternative forced-choice (2AFC) written-word lexical decision test dubbed the Over-regular Word Test (OWT). The test consists of 72 pairs, each containing one real word and one nonword. In each pair, the nonword is a possible pseudohomophone of the word such that the two items of the pair could be said to have the same phonology.[3] The test has two conditions (*N* = 36 pairs in each), and the critical difference between conditions is in the orthographic "goodness" or typicality of the word relative to its nonword mate, as measured by both bigram and trigram frequencies. In condition W>NW (e.g., *grist* vs. *gryst*), the real word is more typical of general English spelling, i.e., it has higher bigram and trigram frequencies, than the nonword. In the NW>W condition (e.g., *tryst* vs. *trist*), this relationship is reversed, and the nonword is more orthographically typical than the real word. The stimuli in the two conditions were yoked to one another, such that (a) each W>NW stimulus pair had a partner in the NW>W condition that differed from it minimally (e.g., *cheese/cheize* was partnered with *seize/seese*, and *node/gnode* with *gnome/nome*), and (b) the target items in the yoked pairs were matched for frequency (e.g., *cheese* and *seize* are comparably frequent words). Thus the yoked pairs in the two conditions were as similar to one another as possible in both orthography and word frequency. All stimulus items are listed in Appendix A.

Figure 1 displays the bigram and trigram frequencies for each target word and its counterpart nonword in each of the two conditions. For each word–nonword pair, the figure shows that both bigrams and trigrams are more frequent for the words in condition W>NW, but for the nonwords in condition NW>W. Bigram and trigram frequencies were calculated from the Kucera and Francis (1967) corpus as follows. Each word in the corpus was divided into its constituent bigrams and

---

[3] Note that the nonwords are possible homophones of their word counterparts in the sense that every nonword's spelling pattern has that pronunciation in some real word(s) in the language, not necessarily in the sense that most people, if asked to pronounce the nonword in isolation, would give it a pronunciation identical to the word member of the pair. For example, the nonword *gryst* might be pronounced /graɪst/ ("griced") by some people; we consider *gryst* a pseudohomophone of *grist* because the real word *tryst* has this spelling pattern and rhymes with *grist*. Likewise, the nonword *nease* might well be pronounced /niz/ ("neeze"), but we selected it as a possible homophone mate for *niece* on the grounds that the spelling pattern _*ease* has an unvoiced consonant in words like *lease* and *grease*.

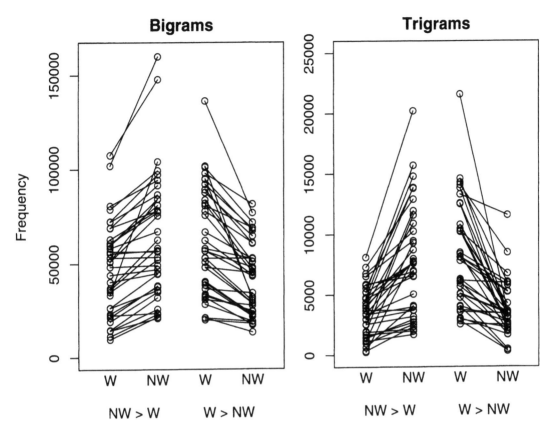

Figure 1. *Bigram and trigram frequencies for the words and nonwords in the W>NW and NW>W conditions of the OWT lexical decision test. The lines join each real word target with its paired nonword distractor.*

trigrams, and each bigram and trigram appearing in the corpus was assigned a weight equivalent to the summed frequency of the words in which it was observed. For example, the word "yacht" appears with frequency 7 in the Kucera and Francis (1967) corpus—hence this word contributed 7 to the frequency of the bigrams "ya," "ac," "ch," and "ht"; and 7 to the frequency of the trigrams "yac," "ach," and "cht." The bigram frequency for each letter string in the OWT was then calculated by summing the frequencies of its constituent bigrams; for example, the pseudo nonword "trist" received a total bigram frequency equal to the sum of the frequencies for "tr," "ri," "is," and "st." Trigram frequencies for all letter strings in the OWT were similarly calculated by summing the frequencies of the constituent trigrams. Word

frequencies for the target items in the two conditions, also from Kucera and Francis, were closely matched: mean log frequency for W>NW = 1.59; for NW>W = 1.68; $F(1, 70) = 0.09$, $p = .77$. The items in each of the two conditions were further subdivided into two groups using a median split on the frequency of the target word, so that performance could be assessed across the 18 higher- and 18 lower-frequency items. Mean word, bigram, and trigram frequencies for the higher- and lower-frequency items are shown in Table 2.

Procedure

The 72 experimental pairs were each printed on a separate sheet of paper, with the real word on the left in half of the pairs and on the right in the remaining half, counterbalanced for condition.

Table 2. *Mean word, bigram, and trigram frequencies calculated separately for higher-frequency and lower-frequency items*

		W > NW	NW > W
Word frequency	High	16	29
	Low	4	2
Bigrams			
High frequency	Word	63023	46286
	Nonword	42118	68682
Low frequency	Word	60312	47023
	Nonword	41935	59476
Trigrams			
High frequency	Word	8062	3452
Low frequency	Nonword	3650	8153
	Word	8274	5876
	Nonword	3664	10307

The order of list presentation was randomised with the sole restriction that pairs of orthographically similar items (e.g., *grist* vs. *gryst* and *tryst* vs. *trist*) did not appear in close proximity. The instruction to participants was "Please point to the real word." In case of potential problems in comprehension of instructions by the SD patients, presentation of the 72 test pairs was preceded by 5 very easy practice pairs of words and nonwords. All of the patients, even the most severely impaired, were able to perform the task.

Results and interim discussion

Eleven age-matched control participants performed near ceiling in both conditions of the OWT. For high-frequency items, proportions correct ranged from 0.94–1.0 with a mean of 0.99 in both conditions. For low-frequency items, proportions correct ranged from 0.82–1.0 with a mean of 0.94 in both conditions. Controls performed slightly better for high-frequency than for low-frequency items, but importantly, they achieved identical scores in the W>NW and NW>W conditions for both high- and low-frequency items.

Table 3 provides individual OWT scores from the SD group (proportion correct out of 18) for the four stimulus subsets created by crossing OWT condition (W>NW vs. NW>W) with word frequency (higher vs. lower) for the 26 individual

Table 3. *OWT performance (proportion correct out of 18) for each of the four subsets of OWT stimulus pairs, for each of 26 administrations of the test to patients with semantic dementia (SD) (N = 22 patients, 4 tested on two occasions), ordered by the patients' scores on a test of Word–Picture Matching (see Table 1), followed by mean proportions correct for the SD cases, the control participants (N = 11) and the patients with Broca's aphasia (N = 5)*

	W>NW		NW>W	
Patient	*Higher freq*	*Lower freq*	*Higher freq*	*Lower freq*
AN	.78	.89	.83	.78
JP-2	.94	.94	.83	.39
LS	.83	1.00	.94	.83
JP-1	.83	.83	.78	.33
ATe-1	.78	.94	.89	.44
MG	.94	.83	1.00	.89
NS-1	.61	.72	.78	.61
MA	.83	.89	.78	.39
JTh	1.00	1.00	.89	.44
WM	.67	.78	.61	.56
SJ	.83	.89	.94	.56
DV	.94	1.00	.83	.50
JC	.78	.78	.67	.50
AT	.94	.67	.61	.22
NS-2	.78	.89	.78	.33
KH	.94	.78	.22	.22
BS	.83	.78	.89	.50
EK	.83	.78	.39	.28
KI	.94	.94	.72	.17
JTw	.83	.78	.78	.44
ATe-2	.72	.94	.56	.28
GT	.72	.83	.61	.56
PS	.94	.89	.83	.50
JG-1	.89	.94	.78	.61
DC	.94	.94	.56	.06
JG-2	.78	.94	.50	.28
SD mean	.84	.87	.74	.46
Control mean	.99	.96	.99	.96
Broca mean	.87	.69	.81	.70

administrations of the test to SD patients. As in Table 1, the patients are ordered by their scores, from highest to lowest, on the word-to-picture matching task from our semantic battery as a measure of degree of semantic deficit. Following the individual-SD OWT scores in Table 3 are the mean proportions correct for each condition for (a) the SD patients, (b) the control participants, and (c) the patients with Broca's aphasia.

Figure 2 displays the OWT results for the SD patients by condition on all items and also split by higher vs. lower frequency. A repeated-measures ANOVA on these results yielded a significant main effect of condition, W>NW vs. NW>W, $F(1, 25) = 58.0$, $p < .001$; a significant main effect of word frequency, higher vs. lower, $F(1, 25) = 40.1$, $p < .001$; and most importantly, a significant interaction between these two factors, $F(1, 25) = 48.4$, $p < .001$.

Figure 3 displays the OWT results as mean proportions correct (with 95% confidence intervals) on the four OWT stimulus subsets but also divided into two SD severity subgroups: OWT performance associated with the 13 best scores on the WPM task (range 0.98–0.72) vs. those associated with the 13 worst WPM scores (range 0.70–0.17). To determine how the severity of semantic impairment interacts with the effects described above, we added this factor (milder vs. more severe impairment, as assessed by a median split on word–picture matching) to the repeated-measures ANOVA described above. As before, the main

effects of word frequency, $F(1, 24) = 82.4$, $p < .001$, and stimulus type, $F(1, 24) = 39.8$, $p < .001$, were reliable, as was their interaction, $F(1, 24) = 46.8$, $p < .001$. The main effect of severity was also significant, $F(1, 24) = 10.7$, $p < .004$, and this effect interacted reliably with word frequency, $F(1, 24) = 11.6$, $p < .003$, but not stimulus type, $F(1, 24) = 0.85$, n.s.

The results in Figure 3 are simple to describe and constitute an excellent match to our prediction for LD performance in semantically impaired patients. So long as the words in this 2AFC LD task had more typical orthographic structure than the nonwords (W>NW), performance was good (though a little below the control range for pairs containing higher-frequency words) and insensitive to both word frequency and degree of semantic degradation. When the nonword members of the pairs were more typical of English orthography than the words, on the other hand, OWT scores were high only when the two other factors affecting performance (word frequency and patient severity) were favourable (high-frequency words

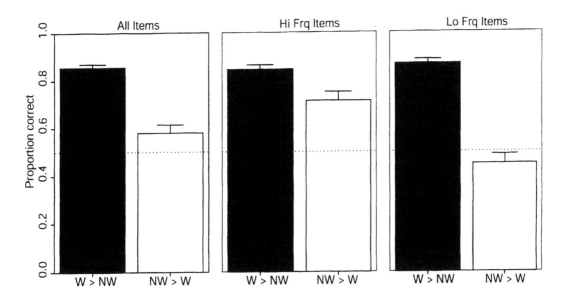

Figure 2. *Average performance for the patients with semantic dementia on the OWT, first as a contrast between all items in each condition (W>NW and NW>W) and then divided into higher- and lower-frequency word targets. The fine dotted line at 0.5 on the Y axis indicates chance performance. Error bars indicate the standard error of the mean.*

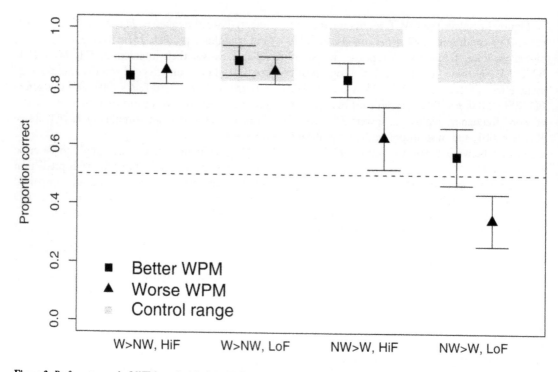

Figure 3. *Performance on the OWT for each of the four subsets of materials, separately for the SD patients with milder comprehension impairment (as measured by Word–Picture Matching: "Better WPM" in the figure legend) and for those with more severe comprehension impairment ("Worse WPM"). Error bars are 95% confidence intervals. The grey shading at the top indicates the range of control performance in the corresponding condition, and the dotted line at 0.5 on the Y axis indicates chance performance.*

and less impaired patients: the square plotted for NW>W, HiF in Figure 3). Either more severe semantic impairment (the triangle for NW>W, HiF) or lower-frequency words (the square for NW>W, LoF) reduced average performance near to chance level; and the combination of these two unfavourable factors (triangle for NW>W, LoF) brought average performance below chance—i.e., under these conditions, the patients on average preferred the nonword to the word. These observations were further bolstered by an informal consideration of the data yielded by the four patients who were tested a second time, approximately 1 year after first assessment. Three of these four patients had lower scores on the second round of testing; but this difference was carried predominantly by NW>W items, and within these items, was larger for low-frequency items (see Table 3).

To judge whether the performance reflected by the farthest-right triangle in Figure 3 was significantly below chance, indicating a reliable preference for the nonwords in this condition, we used the following logic. If a participant were simply responding at random to pairs in this (or any) condition, the likelihood of making 5 or fewer correct responses out of 18 is $p < .048$ from the binomial distribution; thus a score of 5 or less (proportion correct ≤ 0.28) indicates that a participant's performance is likely to be below chance. Of the 13 patients with lower Word–Picture Matching values, 7/13 obtained a score of 5 or less in this NW>W, LoF condition. Furthermore, it is possible to calculate the exact likelihood that 7 or more patients out of 13 would achieve scores as low as these on the basis of chance responding alone. If the probability of a single patient making 5 or fewer correct responses is $p < .048$, then, from the binomial distribution, the likelihood of so many patients achieving such low scores by chance is $p < .0000008$. It therefore seems reasonable to conclude that, as a group, the SD patients with severe semantic deterioration did not just guess at random but reliably preferred the nonword to the word for condition NW>W, LoF.

The same type of repeated-measures ANOVA that we employed for the SD group, when applied to the OWT performance of the Broca's aphasic patients, revealed no reliable main effect of condition, W>NW vs. NW>W, $F(1, 4) < 1$; a significant main effect of word frequency, higher vs. lower, $F(1, 4) = 15.0$, $p < .02$; and no interaction between these two factors, $F(1, 4) < 1$.

It is notable that LD success on the OWT in both control participants and Broca's aphasics was affected by word frequency but not by orthographic typicality. This outcome supports our hypothesis that "natural selection" in word recognition—i.e., a dramatic preference for orthographically typical words—is an abnormal state of affairs engendered by reduced interaction between word meaning and orthographic analysis. As displayed in Figure 3, the fact that lower-frequency words yielded not only a lower mean but also a wider range of performance in control participants means that average SD performance on the W>NW, LoF subset was actually within control bounds. This outcome supports our claim that LD ability in semantically impaired patients can appear to be normal—if and only if the words are more orthographically typical than the nonword stimuli.

EXPERIMENT 2: OBJECT DECISION: THE OVER-REGULAR OBJECT TEST (OOT)

Methods

Participants

Ten patients with a clinical diagnosis of semantic dementia (defined as above), plus 10 age- and education-matched controls, participated in this experiment. Nine of the 10 patients had also participated in Experiment 1 (the OWT). Five of the 10 were from the Cambridge cohort and the other 5 (including 1 who had not participated in

Table 4. *Background data for the OOT participants with semantic dementia, including each patient's sex, age, Mini-Mental State Exam score at (or very close to) the time of experimental testing, Word-Picture Matching as an assessment of comprehension, Object Naming as an assessment of semantic knowledge and word production, and score on copying the complex Rey figure as a measure of visuo-perceptual ability*

Patient	Sex	Age	MMSE	Word–Pic Match[a]	Object Naming[b]	Rey Copy[c]
AN	M	64	29	.98	.91	36
DV	M	64	21	.77	.27	35
NS	F	69	25	.66	.13	36
BS	M	68	25	.63	.45	33
EK	F	60	26	.61	.27	36
KI	M	65	23	.56	.23	35
JTw	M	66	25	.53	.08	34
ATe	M	67	24	.45	.08	36
JG	F	70	19	.17	.03	34
MK	F	67	8	.17	.05	35

[a] Score /30. [b] Proportion correct /64. [c] Score /36.

Experiment 1) were from the Bath cohort. Table 4 gives background data for the OOT participants, ordered by their comprehension scores (from highest to lowest) in word–picture matching. The measures in Table 4 are the same as those in Table 1 for the OWT patients, except that the reading measure has been replaced by scores on the test of copying the complex Rey Figure. As with reading regular words as a "control" task for the early processing component of lexical decision in Experiment 1, Rey scores are included for participants in the Object Decision experiment to establish that—should our prediction of OD impairments be supported by the findings—this will not be attributable to any early visual perceptual deficits: All patients performed well within control limits in perceiving and indeed reproducing this complicated, meaningless figure.

Stimulus materials

We constructed a 2AFC visual object decision test dubbed the Over-regular Object Test (OOT). The test has two conditions, with 30 pairs of items in each condition; each pair contains one line drawing of a real object and one line drawing of a chimeric nonreal version of the same object. As a precise parallel to the OWT in Experiment 1, where the conditions varied in orthographic typicality, the critical difference between the two conditions of the OOT is in the typicality of the real object relative to its nonobject mate: in half the pairs, the real object was more typical than the nonreal object (R>NR), and in the remaining half this relationship was reversed (NR>R). There is no completely objective measure of typicality in the sphere of visual object structure, as was available for orthographic structure in Experiment 1 in the form of bigram and trigram frequencies; but we can at least explain that by typicality here, we refer to the extent to which an object consists of parts that are shared by many other items in the same semantic category. Stimulus items are listed and described in Appendix B.

Typicality can arise either from having a feature in common with most other similar objects or from not having an unusual feature that occurs in very few objects in the category. For example, most familiar animals have modest-sized ears, and one can construct two pairs of items in which the unusual feature of large ears is associated with the real object in one case and with the nonreal object in the other. In the OOT, the former consisted of a line drawing of an elephant with large ears (R) paired with a false elephant with ears scaled down to normal size (NR); this pair then belongs to the NR>R condition, because the nonreal elephant with smaller ears is more typical of the animal domain. Included in the R>NR condition were a real and a chimeric monkey, the real one having normal monkey-sized ears and the false one having large elephant-sized ears; thus for these items, the animal with the more typical appearance is also the real animal. These two pairs of items are illustrated in Figure 4. In the nonanimal

Figure 4. *Examples of stimulus pairs from the NR>R (Nonreal>Real) and R>NR (Real>Nonreal) conditions of the OOT object decision test.*

domain, many tools have a straight, solid handle like the one on a typical screwdriver, but a spanner (wrench in American tool-speak) has an atypical open handle that fits around a nut. In the OOT, two pairs built round this feature were a screwdriver with a straight, solid handle vs. a screwdriver with a handle sporting a spanner-like hole (R>NR), and a spanner with its normal (but domain-atypical) open handle vs. a spanner with a solid screwdriver-like handle (NR>R). We verified our own intuitions about the typicality of such features by asking 10 normal control participants to judge which version of a feature—verbally described—is more typical of objects in the relevant category, e.g., "Do animals typically have large or medium-sized ears?"; "Do animals typically have level or humped backs?"; "Do tools usually have hollow or solid handles?", etc. Their averaged judgments matched our intuitions in all instances.

We have already published data (Rogers et al., 2003) on the performance of SD patients on an Object Decision task designed along these principles. We are introducing a new OD test with additional SD data here for three reasons. First, the previous test, called the OAT (Over-regular Animal Test) contained, as its name suggests, only animals. Although this restriction was employed for a good reason—i.e., that living things have a better-defined typicality structure than manmade artefacts—it nevertheless seemed worthwhile to test the applicability of this principle to the large domain of artefacts as well. Secondly, there were a few "rogue" items in the OAT on which control participants often performed poorly (e.g., many of them preferred the gorilla with a tail to the real, tail-less gorilla: normal people are not *entirely* immune to typicality!), making it hard to conclude that the patients' preference for the nonobject in these few specific NR>R pairs was abnormal. The items in the OOT are a better selection in this regard: out of 10 normal participants, 9 performed perfectly (100% correct choices), and 1 control made one error in each condition (i.e., one error to a R>NR item and one to a NR>R item). Third, the OAT included just 16 pairs per condition, which somewhat limited our power to determine whether individual performance was reliably better

or worse than chance. The OOT has 30 pairs/condition.

Familiarity ratings from UK subjects (Morrison, Chappell, & Ellis, 1997) were available for 53 of the 60 items in the OOT, and we collected ratings for the remaining 7 items. On this basis, we divided the 30 pairs in each condition (R>NR and NR>R) into 15 higher- and 15 lower-familiarity items, just as we had done with regard to word frequency for the OWT in Experiment 1. Mean familiarity ratings (on a 5-point scale) for the high-familiarity items were 3.3 in the R>NR condition and 3.1 in the NR>R condition; for low-familiarity items, the mean ratings were 1.8 in the R>NR condition and 1.9 in the NR>R condition.

Procedure

The 60 experimental pairs of line drawings were each printed on a separate sheet of paper, with the real object on the left in half of the pairs and on the right in the remaining half, counterbalanced for condition. The order of list presentation was randomised, with the sole restriction being that two different pairs of items involving manipulation of the same feature, such as ear size, did not appear in close proximity. The instruction to participants was "Please point to the real thing." In case of potential problems in comprehension of instructions by the SD patients, presentation of the 60 test pairs was preceded by 3 very easy practice pairs of real and nonreal objects. None of the patients, even the most severely impaired, had difficulty following the instructions. Each pair of line drawings in the test consisted of a real and a nonreal version of the same object, and the difference between the two might not always be instantly apparent. In order to ensure that each participant noticed the difference, for each item in the test the experimenter always said (pointing to the relevant feature or part such as the ears on the two elephants or monkeys) "This one looks like this but this one looks like this – which do you think is the real one?", thus drawing the subject's attention to the difference without mentioning the name of the object or the relevant part or giving any specific information about them.

Results and interim discussion

Table 5 provides individual OOT scores (proportion correct out of 15) for the four stimulus subsets created by crossing OOT condition (R>NR vs. NR>R) with object familiarity (higher vs. lower) for each of the 10 SD patients, followed by mean scores. As in Table 4, the patients are ordered by their scores, from highest to lowest, on the word-to-picture matching task from our semantic battery as a measure of degree of semantic deficit. Figure 5 displays the OOT results for the SD patients by condition on all items and also split by higher- vs. lower-familiarity objects. A repeated-measures ANOVA on these results yielded a significant main effect of condition, R>NR vs. NR>R, $F(1, 9) = 25.3, p < .001$; a significant main effect of item familiarity, higher vs. lower, $F(1, 9) = 13.7, p < .005$; and most importantly, a significant interaction between these two factors, $F(1, 9) = 32.6, p < .001$.

To determine how the severity of semantic impairment interacts with the effects described above, we again added this factor (milder vs. more severe impairment, as assessed by a median split on word-picture matching) to the repeated-measures ANOVA described above. As before, the main

Table 5. *OOT performance (proportion correct out of 15) for each of the four subsets of OOT stimulus pairs, for each of 10 patients with semantic dementia, ordered by the patients' scores on a test of Word–Picture Matching (see Table 3), followed by mean proportions correct for the SD cases*

	R>NR		NR>R	
Patient	Higher fam	Lower fam	Higher fam	Lower fam
AN	1.00	1.00	.93	.93
DV	1.00	1.00	.93	.80
EK	1.00	1.00	.67	.60
NS	.87	.80	.93	.67
BS	.87	.87	.73	.47
KI	.80	.93	.33	.13
JTw	.93	1.00	.47	.40
Ate	1.00	1.00	.80	.60
JG	.93	1.00	.60	.47
MK	.93	.93	.53	.27
Mean	.93	.95	.69	.53

effects of familiarity, $F(1, 8) = 12.6, p < .01$, and stimulus type, $F(1, 8) = 38.4, p < .001$, were reliable, as was their interaction, $F(1, 8) = 61.3, p < .001$. The main effect of severity was also significant, $F(1, 8) = 5.3, p < .05$, but did not interact reliably with word frequency, $F(1, 8) < 1$, or stimulus type, $F(1, 8) = 2.6$, n.s. The three-way interaction was statistically reliable, $F(1, 8) = 13.8, p < .001$, indicating that the magnitude of the familiarity-by-regularity interaction itself varied reliably with the severity of the semantic impairment.

Figure 6 displays the OOT results as mean proportions correct, with 95% confidence intervals, on the four OOT stimulus subsets but also divided into two SD severity subgroups: OOT performance associated with the five best scores on the WPM task (range 0.98–0.61) vs. those associated with the five worst WPM scores (range 0.56–0.17). Just as was the case with the OWT results in Figure 3, the OOT results in Figure 6 are simple to describe and constitute an excellent match to our prediction for OD performance in semantically impaired patients. So long as the typicality (with respect to the category to which this object belongs, such as tools or vehicles, or birds or four-legged animals) of the visuospatial structure in an OOT pair was greater for the real object than for its chimeric nonobject counterpart (R>NR), performance was good (though a little below the ceiling-level performance of the control subjects for higher-familiarity objects) and insensitive to both stimulus familiarity and degree of the patients' semantic degradation. When the nonreal members of the pairs were more typical of their object domains than the real things, on the other hand, OOT scores were high only when the two other factors affecting performance (stimulus familiarity and patient severity) were favourable (higher-familiarity objects and less impaired patients: the square plotted for NR>R, HiF in Figure 6). Either more severe semantic impairment (the triangle for NR>R, HiF) or less familiar objects (the square for NR>R, LoF) reduced average performance near to chance level; and the combination of these two unfavourable factors (triangle for NR>R, LoF) brought average perform-

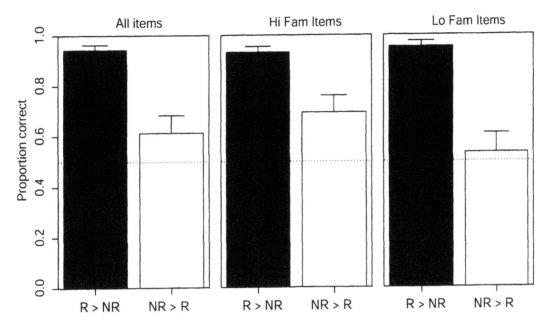

Figure 5. *Average performance for the patients with semantic dementia on the OOT, first as a contrast between all items in each condition (R>NR and NR>R) and then divided into higher- and lower-familiarity object targets. The fine dotted line at 0.5 on the Y axis indicates chance performance. Error bars indicate standard error of the mean.*

ance below chance—i.e., under these conditions, the patients on average preferred the chimera to the real object.

We employed the same logic here as in the OWT study to determine whether the performance reflected by the farthest-right triangle in Figure 6 was significantly below chance, indicating a reliable preference for the nonobjects in this condition; note, however, that with a smaller N for both subjects and items in the OOT than the OWT, there is less power to judge this issue. From the binomial distribution, the likelihood of any individual making 4 or fewer correct responses (out of 15) on the basis of random guessing is $p <$ .06. Of the five patients with lower Word-Picture Matching values, 2/5 obtained a score of 4 or less in this NR>R, LoF condition; the probability of this occurring by chance alone is $p <$ .03. Once again, therefore, it appears that the SD patients with severe semantic deterioration reliably preferred the nonreal chimera to the real object when the typicality relation was NR>R and the

object was in the lower half of the familiarity distribution.

A further two-factor repeated-measures ANOVA was performed to determine whether there might be any (unpredicted) impact of semantic domain—artefacts vs living things—in OOT performance. There was not: Condition, $F(1, 8) =$ 20.7, $p <$ .002; Domain, $F(1, 8) <$ 1; Condition × Domain interaction, $F(1, 8) <$ 1.

And finally, for the $N = 9$ patients who performed both OWT and OOT experiments, we contrasted performance on the two tests. There was, as expected, a highly reliable effect of condition (W>NW and R>NR vs. NW>W and NR>R), $F(1, 8) = 31.3$, $p <$ .001; and there was a marginally significant effect of test, $F(1, 8) = 4.7$, $p =$ .063, reflecting slightly higher scores on the OOT than the OWT. Crucially, however, there was not even a hint of an interaction between condition and test, $F(1, 8) = 0.001$ (yes, that is the F-value, not the p-value), $p =$ .97. This lack of interaction will be obvious from contrasting Figures 2 and 5, or 3 and

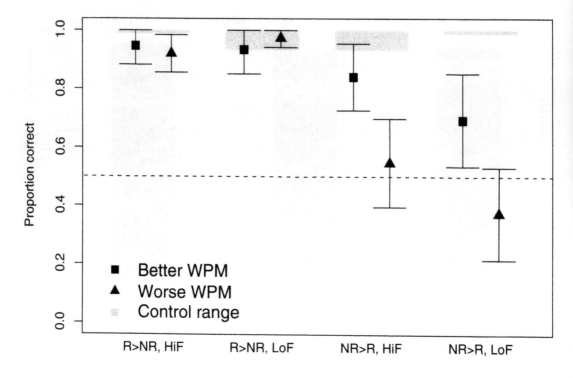

Figure 6. *Performance on the OOT for each of the four subsets of materials, separately for the SD patients with milder comprehension impairment (as measured by Word–Picture Matching: "Better WPM" in the figure legend) and for those with more severe comprehension impairment ("Worse WPM"). The grey shading at the top indicates the range of control performance in the corresponding condition, and the dotted line at 0.5 on the Y axis indicates chance performance.*

6: The patterns of effects in these LD and OD experiments were strikingly identical.

The dramatic interaction between typicality and familiarity characterising the patients' OOT performance is perhaps even more impressive than the same phenomenon for the OWT, for the following reason. Although some of the SD patients in our cohort were highly educated (e.g., one had a PhD, a number had undergraduate degrees), one could worry that at least some patients might never have known the lower-familiarity words in the OWT like *tryst*, and that for such items it might be natural to prefer a more typical spelling like *trist*. Of course we attempted to deal with this issue by having control participants who were not only age- but also education-matched to the patients, and we hope that this has been satisfactory. We are also, however, reassured by obtaining precisely the same

pattern of performance in the OOT, where—although the objects can readily be divided into more and less familiar subsets—objects in the lower-familiarity subset (such as wagon or penguin) would surely have been known to every patient premorbidly.

GENERAL DISCUSSION

We started this investigation with the question of whether word and/or object recognition can be normal in patients whose early structural processing of words and pictures is relatively intact but whose semantic knowledge about the concepts represented by such words and pictures is degraded. Empirically, we have established that this question cannot be answered without a detailed description of the stimulus materials used to test recognition (see Hovius, Kellenbach, Graham, Hodges, & Patterson, 2003, for a similar argument). As previously demonstrated in two single case studies (Bub et al., 1985; Diesfeldt, 1992), accuracy of word recognition as measured by lexical decision can range from normal to chance level depending on the stimuli; and the same is true of object recognition as measured by object decision (Rogers et al., 2003). It is now possible to provide a clear statement of one set of stimulus conditions under which the performance of semantically impaired individuals in these tests may approximate to normal, and of the kinds of changes to these stimulus conditions that will depress the patients' success to a level that is moderately abnormal, or severely impaired, or indeed significantly *below* chance. If the real words or objects are typical of their domains (which in the case of written words means that they are composed of typical, common letter sequences, and in the case of objects means that their visual features are mostly typical of their categories) and the nonreal words or objects are constructed to have atypical characteristics (conditions W>NW in Experiment 1 and R>NR in Experiment 2), then the patients will mainly choose the real words/objects and appear to have normal recognition despite degraded semantics. If the typicality relations of the real vs. nonreal stimuli are reversed, however (conditions NW>W and NR>R), then the patients' performance will be abnormal. The degree to which their accuracy departs from normal then depends on two further factors: the frequency or familiarity of the real word or object, and the extent of the patient's semantic deficit. If both of these factors are favourable (words/objects of high frequency/familiarity, mild semantic impairment), then performance can still be near normal. If one of these factors is auspicious and the other inauspicious, then performance will be markedly impaired and perhaps even fall to near chance. If both factors are detrimental, then performance may well be significantly below chance— that is, the patient will actually prefer the typical nonword or nonobject to the atypical real word or real object.

The conclusions that we draw from this pattern of results are (a) that normal recognition depends on, and indeed is a direct product of, the interaction of perceptual and conceptual processing; and therefore (b) that a degraded semantic system will inevitably impair the ability to "know" a letter string or object-like representation as belonging to the repertoire of real words or objects. It is important to emphasise that, in this conception, the good performance observed when the real stimulus is more typical than the made-up one does not mean that recognition is normal under these conditions. Low accuracy to NW>W or NR>R reflects a perceptual recognition system operating without normal benefit of interaction with semantic knowledge, resulting in "natural selection"; but so does high accuracy to W>NW or R>NR. As demonstrated in a whole host of studies of semantic dementia (e.g., Hodges, Graham, & Patterson, 1995; Rogers et al., in press; Saffran & Schwartz, 1994; Schwartz, Marin, & Saffran, 1979; Warrington, 1975), the hallmark of semantic degradation is a frequency-modulated whittling away of detailed, specific knowledge and a relative preservation of robust information that characterises whole batches of other similar things. In one of our favourite anecdotes demonstrating this point, an SD patient in our cohort looked at a picture of a zebra and said "It's a horse, isn't it?". Then, pointing to the stripes, she added "What are these funny things for?"

Prior to the present study and a very few others in a similar vein (e.g., the beautiful early studies of an SD patient by Schwartz et al., 1979, which included tasks like object name recognition), most of the evidence that semantic degradation has this particular impact (i.e., dissolution of detail, especially for less familiar words/objects) has come from studies of response production, such as object naming (Hodges et al., 1995), word or picture sorting (Rogers et al., in press), concept definitions (Lambon Ralph, Graham, Patterson, & Hodges, 1999), object use (Bozeat, Lambon Ralph, Patterson, & Hodges, 2002), and so on. The current line of research extends this impact into the domain of recognition, and not recognition in the taxing sense of identifying a word or object by naming or defining it, but simply recognition in the sense of "yes, I know this to be a real, familiar thing." In another of our favourite anecdotes (this one from an SD patient studied by M. L. Gorno-Tempini, personal communication), the patient—who was being asked to perform lexical decisions—objected to the test with the query "How can I say whether it's real if I don't know what it means?"

One of our colleagues in Cambridge (A. Marcel, personal communication) is wont to challenge our view of the critical role of conceptual knowledge in object recognition, naming, etc., by pointing out that, although he has no "conceptual" knowledge of a tulip other than what it looks like, he can easily recognise and name it. Our response to this point is simply that his conceptual knowledge of the tulip manifests itself in his ability to produce the name "tulip" when confronted with one, or to draw a sketch of a tulip when given its name. This knowledge is encoded in the network of connections and hidden units that intermediate among visual representations of objects and phonological representations of spoken words (as well as representations in other modalities). Different individual objects or classes of objects have more or less rich and extensive networks of modality-specific information content; and most people (other than flower experts) probably know little about tulips apart from what they look like and what they are called, but much more about the things that they deal with every day, such as trousers or coffee or mobile telephones. But no matter how many different modalities (visual, auditory, tactile, olfactory, verbal: Allport, 1985; Saffran, 2000; Saffran & Schwartz, 1994) represent specific knowledge about a particular concept, our claim is that the function of the semantic system in the brain is to orchestrate the interactions amongst these modality-specific representations; and that this function—crucially—is subserved by modality-independent representations, that allow all of the modality-specific information to communicate and combine so that we can recognise real-world stimuli from many different input modalities and respond to them in many different output modes (see Rogers et al., 2003, in press, for detailed description). Whether the various interacting modality-specific representations are themselves best understood as "perceptual" or as "semantic" may be a bone of contention amongst some theorists; but it is not clear to us that any serious theoretical issues hinge upon this distinction.

Our position is in line with a view that is coming to permeate several different subdisciplines of cognitive psychology, including cognitive development (e.g., Mareschal, 2000; Quinn, 2002; Smith & Samuelson, 1997), visual cognition and expertise in normal adults (e.g., Barsalou, 2003; Tarr & Gauthier, 2000), and category-learning (e.g., Goldstone, Lippa, & Shiffrin, 2001), as well as cognitive neuropsychology: Specifically, that perceiving, recognising, knowing, and remembering constitute mutually interdependent and highly interactive processes, rather than functionally separable and independent cognitive modules. In this vein it is worth briefly mentioning the elegant experiments of Arguin, Bub, Dixon, and colleagues, which provide compelling evidence for the interactive nature of perception and conception (Arguin, Bub, & Dudek, 1996; Dixon, Bub, & Arguin, 1997, 1998). Patient ELM was a visual agnosic who appeared to show particular difficulty in recognising living things from vision, despite normal semantic knowledge about these items in other modalities. ELM's visual impairment extended to the discrimination of simple blob-shapes varying in more than one spatial dimension; but this deficit was dramatically attenuated when ELM learned to associate the blobs with a set of real-world concepts that were semantically unrelated to one another. When taught to associate the same blobs with a set of closely related real-world concepts, ELM showed no benefit. Similar results have been achieved for face recognition in ELM (Dixon et al., 1998), and even for perceptual discrimination in healthy control subjects (Dixon et al., 1997; Gauthier, James, Curby, & Tarr, 2003). The results suggest that semantic knowledge can influence not only the recognition of familiar real-world objects (as in the current study), but also the visual discrimination of simple, novel shapes. These and other studies cited above lead us to agree with the comments of Smith (2000, p. 96), drawn from a complementary literature on the study of conceptual development, who writes:

The agenda for continued progress, then, is the study of the dynamics of perceiving and remembering over multiple time scales, how they combine to make a moment of knowing that is fit to the idiosyncrasies of the here and now, continuous with the just previous past, and wisely informed by a lifetime of perceiving and remembering.

In summary, we predicted—on the basis of a detailed and indeed implemented model of semantic memory—that the consequence of degraded conceptual knowledge in the sphere of word and object recognition would be impaired performance with the specific characteristic of a dramatic preference for typicality, modulated by both item familiarity and degree of semantic deficit. The performance of large-ish groups of patients with semantic dementia in tests of both lexical decision and object decision demonstrated precisely this predicted tendency to select "natural" rather than "real" objects and words.

REFERENCES

Allport, D. A. (1985). Distributed memory, modular systems and dysphasia. In S. K. Newman & R. Epstein (Eds.), *Current perspectives in dysphasia* (pp. 32–60). Edinburgh: Churchill Livingstone.

Arguin, M., Bub, D., & Dudek, G. (1996). Shape integration for visual object recognition and its implication for category-specific visual agnosia. *Visual Cognition, 3*, 221–275.

Barsalou, L. W. (2003). Situated simulation in the human conceptual system. *Language and Cognitive Processes, 18*, 513–562.

Behrmann, M., & Bub, D. (1992). Surface dyslexia and dysgraphia: Dual routes, single lexicon. *Cognitive Neuropsychology, 9*, 209–251.

Bozeat, S., Lambon Ralph, M. A., Graham, K. S., Patterson, K., Wilkin, H., Rowland, J., Rogers, T. T., & Hodges, J. R. (2003). A duck with 4 legs: Investigating the structure of conceptual knowledge using picture drawing in semantic dementia. *Cognitive Neuropsychology, 20*, 27–47.

Bozeat, S., Lambon Ralph, M. A., Patterson, K., Garrard, P., & Hodges, J. R. (2000). Nonverbal semantic impairment in semantic dementia. *Neuropsychologia, 38*, 1207–1215.

Bozeat, S., Lambon Ralph, M. A., Patterson, K., & Hodges, J. R. (2002). When objects lose their meaning: What happens to their use? *Cognitive, Affective and Behavioral Neurosciences, 2*, 236–251.

Breedin, S. D., Saffran, E. M., & Coslett, H. B. (1994). Reversal of the concreteness effect in a patient with semantic dementia. *Cognitive Neuropsychology, 11*, 617–660.

Bub, D., Black, S., Hampson, E., & Kertesz, A. (1988). Semantic encoding of pictures and words: Some neuropsychological observations. *Cognitive Neuropsychology, 5*, 27–66.

Bub, D., Cancelliere, A., & Kertesz, A. (1985). Whole-word and analytic translation of spelling to sound in a nonsemantic reader. In K. Patterson, J. C. Marshall, & M. Coltheart (Eds.), *Surface dyslexia* (pp. 15–34). Hove, UK: Lawrence Erlbaum Associates Ltd.

Diesfeldt, H. F. A. (1992). Impaired and preserved semantic memory functioning in dementia. In L. Backman (Ed.), *Memory functioning in dementia* (pp. 227–263). Amsterdam: Elsevier.

Dixon, M., Bub, D., & Arguin, M. (1997). The interaction of object form and object meaning in the identification performance of a patient with category-specific visual agnosia. *Cognitive Neuropsychology, 14*, 1085–1130.

Dixon, M., Bub, D., & Arguin, M. (1998). Semantic and visual determinants of face recognition in a prosopagnosic patient. *Journal of Cognitive Neuroscience, 10*, 362–376.

Gauthier, I., James, T. W., Curby, K. W., & Tarr, M. J. (2003). The influence of conceptual knowledge on visual discrimination. *Cognitive Neuropsychology, 20*, 507–523.

Gloor, P. (1997). *The temporal lobe and limbic system.* New York/Oxford: OUP.

Goldstone, R. L., Lippa, Y., & Shiffrin, R. M. (2001). Altering object representations through category learning. *Cognition, 78*, 27–43.

Harley, T. A. (1995). *The psychology of language: From data to theory.* Hove, UK: Psychology Press.

Hodges, J. R., Graham, N. L., & Patterson, K. (1995). Charting the progression in semantic dementia: Implications for the neural organisation of long-term memory. *Memory, 3*, 463–495.

Hodges, J. R., Patterson, K., Oxbury, S., & Funnell, E. (1992). Semantic dementia: Progressive fluent aphasia with temporal lobe atrophy. *Brain, 115*, 1783–1806.

Hovius, M., Kellenbach, M. L., Graham, K., Hodges, J. R., & Patterson, K. (2003). What does the object decision task measure? Reflections on the basis of evidence from semantic dementia. *Neuropsychology, 17,* 100–107.

Humphreys, G. W., Riddoch, M. J., & Quinlan, P. T. (1988). Cascade processes in picture identification. *Cognitive Neuropsychology, 5,* 67–103.

Kucera, H., & Francis, W. N. (1967). *Computational analysis of present-day American English.* Providence, RI: Brown University Press.

Lambon Ralph, M. A., Graham, K. S., Patterson, K., & Hodges, J. R. (1999). Is a picture worth a thousand words? Evidence from concept definitions by patients with semantic dementia. *Brain and Language, 70,* 309–335.

Lambon Ralph, M. A., & Howard, D. (2000). Gogi aphasia or semantic dementia? Simulating and assessing poor verbal comprehension in a case of progressive fluent aphasia. *Cognitive Neuropsychology, 17,* 437–465.

Mareschal, D. (2000). Infant object knowledge: Current trends and controversies. *Trends in Cognitive Science, 4,* 408–416.

McClelland, J. L., & Rogers, T. T. (2003). The Parallel Distributed Processing approach to semantic cognition. *Nature Reviews Neuroscience, 4,* 310–322.

Morrison, C. M., Chappell, T. D., & Ellis, A. W. (1997). Age of acquisition norms for a large set of object names and their relation to adult estimates and other variables. *Quarterly Journal of Experimental Psychology, 50A,* 528–559.

Moss, H. E., Tyler, L. K., Hodges, J. R., & Patterson, K. (1995). Exploring the loss of semantic memory in semantic dementia: Evidence from a primed monitoring study. *Neuropsychology, 9,* 16–26.

Patterson, K., & Behrmann, M. (1997). Frequency and consistency effects in a pure surface dyslexic patient. *Journal of Experimental Psychology: Human Perception and Performance, 23,* 1217–1231.

Patterson, K., & Hodges, J. R. (1992). Deterioration of word meaning: Implications for reading. *Neuropsychologia, 30,* 1025–1040.

Patterson, K., Suzuki, T., Wydell, T., & Sasanuma, S. (1995). Progressive aphasia and surface alexia in Japanese. *Neurocase, 1,* 155–165.

Plaut, D. C. (1997). Structure and function in the lexical system: Insights from distributed models of word reading and lexical decision. *Language and Cognitive Processes, 12,* 765–805.

Plaut, D. C., McClelland, J. L., Seidenberg, M. S., & Patterson, K. (1996). Understanding normal and impaired word reading: Computational principles in quasi-regular domains. *Psychological Review, 103,* 56–115.

Quinn, P. C. (2002). Early categorization: A new synthesis. In U. Goswami (Ed.), *Blackwell handbook of child cognitive development* (pp. 84–101). Oxford: Blackwell.

Riddoch, M. J., & Humphreys, G. W. (1987). Visual object processing in optic aphasia: A case of semantic access agnosia. *Cognitive Neuropsychology, 4,* 131–185.

Rogers, T. T., Garrard, P., Lambon Ralph, M. A., Bozeat, S., Hodges, J. R., McClelland, J. L., & Patterson, K. (in press). The structure and deterioration of semantic memory: A neuropsychological and computational investigation. *Psychological Review.*

Rogers, T. T., Hodges, J. R., Lambon Ralph, M. A., & Patterson, K. (2003). Object recognition under semantic impairment: The effects of conceptual regularities on perceptual decisions. *Language and Cognitive Processes, 18,* 625–662.

Rogers, T. T., & Plaut, D. C. (2002). Connectionist perspectives on category-specific deficits. In E. Forde & G. Humphreys (Eds.), *Category specificity in brain and mind* (pp. 251–289). Hillsdale, NJ: Psychology Press.

Saffran, E. M. (2000). The organization of semantic memory: In support of a distributed model. *Brain and Language, 71,* 4–212.

Saffran, E. M., & Schwartz, M. F. (1994). Of cabbages and things: Semantic memory from a neuropsychological perspective—a tutorial review. In C. Umiltà & M. Moscovitch (Eds.), *Attention and performance XV* (pp. 507–535). Hillsdale, NJ: Lawrence Erlbaum Associates Inc.

Schwartz, M. F., Marin, O. S. M., & Saffran, E. M. (1979). Dissociations of language function in dementia: A case study. *Brain and Language, 7,* 277–306.

Seidenberg, M. S., & McClelland, J. L. (1989). A distributed, developmental model of word recognition and naming. *Psychological Review, 96,* 523–568.

Smith, L. B. (2000). From knowledge to knowing: Real progress in infant categorisation. *Infancy, 1,* 91–97.

Smith, L. B., & Samuelson, L. K. (1997). Perceiving and remembering: Category stability, variability, and development. In K. Lamberts & D. Shanks (Eds.), *Knowledge, concepts, and categories* (pp. 93–131). Hove, UK: Psychology Press.

Snowden, J. S., Goulding, P. J., & Neary, D. (1989). Semantic dementia: A form of circumscribed cerebral atrophy. *Behavioural Neurology, 2,* 111–138.

Tarr, M., & Gauthier, I. (2000). FFA: A flexible fusiform area for subordinate-level visual processing automatized by expertize. *Nature Neuroscience, 3,* 754–769.

Tyler, L. K., & Moss, H. E. (1998). Going, going, gone…? Implicit and explicit tests of conceptual knowledge in a longitudinal study of semantic dementia. *Neuropsychologia, 36,* 1313–1323.

Ward, J., Stott, R., & Parkin, A. J. (2000). The role of semantics in reading and spelling: evidence for the "summation" hypothesis. *Neuropsychologia, 38,* 1643–1653.

Warrington, E. K. (1975). Selective impairment of semantic memory. *Quarterly Journal of Experimental Psychology, 27,* 635–657.

APPENDIX A

List of stimulus items in the OWT

Higher frequency				Lower frequency			
W > NW		NW > W		W > NW		NW > W	
Target	*Distractor*	*Target*	*Distractor*	*Target*	*Distractor*	*Target*	*Distractor*
drew	driew	view	vew	nod	knod	knob	nob
nice	knice	knife	nife	amiss	amyss	abyss	abiss
cheese	cheize	seize	seese	hum	humb	numb	num
cope	coap	soap	sope	legion	legeon	pigeon	pigion
pet	pebt	debt	det	grist	gryst	cyst	cist
goat	ghot	ghost	goast	sneer	sneir	weir	weer
dam	damb	lamb	lam	shrewd	shreud	feud	fewd
rot	racht	yacht	yot	nab	gnab	gnash	nash
soak	swoak	sword	sord	node	gnode	gnome	nome
rim	rimb	limb	lim	rile	ruile	guile	gile
garter	gartyr	martyr	marter	lackey	lhaki	khaki	kackey
grease	griece	niece	nease	dollop	dolyp	polyp	pollop
salve	psalve	psalm	salm	sine	scyne	scythe	sithe
fossil	fausil	sausage	sossage	gist	gyst	tryst	trist
vile	vaisle	aisle	ile	coffer	cophyr	zephyr	zeifer
pall	pawl	drawl	drall	booth	beuth	sleuth	slooth
bridal	bridyll	idyll	idal	graphic	grapphic	sapphire	saphire
partake	partaque	opaque	opake	conscript	conscrypt	crypt	cript

APPENDIX B

List of stimulus items in the OOT

R > NR		NR > R	
Target	Chimera	Target	Chimera
Higher familiarity			
fork	fork w/ no handle	kettle	kettle w/ no spout
table	table w/ piano lid added	scissors	scissors w/ straight handle
lorry	lorry w/ train undercarriage	comb	comb w/ handle added
clock	clock w/ spout added	train	train w/ lorry wheels
bus	bus w/ no wheels	umbrella	umbrella handle w/ stick attached
chisel	chisel w/ clothespin-handle	fish	fish w/ legs
cow	cow w/ mane and long neck	grand piano	grand piano w/ lid removed
sheep	sheep w/ seal flippers	bird	bird w/ pig head
hammer	hammer w/ plier-handles	horse	horse w/ short neck and no mane
racquet	racquet w/ umbrella handle	watering can	watering can w/ no spout
screwdriver	screwdriver w/ spanner handle	rabbit	rabbit w/ short ears
chicken	chicken w/ long neck	duck	duck w/ four legs
mouse	mouse w/ long ears	spanner	spanner w/ screwdriver-handle
squirrel	squirrel w/ webbed feet	rooster	rooster w/ four goat legs
fox	fox w/ no ears	goose	goose w/ short neck
Lower familiarity			
drum	drum w/ spout added	frog	frog w/ squirrel feet
pig	pig w/ bird head	pliers	pliers w/ straight handle
axe	axe w/ scissor-handles	swan	swan w/ short neck
monkey	monkey w/ elephant ears	seal	seal w/ sheep legs
goat	goat w/ two chicken legs	elephant	elephant w/ small ears
donkey	donkey w/ hump	turtle	turtle w/ ears added
lion	lion w/ no tail	yacht	yacht w/ wheels added
wagon	wagon w/ runners	eagle	eagle w/ ears added
raccoon	raccoon w/ no ears	helicopter	helicopter w/ wagon wheels
deer	deer w/ six legs	penguin	penguin w/ kangaroo head
leopard	leopard w/ long neck	clothespin	clothespin w/ handle added
giraffe	giraffe w/ seahorse body	camel	camel w/ no hump
kangaroo	kangaroo w/ penguin head	seahorse	seahorse w/ giraffe body
zebra	zebra w/ rhino horn	rhino	rhino w/ no horn
alligator	alligator w/ fins and no legs	ostrich	ostrich w/ tail added

COGNITIVE NEUROPSYCHOLOGY, 2004, 21 (2/3/4) 353–378

TEMPORALLY GRADED SEMANTIC MEMORY LOSS IN ALZHEIMER'S DISEASE: CROSS-SECTIONAL AND LONGITUDINAL STUDIES

Robyn Westmacott
University of Toronto and Baycrest Centre for Geriatric Care, Toronto, Canada

Morris Freedman
Baycrest Centre for Geriatric Care, Mount Sinai Hospital, University Health Network, and University of Toronto, Toronto, Canada

Sandra E. Black
Baycrest Centre for Geriatric Care and Sunnybrook and Women's College Health Sciences Centre, University of Toronto, Toronto, Canada

Kathryn A. Stokes
Baycrest Centre for Geriatric Care, Toronto, Canada

Morris Moscovitch
University of Toronto and Baycrest Centre for Geriatric Care, University of Toronto, Toronto, Canada

Semantic knowledge of famous names and words that entered popular North American culture at different times in the 20th century was examined in 16 patients with mild-to-moderate Alzheimer's disease (AD), 12 of whom were re-tested 1 year later. All patients showed evidence of temporally graded memory loss, with names and words from the remote past being relatively better preserved than recent names and words. There was considerable between-patient variability with respect to severity of semantic impairment. Most patients exhibited losses extending back 30–40 years; however, two mildly impaired (MMSE >28) patients showed deficits restricted to the last 10–15 years. At the 1-year follow-up, patients not only exhibited more severe deficits overall, but the temporally graded period of loss extended further back in time, suggesting that this deficit reflects a loss of previously intact knowledge and not merely faulty encoding or lack of exposure to the material. The extensive period of graded semantic loss exhibited by most patients contrasts with the temporally limited retrograde semantic loss typical of medial temporal lobe amnesia. We propose that short periods of temporally graded semantic memory loss can be explained by damage to medial temporal structures, but that extensive periods of graded loss occur only with additional damage to neocortical tissue. This pattern contrasts with that of autobiographical memory loss, which is often ungraded and extends for the person's entire lifetime, even when damage is restricted to the medial temporal lobes.

Correspondence should be addressed to Robyn Westmacott, Neuropsychology Clinic, 4F-414, Toronto Western Hospital, 399 Bathurst St., Toronto, Ontario, Canada (Email: robyn.westmacott@uhn.on.ca).

This work was funded by Medical Research Council grant MA-6694 to MM and a Canadian Institutes of Health Research Doctoral Scholarship to RW. MF was supported by the Saul A. Silverman Family Foundation, Toronto, Canada, as part of a Canada International Scientific Exchange Program (CISEPO) project. SEB was supported by CIHR grant MT13129. This research was conducted as part of RW's University of Toronto PhD thesis under the supervision of MM. We wish to thank the patients and their families for participating in this study, and to acknowledge gratefully the contributions of Gus Craik and Mary Pat McAndrews to this project. We also thank Matthew Lambon Ralph and one anonymous reviewer for their helpful comments and suggestions.

http://www.tandf.co.uk/journals/pp02643294.html

DOI:10.1080/02643290342000375

Eleanor Saffran's neuropsychological investigations have contributed extensively to our knowledge of the organisation of semantic memory and its neural substrates (for reviews, see Saffran, 1997; Saffran & Schwartz, 1994). One of us (MM) was a graduate student at the University of Pennsylvania when Ellie was a post-doctoral fellow there with Burton Roner, and Myrna Schwartz, Eleanor's long-time collaborator, was also a graduate student. In 1969 or 1970, Oscar Marin, a neurologist interested in cognition, ran a stimulating seminar with Paul Rozin and Burt Rosner on cognitive neurology, a term they coined to refer to the newly revived discipline. As I recall, the seminar met weekly in the evenings at Paul Rozin's house and it was there that many of us were introduced to the wonders and problems of the field, and to the excellent fare that Liz Rozin provided to accompany the discussions. In one of her earliest papers, Eleanor, Oscar Marin, and Myrna Schwartz (1976) documented the progressive deterioration of semantic memory in WLP, a patient who probably had semantic dementia. Although the study was not concerned directly with the nature of remote memory and consolidation, the findings suggested that the loss initially affected more difficult concepts presumably acquired late in life but eventually affected even simple concepts acquired in the remote past. Subsequent investigations of semantic dementia confirmed the generality of this finding (Lambon Ralph, Graham, Ellis, & Hodges, 1998), though it is not known whether it applies also to other forms of dementia. To our knowledge, however, no one has documented systematically the progressive loss of semantic memory longitudinally in Alzheimer's dementia and related it to theories concerning the interaction between the medial temporal lobes and neocortex in remote memory and consolidation. Although this study expands on a topic to which Eleanor's work only hinted, we hope that it will provide useful information for theories on the organisation of semantic memory and the brain, which was central to Eleanor's interests. In doing so, we hope that our paper honours the memory of an old colleague and friend.

Alzheimer's Disease (AD) is a neurodegenerative disorder characterised by anterograde amnesia in addition to severe retrograde memory loss encompassing knowledge of encyclopaedic facts and word meaning, public figures and events, personal facts, and autobiographical episodes (e.g., Greene, Hodges, & Baddeley, 1995; Hodges & Patterson, 1995). Typically, patients display a decline in general intellectual function as well as serious deficits in everyday memory and orientation of the self in time and place. The pathogenesis associated with AD is one of widespread, diffuse atrophy throughout the entire brain accompanied by focal damage to the entorhinal cortex, hippocampus and, in later stages of the disease, regions throughout the temporal, parietal, and frontal neocortex (e.g., Braak & Braak, 1991; Greene, Baddeley, & Hodges, 1996; Gregory & Hodges, 1996; Hodges, Patterson, Ward, Gerrard, Bak, & Perry, 1999). Pathology typically begins in the medial temporal and paralimbic (e.g., cingulate gyrus, basal forebrain) regions, and then extends outward to include widespread regions of neocortex; however, several atypical patterns of progression have been documented (Braak & Braak, 1991; Galton, Patterson, Zuereb, & Hodges, 2000).

The global cognitive decline, progressive course, and widespread pathology characteristic of AD distinguish it from the "classic" medial temporal lobe (MTL) amnesic syndrome. Moreover, there appear to be other, more subtle differences between these two patient populations with respect to patterns of retrograde amnesia. Autobiographical memory tends to be markedly impaired and temporally very extensive in both groups, and may even be more severely impaired in densely amnesic patients relative to AD patients in the early stages of the disease (Dell'Ora, della Salla, & Spinnler, 1989; Kapur, 1999; Moscovitch, 2001). In contrast, however, semantic memory for public figures and events, word meaning, encyclopaedic facts and autobiographical facts (personal semantics) tends to be more severely impaired in AD relative to MTL amnesia. Moreover, although both types of patients have been found to exhibit temporally graded memory loss with better preservation of remote relative to recent memories (e.g., Nadel &

Moscovitch, 1997; Reed & Squire, 1998; Sagar, Cohen, Sullivan, Corkin, & Growdon, 1988; Squire, 1992; Squire & Alvarez, 1995; Westmacott & Moscovitch, 2002), there is evidence to suggest that memory deficits are more likely to be temporally extensive (i.e., dating back 20 or more years) in AD than in MTL amnesia (see Fama et al., 2001; Greene & Hodges, 1996a; Hodges, Salmon, & Butters, 1993; and Kapur, 1999, for reviews). This is particularly true with respect to semantic memory, which, in MTL amnesia, is often impaired only for the 5–15-year time period prior to onset (e.g., Kapur, 1999; Reed & Squire, 1998; Westmacott & Moscovitch, 2002).[1]

Despite a general trend in the literature favouring the view that semantic memory loss is temporally graded in AD, there is considerable variability between patients with respect to the overall severity of the deficit and the extent and slope of the temporal gradient (Beatty, MacInnes, Porphyris, Trosfer, & Cermak, 1988; Fama et al., 2001; Greene & Hodges, 1996a; Hodges et al., 1993; Kapur, 1999; Kopelman, Stanhope, & Kingsley, 1999; Leplow, Dierks, Herrmann, Preper, Annacks, & Ulm, 1997a; Leplow et al., 1997b; Moscovitch, 1982; Sagar et al., 1988; Wilson, Kasdniak, & Fox, 1981). For example, some patients exhibit temporally limited semantic deficits for the last 5–10 years only, whereas others show temporally extensive deficits encompassing 35–40 years or more. Moreover, some studies suggest that semantic memory loss follows a "step-like function" (see Graham, 1999, for use of this term in reference to semantic dementia) as opposed to a true temporal gradient: that is, some patients show selective preservation of very remote semantic knowledge but perform equally poorly across all time periods for which they are amnesic (e.g., Greene & Hodges, 1996a; Leplow et al., 1997a, 1997b; Wilson et al., 1981). However, other studies have found evidence of a more gradual, temporally graded loss such that performance becomes increasingly poor as test items are drawn from more and more recent time periods (Beatty et al., 1988; Fama et al., 2001; Moscovitch, 1982; Sagar et al., 1988).

This variability is difficult to explain in the context of traditional consolidation theory and its assumption that all memories, be they episodic or semantic, become hippocampally independent after a fixed period of time (Alvarez & Squire, 1994; McClelland, McNaughton, & O'Reilly, 1995; Milner, 1966; Murre, 1997; Reed & Squire, 1998; Scoville & Milner, 1957; Squire, 1992; Squire & Zola, 1998; Squire & Zola-Morgan, 1991). According to this view, all post-consolidation memories should be equally vulnerable to neocortical damage. Multiple trace theory (MTT) (Moscovitch & Nadel, 1998; Nadel & Moscovitch, 1997, 2001) offers an alternative to consolidation theory. According to MTT, semantic and episodic memory are treated differently within the hippocampal and neocortical systems. Only episodic memory requires hippocampal complex participation and storage, for as long as the memory trace exists. Consequently, bilateral damage to the hippocampal complex leads to temporally extensive, and often ungraded, autobiographical, episodic memory loss (Nadel & Moscovitch, 1997, 1998, 2001; Nadel, Samsonovich, Ryan, & Moscovitch, 2000). Semantic memory, however, is dependent on the neocortex and can be acquired even with a badly damaged hippocampus as studies on patients with early MTL lesions indicate (by Vargha-Khadem, Gadian, Watkins, Connelly, Van Paesschen, & Mishkin, 1997). Normally, however, acquisition of semantic memory engages the hippocampus and, hence, benefits from the presence of an intact hippocampal system. All aspects of semantic memory are typically stored outside the hippocampal complex. According to MTT, damage to the hippocampal complex leads to a temporally limited and graded semantic memory loss, whereas

---

[1] In contrast, temporally extensive autobiographical memory loss is common in both AD and MTL amnesia (Greene et al., 1995; Kapur, 1999; Nadel & Moscovitch, 1997; Sagar et al., 1988), and often can encompass an entire lifetime (see also recent report by Corkin, 2002, on extensive retrograde amnesia in HM).

damage to the neocortex leads to a temporally extensive memory loss, which should be graded if older semantic memories are re-encoded more often than recent ones.

Other researchers have argued that consolidation should be viewed as a multi-stage process, wherein each stage has its own unique neural substrate (Bergin, Thompson, Baxendale, Fish, & Shorvon, 2000; Blake, Wroe, Breen, & McCarthy, 2000; Kapur, Millar, Colbourn, Abbott, Kennedy, & Docherty, 1997; O'Connor, Sieggreen, Ahern, Schomer, & Mesulam, 1997). However, findings regarding the timescale of this multistage process have been inconsistent, and it is not clear what methodological and/or individual subject factors determine whether a patient will exhibit a step-like or a smooth, temporally graded pattern of memory loss (Kapur, 1999). Furthermore, single-patient analyses examining the correlation between the temporal extent of semantic memory loss and performance on psychometric tests tapping various aspects of cognitive function have been inconclusive. Some studies suggest that semantic memory loss becomes more extensive as overall disease severity increases (e.g., Sagar et al., 1988), whereas others find no evidence of such a correlation (e.g., Fama et al., 2001; Greene & Hodges, 1996a). Understanding the relationships between integrity of semantic knowledge and other aspects of cognitive function is important because it addresses the distinction between global and selective deficits in patients with AD. Although the typical presentation of AD involves a general cognitive decline across many areas of function, atypical cases with very selective deficits (e.g., agnosia, aphasia, or apraxia exclusively) have been documented (e.g., Galton et al., 2000).

Inconsistencies in the neuropsychological literature on AD may reflect, in part, the cross-sectional design of the studies. For example, in a cross-sectional study, it is possible that failure to find a correlation between disease severity and extent of semantic retrograde amnesia reflects between-subject variability in numerous demographic and neurological factors. The longitudinal paradigm is a much more powerful tool for investigating patterns of cognitive decline in patients with neurodegenerative disease. However, few longitudinal studies of semantic memory loss in AD have been conducted (Garrard, Lambon Ralph, Watson, Powis, Patterson, & Hodges, 2001; Greene & Hodges, 1996b; Lambon Ralph, Patterson, & Hodges, 1997), and none has examined changes in temporally graded patterns of performance. Thus, the goal of the present study was to combine cross-sectional and longitudinal paradigms to explore what factors influence the temporal extent of semantic memory loss in AD, and how temporally graded patterns of performance change with disease progression. According to evidence from amnesic patients with damage restricted primarily to the MTL, retrograde amnesia for semantic memory should not extend back for more than 10 years (Westmacott & Moscovitch, 2002). Deficits beyond that time are likely to be a reflection of neocortical damage. If the deficits beyond that time are not graded, it would support the consolidation account, which states that all hippocampally independent memories are equally vulnerable. A graded effect, however, especially one that is exacerbated with disease progression, would suggest that processes intrinsic to the neocortex are primarily responsible for the effect observed beyond the 10-year period, and do not depend on the MTL. The way in which the neocortical component interacts with experience, and the implications of these findings for theories of memory, will be discussed at the end of the paper.

EXPERIMENT 1:
A CROSS-SECTIONAL STUDY OF TEMPORALLY GRADED SEMANTIC MEMORY LOSS IN AD

Semantic knowledge of 20th-century famous names and English vocabulary terms was assessed using the stimuli and experimental tasks described by Westmacott and Moscovitch (2002). The famous names and vocabulary words were categorised into hemi-decades (1940–present) according to when they first entered popular North American culture. The experimental tasks varied along the implicit–explicit continuum with respect to the type of cognitive processing required for performance. Participants began with memory tests involving implicit processing (speeded reading and pronunciation of names and words) and progressed through a series of tasks placing increasingly greater demand upon explicit memory (e.g., recognition, categorisation). In order to obtain the most accurate measure of semantic knowledge possible, all of the tasks were designed to place little demand on the strategic processing and verbal production skills of the participants. This is particularly important when investigating patients with pronounced deficits in language or strategy formation, such as those with AD.

Participants

Sixteen patients who met the NINCDS-ARRDA criteria for probable Alzheimer's disease (McKhann, Drachman, Folstein, Katzman, Price, & Stadlan, 1984) participated in Experiment 1. All of the patients were determined by a neurologist to be in the mild-to-moderate impairment category (i.e., MMSE of 18/30 or greater). Due to the wide range of ages, patients were divided into two groups: Group 1 (61–72 years old) and Group 2 (73–84 years old). However, because there were no significant differences between the groups with respect to task performance, the results were collapsed across age. The demographic and neuropsychological profile of the patient group is presented in Table 1.

Two groups of control subjects were selected to match the two AD groups with respect to age, educational background, and handedness. Control Group 1 consisted of 16 right-handed subjects, 8 male and 8 female, between the ages of 62 and 72 years (M = 65.8 years); on average, subjects had completed 12.3 years of education. Control Group 2 consisted of 16 right-handed subjects, 8 male and 8 female, between the ages of 73 and 85 (M = 77.4); on average, subjects had completed 12.1 years of education. None of the subjects included in the control groups had a history of neurological, medical, or psychological impairment. Again, data were collapsed across age as there were no significant performance differences between the groups.

Materials and experimental tasks

The stimulus set consisted of 480 names of famous people and 360 vocabulary words from the 20th century (1940–1999) classified into 5-year time periods according to when they first became popular. The names were grouped according to the 5-year time period within which they first became famous. An attempt was made to restrict the stimulus set to individuals whose fame was of limited duration such that it did not extend far beyond one particular time period. Prior to data collection, time period classifications were verified by asking a group of 15 healthy individuals (none of whom participated in any of the subsequent experiments) between 50 and 70 years of age to indicate the 5-year time period in which each famous person achieved his or her peak fame. Each of the twelve 5-year time periods from 1940 through to the present contained a total of 40 famous names, 10 associated with each of 4 categories: arts (i.e., actors, musicians, authors), athletics, politics, and miscellaneous. Stimuli were equated for familiarity (frequency) across time periods (see Westmacott & Moscovitch, 2002). In addition, a large set of distracter items was constructed using nonfamous names representing the same range of nationalities as the experimental stimuli (see Westmacott & Moscovitch, 2002). The following tasks were designed to assess semantic memory.

Speeded reading of famous names. Fifteen famous names from each time period were selected for inclusion in the reading times task. A comparison set of 15 nonfamous names was constructed for each time period by scrambling the first and last names within each subset of famous names. Thus, the sets of famous and nonfamous names for each time period contained the exact same set of first and last names; however, these names were arranged into pairs differently for the two sets. This design permitted direct comparisons between the time taken to read famous and nonfamous names.

The subsets of famous and nonfamous (scrambled) names were presented in typed columns on

Table 1. *Demographic and neuropsychological profile of the 16 AD patients, divided into two groups based on age: Group 1 (61–72 yrs) and Group 2 (73–84 yrs)*

	Group mean	SD	Min	Max
Age	74.31	6.05	61	84
Yrs since diagnosis	4.06	1.85	1	8
Yrs education	13.23	3.36	8	21
MMSE (/30)	23.82	3.84	18	30
DRS—total (/144)	115.37	7.45	104	128
Attention (/37)	33.71	1.46	31	36
Initiat./Persev. (/37)	28.47	4.83	21	37
Construction (/6)	5.22	0.79	4	6
Conceptualization (/39)	34.53	3.31	27	39
Memory (/25)	15.06	2.57	11	21
NART [1] (standard score)	108.15	10.54	94	122
WAIS-III Vocab (scaled score)	9.76	2.37	6	14
Boston Naming (/60)	38.59	9.54	24	53
Semantic fluency [2] (raw score)	9.26	4.29	3	20
CVLT				
Acquisition (*T*-score)	29.68	10.05	9	43
Short delay (*Z*-score)	−1.85	0.88	−4	−1
Long delay (*Z*-score)	−2.11	0.96	−4	−0.5
Recog. Discrim. (*Z*-score)	−2.98	1.49	−5	0
Letter fluency [3] (raw score)	33.68	10.73	20	52
WAIS-III				
Digits fwd (%ile)	75.47	10.16	48	99
Digits bkwd (%ile)	31.53	32.32	1	82
WCST				
Categories (/6)	2.32	1.56	0	5
Persev. Resp. (*Z*-score)	2.05	0.37	0.5	5

[1] For five of the patients, NART scores were replaced by scores on the WRAT-III Reading subtest.
[2] Score is based on the number of animal names produced in 1 minute.
[3] Score is based on the total number of words produced for the letters F, A, and S when given 1 minute for each.
MMSE = Mini Mental State Exam; DRS = Dementia Rating Scale; NART = National Adult Reading Test; WAIS-III = Wechsler Adult Intelligence Scale-III; CVLT = California Verbal Learning Test; WCST = Wisconsin Card Sorting Test.

separate sheets of paper. In addition, three practice lists, each consisting of 15 nonfamous names, were constructed from the set of distracters; there was no overlap between the practice items and the experimental items. Participants were asked to read out loud each list of names as quickly and accurately as possible. Reading times, in seconds, were recorded for each list using a stopwatch. Participants' reading accuracy and the ease with which each list was read were also noted. Difference scores were calculated for each time period by subtracting the mean reading time for famous names from the mean reading time for nonfamous names. If the subject hesitated for an extended period of time during the reading because of distractibility or poor attention, timing was stopped and resumed when the subject began reading again. If the subject made an initial pronunciation error but subsequently corrected him or herself, timing continued but no error was recorded.

Recognition of famous names in a three-alternative forced-choice task. The same set of famous names was used. Each of these 180 famous names was paired with 2 nonfamous names matched with respect to gender and ethnicity. These nonfamous distracter names were not scrambled pairs of famous names, thereby rendering the task more sensitive in its ability to detect existing semantic representations of the famous individuals. These 180 name triplets were presented to subjects one at a time and in random order. Subjects were told that only one of the three presented names belonged to a famous individual and were asked to identify which one it was by pointing to the appropriate name. Subjects did not receive any feedback regarding their performance.

Classification of famous names into the correct category. The same set of famous names was used in the famous name classification task. Each name, selected randomly and presented individually, was matched with three category descriptors (e.g., Canadian politician, Hollywood actor, poet) such that only one descriptor provided an accurate description of the famous individual. Participants were asked to point to the most appropriate category descriptor.

Matching of famous last names with the correct first names. Fifteen famous names from each time period were selected from the original stimulus set for inclusion in the matching task. This set of famous names was completely nonoverlapping with respect to the set used in the previous tasks These famous first name–last name pairs were matched with two alternate first names in terms of gender and ethnicity. Subjects were presented with a famous last name (e.g., Clinton) and were asked

to choose the correct first name from a set of three possibilities (e.g., Sam, Bill, Bob).

Matching movies or television programs with the correct actor. One hundred and twenty titles of motion pictures or television programmes were selected, 10 from each time period. Each title was matched with the name of the starring actor along with two other names of famous individuals. One name belonged to another famous actor from the given time period who did not star in the target movie or television show (i.e., incorrect condition); the other name belonged to a famous individual from the given time period who is (was) not an actor (i.e., unrelated condition). The three names were matched with respect to gender. Participants were asked to select the name of the actor starring in the movie or television programme.

Speeded reading of vocabulary terms. Fifteen English vocabulary terms from each time period were selected for inclusion in the reading times task. A comparison set of 15 pseudowords was constructed for each time period by scrambling the syllables within each subset of vocabulary terms. Thus, the sets of real words and pseudowords for each time period contained the exact same set of speech sounds; however, these syllables were arranged differentially into word units for the two sets. This design permitted direct comparisons to be made between the time taken to read real words as opposed to pseudowords.[2] Three practice lists, each consisting of 15 pseudowords, were constructed such that there was no overlap with any of the experimental items. Reading times, in seconds, were recorded for each list using a stopwatch. Participants' reading accuracy and the ease with which each list was read were also noted. Difference scores were calculated for each time period by subtracting the mean reading time for real words from the mean reading time for pseudowords.

---

[2] We acknowledge that the baseline task used for the vocabulary reading task (pseudowords) is considerably more difficult than that used for the famous names reading task (scrambled names), and this may account for the larger difference scores obtained in the vocabulary reading task. However, because we are not attempting to make any comparisons between performance on vocabulary reading and famous name reading, this issue does not affect the interpretation of our findings—namely, the presence of a temporal gradient in patients' performance.

Timing was paused if subjects became distracted during list reading and self-corrected mispronunciations were not scored as errors.

Recognition of vocabulary terms. Each vocabulary word was paired with two pseudowords, and the combination was presented individually and in random order. Subjects were told that only one of the three terms was an actual English word and they were asked to identify it by pointing.

Definitions of vocabulary terms. For each of the English vocabulary terms identified correctly in the forced-choice recognition task, the participant was asked to provide a brief description or definition. Definitions were scored as correct or incorrect; no discrimination was made between responses of different quality, as the goal of the task was to determine whether or not the participant had some knowledge of each word's meaning. Null responses were accepted.

Results

Controls

Means and standard deviations for controls in each of the experimental tasks are presented by time period in Table 2. Three averaged performance scores were calculated: famous name knowledge (average performance across the name recognition, categorisation, matching, and TV/movie tasks); vocabulary knowledge (average performance across the word recognition and definition tasks); and overall performance (average performance across all six tasks included in the first two averaged scores).[3] Performance on the speeded reading tests was analysed separately. Analysis of variance found no significant differences in control subjects' performance across time periods for any of the tasks, $F(1, 13) < 1, p > .05$ for all analyses. Furthermore, time series analysis found no evidence of a linear

trend in performance in any of the experimental tasks, $F(1, 13) < 1, p > .05$ for all analyses.

AD patients

As with controls, average scores for famous name knowledge, vocabulary knowledge, and overall performance were calculated (Figure 1). Average scores on the name and word speeded reading tasks are presented in Figure 2. As a group, AD patients' knowledge of famous names and vocabulary words was markedly impaired relative to controls. Performance followed a smooth temporal gradient, with higher explicit memory scores for remote items than for recent items; this pattern was consistent across tasks (see Table 3 for ANOVAs and time series analyses for each task). However, examination of the individual patient data (see Appendix A) revealed considerable between-subject variability with respect to both the overall severity and the temporal extent of the deficit. Separate analyses of variance performed on each patient's explicit memory performance data for famous names (averaged across the name recognition, name categorisation, name matching, and TV/movie tasks) and words (averaged across the word recognition and word definition tasks) revealed a significant influence of time period for all 16 patients.[4] In three patients, a deficit was apparent for the last 10–15 years only, with performance in, or near, the normal range for all other time periods. Eight patients exhibited a deficit that extended back 20–30 years, with near-normal performance for only the most remote time periods. The five remaining patients demonstrated very extensive temporally graded deficits, affecting items from all time periods. Seven patients demonstrated deficits for famous names and words that were roughly equivalent in terms of severity and temporal extent, whereas eight patients were more impaired for names. Only one patient performed better on words than on names.

---

[3] Data from the two speeded reading tasks were not included in the averaged performance scores because they did not use a percentage scale. Only tasks for which percentage correct could be calculated were included in these averaged scores.

[4] Space restrictions mean that, statistical analyses for each patient individually are not presented; they are available from the authors upon request.

Table 2. *Control subjects' knowledge of famous names and vocabulary words—means and standard deviations by time period*

Task	1940	1945	1950	1955	1960	1965	1970	1975	1980	1985	1990	1995	Average
Speeded name reading[a] *(sec)*													
Mean	6.1	6.3	6.2	6.4	6.2	6.2	6.1	6.3	6.4	6.2	5.9	6.1	6.2
SD	1.2	0.9	1.0	0.8	1.0	1.0	1.1	1.2	0.9	1.1	0.9	0.9	1.0
Name pronunciation errors /15													
Mean	0.7	0.5	0.5	0	0	0.4	0	0	0.4	0.5	0.6	0.7	0.4
SD	0.07	0.03	0.03	0	0	0.01	0	0	0.01	0.03	0.05	0.05	0.02
Name recognition													
Mean	93.2%	94.3%	94.3%	95.3%	94.7%	94.6%	95.6%	95.3%	94.3%	94.1%	93.7%	95.3%	94.5%
SD	4.6%	4.2%	4.2%	4.4%	4.6%	5.0%	4.7%	4.4%	4.8%	4.3%	5.1%	4.2%	4.5%
Name categorisation													
Mean	91.2%	93.8%	93.8%	93.8%	93.5%	94.2%	94.6%	94.9%	93.8%	93.8%	93.2%	94.1%	93.7%
SD	4.4%	4.3%	4.3%	5.2%	4.7%	4.6%	4.4%	5.1%	5.2%	4.9%	4.7%	5.0%	4.7%
First–last name matching													
Mean	92.7%	93.3%	93.3%	94.8%	94.6%	94.1%	94.8%	95.1%	94.8%	94.1%	93.6%	93.8%	94.1%
SD	4.2%	4.4%	4.6%	4.3%	5.2%	4.7%	5.7%	4.4%	5.1%	4.4%	5.1%	4.8%	4.7%
T.V./movie-actor matching													
Mean	89.2%	90.3%	92.1%	91.6%	91.8%	93.3%	92.8%	92.8%	91.7%	90.5%	90.3%	90.7%	91.4%
SD	4.1%	4.6%	4.4%	4.4%	4.6%	4.4%	4.6%	4.9%	4.2%	4.5%	4.9%	5.1%	4.5%
Speeded word reading[b] *(sec)*													
Mean	9.4	9.9	10.2	9 .9	10.2	10.1	9.9	9.8	10.1	10.1	10.0	10.1	10.0
SD	1.1	1	0.9	1.1	1.2	1.2	0.9	1.0	1.3	1.0	1.1	1.1	1.1
Word pronunciation errors													
Mean	0.4	0.2	0	0	0	0.3	0	0	0.4	0.2	0.3	0.2	0.2
SD	0.01	0.01	0	0	0	0.01	0	0	0.02	0.01	0.01	0.01	0.01
Word recognition													
Mean	96.6%	97.5%	97.5%	97.5%	97.5%	98.3%	98.6%	97.5%	97.5%	97.5%	98.3%	97.5%	97.6%
SD	3.3%	4.1%	3.3%	4.3%	4.3%	3.4%	4.2%	2.3%	3.1%	3.3%	3.4%	3.4%	3.5%
Word definition													
Mean	96.0%	96.9%	96.5%	96.9%	95.4%	97.5%	97.5%	95.8%	95.6%	95.6%	96.1%	96.1%	96.3%
SD	4.2%	5.0%	4.3%	4.3%	4.8%	3.4%	3.3%	4.3%	4.8%	4.8%	3.7%	4.5%	4.6%
Averaged name tasks													
Mean	91.6%	92.9%	93.5%	93.8%	93.7%	94.0%	94.4%	94.5%	93.6%	93.1%	92.7%	93.5%	93.4%
SD	4.3%	4.4%	4.4%	4.6%	4.8%	4.7%	4.9%	4.7%	4.8%	4.5%	5.0%	4.8%	4.6%
Averaged words tasks													
Mean	96.4%	97.2%	97.9%	97.2%	96.5%	97.9%	98.0%	96.7%	96.5%	96.5%	97.2%	96.8%	97.0%
SD	3.7%	4.5%	3.8%	4.37%	4.6%	3.4%	3.8%	3.3%	3.9%	4.0%	3.6%	3.9%	4.1%

[a]Scrambled minus famous.
[b]Pseudoword minus word.

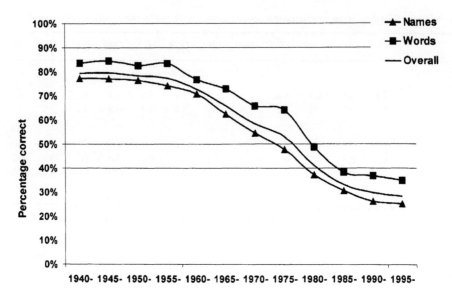

Figure 1. *AD patients' knowledge of famous names and vocabulary terms from across the 20th century: Performance at initial testing.*

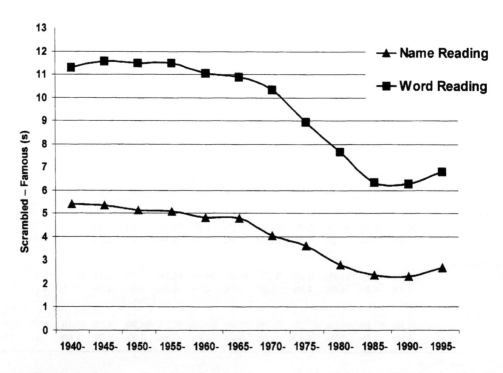

Figure 2. *AD patients' performance on the speeded reading tests for famous names and vocabulary terms. The times presented are difference scores (scrambled minus famous).*

Table 3. *The influence of time period on AD patients' knowledge of famous names and words—results from ANOVA and time series analysis by task*[a]

Task	ANOVA	Time series
Name recognition	12.87	138.91
Name categorisation	14.42	149.87
Name matching	17.61	184.99
TV/movie	17.34	184.62
Word recognition	11.44	115.75
Word definition	11.71	119.62
Name reading	6.49	65.50
Word reading	6.64	62.96

[a] All results significant at the .01 level (2-tailed).

In order to explore the demographic and neuro-psychological factors associated with explicit knowledge of famous names and vocabulary words, correlation and simultaneous multiple regression analyses were performed. In addition to time since diagnosis and education level, performance scores on a number of standardised neuropsychological tests tapping overall mental status, premorbid intellectual capacity, episodic memory, semantic memory, language, and executive function were evaluated as predictor variables (Table 4). Overall performance on the names and words tasks was significantly correlated with time since diagnosis, and performance on the Mini-Mental State Exam, the Dementia Rating Scale (total and Initiation subscale), the National Adult Reading Test, the Vocabulary subtest of the Wechsler Adult Intelligence Scale-III, the Boston Naming Test, semantic fluency (animals), and letter fluency (FAS). After correcting for multiple correlations using the Bonferonni adjustment, years since diagnosis, MMSE, Boston Naming, semantic fluency, and letter fluency remained significantly correlated with overall performance. Correlation patterns were identical when performance for famous names and vocabulary terms were examined separately (Table 4), except that letter fluency was not significantly correlated with famous name performance after correcting for multiple correlations.

Multiple regression analysis on the overall (names and words) explicit memory scores resulted in a two-factor model (R^2 = 0.837), $F(1, 15)$ = 35.98, $p < .0001$, with MMSE (r_p = .720) and Boston Naming (r_p = .696) as predictors. A virtually identical model including MMSE (r_p = .716) and Boston Naming (r_p = .587) was found to predict performance on famous names (R^2 = 0.797), $F(1, 15)$ = 27.50 , $p < .0001$. Performance on vocabulary words was predicted best by a similar model including Boston Naming (r_p = .724) and MMSE (r_p = .620) as predictors (R^2 = 0.786), $F(1, 15)$ = 30.37, $p < .0001$. Finally, AD patients, overall, made few false recognitions and few false word definitions (M = 2.50%, SD = 3.82%; and M = 5.49%, SD = 5.70%, respectively). Despite these low rates overall, patients appeared to make more false recognitions for recent items than remote items. This was confirmed by statistical analysis: for all tasks, percentage of false recognitions/definitions differed significantly across time periods (all $p < .05$), with evidence from time series analyses of a temporal gradient (all $p < .05$). There were no significant correlations between false recognitions/definitions and any of the demographic or neuropsychological factors included in the analysis. Moreover, multiple regression analysis failed to find a significant predictive model.

Discussion

There was no evidence that the integrity of semantic knowledge was temporally graded in control subjects between the ages of 65 and 85 years, nor was there any evidence of age differences in overall performance. Across all tasks, controls performed equally well on famous names and vocabulary words from all time periods. In contrast, as predicted, the AD patients, as a group and individually, exhibited greater knowledge of famous names and vocabulary words from remote time periods than those from recent time periods. The same temporally graded pattern was evident across all tasks, regardless of whether the information was being elicited explicitly (e.g., confident recognition) or implicitly (e.g., speeded reading). However, there was considerable variability between patients with respect to the overall severity and temporal extent of the deficit. Some patients exhibited marked deficits for names and words from the last 10–15 years only, whereas

Table 4. *Correlations between time since diagnosis, years of education, performance on standardised neuropsychological tests in AD patients' knowledge of famous names and vocabulary terms*

Predictor variable	Names	Words	Overall
Yrs since diagnosis	−.618**	−.570**	−.602**
Yrs education	.167	.188	.200
MMSE (/30)	.831**	.779**	.827**
DRS—total (/144)	.553*	.501*	.521*
Attention (/37)	−.407	−.432	−.419
Initiat./Persev. (/37)	.538**	.495*	.547*
Construction (/6)	.081	−.133	−.052
Conceptualisation (/39)	.373	.322	.353
Memory (/25)	.458	.336	.423
NART[1] (standard score)	.523*	.557*	.533*
WAIS-III Vocab (scaled score)	.486*	.551*	.512*
Boston Naming (/60)	.764**	.834**	.813**
Semantic fluency[2] (raw score)	.643**	.726**	.699**
CVLT			
Acquisition (*T*-score)	.180	.303	.255
Short delay (*Z*-score)	.164	.248	.230
Long delay (*Z*-score)	.180	.303	.255
Recog. hits (*Z*-score)	−.017	.062	−.006
Recog. discrim. (*Z*-score)	.133	.063	.109
Letter fluency[3] (raw score)	.540*	.637**	.578**
WAIS-III			
Digits fwd (%[ile])	.171	.274	.230
Digits bkwd (%[ile])	.140	.200	167
WCST			
Categories (/6)	−.004	−.017	−.015
Persev. resp. (*Z*-score)	.040	−.108	−.026

* Correlation is significant at the .05 level (2-tailed); ** Correlation is significant at the .05 level (2-tailed) after Bonferonni adjustment.

other patients exhibited impairments that extended back 35–40 years or more. Still, even the most severely impaired patients demonstrated a *relative* sparing of very remote semantic memories, even if absolute levels of performance were significantly lower than that of controls across all time periods.

If all post-consolidation, hippocampally independent semantic memories were equivalent with respect to vulnerability to damage, then one would predict a "step-like" function with poor performance on recent items and relatively preserved memory (with a flat gradient) across all remote time periods. However, this was not found. Fourteen of the 16 patients exhibited performance patterns that followed a smooth, gradual, temporal gradient extending across all time periods, although there was variation in the slope of this gradient. The other two patients demonstrated more of a step function in their performance, with intact knowledge of names and words except for those from the most recent 10–15 years. Of note, these two patients were least severely impaired on standardised neuropsychological tests.

This finding is consistent with the results of the regression analysis: poorer performance on experimental tasks was associated with lower measures of general cognitive status (DRS, MMSE), language ability (Boston Naming, WAIS-III Vocabulary) and verbal fluency, and with longer time since diagnosis. These findings are intriguing because AD involves a combination of medial temporal and neocortical damage with a typical pattern of progression such that pathology begins in the transentorhinal region and gradually spreads to lateral temporo-parietal and widespread neocortical regions (Braak & Braak, 1991; Galton et al., 2000). There is considerable evidence to suggest that amnesic patients with damage restricted largely to the MTL demonstrate a limited period of semantic retrograde amnesia—typically, 10 years or less for vocabulary and, perhaps, slightly more extensive for famous faces and public events (Fujii, Moscovitch, & Nadel, 2000; Kapur, 1999; Reed & Squire, 1998; Squire, 1992; Squire et al., 1984; Verfaellie, Reiss, & Roth, 1995; Westmacott & Moscovitch, 2002). Our findings (and, to some extent, those of others: Beatty et al., 1988; Fama et al., 2001; Greene & Hodges, 1996a; Hodges et al., 1993, Leplow et al., 1997a, 1997b; Moscovitch, 1982; Sagar et al., 1988) suggest that time-limited semantic retrograde amnesia may also be characteristic of early AD, but that the deficit continues to extend back further in time as the disease progresses, sparing only very remote memories. Thus, even when the disease has progressed to involve widespread neocortical regions, very remote semantic memories may be more resistant to damage than more recent, yet fully consolidated, memories. This interpretation is more consistent with the multi-stage consolidation hypothesis (Bergin et al., 2000; Blake et al., 2000; Kapur et al., 1997; O'Connor et al., 1997) than with traditional consolidation theory (Reed & Squire, 1998; Squire, 1992).

Not all studies, however, have found a relationship between the integrity of semantic knowledge and measures of general cognitive function, language skills, and verbal fluency (e.g., Fama et al., 2001; Greene & Hodges, 1996a; Kapur, 1999). It is possible that inconsistencies in the literature may reflect intersubject variability in disease progression. Although there is considerable evidence for the typical pattern of progression described above, atypical profiles are not uncommon among AD patients and are likely to have unique neuropsychological correlates (Galton et al., 2000). No clear demographic or clinical differences between the present group of patients and those from previous studies are apparent. However, neither our study nor previous studies have examined the integrity of semantic knowledge in individual patients relative to their specific lesion profile. Future research using volumetric and voxel-based morphometric analyses of magnetic resonance imaging (MRI) data would permit further investigation of these hypotheses by attempting to correlate patients' neuropathological and neuropsychological profiles.

EXPERIMENT 2: A LONGITUDINAL STUDY OF TEMPORALLY GRADED SEMANTIC MEMORY LOSS IN AD

In Experiment 2, a longitudinal paradigm was used to examine directly the hypothesis that semantic retrograde amnesia becomes more temporally extensive with the progression of AD. It was predicted that, 1 year after the initial testing session, patients would show a global decline in performance on tests of famous names and vocabulary words, and that their deficits would extend back further in time to involve more remote time periods.

Participants

Twelve of the patients from Experiment 1 participated in a one-year follow-up study. The mean interval between testing sessions was 13.2 months (range = 12.0–14.5 months).

Materials and experimental tasks

The materials and experimental tasks were identical to those of Experiment 1.

Results

The same three averaged performance scores were calculated for each patient at one-year follow-up. Overall, there was a noticeable decline in patients' performance from time one to time two on the famous name tasks (average decline of 12% across patients and name tasks) and the vocabulary word tasks (average decline of 13% across patients and word tasks; Figure 3); $F(1, 11) = 45.87, p < .0001$. However, there was a significant interaction between test session (first or second) and time period, indicating that the extent to which performance declined over time varied depending on the remoteness of the items, $F(11, 121) = 3.63, p < .01$. This interaction is illustrated in Figure 4, which shows the average percentage decline for names and words by time period. Performance declined most for items from 1955–1979, and remained relatively stable across the two testing sessions for items from 1940–1954. Performance on items from 1980 to the present also showed relatively little decline, probably due to poor (near floor) performance on these items at initial testing. Planned comparisons revealed that, for both names and words, this decline in performance was significant for all time periods (all $p < .01$) with the exception of 1940–1944 and 1945–1949.

Analysis of individual subject data (Figure 5)[5] revealed a significant decline in overall performance for famous names in all 12 patients, whereas performance for vocabulary words declined significantly in only 3 patients. Data from the speeded reading tests are not presented but followed a similar pattern. Specifically, there was evidence of decline in famous names for 11 of 12 patients, but

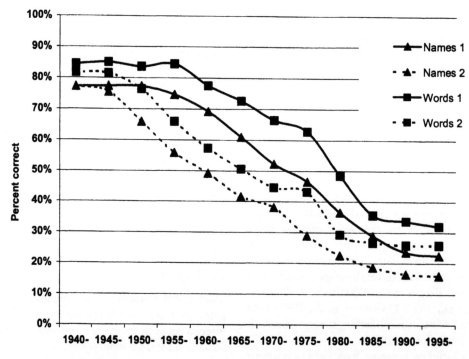

Figure 3. *A comparison of AD patients' knowledge of famous names and vocabulary terms at initial testing (time 1) and at a follow-up session one year later (time 2).*

---

[5] Longitudinal data are presented for only 2 of the 12 patients. Data for the remaining patients are available from the authors.

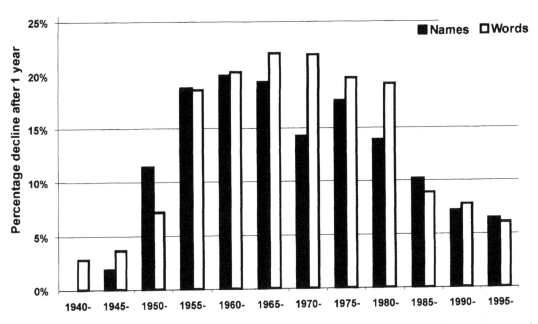

Figure 4. *Percentage decline between time 1 and time 2 in AD patients' knowledge of famous names and vocabulary terms from across the 20th century.*

evidence of decline in vocabulary for only 7 patients. The absence of a significant decline in vocabulary knowledge for the other 9 patients may be due, in part, to lack of statistical power—there were only two indices of vocabulary knowledge (word recognition and definition), whereas there were four indices of famous name knowledge. Moreover, a significant interaction between time period and testing session was found for famous names in all 12 patients, and for words in 11 patients. Consistent with the finding of a significant interaction in the averaged data, the individual patient data suggest that performance decline after 1 year was not equivalent across time periods, which could account for the absence of a significant overall decline in vocabulary knowledge in some patients. Alternatively, because words may be encountered and encoded more frequently than names, they may be more resistant to deterioration.

The longitudinal performance patterns of the individual patients (Figure 5) indicate that the finding of a significant interaction between time period and testing session reflects a trend toward more extensive temporal gradients in performance

at 1-year follow-up. That is, performance was not simply more impaired at follow-up; the impairment appeared to extend back further in time such that time periods that were relatively preserved at the first testing session were noticeably more impaired at the second testing session. In general, across patients, very remote knowledge (1940–1950) remained relatively stable across the two testing sessions, even when performance in other time periods declined markedly. Figure 5a illustrates this pattern in one individual patient. A similar pattern was demonstrated clearly in nine other patients; the remaining two patients exhibited loss after 1 year that was more evenly spread across all time periods (Figure 5).

Discussion

One year after the initial testing session, semantic knowledge of famous names and vocabulary words had declined significantly for most, but not all, of the AD patients. The fact that patients were no longer familiar with names and words that were known 1 year earlier indicates that their deficits do

(a)

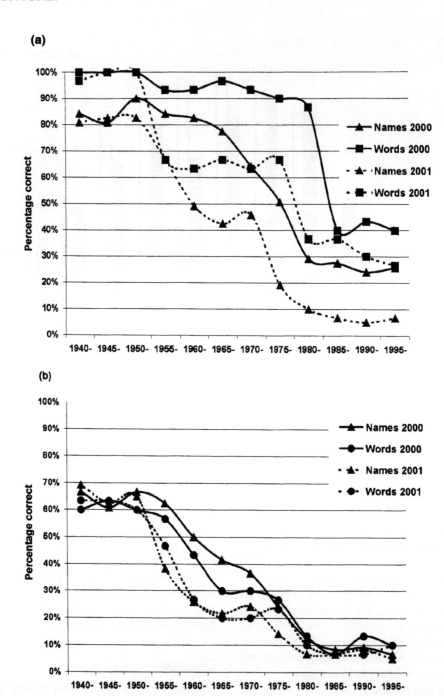

(b)

Figure 5. *The change in individual patients' knowledge of famous names and vocabulary terms after 1 year. (a) The performance of one patient who exhibited a more extensive temporal gradient in knowledge of famous names and vocabulary words at the 1-year follow-up. Nine additional patients showed a similar pattern. (b) The performance of one patient who demonstrated decline in performance across all time periods. Only one other patient showed a similar pattern.*

not merely reflect anterograde memory problems (i.e., faulty encoding of new information) or a lack of exposure to the stimuli. Moreover, performance declined even when information was elicited implicitly (i.e., speeded reading), suggesting that the deficits are not merely due to a failure to access knowledge. Rather, these findings provide clear evidence of a loss or degradation of knowledge that was previously intact. These results are more consistent with those who favour a degradation account of semantic memory impairment in AD (e.g., Butters, 1984; Butters & Cermak, 1996; Chan, Salmon, Butters, & Johnson, 1995; Hodges et al., 1993; Salmon, Butters, & Chan, 1999), than those who believe that the impairment reflects primarily a failure to access the information that remains available, if not wholly intact (e.g., Nebes, 1989; Nebes & Brady, 1990; Nebes & Halligan, 1995).

Of note, the decline in the patients' performance was not consistent for names and words across all time periods. The difference in performance between the two testing sessions was minimal for very remote (i.e., 1940–1954) and very recent (i.e., 1990–present) items, and most pronounced for items from the intermediate time periods. This provides further evidence of the strength and resiliency of very remote semantic memories. Moreover, it is consistent with the hypothesis that post-consolidation semantic memories differ from one another with respect to their vulnerability to damage following brain injury. Specifically, recently consolidated semantic memories, although less vulnerable than newly-acquired pre-consolidation memories, appear to be more susceptible to the effects of brain damage than memories consolidated many years ago. This suggests that semantic memories continue to be strengthened and elaborated throughout the course of their existence, even after the consolidation process is complete. Alternatively, the ability to consolidate and assimilate new information may decline progressively with age and experience, both because the neural structures may be less plastic and because previous learning may bias the system against forming new representations (Ellis & Lambon Ralph, 2000).

GENERAL DISCUSSION

Several important findings emerged from the present studies. First, despite considerable between-subject variability in the severity and temporal extent of semantic memory loss, AD patients were found to exhibit temporally graded semantic memory loss, such that remote information was preserved better than recent information. This is consistent with some previous findings (Beatty et al., 1988; Fama et al., 2001; Greene & Hodges, 1996a; Hodges et al., 1993; Kapur, 1999; Leplow et al., 1997a, 1997b; Sagar et al., 1988; Squire et al., 1984; Wilson et al., 1981) and with the fundamental tenets of all theories reviewed in the introduction (Bergin et al., 2000; Blake et al., 2000; Kapur, 1999; Kapur et al., 1997; Kopelman et al., 1999; Nadel & Moscovitch, 1997, 1998, 2001; Nadel et al., 2000; O'Connor et al., 1997; Reed & Squire, 1998; Squire, 1992; Squire & Zola, 1998). The present findings pertain not only to the initial acquisition and consolidation of semantic memories, but also to the continued transformation of these memories across the lifetime. In addition to being temporally graded, the semantic memory deficits exhibited by most of the AD patients were temporally extensive, covering a period of 40–50 years or more. Because these deficits were found also on implicit (nondeclarative) tests, it suggests a true memory loss rather than mere inaccessibility of semantic representations. When interpreted in the context of studies documenting temporally limited semantic deficits in patients with damage localised to the MTL, these findings provide support for the hypothesis that temporally extensive semantic memory loss occurs only in the presence of neocortical damage. Moreover, they suggest that post-consolidation semantic memories vary in their susceptibility to the effects of brain damage, depending on the length of time since acquisition. Specifically, semantic memories appear to become increasingly resilient over time. We found that the rate of deterioration of semantic memory decreased as information was sampled from more remote time periods.

We offer two interpretations of these findings that are not mutually exclusive, and indeed that may complement each other. The first is that the results can be taken as evidence that semantic memories continue to be strengthened, perhaps due to continued elaboration and re-encoding, even after the initial consolidation process is complete, making them increasingly resilient to the effects of brain damage (Nadel & Moscovitch, 1997, 1998; Squire et al., 1984). The second is that plasticity diminishes with age, either because initial memory representations configure memory systems in their favour and bias them against assimilating new representations (Ellis & Lambon Ralph, 2000) or because the physical neural substrate that comprises these memory systems loses its malleability with time (Moscovitch & Winocur, 1992). We discuss these hypotheses at greater length below.

The second important finding is that AD patients' knowledge of famous names and vocabulary/slang terms was associated with length of illness and measures of overall cognitive status, language ability, and verbal fluency, but not with measures of episodic memory or executive function. The failure to find significant correlations between semantic knowledge and performance on tests of episodic memory and executive function has been consistent across studies. Less consistent, however, have been findings regarding the relationships between semantic knowledge of famous people, time since diagnosis, overall cognitive status, language ability, and verbal fluency (Fama et al., 2001; Greene & Hodges, 1996a; Sagar et al., 1988). Our findings suggest that semantic memory loss in AD occurs as part of a generalised cognitive decline that also impairs language and verbal fluency. In contrast, deficits in episodic memory are less strongly associated with overall cognitive function, and can occur independently of semantic memory deficits. However, in patients with atypical patterns of progression, it may be possible to observe a dissociation between semantic memory and general

cognitive status (Galton et al., 2000); such individual differences in disease progression may account partly for the discrepant findings in the literature. Although our sample did not differ from those of previous studies with respect to demographic and neuropsychological factors, neuroradiological data were not available for all patients, so it is not possible to determine if individual differences in neuropathology were related to behavioural performance. Studying individual differences in AD, and attempting to correlate the neuropathological course of the disease with the manifestation of selective versus global cognitive deficits in individual patients, promises to provide insight into the nature of this disease and into the neural mechanisms mediating various cognitive functions in the healthy brain. Noticeable deficits in semantic memory were apparent also in the early stages of AD. Even the least impaired patients demonstrated significantly lower levels of performance than controls on recent famous names and vocabulary words, consistent with previous studies examining knowledge of famous people and public events (e.g., Greene & Hodges, 1996a; Hodges & Patterson, 1995; Kapur, 1999; Moscovitch, 1982).[6] Knowledge of famous names and vocabulary terms deteriorated markedly over the course of one year for most patients. Declining performance on tests of semantic knowledge, when interpreted in the broader context of a given patient's cognitive-behavioural profile, may be indicative of neurodengenerative disease and, specifically, AD. Psychometric data were not available for the second testing session, so it was not possible to relate changes in performance on standardized neuropsychological tests to deterioration of semantic knowledge. Similarly, lack of quantitative MRI data during the year makes it difficult to ascribe changes in cognitive function to neuroanatomy. We hope to address these issues directly in future studies.

---

[6] However, to our knowledge, this is the first demonstration of temporally graded deficits in vocabulary (common words and slang) in AD patients.

Temporally graded remote semantic memory loss: Implications for theories of memory and consolidation

If semantic memories undergo a relatively short period of hippocampal consolidation, after which they are independent and fully integrated within neocortical networks, as consolidation theory predicts, then why do recently consolidated memories appear to be more vulnerable than those consolidated many years ago? One possibility it that there is a second, more gradual process of integration that takes place within the neocortex aided by the hippocampus (Squire et al., 1984) or after the hippocampally mediated consolidation process is complete. Kapur et al. (1997) and others (Bergin et al., 2000; Blake et al., 2000; O'Connor et al., 1997) have proposed a multiple-stage process of consolidation, with early stages mediated predominately by hippocampus proper and later stages mediated by perihippocampal regions (perirhinal, parahippocampal, entorhinal) and their interactions with surrounding neocortex. However, the timescale of this proposed multi-stage consolidation process was on the order of a few months to a few years, not decades, as in our study.

The present findings suggest that semantic memories undergo an even longer, more gradual process of integration and elaboration such that, throughout the lifetime, semantic memories continue to become stronger and less vulnerable to the effects of brain damage. We do not know if this process is largely dependent upon the passage of time or on continual strengthening and elaboration of memory traces, which are likely to be modulated by factors such as the frequency with which a particular semantic memory is retrieved/reactivated after initial encoding, and the extent to which these reactivated memories are actively processed in relation to newly acquired information. In turn, these retrieval factors are likely to be closely related to the autobiographical significance and emotional salience of the memory, with highly significant and salient information being more likely to be reactivated and processed deeply (Snowden, Griffiths, & Neary, 1996, 1999; Westmacott,

Leach, Freedman, & Moscovitch, 2001; Westmacott, Black, Freedman, & Moscovitch, in press).

This hypothesis is consistent with the multiple trace theory's proposal regarding remote semantic memory. (Moscovitch, 2002; Moscovitch & Nadel, 1998; Nadel & Moscovitch, 1997; Nadel, Ryan, Hayes, Gilboa, & Moscovitch, in press). According to MTT, neocortical structures are sufficient to form domain-specific and semantic representations based on regularities extracted from repeated experiences with words, names, people, objects, and situations. Whereas each autobiographical memory trace is unique, the creation of multiple, related traces facilitates (but is not necessary for) the extraction of the neocortically-mediated information that is common among them, and that is shared with other episodes. This information is then integrated with pre-existing knowledge to form semantic memories that can exist independently of the hippocampal complex. Thus, vocabulary and facts about the world, about people, and events that are acquired in the context of a specific episode are separated from it in neocortex and ultimately stored independently of it. Each encounter with the semantic information adds to this store of knowledge and strengthens it.

As a result, the older semantic memories will have more (or stronger) representations and be more fully integrated into the semantic structure than more recent memories. This process of increased semanticisation may give the impression of prolonged consolidation, though it is a different process. More neocortical damage, therefore, is needed to affect older than newer semantic memories, which accounts for the temporally graded and extensive semantic memory loss observed in our study. Accordingly, remote memories for personal and public semantics, and even for the gist of events and environmental schemata, are not dependent on the continuing function of the hippocampal complex, as are episodic (autobiographical) memories (Rosenbaum, Winocur, & Moscovitch, 2001). Instead, the hippocampal complex is needed only temporarily, until the memory is represented permanently in neocortical structures specialised in processing the information and capable of being modified while doing so.

On the surface, it would seem that, except for timescale, the MTT account of retrograde amnesia for semantic memory is not distinguishably different from that of standard consolidation theory. There are, however, some additional, important differences. According to the standard model, the memory that is held temporarily in the medial temporal lobes is identical to the memory that is stored permanently in neocortex. Indeed, many believe that prolonged consolidation affects a transfer of the same memory from one location to another by strengthening neocortical connections (see Kandel, 2001, p. 1038). MTT assumes, on the other hand, that the temporary, medial temporal memory is fundamentally different from the permanent, neocortical one. The former retains its episodic flavour, such that the semantic content is tied to the temporal-spatial (autobiographical) context in which it was acquired (Rosenbaum et al., 2001). The latter is stripped of its episodic context and retains only the semantic core. By this view, prolonged consolidation refers to the establishment of a neocortical, episode-free semantic trace that can survive on its own; it does not entail the loss of the episodic trace that remains linked to the MTL, nor does it imply that the two traces are identical (see McClelland et al., 1995; Murre, Graham, & Hodges, 2001, for review of models of retrograde amnesia). Indeed, according to MTT, the two types of fundamentally different memories can coexist, so that one can have both an episodic and semantic representation of the same name, event, object, or fact, and one can lose one kind of representation without losing the other. Recent studies on patients with semantic dementia (Graham, Pratt, & Hodges, 1998; Snowden, Griffiths, & Neary, 1994, 1996) and amnesia (Westmacott et al., 2001; Westmacott & Moscovitch, 2003; Westmacott, Black, Freedman, & Moscovitch, in press) supports this prediction (see also review by Rosenbaum et al., 2001, on the application of these ideas to studies of nonhuman species).

Implications for theories of word frequency and age-of-acquisition effects

Our findings also speak to theories concerned with effects of frequency and age-of-acquisition (AoA) in the organisation of the lexicon (Bell, Davies, Hermann, & Walters, 2000; Ellis & Lambon Ralph, 2000; Hirsch & Funnell, 1995; Hodgson & Ellis, 1998; Kremin, Hamerel, Dordain, De Wilde, & Perrer, 1999; Kremin et al., 2001; Lambon Ralph et al., 1998; Silveri, Cappa Paolo, & Maria, 2002; Zevin & Seidenberg, 2002). The interpretation we offer, based on MTT, suggests that it is difficult to disentangle the effects of frequency from the effects of AoA. Older words benefit not only from the effects of time, but also because they are likely to be reactivated more often than recent words and, thereby, form stronger and more extensive representations in semantic memory. At the same time, the older memories have a disproportionately greater influence on the configuration of semantic networks, making it difficult for newer memories to be integrated unless their representations are compatible with the configuration. Ellis and Lambon Ralph (2000) have developed a computational model of reading based on these ideas, and "lesioned" their connectionist network after training by resetting a proportion of the connections to and from hidden units to zero with probabilities ranging from .05 to .20. In simulating the operation of this lesioned network, they found a temporal gradient reflecting errors in generating an output pattern for a given input pattern that is similar to the one we observed in our study.

A recent study by Zevin and Seidenberg (2002) is also consistent with some of the predictions derived from our interpretation, though it is not fully consistent with results obtained by some computational models of reading. They found no AoA effects, if frequency effects are properly controlled. There was also little evidence of AoA in computational models if the words used exhibit normal spelling–sound regularities. If, however, early and late words do not overlap in terms of orthography or phonology, AoA are observed, suggesting that AoA effects are observed when what is learned about early patterns does not carry over to later ones. Because there are no published norms for famous names and for most of the words used in our study, we collected our own by having normal matched controls rate them for familiarity (frequency) and other variables (Westmacott & Moscovitch, 2002). Based on these familiarity ratings, we selected words and names so that familiarity was equated across all time periods. Our finding of a temporal gradient showing that more recent words were more severely affected by dementia suggests that AoA influences performance. Moreover, equivalent gradients were found both in reading and in identification. One interpretation of our finding is that the words and names we used are novel, having entered the language only since 1940, and some much more recently than that. As a result they may not overlap in orthography and phonology with the larger corpus of words in the lexicon. Although this interpretation would account for the reading effect, it cannot account for the effects of identification of the items. Indeed, our results suggest that the word's semantic and lexical representations are highly inter-related. Such an interpretation is compatible with Ellis and Lambon Ralph's (2000) model and simulation for items whose frequency is equivalent across all time periods (their Figure 17, pp. 118–119). Alternatively, what appears to be an AoA effect may actually reflect the accumulated lifetime frequency of the words and names, with older ones having a higher lifetime frequency, though currently they are judged to have the same familiarity as the more recent words. Studies are being conducted to test these hypotheses (Caza & Moscovitch, 2003).

Implications for studies on the reminiscence bump

Memories acquired during late adolescence/early adulthood are particularly robust and easily accessible. Known as the "reminiscence bump," this finding has been discussed extensively in the autobiographical memory literature for years (Crovitz & Schiffman, 1974; Howes & Katz, 1992; Jansari & Parkin, 1996; Rubin & Schulkind, 1997a, 1997b; Rybash & Monaghan, 1999). The present findings suggest that a reminiscence bump may also occur for semantic memory. Memories acquired during the reminiscence bump period may be particularly robust due to more frequent reactivation, more extensive integration within neocortical networks, and/or greater personal or emotional significance. With respect to the last option, in previous studies (Westmacott & Moscovitch, 2003) we found that remote famous names were more likely to hold personal significance for subjects relative to equally familiar recent famous names. Moreover, this "autobiographical significance" resulted in a performance advantage for particular names on tests of episodic and semantic memory. The nature and underlying mechanisms of the reminiscence bump remain unclear, however, and further research is required to determine whether or not it is relevant to the study of semantic memory.

Conclusion

In summary, our findings suggest that recent memories are particularly vulnerable to the effects of early AD pathology; this may be attributable to a combination of encoding deficits and disruption of the consolidation process resulting from MTL damage. Once consolidated, semantic memories may be relatively impervious to MTL damage. However, these consolidated memories still may be susceptible to neocortical damage, with vulnerability decreasing over time as memories continue to be elaborated, strengthened, and more deeply integrated into broader conceptual networks as they are reactivated repeatedly through conscious (and perhaps also unconscious) retrieval processes. The degree to which a particular semantic memory continues to be strengthened may depend on the simple passage of time, the frequency with which it is reactivated, and the proportion of reactivations that are explicit and conscious.

Thus, expanding on the principles of multiple trace theory, we argue that both autobiographical and semantic memories continue to be strengthened, elaborated, and re-encoded in the context of previously acquired and newly acquired memories. The critical difference between autobiographical and semantic memory is that this ongoing process requires the MTL in the case of the former but not the latter. However, semantic memories that have particular autobiographical significance are an exception to this general rule—these semantic memories, like autobiographical memories, depend continually upon the MTL because of their rich contextual details and episodic associations and their heightened emotional salience (Westmacott et al., in press; Westmacott & Moscovitch, 2003).

REFERENCES

Alvarez, P., & Squire, L. R. (1994). Memory consolidation and the medial temporal lobe: A simple neural network model. *Proceedings of the National Academy of Sciences, 91,* 7401–7045.

Beatty, W. W., MacInnes, W., Porphyris, H., Troster, A., & Cermak, L. S. (1988). Preserved topographical memory following right temporal lobectomy. *Brain and Cognition, 8,* 67–76.

Bell, B. D., Davies, K. G., Hermann, B. P., & Walters, G. (2000). Confrontation naming after anterior temporal lobectomy is related to age of acquisition of the object names. *Neuropsychologia, 38,* 83–92.

Bergin, P. S., Thompson, P. J., Baxendale, S. A., Fish, D. R., & Shorvon, S. D. (2000). Remote memory in epilepsy. *Epilepsia, 41,* 231–239.

Blake, R. V., Wroe, S. J., Breen, E. K., & McCarthy, R. A. (2000). Accelerated forgetting in patients with epilepsy: Evidence for impairment in memory consolidation. *Brain, 123,* 472–483.

Braak, H., & Braak, E. (1991). Neuropathological staging of Alzheimer-related changes. *Acta Neuropathologica, 82,* 239–259.

Butters, N. (1984). The clinical aspects of memory disorders: Contributions from experimental studies of amnesia and dementia. *Clinical Neuropsychology, 6,* 17–36.

Butters, N., & Cermak, L. S. (1986). A case study of the forgetting of autobiographical knowledge: Implications for the study of retrograde amnesia. In D. C. Rubin (Ed.), *Autobiographical memory* (pp. 253–272). Cambridge: Cambridge University Press

Caza, N., & Moscovitch, M. (2003). *Cumulative frequency, not age of acquisition, affects lexical decision of older adults and patients with Alzheimer's Disease.* Manuscript submitted for publication.

Chan, A. S., Salmon, D. P., Butters, N., & Johnson, S. A. (1995). Semantic network abnormality predicts rate of cognitive decline in patients with probable Alzheimer's disease. *Journal of the International Neuropsychological Society, 1,* 297–303.

Cipolotti, L., Shallice, T., Chan, D., Fox, N., Scahill, R., Harrison, G., Stevens, J., & Rudge, P. (2001). Long-term retrograde amnesia: The crucial role of the hippocampus. *Neuropsychologia, 39,* 151–172

Corkin, S. (2002). What's new with amnesic patient HM? *Nature Reviews: Neuroscience, 3,* 153–160.

Crovitz, H. F., & Schiffman, H. (1974). Frequency of episodic memories as a function of their age. *Bulletin of the Psychonomic Society, 4,* 519–521.

Dall'Ora, P., della Sala, S., & Spinnler, H. (1989). Autobiographical memory: Its impairment in amnesia syndromes. *Cortex, 25,* 197–217.

Ellis, A. W., & Lambon Ralph, M. A. (2000). Age of acquisition effects in adult lexical processing reflect loss of plasticity in maturing systems: Insights from connectionist networks. *Journal of Experimental Psychology: Learning, Memory, and Cognition, 26,* 1103–1123.

Fama, R., Shear, P. K., Marsh, L., Yesavage, J. A., Tinklenberg, J. R., Lim, K. O., Pfefferbaum, A., & Sullivan, E. V. (2001). Remote memory for public figures in Alzheimer's disease: Relationships to regional cortical and limbic brain volumes. *Journal of the International Neuropsychological Society, 7,* 384–390.

Fujii, T., Moscovitch, M., & Nadel, L. (2001). Consolidation, retrograde amnesia, and the temporal lobe. In F. Boller & J. Grafman (Eds.), L. S. Cermak, (Section Ed.), *The handbook of neuropsychology* (Vol. 4). Amsterdam: Elsevier.

Galton, C. J., Patterson, K., Xuereb, J. H., & Hodges, J. R. (2000). Atypical and typical presentations of Alzheimer's disease: A clinical, neuropsychological, neuroimaging and pathological study of 13 cases. *Brain, 123,* 484–498.

Garrard, P., Lambon Ralph, M. A., Watson, P. C., Powis, J., Patterson, K., & Hodges, J. R. (2001). Longitudinal profiles of semantic impairment for living and nonliving concepts in dementia of Alzheimer's type. *Journal of Cognitive Neuroscience, 13,* 892–909.

Graham, K. S. (1999). Semantic dementia: A challenge to the multiple-trace theory? *Trends in Cognitive Sciences, 3*, 85–87.

Graham, K. S., Pratt, K. H., & Hodges, J. R. (1998). A reverse temporal gradient for public events in a single case of semantic dementia. *Neurocase, 4*, 461–470.

Greene, J. D. W., Baddeley, A. D., & Hodges, J. R. (1996). Analysis of the episodic memory deficit in early Alzheimer's disease: Evidence from the Doors and People Test. *Neuropsychologia, 13*, 537–551.

Greene, J. D. W., & Hodges, J. R. (1996a). Identification of famous faces and famous names in early Alzheimer's disease: Relationship to anterograde episodic and general semantic memory. *Brain, 119*, 111–128.

Greene, J. D. W., & Hodges, J. R. (1996b). The fractionation of remote memory: Evidence from a longitudinal study of dementia of Alzheimer type. *Brain, 119*, 129–142.

Greene, J. D. W., Hodges, J. R., & Baddeley, A. D. (1995). Autobiographical memory and executive function in early dementia of Alzheimer type. *Neuropsychologia, 12*, 1647–1670.

Gregory, C. A., & Hodges, J. R. (1996). Clinical features of frontal temporal lobe dementia in comparison with Alzheimer's disease. *Journal of Neural Transmission, 47*, 103–123.

Hirsch, K. W., & Funnell, E. (1995). Those old familiar things: Age of acquisition, familiarity and lexical access in progressive aphasia. *Journal of Neurolinguistics, 9*, 23–32.

Hodges, J. R., & Patterson, K. (1995). Is semantic memory consistently impaired early in the course of Alzheimer's disease? Neuroanatomical and diagnostic implications. *Neuropsychologia, 33*, 441–459.

Hodges, J. R., Patterson, K., Ward, R., Garrard, P., Bak, T., Perry, R., et al. (1999). The differentiation of semantic dementia and frontal lobe dementia (temporal and frontal variants of frontotemporal dementia) from early Alzheimer's disease: A comparative neuropsychological study. *Neuropsychology, 13*, 31–40.

Hodges, J. R., Salmon, D. P., & Butters, N. (1993). Recognition and naming of famous faces in Alzheimer's disease: A cognitive analysis. *Neuropsychologia, 31*, 775–788.

Hodgson, C., & Ellis, A. W. (1998). Last in, first to go: Age of acquisition and naming in the elderly. *Brain and Language, 64*, 146–153.

Howes, J. L., & Katz, A. N. (1992). Remote memory: Recalling autobiographical and public events from across the lifespan. *Canadian Journal of Psychology, 46*, 92–116.

Jansari, A., & Parkin, A. J. (1996). Things that go bump in your life: Explaining the reminiscence bump in autobiographical memory. *Psychology and Aging, 11*, 85–91.

Kandel, E. R. (2001). The molecular biology of memory storage: A dialog between genes and synapses. *Bioscience Reports, 21*, 565–611.

Kapur, N. (1999). Syndromes of retrograde amnesia: A conceptual and empirical synthesis. *Psychological Bulletin, 6*, 800–825.

Kapur, N., Millar, J., Colbourn, C., Abbott, P., Kennedy, P., & Docherty, T. (1997). Very long-term amnesia in association with temporal lobe epilepsy: Evidence for multiple-stage consolidation processes. *Brain and Cognition, 35*, 58–70.

Kopelman M. D., Stanhope N., & Kingsley, D. (1999). Retrograde amnesia in patients with diencephalic, temporal lobe or frontal lesions. *Neuropsychologia 37*, 939–58

Kremin, H., Hamerel, M., Dordain, M., De Wilde, M., & Perrier, D. (1999). Age of acquisition and name agreement as predictors of mean response latencies in picture naming of French adults. *Brain and Cognition, 41*, 396–401.

Kremin, H., Perrier, D., De Wilde, M., Dordain, M., Le Bayon, A., Gatignol, P., Rabine, C., Corbinuea, M., Lehoux, E., & Arabia, C. (2001). Factors predicting success in picture naming in Alzheimer's disease and primary progressive aphasia. *Brain and Cognition, 46*, 180–183.

Lambon Ralph, M. A., Graham, K. S., Ellis, A., & Hodges, J. R. (1998). Naming in semantic dementia: What matters? *Neuropsychologia, 36*, 775–784.

Lambon Ralph, M. A., Patterson, K., & Hodges, J. R. (1997). The relationship between naming and semantic knowledge for different categories in dementia of Alzheimer's type. *Neuropsychologia, 35*, 1251–1260.

Leplow, B., Dierks, C. H., Herrmann, P., Pieper, N., Annecke, R., & Ulm, G. (1997a). Remote memory in Parkinson's disease and senile dementia. *Neuropsychologia, 35*, 547–557.

Leplow, B., Dierks, C. H., Lehnung, M., Kenkel, S., Behrens, C. H. R., Frank, G., & Mehdorn, M. (1997b). Remote memory in patients with acute brain injuries, *Neuropsychologia, 35*, 881–892.

McClelland, J. L., McNaughton, B. L., & O'Reilly, R. C. (1995). Why there are complementary learning systems in the hippocampus and neocortex: Insights from the successes and failures of connectionist models of learning and memory. *Psychological Review, 102,* 419–457.

McKhann, G., Drachman, D., Folstein, M., Katzman, R., Price, D., & Stadlan, E. M. (1984). Clinical diagnosis of Alzheimer's disease: Report of the NINCDS-ADRDA work group under the auspices of Department of Health and Human Services task force on Alzheimer's disease. *Neurology, 34,* 939–945.

Milner, B. (1966). Amnesia following operation on the temporal lobe. In C. W. M. Whitty & O. L. Zangwill (Eds.), *Amnesia.* London: Butterworth.

Moscovitch, M. (1982). Multiple dissociation of function in the amnesic syndrome. In L. S. Cermak (Ed.), *Human memory and amnesia.* Hillsdale, NJ: Lawrence Erlbaum Associates Inc.

Moscovitch, M. (1995). Recovered consciousness: A hypothesis concerning modularity and episodic memory. *Journal of Clinical and Experimental Neuropsychology, 17,* 276–290.

Moscovitch, M. (2001). Amnesia. In N. J. Smesler, & P. Baltes (Eds.), R. F. Thompson & J. L. McClelland (Section Eds.), *International encyclopaedia of social and behavioural sciences.* Oxford: Elsevier.

Moscovitch, M. (2002). Consolidation: A systems approach to remote memory and the interaction between the hippocampal complex and neocortex. In L. Nadel (Ed.), *The encyclopedia of cognitive science.* New York: MacMillan.

Moscovitch, M., & Nadel, L. (1998). Consolidation and the hippocampal complex revisited: In defense of the multiple-trace model. *Current Opinion in Neurobiology, 8,* 297–300.

Moscovitch, M., & Nadel, L. (1999). Multiple-trace theory and semantic dementia: Response to K. S. Graham. *Trends in Cognitive Sciences, 3,* 87–89.

Moscovitch, M., & Winocur, G. (1992). The neuropsychology of memory and aging. In F. I. M. Craik & T. A. Salthouse (Eds.), *The handbook of aging and cognition* (pp. 315–372). Hillsdale, NJ: Lawrence Erlbaum Associates Inc.

Murre, J. M. J. (1997). Implicit and explicit memory in amnesia: Some explanations and predictions by the Trace Link model. *Memory, 6,* 675–684.

Murre, J. M. J., Graham, K. S., & Hodges, J. R. (2001). Semantic dementia: Relevance to connectionist models of long-term memory. *Brain, 124,* 647–675.

Nadel, L., & Moscovitch, M. (1997). Memory consolidation, retrograde amnesia and the hippocampal complex. *Current Opinion in Neurobiology, 7,* 217–227.

Nadel, L., & Moscovitch, M. (1998). Hippocampal contributions to cortical plasticity. *Neuropharmacology, 37,* 431–439.

Nadel, M., & Moscovitch, M. (2001). The hippocampal complex and long-term memory revisited. *Trends in Cognitive Neuroscience, 5,* 228–230.

Nadel, L., Ryan, L., Hayes, S., Gilboa, A., & Moscovitch, M. (in press). The role of the hippocampal complex in long-term episodic memory. In T. Ono, G. Matsumoto, R. R. Lllinas, A. Berthoz, R. Norgren, H. Nishijo, & R. Tamura (Eds.), *Limbic and association cortical systems—basic, clinical and computational aspects.* Amsterdam: Elsevier Science, Excerpta Medica International Congress Series.

Nadel, L., Samsonovich A., Ryan, L., & Moscovitch, M. (2000). Multiple trace theory of human memory: Computational, neuroimaging, and neuropsychological results. *Hippocampus, 10,* 352–368.

Nebes, R. D. (1989). Semantic memory in Alzheimer's disease. *Psychological Bulletin, 106,* 377–394.

Nebes, R. D., & Brady, C. B. (1990). Preserved organization of semantic attributes in Alzheimer's disease. *Psychology and Aging, 5,* 574–579.

Nebes, R. D., & Halligan, E. M. (1995). Contextual constraint facilitates semantic decisions about object pictures by Alzheimer patients. *Psychology and Aging, 10,* 190–196.

O'Connor, M., Sieggreen, A., Ahern, G., Schomer, D., & Mesulam, M. (1997). Accelerated forgetting in association with temporal lobe epilepsy and paraneoplastic encephalitis. *Brain and Cognition, 35,* 71–84.

Reed, J. M., & Squire, L. R. (1998). Retrograde amnesia for facts and events: Findings from four new cases. *Journal of Neuroscience, 18,* 3943-3954.

Rosenbaum, R. S., Winocur, G., & Moscovitch, M. (2001). New views on old memories: Reevaluating the role of the hippocampal complex. *Behavioral Brain Research, 127,* 183–197.

Rubin, D. C., & Schulkind, M. D. (1997a). Properties of word cues for autobiographical memory. *Psychological Reports, 81,* 47–50.

Rubin, D. C., & Schulkind, M. D. (1997b). Distribution of important and word-cued autobiographical memories. *Psychology and Aging, 12,* 524–535.

Rybash, J. M., & Monaghan, B. E. (1999). Episodic and semantic contributions to older adults' autobiographical recall. *Journal of General Psychology, 126,* 85–96.

Saffran, E. M. (1997). Aphasia: Cognitive neuropsychological aspects. In T. E. Feinberg & M. J. Farah (Eds.), *Behavioral neurology and neuropsychology* (pp. 151–165). New York: McGraw Hill.

Saffran, E. M., & Schwartz, M. F. (1994). Of cabbages and things: Semantic memory from a neuropsychological perspective: A tutorial review. In C. Umiltà & M. Moscovitch (Eds.), *Attention and performance XV: Conscious and non-conscious processes.* Cambridge, MA: MIT Press.

Saffran, E. M., Schwartz, M. F., & Marin, O. S. M. (1976). Semantic mechanisms in paralexia. *Brain and Language, 3,* 255–265.

Sagar, H. J., Cohen, N. J., Sullivan, E. V., Corkin, S., & Growdon, J. H. (1988). Remote memory function in Alzheimer's disease and Parkinson's disease. *Brain, 111,* 185–206.

Salmon, D. P., Butters, N., & Chan, A. S. (1999). The deterioration of semantic memory in Alzheimer's disease. *Canadian Journal of Experimental Psychology, 53,* 108–117.

Schwartz, M. F., Marin, O. S. M., & Saffran, E. M. (1979). Dissociation of language function in dementia. *Brain and Language, 7,* 277–306.

Scoville, W. B., & Milner, B. (1957). Loss of recent memory after bilateral hippocampal lesions. *Journal of Neurology, Neurosurgery and Psychiatry, 20,* 11–21.

Silveri, M. C., Cappa, A., Paolo, M., & Maria, P. (2002). Naming in patients with Alzheimer's disease: Influence of age of acquisition and categorical effects. *Journal of Clinical and Experimental Neuropsychology, 24,* 755–764.

Snowden, J. S., Griffiths, H. L., & Neary, D. (1994). Semantic dementia: Autobiographical contribution to preservation of meaning. *Cognitive Neuropsychology, 11,* 265–288.

Snowden, J. S., Griffiths, H. L., & Neary, D. (1996). Semantic-episodic memory interactions in semantic dementia: Implications for retrograde memory function. *Cognitive Neuropsychology, 13,* 1101–1137.

Snowden, J. S., Griffiths, H. L., & Neary, D. (1999). The impact of autobiographical experience on meaning: Reply to Graham, Lambon Ralph, and Hodges. *Cognitive Neuropsychology, 16,* 673–687.

Squire, L. R. (1992). Memory and the hippocampus: A synthesis from findings with rats, monkeys and humans. *Psychological Review, 99,* 195–231.

Squire, L. R., & Alvarez, P. (1995). Retrograde amnesia and memory consolidation: A neurobiological perspective. *Current Opinion in Neurobiology, 5,* 169–177.

Squire, L. R., & Zola-Morgan, S. (1991). The medial temporal lobe memory system. *Science, 253,* 1380–1386.

Squire, L. R., & Zola, S. M. (1998). Episodic memory, semantic memory, and amnesia. *Hippocampus, 8,* 205–211.

Vargha-Khadem, F., Gadian, D. G., Watkins, K. E., Connelly, A., Van Paesschen, W., & Mishkin, M. (1997). Differential effects of early hippocampal pathology on episodic and semantic memory. *Science, 277,* 376–380.

Verfaellie, M., Reiss, L., & Roth, H. L. (1995). Knowledge of new English vocabulary in amnesia: An examination of premorbidly acquired semantic memory. *Journal of the International Neuropsychological Society, 1,* 443–453

Warrington, E. K. (1996) Studies of retrograde memory: A long-term view. *Proceedings of the National Academy of Sciences, USA, 93,* 13523–13526.

Warrington, E. K., & Sanders, H. I. (1971). The fate of old memories. *Quarterly Journal of Experimental Psychology, 23,* 432–42

Westmacott, R., Black, S. E., Freedman, M., & Moscovitch, M. (in press). The contribution of autobiographical experience to semantic memory: Evidence from Alzheimer's disease, semantic dementia, and amnesia. *Neuropsychologia.*

Westmacott, R., Leach, L., Freedman, M., & Moscovitch, M. (2001). Different patterns of autobiographical memory loss in semantic dementia and medial temporal lobe amnesia: A challenge to the consolidation theory. *Neurocase, 7,* 37–55.

Westmacott, R., & Moscovitch, M. (2002). Temporally graded retrograde memory loss for famous names and vocabulary terms in amnesia and semantic dementia: Further evidence for opposite gradients using implicit memory tests. *Cognitive Neuropsychology, 19,* 135–163.

Westmacott, R., & Moscovitch, M. (2003). The contribution of autobiographical experience to semantic memory. *Memory and Cognition, 31,* 761–774.

Wilson, R. S., Kaszniak, A. W., & Fox, J. H. (1981). Remote memory in senile dementia. *Cortex, 17,* 41–48.

Zevin, J. D., & Seidenberg, M. S. (2002). Age of acquisition effects in word reading and other tasks. *Journal of Memory and Language, 47,* 1–29.

Zola-Morgan, S., Squire, L. R., & Amaral, D. G. (1986). Human amnesia and the medial temporal region: Enduring memory impairment following a bilateral lesion limited to field CA1 of the hippocampus. *Journal of Neuroscience, 6,* 2950–2967.

APPENDIX A

AD patients' knowledge of famous names and vocabulary words at the initial testing session compared to the performance of control subjects (in %)

Patient		1940–	1945–	1950–	1955–	1960–	1965–	1970–	1975–	1980–	1985–	1990–	1995–	Overall
1	Names	51.67	51.67	48.33	40.83	40.00	36.67	26.67	23.34	25.83	15.00	11.67	8.34	31.67
	Words	60.00	63.34	56.67	60.00	53.33	43.34	36.67	40.00	13.34	16.67	13.34	10.00	38.89
2	Names	75.83	71.67	66.67	66.67	55.83	47.50	41.67	29.17	30.83	22.50	16.67	15.00	45.00
	Words	93.34*	93.34*	90.00	93.34*	86.67	83.33	76.67	80.00	53.33	40.00	36.67	36.67	71.94
3	Names	85.00	86.67*	90.00*	92.50*	91.67*	85.84	90.00*	90.84*	84.17	60.84	52.50	52.50	80.21
	Words	96.67*	100.0*	100.0*	96.67*	100.0*	100.0*	100.0*	96.67*	96.67*	86.67	86.67	83.33	95.28*
4	Names	74.17	75.83	71.67	72.50	69.17	55.83	56.67	55.83	39.17	40.84	29.17	29.17	55.83
	Words	86.67	80.00	83.33	86.67	80.00	80.00	76.67	63.33	46.67	46.67	36.67	36.67	66.94
5	Names	61.67	59.17	55.00	52.50	40.83	23.33	20.83	13.33	8.33	13.33	8.33	10.00	30.56
	Words	76.67	73.34	66.67	76.67	70.00	46.67	33.34	30.00	36.67	13.34	16.67	16.67	46.39
6	Names	90.00*	91.67*	92.50*	80.00	71.67	47.50	40.00	33.33	25.83	18.33	10.83	10.83	51.04
	Words	96.67*	100.0*	100.0*	100.0*	76.67	83.33	80.00	46.67	26.67	33.34	23.33	20.00	65.56
7	Names	84.17	80.83	90.00*	84.17	82.50	77.50	64.17	50.83	29.17	27.50	24.17	25.83	60.07
	Words	100.0*	100.0*	100.0*	93.33*	93.33*	96.67*	93.33*	90.00	86.67	40.00	43.33	40.00	81.39
8	Names	85.00	89.17*	90.00*	91.67*	97.50*	95.83*	93.33*	84.17	68.33	66.67	60.00	60.00	81.81
	Words	93.34*	96.67*	96.67*	93.34*	96.67*	100.0*	100.0*	100.0*	83.34	76.67	70.00	66.67	89.44
9	Names	92.50*	94.17*	90.00*	93.33*	97.50*	95.83*	93.33*	91.67*	83.33	75.00	68.33	65.83	86.74
	Words	93.33*	96.67*	100.0*	100.0*	100.0*	100.0*	100.0*	100.0*	100.0*	83.33	76.67	80.00	94.17*
10	Names	80.84	85.00	86.67	85.00	80.00	82.50	42.50	36.67	24.17	12.50	9.17	10.83	52.99
	Words	76.67	80.00	76.67	80.00	83.34	76.67	43.33	43.33	30.00	26.67	16.67	16.67	54.17
11	Names	59.17	57.50	47.50	45.00	44.17	19.17	18.33	17.50	3.33	1.67	3.33	5.00	26.81
	Words	66.67	66.67	60.00	60.00	53.33	53.33	33.33	40.00	13.33	20.00	20.00	20.00	42.22
12	Names	77.50	80.00	80.00	80.00	60.84	52.50	50.83	47.50	45.84	36.67	35.00	22.50	55.76
	Words	93.34*	93.34*	96.67*	100.0*	100.0*	91.67	93.33*	100.0*	50.00	26.67	30.00	26.67	75.14
13	Names	70.00	69.17	67.50	67.50	70.00	68.33	49.17	38.33	25.83	24.17	20.00	17.50	48.96
	Words	73.33	73.33	66.67	73.33	46.67	40.00	33.33	33.34	26.67	13.33	16.67	13.33	42.50
14	Names	86.67	90.83*	90.00*	85.00	90.00*	84.17	63.34	60.84	27.50	15.00	8.33	11.67	59.44
	Words	80.00	76.67	73.33	70.00	43.33	40.00	33.33	36.67	26.67	6.67	10.00	6.67	41.94
15	Names	66.67	60.84	66.67	62.50	50.00	41.67	36.67	24.17	12.50	8.34	9.17	6.67	37.15
	Words	60.00	63.33	60.00	56.67	43.33	30.00	30.00	26.67	13.33	6.67	13.34	10.00	34.44
16	Names	88.33*	88.33*	90.00*	92.50*	91.67*	85.84	90.00*	65.83	64.17	54.17	54.17	51.67	76.39
	Words	96.67*	100.0*	100.0*	93.33*	100.0*	100.0*	90.00	93.33*	76.67	76.67	80.00	73.34	90.00
Control names														
	Mean	91.56	92.92	93.35	93.84	93.65	94.04	94.41	94.51	93.61	93.11	92.66	93.45	93.43
	SD	4.31	4.36	4.36	4.56	4.78	4.67	4.88	4.71	4.82	4.49	4.96	4.78	4.64
Words														
	Mean	96.28	97.20	96.99	97.20	96.46	97.89	98.03	96.65	96.54	96.54	97.18	96.81	96.98
	SD	3.73	4.53	3.76	4.27	4.55	3.44	3.76	3.31	3.94	4.04	3.56	3.94	4.06

* The patient's performance fell within 1 SD of the control group mean.

COGNITIVE NEUROPSYCHOLOGY, 2004, 21 (2/3/4) 379–380

SECTION IV: THREE AS:
ALEXIA, AGRAPHIA, AGNOSIA

A note on Eleanor Saffran's contribution to this area

Eleanor Saffran left almost no topic in cognitive neuropsychology untouched. Although the central focus of her work concerned language, she also ventured further afield and examined more "peripheral" deficits such as agnosia, simultanagnosia, attentional processing in Alzheimer's disease, and pure alexia. In fact, her interests in these topics emerged at many different stages in her illustrious career. For example, in one of her earliest papers, she studied agnosia and complex perceptual processing in collaboration with Oscar Marin (Marin & Saffran, 1975). In this study with a fluent aphasic adult with anomia, they showed that, as long as the patient did not provide commentary on his performance (by remaining silent or counting by rote), his perceptual abilities were preserved. When he did verbalise, however, his misnamings interfered with his perceptual performance. The "power of the word," as they refer to the verbal interference effect, is well captured in their description of the patient's performance on the elephant puzzle of the WAIS Object Assembly task. The patient started successfully and was making good progress until he named the trunk "a mouth". He then proceeded to rearrange the pieces to form a mouth, thereby undoing his initial success, and became unable to complete the task. Eleanor's interest in perceptual matters is also evident in one of the last studies in which she participated. This work documented that pictures, especially those of manipulable objects, elicited stronger associations with action words than did the words naming those pictures (Saffran, Coslett, & Keener, 2003). That pictures and words initially contact somewhat different forms of conceptual information is consistent with the idea that the two formats are associated with different semantic configurations, and that this organisation may reflect the differences in mode of initial acquisition.

Eleanor's interest in the more peripheral domains (visual input and output, as in reading and writing) surfaced at many other points in her career as well. She contributed substantially to our understanding of reading errors in different patterns of acquired dyslexia, both in individuals with focal lesions and in those with progressive degenerative conditions (Saffran, 1980, 1985; Saffran & Coslett, 1996; Saffran, Schwartz, & Marin, 1976). One particular domain in which she contributed significantly was to advance our understanding of pure alexia. In a large series of studies, conducted over the years, with individuals with circumscribed occipital lesions (Shallice & Saffran, 1986) as well as with those with optic aphasia (Coslett & Saffran, 1989), she provided an account of the counterintuitive findings that these patients can perform above chance on covert tasks such as lexical and semantic decision under conditions of rapid presentation, despite being unable to identify the letters in the stimulus. In a comprehensive review paper with the clever title "Implicit vs. letter-by-letter reading in pure alexia: A tale of two systems" (Saffran & Coslett, 1998), she argued, together with Branch Coslett, that the right hemisphere gives rise to covert reading but that letter-by-letter reading is the product of the left hemisphere, operating on the information transmitted from the right.

Eleanor's contributions are numerous and the power of *her* word will be missed.

REFERENCES

Coslett, H. B., & Saffran, E. M. (1989). Preserved object recognition and reading comprehension in optic aphasia. *Brain*, *112*, 1091–1110.

© 2004 Psychology Press Ltd

http://www.tandf.co.uk/journals/pp02643294.html

DOI:10.1080/02643290342000500

Marin, O. S., & Saffran, E. M. (1975). Agnosic behavior in anomia: A case of pathological verbal dominance. *Cortex, 11,* 83–89.

Saffran, E. M. (1980). Reading in deep dyslexia is not ideographic. *Neuropsychologia, 18,* 219–223.

Saffran, E. M. (1985). Lexicalization and reading performance in surface dyslexia. In K. Patterson, J. Marshall, & M. Coltheart (Eds.), *Surface dyslexia: Neuropsychological and cognitive analyses of phonological reading* (pp. 53–72). Hove, UK: Lawrence Erlbaum Associates Ltd.

Saffran, E., & Coslett, H. B. (1996). Attentional dyslexia in Alzheimer's disease: A case study. *Cognitive Neuropsychology, 13,* 205–227.

Saffran, E. M., & Coslett, H. B. (1998). Implicit vs. letter-by-letter reading in pure alexia: A tale of two systems. *Cognitive Neuropsychology, 15,* 141–165.

Saffran, E. M., Coslett, H. B., & Keener, M. T. (2003). Differences in word associations to pictures and words. *Neuropsychologia, 41,* 1541–1546.

Saffran, E. M., Schwartz, M. F., & Marin, O. S. (1976). Semantic mechanisms in paralexia. *Brain and Language, 3,* 255–265.

Shallice, T., & Saffran, E. (1986). Lexical processing in the absence of explicit word identification: Evidence from a letter-by-letter reader. *Cognitive Neuropsychology, 3,* 429–458.

COGNITIVE NEUROPSYCHOLOGY, 2004, 21 (2/3/4) 381–400

LEXICAL INFLUENCES IN GRAPHEMIC BUFFER DISORDER

Karen Sage
University of Manchester, UK

Andrew W. Ellis
University of York, UK

We report the case of patient BH, who misspelled about half of the words she attempted and showed the characteristic features of "graphemic buffer disorder" (an effect of letter length on spelling accuracy, errors involving the substitution, omission, addition, and movement of letters that affect the middles more than the ends of words). Speech comprehension and production were good. Reading of words was, at most, only mildly impaired, though reading of nonwords was more affected. Words were spelled more accurately than nonwords, and BH's ability to spell words correctly was influenced by their imageability, age of acquisition, frequency, and number of orthographic neighbours (N). The effect of length was much reduced once these factors (especially N) were controlled. BH's spelling pattern is discussed in terms of top-down lexical influences on the graphemic buffer. We argue that such effects may be more widespread than has previously been acknowledged.

INTRODUCTION

Miceli, Silveri, and Caramazza (1985) described an Italian patient, FV, with no detectable impairment of reading or spoken language processing, whose attempts at writing were marred by errors involving the substitution, omission, addition, or movement of letters. Several patients have since been reported showing similar patterns of writing errors in English and French as well as Italian. In some patients the dysgraphia was relatively pure, as in FV (see also Jónsdóttir, Shallice, & Wise, 1996; Kay & Hanley, 1994; McCloskey, Badecker, Goodman-Schulman, & Aliminosa, 1994); in other cases the disorder occurred in the context of more widespread language problems. In either situation, the spelling errors were not limited to handwriting but were seen in other forms of spelling output. For example, patient AS of Jónsdóttir et al. made errors in writing to dictation, written object naming, oral spelling and delayed copying that involved omission (e.g., MOULDY → MOUDY), substitution (RELISH → RALISH), addition (LITRE → LIGTRE), or movement (BADGE → BAGDE) of letters, plus combinations of the basic error types. The patients reported to date all made the same types of error when attempting to write nonwords. Errors typically affect the middles of words more than the ends, with the initial position being least affected. In addition, the patients all show an effect of word length on spelling accuracy: The longer the target word (or nonword) is, the less likely they are to spell it correctly.

Many cognitive models of spelling and writing posit separate lexical and sublexical processing

---

Correspondence should be addressed to Karen Sage, Centre for Human Communication and Deafness, Faculty of Education, University of Manchester, Oxford Rd, Manchester M13 9PL, UK (Email: mewsskes@man.ac.uk).

http://www.tandf.co.uk/journals/pp02643294.html
DOI:10.1080/02643290342000438

streams responsible for spelling familiar words and nonwords (e.g., Caramazza, Miceli, Villa, & Romani, 1987; Ellis, 1982; Rapcsak, 1997). Because the deficit in these patients affects both word and nonword spelling, such models must place the locus of the impairment at or beyond the confluence of those two processing streams. At the same time, the fact that the same errors are seen in handwriting and oral spelling suggests that the deficit lies above the point of divergence of processes leading to those different outputs. In many models, the crucial location is occupied by a component usually termed the "graphemic buffer." Figure 1 shows a typical model of this class. According to Houghton, Glasspool, and Shallice (1994), the graphemic buffer makes possible the transition between parallel processing stages at which, for example, semantic and phonological representations of words are used to activate their spellings in the graphemic output lexicon and the serial processes that translate abstract graphemes into the movements required to produce individual letters in the correct order.

We present the case of patient BH, whose spelling problems occurred in the context of good production and comprehension of spoken language. BH's dysgraphia fitted the description of graphemic buffer disorder closely: She showed an effect of letter length on spelling accuracy, with middle letters more affected than end letters, and her errors involved omission, substitution, addition, and movement of letters. Her comprehension and reading aloud of written words was good, though nonword reading was impaired. Spelling of real words was substantially better than nonwords. Importantly, BH's spelling was affected by a number of properties of target words. In addition to the standard length effect, she showed effects of the imageability, age of acquisition, frequency, and number of orthographic neighbours of target words on spelling accuracy. We consider how such lexical influences could be explained within a model like that in Figure 1 and argue that lexical influences may be more widespread in graphemic buffer disorder than is generally acknowledged.

CASE REPORT

BH was born in May 1931. At birth she had two thumbs on her left hand. While she was still a baby, one of the two thumbs was surgically removed. The remaining thumb was an immobile claw about which BH was self-conscious throughout her life. She became used to performing as many tasks as possible with her right hand, including writing. Within her close family there were, however, three left-handers (her brother, her daughter, and her grandson). BH left school at the age of 14 years and worked for most of her adult life in textile manufacturing. She was also an active trades union representative and took full part in local politics. By her own account she was an avid reader of newspapers and novels (approximately three a month). There are only short samples of her premorbid writing available, but these do not suggest any difficulty in grammar or spelling.

In October 1996, BH was admitted to hospital with sudden onset of right hemiparesis and expressive dysphasia. An MRI scan in February 2000 revealed a widespread region of ischaemic damage extending throughout fronto-temporal, parietal,

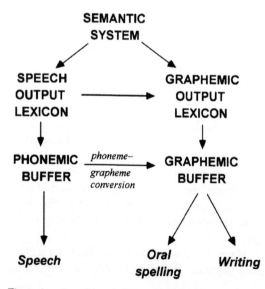

Figure 1. *A tradition dual-route model of spelling in which separate lexical and nonlexical routes converge upon the graphemic buffer.*

and occipital regions of the left cerebral hemisphere. There was relative enlargement of the Sylvian fissure, the sulci of the frontal and parietal lobes, and the lateral ventricle in the left cerebral hemisphere compared to the right, probably reflecting a degree of atrophy related to the infarction. A small ischaemic region was also apparent in the occipital lobe of the right cerebral hemisphere (see Figure 2).

Ten days post-onset BH was able to hold a conversation but complained of word-finding difficulties. She could write her name and address with some effort but letter omissions and substitutions were noted. A few days later her conversational speech was reduced to "Yes" and an extension to the CVA was suspected. BH received 3 months of intensive therapy in a rehabilitation centre. She also underwent audiological testing, which revealed a significant bilateral sensorineural hearing loss. Both ears showed at least a 70 dB loss over the range of frequencies. Bone conduction testing of the right ear also showed 60–70 dB loss over the speech frequencies. BH was fitted with bilateral hearing aids. Visual fields were intact.

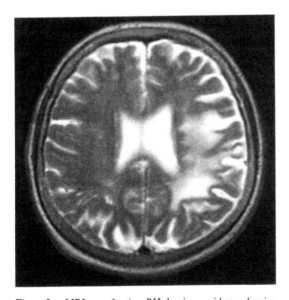

Figure 2. *MRI scan of patient BH showing a widespread region of ischaemic damage extending throughout fronto-temporal, parietal, and occipital regions of the left cerebral hemisphere plus a small ischaemic lesion in the occipital lobe of the right cerebral hemisphere.*

BH was discharged home in January 1997. She lived independently, becoming a founder member and first Chair of a local aphasia self-help group. By this time her conversational speech and understanding were good and she showed only occasional word-finding problems in spontaneous speech. She no longer read books or newspapers for pleasure but was able to read magazines and TV guides for information. She wrote infrequently, saying that writing had become slow and laborious because of the need for constant checking.

The tests reported here were carried out in BH's home between 1998 and 2003, when BH was aged 67 to 72 years. She wore a hearing aid in her right ear throughout all assessments and made full use of lip reading. In spelling to dictation and other tasks involving auditory input BH was always required to repeat a word or nonword correctly before responding. She had no difficulty doing this. Despite a mild right hemiparesis she always wrote with her right hand. She normally wrote in upper case print, saying that she found cursive handwriting difficult.

PERFORMANCE ON NONVERBAL TESTS

BH performed within the normal range on Raven's Progressive Matrices (38/60 in 60 mins; Raven, 1985) and the all-picture version of the Pyramids and Palm Trees Test (52/52; Howard & Patterson, 1992). She scored within the normal range on six of the eight subtests of the Visual Object and Space Perception Battery (VOSP: Warrington & James, 1991), though her score on the progressive silhouettes (12/20) and number location (5/10) subtests fell below the 5% cut-off for people over the age of 50. The most striking aspect of her performance on the Figure of Rey test (Meyers & Meyers, 1995) was that she rotated the figure clockwise through 90 degrees on all three attempts. She seemed unaware of having done this, though we note that her writing was always correctly oriented. If scored without regard to the rotation, her immediate copying fell below the 10th percentile (22.5/36) though her recall after 3 mins (13.5/36) and 40 mins (13.0/36) were normal (at the 50th and 46th percentiles respectively). She performed within the normal range on all the subtests of the Camden Memory Tests battery (Warrington, 1996), showing good recognition memory for visual scenes, unfamiliar faces, and words, and good recall of paired word associates. She had a digit span of 4 and a matching span of 6. She performed simple additions and subtractions without error.

SPEECH PROCESSING

BH's spoken description of the "cookie theft" picture from the Boston Diagnostic Aphasia Examination (Goodglass & Kaplan, 1983) was fluent with a good command of vocabulary. She produced 98 words per minute, with a content: function ratio of .57, which is well within the normal range for age-matched controls (Bird, Lambon Ralph, Patterson, & Hodges, 2000). BH also performed well on tests of spoken naming. Her score of 24/30 on the Graded Naming Test (McKenna & Warrington, 1983) was above average (Warrington, 1997), while her scores on the Boston Naming Test (53/60 in October 1998 and 54/60 in May 2003) were average for the age range 50–59 years (Borod, Goodglass, & Kaplan, 1980).

BH scored well on a variety of tests involving the processing of spoken words and nonwords. These included three tests from the ADA battery (Franklin, Turner, & Ellis, 1992)—minimal pair discrimination of words (39/40) and nonwords (36/40), auditory lexical decision (words: 40/40; nonwords: 34/40), and repetition of mixed words (40/40) and nonwords (38/40). She scored 100/100 on spoken word-to-picture matching with same-category distractors (Lambon Ralph, Ellis, & Sage, 1998a), 51/52 on the spoken word-to-picture matching version of the Pyramids and Palm Trees test (Howard & Patterson, 1992), and 59/60 on auditory synonym judgements from the PALPA battery (Kay, Lesser, & Coltheart, 1992). The auditory synonym judgements test of Warrington, McKenna, and Orpwood (1998) was administered in July 1998 and again in May 2003.

Her combined score for concrete and abstract words (41/50 in 1998; 42/50 in 2003) fell between the 10th and 25th percentile of Warrington et al.'s norms on both occasions. In 1998 her discrepancy between concrete words (24/25) and abstract words (17/25) fell outside the normal range but the discrepancy was within the normal range in 2003 (concrete words: 23/25, abstract words 19/25). In sum, BH's performance on tests of spoken word comprehension was broadly normal.

READING

BH completed a variety of letter discrimination tasks taken from the PALPA battery (Kay et al., 1992) with very few errors. The tests included reversed letter discrimination (correct orientation 18/18, mirror-reversed 17/18), cross-case matching of single letters (upper to lower 26/26; lower to upper 26/26), and sound and letter matching (50/52 and 51/52 respectively). Matching of upper- and lower-case words and nonwords was also performed without error (60/60).

BH read correctly 19/50 of the low-frequency irregular words of the National Adult Reading Test (NART: Nelson, 1982), which equates to a predicted premorbid IQ of 102. She made no errors on visual lexical decision (60/60 on test 25 of the PALPA battery; Kay et al., 1992) or written word-to-picture matching with same-category distractors (100/100; Lambon Ralph et al., 1998a). She scored 56/60 on the written synonym judgement test from the PALPA battery (Kay et al., 1992). On a written version of the synonym judgements test of Warrington et al. (1998) she scored 22/25 on the concrete words and 20/25 on the abstract items. Her total of 42/50 was within the range of 18 age-matched controls (mean 47.2; range 41–50) and her discrepancy score was normal.

BH performed adequately on tests of reading words aloud. Thus she read correctly 79/80 of the words from PALPA test 31 (Kay et al., 1992) that vary on imageability and frequency, 58/60 on the regular and irregular words from test 35 of the same battery, and 240/252 of the words from the "surface list" of Patterson and Hodges (1992) that vary on frequency and regularity. Her reading errors were all visual in nature (e.g., PHASE → "phrase," SEIZE → "size"). We would not want to make a strong claim that BH's word reading was as good as its premorbid level but she was, at most, only very mildly impaired. In contrast, her nonword reading was clearly impaired. Her score on the ADA nonword reading task (24/40) fell outside the normal range for young adults (Franklin et al., 1992). Her score of 22/40 on Hanley and Kay's (1998) nonwords was also well outside the normal range for their adult controls (0–7 errors). She showed a significant effect of letter length on nonword reading accuracy in PALPA test 36 (Kay et al., 1992: 3-*l.* 6/6, 4-*l.* 5/6, 5-*l.* 4/6, 6-*l.* 3/6; Jonckheere trend test, $z = 1.86$, $p < .05$). BH's errors in reading nonwords were again visual, with some lexicalisations (e.g., NENEROUS → "generous") and some nonword errors (DRAVITY → "divority").

SPELLING AND WRITING

BH wrote 26/26 upper-case and 24/26 lower-case letters correctly in response to their spoken names. Her errors in writing lower-case letters involved writing Q for q and being unable to write the letter f. When copying single letters from lower into upper case, she wrote 25/26 correctly, writing J instead of I for i. When copying from upper- to lower-case she wrote 24/26 letters correctly, making errors on F and J by writing them in their upper- rather than lower-case forms. BH was also asked to write to dictation the letter or letters that may be used to represent 32 English phonemes (10 short and long vowels plus 22 consonants that were spoken with a schwa vowel). BH wrote appropriate letters for 23/32 phonemes (72%), making errors on 5/10 vowels and 4/22 consonants.

In two testing sessions BH was asked to write 60 words using upper- or lower-case letters. In each session, half the words were written in upper case and half in lower case using an ABBA design. She wrote 53/60 correctly in upper case and 50/60 in lower case. Thus she was able to write in lower-case print more or less as well as she could in upper case, though she wrote in upper case by preference.

Letter length and spelling

Table 1 shows BH's performance on two tests assessing effects of letter length on spelling accuracy. BH showed an effect of length on writing to dictation in both word sets (PALPA test 39: Jonckheere trend test, $z = 2.64$, $p < .01$; JHUSB: $z = 4.95$, $p < .001$). The difference in performance between high-frequency words (19/35) and low-frequency words (13/35) on the JHUSB test was not significant. BH also showed a significant effect of length in oral spelling of the words from PALPA test 39; Jonckheere trend test, $z = 2.84$, $p < .01$.

Table 1. *Effects of word length on BH's spelling to dictation*

Test	Word length (in letters)					
	3	*4*	*5*	*6*	*7*	*8*
PALPA[a] test 39						
Written spelling to dictation	6/6	6/6	5/6	2/6		
Oral spelling to dictation	6/6	6/6	2/6	2/6		
JHUSB[b]: Written spelling to dictation						
High frequency		7/7	5/7	4/7	3/7	0/7
Low frequency		4/7	6/7	2/7	0/7	1/7

[a] Psycholinguistic Assessments of Language Processing in Aphasia battery (Kay et al., 1992).
[b] Johns Hopkins University Spelling Battery (Goodman & Caramazza, 1994).

Spelling errors

BH made the characteristic errors associated with graphemic buffer disorder. In the course of the assessments reported here and other tests concerned with evaluating effects of therapy, BH was asked to write a total of 1554 words to dictation, involving 1141 different words (some items being presented on more than one occasion). She wrote 853 words correctly (54.9%). Table 2 shows the results of an analysis of her 701 errors. As can be seen, she made substitution, omission, addition, and movement errors as well as compound errors and no response errors.

A number of points may be made about BH's spelling errors. First, although omissions were the largest error category, BH never omitted the initial letter of a word. There were a number of omissions of internal letters (e.g., CHAMBER → CHABER), but there were also a large number of omissions that affected the ends of words. Sometimes BH omitted the last letter only (e.g., DISC → DIS, ELEPHANT → ELEPHAN), but a substantial number of errors involved omission of more of the last part of a word (e.g., ALGAE → ALG, SLEDGE → SLE). These included errors where she was only able to write the first letter (e.g., FALSE → F, TWEED → T). Katz (1991) observed similar errors in his patient HR and suggested that they were evidence of abnormally rapid decay of information from the graphemic buffer (see also Ward & Romani, 1998).

Second, although BH was no more likely to misspell words containing double letters than words without geminates (see below), like other graphemic buffer patients she made some errors in which she doubled the wrong letter in a word, resulting in a letter substitution (e.g., KEEPER → KEPPER). Such errors, which also occur as slips of the pen in normals (Ellis, 1979), have been interpreted as evidence for a separate doubling or geminate process in spelling (Caramazza & Miceli, 1990; Houghton et al., 1994; Jónsdóttir et al., 1996).

Third, inspection of her errors showed that not all letters were equally affected. If we restrict our analysis to substitutions, omissions, and additions of single letters, and movement errors involving simple reversals of pairs of letters, then 29.3% of her errors involved the letter E. That letter was most heavily implicated in movement errors (46%, e.g., NIECE → NEICE) and substitutions (43%, e.g., STINT → STENT) followed by additions (31%, e.g., STOOL → STOOLE) and omissions (12%, e.g., CARAMEL → CARAML). E was more likely to be added than omitted. The remaining 71% of BH's simple errors involved a range of other letters.

Fourth, Jónsdóttir et al. (1996) noted that 16.4% of their patient's errors could be classed as phonologically appropriate (e.g., PLEA → PLEE). A similar proportion of BH's errors (17.8%) could be classed as phonologically correct (by a relatively loose criterion). Such errors were most frequent among substitutions (25%), additions (18%) and omissions (18%), of single letters and among compound errors (24%), with fewer among movement errors (9%) and very few among multiple substitutions, additions, or omissions. Half of the phonological errors (49.6%) involved the letter E, whether as a substituting letter in an unstressed syllable (e.g., CORAL → COREL), an addition (e.g., LENS → LENSE), an omission (e.g., LAPSE → LAPS), or in a movement, which most commonly involved EL/LE transpositions at the ends of words (e.g., KETTLE → KETTEL). Other phonological errors involved an assortment of other letters (e.g., SENSE → SENCE; SWIM → SWIMM; KNOCK → KNOK). Note that these phonologically correct errors can be accommodated comfortably into the categories of Table 2 alongside the nonphonological errors: It is just that in these cases the graphemic errors resulted in something that sounds roughly like the target word. There were few if any outright regularisation errors, like YACHT → YOT or NEPHEW → NEFFUE, of the sort seen in patients with "surface" or "lexical" dysgraphia (e.g., Beauvois & Dérouesné, 1981; Hatfield & Patterson, 1983).

Finally, BH was asked to spell 202 words aloud in the course of testing. She spelled 85 correctly (42.1%). Her errors in oral spelling were of the same type as her errors in writing to dictation (e.g., substitution: SMOKE → "S, H, O, K, E"; omission: WRATH → "W, R, T, H"; addition:

Table 2. *Analysis of errors made by BH in writing to dictation*

Error type	Number (%)	Examples	
		Target	*Error*
Substitution			
Single letters	80 (11.4%)	BURY	BUEY
		LUNCH	LANCH
		MAZE	MASE
		SMASH	SMACH
		CHEESE	CHESSE
		VACUUM	VACUMM
More than one letter	11 (1.6%)	HASTE	HASHI
		QUALM	QUERM
Omission			
Single letters	106 (15.1%)	ALBUM	ALUM
		AMBUSH	ABUSH
		DELTA	DELA
		INSECT	INECT
		SPINACH	SPINCH
More than one letter	143 (20.4%)	LANGUAGE	LANGE
		STUBBORN	STUBON
		OSTRICH	OST
		AREA	AR
		BALLET	B
		YACHT	Y
Addition			
Single letters	42 (6.0%)	ANGER	AUNGER
		MERCY	MERCSY
		TRUNK	THRUNK
		WITNESS	WHITNESS
More than one letter	4 (0.6%)	EDIT	EDITIE
Movement	42 (6.0%)	DENIAL	DEINAL
		THIRD	THRID
		PUZZLE	PUZZEL
		WHARF	WHAFR
Compound errors	207 (29.5%)	AISLE	IALE
		CARBON	CORBINE
		GIRAFFE	GIRRFFA
		PENGUIN	PINGUE
		REIGN	RIANG
		WOLF	WLOFE
No response	52 (7.4%)		
Other	14 (2.0%)	WRATH	ROUG

COFFIN → "C, O, U, F, F, I, N"; movement: BRIDGE → "B, R, I, G, D, E").

Serial position effects

The effect of serial position on BH's errors in writing words to dictation was analysed. Only simple errors involving single substitutions, omissions, additions, or movements were included ($n = 59$). Target words of different lengths were collapsed onto five standardised positions (A–E) using a method introduced by Wing and Baddeley (1980) and employed in several studies of graphemic buffer disorder since then. Points were then assigned to those five positions using the scoring procedure of Caramazza and Miceli (1990). The results are shown in Figure 3. For all simple errors combined, BH showed the characteristic bow-shaped serial position curve, with middle positions being more error-prone than end positions, and initial letters least affected. The individual distributions of substitution and omission errors followed that pattern most closely. Movement errors tended to occur more towards the ends of words while addition errors were more evenly distributed across serial positions.

Phonological spelling

We have noted that BH was able to write appropriate letters for 68% of single phonemes. Her spelling of whole nonwords was poor, however, and considerably less accurate than her spelling of real words. In tests 39 and 45 from the PALPA battery (Kay et al., 1992), BH wrote 20/24 words correctly but only 4/24 nonwords, $\chi^2 = 21.33$, $p < .01$. She showed a significant effect of length on writing the nonwords to dictation (PALPA test 45: 3-*l.* 3/6; 4-*l.* 1/6; 5-*l.* 0/6; 6-*l.* 0/6); Jonckheere trend test, $z = 2.16$, $p < .01$. On another occasion when she was asked to spell aloud the same nonwords, she spelled only 6/24 correctly (3-*l.* 5/6; 4-*l.* 1/6; 5-*l.* 0/6; 6-*l.* 0/6); Jonckheere trend test, $z = 3.10$, $p < .01$.

BH's errors when attempting to spell nonwords orally or in writing were similar in nature to her errors in spelling words (e.g., substitution: GREST → GRASD; omission: DUSP → DUP; addition: OST → OZOST; compound: SQUATE → SCACT).

Additional tests of spelling words to dictation

A number of tests were administered aimed at assessing the effects of different word properties on BH's spelling accuracy. Table 3 shows the results. Unless otherwise stated, the task was written spelling to dictation of words that BH had repeated correctly. The impact of word frequency was quite variable (note also Table 1). Age of acquisition had a more consistent effect, with BH being better able to spell words learned relatively early in life than later-learned words. The effect of imageability was significant in PALPA test 40, though we note that the words are not matched on age of acquisition, which has a high natural correlation with imageability (Bird, Franklin, & Howard, 2000; Gilhooly & Logie, 1980).

An unexpected result in Table 3 was the apparent effect of spelling–sound regularity in PALPA

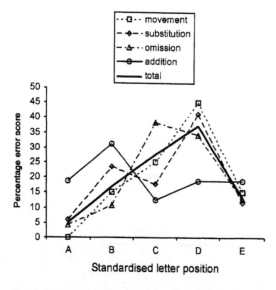

Figure 3. *The effect of serial position on the distributions of total errors and individual error types. Standardisation of positions following Wing and Baddeley (1980); scoring procedure from Caramazza and Miceli (1990).*

Table 3. *BH's performance on tests of writing words to dictation*

Test	Score	
Word varying on frequency (PALPA[a] test 40)	High freq	Low freq
High imageability	8/10	7/10
Low imageability	3/10	2/10
Imageability: $\chi^2 = 7.90$, $p < .01$		
Word varying on frequency (Morrison & Ellis, 1995)	High freq	Low freq
	16/24	17/24
Word varying on AoA (Morrison & Ellis, 1995)	Early	Late
	20/24	10/24
Age of acquisition: $\chi^2 = 7.05$, $p < .01$		
Words varying on AoA, matched on imageability, frequency, and length (unpublished set)	Early	Late
	27/40	14/40
Age of acquisition: $\chi^2 = 7.11$, $p < .01$		
Words varying on AoA and word frequency (Gerhard & Barry, 1998)	Early	Late
Written spelling	13/16	9/16
High frequency	8/16	4/16
Low frequency		
Frequency: $\chi^2 = 5.00$, $p < .05$; AoA: $\chi^2 = 3.03$, $p = .082$	Early	Late
Oral spelling	11/16	8/16
High frequency	11/16	2/16
Low frequency		
Frequency: $\chi^2 = 1.54$, n.s.; AoA: $\chi^2 = 7.44$, $p < .01$		
Words with or without geminate (double) letters (McCloskey et al., 1994)	With	Without
	34/72	34/72
Words varying on spelling–sound regularity (PALPA[a] test 44)	Regular	Irregular
	16/20	8/20
Regularity: $\chi^2 = 7.11$, $p < .01$		
Words varying on orthographic and phonological regularity (Parkin & Underwood, 1983)	Aug 1998	May 1999
Orthographically and phonologically regular	15/24	14/24
Orthographically regular, and phonologically irregular	10/24	10/24
Orthographically and phonologically irregular	2/24	3/24
Aug 1998: $\chi^2 = 15.29$, $p < .01$; May 1999: $\chi^2 = 11.02$, $p < .01$		

[a] Psycholinguistic Assessments of Language Processing in Aphasia battery (Kay et al., 1992).

test 44 and in two administrations of the word sets from Parkin and Underwood (1983). The difference in performance on the Parkin and Underwood word sets was repeated in oral spelling (orthographically and phonologically regular 11/24; orthographically regular but phonologically irregular 12/24; orthographically and phonologically irregular 3/24: $\chi^2 = 8.79$, $p < .01$). An effect of regularity in spelling is usually associated with surface (lexical) dysgraphia (e.g., Beauvois &

Dérouesné, 1981; Hatfield & Patterson, 1983) where patients also make regularisation errors in spelling. We have already noted, however, that while 17.8% of BH's errors could be classed as phonologically correct, she made few if any simple regularisation errors. Irregular words like CASTLE from PALPA test 44 differ from regular words like NEST on more than just the irregularity of their spelling–sound correspondences. In particular, they differ on orthographic distinctiveness; that is, on the extent to which the word spellings are similar to those of other words. The standard measure of orthographic distinctiveness counts the number of words that differ from a given word by a single letter (Coltheart's N: Coltheart, Davelaar, Jonasson, & Besner, 1977). On that measure, CASTLE has only one orthographic neighbour (HASTLE) while NEST has several (BEST, REST, NEAT, etc.). Parkin and Underwood (1983) contrasted "orthographically and phonologically regular" words like MELON with words like DEMON, which they called "orthographically regular and phonologically irregular," and with words like CHOIR which they called 'orthographically and phonologically irregular'. The last set are orthographically distinctive as well as embodying irregular spelling–sound correspondences. As Table 3 shows, BH's problems arose with words with unusual spelling patterns, not with irregular words with more typical spellings.

To assess the possible effect of N on BH's spelling, she was asked to spell to dictation a set of words with many or few orthographic neighbours from Forster and Shen (1996). She showed a trend in favour of high N words like SPEAR over low N words like SPECK (13/25 vs 7/25), $\chi^2 = 2.04$, $p = .153$. When she attempted to spell the same words aloud the difference was significant (high N: 15/25; low N: 6/25), $\chi^2 = 5.15$, $p < .05$. Laxon, Masterson, and Moran (1994) published a set of words that varied N and spelling–sound regularity while being matched on length, frequency, familiarity, and bigram frequency. Regular, consistent words came from families of words with similar spellings that all rhyme (e.g., SIFT, which rhymes with LIFT, RIFT, etc.). Regular, inconsistent words came from families of words where some items are pronounced one way and some another (e.g., COOT, which rhymes with BOOT and ROOT but contrasts with FOOT and SOOT). Exception words had pronunciations that were shared by few, if any, members of their orthographic family (e.g., PINT, whose pronunciation is unique and contrasts with HINT, MINT, STINT, etc.). Within each word set, half the items had high N values (mean 13–15) and half had low

N values (mean 4–5). Table 4 shows the results obtained when BH attempted to write those words to dictation. There was no effect of regularity on spelling once N was controlled, but the effect of neighbourhood size was significant, $\chi^2 = 5.79$, $p < .05$. It seems likely, therefore, that the difference shown by BH on the regular and irregular words of PALPA test 44 and the Parkin and Underwood (1983) word sets can be attributed to differences in number of orthographic neighbours rather than to regularity per se.

Regression analysis of BH's spelling accuracy

It is hard to find or create word sets that vary one of the factors that appears to influence BH's spelling accuracy while being perfectly controlled on all the others. As an alternative to such a factorial approach, a regression analysis was carried out on BH's accuracy in spelling 738 different words to dictation in a variety of assessments between 1998 and 2001. When a word was attempted on more than one occasion, the first attempt was used in this analysis. Overall, she spelled 311 (42%) of those words correctly. The regression analysis examined the ability of 10 properties of the target words, listed below, to predict BH's success or failure in spelling those items.

1. *Imageability*. Ratings of word imageability were available for 562 of the 738 from the MRC Psycholinguistic Database (Quinlan, 1992) and Bird et al. (2000). Ratings for the remaining 176 words were obtained from 25 adult raters who employed the same scale.

Table 4. *BH's performance on writing to dictation the word sets from Laxon et al. (1994)*

	High N	Low N	Total
Exception	10/12	8/12	18/24
Regular, inconsistent	10/12	9/12	19/24
Regular, consistent	11/12	5/12	16/24
Total	31/36	22/36	53/72

2. *Age of acquisition.* Estimates of the age of acquisition (AoA) of 478 of the 738 words were taken from the MRC Psycholinguistic Database (Quinlan, 1992) and from Bird et al. (2000). A new set of 25 adults rated the remaining 260 words using the same scale as in those studies.

3. *Word frequency.* Two frequency measures were taken for each word from Kucera and Francis (1967) and from the CELEX database (combined spoken and written frequency: Baayen, Piepenbrock, & Van Rijn, 1993).

4. *Word length* was measured as the number of letters in a target word.

5. *Number of orthographic neighbours (N)* was defined as the number of words of the same length that differ by a single letter.

6. *Phonological to orthographic (P–O) regularity.* Hanna, Hanna, Hodges, and Rudorf (1966) published data showing which letters are used most often to represent different phonemes (i.e., which are the regular phoneme–grapheme correspondences). This data was to derive a measure of the phonological to orthographic (P–O) regularity of each target word. A word was first given a broad phonemic transcription. For each phoneme we then asked whether it was represented in the word by the most common (regular) letter or letter sequence according to the Hanna et al. (1966) count. If it was, that phoneme was given a value of 1; if not, a value of 0. The total score for each word was then divided by the number of phonemes to give a regularity measure that assigned low scores to CHOIR, PSALM, QUAY, REIGN, THYME, and YACHT, and high scores to ALBUM, BLISTER, INVENT, ROBIN, SAMPLE, and THONG.

7. *Bigram frequency;* and

8. *Trigram frequency.* Mean bigram and trigram frequencies for each word were computed using the norms from Mayzner and Tresselt (1965) and Mayzner, Tresselt, and Wolin (1965).

9. *Geminate/non geminate.* Words containing doubled letters were given a value of 1 on the geminate/nongeminate variable. All other words were given a value of 0.

10. *Orthographic CV structure.* Caramazza and Miceli (1990) argued that their patient LB made more errors to orthographically complex words containing consonant clusters or vowel digraphs than to orthographically simple words. Words were given a value of 1 if they contained a consonant cluster or vowel digraph in their spelling; otherwise they were given a value of 0.

Bigram and trigram frequency counts are only available for words of up to seven letters. The inclusion of that variable reduced the word set from 738 to 615 items. The two frequency measures were subjected to a log $(1 + x)$ transform. Bigram and trigram frequencies were also log transformed while N values were subjected to a square root transformation. At the end of this process the continuous variables all had skew values of less than 1. Outliers were then identified as items lying more than 3.67 *SD*'s from the mean on any of the variables. Four outliers were removed. Table 5 shows the correlations of the independent, predictor variables with each other and with BH's spelling accuracy for the remaining 611 words. With so many items, even low correlations are significant, but the variables correlating most highly with spelling accuracy were age of acquisition, number of orthographic neighbours, imageability, and word length.

When the dependent variable takes the form of 1 (correct) or 0 (incorrect), logistic regression is the appropriate form of analysis. A logistic regression was carried out with Celex word frequency as the frequency measure. Table 6 shows the outcome. The combination of predictors was able to predict success or failure on individual words to a highly significant level. Age of acquisition, imageability, word frequency, word length and number of orthographic neighbours made significant independent contributions to predicting spelling accuracy. P-O regularity, bigram frequency, trigram frequency, geminates, and orthographic CV structure did not. When Kucera and Francis (1967) frequency replaced Celex frequency in a second analysis, the pattern was unchanged. The effect of age of acquisition remained highly significant when both frequency measures were included as predictors, making it highly unlikely that the effect could be a result of a failure to adequately control word frequency (cf. Zevin & Seidenberg, 2002).

Table 5. *Correlation matrix between BH's spelling accuracy and the predictor variables for 611 words*

	1	2	3	4	5	6	7	8	9	10	11	12
1. BH's spelling accuracy	–	–.341	.262	.146	.174	–.256	.309	.105	.175	.110	–.001	–.046
2. Age of acquisition		–	–.568	–.260	–.358	.164	–.272	–.106	–.136	–.171	–.038	–.053
3. Imageability			–	–.116	–.013	.024	.106	.010	.001	–.041	.063	.047
4. Log K-F frequency				–	.846	–.126	.066	–.033	.256	.390	–.010	.038
5. Log Celex frequency					–	–.138	.088	–.025	.205	.349	–.044	–.012
6. Word length (letters)						–	–.590	–.028	–.174	.018	.149	.193
7. Orthographic neighbours ($\sqrt{N}$)								.204	.411	.267	–.048	–.089
8. P–O regularity								–	.158	.083	–.156	–.018
9. Log bigram frequency									–	.615	–.057	.023
10. Log trigram frequency										–	.008	.096
11. Geminate/nongeminate											–	.146
12. Orthographic CV structure												–

Letter length or number of orthographic neighbours?

An influence of word length on spelling is regarded as one of the defining characteristics of graphemic buffer disorder. We note, though, that letter length correlates highly with N (.59 in Table 5) because the longer a word is, the fewer other words tend to differ from it by one letter. We have seen in the regression analysis that the independent contributions of length and N were both significant, suggesting that neither can be completely reduced to an effect of the other. It remains possible, however, that in word sets that vary letter length without controlling N, a substantial part of the apparent length effect is actually due to differences in neighbourhood size. To examine this, BH was asked to write to dictation the five- and eight-letter words from Lavidor and Ellis (2002; Experiment 2) that are matched on N, AoA, imageability, and word frequency. She wrote 16/48 five-letter words correctly and 11/48 eight-letter words. Though there was a trend towards better performance on the shorter words, it was not significant. Figure 4 shows BH's performance on these word sets overlaid on her performance on the items from the JHUSB (Goodman & Caramazza, 1994) and PALPA test 39 (Kay et al., 1992), which are not matched on N. It is clear that once N and other factors are controlled, the independent effect of letter length on BH's spelling performance is considerably reduced.

Table 6. *Results of a logistic regression analysis on 611 items with BH's spelling accuracy as the dependent variable*[a]

	B	Standard error	Wald	p
Age of acquisition	–.003	.001	7.10	< .01
Imageability	.004	.001	13.95	< .001
Log Celex frequency	.333	.163	4.18	< .05
Word length (letters)	–.318	.120	7.04	< .01
Orthographic neighbours ($\sqrt{N}$)	.279	.113	6.09	< .02
P–O regularity	.673	.475	2.01	.156, n.s.
Log bigram frequency	.426	.345	1.52	.217, n.s.
Log trigram frequency	–.059	.292	0.04	.841, n.s.
Geminate/nongeminate	–.086	.119	0.52	.471, n.s.
Orthographic CV structure	.117	.129	0.82	.365, n.s.

[a] Model χ^2 = 133.34, p < .0001.

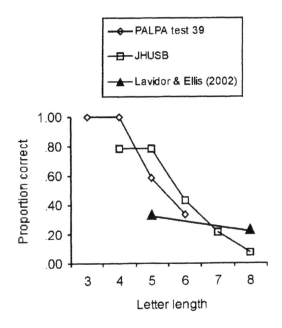

Figure 4. *The effect of letter length on BH's writing to dictation of three sets of words—test 39 from the PALPA battery (Kay et al., 1992), the length test from the JHUSB (Goodman & Caramazza, 1994), and words of five and eight letters from Lavidor and Ellis (2002; Experiment 2) matched on N, AoA, imageability, and word frequency.*

DISCUSSION

BH showed the classic signs of graphemic buffer disorder—an effect of letter length on spelling accuracy, errors in written and oral spelling of words and nonwords that involved the omission, substitution, addition, or movement of letters, and a bow-shaped serial position effect for simple graphemic errors where middle positions in words were more affected than beginnings or ends. But we would note two points in relation to this "classic" profile. The first is that the length effect was greatly reduced once N was controlled (Figure 4). A significant effect of length emerged from the regression analysis in which N was also included, so it appears that letter length exerts a genuinely independent effect in graphemic buffer disorder. But we also suspect that the influence of letter length has been exaggerated in previous studies that have not controlled for neighbourhood size.

The second point is that, as in other studies, the bow-shaped serial position curve shown in Figure 3 is based on the analysis of errors involving simple substitutions, additions, omissions, and movements. We note, though, that 20% of BH's errors involved omissions of more than one letter. Very often, it was the letters toward the end of a word that were omitted. Including such errors in an analysis would shift the serial position distribution to the right, and a patient in whom they were a dominant error type would show a very different serial position curve (cf. Katz, 1991; Schiller, Greenhall, Shelton, & Caramazza, 2001; Ward & Romani, 1998).

BH misspelled over half of the words she was asked to write to dictation, which puts her in the mid-range of severity for word spelling in graphemic buffer patients. Her dysgraphia was a relatively pure one in that her speech production and naming were normal and her comprehension of spoken and written words was good, as was her repetition of both words and nonwords. BH belongs therefore in the category of graphemic buffer patients with (more or less) preserved spoken language processing (e.g., Caramazza et al., 1987; Kay & Hanley, 1994; McCloskey et al., 1994; Miceli et al., 1985; Piccirilli, Petrillo, & Poli, 1992). BH's reading aloud of words was normal or close to normal, though as in many graphemic buffer patients her reading of nonwords was impaired. But whereas an absence of lexical influences on spelling has been held by many authors to be one of the defining characteristic of graphemic buffer disorder (e.g., Caramazza et al., 1987; Jónsdóttir et al., 1996; Schiller et al., 2001), BH showed clear effects of a range of lexical variables. She was better at spelling words than nonwords (a lexicality effect) and her spelling of real words was influenced by their imageability (better spelling of concrete than abstract words), age of acquisition (better spelling of early than late acquired words), frequency (better spelling of high- than low-frequency words, though this effect was very labile), and number of neighbours (better spelling of high than low N words).

Just less than one fifth of BH's spelling errors could be classed as phonologically correct (i.e., sounding like the target word), and initial tests suggested a possible effect of spelling–sound regularity on BH's spelling accuracy. The regularity effect disappeared, however, in word sets where N was controlled, and the effect of phoneme–grapheme regularity did not approach significance in the regression analysis when entered as a predictor alongside N and the other variables. BH had problems spelling individual vowel and consonant phonemes to dictation, and her spelling of even simple nonwords was poor (though she had no difficulty repeating nonwords before attempting to spell them, and would often continue to repeat a nonword as she attempted it). BH's phonologically appropriate errors were not blatant regularisation errors but could readily be classified as the results of substitutions, additions, omissions, and movements of letters, just like her nonphonological errors. Approximately half of them involved the letter E in situations like replacing A in an unstressed syllable or exchanging positions with L at the end of a word. Just occasionally BH seemed to use phonology when struggling to spell a word (as, for example, when she spelled PHOTOGRAPH as PHOTOGRAF), but on balance we would argue that phonology played at most only a minor role in BH's word spelling. We note that patients MC of Annoni, Lemay, de Mattos Pimenta, and Lecours (1998), JES of Aliminosa, McCloskey, Goodman-Schulman, and Sokol (1993), and HE of McCloskey et al. (1994) were all reported to spell regular words better than irregular words but they made few phonologically plausible spelling errors and N was not controlled in the word sets used. We suspect that undetected N effects may have been responsible for the apparent regularity effects in these patients.

Like all graphemic buffer patients, BH made similar errors when spelling words and nonwords. If word and nonword spelling are impaired in the same way, the obvious place to locate the impairment within a traditional model like Figure 1 is at the level of the graphemic buffer itself. As Houghton et al. (1994) observed, if the graphemic buffer is faulty, then the probability of at least one error occurring will increase with the number of letters needing to be produced, so it is quite reasonable to expect a length effect in patients with impaired graphemic buffer functioning. But how could effects of lexical factors like imageability, age of acquisition, word frequency, and N arise? Imageability effects are widely interpreted as reflecting a contribution to performance from semantic representations. For example, the influential account of Hinton and Shallice (1991) and Plaut and Shallice (1993) holds that highly imageable (concrete) words have richer semantic representations than low-imageability (abstract) words, a difference reflected in computational models by assigning more semantic units to concrete than abstract words. The effect of imageability on BH's spelling occurred in the context of good naming and good comprehension of both abstract and concrete words, suggesting that BH's semantic system itself was not significantly impaired. In their computational modelling work, Plaut and Shallice (1993) showed, however, that imageability effects can also occur if the connections between semantic representations and word-forms are damaged. Under such circumstances, the greater number of connections to orthographic representations from concrete compared to abstract semantic representations makes the concrete words better able to survive damage to the connections. We suggest that the imageability effect we observed in BH could also be explained in terms of weakened connections between semantics and the graphemic output lexicon, causing lower activation of lexical units for abstract words with the knock-on consequence that the component letters of abstract words receive less top-down support at the level of the graphemic buffer (cf. Schiller et al., 2001).

Damage to the links between semantics and orthographic word-forms could also explain the effect of age of acquisition on BH's spelling accuracy. Ellis and Lambon Ralph (2000) showed that if an artificial neural network is trained on some ("early") items before other ("late") items are entered into training, then even after extensive additional training the early items can have representations that are stronger and more robust than those of the later items. This happens because early items take advantage of the opportunity they are given to make the large changes to the strength of connections between different representations that happen early in the training of an initially unformed network. Later items manage to be learned by forcing additional changes to connection strengths, but those changes may be resisted by the early items that continue to be trained alongside them. The result is a compromise network structure in which the mappings involved in representing early-learned items are more robust to damage than those representing later-learned items. Damage to the connections between representations in a fully trained network has a more adverse effect on the processing of late than early acquired items (Ellis & Lambon Ralph, 2000, simulation 16), a pattern reflected in the better preservation of early- than late-acquired vocabulary that has been documented in studies of spoken naming in aphasic patients (e.g., Cuetos, Aguado, Izura, & Ellis, 2002; Nickels & Howard, 1995) and in patients with Alzheimer's disease (Silveri, Cappa, Mariotti, & Puopolo, 2002) and semantic dementia (Lambon Ralph, Graham, Ellis, & Hodges, 1998b). The connections between the semantic system and the orthographic output lexicon involved in spelling are built up gradually and cumulatively over the course of childhood and beyond. Their relative strengths would therefore be expected to reflect the age or order of acquisition of different words. We note that Bonin, Fayol, and Chalard (2001) and Bonin, Chalard, Méot, and Fayol (2002) found age of acquisition to be a powerful predictor of the speed with which normal adults can access the spellings of object names in response to pictures and initiate a writing response.

Turning to BH's frequency effect, McCloskey et al. (1994) and Aliminosa et al. (1993) sought to explain a co-occurrence of word frequency effects with other signs of graphemic buffer disorder by proposing two separate loci of impairment—damage at the graphemic output lexicon giving rise to the frequency effect and damage at the graphemic buffer level giving rise to the characteristic errors and the length effect (see also Tainturier & Caramazza, 1996). We would suggest, however, that the same weakening of links from semantics to the graphemic output lexicon that we have postulated to explain the effect of imageability and age of acquisition on BH's spelling could also account

for her frequency effect. There is a long tradition within cognitive modelling of locating frequency effects in the strength of connections between semantic representations and word-forms, with those links that are regularly used because they are involved in processing high-frequency words being stronger than those for low-frequency words that are processed less often (e.g., Plaut, McClelland, Seidenberg, & Patterson, 1996; Coltheart, Rastle, Perry, Langdon, & Zeigler, 2000). Ellis and Lambon Ralph (2000) showed that the strength of connections in their network was influenced by a combination of the point in training at which items were learned (age of acquisition) and the frequency with which they were trained thereafter.

The idea being proposed, then, is that stronger connections between semantics and the graphemic output lexicon for concrete, early-acquired, and high-frequency words will cascade down to the graphemic buffer and result in stronger activation of the component letters of those words, rendering them more resistant to damage to the buffer. Where might effects of N fit into this framework? We are not aware of any previous reports of effects of N in dysgraphic patients, but facilitatory effects of neighbourhood size have been widely reported in normal word recognition (Andrews, 1997; Perea & Rosa, 2000). Those effects have typically been explained in terms of greater top-down activation of letter-level representations by word-level representations for words with more neighbours (e.g., Andrews, 1992; Coltheart & Rastle, 1994). If activation can pass both ways between words in the graphemic output lexicon and letters in the graphemic buffer (cf. McClelland & Rumelhart, 1981), then letters in words with many orthographic neighbours may enjoy more top-down support from the lexicon than words with few orthographic neighbours. Hence we propose that N effects, like effects of imageability, age of acquisition, and word frequency, occur because the letters in some words are more strongly activated than the letters in other words, but the locus of the N effect would be located in the connections between the graphemic output lexicon and the graphemic buffer rather than in the higher-level connections between semantics and the graphemic output lexicon.

Whatever their imageability, age of acquisition, frequency, or neighbourhood size, letters in real words will be more strongly activated than letters in nonwords because of the additional support that letters in words will receive from the graphemic output lexicon. Irrespective of any problems BH may have had in phoneme-to-grapheme conversion, this would contribute to better spelling of words than nonwords (the lexicality effect). We also note that reduced activation of graphemic representations could mean that there may sometimes be only sufficient activation to drive the production of the first few letters, resulting in incomplete, fragmentary response of the sort BH sometimes made and which are more prominent in other patients (e.g., Katz, 1991; Ward & Romani, 1998). We would interpret these as due to insufficient activation of graphemes rather than abnormally rapid decay (Katz, 1991). Sometimes so little activation may reach the graphemic buffer that no letters can be produced at all, resulting in no response errors (7.4% of BH's errors).

The canonical description of graphemic buffer disorder would lead one to believe that graphemic buffer patients are not significantly better at spelling words than nonwords and are not influenced by lexical properties like word frequency and imageability (e.g., Caramazza et al., 1987; Jónsdóttir et al., 1996; Schiller et al., 2001). If that were true, then BH would be a rather unusual case. We believe, however, that she is actually more typical than atypical, particularly among English-speaking patients. Table 7 summarises the available data on effects of lexicality (words vs. nonwords), word frequency, and imageability on spelling to dictation in 17 patients subdivided according to language. Eight of the 17 patients were significantly better at spelling words than nonwords, with a further two showing effects that were close to significance. BH brings the number of patients showing significant or borderline lexicality effects to 11/18. Six of the 14 cases where frequency was manipulated showed a significant advantage for high- over low-frequency words, with another showing two marginal effects. BH brings the total to 9/15. Three of the 13 cases where imageability or concreteness was manipu-

lated showed a significant advantage for high-imageability/concrete over low-imageability/abstract words. Jónsdóttir et al. (1996) state of their patient AS that "concreteness did not significantly affect his performance" (p. 179). The numbers for concrete and abstract words written correctly are not provided, but Jónsdóttir et al. give a chi-squared value of 3.67 for AS's concreteness effect. That equates to a p value of .055, which is very close to significance indeed. BH brings the number of patients showing significant or close-to-significant effects of imageability/concreteness to 5/14.

Overall, 12 of the 17 patients in Table 7 showed signs of lexical influences in their spelling to dictation. BH brings that number to 13/18. Interestingly, that includes 10 of the 11 English-speaking cases now in the literature, the sole exception being patient ML of Hillis and Caramazza (1989), who was unusual in that her errors were skewed towards the beginnings of words and were attributed by Hillis and Caramazza to an effect of neglect on the graphemic buffer. Some of the patients in Table 7 who appear not to show lexical influences were either not tested for one of the effects or were given tests involving too few items for adequate statistical power. Performance in some cases was close to floor or ceiling, making the detection of effects difficult. And none of the patients in Table 7 was tested for effects of age of acquisition or orthographic neighbourhood size (N), both of which had strong influences on BH's spelling. It could be important, though, that lexical influences appear to be stronger in English than Italian patients. It is possible that in languages with transparent orthographies, semantic representations play less of a role in retrieving the spelling of words from the graphemic output lexicon and that the contribution of lexical influences to spelling is reduced in comparison to languages like English. Our main point, though, is that lexical influences in graphemic buffer disorder are much more pervasive than most reviews would lead one to believe. Our account of those influences is that the amount of top-down activation reaching letter representations in the graphemic buffer depends on the strength of connections between the semantic system and the

Table 7. Lexicality, frequency and imageability/concreteness effects in writing to dictation in 17 patients with graphemic buffer disorder

Case	Reference	Lexicality			Word frequency			Imageability/concreteness		
		Words	Nonwords	p	High	Low	p	High	Low	p
Italian										
FV	Miceli, Silveri, and Caramazza (1985)	220/283 (78%)	92/133 (69%)	+	Not reported			Not reported		
LB	Caramazza et al. (1987); Caramazza and Miceli (1990)	438/743 (59%)	179/425 (42%)	**	26/40 (65%)	25/40 (63%)	n.s.	2/20 (10%)	2/20 (10%)	n.s.
SE	Posteraro, Zinelli, and Mazzucchi (1988)	29/40 (73%)	30/40 (75%)	n.s.	13/20 (65%)	16/20 (80%)	n.s.	16/20 (80%)	13/20 (65%)	n.s.
Anon	Piccirilli et al. (1992)	27/40 (68%)	22/40 (55%)	n.s.	12/20 (60%)	15/20 (75%)	n.s.	7/20 (35%)	6/20 (30%)	n.s.
PM	Cantagallo and Bonazzi (1996)	21/40 (52%)	18/40 (45%)	n.s.	12/20 (60%)	9/20 (45%)	n.s.	11/20 (55%)	10/20 (50%)	n.s.
French										
AM	de Partz (1995)	9/20 (45%)	0/20 (0%)	**	28/40 (70%)	19/40 (48%)	+	25/30 (83%)	13/30 (43%)	**
MC	Annoni et al. (1998)	125/260 (48%)	23/56 (41%)	n.s.	39/68 (57%)	34/68 (50%)	n.s.	Not reported		
English										
ML	Hillis and Caramazza (1989)	81/326 (25%)	13/34 (38%)	n.s.	41/146 (28%)	38/146 (26%)	n.s.	3/21 (14%)	3/21 (14%)	n.s.
DH	Hillis and Caramazza (1989); Badecker, Hillis, and Caramazza (1990)	205/326 (63%)	21/44 (48%)	+	109/146 (75%)	72/146 (49%)	**	12/21 (57%)	11/21 (52%)	n.s.
HR	Katz (1991)	30/118 (25%)	0/16 (0%)	*	Not reported			Not reported		
JES	Aliminosa et al. (1993)	91/326 (28%)	0/34 (0%)	**	55/146 (38%)	30/146 (21%)	**	6/21 (29%)	2/21 (10%)	n.s.
HE	McCloskey et al. (1994)	273/326 (84%)	28/34 (82%)	n.s.	127/146 (87%)	114/146 (78%)	+	18/21 (86%)	15/21 (71%)	n.s.
JH	Kay and Hanley (1994); Hanley and Kay (1998)	493/576 (86%)	13/24 (54%)	***	145/152 (95%)	124/152 (82%)	***	38/40 (95%)	36/40 (90%)	n.s.
AS	Jónsdóttir et al. (1996)	954/1646 (58%)	61/115 (53%)	n.s.	Significant effect reported		*	Borderline effect reported		+
FM	Tainturier and Caramazza (1996)	15/84 (18%)	0/34 (0%)	*	32/55 (58%)	10/55 (18%)	*	Not reported		
TH	Schiller et al. (2001)	238/368 (65%)	13/90 (14%)	**	74/111 (67%)	54/111 (49%)	***	30/42 (71%)	18/42 (43%)	**
PB	Schiller et al. (2001)	351/894 (39%)	6/83 (7%)	**	126/251 (50%)	87/258 (34%)	***	38/60 (63%)	21 60 (35%)	**

In some cases the numbers shown have been reconstructed from the % correct and the number of items reported in the original paper.
* $p < .05$; ** $p < .01$; + $.10 < p < .05$.

graphemic output lexicon (influenced by imageability, word frequency, and age of acquisition) and on the strength of connections between the graphemic output lexicon and the buffer (influenced by number of orthographic neighbours). Stronger top-down activation makes letter representations in the graphemic buffer better able to survive the effects of damage.

REFERENCES

Aliminosa, D., McCloskey, M., Goodman-Schulman, R., & Sokol, S. M. (1993). Remediation of acquired dysgraphia as a technique for testing interpretations of deficits. *Aphasiology, 7*, 55–69.

Andrews, S. (1992). Frequency and neighborhood effects on lexical access: Lexical similarity or orthographic redundancy? *Journal of Experimental Psychology: Learning, Memory, and Cognition, 18*, 234–254.

Andrews, S. (1997). The effect of orthographic similarity on lexical retrieval: Resolving neighborhood conflicts. *Psychonomic Bulletin and Review, 4*, 439–461.

Annoni, J.-M., Lemay, M. A., de Mattos Pimenta, M. A., & Lecours, A. R. (1998). The contribution of attentional mechanisms to an irregularity effect at the graphemic buffer level. *Brain and Language, 63*, 64–78.

Baayen, R. H., Piepenbrock, R., & Van Rijn, H. (1993). *The CELEX lexical database (CD-ROM).* Philadelphia: University of Pennsylvania, Linguistic Data Consortium.

Badecker, W., Hillis, A., & Caramazza, A. (1990). Lexical morphology and its role in the writing process: Evidence from a case of acquired dysgraphia. *Cognition, 35*, 205–243.

Beauvois, M.-F., & Dérouesné, J. (1981). Lexical or orthographic dysgraphia. *Brain, 104*, 21–49.

Bird, H., Franklin, S., & Howard, D. (2000). Age of acquisition and imageability ratings for a large set of words, including verbs and function words. *Behavior Research Methods, Instruments and Computers, 33*, 73–79.

Bird, H., Lambon Ralph, M. A., Patterson, K., & Hodges, J. (2000). The rise and fall of frequency and imageability: Noun and verb production in semantic dementia. *Brain and Language, 73*, 17–49.

Bonin, P., Chalard, M., Méot, A., & Fayol, M. (2002). The determinants of spoken and written picture naming latencies. *British Journal of Psychology, 93*, 89–114.

Bonin, P., Fayol, M., & Chalard, M. (2001). Age of acquisition and word frequency in written picture naming. *Quarterly Journal of Experimental Psychology, 54A*, 469–489.

Borod, J. C., Goodglass, H., & Kaplan, E. (1980). Normative data on the Boston Diagnostic Aphasia Examination, Parietal Lobe Battery, and the Boston Naming Test. *Journal of Clinical Neuropsychology, 2*, 209–215.

Cantagallo, A., & Bonazzi, S. (1996). Acquired dysgraphia with selective damage to the graphemic buffer: A single case report. *Italian Journal of Neurological Science, 17*, 249–254.

Caramazza, A., & Miceli, G. (1990). The structure of graphemic representations. *Cognition, 37*, 243–297.

Caramazza, A., Miceli, G. Villa, G., & Romani, C. (1987). The role of the graphemic buffer in spelling: Evidence from a case of acquired dysgraphia. *Cognition, 26*, 59–85.

Coltheart, M., Davelaar, E., Jonasson, J. T., & Besner, D. (1977). Access to the internal lexicon. In S. Dornic (Ed.), *Attention and performance VI* (pp. 535–555). New York: Academic Press.

Coltheart, M., & Rastle, K. (1994). Serial processing in reading aloud: Evidence for dual-route models of reading. *Journal of Experimental Psychology: Human Perception and Performance, 20*, 1197–1211.

Coltheart, M., Rastle, K., Perry, C., Langdon, R., & Ziegler, J. (2001). DRC: A dual route cascaded model of visual word recognition and reading aloud. *Psychological Review, 108*, 204–256.

Cuetos, F., Aguado, G., Izura, C., & Ellis, A. W. (2002). Aphasic naming in Spanish: Predictors and errors. *Brain and Language, 82*, 344–365.

de Partz, M.-P. (1995). Deficit of the graphemic buffer: Effects of a written lexical segmentation strategy. *Neuropsychological Rehabilitation, 5*, 129–147.

Ellis, A. W. (1979). Slips of the pen. *Visible Language, 13*, 265–282.

Ellis, A. W. (1982). Spelling and writing (and reading and speaking). In A. W. Ellis (Ed.), *Normality and pathology in cognitive functions* (pp. 113–146). London : Academic Press.

Ellis, A. W., & Lambon Ralph, M. A. (2000). Age of acquisition effects in adult lexical processing reflect loss of plasticity in maturing systems: Insights from connectionist networks. *Journal of Experimental*

Psychology: Learning, Memory, and Cognition, 26, 1103–1123.

Forster, K. I., & Shen, D. (1996). No enemies in the neighborhood: Absence of inhibitory neighborhood effects in lexical decision and semantic categorisation. *Journal of Experimental Psychology: Learning, Memory, and Cognition, 22,* 696–713.

Franklin, S., Turner, J. M., & Ellis, A. W. (1992). *The ADA comprehension battery.* London: Action for Dysphasic Adults.

Gerhand, S., & Barry, C. (1998). Word frequency effects in oral reading are not merely age-of-acquisition effects in disguise. *Journal of Experimental Psychology: Learning, Memory, and Cognition, 24,* 267–283.

Gilhooly, K. J., & Logie, R. H. (1980). Methods, & designs: Age of acquisition, imagery, concreteness, familiarity, and ambiguity measures for 1,944 words. *Behaviour Research Methods and Instrumentation, 12,* 395–427.

Goodglass, H., & Kaplan, E. (1983). *Assessment of aphasia and related disorders.* Philadelphia: Lea & Febinger.

Goodman, R. A., & Caramazza, A. (1994). *The Johns Hopkins University Dysgraphia Battery.* Baltimore, MD: Johns Hopkins University.

Hanna, R. R., Hanna, J. S., Hodges, R. E., & Rudorf, E. H. (1966). *Phoneme-grapheme correspondences as cues to spelling improvement.* Washington, DC: US Government Printing Office.

Hanley, J. R., & Kay, J. (1998). Does the graphemic buffer play a role in reading? *Cognitive Neuropsychology, 15,* 313–318.

Hatfield, F. M., & Patterson, K. E. (1983). Phonological spelling. *Quarterly Journal of Experimental Psychology, 35,* 451–468.

Hillis, A. E., & Caramazza, A. (1989). The graphemic buffer and attentional mechanisms. *Brain and Language, 36,* 208–235.

Hinton, G. E., & Shallice, T. (1991). Lesioning an attractor network: Investigations of acquired dyslexia. *Psychological Review, 98,* 74–95.

Houghton, G., Glasspool, D. W., & Shallice, T. (1994). Spelling and serial recall: Insights from a competitive queuing model. In G. D. A. Brown & N. C. Ellis (Eds.), *Handbook of spelling: Theory, process and intervention* (pp. 366–404). Chichester, UK: John Wiley.

Howard, D., & Patterson, K. E. (1992). *The Pyramids and Palm Trees test.* Bury St Edmunds, UK: Thames Valley Test Corporation.

Jónsdóttir, M. K., Shallice, T., & Wise, R. (1996). Phonological mediation and the graphemic buffer disorder in spelling: cross-language differences? *Cognition, 59,* 169–197.

Katz, R. B. (1991). Limited retention of information in the graphemic buffer. *Cortex, 27,* 111–119.

Kay, J., & Hanley, R. (1994). Peripheral disorders of spelling: The role of the graphemic buffer. In G. D. A. Brown & N. C. Ellis (Eds.), *Handbook of spelling: Theory, process and intervention* (pp. 295–315). Chichester, UK: John Wiley.

Kay, J., Lesser, R., & Coltheart, M. (1992). *PALPA: Psycholinguistic Assessments of Language Processing in Aphasia.* Hove, UK: Lawrence Erlbaum Associates Ltd.

Kucera, H., & Francis, W. (1967). *Computational analysis of present-day American English.* Providence, RI: Brown University Press.

Lambon Ralph, M. A., Ellis, A. W., & Sage, K. (1998a). Word meaning blindness revisited. *Cognitive Neuropsychology, 15,* 189–200.

Lambon Ralph, M. A., Graham, K. S., Ellis, A. W., & Hodges, J. R. (1998b). Naming in semantic dementia: What matters? *Neuropsychologia, 36,* 775–784.

Lavidor, M., & Ellis, A. W. (2002). Word length and orthographic neighborhood size effects in the left and right cerebral hemispheres. *Brain and Language, 80,* 45–62.

Laxon, V. J., Masterson, J., & Moran, R. (1994). Are children's representations of words distributed? Effects of orthographic neighbourhood size, consistency and regularity in naming. *Language and Cognitive Processes, 9,* 1–27.

Mayzner, M. S., & Tresselt, M. E. (1965). Tables of single-letter and digram frequency counts for various word-length and letter-position combinations. *Psychonomic Monograph Supplements, 1,* 13–31.

Mayzner, M. S., Tresselt, M. E., & Wolin, B. R. (1965). Tables of single-letter and digram frequency counts for various word-length and letter-position combinations. *Psychonomic Monograph Supplements, 1,* 33–78.

McClelland, J. L., & Rumelhart, D. E. (1981). An interactive activation model of context effects in letter perception: Part 1. An account of basic findings. *Psychological Review, 88,* 375–407.

McCloskey, M., Badecker, W., Goodman-Schulman, R. A., & Aliminosa, D. (1994). The structure of graphemic representations in spelling: Evidence from a case of acquired dysgraphia. *Cognitive Neuropsychology, 11,* 341–392.

McKenna, P., & Warrington, E. K. (1983). *Graded Naming Test*. Windsor, UK: NFER-Nelson.

Meyers, J. E., & Meyers, K. R. (1995). *Rey Complex Figure test and recognition trial* (3rd ed.). Odessa, FL: Psychological Test Corporation.

Miceli, G., Silveri, M. C., & Caramazza, A. (1985). Cognitive analysis of a case of pure dysgraphia. *Brain and Language, 25*, 187–121.

Morrison, C. M., & Ellis, A. W. (1995). The roles of word frequency and age of acquisition in word naming and lexical decision. *Journal of Experimental Psychology: Learning, Memory, and Cognition, 21*, 116–133.

Nelson, H. E. (1982). *National Adult Reading Test (NART)*. Windsor, UK: NFER-Nelson.

Nickels, L., & Howard, D. (1995). Aphasic naming: What matters? *Neuropsychologia, 33*, 1281–1303.

Parkin, A. J., & Underwood, G. (1983). Orthographic vs phonological regularity in lexical decision. *Memory and Cognition, 11*, 351–355.

Patterson, K. E., & Hodges, J. R. (1992). Deterioration of word meaning: Implications for reading. *Neuropsychologia, 30*, 1025–1040.

Perea, M., & Rosa, E. (2000). The effects of orthographic neighborhood in reading and laboratory word identification tasks. *Psicológica, 21*, 327–340.

Piccirilli, M., Petrillo, S., & Poli, R. (1992). Dysgraphia and selective impairment of the graphemic buffer. *Italian Journal of Neurological Science, 13*, 113–117.

Plaut, D. C., McClelland, J. L., Seidenberg, M. S., & Patterson, K. (1996). Understanding normal and impaired reading: Computational principles in quasi-regular domains. *Psychological Review, 103*, 56–115.

Plaut, D. C., & Shallice, T. (1993). Deep dyslexia: A case study of connectionist neuropsychology. *Cognitive Neuropsychology, 10*, 377–500.

Postararo, L., Zinelli, P., & Mazzuchi, A. (1998). Selective impairment of the graphemic buffer in acquired dysgraphia: A case study. *Brain and Language, 35*, 274–286.

Quinlan, P. T. (1992). *The MRC Psycholinguistic Database*. London: Oxford University Press.

Rapcsak, S. Z. (1997). Disorders of writing. In L. J. G. Rothi & K. M. Heilman (Eds), *Apraxia: The neuropsychology of action* (pp. 149–172). Hove, UK: Psychology Press.

Raven, J. C. (1985). *Raven's Progressive Matrices* (23rd ed.). London: H. K. Lewis.

Schiller, N. O., Greenhall, J. A., Shelton, J. R., & Caramazza, A. (2001). Serial order effects in spelling errors: Evidence from two dysgraphic patients. *Neurocase, 7*, 1–14.

Silveri, M. C., Cappa, A., Mariotti, P., & Puopolo, M. (2002). Naming in patients with Alzheimer's disease: Influence of age of acquisition and categorical effects. *Journal of Clinical and Experimental Neuropsychology, 24*, 755–764.

Tainturier, M. J., & Caramazza, A. (1996). The status of double letters in graphemic representations. *Journal of Memory and Language, 35*, 53–73.

Ward, J., & Romani, C. (1998). Serial position effects and lexical activation in spelling: Evidence from a single case study. *Neurocase, 4*, 189–206.

Warrington, E. K. (1996). *The Camden Memory Test Battery*. Hove, UK: Psychology Press.

Warrington, E. K. (1997). The Graded Naming Test: A restandardisation. *Neuropsychological Rehabilitation, 7*, 143–146.

Warrington, E., & James, M. (1991). *The Visual Object and Space Perception Battery (VOSP)*. Bury St Edmunds, UK: Thames Valley Test Company.

Warrington, E. K., McKenna, P., & Orpwood, L. (1998). Single word comprehension: A concrete and abstract word synonym test. *Neuropsychological Rehabilitation, 8*, 143–154.

Wing, A. M., & Baddeley, A. D. (1980). Spelling errors in handwriting: A corpus and a distributional analysis. In U. Frith (Ed.), *Cognitive processes in spelling* (pp. 117–133). London: Academic Press.

Zevin, J. D., & Seidenberg, M. S. (2002). Age of acquisition effects in word reading and other tasks. *Journal of Memory and Language, 47*, 1–29.

COGNITIVE NEUROPSYCHOLOGY, 2004, 21 (2/3/4) 401–421

IMPLICIT RECOGNITION IN PURE ALEXIA: THE SAFFRAN EFFECT—A TALE OF TWO SYSTEMS OR TWO PROCEDURES?

Matthew A. Lambon Ralph, Anne Hesketh, and Karen Sage

University of Manchester, UK

Some patients with pure alexia or letter-by-letter reading demonstrate the Saffran effect: residual activation of higher order lexical-semantic representations despite poor word recognition. This study investigated the reading of patient FD, a letter-by-letter reader with a clear Saffran effect. Two alternative explanations for this effect were tested in a series of experiments and through the impact of whole-word and letter-based therapies on FD's reading. One theory assumes that the disparity between overt recognition and implicit activation of word meaning is underpinned by two separate reading systems. An alternative hypothesis argues for a single whole-word reading system supplemented by the deliberate, compensatory strategy of letter-by-letter reading. Under this hypothesis, the Saffran effect reflects partial activation of the single, whole-word system.

FD's results strongly supported the latter hypothesis. FD's reading behaviour was characterised by partial activation of higher word representations, accuracy was graded by word variables known to influence the normal reading system, and most importantly, once the characteristics of the tasks were equated, there was no evidence for a dissociation between word categorisation and recognition. In addition, the whole-word therapy encouraged FD to abandon the letter-by-letter strategy. Without this compensatory technique, FD's emergent deep dyslexia was consistent with a partially activated, whole-word reading system that produces overt reading responses. Comparison of data from this and other studies suggests that the Saffran effect is most likely to be observed in patients with severe pure alexia.

INTRODUCTION

Although reports of "preserved" or "implicit" word recognition in pure and global alexics first appeared in the literature over 40 years ago (Kreindler & Ionasescu, 1961), the first comprehensive investigation of such patients was reported by Shallice and Saffran (1986). This study was followed by a series of papers predominantly by Saffran and her colleagues (Coslett & Saffran, 1989a; Coslett, Saffran, Greenbaum, & Schwartz, 1993; Saffran & Coslett, 1998). The clinical manifestation of this phenomenon (hereinafter referred to as the Saffran effect) is of patients who are able to indicate the meaning of written words, or their lexical status, despite being unable to give the exact identity of the words themselves—i.e., read them aloud. Early studies described patients with very impoverished reading (global alexics) who were able to perform above chance on word–picture

Correspondence should be addressed to Prof M. A. Lambon Ralph, Dept. of Psychology, University of Manchester, Oxford Road, Manchester, M13 9PL, UK (Email: matt.lambon-ralph@man.ac.uk).

We thank Eleanor Saffran not only for the inspiration to conduct this study but also for providing us with materials from her implicit recognition experiments. We are also indebted to FD and his family for their generous donations of time and effort.

DOI:10.1080/02643290342000384

matching tasks or in forced-choice semantic decisions (Albert, Yamadori, Gardner, & Howes, 1973; Caplan & Hedley-Whyte, 1974; Landis, Regard, & Serrat, 1980). While these initial reports are striking, the amount of data presented was minimal. The first detailed investigation of the Saffran effect was on patient ML (Shallice & Saffran, 1986). ML, a slow letter-by-letter reader, was able to perform above chance on a series of forced-choice lexical decision and categorisation tasks even when the words were presented too briefly for ML to report overtly the identity of the word or its constituent letters. Subsequent descriptions of other patients found a similar disparity between above-chance performance under brief presentation and little or no explicit word recognition (for an overview, see Saffran & Coslett, 1998). Having presented each word for a duration of around 250 ms, these patients typically performed in the range of 60–80% correct on various two-alternative forced-choice lexical decision or semantic categorisation tasks. While this level of performance is significantly above that expected by chance, as far as we are aware, no patient has been reported to show normal ability on these simple reading tasks (i.e., at, or close to, perfect performance).

The ability to categorise words without overtly recognising them is, perhaps, the most striking form of the Saffran effect. There is a range of other results that also suggest activation of higher level, lexical-semantic representations in pure alexic patients. For instance, some letter-by-letter readers have exhibited the word superiority effect (better letter recognition under masked presentation if the stimuli correspond to words, or word-like nonwords, than letter strings: Reuter-Lorenz & Brunn, 1990). In addition, pure alexics show influences of variables associated with lexical-semantic processes (frequency and imageability: Behrmann, Plaut, & Nelson, 1998b) and can also demonstrate standard Stroop interference (McKeeff & Behrmann, 2004 this issue).

There is an ongoing debate about the locus of impairment that gives rise to pure alexia (Coltheart, 1998). Some researchers suggest that pure alexia reflects damage to a general visual

system (Behrmann, Nelson, & Sekuler, 1998a; Farah & Wallace, 1991; Mycroft, Behrmann, & Kay, 2003), others argue that there is impaired letter recognition or a breakdown between letter and word representations (e.g., Patterson & Kay, 1982). The explanations all share the notion, however, that pure alexia reflects a relatively early impairment in the visual-orthographic system that leads to poor whole-word recognition. By way of compensation, patients resort to a letter-by-letter reading strategy. At face value, explanations of pure alexia based on early visual impairment seem at odds with the Saffran effect: The early visual deficit is supposed to prevent activation of whole-word representations, thus necessitating the letter-by-letter strategy for word recognition but the Saffran effect is evidence for activation of high-level representations including word meaning.

There are two rival explanations for the Saffran effect in the literature, both of which were first discussed in detail by Shallice and Saffran (1986). The first explanation, championed by Saffran, Coslett, and their colleagues (Saffran & Coslett, 1998), separates the key behavioural elements observed in these patients and posits a separate system for each one. Their theory is based on the notion that there are two parallel reading systems, one in each hemisphere of the brain. The left hemisphere system supports explicit letter and word recognition and, when damaged, uses letter-by-letter reading as a compensatory strategy. The right hemisphere reading system underpins implicit letter and word recognition. When the left hemisphere system is damaged, as it is in pure alexic patients, their letter-by-letter behaviour is derived from the remaining processing in the left hemisphere while the Saffran effect is generated by the right hemisphere. The separation of processing in these systems is further reinforced by the notion that the left hemisphere system can inhibit the right hemisphere. The early report by Landis et al. (1980) noted that their patient's implicit reading disappeared once letter recognition had recovered sufficiently to support letter-by-letter reading. Likewise, Coslett et al. (1993) reported data from patient JWC, who was able to switch between letter-by-letter reading when the task required explicit word identification and whole-word (implicit) recognition for categorisation tasks. In addition, Coslett and Saffran (1989a) were able to demonstrate that performance on categorisation tasks declined as the exposure length was increased from 250 ms to 2 s and it was at this point that the patients were able to engage a letter-by-letter strategy.

Various aspects of the two systems hypothesis have been challenged. The implicit versus explicit distinction was questioned by Feinberg, Dyches-Berke, Miner, and Roane (1994). The patient they described exhibited the Saffran effect but Feinberg et al. argued that her accuracy on various categorisation tasks matched the level of her explicit awareness and was consistent with degraded, partial semantic access from orthography. Coslett and Saffran (1989a) found that with repeated exposure to brief presentation experiments, over several weeks, their patients began to read some words explicitly and without recourse to letter-by-letter reading. Further investigation found that this explicit reading performance (still under brief presentation conditions) was influenced by factors such as imageability and part-of-speech effects—i.e., the patients demonstrated some features of phonological-deep dyslexia, although they did not produce semantic paralexias. A combined pure-deep dyslexic, described by Buxbaum and Coslett (1996), is of added interest because he had a number of features in common with the case described in this study. At unlimited exposure, the patient used a laborious letter-by-letter strategy, exhibited an imageability and part-of-speech effect, and had very poor nonword reading. These effects remained unchanged if the words were presented briefly (100 ms) except that the patient produced a significantly greater number of semantic paralexias.

Although some researchers have argued that the letter-by-letter strategy inhibits the separate reading system that underpins the Saffran effect (Landis et al., 1980; Saffran & Coslett, 1998), other results suggest that these two phenomena can co-occur. For instance, in a thorough review of the pure alexia literature and of newly collected data, Behrmann et al. (1998b) found that pure

alexics' length-reading time function was also influenced by frequency and imageability. The dual influence of length and lexical-semantic factors suggests that, to at least some extent, whole-word reading processes and the letter-by-letter strategy are working in parallel or in conjunction.

These results and the Saffran effect can be explained by an alternative, two "processes" theory. This explanation assumes that impaired visual input drives two processes: a *single* whole-word recognition system and a separate, compensatory letter-by-letter strategy (Behrmann et al., 1998b; Shallice & Saffran, 1986). This contrasts with the two systems hypothesis, which duplicates elements in the left and right hemispheres for whole-word recognition (the two systems) and also includes a separate, compensatory letter-by-letter strategy (which is assumed to be underpinned by the left hemisphere). In effect, there are three processes—left-hemisphere, overt whole-word reading (which is abolished in pure alexia), right-hemisphere reading (that supports covert recognition), and left-hemisphere letter-by-letter reading. Under the two processes/single system hypothesis, patients' reading behaviour, with unlimited exposures, reflects the conjoint action of these two processes. Although slow and laborious, letter-by-letter reading allows for accurate word identification, which is boosted by the whole-word system if the words are common and concrete (Behrmann et al., 1998b). With more severe impairment, the conjoint action of the two processes is reflected in patients who exhibit features of both pure and deep dyslexia (Buxbaum & Coslett, 1996). However, letter-by-letter reading is limited or impossible with brief presentation and, as a deliberate compensatory strategy, patients can learn to avoid or inhibit the technique altogether (Coslett & Saffran, 1989a).

Under this proposal, the Saffran effect simply reflects the partial, remaining activation of the whole-word recognition system (Behrmann et al., 1998b; Feinberg et al., 1994; Shallice & Saffran, 1986). This also explains why performance on lexical decision and categorisation tasks is above chance but never perfect in these cases. The combination of early visual-orthographic impairments and partial semantic access is only surprising if the reading system contains discrete processes. In a cascading or interactive activation system, impaired input will still produce partial, degraded activation in the post-impairment processes (Morton & Patterson, 1980; Shallice & Saffran, 1986). In McClelland and Rumelhart's (1981) interactive activation word recognition model, reduced input to letter features still produced partial letter and word level activation. This was, of course, the basis for their explanation of the word superiority effect in normal readers under masked, brief presentation. Likewise, it explains why pure alexics can also show the word superiority effect (feedback from lexical-semantic knowledge), effects of frequency and imageability (frequent and concrete words are more readily activated even under reduced visual input) and above-chance performance on lexical decision and categorisation tasks (partial activation of lexical and semantic representations). If the Saffran effect does emerge from the normal, premorbid whole-word reading system under reduced or degraded visual input, then this theory also explains why categorisation performance is influenced by the same factors as timed word reading. Shallice and Saffran (1986), for example, demonstrated that patient ML's lexical decision performance was influenced by the wordlikeness of the nonword foils and the frequency of the real words.

A key, unresolved question is why only some patients show the Saffran effect. While a number of patients show above-chance performance on categorisation and lexical decision tasks (Saffran & Coslett, 1998), others do not (e.g., Patterson & Kay, 1982). In a similar vein, Behrmann et al. (1998b) note that the influence of frequency and imageability varies across patients. Three explanations of these differences have been proposed. The first is methodological. Saffran and Coslett (1998) argued that pure alexic patients can be reluctant to relinquish the letter-by-letter strategy and to make a binary decision when the word is merely flashed in front of them. Patients have to be encouraged, therefore, to make responses or even guesses in these somewhat strange, experimental conditions.

While this might be a reason for the failure to find above-chance categorisation in brief presentation tasks, it seems less likely as an explanation for the variation in frequency and imageability effects in pure alexia. Letter-by-letter reading times are presumably boosted automatically by underlying lexical-semantic representations. The second explanation is that the Saffran effect might vary across individual patients according to the presence of other concurrent impairments. So, for example, if some pure alexic patients have additional lexical-semantic deficits, then the functioning of the whole-word recognition system may be compromised and the influence of frequency and imageability reduced or even abolished. The final explanation is based on severity. Behrmann and colleagues (1998b) argued that with very mild visual impairment, word recognition might require little if any assistance from higher-order representations. With very severe impairments, there may be so little input to the whole-word recognition system that the degree of feedback activation is minimal or non-existent. In between, however, moderately degraded visual processing benefits considerably from feedback activation. In support of this hypothesis, Behrmann et al. found that the size of frequency and imageability effects in their pure alexic patients were significantly correlated with the slope of the length-reading time function.

In this study we describe a letter-by-letter reader who demonstrated the Saffran effect. The investigations were designed to test the contrasting predictions of the two systems and two processes hypotheses, and to assess the explanations for why the Saffran effect varies across individual patients.

PATIENT STUDY

Background

Social and medical history

FD was born in 1924. Prior to retirement, he had held a variety of jobs including running a grocer's shop and working for a tyre company. FD was also a Jehovah's Witness. This had two important influences on the present study. First, as reading is a key activity within this faith, FD and his family were highly motivated to undertake extensive assessment and therapy programmes, despite FD's severe alexia. Second, FD's extensive experience of the Jehovah's Witness literature meant that Christian religious terms were extremely familiar to him—a factor made use of in two of the experiments reported below.

In 1995 and 1996, FD had suffered two minor cerebral vascular accidents. These did not lead to hospitalisation but FD was clinically managed at home. In the acute phase FD was noted to have a mild left hemiparesis, which later resolved, and a 24-hour period of "broken sentences" and poor comprehension of simple questions. In August 1997, FD was admitted to hospital with speech difficulty and memory loss. A CT scan (see Figure 1) showed an extensive haemorrhagic infarct in the left parietal lobe extending inferiorly into the temporal lobe. This also revealed evidence of the two previous vascular incidents with old infarcts in the right parietal and right occipital regions. In September 1997, FD underwent a right carotid endocardectomy and was discharged a week later. Unfortunately, FD was readmitted in mid-October with a frontal headache and loss of vision. A new CT scan (see Figure 1) showed an additional left occipital haematoma and a fresh bleed in the occipital horn of the right lateral ventricle. Medical examination revealed right hemianopia, low visual acuity on the right and unsteady gait. FD was discharged in November 1997 with some right visual field difficulties, improving gait with residual unsteadiness, and persisting communication difficulties, for which he was referred for rehabilitation.

Language skills

FD presented with good comprehension and spoken output. His speech revealed mild word-finding difficulties with semantic paraphasias evident in confrontational naming tests and in connected speech. FD also had a severe reading impairment both for comprehension of written text and when reading aloud. FD was asked to complete a comprehensive language assessment and the results are presented below. In particular, we conducted a detailed analysis of FD's reading. Initial assessment revealed FD's prolonged attempts to identify each word with a letter-by-letter strategy (e.g., STOP → "S.T.E.P. … stop"; OPEN → "O.P.E.N. … open").[1] Although FD was able to recognise a minority of words using this strategy, he would most commonly make letter recognition errors and ultimately fail to identify the target word (e.g, TRACK → "T.R.A.Q.D. … … no"; service → "S.E.R.Y. … … no"). Most strikingly, FD would sometimes offer an approximate definition of the target word during his prolonged letter-by-letter attempts (e.g., EXIT → "H., no, D.X.I.P. … notice on a door"; RELIGION → "something religious again … getting better … F.E.Y.I.R.I.O. …").

Letter-by-letter reading

Patients with pure alexia or letter-by-letter reading demonstrate increasing reading times as a function of letter length. In order to test for this central symptom of letter-by-letter reading, FD was presented with 60 high-frequency words that varied in length (two to five letters—matched for frequency across each length). The use of high-frequency vocabulary was essential given that, with less frequent items, FD's omission rate was too high for collecting sufficient timing data. FD's mean correct reading times and error rates are shown in Figure 2. For these words, FD demonstrated a clear effect of word length on both reading times and accuracy. Reading was slow overall and rose from an average of 11 seconds for two letter words up to 38 seconds for five-letter items. FD was relatively accurate for the shorter items but he made considerably more errors on the longest words.

Patients with pure alexia demonstrate poor reading in the context of preserved writing and

---

[1] Target words are denoted in small capitals; letter-by-letter attempts are represented by full capital letters punctuated by full stops; any other comments or spoken responses are shown between inverted commas.

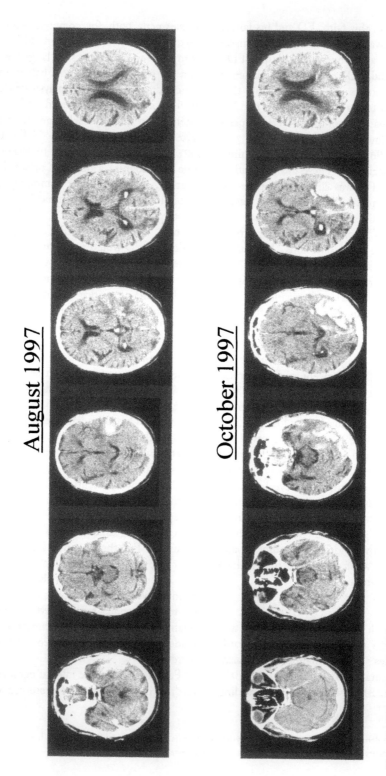

August 1997

October 1997

Figure 1. CT scans for patient FD.

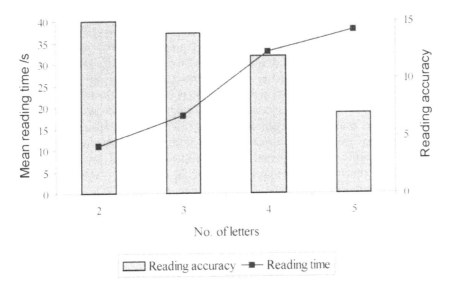

Figure 2. *FD's average reading time and error rate as a function of length.*

the absence of aphasia. This leads to the striking clinical observation of patients who cannot read their own written output. Both aspects were tested in FD. The more general language assessment is reported below. In order to compare spelling and reading, FD was given both words and nonwords that vary in letter length (tests 39 and 36 from the PALPA battery: Kay, Lesser, & Coltheart, 1992). For the words, FD was asked to complete four tasks: reading aloud; "reading" or recognition of the words spoken letter-by-letter by the examiner; oral and written spelling to dictation. For the nonwords, only reading and recognition of orally

spelled words were compared. FD's reading of the words was poor and accuracy did not vary across length. Performance on the other three tasks was no better, although FD tended to be more accurate for the shorter than longer items. There was, however, a significant difference on the nonwords. FD was only able to read two of the shortest non-words but was able to construct the correct pronunciation for a larger number of the items when the letters were spoken by the examiner (McNemar, $p = .001$). It seems likely that FD's poor spelling was due to mild concurrent aphasia (see below).

Table 1. *FD's reading and spelling performance as a function of length*

	Letter length				
Task	*3*	*4*	*5*	*6*	*Overall*
Words (PALPA 39)					
Reading	2/6	3/6	3/6	3/6	14/24
"Reading" of spoken letter strings	6/6	5/6	3/6	3/6	17/24
Oral spelling to dictation	6/6	3/6	4/6	2/6	15/24
Writing to dictation	6/6	2/6	3/6	1/6	12/24
Nonwords (PALPA 36)					
Reading	2/6	0/6	0/6	0/6	2/24
"Reading" of spoken letter strings	6/6	2/6	3/6	2/6	13/24

General visual processing

Table 2 shows FD's results from a range of tests designed to tap letter and number recognition in addition to more general visual perception. Initial reading assessments had found that FD's letter-by-letter attempts commonly contained letter recognition errors. The assessments of letter processing demonstrated the same impairment. Although able to complete cross-case letter matching without error, FD's recognition was impaired for single letters and letter sequences whether presented in upper or lower case. Like other patients in the literature (Behrmann et al., 1998b), FD's impaired reading was associated with a more general, visual perceptual deficit. His scores on

a number of the subtests from the VOSP (Warrington & James, 1991) and BORB (Riddoch & Humphreys, 1992) were abnormal, denoting impaired object recognition and space perception. Although his score on the incomplete letters subtest was within the normal range for accuracy, FD's performance was slow and he often traced the target letter. FD's impaired visual processing also extended to number recognition. In a simple assessment, FD was presented with 30 numbers ranging from two to seven digits in length. His number reading errors contained both digit recognition and syntax errors (e.g., 7456 → "seven thousand, four hundred and twenty-six; 8372 → "eight hundred, three seven two").

General language assessment

FD was given a range of tests designed to assess naming, comprehension, and phonology. The results are summarised in Table 3. On three standard tests of naming to confrontation (Boston Naming Test, Graded Naming Test, and test 54 from the PALPA battery: Goodglass, Kaplan, & Weintraub, 1983; McKenna & Warrington, 1983), FD's scores fell below the normal range. Given the evidence for visuospatial deficits, FD's impaired naming could have been due to poor visual recognition and/or concurrent aphasia. In order to test this further, FD was asked to complete an additional naming task in which items were either presented as spoken definitions or as pictures. This assessment revealed that FD's picture naming was significantly worse than when naming the same items from spoken definitions, suggesting that his poor picture naming was due, in part, to poor visual recognition (McNemar, Exact p = .02). In addition, FD's naming to definition fell slightly below the normal range. Along with the clinical observations of word-finding difficulties in spontaneous speech (see above), this suggests that FD did have mild, additional, aphasic word-finding difficulties.

FD was asked to complete a number of comprehension assessments. These were selected in order to vary the modality of input and difficulty. On a 100-item word–picture matching test with semantic foils (four foils per trial), FD's performance on

Table 2. *Assessment of FD's visual perception and recognition*

Test	FD's score	Norms
VOSP		Normal cut-off
Screen	19	15
Incomplete letters	16	16
Silhouettes	7[a]	15
Object decision	13[a]	14
Progressive silhouettes	15	15
Dot counting	9	8
Position discrimination	14[a]	18
Number location	7	7
Cube analysis	3[a]	6
BORB		Normal range
Minimal feature match	24/25	18.5–25
Foreshortened match	25/25	16.7–25
Object decision (easy)	22/32[a]	28 –32
Object decision (hard)	21/32[a]	22 –30
Item match	30/32	24 –32
Letter recognition		
Single, upper case letter naming	15/26[a]	–
Single, lower case letter naming	18/26[a]	–
Naming of lower case letter sequences	56/80[a]	–
Naming of upper case letter sequences	59/80[a]	–
Cross-case letter matching (PALPA 20)	26/26	26
Number reading	24/30[a]	–

[a] denotes abnormal performance.

VOSP: Visual Object and Space Perception battery; BORB: Birmingham Object Recognition Battery; PALPA: Psycholinguistic Assessments of Language Processing in Aphasia.

Table 3. *FD's background neuropsychological results*

Test	FD's score	Norms
Naming		
Boston Naming Test	11/60[a]	42–60
Graded Naming Test	3/30[a]	*M* = 20.4, S.D. = 4.1
PALPA 54 Picture Naming	51/60[a]	–
Naming		
From definitions	44/51	49–51
Pictures	35/51[a]	50–51
Comprehension		
100-item		
Written word–picture matching	42/100[a]	96–100
Spoken word–picture matching	79/100[a]	96–100
PALPA		
Written word–picture matching	2/15[a]	35–40
Spoken word–picture matching	35/40	35–40
BORB association matching	25/30	21–30
Pyramids and Palm Trees Test		
Pictures	42/52[a]	49–52
Spoken words	46/52*	49–52
Concrete and abstract synonyms		
Concrete	19/25	50–75th %ile
Abstract	18/25	50–75th %ile
PALPA auditory synonyms	55/60	–
ADA auditory synonyms	148/160[a]	152–160
Phonology		
ADA word and nonword repetition	79/80	52–80
PALPA		
Syllable length word repetition	24/24	–
Syllable length nonword repetition	29/30	–
Morphologically complex word repetition	87/90	–
Syllable counting	13/24[a]	22–24
Initial consonant deletion	18/24[a]	21–23
Rhyme judgement	20/24	20–24

[a] Denotes abnormal score.

the spoken and written versions fell below the normal range and the score for written word–picture matching was significantly worse than for the spoken version of the same test (McNemar, Exact, $p < .001$). This is unsurprising given that in this condition both the word and pictures require visual recognition. Indeed, on the PALPA version of the same test, FD's performance was so bad that the assessment had to be discontinued after 15

items. On the other hand, FD's score on the spoken version fell into the normal range published with this test. FD's comprehension was also assessed using the semantic association tasks from the BORB in addition to the picture and spoken word versions of the Pyramids and Palm Trees test (PPT: Howard & Patterson, 1992). For the BORB association test, FD's score fell into the normal range while on the spoken and picture versions of the PPT his performance was mildly abnormal. Given that we had already found evidence for a generalised visual perceptual deficit that impacted on FD's picture naming ability (see above), we also administered three comprehension tests that avoided the visual modality completely. The concrete and abstract synonyms test (Warrington, McKenna, & Orpwood, 1998) contains a series of psychometrically graded word triads that are spoken by the examiner. On both the concrete and abstract items, FD's scores placed him in the normal range. Likewise, on the PALPA auditory synonyms his performance was good and on the ADA version (Franklin, Turner, & Ellis, 1992) his score fell only a few points below the normal range for undergraduates published with this test.

Given FD's poor spelling and aphasic word-finding difficulties, we also asked him to complete a number of tests of phonology. On a series of word and nonword repetition tasks that vary morphological complexity and syllable length, FD's scores were excellent. Evidence for a slight phonological impairment was highlighted, however, in two of three phonological awareness tasks that require deliberate manipulation of word sound (syllable counting and initial consonant deletion).

In summary, FD's very poor reading was accompanied by a general visuospatial deficit in addition to a very mild impairment of phonology plus some aphasic word-finding difficulties (which may have been due to the underlying phonological impairment itself). FD's excellent performance on the tests of spoken word comprehension suggest that there is little or no evidence for a semantic impairment; his poor comprehension of written words and pictures is entirely consistent with his underlying alexia and visuospatial deficit.

FD's Saffran effect

One of the most striking aspects of FD's reading attempts was his ability to indicate the meaning of a word without giving the actual identity of the target itself. Like the patients described by Saffran and Coslett (1998), this suggests that FD was still able to access the partial meaning of written words. In order to test this more formally, FD was asked to complete three two-alternative forced-choice semantic categorisation tasks. For each assessment, a fixation cross was followed by the brief (250 ms) presentation of the target word. FD was encouraged to indicate the correct category (food vs. nonfood; animal vs. nonanimal, male vs. female names) even though he was unable to see the word clearly enough to report its identity. Where FD was uncertain, he was asked to guess. FD's performance is summarised in Table 4. Given that the tests were identical to those administered by Saffran and Coslett, FD's scores are given alongside their patients' for direct comparison.

Table 4 shows that FD did exhibit the Saffran effect: Despite being unable to give the identity of any of these items, his categorisation performance was significantly above chance in all three tests and was comparable in magnitude to the effect found by Saffran and Coslett (1998). Although the combination of above-chance categorisation without overt word recognition is very striking, it should be noted that the scores of FD and all the other patients fell into the mid range. As far as we are aware, no patient has ever demonstrated performance close to ceiling without overt recognition. Likewise, when indicating the meaning of a written word during his letter-by-letter attempts, FD never gave the exact meaning of the target word and he only did this for a subset of the items.

The graded nature of FD's performance was investigated more thoroughly in a second series of brief presentation experiments.

What is the basis of the Saffran effect?

Manipulating FD's accuracy

In the Introduction we laid out two possible explanations for the Saffran effect. The first assumes that the apparent dissociation in brief presentation experiments between good categorisation/lexical decision performance and no overt word recognition reflects two separate reading systems. The alternative explanation suggests that whole-word recognition is still supported by a single reading system, albeit with severely impaired visual input, supplemented by a letter-by-letter strategy. The brief presentation technique prevents any use of letter-by-letter reading and the remaining ability of the impaired, premorbid reading system is laid bare. These two explanations were tested in two investigations: One utilised a specific therapy intervention that discouraged the letter-by-letter approach almost entirely, meaning that FD's reading could be explored without needing the brief presentation method (see below). In addition, prior to therapy intervention, we used a series of further brief presentation tasks to explore the underlying nature of FD's reading.

If the Saffran effect reflects the nature of the single, premorbid reading system, then it should be possible to manipulate the patients' accuracy by varying factors that are known to influence normal and impaired reading performance. In the limit, with the most favourable items, this single reading system might be able to recognise words overtly—that is to say, how much of a word's meaning is

Table 4. *FD's performance on Saffran's 2AFC semantic categorisation tasks*

| Categorisation task | N | Saffran and Coslett (1997) patients | | | | FD | |
		JG	TL	JL	AF	Accuracy	Binomial, p
Food/Non-food	75	80%	67%	79%	76%	61%	.03
Animal/Non-animal	75	75%	69%	85%	71%	71%	<.001
Male/Female names	100	75%	70%	71%	80%	72%	<.001

activated should be a matter of degree rather than the absolute, qualitative difference implied by the two-systems theory. We carried out, therefore, a second series of brief presentation experiments in which the nature of the words and of the forced-choice were manipulated. The method and presentation times were unchanged. The results are summarised in Table 5a for the semantic categorisation tasks and in Table 5b for the lexical decision tests.

Normal and impaired word recognition is influenced by a number of factors including word frequency/familiarity and imageability (Behrmann et al., 1998b). To investigate the role of frequency/familiarity in FD, we utilised the fact that religious words were very familiar to him. In the first experiment, we selected 20 Christian terms and paired them with 20 local place names, which were all highly familiar. FD was required to indicate whether the word was either a religious term or a place name. Although not perfect, FD's score of 79% was the highest of all of the categorisation experiments conducted. Most importantly, with these extremely familiar words, FD was able to recognise six of them even with a 250 ms presentation, suggesting that in these most favourable conditions, FD's reading system was able to recognise words overtly. In order to test our assumption that it was the familiarity of the words that was critical, we repeated the experiment but also included 40 relatively unfamiliar religious words (non-Christian) and place names (towns in southern England). As can be seen in Table 5a, FD's score on the familiar items was almost unchanged but his performance on the unfamiliar terms was significantly worse, $\chi^2 = 3.81$, $p = .05$, and no better than chance.

The third set of categorisation experiments tested our observation that patients who demonstrate the Saffran effect only activate a partial

Table 5. *Manipulation of FD's (a) categorisation accuracy and (b) lexical decision accuracy*

Task	N	Accuracy	Binomial, p
(a) Categorisation accuracy			
Religious terms vs. Local place names	34[a]	79%	<.001
Religious terms vs. Place names	80	69%	<.001
High familiarity	40	78%	<.001
Low familiarity	40	60%	n.s.
4AFC vs. 2AFC			
Birds vs. Animals vs. Tools vs. Vehicles	80	29%	n.s.
Animals vs. Artefacts	80	64%	.01
Birds vs. Animals	40	65%	.04
Tools vs. Vehicles	40	65%	.04
Native/Foreign	40	68%	.02
(b) Lexical decision accuracy			
Lexical decision (PALPA 24) with			
Illegal nonwords	60	88%	<.001
Legal nonwords	60	68%	.003
Imageability by Frequency (PALPA 25)	120	64%	.001
High Imageability/High Frequency	15	93%	<.001
Low Imageability/High Frequency	15	47%	n.s.
High Imageability/Low Frequency	15	53%	n.s.
Low Imageability/Low Frequency	15	60%	n.s.
Nonwords	60	65%	.01

[a] The test contains 40 items but FD was able to recognise 6 words even with a 250 ms brief presentation.

semantic representation that is commensurate with the degree of remaining activation throughout the whole of the reading system. Two types of semantic specificity were tested. First, we manipulated the number of alternatives on offer in the categorisation experiment (4AFC: birds vs. animals vs. tools vs. vehicles; or 2AFC: animals vs. artefacts, etc.). Under our working hypothesis it might be the case that performance would drop in line with the number of alternatives (as Shallice & Saffran, 1986, had found). Second, we manipulated the semantic differentiation required by the categorisation. FD was asked to differentiate at the level of domain (animals vs. artefacts), or between categories (birds vs. animals or tools vs. vehicles) or on the basis of more specific information (native or foreign creatures). As can be seen in Table 5a, the number of alternatives, but not the level of semantic differentiation, influenced FD's accuracy.

The results from the categorisation experiments are consistent with the notion that FD's reading performance reflects the partial remaining activation within a single, damaged reading system. The degree of activation varies in line with the frequency/familiarity of the words. In addition the remaining activation is sufficient to push two-alternative judgements above chance levels but insufficient to support categorisations with more choices. Saffran and Coslett (1998) also explored their patients' reading performance using lexical decision under brief presentation. We included, therefore, two lexical decision experiments that explored related word characteristics. The results are shown in Table 5b.

Assuming that the Saffran effect reflects partial activation within the remaining single reading system, lexical decision—like categorisation—should vary according to word characteristics like frequency and imageability. In addition, partial activation may only be able to support relatively easy decisions. The first experiment was designed to vary the difficulty of the lexical decision (in a similar way to Shallice & Saffran, 1986). Items were taken from the PALPA lexical decision test with illegal nonwords (e.g., CLIP vs. AEMF) and presented under the same brief presentation conditions. In addition, the experiment was repeated but

the illegal items were replaced by legal nonwords derived from the real words (e.g., CLIP vs. CLEP). FD performed above chance on both variants of the experiment but his accuracy was significantly enhanced when he was required to distinguish between words and illegal nonwords, $\chi^2 = 7.07$, $p = .008$.

The previous categorisation tasks found a clear effect of frequency on performance. The second experiment tested whether this was also true for lexical decision while also varying word imageability. Studies of other milder letter-by-letter readers have found evidence for frequency and imageability in reading times (Behrmann et al., 1998b). Items were selected from PALPA test number 25, which orthogonally varies both frequency and imageability and pairs each word with a legal nonword. Overall, FD's lexical decision accuracy (64%) was very similar to the first lexical decision experiment that used legal nonwords (68%). His performance for the words varied, however, in line with the lexical variables. Specifically, FD's recognition of words was only significantly above chance for concrete, high frequency items.

Is there really a dissociation between word identification and "implicit" recognition?

The results from the brief presentation lexical decision and categorisation experiments produced very similar results. Overall, FD's accuracy was influenced by the frequency and imageability of the words and by the difficulty of the decision. This is consistent with the proposal that the Saffran effect is underpinned by the remaining activation of the damaged reading system (Behrmann et al., 1998b; Feinberg et al., 1994; Shallice & Saffran, 1986). This reduced activation will be sufficient to resolve simple discriminations and just like any other normal or impaired system, activation is graded by characteristics such as frequency and imageability. In the limit, with the most favourable items, the remaining activation is sufficient to support near-normal processing—in this case, relatively quick whole-word recognition. These results are consistent with a single system account of the Saffran effect in which there are graded rather than absolute differences in processing. Setting aside

Table 6. *FD's performance on the 2AFC word recognition vs. categorisation task*

Target	Foil type in 2AFC word recognition task			Semantic categorisation
	Shared onset	*Shared end*	*Semantic*	
e.g., duck	dusk	tuck	swan	Living vs.
e.g., bath	bash	path	shower	nonliving
Accuracy (*N* = 40)	70%	90%	90%	45%
Binomial, *p*	.01	<.001	<.001	n.s.

neurological issues (to which we return in the General Discussion), the two system account is based on the observation of a dissociation between poor word identification but good categorisation. FD's results show that categorisation performance varies in a predictable way and occasionally word identification is possible even under brief presentation. One could wonder, therefore, whether there really is a dissociation between word identification and categorisation in these patients—particularly as the two tasks are not equivalent.[2] Word identification is measured simply in terms of reading aloud—i.e., an unconstrained response by the patient. Categorisation (either semantic or lexical), on the other hand, is measured most often by a 2AFC task. It is easy to imagine that a reduced amount of residual activation in the reading system would be sufficient to achieve above-chance accuracy in the 2AFC task (albeit not perfect performance) but that this would be insufficient to derive any overt reading response. We, like Shallice and Saffran (1986), have already demonstrated that FD's accuracy fell significantly in a 4AFC task, so if one extrapolates this to the number of words in an adult's reading vocabulary then it is unsurprising that the system cannot ascertain exactly which word is present.

Our last brief presentation experiment was designed to equate the nature of word identification and categorisation. Forty monosyllabic words were presented in a series of 2AFC conditions that measured either word identification or semantic categorisation (living vs. nonliving). Three types of

foil were included in the 2AFC identification tasks. A foil was derived from each target item by changing either its end (i.e., shared onset and vowel: DUCK vs. DUSK) or beginning (i.e., shared vowel and offset: DUCK vs. TUCK). We also included a semantically-related foil (e.g., DUCK vs. SWAN). The last experimental condition required a living vs. nonliving semantic categorisation. The conditions were counterbalanced across four testing sessions. For each trial, the single target word was presented on the screen for 250 ms, preceded by a fixation cross, and the examiner offered FD either two possible words or categories to choose from.

FD's results across the four conditions are shown in Table 6. A number of important features were highlighted by this experiment. The left-to-right position of the differing letters was important. Although performance in all three versions of the 2AFC identification experiment was significantly above chance, FD's accuracy was significantly better if the words differed at the beginning rather than at the end. His performance was also very good for the semantic foils, which typically shared few if any letters in common, although it is striking that FD accepted the semantic foil in 4/40 trials (for example, FD accepted "shower" for BATH). In this experiment, his semantic categorisation was very poor (at chance) but his 2AFC word identification in the shared onset condition was equivalent to the accuracy he typically achieved on most 2AFC semantic categorisation experiments (around 70%). In conclusion, once the

---

[2] We are indebted to Karalyn Patterson for pointing this fact out to us and for the experimental solution.

nature of the two tasks is made equivalent, there is no evidence to suggest that categorisation is any better than word identification. Based on these results, there is no evidence for a dissociation between the two tasks and thus little motivation for a two systems model. The results from this experiment, taken with those reported above, are consistent with a single system hypothesis.

As noted before, Saffran and Coslett (1998) have argued that above-chance semantic categorisation in these brief presentation experiments is highly dependent on the strategy adopted by the patient. Patients have to be encouraged away from using their letter-by-letter strategy to identify the target word specifically. One could wonder, therefore, whether the 2AFC word identification task used in this experiment discouraged or even inhibited (Landis et al., 1980) the implicit, right-hemisphere reading system leading to poor performance on the semantic categorisation task. While this strategy argument may explain FD's poor semantic categorisation in this specific experiment, the important observation is that his word identification skills, when measured using a 2AFC procedure, are exactly commensurate with his categorisation performance on all the other 2AFC

tasks reported above, none of which emphasised word identity.

Removing the letter-by-letter strategy: FD—the deep dyslexic

The last investigation of FD's reading assessed the impact of a specific therapy intervention. The details of the therapy and its outcome are reported elsewhere (Sage, Hesketh, & Lambon Ralph, 2003) but the key elements are repeated here. It is the particular effect it had on FD's reading that is critical to the present study. The therapy study was split into three phases. Initially, FD was given a baseline assessment for three sets of words, comprising both experimental words (matched across sets for frequency and length) as well as some personally relevant vocabulary. In the second phase, FD was given daily practice on one set of words using an errorless learning approach (Fillingham, Hodgson, Sage, & Lambon Ralph, 2003; Wilson & Evans, 1996) to reinforce whole-word recognition. Specifically, FD was shown each word in turn but to prevent errors, he was given the correct pronunciation by the therapist and he then repeated it five times. This therapy was practiced daily for several weeks and FD was then reassessed

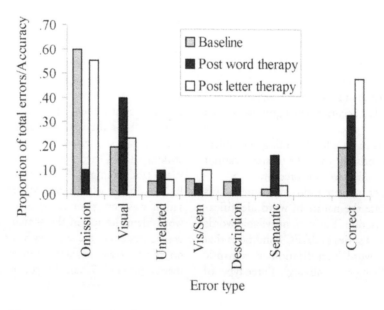

Figure 3. *Influence of therapy type on FD's word reading errors.*

again on all three reading lists. In the final phase, the errorless learning approach was retained but therapy moved from the word to the letter level. This time, the therapist concentrated on individual letters and later, letters within words, again using repetition as the errorless method. After another few weeks of daily practice, FD was assessed again on all three word sets.

The right-hand side of Figure 3 shows the total accuracy for the three word sets at baseline and after each round of therapy. In each case, there was a significant increase in accuracy for the set of therapy items with no significant generalisation to the control words. For the purposes of this study, the two therapies had a dramatic effect on both FD's reading strategy and the distribution of his reading errors. Prior to therapy, FD tried to use an overt letter-by-letter strategy on 68/90 words. Following whole-word therapy he almost completely gave up on this reading strategy, attempting letter-by-letter reading for only 6/90 words and showed a correspondingly (relatively) quicker reading time. Although we did not formally reassess reading times for words of varying lengths, the change in FD's overt reading behaviour was so pronounced that had he presented in this way, he probably would not have been considered to be a letter-by-letter reader. Somewhat surprisingly, although we had expected the letter-based therapy to encourage the return of his letter-by-letter reading, there was no change in FD's reading behaviour after the second therapy. Somewhat serendipitously, FD had almost completely given up on the (rather ineffective) letter-by-letter strategy. This is important for two reasons: First, it reinforces the notion that letter-by-letter reading is a strategy that can be deliberately adopted or discarded (Coslett et al., 1993). Second, and most critically for this study, it meant that FD's reading now reflected his underlying, impaired reading system without compensation by the letter-by-letter approach. In such circumstances, the use of brief presentation to inhibit this strategy was no longer necessary.

In addition to changing his reading style, the two therapy interventions had a dramatic effect on the distribution of FD's reading errors. This is shown in the remainder of Figure 3. As the distribution was very similar for each word set, the error data was combined. At each testing round, FD made a mixture of omissions; visual, semantic, visual-semantic, and unrelated reading errors, together with a handful of responses that gave an indication of the words' meaning (denoted here as description errors). Following each therapy, there was a significant change in the distribution of errors although the distribution following the letter therapy was not significantly different to baseline: baseline vs. post whole-word therapy, $\chi^2(5) = 34.7$, $p < .001$; post whole-word therapy vs. post letter-based therapy, $\chi^2(5) = 27.9$, $p < .001$; base-line vs. post letter-based therapy, $\chi^2(5) = 3.60$, $p = .61$. The whole-word therapy changed the rate of three types of error (as a proportion of total errors): omissions dropped from 60% to 10%; visual errors jumped from 20% to 40%; while, most strikingly, the rate of pure semantic errors climbed dramatically from 3% to 17% (e.g., TRUTH → "faith, no … preach?"; ASPIRIN → "hospital"). In effect, FD had changed from a poor letter-by-letter reader into a deep dyslexic. Although the subsequent, letter-based therapy did not reinvigorate his letter-by-letter reading, it did return his error pattern back to the same as at baseline, with omission errors predominating. His reading, at this stage, would best be described as a form of visual dyslexia (Lambon Ralph & Ellis, 1997).

In order to check the apparent emergence of deep dyslexia after the whole-word therapy, we asked FD to complete three PALPA reading assessments prior to commencing the letter-based therapy. These were selected to test for the symptoms of deep dyslexia (semantic errors, imageability effect, part-of-speech-effect, and abolished nonword reading: Coltheart, Patterson, & Marshall, 1980). In an assessment that varies imageability and frequency (PALPA no. 31), FD only managed to read 11/80 items correctly (with no letter-by-letter attempts). He demonstrated a small but significant imageability effect (high imageability—10/40 vs. low imageability 1/40: $\chi^2 = 8.54$, $p = .003$). On this set of items, omission errors were the most frequent type (51%), with 13% semantic errors (e.g., GRAVY → "stew";

ONION → "apple"), 22% visually related, and 14% unrelated real word errors. FD's reading of words that vary their part of speech (nouns, adjectives, verbs, and functors: PALPA test no. 24) was very poor. He managed to read only 2/10 nouns and 1/10 adjectives, making a variety of errors including semantic paralexias (e.g., HANG → "door", GENTLE → "stroke"). FD was also unable to read any of the short nonwords included in PALPA test no. 24 (though it should be noted that his nonword reading was found to be very poor at initial presentation). In conclusion, FD demonstrated all of the symptoms of deep dyslexia with the exception of a part-of-speech effect—though his reading on this test was close to floor. FD's emergent deep dyslexia is, of course, exactly what one would expect from the two-system hypothesis (Buxbaum & Coslett, 1996; Saffran & Coslett, 1998). Right hemisphere reading is assumed to have overt reading skills that are limited to concrete, real words and might be associated with the production of semantic paralexia (as per the right hemisphere hypothesis for deep dyslexia itself: Coltheart, 2000). This outcome is also consistent, however, with the single-system hypothesis: Damage to computationally-implemented models containing a single reading system produces deep dyslexia (Plaut & Shallice, 1993).

Why does the Saffran effect vary across letter-by-letter readers?

One major unresolved issue in the literature regarding the Saffran effect is why only a proportion of patients with letter-by-letter reading or pure alexia demonstrate the effect (Coltheart, 1998). Even with extensive testing across many patients, other studies have found little or no evidence for above-chance categorisation in brief presentation experiments (e.g., Patterson & Kay, 1982). One possibility is that patients who exhibit the Saffran effect not only have letter-by-letter reading but also some other critical impairment. The background testing revealed that FD was not a pure alexic in that his letter-by-letter reading was accompanied by some mild aphasic symptoms (word-finding difficulties and an impaired ability

to manipulate phonology) along with some spelling problems. One could imagine, therefore, that these subtle language deficits might interfere with the letter-by-letter strategy (which requires letters to be remembered and then blended—i.e., it relies on some phonological skills) and thus reading falls back on the damaged whole-word reading system. This possibility does not seem to hold, however, for Coslett and Saffran's patients (1989). All patients were given the Boston Diagnostic Aphasia Examination, on which their performance (i) was entirely normal (patients TL and AF), or (ii) revealed very subtle degrees of anomia (patient JG), or (iii) slight spelling problems (patient JC).

The second possibility is that the implicit categorisation experiments need to be administered in the correct fashion. Saffran and Coslett (1998) argued that not only brief presentation but also gentle cajoling of the patients was required for them to dispense with their letter-by-letter reading, which otherwise blocks the output of the (right hemisphere) covert reading system. This methodological explanation may be true for certain patients who can switch between efficient letter-by-letter reading and responses based on whole-word reading (patient JWC: Coslett et al., 1993) but it seems unlikely for the majority of cases. Indeed, letter-by-letter reading and the activation of higher-order word and semantic representations are not mutually exclusive. As noted in the Introduction, a number of studies have shown evidence for lexical and semantic effects on the reading times of letter-by-letter readers and the symptoms of pure and deep dyslexia can co-occur (Behrmann et al., 1998b; Buxbaum & Coslett, 1996). Furthermore, the dramatic change in FD's reading style following whole-word therapy suggests that it is possible for some patients to dispense with the letter-by-letter reading strategy altogether. Rather than revealing a simple covert reading system, FD was still able to produce overt responses, albeit of the impoverished type expected for a patient with deep dyslexia.

The third explanation relates to patient severity. Behrmann and colleagues have argued that there may be an inverted U-shaped function that relates

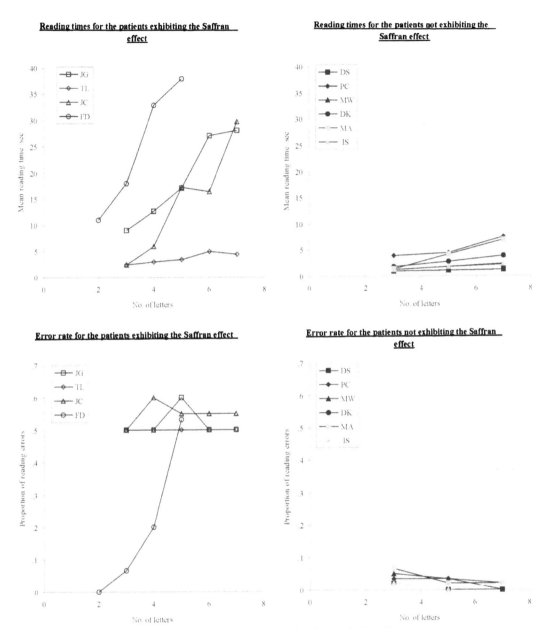

Figure 4. *Comparison of reading times and error rates for patients with and without the Saffran effect.*

severity and the size of lexical-semantic effects in letter-by-letter readers (Behrmann et al., 1998b). In their case series, Behrmann et al. found correlations between the slope of the word length effect (a proxy for the severity of the reading impairment) and the size of the frequency and imageability effects. The question remains, however, as to whether this explanation can be extended from the influences found on reading times in Behrmann's pure alexics to the Saffran effect exhibited by some patients—which is demonstrated in accuracy rather than response time data. There are some hints in the literature that "preserved" reading consistent with the Saffran effect appears at a certain stage during recovery (Landis et al., 1980; Saffran & Coslett, 1998). Initially patients can have extremely poor or non-existent reading (global alexia), followed by partial recognition and finally, reading via letter-by-letter strategy takes over once sufficient recovery has taken place.

The extension of the severity hypothesis to the Saffran effect would be tested best in a case-series design in which the reading behaviour of a set of patients who vary in reading severity could be compared directly on the same set of materials. In a proxy to such data, we combined the reading times and accuracy data for the Saffran and Coslett (1998) patients together with FD—all of whom demonstrate the Saffran effect—and compared this against similar data for a group of patients who do not exhibit the Saffran effect (Behrmann, personal communication).[3] Although these two groups of patient were tested on different materials, the resultant data (see Figure 4) reveal a striking difference. The reading times for the patients who do exhibit the Saffran effect are approximately 10 times slower than the pure alexics who do not show the effect. The exception to this pattern is patient TL (Coslett & Saffran, 1989a), for whom the word length function falls within the same range of quicker reading times. If error rates are also considered, however, then it is clear that the reading accuracy of the Saffran effect patients is considerably worse than the pure alexics without the Saffran effect (who are, in general, very accurate). It would appear that while some of the Saffran effect patients are both slow and errorful, other cases such as TL and FD adopt a different speed-accuracy trade-off. TL's relatively quick reading times came at the cost of poor accuracy while, at least for short words, FD's good accuracy was countered by excessively slow reading times. Furthermore, after the errorless learning therapy, FD's speed-accuracy trade-off actually reversed such that his much quicker reading times came at the cost of many more commission errors (Sage et

al., 2003). Taking reading times and error rates together, these comparative results suggest that reading severity is the key factor that underpins the presence or absence of the Saffran effect.

It might also be possible to extend the severity hypothesis to account for the reading data of two optic aphasics reported by Coslett and Saffran (1989b; Saffran & Coslett, 1998). These patients were completely unable to name letters or words but still exhibited lexical-semantic effects in lexical decision and sorting tasks. These patients might be even further along the severity continuum such that the whole-word reading system is only activated to a minimal extent—too little to support any overt reading ability but sufficient to sustain limited ability in forced-choice procedures such as lexical decision and sorting.

GENERAL DISCUSSION

This study adds another case to the very small number of patients reported in the literature who exhibit the Saffran effect (Feinberg et al., 1994; Saffran & Coslett, 1998; Shallice & Saffran, 1986). FD demonstrated spontaneous, partial access to word meaning during letter-by-letter reading attempts as well as in brief presentation, categorisation experiments. In both situations, FD activated this partial knowledge without overt recognition of the target words. By combining data from this and two other studies, we were able to investigate why only a proportion of pure alexics exhibit the Saffran effect. This comparison revealed that the patients who do demonstrate the effect are considerably slower and less accurate readers. This is consistent, therefore, with the argument that the severity of the patients' impairment is key (Behrmann et al., 1998b).

Two alternative explanations for the Saffran effect were tested in a series of experiments and through the impact of whole-word and letter-based therapies on FD's reading. In their seminal report, Shallice and Saffran (1986) proposed two

---

[3] We are grateful to Marlene Behrmann for sharing her data with us.

theories for this effect. The first was based on the notion that the dissociation between implicit whole-word recognition and explicit, letter-by-letter based reading necessitates two separate reading systems underpinned by neural substrates in the left and right hemispheres (Saffran & Coslett, 1998). The second theory assumes that the patients' behaviour reflects reduced or impaired input to the same single, whole-word reading system that supports normal word recognition, in addition to the deliberate, compensatory strategy of letter-by-letter reading (Behrmann et al., 1998b). Under this alternative hypothesis, the patients' above-chance performance in the brief presentation experiments simply reflects partial, cascading activation within the single, premorbid reading system (Behrmann et al., 1998b; Feinberg et al., 1994).

FD's results strongly support the latter hypothesis. FD's reading behaviour was characterised by partial activation of higher-order word representations, accuracy was graded by word variables known to influence the normal reading system, and, most importantly, once the characteristics of the tasks were equated, there was no evidence for a dissociation between word categorisation and identification—which was, perhaps, the primary motivation for positing two whole-word reading systems. In addition, the whole-word therapy encouraged FD to abandon, almost completely, the letter-by-letter strategy. Without this compensatory technique, FD's reading (a form of either deep or visual dyslexia) was consistent with a partially activated, single, whole-word reading system that produces overt reading responses. These results seem to weaken, or perhaps remove, the need for two whole-word reading systems.

The two systems theory was motivated not only by cognitive but also by neurological factors (Coslett & Monsul, 1994; Saffran & Coslett, 1998). While it is possible to question the nature of the behavioural data, we have said nothing specifi-

cally about the role of the right and left hemispheres. It is well established that pure alexia is associated with lesions in the left occipitotemporal region (Damasio & Damasio, 1983). Although FD had suffered from a series of vascular events, it was only after a left posterior cerebral artery stroke that he presented with severe letter-by-letter reading. There is also the intriguing fact that once his letter-by-letter reading was abandoned, FD turned into a deep dyslexic, which would be predicted by the right hemisphere hypothesis of deep dyslexia (Buxbaum & Coslett, 1996; Coltheart, 1981; Coslett & Saffran, 1989).[4] In addition, Coslett and Monsul demonstrated that transcranial magnetic stimulation (TMS) disrupted the reading of patient JG when it was applied over the right but not the left parietal region. While we cannot draw any firm conclusions about the role of the left hemisphere from a failure to disrupt JG's reading, some kind of role for the right hemisphere is indisputable.

While the neurology of the Saffran-effect patients (including FD) and the TMS results from patient JG are consistent with the two systems hypothesis, this theory is based on the assumption of a relatively transparent relationship between cognitive systems and underlying neural substrates. Behavioural dissociations, however, do not necessarily imply separate neural regions (Plaut, 1995). Likewise a single cognitive system could be supported by more than one neural substrate (Lambon Ralph, McClelland, Patterson, Galton, & Hodges, 2001). Saffran and Coslett (1998) suggest that the visual analysis, lexical, and semantic systems are duplicated in both hemispheres but that only the left is able to convert the words into speech. There are, however, two other legitimate explanations. The first assumes that a single, whole-word recognition system is supported solely by regions in the left hemisphere. When this, or the visual input to it, are impaired by brain damage, performance reflects residual processing in this compromised

---

[4] Although it should be noted that there is an ongoing debate about the right hemisphere hypothesis for deep dyslexia, with neuropsychological and functional neuroimaging data consistent with both sides of the discussion (Coltheart, 2000; Price et al., 1998).

region rather than the functioning of a secondary system. As we have argued above, the Saffran effect is consistent with partial, graded activation of a single word recognition system. At face value, this single system, left hemisphere-only account does not seem to fit readily with the TMS results reported by Coslett and Monsul (1994). One possible explanation is that the right hemisphere TMS either disrupted high-order visual processing of the stimulus or affected communication of this information to the left hemisphere (JG had a right homonymous hemianopia). In either case, a left hemisphere reading system might have been disordered by right hemisphere TMS because the visual input was disrupted or curtailed. The second, alternative explanation assumes that left and right hemisphere regions are involved in visual word recognition but that these bilateral neural substrates are coupled together, thereby producing a single functional system at the behavioural level of analysis. Even if neural processing is equivalent in both hemispheres, the left-hemisphere structures may be more critical for word recognition if these are preferentially connected to left-lateralised language systems (for neuropsychological evidence and an computational implementation of this idea at the semantic level, see Lambon Ralph et al., 2001). As the bilateral substrates are assumed to combine to produce a single function at the behavioural level, this second alternative hypothesis is also consistent with the notion that the Saffran effect reflects partial, graded activation within a single system, and readily explains the Coslett and Monsul's TMS results.

REFERENCES

Albert, M. L., Yamadori, A., Gardner, H., & Howes, D. (1973). Comprehension in alexia. *Brain*, *96*, 317–328.

Behrmann, M., Nelson, J., & Sekuler, E. (1998a). Visual complexity in letter-by-letter reading: "Pure" alexia is not so pure. *Neuropsychologia*, *36*, 1115–1132.

Behrmann, M., Plaut, D. C., & Nelson, J. (1998b). A literature review and new data supporting an inter-

active account of letter-by-letter reading. *Cognitive Neuropsychology*, *15*, 7–52.

Buxbaum, L. J., & Coslett, H. B. (1996). Deep dyslexic phenomena in a letter-by-letter reader. *Brain and Language*, *54*, 136–167.

Caplan, L. R., & Hedley-Whyte, T. (1974). Cueing and memory dysfunction in alexia without agraphia: A case report. *Brain*, *97*, 251–262.

Coltheart, M. (1981). Right-hemisphere reading. *Behavioral and Brain Sciences*, *4*, 67–68.

Coltheart, M. (1998). Seven questions about pure alexia (letter-by-letter reading). *Cognitive Neuropsychology*, *15*, 1–6.

Coltheart, M. (2000). Deep dyslexia is right-hemisphere reading. *Brain and Language*, *71*, 299–309.

Coltheart, M., Patterson, K., & Marshall, J. C. (1980). *Deep dyslexia*. London: Routledge & Kegan Paul.

Coslett, H. B., & Monsul, N. (1994). Reading with the right hemisphere: Evidence from transcranial magnetic stimulation. *Brain and Language*, *46*, 198–211.

Coslett, H. B., & Saffran, E. M. (1989a). Evidence for preserved reading in pure alexia. *Brain*, *112*, 327–359.

Coslett, H. B., & Saffran, E. M. (1989b). Preserved object recognition and reading comprehension in optic aphasia. *Brain*, *112*, 1091–1110.

Coslett, H. B., Saffran, E. M., Greenbaum, S., & Schwartz, H. (1993). Reading in pure alexia—the effect of strategy. *Brain*, *116*, 21–37.

Damasio, A., & Damasio, H. (1983). The anatomical basis of pure alexia. *Neurology*, *33*, 1573–1583.

Farah, M. J., & Wallace, M. (1991). Pure alexia as a visual impairment: A reconsideration. *Cognitive Neuropsychology*, *8*, 313–334.

Feinberg, T., Dyches-Berke, D., Miner, C. R., & Roane, D. M. (1994). Knowledge, implicit knowledge and metaknowledge in visual agnosia and pure alexia. *Brain*, *118*, 789–800.

Fillingham, J. K., Hodgson, C., Sage, K., & Lambon Ralph, M. A. (2003). The application of errorless learning to aphasic disorders: a review of theory and practice. *Neuropsychological Rehabilitation*, *13*, 337–363.

Franklin, S., Turner, J. M., & Ellis, A. W. (1992). *The ADA comprehension battery*. London: Action for Dysphasic Adults.

Goodglass, H., Kaplan, E., & Weintraub, S. (1983). *Boston Naming Test*. Philadelphia: Lea & Febiger.

Howard, D., & Patterson, K. (1992). *The Pyramids and Palm Trees Test: A test of semantic access from words and pictures*. Bury St Edmunds, UK: Thames Valley Test Company.

Kay, J., Lesser, R., & Coltheart, M. (1992). *Psycho-linguistic Assessments of Language Processing in Aphasia (PALPA)*. Hove, UK: Lawrence Erlbaum Associates Ltd.

Kreindler, A., & Ionasescu, V. (1961). A case of pure word blindness. *Journal of Neurology, Neurosurgery and Psychiatry, 24*, 275–280.

Lambon Ralph, M. A., & Ellis, A. W. (1997). "Patterns of Paralexia" revisited: Report of a case of visual dyslexia. *Cognitive Neuropsychology, 7*, 953–974.

Lambon Ralph, M. A., McClelland, J. L., Patterson, K., Galton, C. J., & Hodges, J. R. (2001). No right to speak? The relationship between object naming and semantic impairment: Neuropsychological evidence and a computational model. *Journal of Cognitive Neuroscience, 13*, 341–356.

Landis, T., Regard, M., & Serrat, A. (1980). Iconic reading in a case of alexia without agraphia caused by a brain tumor: A tachistoscope study. *Brain and Language, 11*, 45–53.

McClelland, J. L., & Rumelhart, D. E. (1981). An interactive activation model of context effects in letter perception: Part 1. An account of basic findings. *Psychological Review, 88*, 375–407.

McKeeff, T. J., & Behrmann, M. (2004). Pure alexia and covert reading: Evidence from stroop tasks. *Cognitive Neuropsychology, 21*, 443–458.

McKenna, P., & Warrington, E. K. (1983). *The Graded Naming Test*. Windsor, UK: NFER-Nelson.

Morton, J., & Patterson, K. E. (1980). A new attempt at an interpretation, or, an attempt at a new interpretation. In M. Coltheart, K. E. Patterson, & J. C. Marshall (Eds.), *Deep dyslexia*. London: Routledge & Kegan Paul.

Mycroft, R. H., Behrmann, M., & Kay, J. (2003). *Evidence for a causal role of a visual processing impairment in letter-by-letter reading?* Manuscript submitted for publication.

Patterson, K., & Kay, J. (1982). Letter-by-letter reading: Psychological descriptions of a neurological syndrome. *Quarterly Journal of Experimental Psychology: Human Experimental Psychology, 34A*, 411–441.

Plaut, D. C. (1995). Double dissociation without modularity: Evidence from connectionist neuropsychology. *Journal of Clinical and Experimental Neuropsychology, 17*, 291–321.

Plaut, D. C., & Shallice, T. (1993). Deep dyslexia: A case study of connectionist neuropsychology. *Cognitive Neuropsychology, 10*, 377–500.

Price, C. J., Howard, D., Patterson, K., Warburton, E. A., Friston, K. J., & Wise, R. S. J. (1998). A functional neuroimaging description of two deep dyslexic patients. *Journal of Cognitive Neuroscience, 10*, 303–315.

Reuter-Lorenz, P. A., & Brunn, J. L. (1990). A prelexical basis for letter-by-letter reading: A case study. *Cognitive Neuropsychology, 7*, 1–20.

Riddoch, M. J., & Humphreys, G. W. (1992). *The Birmingham Object Recognition Battery (BORB)*. Hove, UK: Lawrence Erlbaum Associates Ltd.

Saffran, E. M., & Coslett, H. B. (1998). Implicit vs. letter-by-letter reading in pure alexia: A tale of two systems. *Cognitive Neuropsychology, 15*, 141–166.

Sage, K., Hesketh, A., & Lambon Ralph, M. A. (2003). *Using errorless learning to treat letter-by-letter reading: Contrasting whole vs. letter based therapy*. Manuscript submitted for publication.

Shallice, T., & Saffran, E. (1986). Lexical processing in the absence of explicit word identification: Evidence from a letter-by-letter reader. *Cognitive Neuropsychology, 3*, 429–458.

Warrington, E. K., & James, M. (1991). *The Visual Object and Space Perception Battery*. Bury St Edmunds, UK: Thames Valley Test Company.

Warrington, E. K., McKenna, P., & Orpwood, L. (1998). Single word comprehension: A concrete and abstract word synonym test. *Neuropsychological Rehabilitation, 8*, 143–154.

Wilson, B. A., & Evans, J. J. (1996). Error-free learning in the rehabilitation of people with memory impairments. *Journal of Head Trauma Rehabilitation, 11*, 54–64.

COGNITIVE NEUROPSYCHOLOGY, 2004, 21 (2/3/4) 423–441

OBJECT IDENTIFICATION IN SIMULTANAGNOSIA: WHEN WHOLES ARE NOT THE SUM OF THEIR PARTS

M. J. Riddoch and Glyn W. Humphreys
University of Birmingham, UK

We examined object identification in two simultanagnosic patients, ES and GK. We show that the patients tended to identify animate objects more accurately than inanimate objects (Experiments 1 and 4). The patients also showed relatively good identification of objects that could be recognised from their global shape, but not objects whose recognition depended on their internal detail (Experiment 2). Indeed, the presence of local segmentation cues disrupted global identification (Experiment 3). Identification was aided, though, by the presence of surface colour and texture (Experiment 4). We suggest that the patients could derive global representations of objects that served to recognise animate items. In contrast, they were impaired at coding parts-based representations for the identification of inanimate objects.

INTRODUCTION

The term simultanagnosia is used to describe patients who have abnormal deficits in identifying multiple stimuli and in interpreting complex scenes. It was initially described by Bálint (1909), in the context of a disorder affecting also visual reaching to objects (optic ataxia). Bálint's patient was reported as being unable to perceive two or more objects simultaneously although there was no difficulty in identifying single objects. Simultanagnosia has been linked both to bilateral damage of the dorsal visual system (the occipito- parietal region) and to unilateral damage to the ventral visual system in the left hemisphere (the occipito-temporal region) (Bálint, 1909; Coslett & Saffran, 1991; Humphreys & Price, 1994; Luria, Pravdina-Vinaskkaya, & Yarbus, 1963; and Kinsbourne & Warrington, 1962, 1963). However, the impaired localisation and poor spatial coding characteristic of Bálint's syndrome (including abnormal numbers of illusory conjunctions; (see Friedman-Hill, Robertson, & Treisman, 1995) is primarily associated with bilateral parietal damage.

While simultanagnosics, by definition, seem limited to processing one object at a time, the stimulus defined as the "object" can vary in a flexible manner. Luria (1959) was the first to demonstrate that the identification performance of simultanagnosic patients is strongly determined by bottom-up processes of grouping and segmentation. He described a patient who was able to report the star of David when shown the stimulus in a single colour; however, the patient only reported the presence of a triangle when the two triangles making up the star of David were shown in different colours. Identification here is not determined

---

Correspondence should be addressed to M. Jane Riddoch, Brain and Behavioural Sciences, School of Psychology, University of Birmingham, Birmingham, B15 2TT, UK (Email: M.J.Riddoch@bham.ac.uk).

This study was supported by grants from the MRC and the Stroke Association. We thank Marlene Behrmann and an anonymous reviewer for helpful comments on an earlier draft of the manuscript. We are indebted to ES and GK for their time, their patience, and their humour.

423

http://www.tandf.co.uk/journals/pp02643294.html

DOI:10.1080/02643290342000564

by the spatial extent of the stimulus but by how the parts group together (when in the same colour) or segment apart (when in different colours). Similarly, identification performance in simultan-agnosics is typically unaffected by stimulus size (Bálint, 1909; Coslett & Saffran, 1991) or by the distance between the stimuli to be reported (Kinsbourne & Warrington, 1962). Luria's example suggests that the spatial area attended to by simultanagnosic patients is altered by grouping by colour. There is also evidence of grouping by shape. Humphreys and Riddoch (1993) showed that the report of multiple items by simultanagnos-ics was improved by connecting them together (Palmer & Rock, 1994), even when the items were in different colours and the same distance apart when connected or not. Gilchrist, Humphreys, and Riddoch (1996) further showed that connec-tivity per se was not crucial since the report of multiple stimuli by a simultanagnosic patient was improved if edges were locally close and collinear. Boutsen and Humphreys (2000) demonstrated effects of axis alignment and Humphreys et al. (Humphreys, Riddoch, Donnelly, Freeman, Boucart, & Müller, 1994a; Humphreys, Romani, Olaon, Riddoch, & Duncan 1994b) reported effects of closure on identification performance. For instance, when two stimuli were presented, the one with better closure was reported and the one with less closure was not detected (see also Humphreys & Riddoch, 2003a).

These results provide strong evidence that fundamental aspects of object coding continue to operate in simultanagnosia. The limited attention that such patients can bring to bear is determined by the strength of grouping between visual elements. Indeed, competition between perceptual groups may determine both which object is per-ceived (Humphreys et al., 1994b), and the spread of attention across space (Humphreys & Riddoch, 2003a).

As visual scenes become more complex, how-ever, identification in the patients can break down. Classically, when such patients are asked to iden-tify scenes they operate in a piecemeal manner, failing to grasp the relations between different elements. Indeed, even the identification of single objects can be very impaired if the objects are placed on complex backgrounds containing multi-ple segmentation cues. In their detailed description of a simultanagnosic patient, Coslett and Saffran (1992) noted how she could localise a single object shown against a clear background, while localisa-tion was markedly disrupted if the same object was shown against a patterned tablecloth. At least in some cases, then, whether identification and local-isation is achieved is dependent on a complex interaction between visual elements that group into perceptual wholes or that are segmented into separate parts. When segmented into parts, the patients can even identify one part as if it were the whole stimulus (a "partonomic" error).[1] For instance, Humphreys and Price (1994) reported the case of a patient who, when shown a picture of a cup decorated with an apple motif, named the stimulus as an apple and demonstrated no aware-ness of the cup. In part, these detrimental effects of complex contexts can be understood in terms of a failure in spatial filtering, associated with parietal lesions suffered in dorsal simultanagnosia. There is considerable evidence from studies of functional neuroimaging that the parietal lobes subserve both spatial and nonspatial selection of stimuli (Corbetta & Schulman, 1998; Kanwisher & Wojciulik, 2000; Pollman et al., 2003). Damage to parietal lobes may then disrupt visual selection and generate abnormal interference between visual elements. Consistent with this, Friedman-Hill and colleagues (Friedman-Hill, Robertson, Desimone, & Ungerleider, 2003) reported abnormal inter-ference in discriminating a target flanked by distractors, particularly as distractor salience

---

[1] It is possible that the functional deficit can differ across simultanagnosic patients. In some, the disorder affects visual coding (Humphreys & Price, 1994). In others, the problem may be more in developing an integrated representation of multiple objects in short-term visual memory (Coslett & Saffran, 1991). Our concern in this paper is with patients whose problem involves visual coding of objects.

increased. In this instance, there may be inappropriate binding between distractors and targets, disrupting selection and identification.

Along with showing poor attentional selection of stimuli in complex environments, simultanagnosics may also be limited in applying attention across a single stimulus. For example, when presented with compound, hierarchical stimuli, simultanagnosics tend to select the local elements rather than the global shape (Humphreys et al., 1994; Karnath, Ferber, Rorden, & Driver, 1994). In this case, the segmentation cues present (e.g., the spaces between the local elements) can bias attention to local parts, reminiscent of the partonomic errors in object identification. In addition, even when a whole object is encoded, the attentional limitation may lead to the formulation of an impoverished representation. In studies with normal observers, Hummel and Stankiewicz (1998) have presented evidence that objects are coded in a holistic, nondecomposed form when they are not fully attended. Attention is needed in order to derive an articulated parts-based representation. They used an object priming paradigm that examined whether primes facilitated the identification of target objects shown either in the same or a different view. Primes were attended or unattended (when attention was cued to another object in the prime display). Hummel and Stankiewicz found view-independent facilitation effects when primes were attended. In contrast, there were only view-dependent effects when primes were unattended. Hummel and Stankiewicz propose that view-generalisation in priming is contingent on the construction of a parts-based structural description of objects (see also Biederman & Gerhardstein, 1993). This is only achieved when objects are attended and their "parts" bound into the correct spatial relations. In the absence of attention, priming depends on a view-specific holistic representation of objects that facilitates identification of stimuli in the same view but not for stimuli in different views. Shalev and Humphreys (2002), with one of the patients tested here (GK), also reported a deficit in explicitly encoding the positions of parts within objects (do two local circles fall towards the top or the bottom

of a surrounding oval?). However, GK could make discrimination responses based on an identical input if he employed a holistic recognition strategy (e.g., if cued to code the stimulus as an upright or inverted face, when the circles were either towards the top or bottom of the oval). Hall, Humphreys, and Cooper (2001) documented analogous evidence with GK in a reading task.

In this paper we document some of the factors that influence object identification in two simultanagnosic patients, ES and GK. We report, for the first time, a recognition impairment for inanimate relative to animate objects in such patients. Also, for the first time, we show that such a recognition impairment can reflect a pre-semantic deficit affecting the derivation of parts-based representations. We discuss relations between the impairments we report and other disorders of object identification (e.g., within the syndrome of integrative agnosia). We also discuss the implications of the disorder for understanding the relations between global and parts-based object representations, and for understanding category-specific neuropsychological impairments.

CASE REPORTS

ES

ES was a right-handed 59-year-old ex-nursing assistant. Her primary presenting symptom was increased clumsiness of the right arm and increasing inability to perform activities of daily living such as dressing, managing a knife and fork during eating, writing etc. There had been no history of any precipitating injury and there had been a gradual onset of her symptoms over several months. On examination, muscle strength was normal, but sensation and proprioception were bilaterally impaired. There was a very slight increase of tone on the right.

Neuroradiology
The radiological report was based on both MRI and CT scans. The most dramatic structural abnormalities were demonstrated in the left sylvan

fissure, and in the peritrigonal region on the left (see Riddoch, Humphreys, & Edwards, 2000a, for a detailed report).

Neuropsychology

Neuropsychological tests revealed a number of deficits including simultanagnosia, reading deficits, impairments in spontaneous speech, and movement disorders, which included dyspraxia, dysgraphia, and alien hand syndrome.

The Visual Object and Space Perception Test (VOSP; Warrington & James, 1991) was performed when ES was first referred to us. The Space Perception subtests of the VOSP were repeated 18 months later. On the first test occasion, ES fell outside the control range for the screening test (she scored 15/20 correct; scores of 15 or less are considered to indicate severe impairment). The data from the Visual Object and Space Perception subtests are presented in Table 1, together with control data (as given in the VOSP manual). Relative to the control subjects' mean scores, ES performed poorly on all the subtests of the VOSP. Indeed, her score fell within 2 *SD*s for only one of the subtests (Progressive Silhouettes). Taking an overall score for the Space Perception subtests, ES's performance was not significantly worse on the second time of testing relative to the first, $\chi^2(1) = 3.4$.

ES's simultanagnosia was first shown in poor performance in interpreting pictures (which provided a focus for more detailed investigations). For instance, below we present ES's attempt to describe what was happening in the picture of the "Telegraph Boy" (see Kinsbourne & Warrington, 1962). The picture shows a boy holding a bicycle standing by the side of a road. The far side of the road is lined with trees and bushes. A car is approaching from the right. The boy is waving his hat with his right hand in the direction of the approaching car. He is holding a piece of paper (in addition to the bicycle) in his left hand. The front wheel of the bicycle is broken and is lying on the ground. ES's description of this picture is as follows: "He is washing his car . . . not his car, his bike." This description took one minute. "Are these sheep?" (ES was pointing to the bushes). "There's a man. What is he doing? I think he's on his bike." This whole account took 2 minutes 30 seconds.

She also had problems segmenting multiple shapes. For example, in the Overlapping Figures test from the Birmingham Object Recognition Battery (BORB; Riddoch & Humphreys, 1993) she had a ratio of 1.7:1 on the time taken to identify overlapping relative to nonoverlapping letter pairs. The ratio for overlapping relative to nonoverlapping letter triplets was 2.25:1. Age-matched

Table 1. *Performance on the subtests of VOSP (Warrington & James, 1991)*

	ES			Controls	
	Time 1	*Time 2*	*GK*	*Mean*	*SD*
Object perception					
Fragmented letters (*N* = 20)	12[a]		0[a]	18.8	(1.4)
Object decision (*N* = 20)	15[a]			17.7	(1.9)
Progressive silhouettes (*N* = 20)	14			10.8	(2.5)
Object naming (*N* = 30)	10[a]		7[a]	22.2	(4.0)
Space perception					
Dot counting (*N* = 10)	3[a]	5[a]	1[a]	9.9	(0.2)
Position discrimination (*N* = 20)	13[a]	9[a]		19.6	(0.9)
Number location (*N* = 10)	2[a]	0[a]		9.4	(1.1)
Cube analysis (*N* = 10)	6[a]	1[a]		9.2	(1.2)

[a] Impaired performance.

controls have a mean ratio of 1:1 for both letter pairs and triplets (see Riddoch & Humphreys, 1993) (see Table 2).

In addition to showing difficulties with complex scenes and overlapping figures, ES manifested visual extinction. For example, when uppercase letters were exposed for 415 ms she was able to identify 92% (33/36) and 89% (32/36) of single left and right letters respectively, but only 26% (19/72) of simultaneously presented letters (typically identifying only the left-side letter in a pair).[2]

Some impairment was noted in the reading of single words on some of the subtests from PALPA (Kay, Lesser, & Coltheart, 1992). In general, ES made visual errors when reading single words (e.g., check → chick), but text reading was impossible as she found it difficult to scan her attention systematically across the lines. Spontaneous speech was dysarthric. ES exhibited motor impairments including anarchic hand and foot syndrome (Riddoch et al., 2000a; Riddoch, Humphreys, & Edwards, 2000b, 2001). In addition, a bilateral dyspraxia was apparent, which was independent of the modality of testing.

The effects of simultanagnosia on picture naming performance were assessed over a 20-month period. A number of the tests were repeated. ES's performance deteriorated significantly over this time period, so all critical comparisons here were conducted within a session.

GK

GK was a man aged 60 years at the time of testing, who had suffered two strokes in 1986 affecting the right occipitoparietal, and the left and right

Table 2. *Time in seconds to name letters presented either in pairs or triplets (overlapping or not overlapping) (BORB; Riddoch & Humphreys, 1993)*

	Time per item (s)		
	ES	*GK*	*Controls*
Pairs of letters			
Nonoverlapping	1.3	13.3	0.4
Overlapping	2.16	15.0	0.4
Ratio	1:1.66	1:12	1:1
Triplets of letters			
Nonoverlapping	1.6		0.4
Overlapping	3.6		0.4
Ratio	1:2.25		1:1

temporoparietal regions (for scans see Boutsen & Humphreys, 2000). His main symptoms were characteristic of simultanagnosia. He had psychic paralysis of gaze, and his ability to reach to visually presented items was severely impaired. He experienced profound difficulties when describing complex scenes containing multiple objects and, even under free vision, appeared to be unaware of more than one item at a time. He was only able to manage a few of the subtests from VOSP (Warrington & James, 1991), and here his performance was very impaired (see Table 1).

Like ES, his performance when describing the picture of the "Telegraph Boy" was consistent with a diagnosis of simultanagnosia (see Kinsbourne & Warrington, 1962). Thus he starting by saying "seems like bicycles—two bicycles. There are some trees. There is a human, a male … can I see a car?

---

[2] Using a Macintosh DuoDock computer, and VScope software (Rensink & Enns, 1995), letters (6 × 6 mm) were presented for identification, 7 mm either to the left or the right or both sides of fixation following a central fixation cross. The viewing distance was approximately 80 cm. Four different letters were used (upper case A, B, C, and D). Letters were printed in Times font, size 24. There were equal numbers of unilateral and bilateral presentations (i.e., 12 each for unilateral left and unilateral right presentations, and 24 bilateral presentations). The four letters appeared equally often on both left and right sides of the screen. In addition, there were 24 'catch' trials when no letters would appear following presentation of the fixation cross. ES was told to fixate centrally, and that following the fixation cross a letter would appear on either the right or the left side of the screen, or that two letters would appear, one on the left and one on the right side of the screen, or that no letters would appear. She was asked to identify all the letters that she saw.

Could it be an accident? The car has knocked down the bicycle? There appears to be a person holding something, maybe the person could be the police—he seems to be making an alarm of some description. The bicycle has been bashed (I think there is only one bicycle), the car has bashed it. I am presuming a person has been knocked down—but I can't see them. I can see one person—the policeman ... There are two people (one without much hair, the other the policeman with a hat on) and a car ..." This description took 9 minutes.

GK was very slow in identifying letters whether presented in neighbouring pairs or overlapping one another in the Overlapping Figures test from BORB (Riddoch & Humphreys, 1993) (see Table 2). He was more likely to make identification errors in the overlapping condition (33/36 vs. 25/36 correct in the paired and overlapping conditions respectively). GK showed left extinction when stimuli were presented bilaterally, which reduced when contra- and ipsilesional stimuli grouped (Boutsen & Humphreys, 2000; Gilchrist et al., 1996; Humphreys et al., 1994b). When the stimuli varied in "goodness" (e.g., contrasting closed against open figures) the "better" stimulus tended to extinguish the less good item (Humphreys & Riddoch, 2003; Humphreys et al., 1994b). In reading tasks GK showed some evidence of left neglect on single word identification along with a pattern of attentional dyslexia (words could be read but not their constituent letters (see Hall et al., 2001). There was also a word superiority effect on letter report, contrasting two-letter words and non-words (Kumada & Humphreys, 2001). Like ES, text reading was impossible. Simultanagnosic behaviour was also shown in action. Edwards and Humphreys (2002) report that GK made independent, sequential actions to bilateral stimuli even when explicitly instructed to make coordinated reaches. Interestingly, bimanual actions to a single stimulus and to grouped stimuli were coordinated in time.

GK had minor word-finding problems and he tended to produce phonological paraphasias in speech. Comprehension was intact and he was well oriented in time and space.

EXPERIMENTAL STUDY

Under free report conditions, simultanagnosic patients can show relatively good identification of single objects (Coslett & Saffran, 1991; Humphreys & Price, 1994). Nevertheless, as is indicated by data such as those from the Overlapping Figures test (Riddoch & Humphreys, 1993), performance can break down as stimuli become more complex. Under some circumstances, simultanagnosic patients can also manifest partonomic identification of stimuli (Luria, 1959). In the present study we document object identification performance in ES and GK, two patients whose simultanagnosia was relatively severe. We show that, although object naming was relatively good, systematic errors arose under some conditions. First we report that identification tended to be harder for nonliving than for living objects and that, when misidentifications arose, they reflected poor visual access to stored knowledge about the objects. The tendency for better identification of living things could reflect a number of factors including: (1) the patients using global shape for object identification (living things might be identified by their global shape, nonliving things by the relations between their parts), (2) the presence of segmentation cues between the parts of nonliving things, and (3) the presence of texture cues on the surface of living things. These possibilities were tested in the subsequent experiments. The data suggest that each of these factors may play a role in object identification by the patients.

Experiment 1: Effects of animacy on naming line drawings

Both ES and GK were tested on four occasions. ES was assessed over a 20-month period. GK was evaluated over a 5-year time period. Tests 1 and 2 were conducted in 1991 and 1992, Tests 3 and 4 in 1996 and 1997. In each session the patients were presented with the low-frequency items from BORB (Riddoch & Humphreys, 1993, Test 14). Half the items were animate and half inanimate. The stimuli were matched for name frequency across categories. Details of the stimuli are provided in Humphreys, Riddoch, and Quinlan (1988). In the present context it is relevant to note that the animate items were rated as more complex than the inanimate items (on a rating scale of 1 to 5 where 5 is the highest rank, obtained scores were 3.7 vs. 2.6 for animate vs. inanimate items respectively). It was also the case that animate items showed a greater percentage of contour overlap (values 15.7% vs. 12.9% overlap for animate vs. inanimate items respectively, relative to other members of the same category in the Snodgrass & Vanderwart, 1980, norms).

Method

Pictures were taken from BORB (Riddoch & Humphreys, 1993). Each picture was magnified (approximately 2.5 in × 2.5 in square) and mounted separately on a card. There were 19 animate and 19 inanimate items, all with name frequencies less than 10/million in the Kuçera and Francis (1967) norms. They appeared in random order on each occasion.

Results

The results are presented in Table 3. The data were analysed over both sessions and items. Over sessions, patient (ES vs. GK) was treated as a between-subjects factor and animacy (number of correct names for animate vs. inanimate pictures) as a within-subjects factor. Each test session was entered as a separate subject. Over items, patient was treated as a within-items factor and category as a between-items factor. Over sessions there was a reliable main effect of animacy, $F(1, 6) = 49.47$, $p < .001$, but not of patient, $F(1, 6) = 2.99$, $p > .05$. Over items there was again a reliable effect of animacy, $F(1, 36) = 6.93$, and also now an effect of patient, $F(1, 36) = 8.60$, both $p < .025$. Animate objects were named more accurately than inanimate objects, and ES performed better than GK. The interaction (Patient × Category) was not reliable over either sessions or items (both $F < 1.0$).

Errors were classified as either semantic, visual and semantic, visual, partonomic (in which identification seemed to be based on an isolated part of the object), or other (unrelated or "don't know" responses). ES made 32 errors. There were no purely semantic errors, 16 visual/semantic errors (e.g., beetle → spider, chisel → screw), 5 visual errors (e.g., thimble → glass, chisel → cricket bat), 1 partonomic error (naming a helicopter as scissors), and 5 "other" errors. GK made 47 errors. There were 3 semantic errors (e.g., ashtray → pipe, necklace → beads), 17 visual/semantic errors (mouse → squirrel, blouse → coat), 18 visual errors (e.g., celery → chicken, button → plug), 1 partonomic error (naming a helicopter as an aerial), and 8 "other" errors.

Discussion

The patients showed a small but reliable advantage for animate over inanimate objects. This type of advantage has been reported previously in the neuropsychological literature, and it has been associated with either a semantic or a naming disturbance—for example, linked to poor retrieval of functional knowledge about objects (e.g., Cappa, Frugoni, Pasquali, Perani, & Zorat, 1998; Sacchett & Humphreys, 1992; Warrington & McCarthy, 1983, Warrington & McCarthy, 1987). However, neither ES nor GK seemed to suffer any disturbance of semantic knowledge. To test this more formally they were each asked to produce verbal definitions to the names of the objects presented in Experiment 1. Both patients were good at this and generated identifiable definitions for all 38 items. Example definitions are given in Table 4. In addition, the problems were unlikely to reflect poor name retrieval as the patients both made proportionately high numbers of visual misidentifications. These

Table 3. *Percentage correct naming of animate and inanimate items over four test occasions*

	ES		GK	
	Animate	*Inanimate*	*Animate*	*Inanimate*
Time 1	100 (19)	79 (15)	68 (13)	58 (11)
Time 2	89 (17)	68 (13)	58 (11)	53 (10)
Time 3	84 (16)	74 (14)	79 (15)	63 (12)
Time 4	79 (15)	58 (11)	100 (19)	79 (15)
Mean	88 (16.8)	70 (13.3)	76 (14.5)	63 (12.0)

Numbers correct are given in brackets, total per cell = 19.

Table 4. *Examples of definitions produced by ES and GK in response to the names of items they had misnamed when presented as pictures on at least three occasions*

ES	Blouse	It is like a shirt—a woman's shirt
	Tiger	This is an animal—an endangered species which is killed to make medicines. It has orange coloured fur with black stripes. There are also some white bits.
GK	Chisel	There are two types—one for wood, one for metal. The one for wood has a sharp edge made of metal, it has a wooden handle. You use it with a hammer.
	Giraffe	From a hot country—Kenya. It is big, not a meat eater, it eats leaves, its neck is high.

visual errors are consistent with a problem in gaining access to stored knowledge from line drawings.

The majority of patients reported in the literature with "category-specific" deficits tend to find animate objects harder to identify than inanimate ones (see Capitani, Laiacona, Mahon, & Caramazza, 2003; Caramazza & Shelton, 1998; Forde & Humphreys 2002; Humphreys & Forde, 2001; Humphreys & Riddoch, 2003b, for recent reviews). At least one account of such deficits is that they reflect the higher visual similarity within animate compared with inanimate categories (see Humphreys & Forde, 2001). However, were this the only factor, then it is difficult to see how patients with a visual processing deficit (indexed by high numbers of visual naming errors) could name animate objects more accurately than inanimate objects. Indeed, animate objects also tend to be more pictorially complex and to have lower image and name agreement (see Humphreys et al., 1988). All of these factors should contrive to make animate stimuli harder to identify.

Why, then, might the opposite advantage tend to occur with ES and GK? To account for this, we suggest that the nature of the underlying deficit is critical, with contrasting deficits having different effects on animate and inanimate stimuli. The visual errors made by ES and GK generally appeared to reflect the global shape of the objects,

and just a few errors were based on the parts of objects taken in isolation (the partonomic errors). It may be that animate stimuli tend to be identified more from their global shape than inanimate items. For example, animate items tend to have many parts in common (see Humphreys et al., 1988, for evidence) and so are not differentiated easily from parts considered in isolation. In addition, many animate objects can undergo nonrigid self-motion, in which the relative locations of the parts change. This may mean that little weight is placed on a coding of spatial relations between the parts—contrasting with inanimate objects which often undergo rigid transformations in which part-relations are maintained (see Laeng, Carlesimo, Capasso, & Miceli, 2002). The net consequence may be a greater reliance on global shape for animate objects and on partonomic relations for inanimate objects. Some evidence that supports this assertion comes from Gerlach (2001). In a study with normal observers, Gerlach found an advantage for animate over inanimate objects when the stimuli were degraded by presenting them in peripheral vision for short durations, so that high spatial frequency components would be lost (see also Laws & Neve, 1999). Gerlach proposes that, when only low spatial frequency information is available, animate objects may be advantaged because their global shape reveals more of their identity. Also consistent with this, Thomas and Forde (in press) report that nonliving things are harder than living things for control subjects to identify when the stimuli are presented as silhouettes. They too argue that global shape is important for the identification of living things. If ES and GK are dependent on a global "template" type object recognition process, without explicit coding of parts or part-relations, then they may be better with animate objects.

There are also other possibilities. One is that patients benefit from pictorial complexity in an image, since complex images may provide more redundancy as to an object's identity (e.g., multiple parts). However, when we correlated accuracy over the items with their rated pictorial complexity (from Snodgrass & Vanderwart, 1980), there was no evidence of either patient tending to identify the more complex pictures more accurately than less complex pictures, $R(36) = .03$, and $-.12$ for ES and GK respectively, both $p > .05$).[3] Nevertheless, it is also possible that, rather than complexity per se, the patients benefit specifically from textural cues that tend to occur on animate rather than inanimate objects. Surface cues tend to be more diagnostic of the identity of animate compared with inanimate objects (Naor-Raz, Tarr, & Kersten, in press; Price & Humphreys, 1989), and patients reliant on surface cues may find animate objects easier to identify. A further possibility is that inanimate objects, often being built by adding parts together, may contain segmentation cues at the joints between parts (e.g., where the handle connects to the head of an object). If patients are sensitive to these segmentation cues, then they may tend to "over-segment" inanimate objects, generating visual errors. This tendency was noted by Funnell (2000). Funnell's patient was prone to making segmentation errors with line drawings, and this was most evident with inanimate objects. These different accounts are not mutually exclusive. For example, the patients may tend to rely on holistic (nonpartonomic) representations for object recognition, but then use parts-based representations when there are few surface cues present or when there are strong segmentation cues (i.e., with inanimate objects). They may be impaired with parts-based representations.

These proposals were tested in Experiments 2–4, which assessed whether the patients showed (1) differences in the naming of objects that could be identified from their global shape relative to objects for which internal detail was necessary (Experiment 2); (2) abnormal effects of segmentation cues (Experiment 3); and (3) effects of surface cues on object identification (Experiment 4).

Experiment 2: Using global shape vs. internal detail

A number of authors have shown that normal participants generate significantly more distinctive features for nonliving than for living things, suggesting that the identification of local parts may be more critical in the naming of artifacts than of living things (Garrard, Lambon-Ralph, & Hodges, 2001; McRae & Cree, 2002; Moss, Tyler, & Devlin, 2002). Evidence from control subjects naming stimuli under brief, peripheral presentation conditions (Gerlach, 2001), and from naming silhouettes (Thomas & Forde, in press) is consistent with this. To test whether this factor was important for the current patients, Experiment 2 contrasted the identification of pictures of objects that could be named from their outline shape with pictures where the internal detail was needed for identification. Are the patients able to identify "global shape" but not the "internal detail" stimuli?

Method

Test images were created using the Corel Gallery Clipart, Adobe Photoshop, and MacDraw software. There were equal numbers of animate and inanimate items ($N = 33$ in each instance), but they could not be compared directly because they were not matched for factors such as familiarity or name frequency. Instead, matching took place between the items making up the two experimental groups: stimuli that could be recognised from their global shape alone ("global shape" objects, $N = 36$) and objects that needed internal detail to be identified ("internal detail" objects, $N = 30$). Across the groups items were matched for familiarity and frequency and the groups did not differ on either

---

[3] Naming accuracy was based on the number of times each item was identified out of four. The accuracy data were also correlated with the item's name frequency, contour overlap, rated prototypicality (Humphreys et al., 1988), familiarity and image agreement. The only correlation was between accuracy and image agreement. This was statistically significant for ES, $R(36) = .34$, $p < .01$, and marginal for GK, $R(36) = .21$, $p = .07$. The correlation with familiarity also approached significance for GK, $R(36) = .214$, $p = .06$. The patients tended to make more accurate identifications for pictures where there was high agreement on the image representing the object, and objects which were familiar. We note that this is consistent with the patients' object recognition being based on the holistic visual familiarity of the stimuli.

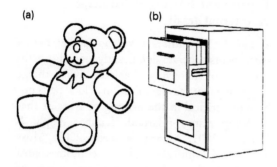

Figure 1. *Examples of stimuli identifiable (a) from global shape and (b) from internal detail.*

factor (both $F < 1.0$)[4]. Assignment of the stimuli into the two experimental categories was based on whether the objects could be identified by normal subjects when presented as silhouettes. Twelve age-matched controls correctly named 34.9/36 of the global shape stimuli from their silhouettes in contrast to 4.7/30 correct in the internal detail condition (there was no consistency across the control subjects as to which items they identified in the internal detail condition). Examples of stimuli from each group are illustrated in Figure 1.

The images were standardised for size (their longest dimension of either height or width was 4.5 inches). Each image was mounted on a separate A4 sheet, and ES and GK were presented with one object at a time, in random order, and asked to identify the stimuli. Their performance was contrasted with that of 12 age-matched controls. The procedure for the control subjects and the simultanagnosic patients was identical.

Results

Performance was scored in terms of the number of items correctly identified. A lenient scoring criterion was adopted. Since the exact name of the items was often difficult to retrieve due to some anomic difficulties with both ES and GK, responses were scored as correct if a correct

description was given. The data are presented in Table 5a. The control subjects scored at or near ceiling with both the global and the internal detail stimuli. The data from the two patients was subjected to a log linear analysis with the factors being patient (ES and GK), stimulus (global vs. internal detail), and accuracy (whether the item was named correctly or not). None of the main effects was significant, but there were two significant two-way interactions: Subject × Accuracy, $\chi^2(1) = 6.13$, $p < .013$ (overall GK had a higher level of accuracy than ES), and Stimulus × Accuracy, $\chi^2(1) = 20.1$, $p < .000$ (the patients were more accurate with the global than in the internal detail stimuli). Naming errors were categorised as visual, visual and semantic, semantic, partonomic, or other (see Experiment 1). The numbers of different error types are given in Table 5b. Both patients made mostly visual or visual/semantic naming errors (81.6% and 61.1% for ES and GK respectively).

Table 5a. *Naming of line drawings where identity is given by global shape or internal detail*

	ES	GK	Controls
Global shape (N = 36)	24	30	36
Internal shape (N = 30)	7	15	28.6

Table 5b. *Categorisation of the naming errors made by ES and GK in Experiment 2*

	ES		GK	
	Internal detail	Global shape	Internal detail	Global shape
Visual	12	11	5	1
Visual/semantic	6	2	2	3
Semantic	2		2	
Partonomic	1		2	1
Other	2	2	1	1

---

[4] Matching was conducted using data from the Oxford Psycholinguistic Database (Quinlan, 1992).

Discussion

Control participants were able to identify both the global shape and internal detail stimuli. The patients, however, showed a clear difference between the stimuli; they found it much easier to name stimuli from their global shapes than those that needed internal detail to be identified. This suggests that the patients can use global shape for object identification. It also indicates that they are relatively poor at using internal details to identify an object. This impoverished use of internal detail may reflect inappropriate segmentation of stimuli when internal segmentation cues are present. Such inappropriate segmentation processes may contribute to their impaired identification of overlapping figures (see Case Descriptions).

As in Experiment 1, the patients mostly made visual errors to objects, and these errors often shared their overall shape with the target picture (e.g., tomato → melon—ES—and apple—GK). However, there were some partonomic errors (camel → snake, based on its neck) and also some visual errors that seemed to reflect the surface texture of the stimulus rather than its overall shape (e.g., Emmenthal cheese → little balls—ES); leopard → raspberry, based on its spots—GK). These occasional partonomic errors may arise when the patients focus attention onto one segmented part of an object, when they seem unaware of the presence of the other parts. The texture errors suggest that, at least on some trials, the patients' attention was focused on the surface features of the objects. The errors are also consistent with texture cues being weighted quite strongly for identification.

In Experiment 3 we attempted to test the idea that the patients showed poor segmentation by comparing the identification of standard line drawings with the identification of the same drawings when some minimal segmentation cues were added. The drawings were all of animate stimuli (animals), which may be identified from their global shapes (Experiment 1). Are the patients abnormally affected by the minimal segmentation cues, which make the animals difficult to identify?

Experiment 3: Naming pictures with and without added segmentation cues

Method

Nineteen pictures of animals were selected from the Snodgrass and Vanderwart picture norms (Snodgrass & Vanderwart, 1980), in order to maximise the chances of identifying the stimuli from their global shape. Each item was approximately 2 × 3 inches in size, and it was presented on two occasions. On one occasion items were displayed as standard. On the other, additional lines were added to the drawings indicating (for instance) the separation of the head from the body and the legs from the trunk. Examples are shown in Figure 2. The standard and segmented drawings were presented using an ABBA design. GK named all the drawings in a single session. ES named all the drawings in two sessions, separated by 2 weeks. The segmented drawings were shown to two age-matched control participants who had no difficulties in identification.

Results

The data are presented in Table 6. Both ES and GK found the standard line drawings easier to name than the artificially segmented line drawings (23/38 vs. 13/38 and 15/19 vs. 8/19 for ES and GK respectively). These effects were statistically significant: McNemar tests of change $\chi^2(1) = 4.8$, $p < .05$ and $\chi^2(1) = 10.1$, $p < .01$ for ES and GK

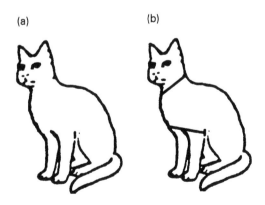

(a)   (b)

Figure 2. *Examples of pictures (a) with and (b) without added segmentation cues.*

Table 6. *Percentage correct naming responses for ES and GK for standard line drawings (Set 1) and artificially segmented line drawings (Set 2) (numbers correct are given in brackets)*

	Set 1	Set 2
ES	63 (24/38)	34 (13/38)
GK	79 (15/19)	42 (8/19)

respectively). All the errors were visual/semantic in nature (e.g., donkey → horse).

Discussion

Both GK and ES were again significantly disrupted by the presence of minimal internal details that segmented the objects into parts. This result occurred even though there is some suggestion that the items were identified from their global shape in the standard condition (cf. Experiments 1 and 2). It appears that the minimal segmentation cues tended to break the objects into separate parts, which the patients then found difficult to identify. Alternatively, the cues may make recognition difficult because they are not segmented but rather bind with the local parts of objects (cf. Friedman-Hill et al., 2003).

Experiment 4: Effects of colour and surface texture

Colour can have an important role in the recognition of some objects. Tanaka and Presnell (1999) have shown that the presence or absence of colour information had a significant effect on the recognition of context-free objects that have a consistent colour (e.g., bananas, carrots), relative to objects with no consistent colour (e.g., cars) (Tanaka & Presnell, 1999). Colour and texture may also prove useful cues in segregating and organising visual input (Blaser & Domini, 2002; Tanaka, Weiskopf, & Williams, 2001). In Experiment 4, we evaluate whether ES and GK were facilitated by surface colour and texture on objects. We compared the identification of line drawings with the identification of grey-level and coloured photographs.

Performance was assessed with animate and inanimate objects. For control subjects, the effects of colour and texture tend to be larger on naming animate relative to inanimate objects, perhaps because colour and texture are more diagnostic of the identity of animate objects (e.g., see Price & Humphreys, 1989). If colour and texture are directly used to help identify stimuli, then any effects maybe particularly strong on animate objects. On the other hand, if the surface details help to prevent stimuli being segmented inappropriately into their parts, then such details may be effective for inanimate as well as animate objects.

Method

The stimuli were taken from the study of Price and Humphreys (1989). GK received 50 animate and 50 inanimate items; ES received 49 animate and 47 inanimate items.[5] The animate and inanimate items were matched for name frequency and number of syllables per item name. Details of the stimuli are provided in Price and Humphreys. It is relevant to note here that animate items had a higher degree of contour overlap and a greater number of common attributes per category than artefacts. Each object was photographed from a prototypical view, against a white background, in both colour and black and white. The object was framed so that its main axis of elongation—either the height (e.g., a refrigerator) or its width (e.g., a banana)—was 2 inches. Outline drawings were produced by tracing the outline and main features of each photograph. The black-and-white line drawings contained no surface texture or shading. Each item was presented individually on a card with no constraints on the time allowed for naming. Items from animate and inanimate categories were presented in random order. The different modes of stimulus presentation were also randomised. Testing spanned three sessions (separated by weekly intervals) in order to ensure that no item was presented more than once in any test occasion. Two age-matched controls had no difficulty in identifying any of the stimuli.

---

[5] Unfortunately, four stimuli were missing from the sessions with ES.

Results

The results are presented in Table 7. The data were analysed using log linear analysis with the factors being patient (ES vs. GK), object (animate vs. inanimate items), picture type (coloured photograph vs. black-and-white photograph vs. line drawing), and accuracy (correct response vs. naming error). There were three significant two-way interactions: Patient × Accuracy, $\chi^2(1) = 26.0$, $p < .000$; Picture Type × Accuracy, $\chi^2(2) = 17.0$, $p < .0002$; and Object × Accuracy, $\chi^2(1) = 6.9$, $p < .008$. GK generally performed better than ES, and animate objects were identified more accurately than inanimate objects. Further analyses of the Picture Type × Accuracy interaction showed that there was no significant difference in performance between coloured and black-and-white photo-

graphs, $\chi^2(1) = 2.5$, $p > .05$. However, both types of photograph were named better than the line drawings, $\chi^2(1) = 3.9$, $p < .05$ and $\chi^2(1) = 6.1$, $p < .01$ for coloured photographs and black-and-white photographs against line drawings, respectively.

As in Experiments 1–3, the patients tended to make visual misidentification errors. This held with the photographs as well as the line drawings, though the errors decreased in magnitude for the photographs (see Table 8).

Discussion

The patients showed strong effects of surface detail on their object identification. Both coloured and grey-level photographs were identified more accurately than line drawings. Control subjects found all the stimuli easy to identify. The effects of surface detail were roughly equal for animate and inanimate objects, though we again found that the patients were worse at identifying inanimate items. Since the effects were equally strong on the two classes of stimulus, we suggest that surface information was not (only) used to directly identify the objects (since surface information should be more diagnostic of animate than inanimate objects; Price & Humphreys, 1989). For inanimate objects, at least, surface details could help to prevent inappropriate segmentation from internal segmentation cues. This improves performance for patients who are abnormally sensitive to such segmentation cues (Experiment 3).

Table 7. *Naming animate and inanimate items presented as photographs (coloured or black-and-white) or black-and-white line drawings*

	ES	GK
Animate		
Coloured photographs	90 (44)	96 (48)
Black-and-white photographs	86 (42)	94 (47)
Black-and-white line drawings	80 (39)	86 (43)
Inanimate		
Coloured photographs	83 (39)	96 (48)
Black-and-white photographs	58 (33)	94 (47)
Black-and-white line drawings	53 (25)	76 (43)

Table 8. *Categorisation of errors for ES and GK in Experiment 4*

	Photographs								Line drawings			
	Coloured				Black-and-white							
	A		I		A		I		A		I	
	ES	GK	ES	GK	ES	GK	ES	GK	ES	GK	ES	GK
Visual	1	1	6	2	2	1	8	1	5	2	15	3
Visual/semantic	4	1	3	–	5	1	4	2	5	3	3	–
Semantic	–	–	–	–	–	1	2	–	–	–	1	3
Other	–	–	1	–	–	–	–	–	–	2	3	1

GENERAL DISCUSSION

We have examined factors determining object identification in two simultanagnosic patients, ES and GK. We showed that the patients have some difficulties in identifying line drawings, particularly of inanimate objects (Experiment 1). The patients also found it easier to identify drawings of stimuli that could be identified from their global shape than stimuli that relied on their internal details being coded correctly (Experiment 2). This suggests that the patients could use global shape information, but they tended to be impaired at using internal details to support object identification. The poor performance with internal detail stimuli may arise because internal details tend to lead to inappropriate object segmentation. This was supported by the data from Experiment 3, where we demonstrated that the presence of a small number of segmentation cues was sufficient to disrupt the identification of animate objects that were otherwise identified correctly (presumably from their global shape). In Experiment 4, we demonstrated relatively strong effects of surface detail on identification performance in the patients. The patients were better at identifying coloured and grey-level photographs compared with line drawings. This held for both animate and inanimate objects, although overall they remained better with animate stimuli.

Our findings indicate that object identification is not necessarily intact in simultanagnosia. Although patients can be good at identifying some objects (e.g., animate stimuli), nonetheless they can have problems with drawings of inanimate stimuli. Previously, different category-specific deficits for inanimate objects have been attributed to deficits in semantic knowledge and naming (see Humphreys & Forde, 2001, for a review). Given that ES and GK primarily suffered occipito-parietal damage, one might conceive that their problems reflect a dorsally mediated route that modulates the identification of inanimate objects used for action (see Kellenbach, Brett, & Patterson, 2003, for recent imaging evidence on the involvement of parietal regions in the processing of objects for action). However, the other experiments presented here indicate that object identification in the patients was modulated by visual rather than semantic factors. For example, the patients had spared semantic knowledge about inanimate objects when tested verbally (Experiment 1). Also, their naming of inanimate objects was improved when the stimuli were shown in photographs rather than as line drawings. Rather than the deficit being semantic, we suggest that it arose because of the impact of the parietal lesions on object coding.

Experiment 2 indicated that the patients could use global shape information for object identification. However, they were impaired at using internal details for identification, and internal segmentation cues also tended to disrupt the identification of objects from their global shape (animate objects, in Experiment 3). These results fit with the idea that damage to the parietal cortex limits a patient's ability to attend to visual stimuli. At least three consequences may follow. One is that the patients tend to identify objects using a holistic representation in which parts, and the spatial relations between parts, are not coded in detail (cf. Hummel & Stankiewicz, 1998; Shalev & Humphreys, 2002). A second is, with limited attention spread across a stimulus, there may be incorrect binding of the stimulus with extraneous, overlapping elements (with the additional lines present, in Experiment 3). A third is that, on some occasions, attention may collapse onto a local part when there are strong segmentation cues present (again with the additional lines, in Experiment 3; or with spaces between the parts of compound stimuli, see Humphreys et al., 1994b; Karnath, Ferber, Rorden, & Driver, 2000). When attention is focused on a local part in this way, the patients can even be unaware of the presence of other visual elements, as when partonomic errors arise (Humphreys et al., 1994b).

Our argument, then, is for a global, ventral recognition process augmented by a parts-based representation that is dependent on more dorsal cortex. This global recognition strategy can underlie the recognition of many objects (Experiment 2), and it may be one of the factors contributing to the advantage for animate over inanimate objects in these patients (Experiments 1 and 4). Animate objects have many parts in common and they tend to undergo nonrigid transformations that may make parts-based structural descriptions unreliable for identification. In contrast, inanimate objects have fewer parts in common (Humphreys et al., 1988), and they tend to undergo rigid transformations across which their structural description is constant (Laeng et al., 2002). They also contain segmentation cues where their parts are joined. All of these factors may emphasise holistic recognition processes with living things and parts-based recognition procedures for nonliving things. Parts-based recognition is difficult for patients with bilateral parietal damage.

One further factor that may also benefit the identification of animate over inanimate objects is the presence of diagnostic colour and texture cues (e.g., Price & Humphreys, 1989). The identification of animate objects ought to be facilitated by colour and texture more than the identification of inanimate objects. We found that ES and GK improved at identifying objects when colour and texture cues were present (Experiment 4). However, the benefit was equally large for inanimate as well as for animate objects. This suggests that surface cues may not have served recognition directly, but rather they may have helped parts cohere together (at least for inanimate objects). Whatever the case, our results indicate that category effects in object recognition do not necessarily arise at a semantic level (see also Humphreys & Riddoch, 2003b). In addition, visual impairments do not necessarily make it harder to identify animate objects. Indeed, the nature of the visual impairment appears to be important. Patients whose visual deficit still enables them to derive global representations of object shape may identify animate objects, even when they are impaired at encoding parts-based representations for the recognition of inanimate objects.

Relation to other forms of recognition deficit

There are several similarities between the recognition disturbances described in GK and ES, here,

and those reported in patients with recognition impairments following more ventral lesions. In particular, we (Riddoch & Humphreys, 1987) have defined a disorder known as integrative agnosia, in which patients with bilateral occipito-temporal lesions are impaired at identifying stimuli in complex backgrounds when there are spatially overlapping forms (see also Behrmann & Kimchi, 2003; Giersch, Humphreys, Boucart, & Kovács, 2000; Ricci, Vaishnavi, & Chatterjee, 1999). Integrative agnosia is also associated with poor encoding of holistic forms from the parts present (Behrmann & Kimchi, 2003), although such patients can respond to some (undifferentiated) aspects of holistic forms. For example, integrative agnosics can show a global advantage when responding to hierarchical compound stimuli (Behrmann & Kimchi, 2003; Humphreys, Riddoch, & Quinlan, 1985). To account for this last result, Humphreys et al. (1985) proposed that there was independent coding of a low spatial frequency representation that the patients responded to with compound stimuli, but that, unlike normal observers, the low spatial frequency description was not elaborated by a description of the parts of the "whole". Recognition failures occur on the many occasions when the unelaborated holistic description is insufficient for object identification. Also, recognition of whole objects is disturbed by the failure in parts-based grouping. Nevertheless, featural properties can be discriminated by attentional scrutiny of local regions, and recognition is thus contingent on the presence of critical, individuating (distinctive) features (see Humphreys & Riddoch, 1984, for evidence).

Although there are similarities between the recognition performance of simultanagnosic and integrative agnosics, there are also important differences. In particular, we suggest that the recognition deficits in each case are caused by contrasting problems: (a) a core deficit in allocating attention to objects (in simultanagnosia), not object coding per se, and (b) a core deficit in grouping and constructing perceptual wholes from multiple visual elements (in integrative agnosia). In integrative agnosia, the ability to control attention can be preserved, as indicated by good performance on serial visual search tasks (Humphreys, Riddoch, Quinlan, Donnelly, & Price, 1992; see also Vecera & Behrmann, 1997). In addition, integrative agnosics are typically aware of the spatial contexts in which stimuli appear. Humphreys (1998) described this as the patients being able to derive a representation of the spatial relations between a small number of separate objects (a "between-object spatial representation"), in a spatially parallel manner. In contrast, this process of rapid, between-object coding is disrupted in simultanagnosia, so that patients only appear aware of the one object being identified (Humphreys, 1998). There is also an impairment of attention; such patients are unable to effect a serial search of a display (see Friedman-Hill et al., 2003; Humphreys & Price, 1994).

These differences in how attention operates influence object recognition. For instance, though features are strongly weighted for object identification in integrative agnosics, the features are typically related to the whole object. Hence, such patients rarely make the partonomic errors found in simultanagnosia, which we attribute to attention collapsing onto a local part which is then coded in isolation from the whole. A further difference may be in the nature of local part coding. In integrative agnosia we suggest that impaired grouping of local elements means that the holistic descriptions are impoverished and do not carry part detail. This can then force their intact attention to a local level. In contrast, the attentional limitation in simultanagnosia may still allow holistic descriptions to carry information about local detail, but the detail is not elaborated into a full parts-based description. This nondecomposed description, carrying part detail, may be better able to sustain object identification than the holistic descriptions derived by integrative agnosics. Moreover, the attentional impairment in simultanagnosia limits the serial scrutiny of local parts, which may not then be strongly weighted for identification. The net result is that identification in simultanagnosia can be affected by the global shape of the stimuli rather than the local detail (Experiment 1 here). Furthermore, the biases towards distinctive local features (in integrative agnosia) and whole shape (in simultanagnosia)

may contribute to the different patterns of category effects in the patient groups. Inanimate objects, dependent on distinctive features, can be relatively spared for integrative agnosics (Riddoch & Humphreys, 1987; Riddoch, Humphreys, Gannon, Blott, & Jones, 1999; Thomas & Forde, in press; Thomas, Forde, Humphreys, & Graham, 2003). Animate objects, dependent on an overall shape, are relatively spared in simultanagnosia (Experiment 1 here). These arguments emphasise that both simultanagnosia and integrative agnosia need to be understood not simply in terms of deficits in visual processing but in terms of interactions between attention and visual coding in object recognition.

REFERENCES

Bálint, R. (1909). Seelenlähmung des "schauens", optische ataxie, räumliche störung der aufmerksamkeit. *Monatschrift für Psychiatrie und Neurologie, 25,* 51–81.

Behrmann, M., & Kimchi, R. (2003). What does visual agnosia tell us about perceptual organisation and its relation to object perception? *Journal of Experimental Psychology: Human Perception and Performance, 29,* 19–42.

Biederman, I., & Gerhardstein, P. C. (1993). Recognising depth-rotated objects: Evidence and conditions for three-dimensional viewpoint invariance. *Journal of Experimental Psychology: Human Perception and Performance, 19,* 1162–1182.

Blaser, E., & Domini, F. (2002). The conjunction of feature and depth information. *Vision Research, 42,* 273–279.

Boutsen, L., & Humphreys, G. W. (2000). Axis-based grouping reduces extinction. *Neuropsychologia, 38,* 896–905.

Capitani, E., Laiacona, M., Mahon, B., & Caramazza, A. (2003). What are the facts of category-specific deficits? A critical review of the clinical evidence. *Cognitive Neuropsychology, 20,* 213–261.

Cappa, S. F., Frugoni, M., Pasquali, P., Perani, D., & Zorat, F. (1998). Category-specific naming impairment for artefacts. *Neurocase, 4,* 391–397.

Caramazza, A., & Shelton, J. R. (1998). Domain-specific knowledge systems in the brain: The animate–inanimate distinction. *Journal of Cognitive Neuroscience, 10,* 1–34.

Corbetta, M., & Shulman, G. L. (1998). Human cortical mechanisms of visual attention during orienting and search. *Philosophical Transactions of the Royal Society, London, Series B* 353, 1241–1244.

Coslett, H. B., & Saffran, E. (1991). Simultanagnosia: To see but not two see. *Brain, 114,* 1523–1545.

Coslett, B., & Saffran, E. (1992). Simultanagnosia in dementia. In M. Schwartz (Ed.), *Cognitive deficits in dementia.* New York: Academic Press.

Edwards, M. G., & Humphreys, G. W. (2002). Visual selection and action in Bálints syndrome. *Cognitive Neuropsychology, 19,* 445–462.

Forde, E. M. E., & Humphreys, G. W. (Eds.). (2002). *Category specificity in brain and mind.* Hove, UK: Psychology Press.

Freeman, E., Driver, J., & Sagi, D. (2003). Top-down modulations of lateral interactions in early vision: Does attention affect integration of the whole or just perception of the parts? *Current Biology, 13,* 985–989.

Friedman-Hill, S. R., Robertson, L. C., Desimone, R., & Ungeleider, L. G. (2003). Posterior parietal cortex and the filtering of distractors. *Proceedings of the National Academy of Sciences, USA, 100,* 4263–4268.

Friedman-Hill, S., Robertson, L. C., & Treisman, A. (1995). Parietal contributions to visual feature binding: Evidence from a patient with bilateral lesions. *Science, 269,* 853–855.

Funnell, E. (2000). Apperceptive agnosia and the visual recognition of object categories in dementia of the Alzheimer type. *Neurocase, 6,* 451–463.

Garrard, P., Lambon-Ralph, M. A., & Hodges, J. R. (2001). Prototypicality, distinctiveness, and intercorrelation: Analysis of the semantic attributes of living and nonliving concepts. *Cognitive Neuropsychology, 18,* 125–174.

Gerlach, C. (2001). Structural similarity causes different category effects depending on task characteristics. *Neuropsychologia, 39,* 895–900.

Giersch, A., Humphreys, G. W., Boucart, M., & Kovács, I. (2000). The computation of occluded contours in visual agnosia: Evidence of early computation prior to shape binding and figure-ground coding. *Cognitive Neuropsychology, 17,* 731–759.

Gilchrist, D., Humphreys, G. W., & Riddoch, M. J. (1996). Grouping and extinction: Evidence for low-level modulation of visual selection. *Cognitive Neuropsychology, 13,* 1223–1249.

Hall, D., Humphreys, G. W., & Cooper, A. (2001). Multi-letter units in reading: Evidence from attentional dyslexia. *Quarterly Journal of Experimental Psychology, 54A,* 439–467.

Hummel, J. E. (2001). Complementary solutions to the binding problem in vision: Implications for shape perception and object recognition. *Visual Cognition, 8,* 489–517.

Hummel, J. E., & Stankiewicz (1998). Two roles for attention in shape perception: A structural description model of visual scrutiny. *Visual Cognition, 5,* 49–79.

Humphreys, G. W. (1998). Neural representation of objects in space: A dual coding account. *Philosophical Transactions of the Royal Society, B353,* 1341–1352.

Humphreys, G. W., & Forde, E. M. E. (2001). Hierarchies, similarity, and interactivity in object recognition: "Category-specific" neuropsychological deficits. *Behavioural and Brain Sciences, 24,* 453–509.

Humphreys, G. W., & Price, C. J. (1994). Visual feature discrimination in simultanagnosia: A study of two cases. *Cognitive Neuropsychology, 11,* 393–434.

Humphreys, G. W., & Riddoch, M. J. (1984). Routes to object constancy: Implications from neurological impairments of object constancy. *Quarterly Journal of Experimental Psychology, 36A,* 385–415.

Humphreys, G. W., & Riddoch, M. J. (1993). Interactions between object and space systems revealed through neuropsychology. In D. E. Meyer & S. Kornblum (Eds.), *Attention and performance XIV* (pp. 143–162). Hillsdale, NJ: Lawrence Erlbaum Associates Inc.

Humphreys, G. W., & Riddoch, M. J. (2003a). From vision to action, and action to vision: A convergent route approach to vision, action and attention. In D. Irwin (Ed.), *The psychology of learning and motivation* (Vol. 42). New York: Academic Press.

Humphreys, G. W., & Riddoch, M. J. (2003b). A case series analysis of "category-specific" deficits of living things: The HIT account. *Cognitive Neuropsychology, 20,* 263–306.

Humphreys, G. W., & Riddoch, M. J. (2003). From what to where: Neuropsychological evidence for implicit interactions between object- and space-based attention. *Psychological Science, 14,* 487–492.

Humphreys, G. W., Riddoch, M. J., & Quinlan, P. T. (1985). Interactive processes in perceptual organisation: Evidence from visual agnosia. In M. I. Posner & O. S. M. Marin (Eds.), *Attention and performance XI.* Hillsdale, NJ: Lawrence Erlbaum Associates Inc.

Humphreys, G. W., Riddoch, M. J., & Quinlan, P. T. (1988). Cascade processes in picture identification. *Cognitive Neuropsychology, 5,* 67–103

Humphreys, G. W., Riddoch, M. J., Donnelly, N., Freeman, T., Boucart, M., & Müller, H. M. (1994a). Intermediate visual processing and visual agnosia. In M. J. Farah & G. Ratcliff (Eds.), *The neuropsychology of high-level vision: Collected tutorial essays.* Hillsdale, NJ: Lawrence Erlbaum Associates Inc.

Humphreys, G. W., Riddoch, M. J., Quinlan, P. T., Donnelly, N., & Price, C. A. (1992). Parallel pattern processing and visual agnosia. *Canadian Journal of Psychology, 46,* 377–416.

Humphreys, G. W., Romani, C., Olson, A., Riddoch, M. J., & Duncan, J. (1994b). Non-spatial extinction following lesions of the parietal lobe in humans. *Nature, 372,* 357–359.

Kanwisher, N., & Wojciulik, E. 2000. Visual attention: Insights from brain imaging. *Nature Reviews (Neuroscience), 1,* 91–100

Karnath, H.-O., Ferber, S., Rorden, C., & Driver, J. (2000). The fate of global information in dorsal simultanagnosia. *Neurocase, 6,* 295–306.

Kay, J., Lesser, R., & Coltheart, M. (1992). *PALPA: Psycholinguistic Assessments of Language Processing in Aphasia.* Hove, UK: Lawrence Erlbaum Associates Ltd.

Kellenbach, M. L., Brett, M., & Patterson, K. (2003). Actions speak louder than functions: The importance of manipulability and action in tool representation. *Journal of Cognitive Neuroscience, 15,* 30–46.

Kinsbourne, M., & Warrington, E. K. (1962). A disorder of simultaneous form perception. *Brain, 85,* 461–486.

Kinsbourne, M., & Warrington, E. K. (1963). Limited visual form perception. *Brain, 86,* 697–705.

Kuçera, H., & Francis, W. N. (1967). *A computational analysis of present-day American English.* Providence, RI: Brown University Press.

Kumada, T., & Humphreys, G. W. (2001). Lexical recovery from extinction: Interactions between visual form and stored knowledge modulate visual selection. *Cognitive Neuropsychology, 18,* 465–478.

Laeng, B., Carlesimo, G. A., Capasso, R., & Miceli, G. (2002). Rigid and nonrigid objects in canonical and noncanonical views. Hemisphere effects on object identification. *Cognitive Neuropsychology, 19,* 697–720.

Laws, K. R., & Neve, C. (1999). A "normal" category specific effect for living things. *Neuropsychologia, 37,* 1263–1269.

Luria, A. R. (1959). Disorders of "simultaneous perception" in a case of bilateral occipito-parietal brain injury. *Brain, 82,* 437–449.

Luria, A. R., Pravdina-Vinaskkaya, E. N., & Yarbus, A. L. (1963). Disorders of ocular movement in a case of simultanagnosia. *Brain, 86,* 219–228.

McRae, K., & Cree, G. S. (2002). Factors underlying category-specific semantic deficits. In M. E. Forde &

G. W. Humphreys (Eds.), *Category-specificity in mind and brain.* Hove, UK: Psychology Press.

Moss, H. E., Tyler, L. K., & Devlin, J. T. (2002). The emergence of category-specific deficits in a distributed semantic system. In E. M. E. Forde & G. W. Humphreys (Eds.), *Category-specificity in mind and brain.* Hove, UK: Psychology Press.

Naor-Raz, G., Tarr, M. J., & Kersten, D. (in press). Is colour an intrinsic property of object representations? *Perception.*

Palmer, S., & Rock, I. (1994). Rethinking perceptual organisation: The role of uniform consecutiveness. *Psychonomic Bulletin and Review, 1,* 29–55.

Pollman, S., Weider, R., Humphreys, G. W., Olivers, C. N. L., Müller, K., Lohmann, G., Wiggins, C. J., & Watson, D. G. (2003). Separating segmentation and target detection in posterior parietal cortex: An event-related fMRI study of visual marking. *NeuroImage, 18,* 310–323.

Price, C. J., & Humphreys, G. W. (1989). The effects of surface detail on object categorisation and naming. *Quarterly Journal of Experimental Psychology, 41A,* 797–828.

Price, C. J., Noppeney, U., Phillips, J., & Devlin, J. T. (2003). How is the fusiform gyrus related to category-specificity? *Cognitive Neuropsychology, 20,* 561–574.

Quinlan, P. T. (1992). *The Oxford Psycholinguistics database.* Oxford: Oxford University Press.

Rensink, R. A., & Enns, J. (1995). Pre-emption effects in visual search: Evidence for low-level grouping. *Psychological Review, 102,* 101–130.

Ricci, R., Vaishnavi, S., & Chatterjee, A. (1999). A deficit of intermediate vision: Experimental observations and theoretical implications. *Neurocase, 5,* 1–12.

Riddoch, M. J., & Humphreys, G. W. (1987). A case of integrative agnosia. *Brain, 110,* 1431–1462.

Riddoch, M. J., & Humphreys, G. W. (1993). *BORB: The Birmingham Object Recognition Battery.* Hove, UK: Lawrence Erlbaum Associates Ltd.

Riddoch, M. J., Humphreys, G. W., & Edwards, M. G. (2000a). Neuropsychological evidence distinguishing object selection from action (effector) selection. *Cognitive Neuropsychology, 17,* 547–562.

Riddoch, M. J., Humphreys, G. W., & Edwards, M. G. (2000b). Visual affordances and object selection. In S. Monsell & J. Driver (Eds.), *Attention and performance XVIII.* Cambridge, MA: MIT Press.

Riddoch, M. J., Humphreys, G. W., & Edwards, M. G. (2001). An experimental analysis of anarchic lower limb action. *Neuropsychologia, 39,* 574–579.

Riddoch, M. J., Humphreys, G. W., Gannon, T., Blott, W., & Jones, V. (1999). Memories are made of this: The effects of time on stored visual knowledge in a case of visual agnosia. *Brain, 122,* 537–559.

Sacchett, C., & Humphreys, G. W. (1992). Calling a squirrel a squirrel but a canoe a wigwam: A category-specific deficit for artefactual objects and body parts. *Cognitive Neuropsychology, 9,* 73–86.

Shalev, L., & Humphreys, G. W. (2002). Implicit location encoding via stored representations of familiar objects: Neuropsychological evidence. *Cognitive Neuropsychology, 19,* 721–744.

Snodgrass, J. G., & Vanderwart, M. A. (1980). A standardised set of 260 pictures: Norms for name agreement, familiarity and name complexity. *Journal of Experimental Psychology: Human Learning and Memory, 6,* 174–215.

Tanaka, J. W., & Presnell, L. M. (1999). Colour diagnosticity in object recognition. *Perception and Psychophysics, 61,* 1140–1153.

Tanaka, J. W., Weiskopf, D., & Williams, P. (2001). The role of colour in high-level vision. *Trends in Cognitive Sciences, 5,* 211–215.

Thomas, R., & Forde, E. M. E. (in press). The role of local and global processing in the recognition of living and nonliving things. *Neurocase.*

Thomas, R., Forde, E. M. E., Humphreys, G. W., & Graham, K. S. (2002). The effects of the passage of time on a patient with category-specific agnosia. *Neurocase, 8,* 466–479.

Vecera, S. P., & Behrmann, M. (1997). Spatial attention does not require preattentive grouping. *Neuropsychology, 11,* 30–43.

Warrington, E. K., & James, M. (Eds.). (1991). *VOSP: The Visual Object and Space Perception Battery.* Bury St Edmunds, UK: Thames Valley Test Company.

Warrington, E. K., & McCarthy, R. A. (1983). Category-specific access dysphasia. *Brain, 106,* 859–878.

Warrington, E. K., & McCarthy, R. A. (1987). Categories of knowledge: Further fractionation and an attempted integration. *Brain, 110,* 1273–1296.

COGNITIVE NEUROPSYCHOLOGY, 2004, 21 (2/3/4) 443–458

PURE ALEXIA AND COVERT READING: EVIDENCE FROM STROOP TASKS

Thomas J. McKeeff and Marlene Behrmann

Carnegie Mellon University, Pittsburgh, PA, USA

Patients with pure alexia (also referred to as letter-by-letter readers) show a marked word-length effect when naming visually presented words, evidenced by a monotonic increase in response time (or decrease in accuracy) as a function of the number of letters in the string. Interestingly, despite the difficulty in overtly reporting the identity of some words, many patients exhibit fast and above-chance access to lexical and/or semantic information for the same words. To explore the extent of this covert reading, we examined the degree of interference afforded by the inconsistent (word identity and colour label do not match) versus neutral condition in a Stroop task in a pure alexic patient, EL. EL shows evidence of covert reading on a semantic categorisation task and a lexical decision task. She also demonstrates covert reading by exhibiting Stroop interference of the same magnitude as a matched control subject, when naming the colour of the ink in which a word is printed. When the word shares some but not all letters with the colour name (BLOW instead of BLUE), neither subject shows interference. In contrast with the control subject, EL does not show Stroop interference when various orthographic changes (degraded visual input, cursive font) or phonological or semantic changes are made to the word. These findings indicate that although some implicit processing of words may be possible, this processing is rather rudimentary. Not surprising, this implicit activation may be insufficient to support overt word identification. We explain these findings in the context of a single, integrated account of pure alexia.

INTRODUCTION

Pure alexia is a neuropsychological disorder in which premorbidly literate adults exhibit severe reading impairments in the absence of other obvious language deficits (for a recent review, see Behrmann, Plaut, & Nelson, 1998b; Coslett & Saffran, 2001). The disorder is a consequence of brain damage typically located in the left occipital lobe but can also result from damage to callosal fibers in the splenium of the corpus callosum or forceps major (Black & Behrmann, 1994; Damasio & Damasio, 1983). The lesion site is also compatible with recent functional imaging data, which point to these regions as implicated in reading (for recent paper, see L. Cohen, Lehericy, Chochon, Lemer, Rivaud, & Dehaene, 2002; Hasson, Levy, Behrmann, Hendler, & Malach, 2002). Patients with this disorder are also termed letter-by-letter (LBL) readers because they appear to process

Correspondence should be addressed to Thomas J. McKeeff, Department of Psychology, Princeton University, Princeton, NJ 08544, USA (Email: tmckeeff@princeton.edu).

This paper is submitted as a special tribute to Dr Eleanor Saffran whose contribution to the field of Cognitive Neuropsychology was immeasurable. She was a true inspiration to us.

This work was supported by funding from the National Institute of Mental Health to MB (MH47566 and MH54246). We thank Matt Lambon Ralph, Rachel Mycroft, and Marie Montant for their useful suggestions.

DOI:10.1080/02643290342000429

letters sequentially when attempting to read a word. This LBL reading behaviour may manifest in the overt articulation of individual letters but, more often, is evident in measures of the accuracy or reaction time of their word processing (for example, in naming or lexical decision tasks). Whereas normal readers require minimal, if any, extra time to read a word as the length increases (up until approximately nine letters; Frederiksen, 1976; Weekes, 1997), suggesting parallel processing of the letters, LBL readers show a linear increase in their reading time and eye movements (Behrmann et al., 2001) as a function of the number of letters in the string. This monotonic relationship between word length and naming latency is assumed to reflect the sequential processing of the individual letters in the string (Warrington & Shallice, 1980).

Covert processing in LBL readers

Despite the apparent failure to process letters in parallel with normal efficiency and the subsequent adoption of the serial processing of letters, some patients with pure alexia demonstrate covert or unconscious processing of words. Although they may not be able to identify a word overtly, they appear to have available to them both lexical and semantic information about the word even when it is presented at exposure durations too brief to support explicit identification. Additionally perplexing is that, when assessed in these covert processing conditions, the word length effect is often absent (Bub & Arguin, 1995; Coslett & Saffran, 1989).

An early demonstration of this implicit reading phenomenon comes from work by Landis, Redard, and Serrat (1980) in a description of a LBL reader who, when shown a word for 30 ms, could not identify it and sometimes denied even seeing the word. Yet, when instructed to match the presented word to an object displayed amidst an array of several objects, he was accurate a significant proportion of the time. Shallice and Saffran (1986), in a more systematic study of covert word reading, described a patient ML who could not explicitly

identify five- and six-letter words at an exposure duration of 2 s. However, ML was able to make a lexical decision to similar five- and six-letter words and nonwords at above-chance levels. This ability was also mediated by the frequency of the words, in that ML was more accurate at classifying high- as opposed to low-frequency words. ML was also able to make semantic classifications (e.g., does the word represent a living or nonliving thing?) of briefly presented words at levels much higher than would be expected by guessing, even though he still could not explicitly identify the target word.

Another surprising finding that is apparent in several LBL readers is the presence of the word superiority effect. The word superiority effect, defined as the increase in accuracy and decrease in response time to detect an individual letter within a word as opposed to a nonword, is thought to arise from the activation of the entire letter string, with greater activation for words than for nonwords. The presence of the word superiority effect in LBL readers is counterintuitive. If LBL reading is accomplished purely in a bottom-up sequential fashion through activating individual letters, there is no obvious reason that lexical status would exert any influence on performance. However, there are now many reports of individuals in whom a word superiority effect has been documented (Bub, Black, & Howell, 1989; Reuter-Lorenz & Brunn, 1990; for the same finding using a different paradigm, see Behrmann & Shallice, 1995).

Although reports of covert processing in LBL are fairly common nowadays, many LBL readers do not show implicit reading, performing at chance levels on lexical and semantic decision tasks (see Arguin et al., 1998, for discussion of this point). It has been suggested that the absence of these covert effects occurs because the individual attempts to read sequentially (even when instructed not to) and that this serial strategy inhibits the output of the covert processing system. According to Coslett and colleagues (Coslett & Saffran, 1994; Coslett, Saffran, Greenbaum, & Schwartz, 1993), there is a fundamental opposition between the strategies involved in covert word processing and those for overt word recognition. The implication is that covert processing is more reliably revealed when the patient is not simultaneously attempting to identify the stimulus explicitly. The use of a paradigm that does not engage explicit reading is therefore advantageous in uncovering covert word processing. One technique that has proven fairly profitable in a number of recent studies is the use of a priming paradigm in which the patient does not respond to the prime (and hence supposedly does not engage in serial processing) but responds to the probe (for example, Arguin et al., 1998). However, given that the probe is also a word and that the patient is engaging in some word processing, one might imagine that the patient is attempting to read the prime too. To better understand the nature of covert processing in LBL reading, the task we adopt in the current paper does not require word reading in the conditions of interest and may be especially useful for revealing implicit reading.

The task we have adopted is a Stroop paradigm and the particular condition of interest is the one in which subjects name the colour of the ink rather than read the word. In the original Stroop task (Stroop, 1935), subjects performed both word and ink naming tasks in blocked fashion. In the *word naming* task, participants read the word presented, while ignoring the ink colour of the words. In the *ink naming* task, participants named the stimulus ink colour, while ignoring the word in which it was presented. Of particular interest is the comparison in naming the ink colour in two conditions: the *control* condition, in which nonword stimuli are used (e.g., several Xs or rectangles) and the *incongruent* condition (for example, the word BLUE, written in red ink). This comparison is especially relevant because, under these conditions, subjects do not name the word but only name the colour ink and therefore do not explicitly engage word recognition processes. Any cost in latency observed in the incongruent over control condition, when subjects are required to name the ink colour, is taken as evidence for the automaticity of word reading (Kahneman & Henik, 1981; but see Besner, 2001). If LBL patients are able to activate any lexical or semantic information covertly, ink colour naming will be significantly slower in the incongruent than in the control condition.

Covert processing and representational precision

Even if one can demonstrate the presence of covert processing using this Stroop paradigm, an open question concerns the extent and precision of the representations activated during implicit reading. Some researchers have argued that the representations activated implicitly are well specified and precise whereas others have suggested that this is not the case. For example, recent studies using the implicit priming paradigm have explored whether words that differ from the target stimulus by a single letter are activated when a word is presented (Bowers, Arguin, & Bub, 1996a; Bowers, Bub, & Arguin, 1996b). If so, this might suggest that a less precise representation is activated. To evaluate the specificity of the representation, these studies use a priming paradigm in which subjects name a briefly presented (100 ms) upper-case word. Prior to the appearance of this target, a prime in lower case, is shown and then backward masked. Even though the exposure duration of the target was brief, substantial reductions in RT (reaction time) were observed when the prime and target were the same compared with when they were different (even if the case was mixed, Arguin et al., 1998). However, if the prime differed from the probe by just a single letter in any position of the word, no priming was evident. Given the absence of priming by a near orthographic neighbour, these studies conclude that the entire string must have been precisely and covertly activated.

A somewhat different result has been obtained in further studies by some of the same investigators. Using the same masked priming task, Arguin et al. (1998) have shown that, in contrast to normal readers, there is no facilitation in the performance of their LBL patient, IH, if the prime is homophonically related to the target. IH also does not show facilitation from increased orthographic neighbourhood size, again suggesting that covert activation is not entirely normal.

Whether or not activation is rich and precisely specified, however, has important theoretical significance. As alluded to previously, at least one account of covert processing in LBL readers, the "right hemisphere account," has argued that the covert reading arises from a different procedure from that used for LBL reading. Whereas the former reflects parallel processing in the right hemisphere, the latter depends on serial and sequential processing generated by the damaged left hemisphere. Additionally, the left hemisphere is responsible for explicit word identification and phonological processing, while the right hemisphere supports covert word processing. Clearly, most LBL readers encode the visual stimuli in the right hemisphere initially due to the right visual field defect, which is present in most, although not all, LBL readers. According to this view, the right hemisphere processing extends beyond perceptually encoding the stimulus and may, in fact, be responsible for all implicit reading. The right hemisphere activation is sufficient to give rise to the covert processing seen in these patients, but cannot mediate the output of the phonological form for overt production, hence the failure to explicitly report the word. On this view, then, the representation activated implicitly is detailed and rich but the information is not transmitted to the left hemisphere for output (Coslett & Monsul, 1994; Coslett & Saffran, 1994; Saffran & Coslett, 1998). Note that, on this account, the sequential processing may interfere with the covert activation and inhibit the ability to derive lexical and semantic representations in the right hemisphere.

An alternative view argues against two separate processes, one for implicit and one for explicit reading, and claims that the covert reading arises from the residual function of the normal reading system. Because of the brain damage, a rather coarse and imprecise representation might be activated implicitly by the conjoint functioning of the right hemisphere and the residual left hemisphere, and this activation may suffice for some tasks but not for others. The failure to report the word explicitly might then arise because naming requires a more precise and refined representation of the input and this is not sufficiently specified. According to this account, even when the patient is not engaged in serial word processing, word processing is mediated by a single unified system that reflects the residual capabilities of the left

hemisphere working in tandem with the intact right hemisphere (Behrmann et al., 1998b). Because of the brain damage, full elaboration of the representation of the word is not possible and any covert effects arise from the partial activation of the input that is derived under the brief exposure conditions.

In addition to using the Stroop paradigm to explore covert processing, the further goal of this paper is to explore the precision of the activated representation. To do so, we compared EL's performance with that of a matched control subject in the control and incongruent conditions of the Stroop ink naming task in a series of experiments in which we manipulate the phonological, lexical, orthographic, and semantic status of the word in an attempt to document the range and extent of implicit reading.

GENERAL METHODS

Participants

Patient EL, previously diagnosed as a LBL reader, participated in this study. A detailed case report of EL (as well as scans of her lesion site) is available in previous publications (Behrmann, Nelson, & Sekuler, 1998a; Montant & Behrmann, 2001). EL is a 50-year-old, native English speaking, right-handed female with 18 years of schooling. She was admitted to the hospital in April 1996 for right arm weakness, blurred vision, and slurred speech caused by two embolic events. A CT scan performed at the time of admission revealed a large infarction in the territory of the left posterior cerebral artery involving the left peristriate infero-temporal visual association cortex, the postero-lateral temporal cortex, and the dorsal parietal cortex in the vicinity of the occipitoparietal cortex. EL does not exhibit any obvious visual agnosia although, in certain experimental conditions, her ability to name pictures is affected by their structural complexity (Behrmann et al., 1998a). EL does not display any writing or spelling difficulties but, as expected, she fails to read easily what she herself has written on a previous occasion. Premorbidly, EL was an avid reader. Ironically and sadly, she was trained as a remedial specialist and worked with children who had developmental reading problems.

EL is able to identify single letters extremely well, even under brief presentation. At the time of this testing, we re-measured EL's word length effect by having her read aloud words of three, five, and seven letters, presented to the left of a fixation cross on a computer screen for an unlimited exposure duration. EL made no errors in reading but required an additional 403.7 ms per letter in the word (calculated by setting string length against RT in a regression analysis). Her mean RT was 1490.81 ms, 2345.07 ms and 3103.70 ms for three-, five-, and seven-letter words, respectively. This linear increase has roughly remained the same for several years now (Behrmann, 1998a; Montant & Behrmann, 2001) and puts her in the class of mild to moderate LBL readers (Behrmann et al., 1998; Shallice, 1988).

To compare EL's performance with that of a non-brain-damaged individual, we tested QK, who was also right-handed and was matched to EL on age, gender, and education.

Apparatus and materials

All experiments were conducted on a Macintosh G3 PowerBook. Stimuli were presented on a 14.1 in (35.8 cm) colour monitor using PsyScope experimental software version 1.2.1 (J. D. Cohen, MacWhinney, Flatt, & Provost, 1993). All voice responses were obtained using a desktop computer microphone (RadioShack, Fort Worth, TX) and voice onset time and key responses were obtained using a Button Box (New Micros, Dallas, TX). Participants were seated approximately 50 cm from the monitor. The experimenter noted the verbal responses made by the participants.

EXPERIMENT 1

Before adopting the Stroop procedure, we first document EL's ability to show covert word processing using the more standard techniques of lexical decision and binary semantic classification.

Methods

Lexical decision. EL completed three blocks of a lexical decision task, using the same set of words used in the naming latency task described above. Each block consisted of randomly presented three-, five-, and seven-letter words and nonwords, derived from the words with one or two vowel changes, for a total of 150 trials in the experiment. A trial was initiated with a centrally located fixation cross, which remained on the screen for 1000 ms. A word or non-word, displayed in Arial 24pt font, then replaced the fixation cross in the same location on the screen, and was presented for 300 ms, an exposure duration far too brief for EL to identify the word (her naming latencies indicate that she requires roughly 400 ms per letter). The stimulus was then replaced by a mask of seven instances of the letter "X" that appeared in the same position as the previous stimuli. This mask remained until response. EL was instructed to determine whether the letter string was a real word or a nonword and to respond with an appropriate button press. Accuracy and RT were recorded.

Semantic classification. This procedure has been used repeatedly to establish whether LBL readers can assign words to a semantic category despite the failure to read them explicitly (Behrmann & Shallice, 1995; Patterson & Kay, 1982; Shallice & Saffran, 1986). This task consisted of 100 words, half of which are food items and half body parts, divided equally into items of four, five or six letters in length. Trials followed the same procedure and timing as the lexical decision task above. EL was instructed to determine whether the word referred to a food item or body part and to respond with an appropriate button press. This task was repeated twice, 2 weeks apart.

Results

Lexical decision. EL performed significantly above chance with 114 out of 150 trials correct (76%), $\chi^2(1, N) = 150) = 20.7$, $p < .0001$. Even under this brief duration, she showed an effect of word length, with higher accuracy for three- compared to five- letter words, $\chi^2(1, N) = 100) = 8.41$, $p < .003$. She also showed an effect of lexicality, with greater accuracy for nonwords than words, $\chi^2(1, N) = 150) = 6.2$, $p < .012$; however, this may reflect a bias to respond "no" when she is uncertain ($d' = 1.58$).

Semantic decision. EL attempted to read aloud 36/200 words. She was incorrect on 26 of these, but all of these were excluded from the analysis of interest. Of the remaining 164 words, she correctly classified 101 (62%), a result suggesting that she performed significantly above chance, $\chi^2(1, N = 164) = 8.8$, $p < .003$, and has access to the semantic information of words that she cannot overtly identify. These findings suggest that EL has some covert processing ability on these more standard implicit tasks. The question is whether we will observe interference in the Stroop colour naming task.

EXPERIMENT 2

The goal of this next experiment is to examine whether EL shows Stroop interference and, if so, whether the interference is comparable in magnitude to that obtained in a normal reader. If this were the case, it would suggest that the extent of the implicit (automatic, in this case) representation is not different from that activated by normal readers.

Methods

Words were printed in capital letters in Chicago 48 pt font. The list of words used in this experiment included the colour words blue, green, purple, red, and yellow. The ink colours chosen were the same as each of the colour words. In this first experiment, we collected data from the word and ink naming task.

In the word naming task, participants were required to read aloud the printed word presented centrally on the screen as quickly and as accurately as possible. In the congruent condition, the ink colour matched the words presented (e.g., the word BLUE printed in blue ink). All words in the control condition were printed in black ink. In the incongruent condition, the words displayed did not match the ink colour but were in one of the other possible ink colours used (e.g., the word BLUE, printed in yellow ink).

In the ink naming task, participants were required to name the ink colour of the words that were presented on the screen. The stimuli used in both the ink naming congruent and incongruent conditions were the same set of stimuli as in the congruent and incongruent word naming task. The control condition for ink naming consisted of a string of the letter "X" (with the Xs printed in the appropriate colour), which varied in length to match the number of letters in each of the colour words used.

The design in this study was entirely within-subject, with the independent variables being task (word naming and ink naming) and congruency condition (congruent, control, and incongruent). This resulted in a total of six different conditions, which were blocked. Each block was prefaced with the task instructions and was followed by 20 randomised trials followed by a short break. Prior to the experiment, participants were given two blocks of 20 practice trials, one each of word and ink naming. The subjects were told to respond as quickly as possible without sacrificing accuracy. RT was measured from the time the words were presented on the screen until a response was made. The experimenter recorded word and ink naming errors. Participants completed the experiment and then, after at least 2 weeks, repeated the entire experiment (with the block order reversed) resulting in a total of 240 trials, 40 in each condition.

Results and discussion

Error trials, trials on which the microphone did not trigger at the correct time, and trials yielding RT values greater than 4 SDs from each subject mean were all excluded from the analysis, resulting in a removal of 5% of the data for QK and 8.3% for EL. No subject made more than two naming errors in any of the conditions, so accuracy performance is not analysed. The data for each subject were entered into a 2 × 3 (Task × Condition) analysis of variance, comparing the tasks of word naming and ink naming. All pairwise comparisons were done using Tukey post hoc comparisons with an alpha level of .05. The results are shown in Figure 1.

The mean RT for the task of word naming for the control subject, QK, (460.1 ms) was faster than the mean RT for ink naming (626.6 ms), $F(1, 222) = 210.8$, $p < .0001$. A main effect of congruency was also observed, $F(2, 222) = 69.8$, $p < .0001$. Importantly, the task by condition interaction for QK was also significant, $F(2, 222) = 49.8$, $p < .0001$. QK did not show any differences between conditions in the word naming task ($p > .05$). She did, however, show the Stroop effect, with ink naming-control (542.8 ms) being faster than ink naming-incongruent (804 ms), an increase of 261.2 ms ($p < .05$). In the ink naming task, QK did not show facilitation in the congruent condition ($p > .05$) compared to the control condition. Overall, EL responded faster for word naming (599.2 ms) than ink naming (724.9 ms), $F(1, 214) = 43.4$, $p < .0001$. EL's word naming in this task is faster compared to her response times for word naming

latency in other reading tasks; however, this is expected given the small set of words used in this Stroop task. EL also showed a main effect of congruency, $F(2, 214) = 17.6$, $p < .0001$, and the task by condition interaction was significant as well, $F(2, 214) = 7.1$, $p < .0001$. Like QK, EL did not show any differences among the three word naming conditions ($p > .05$) but showed significant interference in ink naming, with the RT for the ink naming-incongruent condition (867.2 ms) 194.5 ms slower than for ink naming-control (672.8 ms) ($p < .05$). EL also did not show facilitation in the ink naming-congruent condition ($p > .05$) (see Figure 1). While EL is slower than QK in both tasks, $F(1, 440) = 93.8$, $p < .0001$, there is no task by subject interaction nor a three-way interaction with condition ($p > .05$).

In sum, both subjects showed a similar pattern of data, with no effect in the word naming condition as a function of congruency, but a large Stroop effect as shown by an increase in RTs in the ink naming-incongruent condition compared to the control condition. These results are similar to those typically found in Stroop experiments (see Macleod, 1988). The findings indicate that the

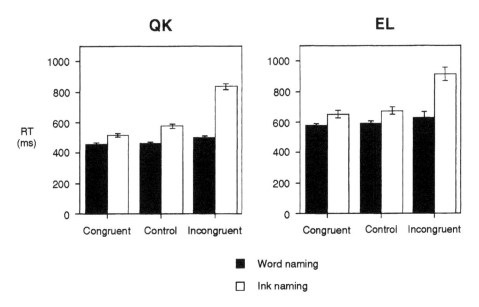

Figure 1. *Response time in a colour Stroop task as a function of task (word naming and ink naming) and condition in EL and control subject QK.*

Stroop paradigm is indeed effective in revealing the covert processing in a LBL reader and that EL appears to activate representations of words implicitly to the same extent as the control subject.

EXPERIMENT 3

Having demonstrated that EL is subject to interference from the incongruent word in the ink naming task, suggesting covert processing of letter strings, we now explore the nature and extent of this interference. This next experiment was designed to replicate the results in Experiment 2. Additionally, this condition was intended to eliminate the possibility that the Stroop interference seen in EL was merely a result of interference caused by reading the first letter(s) and not the entire word. To do this, we included an ink naming onset control condition in which words were chosen to share the first letter(s) with colour words (e.g., BLOW for BLUE and PURITY for PURPLE) (for similar control conditions, see Berti, Frassinetii, & Umiltà, 1994; Patterson & Kay, 1982).

Methods

The onset control words used in this study were chosen to match both the word length and also the first or first few letters of the colour words. The onset control words chosen were BLOW for blue, GROUP for green, PURITY for purple, RAW for red, and YEARLY for yellow. Because both participants failed to show any effect in the word naming task as a function of congruency, and also because we are interested in the extent of Stroop interference in ink naming, we did not collect data for word naming in any of the subsequent experiments. This version of the task has the additional benefit of removing further any interference from serial processing of words as no word naming is involved in any of the conditions.

Stimuli were printed in capital letters in Arial 48 pt font. The experiment was prefaced by instructions and a presentation of the colours used in the task to ensure that the participants knew the

names of the colours. The design in this study was entirely within-subjects, with the independent variables being ink naming condition (standard words and onset control words) and congruency condition (congruent, control, and incongruent). Subjects completed three blocks of each of the ink naming conditions with a long break between each block. Each of the three conditions was balanced so that an equal number appeared in each block. There were 36 trials in each condition, which resulted in a total of 216 trials for each participant, with an equal distribution of both stimulus type and congruency condition.

Each trial began with a centrally positioned fixation cross that appeared for 500 ms. The coloured word stimuli then immediately replaced the cross and remained on the screen until the participant responded. Participants were told to name the colour of the stimuli verbally as quickly as possible without sacrificing accuracy. RT was measured from the time the colour word stimuli was presented on the screen until a voice response was made. The experimenter recorded ink naming errors and microphone errors.

Results and discussion

Trials on which the microphone did not trigger at the correct time and trials with RT values greater than 4 SDs from each subject mean were excluded from the analysis, resulting in a removal of 3.2% of the data for QK and 3.7% for EL. Naming errors occurred infrequently, so accuracy performance is not analysed. The RT data were entered into a 2 × 3 (Word Type × Congruency Condition) analysis of variance. All pairwise comparisons were done using Tukey post hoc comparisons at an alpha level of .05.

For the control subject, QK, an analysis of variance revealed a significant effect of word type (standard, onset control), $F(1, 203) = 21.2$, $p < .0001$, a significant effect of congruency condition, $F(2, 203) = 48.6$, $p < .0001$, and a significant interaction between the two factors, $F(2, 203) = 20.4$, $p < .0001$. She did not show any significant differences when comparing the control and congruent conditions for either standard words or onset control words ($p > .05$). Again, however, she showed evidence of Stroop interference, with ink naming-incongruent (792.5 ms) significantly slower than ink naming-control (588.9 ms), an increase of 203.7 ms ($p < .05$). QK did show interference to some extent based on the first letters of the word, as shown by a longer mean RT in ink naming onset-incongruent (633.8ms) compared to the ink naming onset-control condition (575.5 ms), a difference of 58.2 ms ($p < .05$), but this was less than her interference seen in the standard Stroop task (203.7 ms). This slight interference based on this first letter has been previously demonstrated in the literature (see Macleod, 1981).

An analysis of variance of EL's data revealed a significant effect of word type, $F(1, 202) = 31.1$, $p < .0001$, a significant effect of congruency condition, $F(2, 202) = 9.7$, $p < .0001$, and no interaction. There were no significant differences between the control and congruent conditions ($p > .05$). EL demonstrated Stroop interference, with ink naming-incongruent (961.6 ms) significantly slower than ink naming-control (747.1 ms), an increase of 214.5 ms ($p < .05$) (see Table 1). EL did show an increase of 81.7 ms in RT from ink naming onset-control to ink naming onset-incongruent; however, this difference did not reach significance ($p > .05$) and is much less than her interference seen in the standard ink naming condition

(214.5 ms). Given that EL did not show a significant interference effect with the onset control words and that any interference obtained is considerably less than the extent observed in the standard Stroop task, we can conclude that the covert activation obtained in ink naming for EL is not merely a result of processing the first letter(s) of the word.

EXPERIMENT 4

In this experiment, we manipulated visual/perceptual aspects of the presented words by degrading the stimuli in one condition and by displaying them in cursive font in another condition. The rationale for these manipulations stems from work by Farah and Wallace (1991), who demonstrated that a LBL patient was especially sensitive to stimulus degradation, as evidenced by the disproportionate increase in naming latency across word length when the words were masked. Farah and Wallace (1991) argued that serial letter-by-letter reading results from a deficit in perceptual analysis of visual material and that visual changes to the stimuli exacerbate the serial processing procedure. It is also the case that the performance of LBL readers is slowed, relative to normal subjects, as more visually complex fonts are used (Behrmann

Table 1. *Response times (ms) for control and incongruent (Incog) Stroop conditions, and difference (Diff: incongruent–control) for Experiments 3–6 for EL and control subject QK*

	QK			EL		
	Control	Incong	Diff	Control	Incong	Diff
Experiment 3						
Normal	588.85	792.50	203.65	747.12	961.63	214.51
Onset control	575.53	633.75	58.22	628.48	710.16	81.68
Experiment 4						
Degrade	577.13	678.58	101.44	731.25	765.94	34.68
Cursive	545.22	622.20	116.97	693.86	726.40	32.54
Experiment 5						
Pseudohomophone	626.60	761.37	134.77	661.97	740.02	78.05
Experiment 6						
Uncommon	604.83	687.94	83.11	703.20	757.77	54.57

& Shallice, 1995), that visual similarity among letters influences reading performance (Arguin & Bub, 1993), and that the patients make predominantly visual errors in their word reading. We are interested in whether this vulnerability to visual/perceptual degradation was also evident in EL's covert word processing.

Methods

In the degrade condition, all stimuli were degraded using the PsyScope degrade function at a level of 0.7. This gives the appearance of random noise overlaid on the stimuli, making identification more difficult. In the second condition, we presented all words in cursive Swing 48 pt font. The two visual/perceptual manipulation conditions were presented in separate sessions, each containing 108 randomly presented trials with an equal number from each of the three congruency conditions. All other aspects of this experiment were the same as in the previous experiment.

Results and discussion

We removed 1.4% of the data for QK and 3.7% for EL from the analysis because of naming errors, failure of the microphone to trigger properly, or because RT values were greater than 4 SDs from the mean. Neither subject made more than two naming errors in any of the conditions, so accuracy performance is not analysed. The RT data were entered into two separate one-way analyses of variance. All pairwise comparisons were done using Tukey post hoc comparisons at an alpha level of .05.

The control subject, QK, showed a significant effect of congruency in both the degrade, $F(2, 103) = 16.2$, $p < .0001$ and cursive conditions $F(2, 104) = 22.6$, $p < .0001$. In neither condition was there a significant difference between the control and congruent condition ($p > .05$; however, QK demonstrated a significant increase ($p < .05$) in RT in the incongruent compared to control condition for both the degrade and cursive conditions, an increase of 101.4 ms and 116.9 ms, respectively (see Table 1).

EL showed no effect of congruency in the degrade condition ($p > .05$); however, she did exhibit an effect of congruency in the cursive condition, $F(1, 100) = 3.891$, $p < .024$. Like QK, EL showed no difference in either the degrade or cursive condition when comparing control and congruent conditions. In contrast to QK's performance, EL did not show significant Stroop interference in either the degrade or cursive condition: There is an increase in RT from the control to incongruent condition of 34.68 ms in the degrade condition and 32.54 ms in the cursive condition, but this is not statistically significant ($p > .05$).

When orthographic manipulations are applied to the stimulus, EL no longer demonstrated covert reading, as evidenced by the lack of Stroop interference. In contrast, the control subject QK still showed robust Stroop interference, although this was not as great as in the standard Stroop task. One possible explanation is that the alteration of the visual input renders the stimuli too taxing on the processes used for word recognition. Consequently, in the time required to generate a response for ink naming, the written word is not sufficiently processed to exert an inhibitory effect on the response when the colour and the word identity are incongruent. Because the normal subject is not as dramatically affected by these orthographic manipulations, she processes the written word fast enough for it to have an adverse effect on ink naming performance. EL, on the other hand, does not have enough processing time on the word for its output to have any influence on her speed of ink colour naming. This experiment points out a limitation in the extent of covert activation in EL.

EXPERIMENT 5

To determine whether EL has implicit access to the phonological representation of words, in this experiment we manipulated phonological aspects of the presented words by using pseudohomophones of colour words. Prior studies (Montant & Behrmann, 2001) have demonstrated that EL does benefit from being primed with pseudohomophones, as measured by her decrease in naming latency for associated words; for example, having seen a pseudohomophone prime, her RT is 200 ms faster compared to being primed with an unrelated nonword. Thus, in an explicit word reading task, she is able to derive strong enough phonological representations and to be primed by related representations.

The pseudohomophone Stroop task has three conditions: a congruent condition which paired congruent ink colour and pseudohomophone (e.g., BLOO in blue ink), an incongruent condition (e.g., BLOO in red ink), and a control condition that was the same as in the previous experiments. The word stimuli consisted of WRED for RED, BLOO for BLUE, GREAN for GREEN, and YELOE for YELLOW. All other aspects of the design and procedures for this experiment were the same as in the previous experiments.

Results and discussion

We removed from the analysis all error trials, microphone trigger failure responses, and all trials in which all RT values exceeded 4 SDs from each subject mean. This resulted in a removal of 2.7% of the data for QK and 1.8% for EL. The RT data were entered into a one-way analysis of variance, comparing congruency conditions. All pairwise comparisons were done using Tukey post hoc comparisons at an alpha level of .05.

The control subject QK showed a main effect of condition, $F(2, 101) = 26.5$, $p < .0001$, with no difference between control and congruent conditions ($p > .05$). QK did demonstrate Stroop interference, with an increase in RT of 134.8 ms in the incongruent condition compared to the control condition ($p < .05$) (see Table 1).

EL showed a main effect of condition, $F(2, 103) = 5.5$, $p < .005$, with no difference between control and congruent conditions ($p > .05$). While EL's response times in the incongruent condition are 78.1 ms slower than in the control condition, this difference failed to reach significance ($p > .05$) and is considerably less than the amount of Stroop interference seen in QK. This amount of interference is also much reduced relative to the extent of EL's interference in the

standard Stroop (Experiment 2 and 3) task. EL's apparent failure to show covert activation with a homophonically related prime also points to a boundary condition in her ability to process words implicitly.

We note that, on the right hemisphere account, the right hemisphere is capable of generating lexical and semantic representations and, to a lesser extent (if at all), phonological representations. In light of this, the reduced phonological Stroop effect in EL might not necessarily be a good indicator of right-hemisphere covert processing (even though the task does not require word reading per se) and so, in the next task, we return to an exploration of lexical and semantic interference effects.

EXPERIMENT 6

In this final experiment, we determine whether EL has implicit access to lexical-semantic representations of words. To do so, we examined her Stroop interference from words less common than those used in the previous Stroop experiments. LBL readers, like normal subjects, are slower to name words that are lower in frequency as compared to higher in frequency, although frequency appears to interact with word length such that as length increases, frequency effects are exaggerated (Behrmann et al., 1998). In this frequency Stroop task, common colour words were replaced with words of the same length but of lower frequency. The words used were TAN, PURPLE, BLACK, and GRAY. The mean occurrence of common colour words, as measured by Kuçera and Francis (1967), was 127.8 compared to 76.3 in the uncommon colour word condition. All other aspects of the design and procedures for this experiment were the same as in the previous experiments.

Results and discussion

Two trials were removed from EL's analysis, one for a naming error, and the other because of microphone trigger problems, resulting in a removal of 1.8% of the data. Neither subject had responses that exceeded 4 *SD*s from each subject mean. QK did not have any data removed because there were no naming errors or microphone trigger problems. The data for each subject were entered into a one-way analysis of variance, comparing conditions. All pairwise comparisons were done using Tukey post hoc comparisons at an alpha level of .05.

QK showed a main effect of congruency, $F(2, 105) = 17.17$, $p < .0001$, with no difference between the control and congruent conditions ($p > .05$). QK demonstrated Stroop interference, with an increase of 83.11 ms from the control condition to the incongruent condition ($p < .05$) (see Table 1). However, this interference is less than that she exhibited to the more common words (Experiment 2, 261.2 ms; Experiment 3, 203.7 ms). This reduction in Stroop interference is compatible with the results reported in the literature (Macleod, 1991).

EL also showed a main effect of congruency, $F(2, 103) = 3.077$, $p < .05$. There was no significant difference between the control and congruent condition ($p > .05$). EL failed to show Stroop interference, with a 54.6ms increase from the control to the incongruent condition ($p > .05$). This is much less compared to the Stroop interference seen in common colour words (Experiment 2, 194.5 ms; Experiment 3, 214.5 ms). This difference is also less than the interference effect seen in QK, which was statistically significant.

GENERAL DISCUSSION

Patients with pure alexia, also known as LBL readers, read in a laborious and sequential manner, as is evident in their increase in naming latency as a function of the number of letters in a word string. However, counterintuitive and perplexing evidence has amassed showing that some of these patients do in fact exhibit some level of covert reading in which words are processed rapidly and perhaps even in parallel. Indeed, under some circumstances, the patients appear to have considerable information about a word (for example, its semantic category) despite being unable to identify it explicitly. But not all patients show this covert

processing and, even when they do, the extent and nature of the implicit representation is not particularly well understood. While some researchers have suggested that this covert processing gives rise to rich and detailed representations, others have argued that this is not so and that the representation is, at best, partial and imprecise. On this latter account, the failure of the patients to explicitly identify the word is a direct consequence of the partial and impoverished representation, which arises from the residual function of the normal reading system.

We have adopted a Stroop interference paradigm with a LBL patient, EL, with two major goals. The first is to explore whether, using a procedure in which subjects are required to name the colour of the ink of a letter string without reading the word, we can elicit evidence of covert processing in an individual who does show some covert processing in the more standard implicit tasks (such as lexical decision and binary semantic classification) although this is not as strong as that observed in some other LBL readers (see Coslett & Saffran, 1989). The critical finding is that this procedure, which does not engage word recognition (and serial processing), produces Stroop interference in EL of the same magnitude as in the matched control subject. Moreover, as with the control subject, when only the first letter(s) of the word matches the colour name, very little interference is obtained, indicating that more than the first letter must be activated implicitly in order to give rise to the Stroop interference effect. The implication of this is that EL must be processing more than the first letter of the word covertly.

The second goal is to explore the nature and extent of the representations that are activated covertly. To this end, we explore whether the Stroop interference is of the same magnitude as in the normal reader when we manipulate various aspects of the word stimulus in relation to the colour of the ink. Understanding this will allow us to determine the extent of the orthographic, phonological, and semantic activation that is possible at an implicit level in a LBL reader. We found that, first, the extent of the Stroop interference is reduced in the matched control subject under these various conditions but that in all cases, she still showed a significant difference between ink naming speed in the control versus the incongruent condition. Second, and perhaps more relevant, EL did not show Stroop interference when the written words are less frequent than the common colour words, when the written words are degraded or presented in cursive font, or when the written words are homophonically related to the colour word.

That we observe Stroop interference in only some conditions for EL, in contrast with the control subject, suggests that while some aspects of the written word are activated, not all aspects are adequately represented to support covert processing. Many interpretations of the interference effect in Stroop tasks rely on the finding that word reading proceeds at a faster pace than ink naming (due to the increased experience with word reading) and, hence, the processed written word can adversely impact the ink naming when the outputs are incongruent (see, for example, J. D. Cohen, Servan-Schreiber, & McClelland, 1991). The presence or absence of the Stroop effects in EL, then suggests that in the amount of time the word is present before the ink colour is read, only a limited amount of word processing can be completed. It is only the standard Stroop task, in which word processing conditions are ideal and the most information can be extracted from the word, which may offer sufficient time for word processing for EL. We also note that in the standard Stroop task, only a small number of highly common words are used and this, too, can facilitate the speed of word processing in EL. But of great relevance is that manipulating aspects of the word, including frequency, visual input, or the relationship between orthography and phonology, no longer provides sufficient time for word processing and the automatic inhibition of ink naming in the incongruent case. In sum, when all components of the word are favourable (high frequency, small set of items, accessible font, consistent phonology and semantics), enough factors can combine to activate a covert representation that can influence ink naming. When one explores further, however, the representation that is activated covertly is found to

be weaker or less precise than that activated by a normal control and so this underlying representation may not be sufficiently robust to support word naming, which requires precision.

Before discussing the theoretical implications of these findings, we need to point out that we are not the first to run a Stroop experiment with a LBL reader: Patterson and Kay (1982) ran a Stroop experiment using ink naming with one of their LBL readers, MW, but obtained no evidence of Stroop interference. Surprisingly, and in contrast with our results, they observed a congruency effect (better performance on congruent than control condition); however, as we suggest below, they too argued that this covert facilitation might arise from partial processing of the word. The absence of an interference effect in their patient, however, is somewhat surprising given that we have claimed that it is a particularly useful paradigm, which does not evoke sequential processing of letters. That MW did not show this effect may suggest that this might not be as watertight and robust a procedure as we have proposed. Alternatively, it may still be possible that even if the procedure is robust, covert word reading might not be evident in all individuals. In particular, because MW was so severely impaired (she took 12.8 seconds to read a three- to four-letter word), covert effects may not be possible in very profoundly impaired LBL readers. These suggestions are speculative, however, and remain to be explored further.

As mentioned previously, one prominent theory about pure alexia argues for two different modes of word processing: a right-hemisphere based parallel mode that is the source of covert processing, and a left-hemisphere based sequential mode that is the source of the laboured serial reading pattern. Given that covert processing is mediated by the right hemisphere and that the letters are processed in parallel, one might expect that the extent of this covert activation would be normal (the hemisphere is intact) if it is not subject to any interference by the sequential word process that usually opposes it. The alternative perspective does not differentiate between two modes of processing and presupposes that all forms of reading emerge from the residual function of the normal reading system, which has been damaged. Any covert processing, then, will reflect whatever activation the system is capable of generating given the exposure duration of the stimulus and it will probably be partial and imprecise.

Given the abnormal covert activation observed in EL, the findings seem more compatible with the latter perspective of a single, integrated, reading system. This perspective has been fleshed out in some detail recently by Behrmann and colleagues (Behrmann et al., 1998b; Montant & Behrmann, 2001). This view holds that a general visual perceptual deficit, which degrades the quality of the input, sustained by virtue of the left posterior hemisphere damage, is fundamental to LBL reading. As a result of this perceptual deficit, only weak parallel activation is possible and, to increase this activation, patients need to make multiple fixations to allow the higher spatial resolution of the fovea to be applied to the input. Indeed, a recent study has documented that LBL readers make more frequent fixations on longer than shorter words than do normal readers (Behrmann, Shomstein, Black, & Barton, 2001). Any covert effects emerge from whatever weak parallel activation is possible under the limited exposure duration used for stimulus presentation.

The notion that there may be some parallel activation, which is weak and insufficient to mediate reading, also derives support from several very recent studies on the topic. Lambon Ralph, Hesketh, and Sage (2004 this issue) present data from pure alexic patient FD, who demonstrated decreased performance in a brief presentation lexical decision and semantic categorisation task as a function of decreasing word frequency, image-ability, and familiarity. These data led the authors to conclude that FD's fast access to lexical and semantic aspects of words is evidence for a weak parallel activation of words: however, this is insufficient to drive normal word processing, which is the reason for the severe LBL reading.

Arguin, Fiset, and Bub (2002) demonstrated that their LBL reader IH, like controls, was faster at naming words that had many as compared to few orthographic neighbors (i.e., words of the same length that differ by one letter) and that this was independent of word length. The authors conclude that a decreased naming latency for words with many orthographic neighbours is evidence for an intact parallel letter processor. However, unlike controls, IH was slower at naming words that contained many versus a few confusable letters (i.e., a similarity of letters within a word with other letters of the alphabet). The claim is that parallel letter processing may still be possible but that it gives rise to considerable background noise and that this noise prevents the system from resolving differences between visually similar letters. It is this noise that makes the sequential processing of letters mandatory. The relevant aspect of this is that the parallel activation that arises is simply too weak and it is possible that it may only support rudimentary covert processing.

Consistent with this is the claim by Osswald, Humphreys, and Olson (2002) that attempts to read at the supra-letter level (in parallel even if to a limited extent) has detrimental consequences for word recognition in LBL readers. Their patient, DM, who appears to be very similar in severity to EL as defined by the slope of the naming latency function (roughly 400 ms in both cases), performed better when letters were presented sequentially than simultaneously. The interpretation of this is that simultaneous letters give rise to increased lateral masking and disrupt the extraction of individual letters. Interestingly, DM also performed better when a few letters, corresponding to a functional spelling unit, are presented at a time than under simultaneous conditions, suggesting that some supra-letter processing is possible but that it breaks down when larger units are presented. Again, the relevant finding here is that parallel activation of visual input may not only be too weak but can also be detrimental.

The data from FD, IH, and DM, like EL, suggest that parallel activation of many letters is not sufficiently strong to mediate covert processing. Rather, the output of these individuals suggest that there may be some limited parallel activation, which is insufficient and which compels a sequential procedure. Rather than thinking about two independent reading routes, then, the findings from EL might more profitably be explained as reflecting the residual capabilities of an integrated reading system struggling to produce a coherent response. When all factors point in the same direction, there is sufficient activation to support covert reading. When one digs a little deeper, however, it becomes more apparent that the covert representations are not sufficiently detailed or rich. Instead of conceptualising LBL reading as arising from two distinct sources, a sequential left hemisphere processor and an intact parallel right hemisphere processor, the pattern of findings might well be accounted for by a single reading system that, following damage, is only partially functional.

REFERENCES

Aglioti, S., Bricolo, E., Cantagallo, A., & Berlucchi, G. (1999). Unconscious letter discrimination is enhanced by association with conscious color perception in visual form agnosia. *Current Biology, 9,* 1419–1422.

Arguin, S., Fiset, S., & Bub, D. (2002). Sequential and parallel letter processing in letter-by-letter dyslexia. *Cognitive Neuropsychology, 19,* 535–555.

Behrmann, M., Nelson, J., & Sekuler, E. (1998a). Visual complexity in letter-by-letter reading: "Pure" alexia is not so pure. *Neuropsychologia, 36,* 1115–1132.

Behrmann, M., Plaut, D. C., & Nelson, J. (1998b). A literature review and new data supporting an interactive account of letter-by-letter reading. *Cognitive Neuropsychology, 15,* 7–51.

Behrmann, M., Shomstein, S., Black, S. E., & Barton, J. J. S. (2001). Eye movements of letter-by-letter readers during reading: Effects of word length and lexical variables. *Neuropsychologia, 39,* 983–1002.

Berti, A., Frassinetti, F., & Umiltà, C. (1994). Nonconscious reading? Evidence from neglect dyslexia. *Cortex, 30,* 181–197.

Besner, D. (2001). The myth of ballistic processing: Evidence from Stroop's paradigm. *Psychonomic Bulletin and Review, 8,* 324–330.

Black, S. E., & Behrmann, M. (1994). Localization in alexia. In A. Kertesz (Ed.), *Localization and neuroimaging in neuropsychology* (pp. 331–376). San Diego: Academic Press.

Bowers, J. S., Arguin, M., & Bub, D. N. (1996a). Fast and specific access to orthographic knowledge in a case of letter-by-letter reading. *Cognitive Neuropsychology, 13,* 525–567.

Bowers, J. S., Bub, D. N., & Arguin, M. (1996b). A characterisation of the word superiority effect in a case of letter-by-letter surface alexia. *Cognitive Neuropsychology, 13,* 415–442.

Bub, D., & Arguin, M. (1995). Visual word activation in pure alexia. *Brain and Language, 47,* 77–103.

Bub, D., Black, S. E., & Howell, J. (1989). Word recognition and orthographic context effects in a letter-by-letter reader. *Brain and Language, 36,* 357–376.

Cohen, J. D., MacWhinney, B., Flatt, M., & Provost, J. (1993). PsyScope: A new graphic interactive environment for designing psychology experiments. *Behavioral Research Methods, Instruments and Computers, 25,* 257–271.

Cohen, J. D., Servan-Schreiber, D., & McClelland, J. L. (1992). A parallel distributed processing approach to automaticity. *American Journal of Psychology, 105,* 239–269.

Cohen, L., Lehericy, S., Chochon, F., Lemer, C., Rivaud, S., & Dehaene, S. (2002). Language-specific tuning of visual cortex? Functional properties of the visual word form area. *Brain, 125,* 1054–1069.

Coslett, H. B., & Monsul, N. (1994). Reading with the right hemisphere: Evidence from transcranial magnetic stimulation, *Brain and Language, 46,* 198–211.

Coslett, H. B., & Saffran, E. M. (1989). Evidence for preserved reading in "pure" alexia. *Brain, 112,* 327–359.

Coslett, H. B., & Saffran, E. M. (1992). Optic aphasia and the right hemisphere: A replication and extension. *Brain and Language, 43,* 148–161.

Coslett, H. B., & Saffran, E. M. (1994). Mechanisms of implicit reading in alexia. In M. J. Farah & G. Ratcliff (Eds.), *The neuropsychology of high-level vision* (pp. 299–330). Hillsdale, NJ: Lawrence Erlbaum Associates Inc.

Coslett, H. B., & Saffran, E. M. (2001). Peripheral dyslexias. In M. Behrmann (Ed.), *Handbook of neuropsychology* (2nd ed.). Amsterdam: North Holland/ Elsevier Science.

Coslett, H. B., Saffran, E. M., Greenbaum, S., & Schwartz, H. (1993). Reading in pure alexia: The effect of strategy. *Brain, 116,* 21–27.

Damasio, A., & Damasio, H. (1983). The anatomic basis of pure alexia. *Neurology, 33,* 1573–1583.

Farah, M. J., & Wallace, M. (1991). Pure alexia as a visual impairment: A reconsideration, *Cognitive Neuropsychology, 8,* 313–334.

Fiez, J. A., & Petersen, S. E. (1998). Neuroimaging studies of word reading. *Proceedings of the National*

Academy of Sciences of the United States of America, 95, 914–921.

Friedman-Hill, S. R., Robertson, L. C., & Treisman, A. (1995). Parietal contributions to visual feature binding: Evidence from a patient with bilateral lesions. *Science, 269,* 853–855.

Hanley, J. R., & Kay, J. (1996). Reading speed in pure alexia. *Neuropsychologia, 34,* 1165–1174.

Hasson, U., Levy, I., Behrmann, M., Hendler, T., & Malach, R. (2002). Center-biased representation for characters in the human ventral visual stream. *Neuron, 34,* 479–490.

Howard, D. (1991). Letter-by-letter readers: Evidence for parallel processing. In D. Besner & G. W. Humphreys (Eds.), *Basic processes in reading: Visual word recognition* (pp. 34–76). Hove, UK: Lawrence Erlbaum Associates Ltd.

Kahneman, D., & Henik, A. (1981) Perceptual organization and attention. In M. Kubovy & J. R. Pomerantz (Eds.), *Perceptual organization* (pp. 181–211). Hillsdale, NJ: Lawrence Erlbaum Associates Inc.

Kay, J., & Hanley, R. (1991). Simultaneous form perception and serial letter recognition in a case of letter-by-letter reading. *Cognitive Neuropsychology, 8,* 249–273.

Kuçera, H., & Francis, W. (1967). Computational analysis of present-day American English. Providence, RI: Brown University Press.

Lambon Ralph, M., Hesketh, A., & Sage, K. (2004). Implicit recognition in pure alexia: The Saffran effect—a tale of two systems or two procedures? *Cognitive Neuropsychology, 21,* 401–421.

Landis, T., Redard, M., & Serrat, A. (1980). Iconic reading in a case of alexia without agraphia caused by a brain tumor. *Brain and Language, 11,* 45–53.

Leff, A. P., Crewes, H., Plant, G. T., Scott, S. K., Kennard, C., & Wise, R. J. (2001). The functional anatomy of single-word reading in patients with hemianopic and pure alexia, *Brain, 124,* 510–521.

MacLeod, C. M. (1991). Half a century of research on the Stroop effect: An integrative review. *Psychological Bulletin, 109,* 163–203.

McClelland, J. L., & Rumelhart, D. E. (1981). An interactive activation model of context effects in letter perception: Part 1. An account of basic findings. *Psychological Review, 88,* 375–407.

Montant, M., & Behrmann, M. (2001). Phonological activation in pure alexia. *Cognitive Neuropsychology, 18,* 8, 697–727.

Osswald, K., Humphreys, G. K., & Olson, A. (2002). Words are more than the sum of their parts: Evidence for detrimental effects of word-level information in alexia. *Cognitive Neuropsychology, 19,* 675–695.

Patterson, K. E., & Kay, J. (1982). Letter-by-letter reading: Psychological descriptions of a neurological syndrome. *Quarterly Journal of Experimental Psychology, 34A,* 411–441.

Price, C. J., & Humphreys, G. W. (1992). Letter-by-letter reading? Functional deficits and compensatory strategies. *Cognitive Neuropsychology, 9,* 427–457.

Reuter-Lorenz, P., & Brunn, J. (1990). A prelexical basis for letter-by-letter reading: A case study. *Cognitive Neuropsychology, 7,* 1–20.

Saffran, E. M., & Coslett, H. B. (1998). Implicit vs. letter-by-letter reading in pure alexia: A tale of two systems. *Cognitive Neuropsychology, 15,* 141–165.

Shallice, T. (1988). *From neuropsychology to mental structure.* Cambridge: Cambridge University Press.

Shallice, T., & Saffran, E. (1986). Lexical processing in the absence of explicit word identification: Evidence from a letter-by-letter reader. *Cognitive Neuropsychology, 3,* 429–458.

Stroop, J. R. (1935). Studies of interference in serial verbal reactions. *Journal of Experimental Psychology, 18,* 643–662.

Warrington, E. K., & Shallice, T. (1980). Word-form dyslexia. *Brain, 103,* 99–112.

COGNITIVE NEUROPSYCHOLOGY, 2004, 21 (2/3/4), 459–462

SUBJECT INDEX